**SEVENTH
EDITION**

Procedures in the Justice System

GILBERT B. STUCKEY

CLIFF ROBERSON, LLM, PH.D.
Department of Criminal Justice
Washburn University

HARVEY WALLACE, J.D.
Department of Criminology
California State University, Fresno

PEARSON
Prentice
Hall

Upper Saddle River, New Jersey 07458

OCT 0 6 2004

Library of Congress Cataloging-in-Publication Data

Stuckey, Gilbert B.
  Procedures in the justice system / Gilbert B. Stuckey, Cliff Roberson,
Harvey Wallace.— 7th ed.
     p. cm.
Includes bibliographical references and index.
  ISBN 0-13-112295-9
  1. Criminal procedure—United States. 2. Criminal justice,
Administration of—United States. I. Roberson, Cliff, 1937-
II.
Wallace, Harvey. III. Title.
  KF9619 .S8 2004
  345.73'05—dc21

                                        2003007011

Editor-in-Chief: Stephen Helba
Director of Production and Manufacturing:
  Bruce Johnson
Executive Editor: Frank Mortimer, Jr.
Assistant Editor: Sarah Holle
Editorial Assistant: Barbara Rosenberg
Marketing Manager: Tim Peyton
Managing Editor — Production: Mary Carnis
Manufacturing Buyer: Cathleen Petersen
Production Liaison: Denise Brown

Full Service Production and Production:
  Nick Angelides/Pine Tree Composition, Inc.
Design Director: Cheryl Asherman
Design Coordinator: Miguel Ortiz
Cover Designer: Carey Davies
Cover Printer: Coral Graphics
Cover Image Photographer: John Neubauer,
  PhotoEditinc.com
Printer/Binder: Courier Westford

Pearson Education LTD.
Pearson Education Singapore, Pte. Ltd
Pearson Education, Canada, Ltd
Pearson Education–Japan
Pearson Education Australia PTY, Limited
Pearson Education North Asia Ltd
Pearson Educaçion de Mexico, S.A. de C.V.
Pearson Education Malaysia, Pte. Ltd

10 9 8 7 6 5 4 3 2 1
ISBN 0-13-112295-9

Contents

CHAPTER 3
The Arrest
53

CHAPTER 4
The Initial Appearance
78

CHAPTER 5
Pretrial Proceedings
101

CHAPTER 10
The Trial: Roles of Major Participants   207

CHAPTER 11
The Jury   228

CHAPTER 12
Trial Procedure   254

Preface

This edition, like the three previous editions, is dedicated to our colleague, the late Gilbert B. Stuckey.

The seventh edition of *Procedures in the Justice System* continues the tradition of providing the reader with a thorough understanding of our justice system from the time of arrest through the sentencing of the criminal offender. Legal rules of procedure are presented in language that is easy to understand. The crime rate continues as one of society's major problems, not only in the United States but also throughout the world. It is the primary responsibility of those directly connected with the justice system, such as members of law enforcement agencies, the courts, and correctional officers, to fight crime. Yet to effectively curb crime, society needs the assistance of every law-abiding person.

By studying history, we often see the mistakes of the past and thus can make efforts not to repeat those mistakes in the future. One past mistake was the failure to recognize that the members of the justice system are a team who must work together. Yet, to work as a team, it is necessary for each member to understand his or her own responsibility as well as that of each of the other members.

In this seventh edition, the coverage of victims' rights and of the effects of gangs on the crime problem has been expanded. The discussions of constitutional and civil rights of an accused, of the laws of arrest, and of search and seizure have also been expanded. In addition, we have included selected court cases to provide the reader with experience in reading court decisions and to assist the reader in understanding the legal issues involved. Also included in the seventh edition are motions and reports taken from actual trial records and other supplemental material. These are submitted to provide the reader with a better idea of the practical issues involved in trying criminal cases.

This book was written for those interested in our justice system, particularly for police and correctional science students. It explains the duties and responsibilities of the law enforcement agencies, courts, and correctional departments, in relation to law violators, from the time of accusation until completion of sentence. Criminal justice students should, however, study more than just judicial procedures. The student should have some knowledge of why we have laws and why those laws are broken, should be cognizant of the constitutional rights of an accused, and should have a better understanding of the philosophy of correctional endeavors. Thus, material on these subjects is incorporated into this text. The information in this text will help the student, as well as others, attain a more thorough knowledge of our justice system and of the role that each member must play to achieve, through teamwork, law and order for all.

Special thanks goes out to the following reviewers for their hard work and assistance on this edition; Wojciech Cebulak, Minot State University, Minot, N.D.; Mark Stetler, Montgomery College, Spring, TX; Chris DeLay, University of Louisiana, Lafayette, LA.

To assist the instructor in presenting the material in this edition, an Instructor's Manual contains objectives, chapter outlines, teaching aids, and examination questions and answers, including true-false, multiple-choice, and fill-in questions. A selection of federal forms and a powerpoint presentation for each chapter will also be included.

Suggestions for improvement, corrections, and other comments are invited and may be forwarded to Cliff Roberson, P.O. Box 2267, Stafford, Texas 77497, or via e-mail to ceroberso@aol.com

Cliff Roberson, LLM, Ph.D.
Professor of Criminal Justice
Washburn University
Professor of Criminology (Retired),
California State University, Fresno

Harvey Wallace, J.D.
Professor of Criminology
California State University, Fresno

CHAPTER 1

Historical Development of Law and the Justice System

The law embodies the story of a nation's development through many centuries, and it cannot be dealt with as if it contained only the axioms and corollaries of a book of mathematics.
—Oliver Wendell Holmes, *The Common Law,* 1881

Since participation in the justice system begins with the breaking of a criminal law, we should understand what is law and whether laws are necessary in our form of society.

THE EARLY DEVELOPMENT OF LAWS

A law in its simplest form is merely a guideline for human behavior. Its purpose is to encourage people to do what is right and discourage them from doing what is wrong. A law has been described as a social tool to mold and regulate human conduct. Legally, a law is defined as an act of a legislative body written and recorded in some public repository, informing people of what is right and wrong. In the case of *Koenig* v. *Flynn,* it was stated as "that which must be obeyed and followed by citizens, subject to sanctions or legal consequences, is a law."[1]

The next question to be answered is, Are laws necessary today? It has been stated frequently that laws are made to be broken. Also, it has been alleged that if there were no laws, they would not be broken. In fairness to the declarant of this statement, it is only logical to assume that if there were nothing to break, nothing would be broken. So we return to the question, Are laws necessary? Before answering, it may be well to consider what the origin of laws is and why they came into being.

A human being comes into the world with certain basic needs that remain throughout his or her life. These are the needs for food, shelter, companionship, and sexual gratification. If untrained and uncontrolled, a person may attempt to satisfy these needs in a most animalistic manner. If one were completely isolated from all other human beings, the fashion in which he or she might try to accomplish satisfaction of personal needs would be relatively unimportant. However, the moment one comes in contact with another person, the needs of each individual must be considered, and each must respect the desires of the other. Each person must learn to realize that his or her liberties cease where the other's begin. Certain restraints upon activity must be imposed. Thus, there is a necessity for some guidelines about satisfying personal needs without infringing upon the rights of others.

People may agree upon a division of territory, and each will confine his or her activities to that territory. If this arrangement takes place, there is little reason for other guidelines, but if they should agree to combine their efforts, further regulations must be made. It must be decided who will do what and how they will share. As more and more persons enter the picture, the necessity for more rules becomes apparent. Eventually, it will be necessary to choose a leader or chief to see that the rules are followed and to keep order within the tribe or society.

Undoubtedly, many of the early established guidelines came about through trial and error. When it was recognized that a tribal member committed an act that threatened the existence of the tribe, a restraint against that act was created, and a violation of that restraint was what we now know as a crime. It probably did not take long for members of a primitive tribe to learn that they could not go about killing each other and still have the tribe continue to exist. Therefore, rules against murder were established. To satisfy a person's need for food and shelter, that person devised certain tools that became his or her property. The taking of these tools by another, depriving the owner of their use, was a serious act, so that a rule against theft was enacted. People took mates to satisfy their needs for companionship and sexual gratification. The mate was also personal property, and to violate that property right was an offense, so that rules against adultery were formed.

As tribes, or societies, grew in number and became somewhat more sophisticated, so did their regulations. As time passed, people developed the belief in a deity. Regulations respecting these beliefs were also established, and the violation of these rules was a serious offense against the society.

Code of Hammurabi

The Code of Hammurabi is considered one of the first-known attempts to establish a written code of conduct. King Hammurabi ruled Babylon at approximately 2000 B.C. He was the sixth king of the First Dynasty of Babylonia for about fifty-five years. Babylon during that period of time was a commercial center for most of the known and civilized world. Since its fortune lay in trade and other business ventures, the Code of Hammurabi provided a basis for the order and certainty that were essential for commerce. The code established rules regarding theft, sexual relationships, and interpersonal violence. It was intended to replace blood feuds with a system sanctioned by the state.

The Code of Hammurabi was divided into five sections:

A penal or code of laws.
A manual of instruction for judges, police officers, and witnesses.
A handbook of rights and duties of husbands, wives, and children.
A set of regulations establishing wages and prices.
A code of ethics for merchants, doctors, and officials.

The code established certain obligations and objectives for the citizens of Babylon to follow. These included the following elements.

An Assertion of the Power of the State. This was the beginning of state-administered punishment. The blood feuds that had occurred previously between private citizens were barred under the code.

Protection of the Weaker From the Stronger. Widows were to be protected from those who might exploit them, elder parents were protected from sons who would disown them, and lesser officials were protected from higher officials.

Restoration of Equity Between the Offender and the Victim. The victim was to be made as whole as possible and, in turn, he or she was required to forgive vengeance against the offender.

Stele of Hammurabi—detail of upper part. The sun god dictating his laws to King Hammurabi. Babylon relief from Susa c. 1760 B.C (diorite, height of Stele c. 2.1. m height of relief 71 cm). Louvre, Paris, France. (*Source:* Copyright Giraudon/Art Resource, N.Y.)

Of noteworthy importance in the code was its concern for the rights of victims. In reality, this code may have been the first "victims' rights statute" in history. Unfortunately, as will be seen, society began to neglect victims in its rush to punish the offender, with the result that victims' rights would not resurface until the present century.

Biblical historians tell us that when Moses led the Israelites out of Egypt, some thirteen hundred years before Christ, he quickly realized that these people must have some guidelines to follow if they were to continue to exist. Through an inspiration from God, ten basic rules known as the Ten Commandments were established. Included were not only those laws that earlier tribes found necessary for existence, that is, rules against murder, theft, and adultery, but also more sophisticated rules that pertained to admonitions against not respecting God. In addition were admonitions against certain thoughts that people may conceive that might lead them into greed. Thus, a person should not covet his or her neighbor's property. When Moses gave these guidelines to the people of Israel, he commanded that they obey them, since they would ensure life and entrance into the possession of the land. He further indicated that these laws were not to be tampered with in the interest of human weakness. There was no mention that these laws were made to be broken. Nor has there been any such suggestion by anyone in authority since that time that laws are made to be broken.

Because of the effect of ecclesiastical law on the nations of Europe, most of these commandments were incorporated into their laws and, in turn, were brought to this country by the colonists. Our early criminal laws included rules against murder, theft, adultery, working on Sunday ("blue laws"), profanity, and perjury, as well as rules describing family responsibilities. Although we have become a more permissive society and take some of the earlier guidelines less seriously, a few of the Ten Commandments are still found in the criminal laws of all the states of this nation, because they are necessary for the existence of any society. These are the laws against murder, theft, perjury, and adultery; other laws are added to these from time to time.

As societies become more complex, so do their laws. New restraints are placed upon people's activities. These laws are designed with the hope that people can and will live more peacefully and pleasantly with their fellow human beings. Again we see, from a sociological standpoint, that laws are necessary for humankind's existence. From a legal standpoint, laws are necessary to inform people what is right and what is wrong. People must be made aware of the acts for which, if committed, they may be prosecuted. In our form of government, each criminal law must be spelled out in detail so that a person may know the exact act that, if committed, is a violation of the law. If a law is considered too vague, it will be declared null and void.

THE COMMON LAW

Much of the basic criminal law of this country originated from the common law of England. Originally, the common law of England was nothing more than a set of unwritten regulations and customs that acted as guidelines in settling disputes, determining the inheritance of property, and dealing with persons who committed misdeeds of a serious antisocial nature. As time passed, court decisions were made a part of the common law. Thereafter, the common law was further enlarged by legislative enactments and was brought to this country by the colonists to act as guidelines for conduct.

MODERN CRIMINAL LAW

Today, the criminal law of the various states is a written set of regulations that is largely the result of legislative action. These regulations are recorded in some official record within the states and are often referred to as the penal code. Criminal laws vary somewhat between the states. In some states, there is no reliance upon the common law to determine what is right and wrong. The statutes spell out specifically the act that is made a crime and the punishment that may be inflicted for the commission of such an act. For example, the code may state that manslaughter is the unlawful killing of a human being without malice. This definition will be followed by a statement that one convicted of manslaughter may be imprisoned for a period not to exceed four years. The statutes of other states provide that "manslaughter" is punishable by imprisonment not to exceed a prescribed number of years. But this statute does not define what act constitutes manslaughter. The courts must then look to the common law to determine the interpretation of manslaughter.

CLASSIFICATION OF CRIMES AND PUNISHMENT

In our present form of jurisprudence, not only do we tell people what a criminal act is, but we also tell them the punishment they may be subjected to if they commit the act. The following definition is generally found in the statutes of the states: A crime or public offense is an act committed or omitted in violation of a law forbidding or commanding it and to which is annexed, upon conviction, one or more of several punishments. The basic forms of punishment are death, imprisonment, fines, removal from office, or disqualification to hold and enjoy any office of honor, trust, or profit. We have classified criminal laws in accordance with their seriousness to society and have stated the punishment that could be inflicted upon conviction. Earlier in our history, we classified criminal laws as treason, felonies, and misdemeanors. Most states eliminated treason as a category of crime and listed it merely as another felony violation. Thus, two classifications remained: felonies and misdemeanors. However, in recent years, many states have added a third and a fourth classification, an infraction and a state jail felony.

With the felony being the most serious crime, the violator is subjected to the most severe punishment either by death, imprisonment in a state prison, or carrying a sentence of more than one year. The misdemeanor, being a less serious threat to the existence of a society, carries a lesser punishment, the most severe of which is usually not more than a year in jail. The infraction is the least serious crime, carrying a fine or probation but, in most states, no imprisonment. The state jail felony is a crime that is more serious than a misdemeanor but not as serious as a felony.

The procedure by which one accused of a crime is brought to trial and punished is known as a criminal action, and the one prosecuted is known as the defendant. Criminal actions are commenced with the filing of a formal written document with the appropriate court. In some states, there is no requirement to file a formal written document in cases involving infractions. The charging document is referred to as an accusatory pleading. In most felony prosecutions, the document will be an indictment or an information. In misdemeanor prosecutions, the accusatory pleading is generally a complaint, as explained in Chapter 4. When a criminal law is broken, it is done against society as a whole, so that the prosecutive action is brought in the name of the people; thus, the action is generally entitled "People versus [the defendant]," "State versus [the defendant]," or "Commonwealth versus [the defendant]," stating the defendant's name.

THE JUSTICE SYSTEM

When examining the criminal justice system, we will discover many technical rules and procedures that must be followed. These procedures are the result of a long evolutionary process. The process is interesting, particularly the development of the right of an accused to a trial by jury. The trial by jury, for example, is regarded by many as one of the greatest achievements of our justice system.

When considering trial by jury, we immediately visualize a comfortable courtroom with a judge sitting behind a desk on a raised platform and presiding over the trial proceedings in a dignified and formal manner. We see the jury sitting in the jury box listening to the testimony of witnesses who have some knowledge about the facts of the case, and the prosecuting attorney presenting evidence in an effort to prove the defendant guilty beyond a reasonable doubt. We also tend to see the defense attorney as a Perry Mason or Ben Matlock. We may also picture the defendant conferring with the attorney throughout the trial. At the conclusion of the trial, we visualize the jury deliberating on the evidence that has been presented, and their returning a verdict of guilt or innocence. The actual practice may, however, be quite different.

Guilt or innocence has not always been decided by a jury trial. In fact, the jury system as we know it today is of comparatively recent origin, coming into existence at the start of the eighteenth century. The early history of jurisprudence efforts to determine guilt or innocence were primarily calls upon the supernatural or for signs from God.

As we trace the development of the trial by jury, our concentration centers primarily on England, from which most of our judicial system came. Many blank spots are encountered in tracing the history of a jury trial because of the lack of records. But it is known that the Christian church played an important role in the development of much of the law and procedure of early England. Most of the early records available for study of the beginnings of the judicial system were prepared by the clergy and are largely incomplete. These records were not compiled as a history of the time but were merely a documentation of certain customs and events of the era.

The Invasion of England

History states that Julius Caesar invaded England in 55 B.C. and that Christianity was taught there as early as A.D. 64. At that time, Christianity was not accepted by the Romans, and any activity of the Christian church throughout the Roman Empire had to be underground. Yet despite the persecution of Christians, their church continued to grow. Religious societies and new congregations were being formed. Rules, regulations, and laws were being established to be followed by the Christians, but they were unlawful in the eyes of the Romans. However, these laws were soon to become the laws of the continent of Europe and England. By the year A.D. 200, Roman jurisprudence had reached its peak, and from that time on, Roman law began to decline. Instead of looking forward, the Roman leaders were looking backward to what had been. The Roman persecution of Christians terminated in A.D. 303; and in A.D. 313, Christianity was established as a lawful religion. Almost immediately the bishops of the Christian church involved themselves in politics, and they soon became as powerful as the emperor. The Church law, also known as the canon or ecclesiastical law, began to dominate the lives of people throughout Europe.

There is little doubt that Julius Caesar imported much of the Roman law to England, but the Romans did not have an easy life there because other peoples invaded England. The Saxons conducted raids on the coastal plains as early as the third century and continued to do so thereafter. The Romans are said to have abandoned England sometime before A.D. 429, and the Anglo-Saxon invasions began on a large scale in A.D. 449. The Anglo-Saxons are believed to have established laws, since they were known to have existed on the continent of Europe at the time, but records of the Anglo-Saxon laws and procedures are mostly fragmentary. Those that are available shed little light upon the judicial procedures of that time. It is known that kings established themselves and ruled until they were overthrown or died. A king formulated his own laws, which were known as the king's laws, laws of the land, temporal laws, or secular laws. The Anglo-Saxons held reign in England until the Norman Conquest in A.D. 1066. Prior to this time, England was experiencing considerable strife. Much of the administration of justice was left to the bishops of the church to be processed through the ecclesiastical courts, and the canon law continued to play a dominant role. But as kings began to establish themselves more securely, they continued to formulate more and more laws affecting the people.

These laws were enforced through the king's courts, known as secular or temporal courts. The king's court was presided over by the king's justices.

Although there was an effort made to separate the jurisdiction of the secular courts and the ecclesiastical courts, rivalry still arose, particularly as it related to appeals. The ecclesiastical courts had jurisdiction over all matters pertaining to people's souls and church-related matters, including violations by the clergy. All laypeople were subject to both the ecclesiastical laws and the secular laws. The ecclesiastical laws regulated many affairs of the layperson's life, such as marriage, divorce, and the distribution of property after death. Through the ecclesiastical courts, laypeople could be tried and punished for various offenses, including such crimes as adultery, fornication, incest, bigamy, defamation, and blasphemy. Originally, the ecclesiastical courts were presided over by the bishops of the church, but as the caseload increased, charges were often heard by the bishops' assistants, known as archdeacons. Crimes of murder or theft and attacks on property or persons were violations of the secular laws, and the offender was tried and punished by the secular courts.

The Magna Charta

When an offender was convicted, his or her property was usually forfeited. This forfeiture became a source of great revenue to the church or king, depending upon what law was broken. In order to increase their revenue, kings frequently made various acts a crime in order to confiscate the property of a landowner or merchant. How the people fared depended largely on the compassion of the king at the time. In tracing our judicial procedure, frequent mention is made of the Magna Charta (also spelled Magna Carta) and its influence on people's rights. This document is considered to be the forerunner of the present "due process" rights, since the Magna Charta granted to the people of England certain political and civil rights. The Magna Charta, which is the result of a king's being unduly oppressive to the people of England, was signed during the reign of King John, who was known as the "cruel ruler."

King John took over the reign of England in A.D. 1199 after the death of his brother, King Richard, the "Lion Hearted." King John was described as being clever but greedy and tyrannical in ruling his people. Conditions under him became unbearable for both the nobleman and the commoner. In an effort to improve the situation, the noblemen gathered and prepared a document containing certain resolutions that they felt were in the best interest of the people. King John was maneuvered onto the Plains of Runnymede on June 15, 1215, where he

King John shown signing the Magna Carta (1215). Undated illustration, after a painting by Chapel. (*Source:* CORBIS)

was forced to sign the Magna Charta. Among other resolutions in the Magna Charta was the guarantee that, stated briefly, held that no free man shall be seized and imprisoned except by judgment of his peers or by the law of the land. Contrary to the beliefs of many, this guarantee did not give to people the right to a trial by jury. Trial by jury, as we know it today, did not come into existence until the latter part of the seventeenth century. It merely meant that when a criminal accusation was made against a person, he or she was entitled to have the charge reviewed by a council consisting of members of the community. If the council concluded that the charge was well-founded, they would command that the accused be held to answer for trial. Guilt or innocence was decided by the procedures of the time—trial by ordeal or trial by battle. This council, which became known as a grand jury, comprised between sixteen and twenty-four persons.

The right of an accused to appeal his or her case was practically unknown in early judicial procedure. But as time passed, a limited right of appeal was granted. Appeals in the ecclesiastical courts, in the twelfth century particularly, were taken to the bishop from the court presided over by an archdeacon, and from the bishop to the archbishop. The final appeal was to the pope in Rome. The final appeal from the king's court was to the king. Although the kings for the most part respected the jurisdiction of the ecclesiastical courts, this final appeal to the pope was upsetting to the kings. The inevitable result of this final appeal to the pope was to give recognition to the fact that the canon law was a worldwide system and was not limited to any national boundary. The kings were jealous of the pope's outside influence, over which the kings had little control, so that they often tried to restrict this influence. King William I declared that no one was to receive a letter from the pope unless it was first shown to him. Later, other kings declared that there should be no appeal to the pope without consent of the king. Yet with all the kings' jealousy of the pope, King John, in his desperation, sought the assistance of Pope Innocent III after he was forced to sign the Magna Charta on June 15, 1215. King John requested that the pope annul the Magna Charta, which he did on August 25, 1215. The pope further forbade the king to enforce the Magna Charta upon the grounds that this charter was extorted from King John by force and that the terms of the charter were "dishonorable, unjust, unlawful, and derogatory" to the king. But after the death of King John in October 1216, the Magna Charta was revised, and its provisions were again placed into operation. It was expected that kings thereafter would comply with these provisions.

Early Treatment of Offenders

With the church playing the paramount role in the administration of justice in the early history of England, it is only natural that the deity was called upon to assist when efforts were made to determine the guilt or innocence of one accused of a crime. From the time of the invasion of England by the Romans until the Norman Conquest, a person accused of breaking the law could be handled in one of four ways:

- The community could make war on the offender;
- the offender might be exposed to the vengeance of those he had offended;
- the offender might be permitted to make atonement for his crime; or
- the community might inflict upon the offender the penalty already established for the particular crime after his or her guilt had been determined.

Outlawry

Perhaps the earliest method of handling one who was accused of committing a crime was to wage war upon the accused. It was held that when one had gone to war with the community by committing a crime, the community was not only entitled to, but bound to, make war upon the offender. The accused was declared "outlawed," or without the protection of the law. Thus, the community was to pursue and slay the offender, burn the offender's house, ravage his or her land, and take his or her possessions. As time passed, this form of punishment was inflicted upon only the person of lowest status, the slave. The declaration was, in effect, the imposition of the death penalty, because without the protection of the community, the individual would soon be killed by others or by wild beasts.

The Blood Feud

If the accused was not outlawed, the community might leave the accused unprotected against those he or she had offended, whereupon they might avenge themselves by taking whatever action they deemed appropriate in accordance with the crime committed, even to the slaying of the offender. Some of the offender's relatives might be slain also, since not all persons were of the same status in the early history of England. The lowest status was that of slave; next was the serf, who was bound to native soil instead of being the absolute property of a master such as the slave; then status continued up to the highest, that of king. In between were a number of other classes of persons, such as the barons and knights, who were referred to as "thegns"; the freeman workers were known as "ceorls." It was alleged that six ceorls were the equivalent of one thegn. Thus, if a ceorl should slay a thegn, the slayer and five of his or her kinsfolk also would have to be slain. However, it might take time to locate the kinsfolk in order to slay them, and other members of the family might inherit the responsibility of avenging the crime; thus, the blood feud took place.

Atonement

There is no doubt that blood feuds were not the most popular method of settling a crime that had been committed, particularly when the blood feud reached a point when relatives of the offended or offender became involved in avenging the crime. It is only natural that the relatives would prefer to conduct some type of financial bargaining rather than engage in a lengthy hunt for the offender or the offender's relatives and then become involved in a bloody entanglement to avenge a crime. Frequently, a price of so many cows or horses, or a sum of money, was agreed upon, which the offender or the relatives could pay in order to bring about peace in the community. Thus, the system of atonement was established. Each particular crime developed a designated price that had to be paid when that crime was committed. Even murder could be atoned under certain circumstances depending upon the status of the offender and the offended. Atonement was an accepted procedure in most instances, not only by the offended but also by the church and the king, since each would receive a portion of the atonement depending upon the crime. For example, if a couple were caught committing adultery, the man paid the king in order to regain his peace in the community, whereas the woman would pay the church for the sin she had committed. If the offender was without possessions, in order to make atonement, he or she might have to go into bondage or be subjected to a prescribed punishment. The system of atonement is the forerunner of the present procedures of fining persons for having committed certain crimes.

Trial by Ordeal

Since not all persons were permitted to make an atonement, other procedures had to be devised to bring those guilty of having committed a crime to justice. One of the most prevalent methods utilized in determining guilt or innocence of an accused was the trial by ordeal. The accused would be required to perform some physical feat. This procedure was a call to the deity for assistance in determining the guilt or innocence of the accused. The theory was that if the accused were innocent, God would enable him or her to perform the required ordeal. If guilty, the accused would fail in his or her performance. The accused would then be subjected to the prescribed punishment for the crime committed. When punishment was inflicted, it was usually severe. The punishment may have been death by hanging, beheading, stoning, burning, or drowning. If the punishment did not amount to death, the guilty one might have one or both ears cut off, have the nose or upper lip severed, have a hand or foot cut off, be castrated, or be flogged, tarred and feathered. People who had falsely accused someone might lose their tongues. In addition, they might be banished from the land (a punishment that was later referred to as outlawry) or be sold into slavery.

The ordeal that the accused might be subjected to varied greatly in procedure, but whatever it may have been, it was preceded by an oath by the accused; this was an oath of innocence to God. If found guilty by failing in the ordeal, the accused would not only suffer the punishment inflicted upon him or her but also would receive divine punishment according to the belief of the time. Most of the ordeals were supervised by priests.

The most prevalent ordeal used was that of the "hot iron." The accused would appear before the altar, give the oath, and then have a hand sprinkled with holy water. A red-hot iron would be laid across the hand, and the accused would take nine paces and drop the iron. The accused would return to the altar where a priest would bind the burned hand. Three days later, the accused would return to the priest and have the hand unbound. If the wound had healed, the accused was found innocent; if it had not healed, the accused was adjudged guilty and would then be subjected to the prescribed punishment in accordance with the crime committed.

Another type of ordeal was that of the "boiling pot of water" from which the accused might be required to remove a large rock. The same binding procedure would be followed as in the instance of the hot iron. It would seem that under this system there would be few acquittals, but apparently many priests would feel compassion for those accused and would assist God in determining guilt or innocence. Records reveal that in one period there were eighty-three acquittals out of eighty-four trials by ordeal. Upon viewing the wound, the priest declared that it had healed. This record of acquittals caused the king much displeasure because of the loss of revenue.

The accused might be subjected to other types of ordeals in addition to the hot iron and boiling pot of water. For example, the accused might be required to walk barefoot and blindfolded over nine red-hot ploughshares laid lengthwise at unequal distances, or the accused might have his or her thumbs tied to the toes and be thrown into a lake or pond. If the accused did not sink, he or she was declared innocent. Also used was the "ordeal of the accursed morsel," whereby a piece of bread was prayed over. It was then given to the accused, who was to swallow it. If the person choked, he or she was found guilty. The "decision of the cross" involved the laying of two pieces of wood on an altar, one of which had been marked with a cross. After a prayer asking for a sign from God, a priest or young boy would pick up one of the pieces of wood without looking at it. If it bore the mark of a cross, the accused was deemed to be innocent.

Trial by Battle

Another method of determining guilt or innocence was trial by battle. In this method, the accused and the accuser would go into actual combat with each other, usually using battle axes. Before the battle took place, both participants would swear to God that they were right. It is believed that the trial-by-battle procedure was brought to England by the Normans. It is known that trial by battle was used as a method of determining guilt on the continent before the Norman Conquest, and there is no record of its use in England before the Norman invasion. The church displayed less favor to trial by battle than to trial by ordeal because it involved a certain amount of pagan ceremony. However, trial by battle was tolerated because it also involved a call to God, and the one who came forth the victor did so not from brute force but through the assistance of God.

Trial by Compurgation

The church was always seeking ways to determine the guilt or innocence of an accused person without the tortures of the ordeal or the bloodshed of the battle, particularly when its own hierarchy was involved. It is believed that determining guilt by compurgation, through oath helpers or wager of the law, by which terms it was also known, originated within the church, but the method was not confined to church personnel. For a time, it was used for the laypeople, since it related to violations of the secular and ecclesiastical laws. Trial by compurgation originated on the continent of Europe, but there are records indicating its existence in England before the Norman Conquest.

In the trial by compurgation, both the accused and the accuser would take an oath to God. The accused would swear to his or her innocence, and the accuser would swear that the accusation was true. Each would be assisted by oath helpers, or compurgators. The compurgators of the accused would swear to God that the oath given by the accused was a true oath. The accuser would be accompanied by oath helpers who would swear to his or her truthfulness.

Initially, the accused's oath helpers were often relatives, and if the accused should fail in the oath-taking experience, the matter might turn into a blood feud; consequently, the relatives were usually very willing to assist, although their assistance frequently led to perjury. Because of the unreliability of the relatives as oath helpers, the accused soon had to select oath helpers from persons in the community who were not relatives. If the accused had a bad reputation, he or she might experience difficulty in getting oath helpers. An oath helper might be compared with a character witness in our present judicial system. In some instances, the accused had to select oath helpers from a list supplied to him or her by the accuser or by one of the priests or justices involved. Many times the accused would be unknown to these persons, so that they were permitted to swear to the truthfulness of the accused's oath to the best of their knowledge and belief. The number of oath helpers that was called to assist varied considerably. Any number between four and sixty-six was called, but most frequently the number was twelve.

Although trial by compurgation was used for a time, it did not replace the trial by ordeal or the trial by battle. As time passed, the wording of the oath to be taken by the accused and the oath helpers became so complex that repeating it without error was almost impossible. If an error was made, the accused was automatically declared guilty, and the prescribed punishment was inflicted. Thus, with the technical language of the oath and the general unreliability of the oath helpers, trial by compurgation was somewhat of a farce. It therefore soon fell into decay and disuse, and other methods were adopted to determine guilt or innocence.

The Establishment of Juries

As early as the ninth century, Frankish kings on the European continent would summon, through a public officer, the most trustworthy people of a community. These people were then placed under oath to answer truthfully all questions directed at them during sessions with the king. These sessions, which were called inquests, did not necessarily arise out of criminal activity or litigation but were often merely fact-finding meetings in which the king could gather information about the community. During the inquest, the king might ask the following kinds of questions: What were the rights of the king in their particular community? Who were the landowners, and how much land did they own? What were the customs of their area? Who had a better title to a piece of property, John or James? The number of people summoned to serve on this body varied from three to seventy-two, but twelve was the number most frequently called.

In addition to seeking the answers to these kinds of questions, the king would ask this body whom they suspected of having committed murder, rape, or robbery. This body was the first crude form of an accusatory jury. But the Frankish kings did not always confine the use of the jury merely to accuse a person of a crime; in fact, they often called upon the jury to render a verdict of guilt or innocence. In order to collect their revenue for crimes committed, these kings frequently preferred the verdict of this body of people over that of a trial by ordeal, battle, or compurgation. During the early use of the jury held by kings, it is not inconceivable that people may have found themselves accused and convicted without even knowing that an accusation had been directed toward them.

To collect the wages of sin, the Frankish bishops were also known to have used the inquest to determine who had committed crimes against the church. Records reflect that certain Frankish bishops selected a number of trustworthy men from an assembled laity, or congregation, who were administered an oath to tell the truth and conceal nothing for love or hate, reward or kinship, and to report their suspicions about their neighbors who might have sinned against the church. These suspected sinners then would be put through the ordeal.

There is little record of the inquest being used in England until after the Norman Conquest. However, Ethelred the Unready, King of England, is alleged to have decreed early in the eleventh century that a "moot" was to be held in every "wapentake," and that the twelve eldest "thegns" were to go out with the "reeve" and swear on a "relic" that they would neither accuse an innocent person nor conceal a guilty person. In our terminology, a meeting was to be held in every county subdivision where the eldest trustworthy members of that community were to go out with a local representative of the king and swear on some religious object that they would neither accuse an innocent person nor conceal one guilty of a crime.

Accusatory Juries

Hardly had England been conquered in A.D. 1066 when William the Conqueror summoned bodies of people from all the communities to assist him in obtaining general as well as criminal information concerning their respective areas. In the mid–twelfth century, King Henry II made great use of the juries to determine what cases his justices should hear as they rode their circuits through the kingdom. He would summon twelve of the most trustworthy noblemen of a hundred (or county) and four men from each township, who were sworn to hear accusations and determine whether they were well founded. If so, the accused would be given an opportunity to prove his or her innocence by one of the various trial procedures.

King Henry II also suggested that the bishops of the ecclesiastical courts should not rely merely upon an accuser's unsworn suggestion that one had committed a crime before subjecting the accused to the ordeal, battle, or compurgation. Rather, the bishops should have the sheriff summon twelve of the most lawful men of the neighborhood to hear an accusation to determine its reliability before the accused be put on trial.

The accusatory jury had become such an important part of justice by the beginning of the thirteenth century that when King John ignored its use and acted upon his own knowledge of accusations, the right to an accusatory jury was made a part of the Magna Charta. Included in the provisions of the Magna Charta was this guarantee: "No freeman shall be taken, or imprisoned, or disseized, or outlawed, or exiled, in any way harmed—nor will we go upon or send upon him—save by the lawful judgment of his peers or by the law of the land." It was expected that King John and all following kings would comply with this guarantee—the forerunner of our grand jury system.

The Development of Trial by Jury

As time passed, greater use of the jury was made. It was called upon not only to decide whether an accusation was well founded but also, as in the case of some of the Frankish kings' juries, to render a verdict of guilt or innocence. It was eventually believed that a jury should not be both an accusatory jury and a trial or verdict jury. Consequently, one jury would be summoned to hear the accusation (later referred to as the grand jury), and another jury was summoned to render a verdict of guilt or innocence (known as the petit jury). The petit, or trial, jury, which usually consisted of twelve persons initially functioned entirely differently from the juries of today. These early trial juries assembled and stated what they knew about a particular crime, or they might be assembled and commanded to go forth into the countryside and ascertain facts about the alleged crime. Then the jurors would talk to neighbors, pick up hearsay information and rumors, and would undoubtedly be contacted by the accused and the accuser. After gathering their evidence, they would reassemble and draw a conclusion as to guilt or innocence. If the accused was found guilty, the prescribed punishment for the crime was inflicted upon him or her. Soon it was not just the jurors who expressed what they had learned about the crime: witnesses might appear before the jury and relate what they knew about the accusation. Since the knowledge of the witnesses was often no more than rumor or hearsay, the jury might give little weight to the testimony of the witnesses and decide contrary to the general consensus of the witnesses. This outcome was particularly true if the witnesses believed the accused to be innocent. The reason that the jury might decide contrary to the belief of the witnesses was that the jury was fearful of rendering a false verdict, thus denying the king his revenue. The jurors knew that the king's justices often had advance information about a crime because of reports from the sheriffs and the coroners. If the jurors made a false verdict in the eyes of the justices, they would be required to make atonement and were even punished in some instances.

Because of the danger of conviction in a trial by jury, an accused would frequently revert to the trial by ordeal. However, after the ordeal was abolished around A.D. 1215 and trial by compurgation had met with disfavor, the only procedure remaining was trial by battle. But if the accuser was a woman or a noncombatant, trial by battle was impossible, so it was unknown what should be done with the accused who refused a trial by jury or who put himself or herself upon the country, as the jury trial was sometimes referred to. Occasionally, under the circumstances, the accused was hanged immediately, or in other instances, was imprisoned for a year and given only a sip of water daily and a small morsel of bread. Sometimes the accused would be imprisoned and weights would be placed upon his or her chest in increasing amounts until the person submitted to a trial by jury. Often the accused would prefer being crushed to death in an effort to save his or her possessions for his or her family, rather than having them confiscated by the king, should the jury pass a conviction.

As time passed and the king could no longer confiscate property as payment for crimes and jurors were no longer punished or required to make atonement for possible erroneous verdicts, greater reliability was placed on the testimony of witnesses. Accordingly, the development of trial by jury progressed to what we know today. However, it still had a way to go even when the colonists settled in this country. The Maryland Archives reveal that on September 22, 1656, a judge in Patuxent, Maryland, impaneled a jury of seven married women and four single women to determine the guilt of one Judith Catchpole, who was accused of murdering her child. She denied guilt and even denied having a child. The judge then commanded the jury to go forth and determine first whether Judith had a child and, if so, whether she murdered it. At this time, the jury was to "go forth into the countryside and seek information" rather than depend upon the sworn testimony of witnesses. It is also interesting that a jury of eleven instead of twelve was impaneled, because long before that time, the number of twelve jurors for a trial was well established in England. By the thirteenth century, the usual number for a petit jury in England was twelve. By the fourteenth century, a jury of twelve persons was firmly established, and thereafter the number of twelve persons composing a trial jury seems to have developed some superstitious reverence.

Why a jury of twelve evolved is lost in the annals of history, but it is believed to have been based upon Christ's having chosen twelve apostles. It has been alleged that twelve was a popular number at the time of Christ, as witnessed by the twelve tribes of Israel, the twelve tablets, Solomon's twelve judges, and the twelve signs of the zodiac. Thus, it is highly likely that the jury comprising twelve persons is based upon that fact, especially since the church played a dominant role in the development of the judicial systems in both Europe and England. One of the ancient kings of Europe, Morgan of Gla-Morgan, is alleged to have adopted a form of trial by jury called the Apostolic Law, which declared that since Christ and his twelve apostles were finally to judge the world, so human tribunals should comprise the king and twelve wise men. Also at a later time, the following oath is alleged to have been required of a trial jury of twelve: "Hear this, ye justices, that I will speak of that which ye shall ask of me on the part of the king, and I will do faithfully to the best of my endeavor. So help me God, and these holy Apostles."

When the colonists came to North America, they were well indoctrinated with the view that a trial jury should comprise twelve persons, although it is known that one or two of the colonies permitted a jury to comprise fewer than twelve. It is not entirely clear from historical data whether permitting fewer than twelve was a conscious effort to break from tradition, a defiance of the king and England, or whether it was because of the small number of people in the colonies involved, making it difficult to find twelve qualified jurors. This situation may have accounted for the fact that the judge in the Catchpole case impaneled only eleven women instead of twelve. It was also a break with tradition to impanel women instead of men on the jury, since women were not generally considered to be qualified as jurors.

Historical Development of the Bill of Rights

As we approach the study of the judicial procedure followed today, it is important to review some of the rights and guarantees granted to one accused of a crime. These rights and guarantees are to be found either in the Constitution of the United States or in the constitutions and statutes of the various states. Some of these rights are based upon the common law of England, but others were developed over time as a result of dealing with accused persons.

Returning now to the Magna Charta, we find that it created no panacea, but it did ensure to the people certain liberties, which they had been denied previously, and made way for the establishment of due process of law. But the people of England continued to be subjected to many oppressive practices, and many were persecuted because of their religious beliefs. To escape these practices, a number of people left for North America to establish colonies. The king considered these colonies to be his possessions; the colonists were still under the rule of the king, and all too often that rule lay heavily upon them. They were taxed excessively and were generally oppressed. When they objected, they were often taken to England for trial. As time passed, the colonists increased their opposition. This became a source of irritation to the king, who sent his armies to enforce his rule. Suspected objectors were frequently subjected to searches and seizures without cause and imprisoned without justification.

As a result of the king's extreme actions, the colonists banded together and adopted a resolution declaring their political independence from England. This document is the Declaration of Independence, which announced to the world that the colonists were serious in their aim to become an independent nation, and it asked for understanding and compassion from other nations. The Declaration of Independence set forth the reasons for their actions and grievances against the king. Among the charges were that the king

> . . . has refused to assent to laws, the most wholesome and necessary for the public good; . . . has obstructed the administration of justice; . . . has kept among us, in times of peace, standing armies without the consent of our legisla-

tures; . . . has deprived many of the benefits of trial by jury; . . . has transported us beyond seas to be tried for pretended offenses.

By reviewing the Declaration of Independence, we are able to appreciate the conditions of the time and the conflicts experienced by the people of America. The Declaration became the basis of the guarantees later to be embodied in our Constitution.

The king did not take this Declaration of Independence lightly. He sent additional armies to subdue the colonies, resulting in the Revolutionary War. When peace was restored in 1783, the colonies became a self-governing nation. A governmental structure had to be formed, and laws had to be made for governing the people. Although various efforts at governmental structures were attempted, each revealed weaknesses. In 1787, representatives of the colonies, now referred to as states, met in Philadelphia to attempt again to formulate an acceptable and a workable governmental structure. The result of this conference, known as the Constitutional Convention, was the United States Constitution, which was finally adopted in 1789. It established three branches of government: executive, legislative, and judicial.

As the various state representatives reviewed this document, they felt that a vital weakness still remained in its structure: The people were not guaranteed protection against oppression should this central government become too strong and powerful. Therefore, it was agreed that certain additions should be made to the Constitution. Again representatives of the states met in Congress during 1789 and proposed twelve amendments to the Constitution. Ten of there were adopted in 1791 and are known as the Bill of Rights, which guarantees certain rights to the people. The two amendments that were not adopted did not pertain to guarantees but were related to the legislative structure of the government. Because of the importance of these amendments to the administration of justice, we review them next.

The Bill of Rights

Amendment I: Restriction on Powers of Congress. Congress shall make no law respecting an establishment of religion, or prohibiting the free exercise thereof, or abridging the freedom of speech, or of the press; or the right of the people peaceably to assemble, and to petition the government for a redress of grievances.

Amendment II: Right to Bear Arms. A well-regulated militia being necessary to the security of a free State, the right of the people to keep and bear arms shall not be infringed.

Amendment III: Billeting of Soldiers. No soldier shall, in time of peace, be quartered in any house without the consent of the owner; nor in time of war, but in a manner to be prescribed by law.

Amendment IV: Seizures, Searches and Warrants. The right of the people to be secure in their persons, houses, papers, and effects, against unreasonable searches and seizures shall not be violated, and no warrants shall issue but upon probable cause, supported by oath or affirmation, and particularly describing the place to be searched and the persons or things to be seized.

Amendment V: Criminal Proceedings, Condemnation of Property. No person shall be held to answer for a capital or otherwise infamous crime, unless on a presentment or indictment of a grand jury, except in cases arising in the land or naval forces, or in the militia, when in actual service in time of war or public danger; nor shall any person be subject for the same offense to be twice put in jeopardy of life or limb; nor shall be compelled in any criminal case, to be a witness against himself; nor be deprived of life, liberty, or property, without due process of law, nor shall private property be taken for public use without just compensation.

Amendment VI: Mode of Trial in Criminal Proceedings. In all criminal prosecutions the accused shall enjoy the right to a speedy and public trial, by an impartial jury of the State and district wherein the crime shall have been committed, which district shall have been previously ascertained by law; and to be informed of the nature and cause of the accusation; to be confronted with the witnesses against him; to have compulsory process for obtaining witnesses in his favor, and to have the assistance of counsel for his defense.

Amendment VII: Trial by Jury. In suits at common law, where the value in controversy shall exceed twenty dollars, the right of trial by jury shall be preserved; and no fact tried by jury, shall be otherwise reexamined in any court of the United States than according to the rules of common law.

Amendment VIII: Involuntary Servitude. Excessive bail shall not be required, nor excessive fines imposed, nor cruel and unusual punishment inflicted.

Amendment IX: Certain Rights Not Denied to the People. The enumeration in the Constitution of certain rights shall not be construed to deny or disparage others retained by the people.

Amendment X: State Rights. The powers not delegated to the United States by the Constitution, nor prohibited by it to the States, are reserved to the states, respectively, or to the people.

Due Process of Law

As we study these amendments, we must remind ourselves that when they were adopted, the oppressive conditions that brought them into being were still vivid in the memory of the people. Thus, these guarantees were to protect the people against any action that might be attempted by the federal government and as such were applicable only to federal officers. The states, as provided in the Ninth and Tenth Amendments, were free to establish their own guarantees relating to the actions permitted by state and local officials. We will find that the Fourth, Fifth, Sixth, and Eighth Amendments are most significant in the administration of justice.

As time passed, slavery and involuntary servitude, such as forcing men to build public roads or to serve in a state militia without pay, were permitted in some states. After the Civil War, the Thirteenth Amendment, abolishing slavery, was added to the United States Constitution. To prohibit other oppressive and arbitrary actions by the states, the Fourteenth Amendment was adopted in 1868. This amendment held that:

> All persons born or naturalized in the United States, and subject to the jurisdiction thereof, are citizens of the United States and of the State wherein they reside. No State shall make or enforce any law which shall abridge the privileges or immunities of citizens of the United States; nor shall any State deprive any person of life, liberty, or property, without due process of law; nor deny to any person within its jurisdiction the equal protection of the laws.

It should be emphasized that this amendment was directed to the states to prevent them from depriving any person of life, liberty, or property without due process of law. However, the amendment raised a question regarding the interpretation of the term "due process of law" as it related to the administration of justice. The courts later concluded that if an accused had his "day in court" with the right to appeal a conviction, the due process of law clause of the Fourteenth Amendment had been satisfied. We will find in our study of the judicial procedure throughout this text that the United States Supreme Court has since placed a different interpretation on the meaning of the due process of law clause of the Fourteenth Amendment. The Supreme Court has ruled that the following particular Bill of Rights guarantees are applicable to the states: the Fourth Amendment right to be free from unreasonable searches and seizures and to have any illegally seized evidence excluded from criminal trials;[2] the Fifth Amendment privilege against self-incrimination[3] and the guarantee against double jeopardy,[4] and the Sixth Amendment rights to counsel,[5] to a speedy trial,[6] to a public trial,[7] to confront opposing witnesses,[8] and to an impartial jury.[9] Decisions making these guarantees applicable to the states will be discussed as the judicial procedure is further explained. For practical purposes, these amendments are as applicable to state and local officers as they are to federal officers.

In addition to the guarantees provided by the Bill of Rights, each state has furnished to the people within that state additional guarantees and rights, which are

**RELATIONSHIP OF THE BILL OF RIGHTS
AND THE FOURTEENTH AMENDMENT
TO THE CONSTITUTIONAL RIGHTS OF THE ACCUSED**

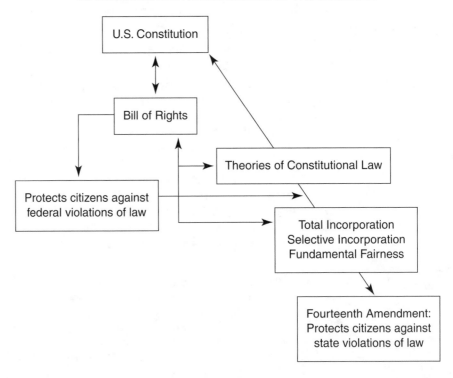

contained in the state statutes on the state constitution. To ensure that the guarantees of the Bill of Rights and the state statutes are properly afforded the people, court structures have been established.

COURT STRUCTURES

The court system in the United States is based upon the principle of federalism.[10] The first Congress established a federal court system, and the individual states were permitted to continue their own judicial structure. There was general agreement among our nation's founding fathers that individual states needed to retain significant autonomy from federal control. Under this concept of federalism, the United States developed as a loose confederation of semi-independent states, with the federal court system acting in a very limited manner. In the early history of our nation, most cases were tried in state courts, and it was only later that the federal government and the federal judiciary began to exercise jurisdiction over crimes and civil matters. Jurisdiction in this context simply means the ability of the court to enforce laws and punish individuals who violate those laws.

As a result of this historical evolution, a dual system of state and federal courts exists today. Therefore, federal and state courts may have concurrent jurisdiction over specific crimes. For example, a person who robs a bank may be tried and convicted in state court for robbery and then tried and convicted in federal court for the federal offense of robbery of a federally chartered savings institution.

A second characteristic of the American court system is that it performs its duties with little or no supervision. A supreme court justice does not exercise supervision over lower court judges in the same way that a government supervisor or manager exercises control over his or her employees. The U.S. Supreme Court and the various state supreme courts exercise supervision only in the sense that they hear appellate cases from lower courts and establish certain procedures for these courts.

A third feature of our court system is that of specialization that occurs primarily at the state and local level. In many states, courts of limited jurisdiction hear misdemeanor cases. Other state courts of general jurisdiction try felonies. Still other courts may be designated as juvenile courts and hear only matters involving juveniles. This process also occurs in certain civil courts that hear only family law matters, probate matters, or civil cases involving damages. At the federal level, there are courts, such as bankruptcy court, that hear only cases dealing with specific matters.

The fourth characteristic of the American court system is the organization of state and federal courts into geographic areas. In many jurisdictions, these are called judicial districts and contain various levels of courts. For example, on the federal level, the Ninth Circuit Court of Appeals has district (trial) courts that hear matters within certain specific boundaries and an appellate court that hears all appeals from cases within that area. Several studies have been conducted regarding the difference in sentences for the same type of crime in geographic district courts. For instance, in Iowa the average sentence for motor vehicle theft was forty-seven months, whereas the average sentence for the same offense in New York was fourteen months.[11] This observation shouldn't be taken as a criticism;

rather, it may reflect different social values and attitudes within specific geographic areas.

After a person is arrested, unless the charge against him or her is dismissed, some prosecutive action must be taken, which will occur in the appropriate court. In order for students to have a clearer understanding of the judicial proceedings from the time of arrest through sentencing, a discussion of the court system follows. Although the court system may vary somewhat among the states, it is basically the same. The states are divided into territorial divisions known as counties, except in Louisiana, where they are called parishes, and in Alaska, which is divided into four judicial districts. Each county, parish, or district has its own trial court system. The chief trial court is known as the superior court, district court, or circuit court, depending upon the title that the court is given in a particular state. This court, in addition to trying civil matters, will hear trials involving felony cases and possibly some more serious, or high, misdemeanor charges. Generally, this court holds forth in the county seat. Although these courts are technically county courts, they are referred to in many books on judicial procedures as state courts, as distinguished from federal courts.

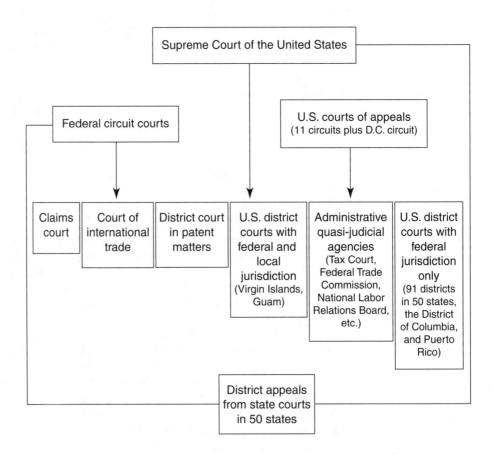

THE STATE COURT SYSTEM

Historically, each of the thirteen states had its own unique court structure. This independence continued after the American Revolution and resulted in widespread differences among the various states; some of these differences still exist today. Because each state adopted its own system of courts, the consequence was a poorly planned and confusing judicial structure. As a result, there have been several reform movements whose purpose has been to streamline and modernize this system.

Many state courts can be divided into three levels: trial courts, appellate courts, and state supreme courts. It is in trial courts that criminal cases start, evidence is presented, the defendant is found guilty or not guilty, and a sentence is imposed if the defendant is found guilty. The trial court conducts the entire series of acts that culminate in either the defendant's release or sentencing. State trial courts can be further divided into courts of limited or special jurisdiction and courts of general jurisdiction.

The nature and type of case determines which court will have jurisdiction. Courts that hear and decide only certain limited legal issues are courts of limited jurisdiction. Typically, these courts hear certain types of minor civil or criminal cases. Approximately 13,000 local courts are in the United States. They are county, magistrate, justice, or municipal courts. Judges in these courts may be either appointed or elected. In many jurisdictions, these are part-time positions, and the incumbent may have another job or position in addition to serving as a judge.

Coming to the county seat from outlying areas of the county has often presented hardship and expense to many of those involved in a trial. To accommodate these persons and to relieve part of the caseload of the superior court, some counties have been divided into judicial districts, each containing a lower court. This lower court is often referred to as an inferior court, as opposed to the superior court, and is known in many places as the justice court. The judge is frequently called the justice of the peace. This court has limited jurisdiction, hearing certain misdemeanor charges and civil matters involving small amounts of money. Usually the judge is elected by the people within the district, and generally in the past there was no requirement that he or she have legal training. The reason for no such requirement was that in many outlying judicial districts, there were no attorneys; however, the people of those districts were entitled to some judicial assistance. Today, as more attorneys are available, many states have phased out the judges of the inferior courts who are not attorneys. However, the elimination of the layperson judge has met with resistance. Some contend that the local inferior, or lower, court can provide a form of justice that is convenient for both the accused and the accuser and that the layperson justice of the peace is part of the American heritage. Others contend that to subject an accused to possible imprisonment after a conviction in a trial presided over by a layperson judge is denying the accused the right to due process of law. This matter was brought before the U.S. Supreme Court in the case of *North* v. *Russell,* after North was convicted of drunk driving and sentenced to thirty days in jail by a lawperson sitting as a police court judge.[12] North contended that his conviction for drunk driving and sentencing to thirty days in jail was a violation of his right to due process of law as provided in the Fourteenth Amendment. The Court upheld the conviction upon the grounds that North could have taken his case to a higher court and had it completely tried again by a court presided over by an attorney judge. Therefore, North was not denied due process of law. The Court pointed out that there was an advantage to the accused in having the trial in a community near his residence rather than traveling to a distant court where a law-trained judge was provided. The decision did not rule out all layperson judges as being a denial of due process of law, but it should be noted that the judicial structures of some states do not provide for a conviction in a lower court to be taken to a higher court and the case started anew. Where such a procedure is not available, courts could hold that an accused would be denied the right of due process of law in a proceeding before a layperson judge.

However, simply because they handle minor civil and criminal matters does not mean these courts do not perform important duties. Many times the only contact the average citizen will have with the judicial system occurs at this level. Courts

KANSAS COURT SYSTEM

Sample of a State Court System

Sample of a State Court System

of limited jurisdiction hear and decide issues such as traffic tickets or set bail for criminal defendants.

In addition, courts of limited jurisdiction may hear certain types of specialized matters such as probate of wills and estates, divorces, child custody matters, and juvenile hearings. These types of courts may be local courts or, depending on the state, courts of general jurisdiction that are designated by statute to hear and decide specific types of cases. For example, in California, a superior court is considered a court of general jurisdiction; however, certain superior courts are designated to hear only juvenile matters, thereby becoming a court of limited jurisdiction when sitting as a juvenile court.

Courts of general jurisdiction are granted authority to hear and decide all issues that are brought before them. These are the courts that normally hear all major civil or criminal cases. These courts are known by a variety of names, such as superior courts, circuit courts, district courts, or courts of common pleas. Since they are courts of general jurisdiction, they have authority to decide issues that occur anywhere within the state. Some larger jurisdictions such as Los Angeles or New York may have hundreds of courts of general jurisdiction within the city limits. Typically, these courts hear civil cases involving the same types of issues that courts of limited jurisdiction hear, although the amount of damages will be higher and may reach millions. These courts also hear the most serious forms of criminal matters, including death penalty cases.

Courts of general jurisdiction traditionally have the power to order individuals to do or refrain from doing certain acts. These courts may issue injunctions prohibiting certain acts or requiring individuals to do certain functions or duties. This authority is derived from the equity power that resides in courts of general jurisdiction. Equity is the concept that justice is administered according to fairness as contrasted to the strict rules of law. In early English common law, such separate courts

---

A Comparison of Criminal and Tort Law

Similarities

- Goal of controlling
- Imposition of sanctions
- Some common areas of legal action—for example, personal assault, control of white-collar offenses such as environmental pollution

Differences

Criminal Law	Tort Law
Crime is a public offense.	Tort is a civil or private wrong.
The sanction associated with criminal law is incarceration or death.	The sanction associated with tort law is monetary damages.
The right of enforcement belongs to the state.	The individual brings the action.
The government ordinarily does not appeal.	Both parties can appeal.
Fines go to the state.	The individual receives damages as compensation for harm done.

---

of equity were known as Courts of Chancery. These early courts were not concerned with technical legal issues; rather, they focused on rendering decisions or orders that were fair or equitable. In modern times, the power of these courts has been merged with courts of general jurisdiction, allowing them to rule on matters that require fairness as well as the strict application of the law. The power to issue temporary restraining orders in spousal abuse cases comes from this authority.

Appellate Courts

Appellate jurisdiction is reserved for courts that hear appeals from both limited and general jurisdiction courts. Except for appeals from minor courts that are heard "de novo" (as a new trial), these courts do not hold trials or hear evidence. Instead, they decide matters of law on the basis of the record of trial and appellate briefs, and they issue formal written decisions, or "opinions." In a few states, the intermediate-level appellate courts have limited authority to make findings of fact. There are two classes of appellate courts: intermediate and final.

The intermediate appellate courts are known as courts of appeals. Approximately half the states have designated intermediate appellate courts. These courts may be divided into judicial districts that hear all appeals within their district. They will hear and decide all issues of law that are raised on appeal in both civil and criminal cases. Since these courts deal strictly with legal or equitable issues, there is no jury to decide factual disputes. These courts accept the facts as determined by the trial courts. Most criminal cases end at either the trial or intermediate appellate court level; less than one percent of the cases are appealed to the state highest appellate court. However, whereas all states have appellate courts for criminal appeals, there appears to be no constitutional duty for states to have appellate courts. Intermediate appellate courts have the authority to reverse the decision of the lower courts and to send the matter back with instructions to retry the case in accordance with their opinion. They also may uphold the decision of the lower court. In either situation, the party who loses the appeal at this level may file and appeal with the next higher appellate court.

Supreme Courts

Final appellate courts are the highest state appellate courts. They may be known as supreme courts or courts of last resort. There may be five, seven, or nine justices sitting on this court depending on the state. This court has jurisdiction to hear and decide issues dealing with all matters decided by lower courts, including ruling on state constitutional or statutory issues. This decision is binding on all other courts within the state. In two states, Oklahoma and Texas, the state supreme courts do not have jurisdiction over criminal matters. In these two states, the highest courts of appeal for criminal matters is the Court of Criminal Appeals.

Once the highest state appellate court decides an issue, the conviction is considered final. The defendant may attack the judgment of a state court by filing a writ with a federal court. But before the federal court will accept a writ attacking a state court judgment, a federal issue must be involved. Normally, the federal issue is that the state court violated the federal constitutional rights of the defendant. This is regarded as a collateral attack.

THE FEDERAL COURT SYSTEM

Although state courts had their origin in historical accident and custom, federal courts were created by the U.S. Constitution. Section 1 of Article III established the federal court system with the words providing for "one supreme Court, and . . . such inferior Courts as the Congress may from time to time ordain and establish." From this beginning, Congress has engaged in a series of acts that have resulted in today's federal court system. The Judiciary Act of 1789 created the U.S. Supreme Court and established district and circuit courts of appeals.

Federal District Courts are the lowest level of the federal court system. These courts have original jurisdiction over cases involving a violation of federal statutes. Because these district courts handle thousands of criminal cases per year, questions have been raised regarding the quality of justice that can be delivered by overworked judges.

Federal Circuit Courts of Appeals are the intermediate-appellate courts within the federal system. These courts are called circuit courts because the federal system is divided into eleven circuits. A twelfth circuit court of appeals serves the Washington, D.C., area. These courts hear all criminal appeals from the District Courts. These appeals are usually heard by panels of three of the appellate court judges rather than by all the judges of each circuit.

The United States Supreme Court is the highest court in the land. It has the capacity for judicial review of all lower court decisions involving federal issues or federal questions. By exercising this power, the Supreme Court determines what laws and what lower court decisions conform to the mandates set forth in the U.S. Constitution, national treaties, and federal law. The concept of judicial review was first referred to by Alexander Hamilton in the *The Federalist* papers, where he referred to the Supreme Court as ensuring that the will of the people will be supreme over the will of the legislature.[13] This concept was firmly and finally established in

ORGANIZATION OF FEDERAL COURTS HANDLING CRIMINAL MATTERS

our system when the Supreme Court asserted its power of judicial review in the case of *Marbury* v. *Madison.*[14]

The U.S. Supreme Court has original jurisdiction in the following cases:

- cases between the United States and a state;
- cases between states; cases involving foreign ambassadors, ministers, and consuls; and
- cases between a state and a citizen of another state or country.

The Supreme Court hears appeals from lower courts, including the various state supreme courts (on issues involving federal questions). If four justices of the U.S. Supreme Court vote to hear a case, the Court will issue a writ of certiorari, which is an order to a lower court to send the records of the case to the Supreme Court for review. The Court meets on the first Monday of October and usually remains in session until June. The Court may review any case it deems worthy of review, but it actually hears very few of the cases filed with it. Of approximately 5,000 appeals each year, the Court hears about 100.

VENUE

Defined simply, venue is the geographic area in which a case may be heard. It is the place where a case is brought to trial and the area from which the jurors are selected. Usually, venue will lie within the county or judicial district in which a crime is committed. Venue may be waived by the defendant. There are times when a defendant may request that a trial be held in a county other than where the crime was committed.

Occasionally, situations arise when it is difficult to determine in which county a crime was committed in order to have venue established. Many states have set

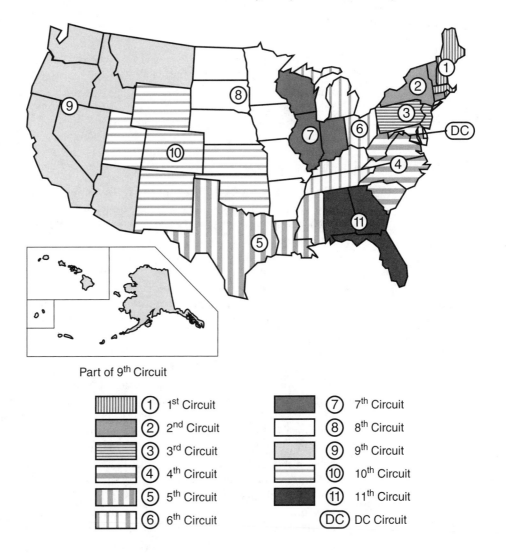

Part of 9th Circuit

	1st Circuit		7th Circuit
②	2nd Circuit	⑧	8th Circuit
③	3rd Circuit	⑨	9th Circuit
④	4th Circuit	⑩	10th Circuit
⑤	5th Circuit	⑪	11th Circuit
⑥	6th Circuit	DC	DC Circuit

forth guidelines to overcome this dilemma. They include such provisions as the following:

- When an offense is committed in part in one county and in part in another, the trial may be held in either county, and
- when an offense is committed on the boundary of two or more counties, or within 500 yards (this distance may vary among states) of the boundary, the trial may be held in either jurisdiction.

Prior to the passage of such provisions, there was a joke among old-time sheriffs and prosecutors about wearing out bodies by dragging them across county lines to avoid the responsibility of investigations and prosecutions. It has also been held that when a crime is committed within the state in a boat, a motor vehicle, an aircraft, or a common carrier, the trial may be held in any county through which the trip passed or was terminated.

JURISDICTION

Jurisdiction is the inherent power of a court to hear and decide a case, whereas venue designates a particular area in which a case may be heard and decided. Unfortunately, the statutes of some states use "jurisdiction" when in fact the statute refers to "venue," thus leading to confusion to the layperson. This dual use of the term "jurisdiction" stems from the fact that it is an all-encompassing word, embracing every kind of judicial action.

Federal Versus Local Jurisdiction

Since we have learned that there are two court systems, that is, the state system and the federal system, it may be useful at this point to compare the jurisdiction of each. As we have previously stated, criminal laws enacted by the U.S. Congress are known as federal criminal laws and are enforced by federal officers. Criminal laws passed by the state legislatures are generally enforced by city police departments or sheriffs and their deputies, and assisted by state officers where they have the authority to do so. Although most of the criminal laws within a state are state enacted, the violators are prosecuted in the county court or local system, since that is where the trial courts are located. Thus, our discussion of the jurisdiction of the two systems is directly related to the trial jurisdiction of the federal and county courts.

When a crime is committed, the violator may have broken either a federal law or a state law, depending upon the act. For example, a person may rob a liquor store, an act that would be a violation of a state statute, since all states have laws making robbery a crime. Or a person may violate the Sherman Antitrust Law, an act that would be a federal violation. The county court would have exclusive jurisdiction to try the case of robbery, whereas the federal government would have exclusive jurisdiction to try the antitrust violation. It is possible for a person to commit both a federal and a state violation with a series of acts arising out of a sequence of events. For example, a person may steal an automobile in one state and transport it to another state. Such an individual could be prosecuted in the local courts for the theft of the vehicle and prosecuted in the federal courts because it is a federal crime to transport a vehicle from one state to another knowing that it has been stolen. In this example, the offender has actually committed two violations as a result of two different acts—one being the theft and the other the transportation of the vehicle while knowing that it has been stolen. In these two examples, each court has its own trial jurisdiction exclusive of the other.

As stated, it is possible for an individual to violate both a federal and a state law by the same act. For example, an individual may kill a federal officer, thereby violating a federal statute, and the killing may also violate a state homicide statute. Under these circumstances, "concurrent" jurisdiction would exist. The question then would be whether the accused could be prosecuted in both the federal and the state courts. This question can best be discussed in Chapter 5, which deals with the plea of once in jeopardy.

Although most crimes committed on government reservations are also local or state violations, the federal courts have exclusive jurisdiction to try those matters because they were committed on a government reservation. It should be pointed out that government reservations are comparatively few in number. In order for a

The Interrelationship of the Criminal Justice System and the Criminal Justice Process

The System: Agencies of Crime Control	The Process
1. Police	1. Contact
	2. Investigation
	3. Arrest
	4. Custody
2. Prosecution and defense	5. Complaint/charging
	6. Grand jury/preliminary hearing
	7. Arraignment
	8. Bail/detention
	9. Plea negotiations
3. Court	10. Adjudication
	11. Disposition
	12. Appeal/postconviction remedies
4. Corrections	13. Correction
	14. Release
	15. Postrelease

territorial area to be a government reservation, the land must have always been U.S. property, with the title still retained by the United States, or property acquired from a state for which all right and title was relinquished. Most military installations and national parks are government reservations; most post offices are not. Scattered throughout the United States are many national forests, but most of these are not government reservations, so that any crimes committed in these forests are within the jurisdiction of the local courts. However, any theft of the trees from these forests is a theft of government property, which would be a federal violation.

In review, jurisdiction—as it relates to the administration of justice—refers to the right and the power of a particular court to try a case. It includes jurisdiction over the person and the subject matter of the issue to be tried. For example, inferior courts have jurisdiction, or the right, to hear misdemeanor matters. The superior or district court has jurisdiction, or the right, to hear felony cases. Jurisdiction is basic to the trial of a case, and it cannot be waived. It is a right of the court established by law.

CAPSTONE CASES

Harmelin v. Michigan
111 S.Ct. 2680 (1991)

[The excerpts from this case provide the reader with a historical background of the "cruel and unusual" clause of the Eighth Amendment to the U.S. Constitution. The U.S. Supreme Court decided the case of *Ronald Allen Harmelin, Petitioner* v. *Michigan* on June 27, 1991.]

Justice Scalia announced the judgment of the Court. . . . [In this case, the defendant claims that his sentence was disproportionate and therefore in violation of the "cruel and unusual" clause of the Eighth Amendment. The Court denied his claim.]

There is no doubt that the Declaration of Rights is the antecedent of our constitutional text. (This document was promulgated in February 1689 and was enacted into law as the Bill of Rights.) In 1791, five State Constitutions prohibited "cruel or unusual punishments," and two prohibited "cruel" punishments. The new Federal Bill of Rights, however, tracked Virginia's prohibition of "cruel and unusual punishments," which most closely followed the English provision. In fact, the entire text of the Eighth Amendment is taken almost verbatim from the English Declaration of Rights, which provided "[t]hat excessive Baile ought not to be required nor excessive Fines imposed nor cruell and unusuall Punishments inflicted."

Compare this case with a recent United States Supreme Court decision dealing with cruel and unusual punishment in the 21st Century.

Perhaps the Americans of 1791 understood the Declaration's language precisely as the Englishmen of 1689 did—though as we shall discuss later, that seems unlikely. Or perhaps the colonists meant to incorporate the content of that antecedent by reference, whatever the content might have been. Solem suggested something like this, arguing that since Americans claimed "all the rights of English subjects," "their use of the language of the English Bill of Rights is convincing proof that they intended to provide at least the same protection," . . . Thus, not only is the original meaning of the 1689 Declaration of Rights relevant, but also the circumstances of its enactment, insofar as they display the particular "rights of English subjects" it was designed to vindicate. . . . The Magna Carta provided that "[a] free man shall not be fined for a small offence, except in proportion to the measure of the offence; and for a great offence he shall be fined in proportion to the magnitude of the offence, saving his freehold. . . ." Most historians agree that the "cruell and unusual Punishments" provision of the English Declaration of Rights was prompted by the abuses attributed to the infamous Lord Chief Justice Jeffreys of the King's Bench during the Stuart reign of James II. . . . They do not agree, however, on which abuses.

Justices Jeffreys is best known for presiding over the "Bloody Assizes" following the Duke of Monmouth's abortive rebellion in 1685; a special Commission led by Jeffreys tried, convicted, and executed hundreds of suspected insurgents. Some have attributed the Declaration of Rights provision to popular outrage against those proceedings.

But the vicious punishments for treason decreed in the Bloody Assizes (drawing and quartering, burning of women felons, beheading, disemboweling, etc.) were common in that period—indeed, they were specifically authorized by law and remained so for many years afterwards. Thus, recently historians have argued, and the best historical evidence suggests, that it was not Jeffreys' management of the Bloody Assizes that led to the Declaration of Rights provision, but rather the arbitrary sentencing power he had exercised in administering justice from the King's Bench, particularly when punishing a notorious perjurer. Jeffreys was widely accused of "inventing" special penalties for the King's enemies, penalties that were not authorized by common-law precedent or statute.

The preamble to the Declaration of Rights, a sort of indictment of James II that calls to mind the preface to our own Declaration of Independence, specifically referred to illegal sentences and King's Bench proceedings. "Whereas the late King James the Second, by the Assistance of diverse Evil Councellors, Judges and Ministers imployed by him did endeavour to subvert and extirpate the Protestant Religion, and the Lawes and Liberties of this Kingdome."

"By Prosecutions in the Court of King's Bench for Matters and Causes cognizable onely in Parlyament and by diverse other Arbitrary and Illegall Courses. [E]xcessive Baile hath beene required of Persons committed in Criminal Cases to elude the Benefit of the Lawes made for the Liberty of the Subjects. And excessive Fines have been imposed. And illegall and cruell Punishments have been inflicted. All which are utterly and directly contrary to the knowne Lawes and Statutes and Freedome of this Realme."

The only recorded contemporaneous interpretation of the "cruell and unusuall Punishments" clause confirms the focus upon Jeffreys' King's Bench activities, and upon the illegality rather than the disproportionality of his sentences. In 1685 Titus Oates, a Protestant cleric whose false accusations had caused the execution of 15 prominent Catholics for allegedly organizing a "Popish Plot" to overthrow King Charles in 1679, was tried and convicted before the King's Bench for perjury. Oates' crime, "bearing false witness against another, with an express premeditated design to take away his life, so as the innocent person be condemned and executed" had, at one time, been treated as a species of murder, and punished with death. At sentencing, Jeffreys complained that death was no longer available as a penalty and lamented that "a proportionable punishment of that crime can scarce by our law, as it now stands, be inflicted upon him." The law would not stand in the way, however. The judges met, and, according to Jeffreys, were in unanimous agreement that "crimes of this nature are left to be punished according to the discretion of this court, so far as that the judgment extend not to life or member." Another Justice taunted Oates that "we have taken special care of you," . . . The court then decreed that he should pay a fine of "1000 marks upon each Indictment," that he should be "stript of [his] Canonical Habits," that he should stand in the pillory annually at certain specified times and places, that on May 20 he should be whipped by "the common hangman" "from Aldgate to Newgate," that he should be similarly whipped on May 22 "from Newgate to Tyburn," and that he should be imprisoned for life.

"The judges, as they believed, sentenced Oates to be scourged to death." Oates would not die, however. Four years later, and several months after the Declaration of Rights, he petitioned the House of Lords to set aside his sentence as illegal. "Not a single peer ventured to affirm that the judgment was legal; but much was said about the odious character of the appellant" and the Lords affirmed the judgment. A minority of the Lords dissented, however, and their statement sheds light on the meaning of the "cruell and unusuall Punishments" clause: "1st, [The King's Bench] being a Temporal Court, made it a Part of the judgment, That Titus Oates, being a Clerk, should, for his said Perjuries, be divested of his canonical and priestly Habit. . . ; which is a Matter wholly out of their Power, belonging to the Ecclesiastical Courts only. 2dly, [S]aid Judgments are barbarous, inhuman, and unchristian; and there is no Precedent to warrant the Punishments of whipping and committing to Prison for Life, for the Crime of Perjury; which yet were but Part of the Punishments inflicted upon him. 4thly, [T]his will be an Encouragement and Allowance for giving the like cruel, barbarous and illegal Judgments hereafter, unless this Judgment be reversed. 5thly, . . . [T]hat the said Judgments were contrary to Law and ancient Practice, and therefore erroneous, and ought to be reversed. 6thly, Because it is contrary to the Declaration on the Twelfth of February last that excessive Baile ought not to be required, nor excessive Fines imposed, nor cruel nor unusual Punishments afflicted."

Unless one accepts the notion of a blind incorporation, however, the ultimate question is not what "cruell and unusuall punishments" meant in the Declaration of Rights, but what its meaning was to the Americans who adopted the Eighth Amendment. Even if one assumes that the Founders knew the precise meaning of that English antecedent, a direct transplant of the English meaning to the soil of American constitutionalism would in any case have been impossible.

There were no common-law punishments in the federal system, so that the provision must have been meant as a check not upon judges but upon the Legislature.

Wrenched out of its common-law context, and applied to the actions of a legislature, the word "unusual" could hardly mean "contrary to law." But it continued to mean (as it continues to mean today) "such as [does not] occu[r] in ordinary practice," "[s]uch as is [not] in common use," . . . According to its terms, then, by forbidding "cruel and unusual punishments."

The Eighth Amendment received little attention during the proposal and adoption of the Federal Bill of Rights. However, what evidence exists from debates at the state ratifying conventions that prompted the Bill of Rights as well as the Floor debates in the First Congress which proposed it "confirm[s] the view that the cruel and unusual punishments clause was directed at prohibiting certain methods of punishment."

Atkins v. *Virginia*
122 S.Ct. 2242 (2002)

[Compare and contrast this case with *Harmelin v. Michigan.* Has the Supreme Court changed its fundamental position on Cruel and Unusual Punishment? What is the effect of society's perception on the execution of the mentally retarded on the court's decision?]

Those mentally retarded persons who meet the law's requirements for criminal responsibility should be tried and punished when they commit crimes. Because of their disabilities in areas of reasoning, judgment, and control of their impulses, however, they do not act with the level of moral culpability that characterizes the most serious adult criminal conduct. Moreover, their impairments can jeopardize the reliability and fairness of capital proceedings against mentally retarded defendants. Presumably for these reasons, in the 13 years since we decided Penry v. Lynaugh, 492 U.S. 302 (1989), the American public, legislators, scholars, and judges have deliberated over the question whether the death penalty should ever be imposed on a mentally retarded criminal. The consensus reflected in those deliberations informs our answer to the question presented by this case: whether such executions are "cruel and unusual punishments" prohibited by the Eighth Amendment to the Federal Constitution.

Petitioner, Daryl Renard Atkins, was convicted of abduction, armed robbery, and capital murder, and sentenced to death. At approximately midnight on August 16, 1996, Atkins and William Jones, armed with a semiautomatic handgun, abducted Eric Nesbitt, robbed him of the money on his person, drove him to an automated teller machine in his pickup truck where cameras recorded their withdrawal of additional cash, then took him to an isolated location where he was shot eight times and killed.

Jones and Atkins both testified in the guilt phase of Atkins' trial. Each confirmed most of the details in the other's account of the incident, with the important exception that each stated that the other had actually shot and killed Nesbitt. Jones' testimony, which was both more coherent and credible than Atkins', was obviously credited by the jury and was sufficient to establish Atkins' guilt. At the penalty phase of the trial, the State introduced victim impact evidence and proved two aggravating circumstances: future dangerousness and "vileness of the offense." To prove future dangerousness, the State relied on Atkins' prior felony convictions as well as the testimony of four victims of earlier robberies and assaults. To prove the second aggravator, the prosecution relied upon the trial record, including pictures of the deceased's body and the autopsy report.

In the penalty phase, the defense relied on one witness, Dr. Evan Nelson, a forensic psychologist who had evaluated Atkins before trial and concluded that he was "mildly mentally retarded." His conclusion was based on interviews with people who knew Atkins, a review of school and court records, and the administration of a standard intelligence test which indicated that Atkins had a full scale IQ of 59.

[The American Psychiatric Association, Diagnostic and Statistical Manual of Mental Disorders 41 (4th ed. 2000) defines "Mild" mental retardation as typically used to describe people with an IQ level of 50–55 to approximately 70.]

The Supreme Court of Virginia affirmed the imposition of the death penalty. Because of the gravity of the concerns expressed by the dissenters at the state supreme court, and in light of the dramatic shift in the state legislative landscape that has occurred in the past 13 years, we granted certiorari to revisit the issue that we first addressed in the Penry case.

The Eighth Amendment succinctly prohibits "excessive" sanctions. It provides: "Excessive bail shall not be required, nor excessive fines imposed, nor cruel and unusual punishments inflicted." In *Weems* v. *United States*, 217 U.S. 349 (1910), we held that a punishment of 12 years jailed in irons at hard and painful labor for the crime of falsifying records was excessive. We explained "that it is a precept of justice that punishment for crime should be graduated and proportioned to the offense." We have repeatedly applied this proportionality precept in later cases interpreting the Eighth Amendment. See *Harmelin* v. *Michigan*, 501 U.S. 957,(1991)].

As Chief Justice Warren explained in his opinion in *Trop* v. *Dulles*, 356 U.S. 86 (1958): "The basic concept underlying the Eighth Amendment is nothing less than the dignity of man. . . . The Amendment must draw its meaning from the evolving standards of decency that mark the progress of a maturing society."

Proportionality review under those evolving standards should be informed by " 'objective [**16] factors to the maximum possible extent,'" see *Harmelin*, 501 U.S., at 1000. We have pinpointed that the "clearest and most reliable objective evidence of contemporary values is the legislation enacted by the country's legislatures."

Thus, in cases involving a consensus, our own judgment is "brought to bear," by asking whether there is reason to disagree with the judgment reached by the citizenry and its legislators.

Guided by our approach in these cases, we shall first review the judgment of legislatures that have addressed the suitability of imposing the death penalty on the mentally retarded and then consider reasons for agreeing or disagreeing with their judgment.

The parties have not called our attention to any state legislative consideration of the suitability of imposing the death penalty on mentally retarded offenders prior to 1986. In that year, the public reaction to the execution of a mentally retarded murderer in Georgia apparently led to the enactment of the first state statute prohibiting such executions. In 1988, when Congress enacted legislation reinstating the federal death penalty, it expressly provided that a "sentence of death shall not be carried out upon a person who is mentally retarded." In 1989, Maryland enacted a similar prohibition. Responding to the national attention [regarding this issue], state legislatures across the country began to address the issue.

It is not so much the number of these States that is significant, but the consistency of the direction of change. The practice [of executing the mentally retarded], therefore, has become truly unusual, and it is fair to say that a national consensus has developed against it.

Our independent evaluation of the issue reveals no reason to disagree with the judgment of "the legislatures that have recently addressed the matter" and concluded that death is not a suitable punishment for a mentally retarded criminal. We are not persuaded that the execution of mentally retarded criminals will measurably advance the deterrent or the retributive purpose of the death penalty. Construing and applying the Eighth Amendment in the light of our "evolving standards of decency," we therefore conclude that such punishment is excessive and that the Constitution "places a substantive restriction on the State's power to take the life" of a mentally retarded offender.

The judgment of the Virginia Supreme Court is reversed and the case is remanded for further proceedings not inconsistent with this opinion.

It is so ordered.

DISSENT:

[Chief Justice Rehnquist] The question presented by this case is whether a national consensus deprives Virginia of the constitutional power to impose the death penalty on capital murder defendants like petitioner, i.e., those defendants who indisputably are competent to stand trial, aware of the punishment they are about to suffer and why, and whose mental retardation has been found an insufficiently compelling reason to lessen their individual responsibility for the crime. The Court pronounces the punishment cruel and unusual primarily because 18 States recently have passed laws limiting the death eligibility of certain defendants based on mental retardation alone, despite the fact that the laws of 19 other States besides Virginia continue to leave the question of proper punishment to the individuated consideration of sentencing judges or juries familiar with the particular offender and his or her crime.

In making determinations about whether a punishment is "cruel and unusual" under the evolving standards of decency embraced by the Eighth Amendment, we have emphasized that legislation is the "clearest and most reliable objective evidence of contemporary values." The reason we ascribe primacy to legislative enactments follows from the constitutional role legislatures play in expressing policy of a State. "'In a democratic society legislatures, not courts, are constituted to respond to the will and consequently the moral values of the people.'" Our opinions have also recognized that data concerning the actions of sentencing juries, though entitled to less weight than legislative judgments, "'is a significant and reliable index of contemporary values.'"

To further buttress its appraisal of contemporary societal values, the Court marshals public opinion poll results and evidence that several professional organizations and religious groups have adopted official positions opposing the imposition of the death penalty upon mentally retarded offenders. In my view, none should be accorded any weight on the Eighth Amendment scale when the elected representatives of a State's populace have not deemed them persuasive enough to prompt legislative action. Even if I were to accept the legitimacy of the Court's decision to reach beyond the product of legislatures and practices of sentencing juries to discern a national standard of decency, I would take issue with the blind-faith credence it accords the opinion polls brought to our attention. An extensive body of social science literature describes how methodological and other errors can affect the reliability and validity of estimates about the opinions and attitudes of a population derived from various sampling techniques. Everything from variations in the survey methodology, such as the choice of the target population, the sampling design used, the questions asked, and the statistical analyses used to interpret the data can skew the results.

Justice Scalia, with whom the Chief Justice and Justice Thomas join, dissenting.

Today's decision is the pinnacle of our Eighth Amendment death-is-different jurisprudence. Not only does it, like all of that jurisprudence, find no support in the text or history of the Eighth Amendment; it does not even have support in current social attitudes regarding the conditions that render an otherwise just death penalty inappropriate. Seldom has an opinion of this Court rested so obviously upon nothing but the personal views of its members.

Under our Eighth Amendment jurisprudence, a punishment is "cruel and unusual" if it falls within one of two categories: "those modes or acts of punishment that had been considered cruel and unusual at the time that the Bill of Rights was adopted," *Ford* v. *Wainwright*, 477 U.S. 399 (1986), and modes of punishment that are inconsistent with modern "standards of decency," as evinced by objective indicia, the most important of which is "legislation enacted by the country's legislatures."

The Court makes no pretense that execution of the mildly mentally retarded would have been considered "cruel and unusual" in 1791. Only the severely or profoundly mentally retarded, commonly known as "idiots," enjoyed any special status under the law at that time. They, like lunatics, suffered a "deficiency in will" rendering them unable to tell right from wrong. 4 W. Blackstone, Commentaries on the Laws of England 24 (1769).

The Court is left to argue, therefore, that execution of the mildly retarded is inconsistent with the "evolving standards of decency that mark the progress of a maturing society." Before today, our opinions consistently emphasized that Eighth Amendment judgments regarding the existence of social "standards" "should be informed by objective factors to the maximum possible extent" and "should not be, or appear to be, merely the subjective views of individual Justices."

[T]he Prize for the Court's Most Feeble Effort to fabricate "national consensus" must go to its appeal (deservedly relegated to a footnote) to the views of assorted professional and religious organizations, members of the so-called "world community," and respondents to opinion polls. I agree with the CHIEF JUSTICE, (dissenting opinion), that the views of professional and religious organizations and the results of opinion polls are irrelevant. Equally irrelevant are the practices of the "world community," whose notions of justice are (thankfully) not always those of our people. "We must never forget that it is a Constitution for the United States of America that we are expounding. . . . Where there is not first a settled consensus among our own people, the views of other nations, however enlightened the Justices of this Court may think them to be, cannot be imposed upon Americans through the Constitution."

Nothing has changed the accuracy of Matthew Hale's endorsement of the common law's traditional method for taking account of guilt-reducing factors, written over three centuries ago:

> "[Determination of a person's incapacity] is a matter of great difficulty, partly from the easiness of counterfeiting this disability . . . and partly from the variety of the degrees of this infirmity, whereas some are sufficient, and some are insufficient to excuse persons in capital offenses. . . .
>
> "Yet the law of England hath afforded the best method of trial, that is possible, of this and all other matters of fact, namely, by a jury of twelve men all concurring in the same judgment, by the testimony of witnesses . . . and by the inspection and direction of the judge." 1 Hale, *Pleas of the Crown*, at 32–33.

REVIEW QUESTIONS

1. Why are laws necessary?
2. Define Common Law.
3. How do we classify laws?
4. What is civil law?
5. What is ecclesiastical law?
6. In what year was the Magna Charta signed?
7. What significant contribution did the Magna Charta make in reference to the administration of justice?
8. How did the trial by ordeal and the trial by battle differ from each other?
9. Describe a trial by compurgation.
10. How did the English kings use early juries?
11. What was the accusatory jury?
12. The United States' Bill of Rights is what part of what document?
13. What portions of the Bill of Rights are of particular significance to the administration of justice?
14. What amendment makes the Bill of Rights applicable to the states?
15. Define venue.
16. Define jurisdiction.
17. How do jurisdiction and venue differ from each other?

LOCAL PROCEDURE

Since judicial procedure differs slightly from state to state, the reader may wish to consult the local prosecuting attorney for the procedure within his or her state.

1. By what names are trial courts known in your state?
2. What are the trial jurisdictions of the trial courts in your state?
3. What are the qualifications of the judges presiding over the trial courts in your state?

ENDNOTES

1. 258 NY 292 (1932).
2. *Mapp* v. *Ohio*, 367 U.S. 643 (1961).
3. *Malloy* v. *Hogan*, 378 U.S. 1 (1964).
4. *Benton* v. *Maryland*, 95 U.S. 784 (1969).
5. *Gibdeon* v. *Wainwright*, 372 U.S. 335 (1963).
6. *Kloper* v. *N.C.*, 386 U.S. 335 (1967).
7. In re *Oliver*, 330 U.S. 257 (1942).
8. *Pointer* v. *Texas*, 380 U.S. 400 (1965).
9. *Duncan* v. *Louisiana*, 391 U.S. 145 (1968).

10. Portions of this section have been adapted from Harvey Wallace, "The Roles of Federal and State Law: The Judicial System and Victims of Crime in *The National Victim Assistance Academy Text* (OVC, Washington D.C.), 2001.

11. Pursley, *Introduction to Criminal Justice,* 6th ed. (Macmillan, New York), 1994.

12. 437 U.S. 328 (1976).

13. *The Supreme Court of the United States* (U.S. Government Printing Office, Washington, D.C.).

14. 1 Cranh 137 (1803).

Search and Seizure

CHAPTER 2

The right of the people to be secure in their persons, houses, papers, and effects, against unreasonable searches and seizures, shall not be violated, and no Warrants shall issue, but upon probable cause, supported by Oath or affirmation and particularly describing the place to be searched, and the persons or things to be seized.

—Fourth Amendment of the U.S. Constitution (1791)

HISTORY AND PURPOSE OF THE FOURTH AMENDMENT

From a criminal procedure perspective, the Fourth Amendment contains the most important language in existence within the United States legal structure. It must be stressed that not all searches are prohibited, only those that are unreasonable. The issues surrounding searches and seizures can become quite complex, and many times students or even professionals in the field lose sight of the rationale and reasons for the Fourth Amendment. Asking the following questions any time that a search or seizure situation arises will assist in analyzing this complex area of constitutional law:

1. **Does the Fourth Amendment apply?** If it does not apply, the question of reasonableness and warrants and probable cause are irrelevant. For example, as will be discussed later in this chapter, there are certain situations such as evidence found in open fields that can be seized because the Fourth Amendment does not apply to property found in open fields.
2. **If the Fourth Amendment does apply, has it been complied with?** If all the requirements have been satisfied, then any evidence will be admitted. If it has not been complied with, go to question 3.
3. **If the Fourth Amendment does apply and it has not been complied with, what sanctions will the court impose on any evidence seized in violation of the amendment?** The court has a range of options available to it if it determines that the officers or agents have violated the Fourth Amendment.

Fourth Amendment Diagrammed

1. The right of the people to be secure in their
   a. persons,
   b. houses,
   c. papers,
   d. and effects

   against unreasonable searches and seizures, shall not be violated, and

2. No warrants shall issue, but
   a. upon probable cause
   b. supported by oath or affirmation and

3. Particularly describing the
   a. place to be searched
   b. and the persons or things to be seized.

Source: U.S. Constitution, Fourth Amendment (designations added)

These are simple questions and a seemingly simple approach to the concepts of search and seizure, but using this approach will enable students to focus on the correct issues within this area of criminal procedure.

When the U.S. Constitution was being drafted and considered by our forefathers, there was very little, if any, thought given to including a declaration of rights for individual citizens. At that time, the original state constitutions contained language that purported to protect individuals from undue oppression by the government. However, the ratification process produced a movement to include amendments in the form of a Bill of Rights, which would address individual rights and restrict government action in the area of the criminal justice process. The drafters of the U.S. Constitution and the Bill of Rights were influenced by a number of factors, including our English heritage, the misuse of the criminal justice process within the colonies during English rule, and a belief in the limited role of government.[1] Thus, the Fourth Amendment was based upon a distrust of government and a desire to prevent arbitrary actions by that government or its agents into personal areas such as the unreasonable seizure of persons, property, or other items without proper justification.

However, before the rights that are guaranteed in the Bill of Rights were to have an impact on individuals within the criminal justice system, two critical events would have to occur: First, since most criminal prosecutions take place at the local or state level, the U.S. Supreme Court would have to make the Bill of Rights apply to local criminal justice procedures; and second, the Court would have to interpret those rights and the way that they impact local government and individual citizens. As will be seen later in this chapter, both of those events would occur with the result that individuals are protected from invasive governmental action.

The Fourth Amendment deals with both the "seizures" of persons and property. To properly understand its scope and ramifications within the criminal justice system, we should examine a concept known as the Exclusionary Rule.

EXCLUSIONARY RULE

In 1914, the U.S. Supreme Court decided *Weeks* v. *United States* that established the exclusionary rule and its applicability to the federal government.[2] In *Weeks,* local and federal law enforcement officers seized evidence from the home of the defendant. The court excluded the evidence seized by the federal officers, holding that to allow it would defy the prohibitions of the Constitution that were intended to protect the people against such unauthorized actions. While the federal prohibition remained in effect, local police were still able to conduct searches and seizures according to the rules established by the individual states, since the Fourth Amendment applied only to federal action for the next 35 years.

In 1949, the court issued its ruling in *Wolf* v. *Colorado.*[3] This was the first time the Supreme Court considered whether the Fourth Amendment should be imposed upon state proceedings by using the Fourteenth Amendment Due Process Clause. In *Wolf,* the court addressed the question of whether a conviction by a state court for a state offense denies "due process" of law as required by the Fourteenth Amendment, solely because evidence admitted at the trial was obtained in a manner that would have rendered it inadmissible in a federal court, since such evidence would have been obtained in violation of the Fourth Amendment. Although acknowledging that individuals should be secure from arbitrary intrusion by police and that such security is basic to a free society, the *Wolf* court reviewed the states' acceptance of the *Weeks* doctrine and pointed out that at the time of the decision, 30 states rejected the concept. The justices therefore held that the Fourteenth Amendment does not forbid admission of evidence obtained in violation of the Fourth Amendment. It would take another 12 years before the court would overrule *Wolf* when it decided its landmark case of *Mapp* v. *Ohio.*[4]

In *Mapp* v. *Ohio,* the court expressly overruled *Wolf* by acknowledging that *Wolf* was founded on factual considerations that lacked validity in today's society. The court found that in the intervening years [since its decision in *Wolf*], a number of states had accepted the validity of the Exclusionary Rule, and experience had demonstrated that other options and remedies to prevent illegal searches were worthless and futile.

In *Mapp,* three Cleveland police officers arrived at Mapp's home to search for a person who was wanted for questioning in connection with a recent bombing. Miss Mapp and her daughter lived on the second floor of the two-family dwelling. Upon arrival at the home, the officers knocked on the door and demanded entry, but Miss Mapp, after telephoning her attorney, refused to admit them without a search warrant. Three hours later, after additional officers were on the scene, the officers forced a door in the house. By that time, Miss Mapp's attorney arrived, but the officers would not allow him to enter the house or consult with Miss Mapp. Meanwhile, as the officers entered the house, Miss Mapp demanded to see their search warrant. One of the officers held out a paper and claimed that it was the warrant. Miss Mapp grabbed the paper and placed it in her bosom. The officers struggled with her and regained possession of the "warrant" and placed her under arrest. The officers searched the house, dressers, and trunks, finding some obscene material in a trunk. Miss Mapp was charged and convicted of possession of obscene material. At the trial no search warrant was produced, nor was the failure to produce one explained. Miss Mapp was convicted, and she appealed.

In overturning her conviction, the Supreme Court stated:

> Moreover, our holding . . . is not only the logical dictate of prior cases but it also makes very good sense. There is no war between the Constitution and common sense. Presently, a federal prosecutor may make no use of evidence illegally seized [because of Weeks], but a State's attorney across the street may. . . . Thus the State, by admitting evidence unlawfully seized, serves to encourage disobedience to the Federal Constitution which it is bound to uphold. . . .
>
> Our decision, founded on reason and truth, gives to the individual no more than that which the Constitution guarantees him, to the police officer no less that that to which honest law enforcement is entitled, and, to the courts, that judicial integrity so necessary in the true administration of justice. . . .

The deterrence effect on unreasonable searches and seizure is a major purpose of the Exclusionary Rule. However, the rule also serves at least two other purposes. The judicial integrity approach is to ensure that courts will not become accomplices in violating the rules they were sworn to uphold. Another purpose is to ensure that citizens understand that the government will not profit by unlawful activity, thereby minimizing the lack of trust in our government.

What happens if the officers conducting the search were acting in good faith? This is exactly the situation in *United States* v. *Leon*.[5] The Supreme Court created a "good faith" exception to the exclusionary rule by holding that the Fourth Amendment Exclusionary Rule should be modified so as not to bar use of evidence obtained by officers acting in good faith reliance on a search warrant issued by a magistrate that is later found to be unsupported by probable cause. The court reasoned that the Exclusionary Rule was designed to safeguard Fourth Amendment rights through its deterrence effect on police and that it should not apply to magistrates.

FOCUS: *What if the wrong warrant is used in a search and seizure case?*

Suppose a detective investigating a homicide case needed a search warrant, but because it was Sunday, he could find only one that was used for controlled substances. He took it to a magistrate and pointed out the problems. The magistrate told him to cross out the language regarding controlled substances and to use the warrant; however, the detective neglected to make some of the changes. After the warrant was served, the defendant challenged its validity.

Should the warrant be declared valid under the principles set forth in *Leon?* In *Massachusetts* v. *Sheppard*, the court upheld such a process and allowed the seized evidence to be used against the defendant.

468 U.S. 981 (1984)

FRUITS OF THE POISONOUS TREE DOCTRINE

What happens if law enforcement violates the protections offered by the Fourth Amendment? The most straightforward explanation of the Fruits of the Poisonous Tree Doctrine is that courts will not allow the "fruit," or evidence obtained as a result of an illegal search, to be used against the accused. In explaining this doctrine, one court stated: "The essence of a provision forbidding the acquisition of evidence in a certain way is that not merely evidence so acquired shall not be used before the Court, but that it shall not be used at all."[6]

The Fruits of the Poisonous Tree Doctrine applies to searches, arrests, confessions, and other evidence-gathering activities of law enforcement. However, not all evidence is automatically barred simply because it may have initially been gathered in violation of the Constitution. In *Wong Sun* v. *United States,* the Supreme Court held that the issue was whether the originally obtained illegal evidence can be admitted because it could or was obtained by means sufficiently distinguishable to be purged of the primary taint of illegality.[7] *Wong Sun* also restated the rule that the exclusionary rule has no, application when the government learned of the evidence from a source independent of any taint. Another theory used to "cleanse" or avoid the Fruits of the Poisonous Tree Doctrine is the so-called "Inevitable Discovery Rule," which allows the admission of evidence if it would have been found and discovered legally at a later time.

PROTECTED AREAS AND INTERESTS

Exactly what interest is protected by the Fourth Amendment? The language in the Amendment states that persons, houses, papers, and effects shall be protected or secure against unreasonable searches. Does that mean a person can carry a bomb on an airplane without being searched? Can a person commit a crime inside his or her home and be secure against a search? The courts have established a "zone of constitutional protection" that surrounds a person and moves with that person wherever he or she travels.

EXPECTATION OF PRIVACY ZONE

The older view was that a search required a physical intrusion into a "constitutionally protected area."[8] In the leading case of *Katz* v. *United States,* the Supreme Court expanded the scope of the Fourth Amendment by establishing an "expectation of privacy zone" that is protected by the Constitution.[9] In *Katz,* FBI agents had attached an electronic listening device to the outside of a public phone booth that the defendant used to make wagering call. The court held that the Fourth Amendment protects people, not places. The Justice Harlen in a concurring opinion went on to state that the test for any expectation of privacy is based upon two requirements: (1) that a person exhibit an actual or subjective expectation of privacy and (2) that the expectation is one that society is prepared to recognize as reasonable. In this case, the defendant went to a public phone booth, closed the glass door, and made a call. It is clear that while people could see him in the booth, he had an actual expectation that the phone call itself would not be overheard. It is also clear that society would deem that making any calls from a public phone booth with the door closed as a situation in which there is a reasonable expectation of privacy.

PRACTICUM

Using Justice Harlan's two-prong test for a citizen's expectation of privacy, answer the following questions regarding search and seizure:

If a person leaves narcotics on his desk at work and that location is open to the public, is there any expectation of privacy?

What if a criminal leaves plans for a burglary in a hotel room after she checks out of the hotel?

If a person were to leave a murder weapon in an open field, is there any expectation of privacy?

These and other questions will be discussed in the following section.

EXCEPTIONS TO THE FOURTH AMENDMENT

If the police activity is not a search, the Fourth Amendment does not apply. Therefore, the question becomes, How far does the protection of the Fourth Amendment extend? This section deals with areas and interests that are considered exceptions to the Fourth Amendment and therefore are considered outside the scope of protection of the Fourth Amendment.

Consent

If a party consents to a search, there are no Fourth Amendment protections. The question of whether the consent is valid is a question of fact to be determined from the totality of the circumstances.[10] The Supreme Court in *Schneckloth* v. *Busta-monte* held that although the subject's knowledge or a right to refuse is a factor to be taken into account, it is not a requirement to establishing a voluntary search.[11]

Another issue that sometimes arises concerns consent obtained by deception. What if an undercover officer is invited into a home that is being used to distribute narcotics? When a criminal gives consent to another person to enter an area normally protected by the Fourth Amendment, knowing that as a result he will reveal to that person criminal activity, such consent is not invalid merely because the consent was given to an undercover police officer.[12]

What happens when a third party gives consent? The Supreme Court has adopted a common authority test for consent by third parties. Common authority rests upon the mutual use of the property by persons generally having joint access or control for most purposes, so that it is reasonable to recognize that any of the coinhabitants has the right to permit the inspection in his own right and that the others have assumed the risk that one of their number might permit the common area to be searched.[13]

Who can give consent? It is generally agreed that one spouse can give consent to search the family residence. If a son or daughter is a minor, parents are presumed to be able to consent to a search of the child's room. What happens if a child consents to a search of the parents' home? If the child is older, courts generally uphold such consent on the theory that older children acquire authority and discretion to admit whom they want into the family house. Property relationships raise special issues regarding consent. An owner may not consent to a search of the renter when the owner has given the renter exclusive possession of the property.

Plain View Doctrine

The Supreme Court has established an exception to the Fourth Amendment in the form of the Plain View Doctrine. This concept holds that the Plain View Doctrine authorizes seizure of illegal evidence visible to a police officer if the officer's access

Notable Case Doctrines and Exceptions to the Fourth Amendment (Search and Seizure) and Fifth Amendment (Self-incrimination) Clauses

	Case Decision	*Holding*
Fourth Amendment Doctrine		
Expectation of privacy	*Katz* v. *United States* (1968)	Electronic eavesdropping is a search.
Plain view	*Arizona* v. *Hicks* (1967)	Fourth Amendment may not apply when the object is in plain view.
Open fields	*Oliver* v. *United States* (1984)	To what extent can police search a field and curtilage?
Warrant Requirements		
Probable cause	*Illinois* v. *Gates* (1983)	Probable cause to issue a warrant is based on a "totality of circumstance."
Stop and frisk	*Terry* v. *Ohio* (1967)	Police are authorized to stop and frisk suspicious persons.
Consent	*Schneckloth* v. *Bustamonte* (1973)	There is consent to search and seizure.
Bus sweep	*Florida* v. *Bostick* (1991)	Police, after obtaining consent, may conduct a search of luggage without a search warrant or probable cause.
Exceptions to the Warrant Requirement		
Federal requirement of exclusionary rule	*Weeks* v. *United States* (1914)	U.S. Supreme Court applied the exclusionary rule to federal prosecutions.
State application	*Mapp* v. *Ohio* (1961)	U.S. Supreme Court applied the exclusionary rule to state prosecutions.
Automobile search	*United States* v. *Ross* (1982)	Warrantless search of an auto is permissible when it is based on probable cause.
Search incident to arrest	*Chimel* v. *California* (1969)	Permissible scope for a search is the area "within the arrestee's immediate control."
Exceptions to the Exclusionary Rule		
Good faith	*United States* v. *Leon* (1984)	When police rely on "good faith" in a warrant, the evidence seized is admissible even if the warrant is subsequently deemed defective.
Good faith	*Arizona* v. *Evans* (1995)	Even though police arrested a man on the basis of an erroneous warrant that resulted from a court employee's computer error, the evidence they found in a subsequent search is admissible.
Fifth Amendment Doctrine		
Self-incrimination	*Miranda* v. *Arizona* (1966)	Defendant must be given the *Miranda* warning before questioning begins.
Miranda warning	*Dickerson* v. *United States* (2000)	Congress cannot overrule the requirements that *Miranda* rights be read to criminal suspects.

to the object has a Fourth Amendment justification. In *Horton* v. *California* the court summed up this doctrine by stating, ". . . not only must the officer be lawfully located in a place from which the object can be plainly seen, but he or she must also have a lawful right to access to the object itself."[14] Compare and contrast the following situations: (1) The officer is standing on a public sidewalk and can see inside a home through an open window. He observes narcotics on a table. (2) The officer is responding to a loud party complaint, and after identifying herself to the owner, the officer is invited into the house. Once inside, she observes narcotics lying on the table in the room where she is standing. In the first situation, the officer is on a public sidewalk and therefore lawfully in a place from which he can observe the object, but to gain entrance to the house, he must obtain a search warrant.[15] In the second situation, the officer is lawfully located in a place from which the object can be seen, since she was given consent to enter the home; and once in the home, she has a lawful right to access to the object itself.

How far does the expectation of privacy extend when dealing with the Plain View Doctrine? Does a defendant who is growing marijuana in a fenced backyard have a right of privacy from a plane flying over the property? In *California* v. *Ciraolo,* the Supreme Court held that the defandant did not have any reasonable expectation of privacy.[16] The officers were in a private plane flying at 1,000 feet when they saw the marijuana. They obtained a search warrant, seized the property, and charged the defendant. The court upheld the procedure, explaining there was no reasonable expectation of privacy from aircraft flying overhead. This concept has been expanded to include helicopters flying at 400 feet over a partially enclosed greenhouse. In that case, the court upheld the search, reasoning that helicopters can lawfully fly lower than planes and that again there was no reasonable expectation of privacy.[17]

Abandonment

If a person abandons property, is there any continuing expectation of privacy regarding that property? Abandonment requires intent by the party abandoning the property to give up all claim of ownership to the item or items.[18] In *California* v. *Greenwood,* the Supreme Court held that evidence of the defendant's narcotic use obtained from his garbage bags left on the sidewalk for pickup by the trash collector was properly admitted, since the defendant had evidenced an intent to abandon the property.[19] The court held that the defendants had no subjective expectation of privacy for garbage bags left on the sidewalk that society deems as reasonable. It went on to state that such bags were readily accessible to animals, children, snoops, and other members of the public. What if a person checks out of a hotel room and leaves incriminating evidence in the trash container in the hotel room? Does the person have any expectation of privacy? Would the manager or a maid have a right to observe the material in the container? Could the manager of the hotel authorize the police to enter the vacant hotel room and seize the evidence? When someone checks out of a hotel and leaves property behind, there is no reasonable expectation of privacy. Furthermore, once having checked out, the person has no authority to prevent any member of the public or employee from entering that room to clean it for the next guest or to inspect it for damage. Since technically the manager now controls the room, that person can grant police access to the abandoned room and any evidence in the trash container.[20]

Open Fields

In an early case dealing with the Fourth Amendment and seizure of evidence from an open field, Justice Holmes pointed out in *Hester* v. *United States* that the special protection offered by the Fourth Amendment to citizens in their persons, places, papers, and effects does not extend to open fields. He went on to point out that the distinction between open fields and the home is as old as the common law.[21]

The concept of the sanctity of a person's home developed during early times. Curtilage includes the home and the land immediately surrounding it.

What effect did *Katz* have on *Hester? Hester* was decided in 1924, and *Katz* established the expectation of privacy in 1967. Did *Katz,* by implication, overrule *Hester? Oliver* v. *United States* addressed this issue.[22] The court in *Oliver* held that open fields do not provide the setting for those intimate activities that the Fourth Amendment was designed to protect.

Businesses

Does a business owner have any protection or expectation of privacy within a commercial establishment open to the general public? The question revolves around whether or not the activity engaged in by the police is classified as a search. This in turn depends on the physical characteristics of the business. An officer may enter a commercial business during the time it is open to the public and may go anywhere within that business that members of the public go, and that access will not be considered a search. However, if the officer opens a door marked private and observes criminal activity, that activity falls under the *Katz* zone of privacy rule, and it would be deemed an illegal search.

Vehicles

There is a lesser expectation of privacy when dealing with vehicles. If the officer is lawfully present at the vehicle (issuing a traffic ticket, for example) and the officer observes or smells what is inside the vehicle, or even examines the exterior of the vehicle, such activity is not considered a search within the meaning of the Fourth Amendment. However, if the officer intrudes into "protected" places, that activity may be classified as a search. Automobile Inventory Searches raise special issues.

Automobiles or motorcycles by their very nature are mobile and can be moved or relocated very easily. The court addressed the issue of the scope of a search incident to a lawful arrest in *New York* v. *Belton*, where it held that when an officer has made an arrest, he may search the passenger compartment of that automobile including the contents of any containers found within the passenger compartment.[23] The courts have relied upon the fact that automobiles stopped on highways are movable (the so-called mobility factor), as well as stating that there is a lesser expectation of privacy for items carried within an automobile.

Tracking of Movements

Is it a search for law enforcement to monitor the movements of a suspect? Clearly, law enforcement officers may surveil or follow a suspect without his or her knowledge or consent on public roads and public property. The courts have stated that persons traveling in an automobile on public roads have no reasonable expectation of privacy in their movements from one place to another.[24] Additionally, the courts allow officers to attach electronic beepers to the exterior of cars and to follow the movement of those cars from a distance. In *United States* v. *Karo,* the Supreme Court held that the use of a beeper attached to the suspect's car was not a search within the scope of the Fourth Amendment because it does not infringe on any privacy interest and conveys no protected information.[25] The court went on to state that no possessory interest had been interfered with in any meaningful way.

Random Drug Testing

In *Board of Education of Independent School Dist. No. 92 of Pottowotomie County* v. *Earls,* the Supreme Court upheld a school district's policy of requiring random drug testing as a condition for participating in interscholastic activities.[26] The court held that the Fourth Amendment was not violated because the school's interest in protecting its students' health and safety and in deterring drug usage serves an important governmental concern. The court went on to state that there was a minimal invasion of privacy caused by the tests. The court relied upon its earlier decision of *Vernonia School District* v. *Action* that allowed suspicionless drug testing of athletes.[27]

INSPECTIONS AND REGULATORY SEARCHES

These are administrative searches that fall outside the scope of the day-to-day activities normally associated with law enforcement activities. They have are considered outside the scope of the protection of the Fourth Amendment and therefore are judged by a different standard. The courts have established a reasonable legislative or administrative standard for use in these situations. This standard is less than probable cause requirement used in Fourth Amendment situations. It is a test that balances the need to search against the invasion that the search entails. This balancing test considers (1) whether the practice has a long history of judicial and public acceptance, (2) whether the practice is necessary to achieve acceptable results, and (3) whether the practice involves a relatively limited invasion of privacy.[28]

Welfare Inspections

The courts have considered that a visit by caseworkers to a welfare recipient's home does not constitute a search within the meaning of the Fourth Amendment. In *Wyman* v. *James,* the court reasoned that a welfare recipient may be required to consent to such visits as a condition of continued receipt of benefits.[29]

Inspections at Fire Scenes

Can a fire inspector or an arson inspector remain in a building after a fire to conduct an investigation without obtaining a search warrant? Clearly, fire personnel can enter a building to put out a fire. This is a form of emergency that is outside the protection of the Fourth Amendment. The courts have stated that whereas inspectors or fire fighters can remain in a building once the fire is extinguished, if they leave and desire to reenter, they must obtain a warrant.

Border Searches

The Supreme Court addressed the issue of competing rights and value in a border search in *United States* v. *Ramsey*.[30] The court held that searches at the border are per se reasonable because of the right of the sovereign nation to protect itself by stopping and searching persons and property entering its soil. Therefore, searches of persons and property entering the country may be made without obtaining a warrant or establishing probable cause. This activity is a form of balancing the national interest in preventing illegal persons and goods from entering the United States against the limited intrusion that occurs when a person decides to cross the border.

Airport Searches

In the late 1960s, we began limited searches of persons traveling on airlines if they met a predetermined profile. This process was abandoned in 1973, and then all persons traveling on airlines were required to pass through a magnetometer and have their carry-on luggage X-rayed and/or inspected. The courts have upheld such airport searches on the basis of balancing the need for the search with its limited scope. Additionally, the search is limited to a certain process, and passengers have advance notice of its existence. This notice allows them to avoid the search simply by choosing not to fly.

Searches of Prisoners

It has been said that prisoners do not lose all their Fourth Amendment rights simply because they are incarcerated. However, the courts have ruled in favor of correctional institutions in a number of situations. For example, a prisoner's mail may be read; after a visit with friends or family, they may be searched; and their religious practices may be curtailed. The courts balance the security of the institution against the rights of the inmate and in most situations find for the institution. It is said that courts are loath to second-guess prison administrators.

PROBABLE CAUSE

There are two parts to the Fourth Amendment. In the event a warrant is not used, then the first part of the amendment comes into play and requires that the people be secure "against unreasonable searches and seizures." However, when a warrant is used, the second part of the amendment requires that "no Warrants shall issue, but upon probable cause." Therefore, for a search warrant to be valid, the issuing authority must find that there are statements or other evidence that establishes probable cause.

The Supreme Court has a long history of expressing a strong preference for the use of search warrants. Warrants impose an orderly process with an independent review by the judiciary. This process has resulted in a slight shading or difference in evaluating searches with or without a warrant. The court gives more deference to searches conducted with a warrant, holding that the reviewing court is not to conduct a de novo or an independent evaluation of the magistrate's probable cause determination; rather, the review is merely intended to decide whether the evidence taken as a whole forms a substantial basis for the magistrate's finding of probable cause.[31]

Probable cause is an objective test that requires the facts to be such as would warrant a belief by a reasonable person that criminal conduct has occurred or is about to occur.

Information received from informants can complicate evaluations by the courts of whether or not probable cause exists. An informant is a person who learns of criminal conduct by being involved in the criminal culture. The term does not refer to a citizen who is a witness or victim. In *Aguilar* v. *Texas,* the Supreme Court set forth a two-prong test to determine whether probable cause existed when dealing with information from an informant.[32] This test requires (1) that the informant have a basis of knowledge for his or her allegations that someone is committing a criminal act and (2) that there must be facts to support the credibility of the informant or his or her information.

In *Illinois* v. *Gates,* the Supreme Court later adopted a "totality of the circumstances" analysis that traditionally has been used in probable cause determinations.[33] The *Gates* court continued to state that an informant's veracity, reliability, and basis of knowledge are critical in determining whether probable cause exists in any given situation.

The court views witnesses or victims in a different light. Witnesses or victims are not passing on rumor; rather, they are reciting information that they observed regarding criminal activity. The knowledge or veracity of witnesses or victims is seldom questioned for purposes of probable cause. Courts look at a variety of factors in determining whether statements by victims/witnesses establish probable cause, including the particularity of the description of the perpetrator.

SEARCH WITH A WARRANT

As indicated earlier in this chapter, the courts prefer that a law enforcement officer obtain a search warrant. The warrant process involves (1) a neutral and detached magistrate, (2) an oath or affirmation, (3) establishment of probable cause, (4) particular description of the place to be searched, (5) particular description of the items to be seized, and (6) the time of execution.

A Neutral and Detached Magistrate

The court has stated that police and prosecutors cannot be expected to remain neutral when dealing with their own investigations. A neutral and detached magistrate provides a fresh and an unbiased determination regarding the sufficiency of the evidence supporting the request for the warrant. The magistrate cannot receive any funds for issuing the warrant; otherwise, he or she has a financial interest in the case. Nor can the magistrate be involved in the execution of the warrant.

An Oath or Affirmation

Typically, warrants require a written record under an oath or affirmation. Courts are reluctant to allow other information to be brought in at a later date to rehabilitate an otherwise defective warrant. This rule should be distinguished from the oral or the telephonic issuance of warrants that is now common in many jurisdictions.

Whether the information is presented in writing or over the telephone, it must be attested to by an oath or affirmation.

Establishment of Probable Cause

Once probable cause has been established in the warrant, it can be issued. What happens if the facts supporting the probable cause are false? In *Franks* v. *Delaware,* the Supreme Court allowed the defendant to present evidence to show that the information contained in the search warrant was false and therefore that no probable cause had been established.[34] The court stated that banning such a process would destroy the probable cause requirement in a warrant because an officer could lie about the facts and there would be no way or method to counter such false allegations.

Particular Description of the Place to be Searched

The warrant does not have to describe every detail of the place to be searched. In urban areas, for single family residences, the street address is usually sufficient. However, warrants must be more specific when dealing with multiple-family apartments. For example, there may be an apartment No. 3 on each floor, and if the warrant simply states "425 S. Swift, Apt 3" without describing which floor, the warrant may well be defective, since it does not describe the particular place to be searched. As a practical matter, many jurisdictions require that officers describe the place to be searched to avoid mistakes. "The address of the premise to be searched is 323 N. Apple Street. It is a single-family residence, with an attached two-car garage. The premise has white exterior stucco walls and a brown shingle roof with two tall trees in the front yard. It is the third house on the western side of the street in a northern direction from the cross street of S. Apple."

Particular Description of the Items to Be Seized

The leading case in this area is *Marron* v. *United States.*[35] Marron required that any item sized be particularly described in the warrant. However, in *Coolidge* v. *New Hampshire,* this concept was broadened to allow officers to seize evidence that was not described in the warrant if (1) it was in plain view and (2) it was of an incriminating nature.[36] Although *Coolidge* does not allow officers to go on a fishing expedition searching for evidence, if they are conducting a search of a premise and during the search observe other items that are incriminating, they may lawfully seize those items. For example, officers may have a warrant that allows them to search for bank records that show the commission of a mail fraud, and after opening a desk drawer they observe narcotics, they may seize the narcotics.

The Time of Execution

Some jurisdictions allow warrants to be executed only within a limited number of days after issuance. For example, a warrant might be issued on October 15 and can be served any time within the next ten days. Approximately half the states require that warrants be executed only during the daylight hours unless the officers can show some special need to serve the warrant at other times, such as during the evening hours.

REVIEW QUESTIONS

1. Explain the purpose of the Fourth Amendment. Is it an absolute bar to all searches? Why? Why not?

2. What principle is the Exclusionary Rule based upon? Does it work? Can you list other ways that the objective of the Exclusionary Rule could be accomplished?

3. What is the zone of privacy? How does it work? Does it attach to places or persons?

4. List some of the exceptions to the Fourth Amendment. Which one is the most important in your opinion?

5. Describe the requirements for the issuance of a search warrant. Which one is the most important, and which the least important? Justify your answer.

ENDNOTES

1. Wayne LaFave et al., *Criminal Procdure,* 3rd ed. (West, St. Paul, Minn.) 2000.
2. 232 U.S. 383 (1014).
3. 338 U.S. 25 (1949).
4. 367 U.S. 643 (1961).
5. 468 U.S. 897 (1984).
6. *Silverhorne Lumber Co.* v. *United States,* 251 U.S. 385 (1920).
7. 371 U.S. 471 (1963).
8. See *Silverman* v. *United States,* 365 U.S. 505 (1961).
9. 389 U.S. 347 (1967).
10. *Schneckloth* v. *Bustamonte,* 412 U.S. 218 (1973).
11. Ibid.
12. See for example, *On Lee* v. *U.S.,* 343 U.S. 747 (1952) and *Hoffa* v. *U.S.,* 385 U.S. 293 (1966).
13. *United States* v. *Matlock,* 415 U.S. 164 (1974).
14. 496 U.S. 128 (1983).
15. There are some situations in which police officers may enter the house without a warrant, but these are exceptions to the general rule.
16. 476 U.S. 207 (1986).
17. *Florida v. Riley,* 488 U.S. 445 (1989).
18. *Abel* v. *United States,* 362 U.S. 217 (1960).
19. 486 U.S. 35 (1988).
20. *Abel* v. *United States,* 362 U.S. 217 (1960).
21. 265 U.S. 57 (1924).
22. 466 U.S. 170 (1984).
23. 453 U.S. 454 (1981).
24. 460 U.S. 276 (1983).
25. 468 U.S. 705 (1984).
26. 122 S.Ct. 2559 (2002).
27. 515 U.S. 646 (1995).
28. See *Camara v. Municipal Court,* 387 U.S. 523 (1967).
29. 400 U.S. 309 (1971).
30. 431 U.S. 606 (1977).
31. *Massachusetts* v. *Upton,* 466 U.S. 727 (1984).

32. 378 U.S. 108 (1964).
33. 462 U.S. 213 (1983).
34. 438 U.S. 154 (1978).
35. 275 U.S. 192 (1927).
36. 403 U.S. 443 (1971).

CHAPTER 3

The Arrest

He always has an alibi, and one or two to spare: At whatever time the deed took place—Macavity wasn't there.

—T. S. Eliot, "Macavity: The Mystery Cat"

ARREST OF THE LAW VIOLATOR

When a person violates a criminal law, society should take some action against that person: An arrest should be made. Originally, the members or citizens of society were responsible for taking the violator into custody. In fact, it was such a responsibility for members of society to make the arrest that failure to do so was a violation. Even withholding information about a known crime from the authorities was a violation. In both instances, the violation was called a "misprision of a felony." As law enforcement agencies were created, the citizen was relieved of much of the responsibility for making arrests. Yet the citizen, or "private person," has not given up this right to make an arrest.

Private Person Arrest

The arrest by a private person is sometimes referred to as a "citizen's arrest," but the private person does not have to be a citizen to make an arrest. The private person may make arrests under certain conditions, which are restrictive in order to discourage the private person from making unnecessary arrests. Arrests should be made by the professional, that is, the law enforcement officer. Even though arrests by a private person are discouraged, thousands of private person arrests are made annually in this country. These arrests are made primarily by security guards employed by private industries to curb shoplifting and employee thefts. The records of one drug store chain reflect that the security guards of that chain average more than twelve thousand private person arrests annually. It is important, therefore, that the private person know his or her rights and limitations in making a private person arrest. A private person arrest generally requires that the crime for which the arrest is made has been committed or attempted in the presence of the arresting person. The statutes of some states provide for the arrest of a felon even though the crime occurred in the absence of the private party. A felony must have in fact been committed, and the private person must have had reasonable cause to believe that the person arrested committed the felony.

Although the powers of arrest and the procedure in making arrests may have been covered in other areas of study, a brief discussion of arrests is useful because of their importance in the prosecution of cases. If an arrest is not made lawfully, any information learned or physical evidence obtained will in most instances be inadmissible in court, and it is likely that the offender will never be brought to trial. In *Legrand* v. *Bedinger,* the court stated the following:

> The term "arrest" is derived from the French, arrester, to stop or stay, and signifies a restraint of a man's person; depriving him of his own will and liberty, and binding him to become obedient to the will of the law. It is called the beginning of imprisonment.[1]

Legally, an arrest has been defined as the taking of a person into custody in the manner authorized by law. The arrest is made by actual restraint of the person or by submission of the offender to the custody of an officer. The person arrested may be subjected to such restraint as is reasonable for the arrest and detention. There must be sufficient probable cause for the arrest to be made. Briefly, it has been held that probable, or reasonable, cause is shown if a person of ordinary prudence would be led to believe that a crime had been committed. Reasonable cause may exist even though there may be some room for doubt, but it must be more than a mere suspicion that a crime had been committed. It is difficult to set forth guidelines in determining probable cause. One might ask what facts would cause an ordinary, prudent person to believe that a crime had been committed. The test for probable cause must be determined by the circumstances of each individual case on the basis of the situation confronting the officer at the time that the arrest is made. The ordinary, prudent person test has been criticized as being unrealistic because the officer, through training and experience, could recognize certain facts that would cause him or her to believe that a crime had been committed. Such facts may not be of a suspicious nature to the ordinary, prudent person. Yet the courts have consistently adhered to this test. However, most courts will consider the facts as seen by the officer before dismissing a charge because of lack of probable cause.

Arrest by a Law Enforcement Officer

We should define the terms *law enforcement officer* or *peace officer* before continuing this discussion. A law enforcement officer or peace officer is a person employed by some branch of the government and is sworn to uphold the laws of the United States, the state, county, or city by which he or she is employed. The statutes of some states specifically spell out who are law enforcement or peace officers within that state; if not listed in the statutes, a person is not a law enforcement officer within that state. Law enforcement or peace officers may be placed in four basic categories: federal officers, employed by the U.S. government; state officers, employed by the state; sheriffs, employed by the county or parish; and city police officers, employed by their respective cities.

ARRESTS AND WARRANTS

As we indicated earlier, the Fourth Amendment protects against unreasonable searches and seizures. This language makes it clear that the amendment applies both to searches of persons and places and to arrests of persons. An arrest may be made in two ways: with or without a warrant. As indicated, in both situations the arresting officer must have probable cause to arrest. There are two elements to probable cause to arrest: (1) that a crime has been committed and (2) that the person to be arrested committed the offense.[2]

Arrest without a Warrant

An arrest without a warrant is the most common form of arrest. Historically, warrantless arrests have always been allowed under the common law. The courts have held that requiring a warrant for every arrest is impractical.[3] However, there is one situation in which an arrest warrant is required. The Supreme Court held that unless there are exigent or emergency circumstances, the police may not enter a private home to make a warrantless arrest.[4]

The courts have held that entry into a home is an extreme intrusion and that entry to make an arrest is very similar to entry to search a home, and therefore the Fourth Amendment requires that a neutral magistrate make a determination that there is probable cause to make the arrest before such an intrusion is allowed. The exception to this warrant requirement is exigent or emergency circumstances. Courts have ruled that fresh or hot pursuit of a suspect as he or she runs into a home does not require a warrant.[5] Additionally, if the police believe that if they wait for the issuance of a warrant the suspect will destroy the evidence, they may enter and make an arrest without a warrant.[6]

Arrest with a Warrant

Even though officers may arrest a suspect without a warrant, there is legal preference for arrests made with a warrant. This is the case because it places the determination of finding of the existence of probable cause in the hands of a neutral magistrate. The Supreme Court, though upholding warrantless arrests, has stated that the deliberate determination of magistrates is preferred over the hurried actions of police officers.[7]

An arrest warrant is a written order issued by the proper judicial officer upon a showing of probable cause directing the arrest of a particular person. Arrest warrants must conform to certain requirements. Although these vary from jurisdiction to jurisdiction, most warrants require the following information:

- The caption or title of the court from which the warrant is issued.
- The name of the person to be arrested. The warrant must describe with particularity the person to be seized. (Many warrants also require a detailed description of the person, including height, weight, and hair color.)
- A description of the offense. This normally is described in the language of the statute or law that the suspect violated.
- The date of issuance of the warrant.
- A command that officers take the suspect into custody and bring him or her before the proper judicial officer.
- A signature of the issuing official.

Many states require officers to have warrants of arrest for misdemeanors committed outside their presence. This circumstance usually means that the officer must witness the criminal act. The officer doesn't have to see the offense; the courts have ruled that use of any of the officer's senses is sufficient. The officer may hear the offense (sounds of gun fire) or even smell the offense (marijuana burning). Recently, some states have enacted statutory exceptions to this requirement. Most notable is the authority of officers to arrest suspects in domestic violence cases, even if the officer did not see the suspect strike the victim.

Some jurisdictions allow for the use of telephonic arrest warrants. These warrants are most often used when it is after normal working hours and when it is considered necessary to arrest the suspect immediately. In these jurisdictions, officers telephone a prosecuting attorney and explain why they need a warrant. The prosecutor then calls a judge at his or her home, who listens to the officer's testimony over the phone. The judge may authorize the issuance of a warrant and direct the officer to fill in the blanks on the warrant and print the judge's name. A copy of this warrant is then given to the judge when he or she comes to work.

STOP AND FRISK AND OTHER DETENTIONS

Until 1967, a "search" was an all-or-nothing concept. Either it was a search subject to the probable cause and warrant requirements, or it was not a search. This situation often was referred to as the bright-line approach. In 1967 and 1968, the Supreme Court devised nontraditonal definitions of probable cause on the basis of the concept of a floating reasonableness standard. The 1967 case of *Camara* v. *Municipal Court of City and County of San Francisco* (387 U.S. 523) involved administrative inspections. The 1968 case was *Terry* v. *Ohio* (392 U.S. 1). Terry developed the concept of searches of differential intrusiveness, and in those cases in which the intrusiveness is minimal, the standard of "reasonable suspicion" was deemed sufficent. The Supreme Court in *Terry* stated that "there is no ready test for determining the reasonableness other than by balancing the need to search against the invasion which the search entails. The procedures used by the police in these situations must be governed by the exigencies which justify its initiation."

The *Terry* case developed the concept of stop and frisk. A stop and frisk is less than an arrest. The rules applying to temporary detention also apply to stop-and-frisk situations. It was a standard police practice to stop suspicious persons in public places for the purposes of questioning them or conducting an investigation. Until the *Terry* case, there was a question as to whether this procedure constituted a violation of the Fourth Amendment, since the officers generally do not have probable cause to detain and question the individuals.

In *Terry* v. *Ohio,* an officer observed Terry and two other men walking back and forth in front of a store. The officer decided that the men were casing the store for a possible robbery. When he approached them and asked for identification, he received only mumbled replies. He then grabbed Terry, turned him around, and patted him down. The officer found a pistol in Terry's pocket. Terry, an excon, was arrested for carrying a concealed weapon. The Court upheld the search and found no Fourth Amendment violation.

The Court held that a police officer may temporarily detain a person for questioning if the officer has a reasonable suspicion that criminal activity may be involved. The officer may pat down for weapons only if the officer has the additional reasonable suspicion that the pat down is necessary for safety reasons.

Temporary Detention

Mere temporary detention for questioning is not considered to be an arrest (50 Cal. Rev. 99). If, however, police restraint goes beyond that which is reasonably necessary for questioning, an arrest may result. For example, handcuffing an alleged drug dealer and moving to another area of the airport for questioning is considered to be an arrest (*People* v. *Campbell,* 118 C.A. 3rd 588, 1981).

A temporary detention of a vehicle is less of a full arrest, and, accordingly, the level of probable cause necessary to support a temporary detention is less than that required for a full arrest. A detention starts the moment that the officer directs the vehicle to stop, for example, when an officer turns on the red lights. It is not a detention if the vehicle is already parked and the officer asks the driver for his or her license or other identification (*People* v. *Gonzales,* 164 C.A. 3rd 1194, 1981).

Reasonable Suspicion

A detention requires at least reasonable suspicion. (*Note:* Reasonable suspicion is less than probable cause. The officer must have reasonable suspicion that criminal activity is occurring, is about to occur, or has recently occurred and that the vehicle or a person in the vehicle is connected with that criminal activity.) The reasonable suspicion must be based on specific facts that can be articulated to a court. If the suspicion relates to any person in the vehicle (including a passenger), the officer may stop the vehicle.

In *People v. Remiro,* 89 C.A. 3rd 809 (1979), an appellate court upheld the stop of the vehicle on the basis of the officer's reasonable suspicion. In this case, the officer saw a van he did not recognize that was driving slowly in a residential neighborhood at 1:30 A.M. The officer followed the van and noticed that it was traveling in a circle. He stopped the van. His stop was upheld on the basis of the following articulable facts:

1. The van's speed and route were suggestive of a "casing" operation.
2. The officer was familiar with the neighborhood, its vehicles, and driving patterns.
3. He did not recognize the vehicle.
4. He knew that many residential burglaries had occurred in the neighborhood.
5. He knew that vans were frequently used in such burglaries.

In *People v. Dominguez,* 118 C.A. 3rd 1315 (1985), the court upheld a detention of the vehicle when the identities of the persons within the vehicle were unknown and a warrant existed for the registered owner. The court indicated that if none of the people could be the registered owner, that is, of a different race, then the legality of the detention would be questionable.

A stop based on a "wanted flyer" or a similar notice or bulletin issued by another jurisdiction and related to completed criminal activity is sufficient basis to detain a vehicle and its occupants if the other jurisdiction had a valid basis to issue the flyer, and so forth (*U.S.* v. *Hemsley,* 105 S Ct. 675, 1985).

Distinguishing an Arrest from a Terry-Type Detention

Often it is necessary to distinguish an arrest from a stop-and-frisk situation, especially if evidence is found during the detention. The leading Supreme Court decision on this question is *United States* v. *Sharp,* 470 U.S. 675 (1990). In that case, the length of the detention was considered. The Court indicated that a Terry-level stop will ordinarily be for a fairly short duration and that the detention will be no longer than necessary to effectuate the purpose of the detention. Other factors considered include the following: Did the police pursue the investigation diligently? Was the method of investigation likely to confirm or dispel the officer's suspicions quickly?

A warrantless "protective sweep" of a residence by the police who are making a lawful arrest in the residence is considered to be legal if the police have a reasonable suspicion that the residence may contain an individual who poses a danger to the officers or to others (*Maryland* v. *Buie,* 494 U.S. 325, 1985). The protective sweep should be a quick and limited search of the premises and narrowly confined to a cursory visual inspection of those places where an individual may be hiding.

TERRITORIAL JURISDICTION TO MAKE AN ARREST

From a procedural standpoint, it is important to determine if an officer has the authority to make an arrest, particularly when he or she has no warrant. If the officer does not have the authority, the arrest will be declared unlawful. One factor that becomes significant in determining the officer's authority is whether the officer was in his or her territorial jurisdiction. In most states, the territorial jurisdiction of the city police is confined to the city limits. Any arrest without a warrant made beyond the city limits would have to be made as a private person and to meet the restrictions of a private person arrest. Similarly, the territorial authority of the sheriff of a county or parish is limited to the county or parish line. Some states limit the jurisdiction of the sheriff within the county, allowing arrests only in unincorporated areas. These states remove the sheriff's authority to make arrests within an incorporated city. However, in most states the sheriff is considered to be the chief law enforcement officer of the county and has authority to make arrests anyplace within the county. The sheriff, when within city limits, would have concurrent authority with the city police.

It was held for a long time that if an outlaw was able to outdistance a sheriff to the county line, the sheriff had to discontinue the pursuit since he had no authority to make an arrest in the adjoining county. To prevent the escape of an outlaw under these circumstances, the "hot pursuit" rule was developed. This rule provided that if an officer was in "hot" or "fresh" pursuit of an offender, the officer could follow the offender into another jurisdiction to make an arrest. The problem presented by this rule was, What would be interpreted as fresh pursuit? In early times when the local officer made the pursuit on horseback, it was concluded that if the officer could keep the outlaw in sight or still see the dust kicked up by the outlaw's horse, the officer was in fresh pursuit. With the advent of the motor vehicle as a means of escape, as well as pursuit, the "in sight" theory became impractical. Therefore, it is generally held today that if a pursuit is uninterrupted and continuous, it is a fresh pursuit. But even with this concept of fresh pursuit, the local officer had no authority to cross a state line to make an arrest. Thus, if the fleeing offender was able to reach the state line before apprehension, he or she had sanctuary in the next state. With rapid transportation available to criminals, new rules and regulations concerning the extent of pursuit had to be formulated.

Uniform Act of Fresh Pursuit

Today, most states have adopted what is known as the Uniform Act of Fresh Pursuit. This act provides that a peace officer of one state may enter another state in fresh pursuit to arrest one who has committed a felony in the state from which the offender fled. In adopting the Uniform Act of Fresh Pursuit, a few states have not only made the act applicable to felonies but also to certain misdemeanors, usually those involving moral turpitude. Moral turpitude has been defined as conduct contrary to justice, honesty, modesty, or good morals. There is no specific distance set forth in the act that the officer may proceed within the state in order to make the arrest. The act does provide that after the arrest is made, the officer must take the arrested person before a local magistrate, without unnecessary delay, for a hearing to determine the lawfulness of the arrest. If the magistrate concludes that the arrest was lawful, the magistrate will either commit the accused or release him or her on bail pending extradition proceedings.

Limited Arrest Powers

A few states do grant local officers the right to make an arrest without a warrant anywhere in the state. This right is based on the theory that, when sworn as a peace officer within a city or county, the officer swears to uphold the constitution and laws of the state as well as local ordinances, thereby giving the officer statewide arrest powers. But as stated, in most states the local officer has authority to make arrests without a warrant only within the territorial jurisdiction in which he or she is employed, except in fresh pursuit instances. Some people in the justice system believe that this limited arrest power by local officers hampers law enforcement. As a result, statutes have been passed in some states extending the arrest power of local officers.

Although the extended authority differs among states, the power to make arrests without a warrant beyond the territorial area in which an officer is employed is usually confined to any one of three situations. Authority has been granted in some states permitting an officer to make a lawful arrest beyond the officer's area if the officer has prior permission from the chief or sheriff of the area in which the arrest is to be made. This granted authority is based upon an old posse comitatus right of a sheriff. The posse comitatus right came into being early in the history of this country and particularly in the western part of the United States. The sheriff was often the only law enforcement officer within the county and therefore frequently needed assistance in locating and apprehending a criminal. To obtain this assistance, the sheriff was authorized by law to call on citizens of the county and deputize them to assist in the location and apprehension of a dangerous felon. These deputies were formed into a posse. Under posse comitatus, the officer making the arrest, in a sense, is a temporary officer of the jurisdiction in which the arrest is made. Further, the right to make an arrest beyond the officer's area of employment has been granted in instances when the offender is wanted for a crime committed in the officer's area of employment. In other instances, authority has been granted to an officer to make arrests beyond the officer's jurisdiction on an extended private person arrest power. This extended right permits the officer to arrest a person who has committed a crime or where there is reasonable cause to believe that a crime was committed in the presence of the officer and that lives may be in danger, property may be immediately damaged, or the offender may escape.

State Police Agencies

All states except Hawaii have some type of state police or law enforcement system. The state police agencies have statewide territorial jurisdiction, but states vary considerably as to the power of its state police to make arrests. In some states, the state police have the power to enforce all state laws and have concurrent power throughout the state with local law enforcement agencies. In other states, the state police have limited jurisdiction that confines them to enforcing criminal laws only on state property. In addition to the state police, a number of investigative agencies in most states have limited authority and arrest powers and are employed to perform specific duties. Examples of limited investigative authority and arrest powers are game wardens and drug administrations. In some states, the state police not only enforce state laws generally but also patrol the highways; other states have a separate agency for this purpose, a highway patrol. Although the territorial jurisdiction of state police is restricted to the state boundaries, the Uniform Act of Fresh Pursuit is applicable to these agencies as well as to local officers.

Federal Law Enforcement Agencies

Technically, the only peace officers of the U.S. government are the U.S. Marshals within the Department of Justice. But as with the states, a number of federal investigative agencies have emergency arrest powers. All federal officers have territorial jurisdiction throughout the United States and possessions. Also within the U.S. Department of Justice is the Federal Bureau of Investigation (FBI), which was established in 1908 and has investigative jurisdiction over all federal violations not specifically assigned to some other federal agency. The FBI began in 1908 as the Bureau of Investigation.[8] It was created in part because of other law enforcement agencies' inability to investigate and arrest corrupt politicians and business leaders. The Bureau began as a small organization; however, it grew and became a household name under the guidance of J. Edgar Hoover. The FBI investigates a wide range of violations. Examples of FBI investigations include bank robberies; kidnapping when the victim has been, or is presumed to have been, transported across a state line; theft from interstate shipment; internal security matters; and interstate organized crime activities. The Federal Drug Enforcement Administration is now a part of the Federal Bureau of Investigation. The Immigration and Naturalization Service, of which the Border Patrol is a part, is within the Department of Justice.

Within the U.S. Treasury Department is the Secret Service, created in 1865 to investigate and curtail counterfeiting of the U.S. currency. After the assassination of President William McKinley in 1901, the Secret Service was charged with the duty of protecting the president of the United States. This duty has been expanded to include not only the president but also his immediate family, certain other high governmental officials, and some foreign dignitaries. Other agencies within the U.S. Treasury Department are the Customs Service; the Alcohol, Tobacco, and Firearms Service; the Internal Revenue Service; and the U.S. Postal Service.

Among the duties of the Customs Service are investigations of smuggling operations. The Alcohol, Tobacco, and Firearms Service investigates violations pertaining to the illegal manufacture of alcoholic beverages, illegal possession of certain firearms, and tobacco infractions. The Internal Revenue Service oversees the collection of federal income taxes and violations of federal income tax law. U.S. Postal Service inspectors investigate violations pertaining to the mail, such as use of the mails to defraud and mail theft. There are a number of other investigative agencies of the federal government, but the foregoing are the ones most frequently encountered in law enforcement.

After the events of September 11, 2001, and in response to a number of factors, President George W. Bush created the Office of Homeland Security. He appointed Tom Ridge as its first director. The mission of the Department of Homeland Security is to do the following:

- Prevent terrorist attacks within the United States;
- Reduce America's vulnerability to terrorism, and;
- Minimize the damage and recover from attacks that do occur.

The Department of Homeland Security has a clear and an efficient organizational structure with four divisions:

Border and Transportation Security. The Department of Homeland Security is responsible for securing our nation's borders and transportation systems, would manage who and what enters our homeland, and work to prevent the entry of terrorists and the instruments of terrorism while ensuring the speedy flow of legitimate traffic.

Emergency Preparedness and Response. The Department of Homeland Security will ensure the preparedness of our nation's emergency response professionals, provide the federal government's response, and aid America's recovery from terrorist attacks and natural disasters.

Chemical, Biological, Radiological, and Nuclear Countermeasures. The Department of Homeland Security leads the federal government's efforts in preparing for and responding to the full range of terrorist threats involving weapons of mass destruction.

Information Analysis and Infrastructure Protection. The Department of Homeland Security merges under one roof the capability to identify and assess current and future threats to the homeland, map those threats against our current vulnerabilities, inform the president, issue timely warnings, and immediately take or effect appropriate preventive and protective action.

FORCE IN EFFECTING AN ARREST

The laws among the states are comparatively uniform as to the amount of force that may be used by a peace officer in making an arrest, but there seems to be some doubt as to the degree of force that may be used by a private person. The statutes of most states provide that any peace officer who has reasonable cause to believe that the person to be arrested has committed a public offense may use reasonable force to effect the arrest, to prevent escape, or to overcome resistance. It is also generally held that the officer may break open a door or window of a house in which the person to be arrested is, or is believed to be, located. Unless there is a danger to the life of the officer or others, the officer must first demand admittance and explain the purpose for which the admittance is desired.

Although the officer may use whatever force is reasonably necessary to overcome the resistance of the accused, the officer may not use force that is disproportionate to the resistance met. If undue force is used, the officer could be guilty of violating the civil rights of the accused and be prosecuted in a federal court under the Civil Rights Acts (see Title 18 U.S. Code, section 242, and Title 42 U.S. Code, section 1983). That treatment is exactly what happened in *Tennessee v. Garner.*[9] In that case, Memphis police officers responded to a call of a burglary in progress. One of the officers went into the backyard of the house and saw Edward Garner flee from the house and attempt to climb a chain-link fence. The officer fired his weapon and killed the suspect. The perpetrator's father filed a federal civil rights lawsuit, and the U.S. Supreme Court held that the use of deadly force was a form of seizure protected by the Fourth Amendment and that it was unreasonable under these circumstances. The court reasoned that the officer was not in fear for his safety and had no evidence that the suspect was armed or a danger to any other person.

Whether excessive force was used in a particular instance is a matter of fact that would be determined by some board of inquiry, jury, or judge. The question to be determined is whether the force used was that which an ordinary, prudent person would have used under the circumstances. Any mistreatment of an accused person once he or she is under control could also be a violation of the accused's civil rights. In addition to having violated the federal laws on civil rights, the officer could possibly be charged with assault and battery under a state statute.

FOCUS: *Excessive Force and Videotapes*

In March 1991, several Los Angeles police officers were videotaped beating an African American male named Rodney King with their batons as he lay on the ground. The officers were charged with state crimes and tried in a Superior Court in Simi Valley, a suburb of Los Angeles. The state jury acquitted the officers, and they were then tried and found guilty of federal crimes of violating Mr. King's civil rights.

The videotape that was broadcast across the world shows the officers beating Mr. King for 19 seconds. The tape does not show that the officers had chased Mr. King for 8 miles, surrounded him, and used electronic darts carrying 50,000 volts that failed to subdue him. When he ran for the nearby park, the officers began to wildly beat on Mr. King. That was the portion that was captured on videotape and shocked the world.

Approximately 11 years later, on July 6, 2002, Inglewood police officers were involved in an altercation with a young African American male that was also videotaped. The tape shows the officers pulling the handcuffed male to his feet and slamming his body onto the top of the police cruiser. Officer Jeremy More is then shown striking the male with his fist as he lay on the vehicle. The officer claims that the male was squeezing his testicles and so he had to apply force to make him let go.

> When should an officer be able to use force to effect and arrest?
> When does force become excessive?
> What can be done to prevent officers from using excessive force?

More and more law enforcement agencies are using dogs in the location and capture of suspects. To avoid a possible excessive force accusation in the capture of a suspect, the dog handler should warn the suspect that a dog will be released unless the suspect surrenders peacefully. Also, the dog should be restrained once the suspect is under control.

But what about the private person? How much force may he or she use to effect the arrest? The statutes of many states are silent on this issue. Although it is generally conceded that a private person may also use that degree of force reasonably necessary to make the arrest and to overcome resistance, most states do not give a private person the right to break into a dwelling to make an arrest for a misdemeanor violation.

Calling for Assistance

In making an arrest, an officer or a private person may call upon as many persons as are deemed necessary for assistance in making the arrest. In general, no prosecutive action can be taken against anyone for refusing to assist the private person in making an arrest. However, the statute of one state provides that any person making an arrest may orally summon as many people as he or she finds necessary, and that all those failing to obey such a summons for assistance will be guilty of a misdemeanor. This provision implies that anyone failing to assist a private person will be subject to prosecution. Most states make it a violation for certain persons to refuse to assist an officer in making an arrest when summoned to do so. As was the case with states that allow officers to arrest outside their jurisdiction, this provision is based upon the old posse comitatus policy that a sheriff had the authority to deputize members of a community and demand that they assist him in the location and apprehension of an outlaw. In modern practice, it is not necessary in an emergency situation to deputize a person before requesting assistance. Many times an officer is confronted with circumstances in which immediate help is needed in making an arrest. Under these circumstances, an officer may orally summon those present to assist him or her, and a failure to come to the officer's aid may subject those persons to prosecution.

States differ considerably in who must assist an officer in making an arrest. The statutes of several states provide that an officer making a lawful arrest may command the aid of every male person over eighteen years of age to assist him or her, and any male failing to obey the command for assistance shall be guilty of a misdemeanor. This provision makes no mention of the male's being "able-bodied." This provision was excluded purposely. When an officer is presented with an emergency situation, he or she should not have to spend time determining who is physically capable of assisting him or her. It also prohibits an individual from using the excuse that he is not physically able to assist. Not all requests for assistance entail a physical encounter with the accused. The assistance may be only a request that the individual radio for other police units to come to the aid of an officer, a task that could be performed by a person in a wheelchair.

The statutes of some states provide that every able-bodied person over the age of eighteen years who refuses to aid an officer in making an arrest after being commanded to do so is guilty of a misdemeanor. Such a provision makes both men and women subject to prosecution should they fail to assist in making an arrest after being summoned to do so by an officer. The problem created with the provision that the person be able-bodied is how you determine whether the person summoned was able-bodied. It has been held that the mere fact that there may be some danger involved in rendering assistance is not sufficient reason to refuse to assist. The statutes of a few states provide that every person who fails to obey a command by an officer to assist him or her in making an arrest shall be guilty of a misdemeanor. Such a provision is all-encompassing, since no mention is made of the person being able-bodied, male or female, or within a specific age designation.

The statute of one state provides that the officer requesting assistance must be in uniform for prosecutive action to be applicable. This requirement is again to eliminate the possibility of an individual's using the excuse that he or she did not know that the person requesting assistance was an officer. However, this restriction is not without complications. In view of the wording of the statute, even if an individual knows that the person summoning assistance is an officer, unless the officer is in uniform when summoning aid, the individual cannot be prosecuted if he or she fails to assist the officer. This provision also raises the question, What is a uniform? Some law enforcement agencies have adopted the sport coat or blazer and sport pants style of uniform, which gives the appearance of civilian clothing. Would this be considered a uniform within the meaning of the statute?

When a person responds to an officer's call or demand for assistance, he or she has the same rights and privileges as the officer. Such a person is, in effect, a temporary law enforcement officer and has the right to use reasonable force to effect the arrest. If the person called upon to assist the officer acts in good faith, he or she is protected from civil liability.[10]

Resisting Arrest

Generally, it is a violation to willfully resist, delay, or obstruct a peace officer in the performance of his or her duty, including making an arrest. Yet, may an individual who is being arrested by a private person resist that arrest without being subjected to prosecution for the resistance? Most state statutes are silent on this point. Since there is no provision that an individual can be charged with an act of resisting arrest by a private person, presumably one is not subject to any additional charge except the one for which the arrest is being made, and the only peril is in meeting the resistance of the private person.

In this discussion, a question regarding the right of a person to resist an unlawful arrest must also arise. As previously stated, it is generally held that resisting an officer in the performance of his or her duty is a violation. But is an officer performing his or her duty by making an unlawful arrest? It was previously held at common law that a person could resist an unlawful arrest, and this view is followed in some of the states whether the arrest is being made by an officer or a private person. This situation results in many curbside court sessions and brawls between the accused and the arresting person, with each claiming to be right and with violent resistance taking place. Other states have provided that if a person is being arrested or has reasonable cause to believe that he or she is being arrested by an officer, the person is under the duty to refrain from using force or any weapon to resist such arrest. By court interpretation, it has been held that this provision refers to unlawful arrests as well as lawful ones. Note, however, that the provision pertains only to officers and is still silent about resisting arrest by a private person.

Although a person may not resist an unlawful arrest in some states, he or she is not without recourse. One is entitled to seek immediate release from custody by a writ of habeas corpus proceeding and may sue those responsible for the illegal arrest for damages in civil court. Once the arrest of a suspect is completed, he or she should be searched for weapons and evidence. Depending upon the circumstances of the case, it may be advisable to search the immediate area where the arrest took place for any additional evidence, including instruments that may have been used in committing the crime. A search may also be made for any hidden weapons that the suspect might use to attempt an escape or to harm the arresting officer or others. These searches are considered reasonable as incidental to the arrest because if the search were not done at the time, evidence could be lost or destroyed.

MIRANDA AND ITS EFFECT

Before the U.S. Supreme Court decided *Miranda* v. *Arizona,* confessions and the accompanying interrogations were decided on a case-by-case method.[11] This approach reviewed the circumstances surrounding the interrogation to determine whether the suspect's will was broken by the police. The interrogation was considered improper if it violated the suspect's due process rights.

Pre-Miranda Techniques

In *Brown* v. *Mississippi,* the defendant was taken to the crime scene, where he was questioned regarding his involvement in a murder.[12] After denying guilt, he was hung by a rope from a tree. He continued to claim innocence and was tied to the tree and whipped. Brown was released but subsequently seized again and whipped until he finally confessed. The court held that the confession was a product of coercion and brutality and therefore violated the defendant's Fourteenth Amendment due process rights.

In *Ashcraft* v. *Tennessee,* the defendant was taken to the police station and questioned continuously for two days regarding the murder of his wife.[13] The officers questioned Ashcraft in relays because they became exhausted during the interrogation; however, the defendant was denied rest and sleep during the entire time. The court held that the prolonged interrogation of Ashcraft was coercive, and therefore the confession was involuntary and inadmissible.

In *Spano* v. *New York,* the defendant was suspected of a murder.[14] Spano informed a friend who was a rookie police officer that he had in fact killed the victim. Spano was arrested, and the rookie officer was instructed to tell Spano that he (the officer) was in trouble and might lose his job unless Spano confessed. Spano finally confessed to the killing. The Supreme Court held that the use of deception as a means of psychological pressure to obtain a confession was a violation of the defendant's constitutional rights and that therefore the confession was involuntary and suppressed.

In *Escobedo* v. *Illinois,* the defendant was arrested for murder and interrogated for several hours at the police station.[15] During the interrogation, Escobedo repeatedly requested to see his attorney, who was also at the police station demanding to see his client. The police refused both requests and finally obtained the confession. The court held that Escobedo was denied his right to counsel and that therefore no statement obtained from him could be used at a criminal trial.

The *Escobedo* decision was confusing because it is not clear when the right to counsel attaches during the interrogation. Trial courts began interpreting the meaning of *Escobedo* differently. Thus, the stage was set for the U.S. Supreme Court to clear up the confusion that had resulted from its previous rulings.

Miranda Safeguards

In *Miranda* v. *Arizona,* the U.S. Supreme Court established certain safeguards for individuals who are being interrogated by police.[16] Most people know that the *Miranda* decision requires police officers to advise defendants of their constitutional rights. In reality, *Miranda* established a four-prong test that must be satisfied before a suspect's statements can be admitted into evidence. The test requires affirmative answers to all four of the following questions:

1. Was the statement voluntary?
2. Was the Miranda warning given?
3. Was there a waiver by the suspect?
4. Was the waiver intelligent and voluntary?

Unless all these questions are answered in the affirmative, none of the suspect's statements can be admitted into evidence. In *Miranda,* the defendant was arrested at home in Phoenix, Arizona, in connection with the rape and kidnapping of a female and was taken to a police station for questioning. At the time, he was twenty-three years old, poor, and basically illiterate. After being questioned for two hours, he confessed to the crime. The Supreme Court issued its now famous Miranda warning requirement stating the following:

> We hold that when an individual is taken into custody or otherwise deprived of his freedom . . . the privilege against self-incrimination is jeopardized. . . . He must be warned prior to any questioning that he has a right to remain silent, that anything he says can be used against him in a court of law, that he has a right to an attorney, and that if he cannot afford an attorney one will be appointed for him prior to any questioning if he so desires.

The *Miranda* decision has drawn a bright line for admissibility of confessions and admissions obtained during investigations. It changed the way police interrogated suspects. The decision was sweeping in its scope, but it still left questions unanswered.

In *Berkemer* v. *McCarty,* the Supreme Court held that the Miranda warning must be given during any custodial interrogation.[17] The court held that a person subjected to a custodial interrogation must be given the warning regardless of the severity of the offense, but questioning a motorist at a routine traffic stop does not constitute custodial interrogation.

The *Miranda* decision has generated both support and criticism since its inception. Supporters argue that it protects the rights of those accused of crimes, whereas detractors claim that it allows the guilty to go free because the officer may not have followed all the rules. In recent years, the courts have begun to allow statements to be admitted into evidence despite the absence of the Miranda warning.

The Eroding of Miranda

Miranda did not prevent statements obtained in violation of its rules from being used to impeach the credibility of a defendant who takes the witness stand. In *Harris* v. *New York,* the court held that it was proper to use such statements so long as the jury was instructed that the confession was not to be considered evidence of guilt but only to determine whether the defendant was telling the truth.[18] Voluntary statements made by the defendant without having received the Miranda warning are admissible even though the defendant is later advised of his or her rights and waives those rights. In *Oregon* v. *Elstad,* the defendant was picked up at his home as a suspect in a burglary and made incriminating statements without receiving his Miranda warning.[19] After being advised of his rights, he waived them and signed a confession. The Supreme Court held that the self-incrimination clause of the Fifth Amendment did not require suppression of the written confession because of the earlier unwarned admission.

In *Illinois* v. *Perkins,* the Supreme Court held that an undercover officer posing as an inmate need not give a jailed defendant the Miranda warning before asking questions that produce incriminating statements.[20] The court held that there is no coercive atmosphere present when an incarcerated person speaks freely to someone who he believes is a fellow inmate. The court added that the Miranda warning does not forbid strategic deception by taking advantage of a suspect's misplaced trust.

In *Arizona* v. *Fulminante,* the U.S. Supreme Court held that the harmless error rule is applicable to cases involving involuntary confessions.[21] The harmless error rule holds that an error made by the trial court in admitting illegally obtained evidence does not require a reversal of the conviction if the error was determined to be harmless. The burden of proving harmless error rests with the prosecution and must be proved beyond a reasonable doubt.

In *Davis* v. *United States,* the U.S. Supreme Court considered the degree of clarity that was necessary for a suspect to invoke his Miranda rights.[22] Agents of the Naval Investigative Service were questioning the defendant in connection with the death of a sailor. The defendant initially waived his rights, but approximately ninety minutes later he stated, "Maybe I should talk to a lawyer." The agents asked clarifying questions, and when the defendant stated he did not want an attorney, the interrogation resumed and elicited incriminating statements. The court held that an equivocal request for a lawyer is insufficient to invoke the right to counsel and that there is no need for clarifying questions before proceeding with the interrogation.

Two years after *Miranda* was decided, Congress passed 18 U.S.C. § 3501, which set forth only voluntariness as the touchstone of admissibility for statements. In 2000, the Supreme Court finally had a case before it that allowed it to examine this law. In *Dickerson* v. *United States,* the court held that the Miranda decision was of constitutional orgin and that therefore Congress my not overrule its scope or effect.[23]

After years of allowing suspects to avoid police interrogation by invoking their Miranda rights, the Supreme Court is beginning to take a more reasonable and practical approach to this controversial issue.[24] However, police officers must still carefully tailor their interrogations so that they obtain information from the suspects while protecting their constitutional rights.

IMMUNITY FROM ARREST

Certain classes of persons are immune from arrest because of statutory regulations. These include representatives from foreign countries, legislators, and out-of-state witnesses.

Diplomatic Immunity

International law and various agreements between nations exchanging representatives are the bases for diplomatic immunity. For example, in the United States, as provided by international law, diplomatic officers, their staff, members of their families, and their servants are free from local jurisdiction, and as such they should not be arrested or detained for any offense unless they are citizens of or permanent residents of the United States (Title 22 U.S. Code, section 252). The diplomatic officers who enjoy this unlimited immunity are ambassadors, ministers, their assistants, and attachés. The purpose behind the doctrine of diplomatic immunity is to contribute to the development of friendly relations between nations and to ensure the efficient performance of the diplomatic missions.

Although these persons have complete immunity from arrest, detention, or prosecution, the immunity does not give them blanket authority to disregard the laws of the United States and of the individual states. As established by international law, it is the duty of all foreign representatives to respect the laws and regulations of the land. If a member of the diplomatic corps commits a crime, the offense should be brought to the attention of the United States Department of State, and if the crime is a serious one, the State Department may request that the member be recalled from the country.

Consular Immunity

Consuls and their deputies are also representatives of foreign nations but have only limited immunity. In all cases, however, they are to be treated with due respect. The consular officers are not liable for arrest or detention pending a trial except in cases of a serious felony having been committed. Since consular officers' immunity is limited to acts in performance of their duties, the immunity does not include members of their families or servants, but they too should be treated with proper respect. A police officer may treat a consular officer who commits a traffic violation the same as he or she does anyone else. The police officer may simply warn the consular officer, or the police officer may issue a citation, since this is not considered in violation of the immunity of arrest and detention.

Most diplomatic corps are stationed either in Washington, D.C., or with the United Nations in New York, but consular officers are assigned to stations in many large cities throughout the United States. Peace officers in the United States may encounter members of these groups anywhere, since many of them travel extensively. Each member of these groups should have official identification in his or her possession, whereby a peace officer may determine the official status of the member and the immunity to which he or she is entitled.

Legislative Immunity

Most states have some type of provision in their statutes granting immunity to legislative members, but this immunity is limited. Many of the states hold that the immunity relates only to arrest arising out of some civil matter and that there is no immunity from arrest on a criminal charge.

Out-of-State Witnesses

The Uniform Act to Secure the Attendance of Witnesses from Without the State in Criminal Cases has been adopted by most of the states. This act provides that if a person goes into a state in obedience of a subpoena to testify in that state, he or she shall not be subject to arrest in connection with any crime committed in the state prior to his or her entrance into the state to testify. The person is also granted a reasonable time to leave the state after testifying without being subject to such an arrest but is not granted any immunity from arrest for a crime that he or she may commit while in the state to testify. A similar immunity is given to persons passing through a state to testify in another state in obedience of a subpoena. One might question this immunity from arrest given to a witness. The reason is that the testimony is more important to a particular case than is the prosecution of a witness for some past violation of the law. In addition, if the prosecution were significant, there is no reason that extradition proceedings could not be brought against the witness.

BOOKING

When people are arrested, the usual procedure is to take them to the police station for booking. Booking consists of recording the arrest in official law enforcement records, fingerprinting, and photographing the accused. If the charge is a bailable offense, the accused is entitled to post bail at this time. If bail is not posted, the accused will be searched and placed in jail until he or she does post bail or until final prosecution takes place. Even though the accused was searched in the field at the time of the arrest, a more thorough search may be made at the time of booking for weapons or evidence that may have been missed during the field search.

Right to Telephone Calls

Whether an arrest is made by a law enforcement officer or by a private person, the accused is entitled to certain rights. One of these rights is to be informed of the offense for which the accused is being arrested. Another right provided by the statutes of some states is the right to make telephone calls. This right has been incorporated into the laws to prohibit individuals from being held indefinitely without anyone knowing that they have been arrested—in other words, to prevent them from being held incommunicado.

In those states in which the arrested person is permitted to make telephone calls, there are considerable differences in the rights afforded the arrested person. These rights differ as to the number of calls that may be made; to whom, how soon after the arrest, and at whose expense they may be made; whether the calls can be monitored; and whether the arrested person must be advised of the right to make the calls. It is generally held that the arrested person is entitled to make the calls immediately after being booked, or, except where physically impossible, within a prescribed time, such as three hours, after the arrest. It is also generally provided that the arrested person is entitled to make at least one or more completed calls to an attorney, bail bondsman, relative, or other person. The calls are to be made free of charge if to a local area; otherwise, they are made at the expense of the arrested person. Some jurisdictions require that the arrested person be advised of the right to make the calls; others merely require that the right be posted in a conspicuous place in the area of detention. This right is a continuing one and is not waived if the arrested person does not request to make the calls immediately after being booked. Some states also require that if the arrested person is physically unable to make the call, he or she is entitled to the assistance of an officer.

ISSUANCE OF A CITATION

At one time in our history, all criminal offenders were brought to court with force. Even in civil matters, an arrest was frequently used to bring the defendant to court. Today, the defendant in a civil matter is not forced to appear in court. If the defendant fails to appear as requested, the person bringing the suit, who is known as the plaintiff, is given the judgment by default. Even in criminal matters, particularly involving minor violations, efforts are made to persuade the accused to come to court with as little inconvenience to all as is possible. But when a warrant of arrest is issued, the person named in the warrant must be taken into custody, booked, and transported for arraignment unless he or she posts bail before arraignment. This same procedure is followed in most arrests made without a warrant. Each of these steps is time-consuming, and if the person does not post bail, he or she must be confined to jail pending the judicial proceedings. This detention often causes overcrowding of the jail facilities, and in some instances, an injustice to the accused. To alleviate this situation, many states have adopted legislation whereby an officer may issue a citation for a misdemeanor or an infraction violation instead of taking the person into custody.

A citation (sometimes referred to as a summons) is a written notice issued to a violator to appear in court. The citation lists the violator's name, address, and the offense committed. It also sets forth the time, place, and date that the violator is to appear in court. If the arrested person signs the citation agreeing to appear in court as directed, he or she is entitled to be released without further action being taken at that time.

In most instances, a citation will be issued for an infraction and for a traffic violation. But it is generally within the discretion of the law enforcement officer whether a citation will be issued for a misdemeanor violation. Many law enforcement agencies have established guidelines on which misdemeanor violations a citation may be issued for in lieu of taking the offender into custody. One reason for the selective practice is that it may be felt that the violator would not appear in court and that booking and confinement until he or she posts bail is the preferable procedure. Some law enforcement agencies have established a policy of taking an offender into custody, booking him or her, and then releasing the offender on a citation. This procedure defeats part of the purpose of issuing the citation in that the offender is taken into custody, transported to the station, and booked. Those following this process feel that the identifying data obtained from the booking justifies the time consumed, particularly if the violator does not appear as agreed and must be sought on a bench warrant. To discourage the book-and-then-release practice, some jurisdictions require that the arresting agency conduct a background investigation to determine whether the person should be released on a citation. The investigation should include the person's name, address, length of residence at that address, length of residence in the state, marital and family status, current employment, length of current employment, prior arrest record, and such other facts as would bear on the question of the release of the individual.

Even though the violator is released in the field by signing the citation, most jurisdictions permit the law enforcement agency involved to request that the violator be booked prior to commencement of final judicial proceedings in order to get identifying data for future reference.

Citation Court Procedure

In some jurisdictions, a copy of the citation is filed with the appropriate court. This citation will become the accusatory document eliminating the necessity of the officer's filing a complaint. In other jurisdictions, a copy of the citation is furnished to the prosecuting attorney, and on the basis of this citation, a complaint will be filed with the court that is to hear the case. After the citation has been issued and before the arraignment, the violator may post bail for his or her appearance. If the violator should fail to appear as agreed, the bail may be forfeited. The judge, at his or her discretion, either may order that no further proceedings shall take place on the matter or may issue a bench warrant for the arrest of the violator. The judge will then proceed on the original charge for which the citation was issued, and in most jurisdictions, the violator can be charged with a misdemeanor for failure to appear.

CHARGING THE DEFENDANT WITH A CRIME

Misdemeanor—Brief judicial hearing and trial

```
                        ┌──────────┐
                        │  Felony  │
                        └──────────┘
              ┌──────────────┴──────────────┐
```

Grand Jury

- Some states refer defendant.
- Other states have the option of bypassing a preliminary hearing and referring to the grand jury.
- Powers include investigation and charging.
- Witnesses presented by prosecution; defendant not present and doesn't testify.
- Product of grand jury is indictment.

Preliminary Hearing

- Some states use hearing as a step to trial.
- Others use hearing to bind over to a grand jury.
- Product of preliminary hearing is "information."
- Standard of proof is probable cause.

THE SUMMONS

Although a citation is sometimes referred to as a summons, technically a summons differs from a citation. The true summons is issued by a judge in lieu of a warrant of arrest. The summons commands the accused to appear in court at a specified time and eliminates the need of arresting the accused and bringing him or her before the court. The summons may be issued by a judge when he or she feels that the accused will appear as commanded without the need to make an arrest. The summons, like the warrant of arrest, is based upon a complaint filed with the court. After the summons is issued, it may be personally delivered or mailed to the accused. If the person named in the summons fails to appear as commanded, a warrant of arrest will be issued. A summons differs from a citation in that a summons is issued by a judge and either mailed to or served upon the accused personally, commanding his or her appearance; a citation is generally issued by an officer in the field.

Capstone Case ———————————————————

Tennessee v. *Garner*
471 U.S. 1, 105 S.Ct. 1694, 85 L.Ed.2d 1 (1985)

Justice White delivered the opinion of the Court.

At about 10:45 P.M. on October 3, 1974, Memphis Police Officers Elton Hymon and Leslie Wright were dispatched to answer a "prowler inside call." Upon arriving at the scene they saw a woman standing on her porch and gesturing toward the adjacent house. She told them she had heard glass breaking and that "they" or "someone" was breaking in next door. While Wright radioed the dispatcher to say that they were on the scene, Hymon went behind the house. He heard a door slam and saw someone run across the back yard. The fleeing suspect, who was appellee-respondent's decedent, Edward Garner, stopped at a 6 feet-high chain link fence at the edge of the yard. With the aid of a flashlight, Hymon was able to see Garner's face and hands. He saw no sign of a weapon, and, though not certain, was "reasonably sure" and "figured" that Garner was unarmed. He thought Garner was 17 or 18 years old and about 5'5" or 5'7" tall. While Garner was crouched at the base of the fence, Hymon called out "police, halt" and took a few steps toward him. Garner then began to climb over the fence. Convinced that if Garner made it over the fence, he would elude capture, Hymon shot him. The bullet hit Garner in the back of the head. Garner was taken by ambulance to a hospital, where he died on the operating table. Ten dollars and a purse taken from the house were found on his body.

In using deadly force to prevent the escape, Hymon was acting under the authority of a Tennessee statute and pursuant to Police Department policy. The statute provides that "if, after notice of the intention to arrest the defendant, he either flee or forcibly resist, the officer may use all the necessary means to effect the arrest." The Department policy was slightly more restrictive than the statute, but still allowed the use of deadly force in cases of burglary. . . .

Garner's father then brought this action in the Federal District Court for the Western District of Tennessee, seeking damages under 42 U.S.C. 1 983 for asserted violations of Garner's constitutional rights. . . . The District Court . . . found that the statute, and Hymon's actions, were constitutional. . . . The Court of Appeals reversed and remanded. . . . The State of Tennessee, which had intervened to defend the statute, appealed to this Court.

Whenever an officer restrains the freedom of a person to walk away, he has seized that person. While it is not always clear just when minimal police interference becomes a seizure, there can be no question that apprehension by the use of deadly force is a seizure subject to the reasonableness requirement of the Fourth Amendment.

A police officer may arrest a person if he has probable cause to believe that person committed a crime. Petitioners and appellant argue that if this requirement is satisfied the Fourth Amendment has nothing to say about how that seizure is made. This submission ignores the many cases in which this Court, by balancing the extent of the intrusion against the need for it, has examined the reasonableness of the manner in which a search or seizure is conducted. . . . Because one of the factors is the extent of the intrusion, it is plain that reasonableness depends on not only when a seizure is made, but also how it is carried out. . . .

The same balancing process applied in the cases cited above demonstrates that, notwithstanding probable cause to seize a suspect, an officer may not always do so by killing him. The intrusiveness of a seizure by means of deadly force is unmatched. The suspect's fundamental interest in his own life need not be elaborated upon. The use of deadly force also frustrates the interest of the individual, and of society, in judicial determination of guilt and punishment. Against these interests are ranged governmental interests in effective law enforcement. It is argued that overall violence will be reduced by encouraging the peaceful submission of suspects who know that they may be shot if they flee. Effectiveness in making arrests requires the resort to deadly force, or at least the meaningful threat thereof. "Being able to arrest such individuals is a condition precedent to the state's entire system of law enforcement."

Without in any way disparaging the importance of these goals, we are not convinced that the use of deadly force is a sufficiently productive means of accomplishing them to justify the killing of nonviolent suspects. The use of deadly force is a self-defeating way of apprehending a suspect and so setting the criminal justice mechanism in motion. If successful, it guarantees that that mechanism will not be set in motion. And while the meaningful threat of deadly force might be thought to lead to the arrest of more live suspects by discouraging escape attempts, the presently available evidence does not support this thesis. The fact is that a majority of police departments in this country have forbidden the use of deadly force against nonviolent suspects. If those charged with the enforcement of the criminal law have abjured the use of deadly force in arresting nondangerous felons, there is a substantial basis for doubting that the use of such force is an essential attribute of the arrest power in all felony cases. Petitioners and appellant have not persuaded us that shooting nondangerous fleeing suspects is so vital as to outweigh the suspect's interest in his own life.

The use of deadly force to prevent the escape of all felony suspects, whatever the circumstances, is constitutionally unreasonable. It is not better that all felony suspects die than that they escape. Where the suspect poses no immediate threat to the officer and no threat to others, the harm resulting from failing to apprehend him does not justify the use of deadly force to do so. It is no doubt unfortunate when a suspect who is in sight escapes, but the fact that the police arrive a little late or are a little slower afoot does not always justify killing the suspect. A police officer may not seize an unarmed, nondangerous suspect by shooting him dead. The Tennessee statute is unconstitutional insofar as it authorizes the use of deadly force against such fleeing suspects.

It is not, however, unconstitutional on its face. Where the officer has probable cause to believe that the suspect poses a threat of serious physical harm, either to the officer or to others, it is not constitutionally unreasonable to prevent escape by using deadly force. Thus, if the suspect threatens the officer with a weapon or there is probable cause to believe that he has committed a crime involving the infliction or threatened infliction of serious physical harm, deadly force may be used if necessary to prevent escape, and if, where feasible, some warning has been given. As applied in such circumstances, the Tennessee statute would pass constitutional muster.

It is insisted that the Fourth Amendment must be construed in light of the common-law rule, which allowed the use of whatever force was necessary to effect the arrest of a fleeing felon, though not a misdemeanant.

The State and city argue that because this was the prevailing rule at the time of the adoption of the Fourth Amendment and for some time thereafter, and is still in force in some States, use of deadly force against a fleeing felon must be "reasonable." It is true that this Court has often looked to the common law in evaluating the reasonableness, for Fourth Amendment purposes, of police activity. On the other hand, it "has not simply frozen into constitutional law those law enforcement practices that existed at the time of the Fourth Amendment's passage." Because of sweeping change in the legal and technological context, reliance on the common-law rule in this case would be a mistaken literalism that ignores the purposes of a historical inquiry.

It has been pointed out many times that the common-law rule is best understood in light of the fact that it arose at a time when virtually all felonies were punishable by death. . . . Courts have also justified the common-law rule by emphasizing the relative dangerousness of felons.

Neither of these justifications makes sense today. Almost all crimes formerly punishable by death no longer are or can be. And while in earlier times "the gulf between the felonies and the minor offenses was broad and deep," today the distinction is minor and often arbitrary. Many crimes classified as misdemeanors, or nonexistent, at common law are now felonies. These changes have undermined the concept, which was questionable to begin with, that use of deadly force against a fleeing felon is merely a speedier execution of someone who has already forfeited his life. They have also made the assumption that a "felon" is more dangerous than a misdemeanant untenable. Indeed, numerous misdemeanors involve conduct more dangerous than many felonies.

There is an additional reason why the common-law rule cannot be directly translated to the present day. The common-law rule developed at a time when weapons were rudimentary. Deadly force could be inflicted almost solely in a hand-to-hand struggle during which, necessarily, the safety of the arresting officer was at risk. Handguns were not carried by police officers until the latter half of the last century. Only then did it become possible to use deadly force from a distance as a means of apprehension. As a practical matter, the use of deadly force under the standard articulation of the common-law rule has an altogether different meaning—and harsher consequences—now than in past centuries.

One other aspect of the common-law rule bears emphasis. It forbids the use of deadly force to apprehend a misdemeanant, condemning such action as disproportionately severe.

In short, though the common law pedigree of Tennessee's rule is pure on its face, changes in the legal and technological context mean the rule is distorted almost beyond recognition when literally applied.

In evaluating the reasonableness of police procedures under the Fourth Amendment, we have also looked to prevailing rules in individual jurisdictions. The rules in the States are varied. Some 19 States have codified the common-law rule, though in two of these the courts have significantly limited the statute. Four States, though without a relevant statute, apparently retain the common-law rule. Two States have adopted the Model Penal Code's provision verbatim. Eighteen others allow, in slightly varying language, the use of deadly force only if the suspect has committed a felony involving the use or threat of physical or deadly force, or is escaping with a deadly weapon, or is likely to endanger life or inflict serious physical injury if not arrested. Louisiana and Vermont, though without statutes or case law on point, do forbid the use of deadly force to prevent any but violent felonies. The remaining States either have no relevant statute or case-law, or have positions that are unclear.

It cannot be said that there is a constant or overwhelming trend away from the common-law rule. In recent years, some States have reviewed their laws and expressly rejected abandonment of the common-law rule. Nonetheless, the long term movement has been away from the rule that deadly force may be used against any fleeing felon, and that remains the rule in less than half the States.

This trend is more evident and impressive when viewed in light of the policies adopted by the police departments themselves. Overwhelmingly, these are more restrictive than the common-law rule. . . . Overall, only 7.5% of departmental and municipal policies explicitly permit the use of deadly force against any felon; 86.8% explicitly do not. In light of the rules adopted by those who must actually administer them, the older and fading common-law view is a dubious indicium of the constitutionality of the Tennessee statute now before us.

Actual departmental policies are important for an additional reason. We would hesitate to declare a police practice of long standing "unreasonable" if doing so would severely hamper effective law enforcement. But the indications are to the contrary. There has been no suggestion that crime has worsened in any way in jurisdictions that have adopted, by legislation or departmental policy, rules similar to that announced today.

Nor do we agree with petitioners and appellant that the rule we have adopted requires the police to make impossible, split-second evaluations of unknowable facts. We do not deny the practical difficulties of attempting to assess the suspect's dangerousness. However, similarly difficult judgments must be made by the police in equally uncertain circumstances. Nor is there any indication that in States that allow the use of deadly force only against dangerous suspects, the standard has been difficult to apply or has led to a rash of litigation involving inappropriate second-guessing of police officers' split-second decisions. Moreover, the highly technical felony/misdemeanor distinction is equally, if not more, difficult to apply in the field. An officer is in no position to know, for example, the precise value of property stolen, or whether the crime was a first or second offense. Finally, as noted above, this claim must be viewed with suspicion in light of the similar self-imposed limitations of so many police departments.

Officer Hymon could not reasonably have believed that Garner—young, slight, and unarmed—posed any threat. Indeed, Hymon never attempted to justify his actions on any basis other than the need to prevent an escape.

The dissent argues that the shooting was justified by the fact that Officer Hymon had probable cause to believe that Garner had committed a nighttime burglary. While we agree that burglary is a serious crime, we cannot agree that it is so dangerous as automatically to justify the use of deadly force. The FBI classifies burglary as a "property" rather than a "violent" crime. Although the armed burglar would present a different situation, the fact that an unarmed suspect has broken into a dwelling at night does not automatically mean he is physically dangerous. This case demonstrates as much. In fact, the available statistics demonstrate that burglaries only rarely involve physical violence. During the 10-year period from 1973–1982, only 3.8% of all burglaries involved violent crime.

The judgment of the Court of Appeals is affirmed.

Justice O'Connor, with whom the chief justice and Justice Rehnquist join, dissenting. . . .

Because burglary is a serious and dangerous felony, the public interest in the prevention and detection of the crime is of compelling importance. Where a police officer has probable cause to arrest a suspected burglar, the use of deadly force as a last resort might well be the only means of apprehending the suspect. With respect to a particular burglary, subsequent investigation simply cannot represent a substitute for immediate apprehension of the criminal suspect at the scene. Indeed, the Captain of the Memphis Police Department testified that in his city, if apprehension is not immediate, it is likely that the suspect will not be caught. Although some law enforcement agencies may choose to assume the risk that a criminal will remain at large, the Tennessee statute reflects a legislative determination that the use of deadly force in prescribed circumstances will serve generally to protect the public. Such statutes assist the police in apprehending suspected perpetrators of serious crimes and provide notice that a lawful police order to stop and submit to arrest may not be ignored with impunity. . . .

[The dissent notes also that three-fifths of all rapes in the home, three-fifths of all home robberies, and about a third of home assaults were committed by burglars.]

REVIEW QUESTIONS

1. Define an arrest.
2. Define probable cause for an arrest.
3. Who are peace officers?
4. What is meant by fresh pursuit?
5. What charges may be brought against an officer who uses excessive force in making an arrest?
6. What is meant by diplomatic immunity?
7. Which officials fall within the diplomatic immunity provisions?
8. For what reason is an arrested person entitled to make telephone calls?
9. What is a citation?
10. How does the procedure followed in the issuing of a citation differ from executing a warrant of arrest?

LOCAL PROCEDURE

1. Do peace officers have statewide arrest powers?
2. Who, if anyone, must come to the aid of an officer in making an arrest when called upon to do so or else be subject to prosecution?
3. Does an arrested person have the right to make telephone calls, and, if so, to whom and how many calls may he or she make? Must the person under arrest be advised of this right to make the calls?
4. Has your state adopted the Uniform Act of Fresh Pursuit? If so, does the act apply to felony violations only, or has it been made applicable to misdemeanors? If applicable to misdemeanors, what types?

ENDNOTES

1. 20 Ky. 539.
2. *Wong Sun* v. *U.S.,* 371 U.S. 471 (1963).
3. *U.S.* v. *Watson,* 423 U.S. 411 (1976).
4. *Payton* v. *New York,* 445 U.S. 573 (1980).
5. *U.S.* v. *Santana,* 427 U.S. 38 (1976).
6. *U.S.* v. *Davis,* 461 F.2d 1026 (3d Cir. 1972).
7. *Aguilar* v. *Texas,* 378 U.S. 108 (1964).
8. See Wallace, Roberson, and Steckler, *Fundamentals of Police Administration* (Prentice-Hall, New Jersey), 1995.
9. 471 U.S. 1 (1985).
10. See *Peterson* v. *Robison,* 277 P.2d 19, 24 (Cal. 1954).
11. This section has been adapted from Wallace, Roberson, and Steckler, *Written Interpersonal Communication Methods for Law Enforcement* (Prentice-Hall, New Jersey), 1997.
12. 297 U.S. 278 (1936).
13. 322 U.S. 143 (1944).
14. 360 U.S. 315 (1959).
15. 378 U.S. 748 (1964).
16. 384 U.S. 436 (1966).
17. 468 U.S. 420 (1984).
18. 401 U.S. 222 (1971).
19. 470 U.S. 298 (1985).
20. 495 U.S. 292 (1990).
21. 111 S.Ct. 1246 (1991).
22. 114 S.Ct. 2350 (1994).
23. 539 U.S. 428 (2000).
24. Kimberly A. Crawford, "Invoking the Miranda Right to Counsel." FBI Law Enforcement Bulletin 27 (March 1995).

CHAPTER 4

The Initial Appearance

To implement the Fourth Amendment's protection against unfounded invasions of liberty and privacy, the Court has required that the existence of probable cause be decided by a neutral and detached magistrate whenever possible.

—Justice Powell in *Gerstein* v. *Pugh* 420 U.S. 103 (1975)

It's better to enter the mouth of a tiger than a court of law.

—Old Chinese proverb

PURPOSE OF THE INITIAL APPEARANCE

Although there is no mention of the "initial appearance" in our Bill of Rights, it is a basic right of an arrested person to be taken before a magistrate without unnecessary delay. This right is included in the federal rules of procedure and in the laws of the states. The initial appearance consists of the accused's appearing before a magistrate to be advised of certain rights to which he or she is entitled. A magistrate may be defined as anyone having the authority to issue an arrest warrant or a search warrant. From a practical standpoint, a magistrate generally is a judge of one of the inferior courts who spends much of his or her time conducting initial appearance hearings. The initial, or "first," appearance is sometimes referred to as an "arraignment." The term *arraignment* is used in many areas, and even the U.S. Supreme Court in the landmark cases of *McNabb* v. *United States*[1] and *Mallory* v. *United States*[2] referred to the initial appearance as an "arraignment." In some states, the accused is permitted to enter a plea at the initial appearance, which adds to the tendency to call the initial appearance an arraignment.

At the initial appearance, the accused will be officially informed of the charge against him or her. Although the person is entitled to be informed of the charge at the time of the arrest, the charge is often changed between the time of the arrest and the initial appearance. For example, a person may be arrested on a charge of aggravated assault, but between the time of the arrest on that charge and the initial

---

Steps in the Pretrial Process

1. **Arrest:** suspect taken into custody.
2. **Booking:** administrative record of arrest.
3. **Initial appearance:** notice of charge, advice of rights, setting of bail.
4. **Preliminary hearing:** test of evidence against defendant.
5. **Grand jury/information:** review of evidence by grand jury; charge filed by prosecution.
6. **Arraignment:** appearance for plea; defendant elects trial by jury or judge.
7. **Guilty plea/trial:** plea accepted, or trial scheduled.

---

appearance, the victim dies. The charge is usually changed from aggravated assault to homicide. Further, at the initial appearance, if the offense is one for which bail may be posted, the accused will be informed of the right to make bail if he or she is not already out on bail. If the accused is not represented by an attorney, the rights to the assistance of counsel and to remain silent will be explained. Each of these rights are discussed in detail.

Time of the Initial Appearance

One of the more troublesome problems involved in an initial appearance concerns when it must be held once the arrest is made. For many years, neither the courts nor law enforcement agencies were particularly concerned about the timing of the initial appearance. As a result, many arrested persons were held incommunicado in jail for days and sometimes weeks before being taken before a magistrate. To overcome the injustice of this procedure, it is now provided that an arrested person must be taken before a magistrate without unnecessary delay. However, this provision is not without its complications. What will the courts accept, if anything, as necessary or reasonable delay in taking the defendant before a magistrate, and what penalties will be attached if there is an unnecessary delay deemed in the initial appearance? To assist officers in determining time limits, most states have enacted provisions setting forth the time within which the initial appearance must take place. The time limit varies considerably among the states, but the following is typical of the wording of such statutes:

> The arrested person must be taken before a magistrate without unnecessary delay, and in any event no longer than two days, Sundays and holidays excluded. If the two-day period expires when the Court is not in session, the time for the initial appearance will be extended until the next regular court session.

This provision implies that the two-day period is actually based on a forty-eight-hour limit. It is pointed out that the forty-eight-hour restriction is not a blanket authority to hold all arrested persons for that time without taking them before a magistrate. A delay in the initial appearance for a much shorter time could be interpreted as an unnecessary delay. Some states have a seventy-two-hour limit, and a few states merely provide that an arrested person must be taken before a magistrate without unnecessary delay. If an arrested person is not taken before a magistrate within the prescribed time, he or she must be released. Whether the person could be arrested again after the release is doubtful; much would depend on the facts of the particular case and the reason for the delay in the initial appearance. In some instances, the release of the accused will result in a dismissal of the charge and will bar further prosecutive action, particularly in misdemeanor cases.

The time within which an initial appearance must be held and the penalties that may be attached for the delay were placed in particular emphasis by the landmark decision handed down by the U.S. Supreme Court in 1943 in the case of *McNabb* v. *United States*. The facts of that case reveal that some of the defendants were held for six days after the arrest before being arraigned, during which time confessions were obtained from them. These confessions were introduced against the defendants in their trial for the murder of a federal officer. The conviction was appealed to the U.S. Supreme Court upon the grounds that the confessions had been involuntarily given. The Court concluded that there was an unnecessary delay in the arraignment, during which time these confessions were obtained. To discourage unnecessary delay in arraignments, the Court held that any confession obtained during an unnecessary delay would be inadmissible as evidence in a court proceeding. This was an entirely new approach to the admissibility of confession. Prior to the *McNabb* decision, the test of admissibility was voluntariness in the giving of the confession. So the Court, in that case, attached a very significant penalty to a delay in arraigning an arrested person.

Although this decision pertained only to federal officers, several states have adopted the rule set forth in the *McNabb* decision by maintaining that confessions obtained by local officers during a delay in arraignment are inadmissible as evidence. It becomes important to determine what, if anything, might be considered a necessary delay in arraigning an arrested person. Following the *McNabb* case, the U.S. Supreme Court handed down other decisions relative to the time factor in arraignments. It was indicated in one case that the Court took into consideration that an arrested person should be booked before being arraigned. In another case, it was held that some investigative activity to verify information furnished by the defendant before being arraigned would be tolerated (see *Mallory* v. *United States*).

The U.S. Supreme Court cases mentioned are of little assistance in furnishing guidelines for how long an accused may be held within the prescribed time limit before the initial appearance and still have the delay considered necessary. It has been held by the courts that if the delay is solely for the purpose of interrogating the accused, such delay is not considered necessary. Yet it is recognized that some questioning after an arrest may be in order, followed by a reasonable investigation to verify or refute information given by the arrested person. Such questioning could assist in the early release of an innocent person or could act as a justification for the arrest. For example, in one case, the delay in initial appearance for almost the entire prescribed time was upheld. In that case, the owner of an old model car took the car to a garage to be repaired. The mechanic told the owner that the car would be ready in three days. When the owner did not return for the car for more than a week, the mechanic checked the car in an effort to locate some identification in order to notify the owner that the car was ready. The mechanic found no identification, but he did find $1,500 in the glove compartment. He became suspicious and notified the local authorities. The officers were also unable to determine the owner and asked to be called if he should return for the car. Upon returning for the car a few days later, the owner was questioned by the officers but gave evasive answers.

He was arrested for reasonable cause to believe that a crime had been committed since it was thought that an ordinarily prudent person would hold such a belief under the circumstances. But what crime should he have been booked for? Had he committed robbery, burglary, grand theft, or some other crime? He was charged with grand theft, but there were no facts to verify such a crime in the area. He was further questioned by the officers but refused to reveal his identity or place of residence. The investigation revealed no damaging evidence. As the forty-eight hour limit approached, the authorities realized that the accused would have to be released, yet they believed that he had been involved in some type of crime because an innocent person would have assisted in getting his own release much earlier. Just before the time limit was reached, the officers received a call from a woman reporting her husband as missing. The description of the missing husband fit that of the man in custody. It was learned that the accused had cashed a number of forged checks and that the money in the glove compartment was from his check-cashing activity. He had forgotten that it was in the glove compartment when he took the car to the garage. It is interesting that he stated that he was cashing the forged checks to get enough money to buy a small ranch where he could raise his children in a wholesome atmosphere.

Generally, a delay in an initial appearance or in an arraignment is not sufficient grounds for a reversal of a conviction on appeal unless it can be shown that the delay deprived the defendant of a fair trial. A few states have adopted the *McNabb* rule of excluding a confession obtained during a delay in arraignment. But there are other penalties besides the procedural one pertaining to the admissibility of confession that may be attached to a delayed arraignment. Many states hold that a public officer who willfully delays bringing a defendant before a magistrate for the arraignment is guilty of a misdemeanor. It has also been held that once the time limit has been reached wherein an arrested person must be taken before a magistrate, any detention beyond that period is illegal, and that the officer responsible for such detention is subject to a civil suit for damages on a false imprisonment allegation.

Accepting the Accused for the Initial Appearance

Whether the accused was arrested by a private person or by an officer, he or she must be taken before a magistrate. The laws of many states provide that a private person who arrests another must take that person before a magistrate without unnecessary delay or deliver the arrested person to a peace officer who will in turn see that the accused is taken before a magistrate. The usual procedure is that the private person will deliver the arrested person to a peace officer rather than take the person before a magistrate himself or herself. This situation creates the problem of how far the officer should go in determining the legality of the arrest before accepting the accused. There seems to be no uniformity in the answer to this problem. The courts of some states have held that if a competent private person informs the officer of the charge for which the arrest was made and demands that the officer take the accused, the officer has no right to refuse acceptance of the arrested person. This approach is reinforced by the further provision in some states that an officer who willfully refuses to accept one who has been charged with a crime is also subject to prosecution. Under the circumstances, an officer is not civilly liable for false arrest by accepting one arrested by a private person. The officer in reality is only a transportation officer and not an arresting one.[3] Other states permit the officer to make a determination concerning the legality of the arrest by the private citizen before accepting the accused. Such a ruling places a tremendous burden upon the officer. The officer is partially acting as a court in making a determination as to the legality of the arrest. If the officer incorrectly concludes that the arrest was legal, he or she could possibly be held civilly liable for accepting the accused.

THE COMPLAINT

Prior to the initial appearance, a legal document must be filed with the court setting forth the charge against the accused, who will be referred to as the defendant hereinafter in relation to the judicial procedure. In most instances, this legal document will be a complaint. The complaint is comparatively simple. It sets forth the name of the defendant, the date and place that the offense took place, and the nature of the offense. The complaint must contain enough facts to enable the judge to determine whether a crime has been committed and whether there is reasonable cause to believe that the defendant committed it. If the defendant is not in custody, a warrant of arrest will be issued on the basis of this complaint. The complaint is sometimes referred to as an accusatory pleading. As we progress further into the judicial procedure, it will be determined that other accusatory pleadings follow the complaint in felony cases, but in misdemeanor matters, it is usually the only accusatory pleading filed with the court.

What Are the Most Common Reasons for Rejection or Dismissal of a Criminal Case?

Many criminal cases are rejected or dismissed because of:

1. **Insufficient evidence**—a failure to find sufficient physical evidence linking the defendant to the offense.
2. **Witness problems**—for example, when a witness fails to appear, gives unclear or inconsistent statements, is reluctant to testify, or is unsure of the identity of the offender, or when a prior relationship exists between the victim/witness and the offender.
3. **The interests of justice**—deciding not to prosecute certain types of offenses, particularly those that violate the letter but not the spirit of the law (for example, offenses involving insignificant amounts of property damage).
4. **Due process problems**—violations of the constitutional requirements for seizing evidence and for questioning the accused.
5. **A plea on another case**—for example, when the accused is charged in several cases and the prosecutor agrees to drop one or more of the cases in exchange for a plea of guilty on another case.
6. **Pretrial diversion**—agreeing to drop charges with the accused successfully meets the conditions for diversion, such as completion of a treatment program.
7. **Referral for other prosecution**—when there are other offenses, perhaps of a more serious nature, in a different jurisdiction, or deferring to a federal prosecution.

Bound Over for Trial

If the magistrate concludes that the evidence presented establishes probable cause that the defendant committed the crime(s) charged, the magistrate will bind the defendant over for trial. If the magistrate concludes that the evidence supports only a misdemeanor charge, the magistrate will reduce the charges to the lesser offense. In some states, the magistrate has the authority to then handle the misdemeanor. In some states, if the defendant pleads guilty, the magistrate has the authority to accept the guilty plea in a felony case and then forwards the case to the felony trial court for sentencing. If the magistrate determines that probable cause does not exist to hold the defendant over for trial, the magistrate will dismiss the charges. *Note:* When the magistrate dismisses the charges, double jeopardy has not attached and the prosecutor may refile in another court. In general, the magistrate dismisses the charges in about 15 percent of the cases and reduces the charges to misdemeanors in about 10 percent of the cases.

BAIL

The Right to Post Bail

The right of an arrested person to post bail to obtain release from custody is an inherent right. As stated in the case of *Stack* v. *Boyle:*[4]

> This traditional right to freedom [by posting bail] before conviction permits the unhampered preparation of a defense, and serves to prevent the infliction of punishment prior to conviction. . . . Unless this right to bail before trial is preserved, the presumption of innocence, secured only after centuries of struggle, would lose its meaning.

But the right to post bail is not a guarantee included in our Bill of Rights. The Eighth Amendment to the Constitution merely provides that "excessive bail shall not be required," implying that not all offenses are bailable. By constitutional provision or by statute, the right to post bail by someone arrested under certain conditions is granted by all states. If the defendant has not been released on bail by the time of the initial appearance, the right to post bail will be explained to him or her at that time.

Historical Development of Bail

The origin of the term *bail* has been obscured by time. Some believe that the term is from the old French word *baillier,* meaning "to deliver." Others hold that it originated from the common law procedure of bailments. A bailment is the deposit of something of value with another for a particular purpose. In the case of bail, the deposit was for the release of one in custody. The right to post bail is found in the early history of England. By the time of the Norman Conquest in A.D. 1066, the posting of a form of security to obtain the release of an accused was a common practice on the continent of Europe, and it became a part of the common law of England. It was developed as a humanitarian procedure. Previously, people accused of crimes were thrown into the dungeons of local noblemen to make sure that they would be available for trial when the judge made his or her circuit. This custom was important to the king. If the charge was serious and the accused was convicted, his or her property was confiscated, thus providing a lucrative source of revenue for the king. Often by the time of the trial, the accused would have died from malnutrition and neglect. To prevent this outcome from happening, relatives or friends of the accused would seek his or her release to their custody upon a promise that they would produce the accused for the trial. To make certain that the relatives or friends would fulfill their promise, they were required to post some security in the form of chattels or objects of value. If the accused was not produced for trial, these chattels would be confiscated by the king. In addition, the persons posting the security had to suffer the punishment that the accused would have been subjected to had he or she been convicted. As time passed, the practice of punishing those who had posted security was discontinued, and they lost only the security.

Purpose of Bail

Today, we continue to place persons who are arrested into jail. We do so not as a form of punishment, because one cannot be punished or imprisoned until found guilty of a crime. We confine arrested persons to make sure that they will be available for trial. If we can obtain that surety by permitting accused persons to post bail, they are entitled to be released from custody until found guilty of the accusation. "Thus, the only purpose of bail is to secure the release from custody of one who has been arrested upon his or her promise to appear at the various court proceedings related to the offense. These may include the arraignment, the preliminary hearing, the trial, and other such proceedings that the court may direct.

At common law, it was felt that there was no way to ensure the trial presence of one who was charged with a capital offense, so bail was denied to that type of offender. A capital offense is one for which the death penalty may be inflicted. The statutes of many states have included similar provisions, holding that one charged with a capital offense may be denied bail if the proof of guilt is great. Even in those states in which capital punishment has not been made a penalty, bail may be denied to one arrested for murder if the proof of guilt is evident.

Denial of Bail for Protective Reasons

In the past, a few jurisdictions have provided that bail may be denied to an arrested person if his or her release on bail would cause a danger to the public. This policy is based upon an interpretation of the Eighth Amendment to the Constitution by the U.S. Supreme Court in the case of *Carlson* v. *Lando.*[5] In review, the Eighth Amendment guarantees that "excessive bail shall not be required." In the *Carlson* case, the Court rested its interpretation of the Eighth Amendment on the common law, stating the following:

> The bail clause was lifted with slight changes from the English Bill of Rights Act. In England that clause has never been thought to accord a right to bail in all cases, but merely to provide that bail shall not be excessive in those cases where it is proper to grant bail. When this clause was carried over into our Bill of Rights, nothing was said that indicated any different concept. The Eighth Amendment has not prevented Congress from defining the classes of cases in which bail shall be allowed in this country. Thus in criminal cases bail is not compulsory where the punishment may be death. Indeed, the very language of the Amendment fails to say all arrests must be bailable.

Thus, it was concluded that the Eighth Amendment does not grant the right to bail. The Eighth Amendment can be construed to mean only that bail shall not be excessive in those cases in which it is proper and that the denial of bail in certain cases is permissible. In recognition of the Court's interpretation of the Eighth Amendment and in response to the alarming problem of crimes committed by persons released on bail, Congress enacted an elaborate plan of preventive detention by enactment of the Bail Reform Act of 1987 (Title 18 U.S. Code, section 3242). This act provides that a federal officer may detain, pending trial, an arrestee who may be a danger to another person or a community. But before such an arrestee can be detained, a hearing must be held to determine "by clear and convincing evidence" that no condition exists that will assure the safety of a person or community if the arrestee were released on bail.

The constitutionality of this act was questioned by the defendant in the case of *United States* v. *Salerno.*[6] The defendant Salerno alleged that the act violated his right to the "Due Process of Law" clause embodied in the Fifth Amendment of the Constitution, which provides that "No person shall . . . be deprived of life, liberty or property without due process of law. . . ." The U.S. Supreme Court did not agree with this contention and stated that the act limits its application to those arrested on the most serious offenses and that the arrestee is entitled to a prompt hearing. During this hearing, the arrestee has the right to be represented by an attorney, to cross-examine witnesses, and to testify in his or her own behalf. In the opinion of the Court, this procedure fulfills the Due Process Clause of the Constitution.

The defendant also alleged that the act violated his right against excessive bail provided in the Eighth Amendment of the Constitution. To this allegation, the Court reiterated that the Eighth Amendment does not guarantee bail in all instances. When community safety is at stake, the government may deny bail and detain individuals believed to be dangerous to society.

Since the U.S. Supreme Court has upheld the "protective detention" of certain individuals arrested by federal officers, many states have enacted similar statutes permitting the detention pending trial of individuals arrested by state officers, who are believed to be dangerous. However, to abide by the Due Process Clause, those acts are required to provide for a prompt detention hearing similar to the Bail Reform Act of 1987.

Form of Bail

To post bail is to deposit an acceptable object of value with the appropriate court to ensure the appearance of the accused in court. Generally, the acceptable object of value is cash, U.S. or state bonds, or an equity in real property. If real property is pledged as security, most states require that the value of the property be twice that of the amount of bail. This requirement is made because of the possible fluctuation of real estate values and the difficulty of converting the real property into cash.

Since most arrested persons do not have these forms of security, they must rely upon someone to post bail for them. This person, known as a surety, may be a friend or relative, but in many cases, the person depositing the security will be one in the business of posting bail—a bail bondsperson. For a fee, the bail bondsperson will post the required security, which is usually a surety bond issued by some reliable company. Should the accused fail to appear as promised, the surety bond guarantees the bail payment in cash to the appropriate court. The fee that the bail bondsperson charges for this service is about 10 percent of the amount of the bail. A bail bondsperson who has some doubt whether the accused will appear if released on bail may request relatives of the accused to deposit collateral funds to reimburse him or her if the accused does not appear. If the risk of the accused's not appearing is too great and no one will come to the aid of the accused by depositing collateral funds, the bail bondsperson may refuse to post the bail, and the accused will be detained until the judicial proceedings are completed. But once bail has been deposited, the accused is entitled to immediate release from custody. The law is silent in most jurisdictions on the extent of time that a defendant may be free on bail, but it is generally assumed that he or she is entitled to be free throughout all the proceedings up to conviction. However, at his or her discretion, a judge may commit a defendant during the trial. Also, the defendant is not guaranteed the right to be free during an appeal time. Upon conviction, the defendant is no longer presumed to be innocent but is presumed to be guilty. But again, a judge, at his or her discretion, may permit a defendant to post bail during the appeal proceedings.

Amount of Bail

The bail that is required to be posted is that amount that will ensure the court appearance of the accused. Anything above that amount could be considered excessive. Determining this amount is not easily accomplished. The amount that would guarantee the appearance of one person may be entirely different for another. Also, the amount that would ensure the appearance on one charge may differ from another charge. In determining the amount of bail, a judge may consider the seriousness of the crime; the criminal record of the defendant; his or her employment record; family ties; whether the defendant was a fugitive at the time of arrest; whether he or she is wanted in any other jurisdiction; how great the evidence of guilt may be; the financial burden that he or she may suffer by not appearing; and whether the defendant has more to gain than to lose by not appearing.

The amount of bail set by a judge will not necessarily remain the same throughout the proceedings. Circumstances may arise that justify an increase or decrease in the amount. If the defendant has been released on bail and the amount is increased, he or she must post the amount of the increase or be placed in custody again.

Excessive Bail

As has been stated, the Eighth Amendment to the Constitution provides that "excessive bail shall not be required"; however, what constitutes excessive bail is not easily determined. What is excessive for one defendant may not be excessive for another. Whether the wealth or poverty of a defendant should be considered in determining the amount of bail is a difficult question to answer. There is no doubt that a wealthy defendant could more readily post bail, flee the country, and live elsewhere in comfort, whereas the poverty-stricken defendant may be unable to post even the smallest amount of bail. However, the mere fact that one cannot post bail does not mean that it is excessive. The courts have held that for bail to be excessive, it must be unreasonably great and clearly disproportionate to the offense involved. A defendant who believes that his or her bail is excessive may apply to the court for a reduction and, if this attempt fails, may appeal the matter to an appellate court for review on a writ of habeas corpus.

Bail Schedule

Since the amount of bail required largely depends on judicial discretion, the amount varies extensively. To establish uniformity in the amounts required, many states have adopted a procedure whereby judges of a county agree upon the amount of bail that is considered to be equitable on each misdemeanor violation. These amounts are listed in a schedule and act as guidelines for judges of the county. The amounts may still vary between counties. It has been recommended that a similar schedule be prepared for felony charges. But as we have pointed out, it is difficult to determine the amount that will ensure the appearance of a defendant in court, particularly in felony matters, so that such a schedule could be most unrealistic. A few states, however, have adopted a schedule for felony charges.

Forfeiture of Bail

Once the defendant is released on bail, and if, without sufficient cause, he or she fails to appear when lawfully required to do so, the bail will be forfeited. Forfeiting bail means that the security posted by the defendant, or someone in his or her behalf, is confiscated by the court and deposited in an official fund. The confiscation is justified on the grounds that the security will be used to pay additional court costs and costs involved in locating the defendant. In felony cases particularly, if the defendant does not appear as agreed, the court will issue a bench warrant for the immediate arrest of the accused. When arrested, the defendant will be tried on the original charge, and in some jurisdictions, can also be charged with violation of "failing to appear" or, as it is more commonly known, "bail-jumping." If a defendant does not appear on some minor misdemeanor charges or on most traffic violations, a judge may forfeit the bail, considering it the equivalent of the fine, dismiss the charge; and order that no further action be taken on the matter.

Surrender of Defendant by Surety

The surety who posted bail for a defendant may surrender him or her to the court having jurisdiction over the case any time before bail is forfeited. Upon surrendering the defendant, the surety is relieved of all responsibility and is entitled to have the security returned to him or her. For the purpose of surrendering the defendant, the surety may arrest the defendant. This arrest is an extension to the power of arrest by a private person. It is given upon the old theory that one posting bail has indirect custody of a defendant, and the surety may be relieved of that obligation by seizing the defendant and surrendering him or her to the court.

Exoneration of Bail

If the defendant appears in court at all times required, the bail has served its purpose, and the surety is entitled to have it returned. This return is known as the exoneration of bail.

Release on Own Recognizance

In the past, judges developed a practice of releasing defendants charged with minor offenses without posting bail—merely upon their promise to appear. This procedure became known as releasing one on his or her own recognizance, or OR release. The statutes of most states have extended this practice to any bailable

Pretrial Release Mechanisms

Stage	Mechanism	Description
Police	Field citation release	An arresting officer releases the arrestee on a written promise to appear in court, at or near the actual time and location of the arrest. This procedure is commonly used for misdemeanor charges and is similar to issuing a traffic ticket.
Police	Station house citation release	The determination of an arrestee's eligibility and suitability for release and the actual release of the arrestee are deferred until after he or she has been removed from the scene of an arrest and brought to the station house or police headquarters.
Police/pretrial	Jail citation release	The determination of an arrestee's eligibility and suitability for citation release and the actual release of the arrestee are deferred until after he or she has been delivered by the arresting department to a jail or other pretrial detention facility for screening, booking, and/or admission.
Pretrial/court	Direct release authority by pretrial program	To streamline release processes and reduce the length of stay in detention, courts may authorize pretrial programs to release defendants without direct judicial involvement. Where court rules delegate such authority, the practice is generally limited to misdemeanor charges, but felony release authority has been granted in some jurisdictions.
Police/court	Bail schedule	An arrestee can post bail at the station house or jail according to amounts specified in a bail schedule. The schedule is a list of all bailable charges and a corresponding dollar amount for each. Schedules may vary widely from jurisdiction to jurisdiction.
Court	Judicial release	Arrestees who have not been released either by the police or the jailer and who have not posted bail appear at the hearing before a judge, magistrate, or bail commissioner within a set period of time. In jurisdictions with pretrial release programs, program staff often interview arrestees detained at the jail prior to the first hearing, verify the background information, and present recommendations to the court at arraignment.

offense, including felony charges. The laws provide that a judge may release a defendant on his or her own recognizance if it appears that the defendant will comply with the agreement to appear as directed. However, these laws do not give the defendant the right to be released merely on his or her own recognizance. Even though a defendant is released on his or her own recognizance, a judge may later require the defendant to post bail or even to be committed to actual custody.

Prior to being released on his or her own recognizance, the defendant must agree in writing to appear at all times and places as ordered by the court, and if he or she does not appear and is apprehended in another state, the defendant waives extradition proceedings. In most states, it is provided that if the defendant who is released on his or her own recognizance fails to appear as agreed, he or she can be charged with the failure to appear. If the original charge was a felony, the defendant can be charged with a felony for failure to appear. If the original charge was a misdemeanor, the defendant can be charged with a misdemeanor for failure to appear. It has been recommended that greater use be made of OR releases, particularly in minor offenses, so as to obtain the release of those who are unable to post bail for financial reasons.

Bail for a Material Witness

The laws of most states permit a judge to demand that a material witness to a felony violation deposit security for his or her appearance at the trial if the judge believes that the witness will otherwise not appear. If the witness is unable to post the security (bail) for his or her appearance, the witness may be held in custody. The detention of a witness who is unable to post bail is unusual in our form of judicial procedure, since it permits the incarceration of one not charged with a crime. For this reason, it is not used extensively. To further overcome the inconvenience of a material witness's being detained, many jurisdictions provide that if a material witness cannot deposit security to ensure his or her appearance at the trial, his or her testimony may be incorporated into a deposition. A deposition is a written statement of a witness taken under oath before a magistrate, with both the prosecution and the defense having the right to be present.

BOUNTY HUNTERS

Bounty hunter Michael Kole has nabbed more than 100 fugitives from justice. But he was arrested on burglary charges when he went into the home of a third party without permission. The state law (Ohio) provided that a bounty hunter could arrest a defendant at any time and any place. One of the prosecutors in the case stated that "the sancity of the American home just doesn't go out the window when somebody gets out on bond." The Ohio court will rule on the right of Mr. Kole to enter the home of a third party to arrest a defendant. Recently courts in Indiana, Iowa, Maryland, Minnesota, Missouri, New Mexico, New York, and North Carolina have ruled against the rights of bounty hunters and in favor of third-party rights (as reported in the *Dayton Daily News,* Dayton, Ohio, Monday, April 16, 2001).

Bail bondspersons provide criminal defendants a bond to get them out of jail pending trial. They hire bounty hunters to track down defendants who skip out on court appearances and leave the bondsperson liable for the bond money. Bounty hunters may pursue a fugitive into another state; may arrest him or her; and if necessary, may break and enter his or her house for that purpose according to the 1872 U.S. Supreme Court case of *Taylor* v. *Taintor.* The common law dating to Medieval England included the right of bounty hunters to arrest bail-jumpers.

Most states require bounty hunters to receive state-approved training of arrest procedures and the use of firearms. Excons are excluded from being bounty hunters. In some states, the bounty hunter must give the police advance warning before making an arrest. The actual number of bounty hunters is unknown. Most are part-timers with past law enforcement experience. Bounty-hunting information may be found on the internet. For example, one company sells a computer program "Bounty Hunter Computer Tracking & Recovery Software" to help bounty hunters.

Appendix A contains an outline of trial procedure. This outline should help the reader see the overall picture as we discuss the various segments of the trial in the text.

Capstone Case

United States v. *Salerno*
481 U.S. 739 107 5 Ct. 2095, 95 L.Ed.2d 697 (1987)

Chief Justice Rehnquist delivered the opinion of the Court.

I

Responding to "the alarming problem of crimes committed by persons on release," Congress formulated the Bail Reform Act of 1984, 18 U.S.C.3141 et seq., as the solution to a bail crisis in the federal courts. The Act represents the National Legislature's considered response to numerous perceived deficiencies in the federal bail process. By providing for sweeping changes in both the way federal courts consider bail applications and the circumstances under which bail is granted, Congress hoped to "give the courts adequate authority to make release decisions that give appropriate recognition to the danger a person may pose to others if released."

To this end, Section 3141(a) of the Act requires a judicial officer to determine whether an arrestee shall be detained. Section 3142(e) provides that "if after a hearing pursuant to the provisions of subsection (f), the judicial officer finds that no condition or combination of conditions will reasonably assure the appearance of the person as required and the safety of any other person and the community, he shall order the detention of the person prior to trial." Section 3142(f) provides the arrestee with a number of procedural safeguards. He may request the presence of counsel at the detention hearing, he may testify and present witnesses in his behalf, as well as proffer evidence, and he may cross-examine other witnesses appearing at the hearing. If the judicial officer finds that no conditions of pretrial release can reasonably assure the safety of other persons and the community, he must state his findings of fact in writing, and support his conclusion with "clear and convincing evidence."

The judicial officer is not given unbridled discretion in making the detention determination. Congress has specified the considerations relevant to that decision. These factors include the nature and seriousness of the charges, the substantiality of the government's evidence against the arrestee, the arrestee's background and characteristics, and the nature and seriousness of the danger posed by the suspect's release. Should a judicial officer order detention, the detainee is entitled to expedited appellate review of the detention order.

Respondents Anthony Salerno and Vincent Cafaro were arrested on March 21, 1986, after being charged in a 29-count indictment alleging various Racketeer Influenced and Corrupt Organizations Act (RICO) violations, mail and wire fraud offenses, extortion, and various criminal gambling violations. The RICO counts alleged 35 acts of racketeering activity, including fraud, extortion, gambling, and conspiracy to commit murder. At respondents' arraignment, the Government moved to have Salerno and Cafaro detained pursuant to Section 3142(e), on the ground that no condition of release would assure the safety of the community or any person. The District Court held a hearing at which the Government made a detailed proffer of evidence. The Government's case showed that Salerno was the "boss" of the Genovese Crime Family of La Cosa Nostra and that Cafaro was a "captain" in the Genovese Family. According to the Government's proffer, based in large part on conversations intercepted by a court-ordered wiretap, the two respondents had participated in wide-ranging conspiracies to aid their illegitimate enterprises through violent means. The Government also offered the testimony of two of its trial witnesses, who would assert that Salerno personally participated in two murder conspiracies. Salerno opposed the motion for detention, challenging the credibility of the Government's witnesses. He offered the testimony of several character witnesses as well as a letter from his doctor stating that he was suffering from a serious medical condition. Cafaro presented no evidence at the hearing, but instead characterized the wiretap conversations as merely "tough talk."

The District Court granted the Government's detention motion, concluding that the Government had established by clear and convincing evidence that no condition or combination of conditions of release would ensure the safety of the community or any person. . . .

Respondents appealed, contending that to the extent that the Bail Reform Act permits pretrial detention on the ground that the arrestee is likely to commit future crimes, it is unconstitutional on its face. Over a dissent, the United States Court of Appeals for the Second Circuit agreed. Although the court agreed that pretrial detention could be imposed if the defendants were likely to intimidate witnesses or otherwise jeopardize the trial process, it found Section 3142(e)'s authorization of pretrial detention [on the ground of future dangerousness] repugnant to the concept of substantive due process, which we believe prohibits the total deprivation of liberty simply as a means of preventing future crimes. The court concluded that the Government could not, consistent with due process, detain persons who had not been accused of any crime merely because they were thought to present a danger to the community. It reasoned that our criminal law system holds persons accountable for past actions, not anticipated future actions. Although a court could detain an arrestee who threatened to flee before trial, such detention would be permissible because it would serve the basic objective of a criminal system—bringing the accused to trial. The court distinguished our decision in *Gerstein* v. *Pugh* in which we upheld police detention pursuant to arrest. The court construed Gerstein as limiting such detention to the "administrative steps incident to arrest." The Court of Appeals also found our decision in *Schall* v. *Martin*, 467 U.S. 253 (1984), upholding post arrest pretrial detention of juveniles, inapposite because juveniles have a lesser interest in liberty than do adults.

A facial challenge to a legislative Act is, of course, the most difficult challenge to mount successfully, since the challenger must establish that no set of circumstances exists under which the Act would be valid. The fact that the Bail Reform Act might operate unconstitutionally under some conceivable set of circumstances is insufficient to render it wholly invalid, since we have not recognized an "overbreadth" doctrine outside the limited context of the First Amendment. We think respondents have failed to shoulder their heavy burden to demonstrate that the Act is "facially" unconstitutional.

Respondents present two grounds for invalidating the Bail Reform Act's provisions permitting pretrial detention on the basis of future dangerousness. First, they rely upon the Court of Appeals' conclusion that the Act exceeds the limitations placed upon the Federal Government by the Due Process Clause of the Fifth Amendment. Second, they contend that the Act contravenes the Eighth Amendment's proscription against excessive bail. We treat these contentions in turn.

A

The Due Process Clause of the Fifth Amendment provides that "No person shall . . . be deprived of life, liberty, or property, without due process of law. . . ." This Court has held that the Due Process Clause protects individuals against two types of government action. So-called "substantive due process" prevents the government from engaging in conduct that "shocks the conscience," or interferes with rights "implicit in the concept of ordered liberty." When government action depriving a person of life, liberty, or property survives substantive due process scrutiny, it must still be implemented in a fair manner. This requirement has traditionally been referred to as "procedural" due process.

Respondents first argue that the Act violates substantive due process because the pretrial detention it authorizes constitutes impermissible punishment before trial. The Government, however, has never argued that pretrial detention could be upheld if it were "punishment." The Court of Appeals assumed that pretrial detention under the Bail Reform Act is regulatory, not penal, and we agree that it is.

As an initial matter, the mere fact that a person is detained does not inexorably lead to the conclusion that the government has imposed punishment. To determine whether a restriction on liberty constitutes impermissible punishment or permissible regulation, we first look to legislative intent. Unless Congress expressly intended to impose punitive restrictions, the punitive/regulatory distinction turns on "whether an alternative purpose to which the restriction may rationally be connected is assignable for it, and whether it appears excessive in relation to the alternative purpose assigned. . . ."

We conclude that the detention imposed by the Act falls on the regulatory side of the dichotomy. The legislative history of the Bail Reform Act clearly indicates that Congress did not formulate the pretrial detention provisions as punishment for dangerous individuals. Congress instead perceived pretrial detention as a potential solution to a pressing societal problem. There is no doubt that preventing danger to the community is a legitimate regulatory goal.

Nor are the incidents of pretrial detention excessive in relation to the regulatory goal Congress sought to achieve. The Bail Reform Act carefully limits the circumstances under which detention may be sought to the most serious of crimes. See 18 U.S.C.3142(f) (detention hearings available if case involves crimes of violence, offenses for which the sentence is life imprisonment or death, serious drug offenses, or certain repeat offenders). The arrestee is entitled to a prompt detention hearing, and the maximum length of pretrial detention is limited by the stringent time limitations of the Speedy Trial Act. Moreover, as in *Schall* v. *Martin,* the conditions of confinement envisioned by the Act appear to reflect the regulatory purposes relied upon by the government. As in Schall, the statute at issue here requires that detainees be housed in a "facility separate, to the extent practicable, from persons awaiting or serving sentences or being held in custody pending appeal." We conclude, therefore, that the pretrial detention contemplated by the Bail Reform Act is regulatory in nature, and does not constitute punishment before trial in violation of the Due Process Clause.

The Court of Appeals nevertheless concluded that "the Due Process Clause prohibits pretrial detention on the ground of danger to the community as a regulatory measure, without regard to the duration of the detention." Respondents characterize the Due Process Clause as erecting an impenetrable "wall" in this area that "no governmental interest—rational, important, compelling or otherwise—may surmount."

We do not think the Clause lays down any such categorical imperative. We have repeatedly held that the government's regulatory interest in community safety can, in appropriate circumstances, outweigh an individual's liberty interest. For example, in times of war or insurrection, when society's interest is at its peak, the government may detain individuals whom the government believes to be dangerous. Even outside the exigencies of war, we have found that sufficiently compelling governmental interests can justify detention of dangerous persons. Thus, we have found no absolute constitutional barrier to detention of potentially dangerous resident aliens pending deportation proceedings. We have also held that the government may detain mentally unstable individuals who present a danger to the public, and dangerous defendants who become incompetent to stand trial. We have approved of post arrest regulatory detention of juveniles when they present a continuing danger to the community. . . . Even competent adults may face substantial liberty restrictions as a result of the operation of our criminal justice system. If the police suspect an individual of a crime, they may arrest and hold him until a neutral magistrate determines whether probable cause exists. *Gerstein* v. *Pugh*. Finally, respondents concede and the Court of Appeals noted that an arrestee may be incarcerated until trial if he presents a risk of flight or a danger to witnesses.

Respondents characterize all of these cases as exceptions to the "general rule" of substantive due process that the government may not detain a person prior to a judgment of guilt in a criminal trial. Such a "general rule" may freely be conceded, but we think that these cases show a sufficient number of exceptions to the rule that the congressional action challenged here can hardly be characterized as totally novel. Given the well-established authority of the government, in special circumstances, to restrain individuals' liberty prior to or even without criminal trial and conviction, we think that the present statute providing for pretrial detention on the basis of dangerousness must be evaluated in precisely the same manner that we evaluated the laws in the cases discussed above.

The government's interest in preventing crime by arrestees is both legitimate and compelling. In Schall, we recognized the strength of the State's interest in preventing juvenile crime. This general concern with crime prevention is no less compelling when the suspects are adults. Indeed, "the harm suffered by the victim of a crime is not dependent upon the age of the perpetrator." The Bail Reform Act of 1984 responds to an even more particularized governmental interest than the interest we sustained in Schall. The statute we upheld in Schall permitted pretrial detention of any juvenile arrested on any charge after a showing that the individual might commit some undefined further crimes. The Bail Reform Act, in contrast, narrowly focuses on a particularly acute problem in which the government interests are overwhelming. The Act operates only on individuals who have been arrested for a specific category of extremely serious offenses. Congress specifically found that these individuals are far more likely to be responsible for dangerous acts in the community after arrest. Nor is the Act by any means a scattershot attempt to incapacitate those who are merely suspected of these serious crimes. The government must first of all demonstrate probable cause to believe that the charged crime has been committed by the arrestee, but that is not enough. In a full-blown adversary hearing, the government must convince a neutral decision maker by clear and convincing evidence that no conditions of release can reasonably assure the safety of the community or any person. While the government's general interest in preventing crime is compelling, even this interest is heightened when the government musters convincing proof that the arrestee, already indicted or held to answer for a serious crime, presents a demonstrable danger to the community. Under these narrow circumstances, society's interest in crime prevention is at its greatest.

On the other side of the scale, of course, is the individual's strong interest in liberty. We do not minimize the importance and fundamental nature of this right. But, as our cases hold, this right may, in circumstances where the government's interest is sufficiently weighty, be subordinated to the greater needs of society. We think that Congress' careful delineation of the circumstances under which detention will be permitted satisfies this standard. When the government proves by clear and convincing evidence that an arrestee presents an identified and articulable threat to an individual or the community, we believe that, consistent with the Due Process Clause, a court may disable the arrestee from executing that threat. Under these circumstances, we cannot categorically state that pretrial detention "offends some principle of justice so rooted in the traditions and conscience of our people as to be ranked as fundamental."

Finally, we may dispose briefly of respondents' facial challenge to the procedures of the Bail Reform Act. To sustain them against such a challenge, we need only find them "adequate to authorize the pretrial detention of at least some persons charged with crimes," whether or not they might be insufficient in some particular circumstances. We think they pass that test. As we stated in Schall, "there is nothing inherently unattainable about a prediction of future criminal conduct."

Under the Bail Reform Act, the procedures by which a judicial officer evaluates the likelihood of future dangerousness are specifically designed to further the accuracy of that determination. Detainees have a right to counsel at the detention hearing. They may testify in their own behalf, present information by proffer or otherwise, and cross-examine witnesses who appear at the hearing. The judicial officer charged with the responsibility of determining the appropriateness of detention is guided by statutorily enumerated factors, which include the nature and the circumstances of the charges, the weight of the evidence, the history and characteristics of the putative offender, and the danger to the community. The government must prove its case by clear and convincing evidence.

Finally, the judicial officer must include written findings of fact and a written statement of reasons for a decision to detain. The Act's review provisions provide for immediate appellate review of the detention decision.

We think these extensive safeguards suffice to repel a facial challenge. The protections are more exacting than those we found sufficient in the juvenile context, see Schall, and they far exceed what we found necessary to effect limited post arrest detention in *Gerstein* v. *Pugh*. Given the legitimate and compelling regulatory purpose of the Act and the procedural protections it offers, we conclude that the Act is not facially invalid under the Due Process Clause of the Fifth Amendment.

B

Respondents also contend that the Bail Reform Act violates the Excessive Bail Clause of the Eighth Amendment. . . .

The Eighth Amendment addresses pretrial release by providing merely that "Excessive bail shall not be required." This Clause, of course, says nothing about whether bail shall be available at all. Respondents nevertheless contend that this Clause grants them a right to bail calculated solely upon considerations of flight. They rely on *Stack* v. *Boyle* in which the Court stated that "Bail set at a figure higher than an amount reasonably calculated to ensure the defendant's presence at trial is excessive under the Eighth Amendment." In respondents' view, since the Bail Reform Act allows a court essentially to set bail at an infinite amount for reasons not related to the risk of flight, it violates the Excessive Bail Clause. Respondents concede that the right to bail they have discovered in the Eighth Amendment is not absolute. A court may, for example, refuse bail in capital cases. And, as the Court of Appeals noted and respondents admit, a court may refuse bail when the defendant presents a threat to the judicial process by intimidating witnesses. Respondents characterize these exceptions as consistent with what they claim to be the sole purpose of bail—to ensure integrity of the judicial process.

While we agree that a primary function of bail is to safeguard the courts' role in adjudicating the guilt or innocence of defendants, we reject the proposition that the Eighth Amendment categorically prohibits the government from pursuing other admittedly compelling interests through regulation of pretrial release. The above-quoted dicta in *Stack* v. *Boyle* is far too slender a reed on which to rest this argument. The Court in Stack had no occasion to consider whether the Excessive Bail Clause requires courts to admit all defendants to bail, because the statute before the Court in that case in fact allowed the defendants to be bailed. . . .

The holding of Stack is illuminated by the Court's holding just four months later in *Carlson* v. *Landon*, 342 U.S. 524 (1952). In that case, remarkably similar to the present action, the detainees had been arrested and held without bail pending a determination of deportability. The Attorney General refused to release the individuals, "on the ground that there was reasonable cause to believe that release would be prejudicial to the public interest and would endanger the welfare and safety of the United States." The detainees brought the same challenge that respondents bring to us today: the Eighth Amendment required them to be admitted to bail. The Court squarely rejected this proposition:

> The bail clause was lifted with slight changes from the English Bill of Rights Act. In England that clause has never been thought to accord a right to bail in all cases, but merely to provide that bail shall not he excessive in those cases where it is proper to grant bail. When this clause was carried over into our Bill of Rights, nothing was said that indicated any different concept. The Eighth Amendment has not prevented Congress from defining the classes of cases in which bail shall be allowed in this country. Thus, in criminal cases bail is not compulsory where the punishment may be death. Indeed, the very language of the Amendment fails to say all arrests must be bailable.

Carlson v. *Landon* was a civil case, and we need not decide today whether the Excessive Bail Clause speaks at all to Congress' power to define the classes of criminal arrestees who shall be admitted to bail. For even if we were to conclude that the Eighth Amendment imposes some substantive limitations on the National Legislature's powers in this area, we would still hold that the Bail Reform Act is valid. Nothing in the text of the Bail Clause limits permissible government considerations solely to questions of flight. The only arguable substantive limitation of the Bail Clause is that the government's proposed conditions of release or detention not be "excessive" in light of the perceived evil. Of course, to determine whether the government's response is excessive, we must compare that response against the interest the government seeks to protect by means of that response. Thus, when the government has admitted that its only interest is in preventing flight, bail must be set by a court at a sum designed to ensure that goal, and no more. We believe that when Congress has mandated detention on the basis of a compelling interest other than prevention of flight, as it has here, the Eighth Amendment does not require release on bail.

II

In our society liberty is the norm, and detention prior to trial or without trial is the carefully limited exception. We hold that the provisions for pretrial detention in the Bail Reform Act of 1984 fall within that carefully limited exception. We are unwilling to say that this congressional determination, based as it is upon that primary concern of every government's concern for the safety and indeed the lives of its citizens, on its face violates either the Due Process Clause of the Fifth Amendment or the Excessive Bail Clause of the Eighth Amendment.

Justice Marshall, with whom Justice Brennan joins, dissenting.

. . . The majority approaches respondents' challenge to the Act by dividing the discussion into two sections, one concerned with the substantive guarantees implicit in the Due Process Clause, and the other concerned with the protection afforded by the Excessive Bail Clause of the Eighth Amendment. This is a sterile formalism, which divides a unitary argument into two independent parts and then professes to demonstrate that the parts are individually inadequate.

On the due process side of this false dichotomy appears an argument concerning the distinction between regulatory and punitive legislation. The majority concludes that the Act is a regulatory rather than a punitive measure. The ease with which the conclusion is reached suggests the worthlessness of the achievement. The major premise is that "unless Congress expressly intended to impose punitive restrictions, the punitive/regulatory distinction turns on whether an alternative purpose to which it may rationally be connected is assignable for it, and whether it appears excessive in relation to the alternative purpose assigned to it. . . ." The majority finds that "Congress did not formulate the pretrial detention provisions as punishment for dangerous individuals," but instead was pursuing the "legitimate regulatory goal" of "preventing danger to the community." Concluding that pretrial detention is not an excessive solution to the problem of preventing danger to the community, the majority thus finds that no substantive element of the guarantee of due process invalidates the statute.

This argument does not demonstrate the conclusion it purports to justify. Let us apply the majority's reasoning to a similar, hypothetical case. After investigation, Congress determines (not unrealistically) that a large proportion of violent crime is perpetrated by persons who are unemployed. It also determines, equally reasonably, that much violent crime is committed at night. From amongst the panoply of "potential solutions," Congress chooses a statute which permits, after judicial proceedings, the imposition of a dusk-to-dawn curfew on anyone who is unemployed. Since this is not a measure enacted for the purpose of punishing the unemployed, and since the majority finds that preventing danger to the community is a legitimate regulatory goal, the curfew statute would, according to the majority's analysis, be a mere "regulatory" detention statute, entirely compatible with the substantive components of the Due Process Clause.

The absurdity of this conclusion arises, of course, from the majority's cramped concept of substantive due process. The majority proceeds as though the only substantive right protected by the Due Process Clause is a right to be free from punishment before conviction. The majority's technique for infringing this right is simple: merely redefine any measure which is claimed to be punishment as "regulation," and, magically, the Constitution no longer prohibits its imposition. Because, as I discuss in Part III, infra, the Due Process Clause protects other substantive rights which are infringed by this legislation, the majority's argument is merely an exercise in obfuscation.

The logic of the majority's Eighth Amendment analysis is equally unsatisfactory. The Eighth Amendment, as the majority notes, states that "excessive bail shall not be required." The majority then declares, as if it were undeniable, that: "this Clause, of course, says nothing about whether bail shall be available at all." If excessive bail is imposed the defendant stays in jail. The same result is achieved if bail is denied altogether. Whether the magistrate sets bail at $1 billion or refuses to set bail at all, the consequences are indistinguishable. It would be mere sophistry to suggest that the Eighth Amendment protects against the former decision, and not the latter. Indeed, such a result would lead to the conclusion that there was no need for Congress to pass a preventive detention measure of any kind; every federal magistrate and district judge could simply refuse, despite the absence of any evidence of risk of flight or danger to the community, to set bail. This would be entirely constitutional, since, according to the majority, the Eighth Amendment "says nothing about whether bail shall be available at all."

But perhaps, the majority says, this manifest absurdity can be avoided. Perhaps the Bail Clause is addressed only to the judiciary. "We need not decide today," the majority says, "whether the Excessive Bail Clause speaks at all to Congress' power to define the classes of criminal arrestees who shall be admitted to bail." The majority is correct that this question need not be decided today; it was decided long ago. Federal and state statutes which purport to accomplish what the Eighth Amendment forbids, such as imposing cruel and unusual punishments, may not stand. The text of the Amendment, which provides simply that "excessive bail shall not be required, nor excessive fines imposed, nor cruel and unusual punishments inflicted," provides absolutely no support for the majority's speculation that both courts and Congress are forbidden to inflict cruel and unusual punishments, while only the courts are forbidden to require excessive bail.

. . . The majority concedes, as it must, that "when the government has admitted that its only interest is in preventing flight, bail must be set by a court at a sum designed to ensure that goal, and no more." But, the majority says, "when Congress has mandated detention on the basis of a compelling interest other than prevention of flight, as it has here, the Eighth Amendment does not require release on bail." This conclusion follows only if the "compelling" interest upon which Congress acted is an interest which the Constitution permits Congress to further through the denial of bail. The majority does not ask, as a result of its disingenuous division of the analysis, if there are any substantive limits contained in both the Eighth Amendment and the Due Process Clause which render this system of preventive detention unconstitutional. The majority does not ask because the answer is apparent and, to the majority, inconvenient.

III

The essence of this case may be found, ironically enough, in a provision of the Act to which the majority does not refer. Title 18 U.S.C.31 42 provides that "nothing in this section shall be construed as modifying or limiting the presumption of innocence." But the very pith and purpose of this statute is an abhorrent limitation of the presumption of innocence. The majority's untenable conclusion that the present Act is constitutional arises from a specious denial of the role of the Bail Clause and the Due Process Clause in protecting the invaluable guarantee afforded by the presumption of innocence. "The principle that there is a presumption of innocence in favor of the accused is the undoubted law, axiomatic and elementary, and its enforcement lies at the foundation of the administration of our criminal law." Our society's belief, reinforced over the centuries, that all are innocent until the state has proven them to be guilty, like the companion principle that guilt must be proved beyond a reasonable doubt, is "implicit in the concept of ordered liberty," and is established beyond legislative contravention in the Due Process Clause.

The statute now before us declares that persons who have been indicted may be detained if a judicial officer finds clear and convincing evidence that they pose a danger to individuals or to the community. The statute does not authorize the government to imprison anyone it has evidence is dangerous; indictment is necessary. But let us suppose that a defendant is indicted and the government shows by clear and convincing evidence that he is dangerous and should be detained pending a trial, at which trial the defendant is acquitted. May the government continue to hold the defendant in detention based upon its showing that he is dangerous? The answer cannot be yes, for that would allow the government to imprison someone for uncommitted crimes based upon proof not beyond a reasonable doubt. The result must therefore be that once the indictment has failed, detention cannot continue. But our fundamental principles of justice declare that the defendant is as innocent on the day before his trial as he is on the morning after his acquittal. Under this statute an untried indictment somehow acts to permit a detention, based on other charges, which after an acquittal would be unconstitutional. The conclusion is inescapable that the indictment has been turned into evidence, if not that the defendant is guilty of the crime charged, then that left to his own devices he will soon be guilty of something else.

To be sure, an indictment is not without legal consequences. It establishes that there is probable cause to believe that an offense was committed, and that the defendant committed it. Upon probable cause a warrant for the defendant's arrest may issue; a period of administrative detention may occur before the evidence of probable cause is presented to a neutral magistrate. . . . Once a defendant has been committed for trial he may be detained in custody if the magistrate finds that no conditions of release will prevent him from becoming a fugitive. But in this connection the charging instrument is evidence of nothing more than the fact that there will be a trial, and release before trial is conditioned upon the accused's giving adequate assurance that he will stand trial and submit to sentence if found guilty. Like the ancient practice of securing the oaths of responsible persons to stand as sureties for the accused, the modern practice of requiring a bail bond or the deposit of a sum of money subject to forfeiture serves as additional assurance of the presence of an accused.

The finding of probable cause conveys power to try, and the power to try imports of necessity the power to assure that the processes of justice will not be evaded or obstructed. "Pretrial detention to prevent future crimes against society at large, however, is not justified by any concern for holding a trial on the charges for which a defendant has been arrested." The detention purportedly authorized by this statute bears no relation to the government's power to try charges supported by a finding of probable cause, and thus the interests it serves are outside the scope of interests which may be considered in weighing the excessiveness of bail under the Eighth Amendment.

IV

Honoring the presumption of innocence is often difficult; sometimes we must pay substantial social costs as a result of our commitment to the values we espouse. But at the end of the day the presumption of innocence protects the innocent; the shortcuts we take with those whom we believe to be guilty injure only those wrongfully accused and, ultimately, ourselves.

I dissent.

Justice Stevens, dissenting:

There may be times when the government's interest in protecting the safety of the community will justify the brief detention of a person who has not committed any crime. . . . It is clear to me that a pending indictment may not be given any weight in evaluating an individual's risk to the community or the need for immediate detention.

If the evidence of imminent danger is strong enough to warrant emergency detention, it should support that preventive measure regardless of whether the person has been charged, convicted, or acquitted of some other offense. In this case, for example, it is unrealistic to assume that the danger to the community that was present when respondents were at large did not justify their detention before they were indicted, but did require that measure the moment that the grand jury found probable cause to believe they had committed crimes in the past. It is equally unrealistic to assume that the danger will vanish if a jury happens to acquit them. Justice Marshall has demonstrated that the fact of indictment cannot, consistent with the presumption of innocence and the Eighth Amendment's Excessive Bail Clause, be used to create a special class the members of which are, alone, eligible for detention because of future dangerousness.

REVIEW QUESTIONS

1. What is the purpose of the initial appearance?
2. Why is the initial appearance important?
3. How soon after an arrest must the accused be furnished with an initial appearance?
4. What is the purpose of bail?
5. In what form may bail be posted?
6. How much bail is a defendant required to post?
7. What does forfeiture of bail signify?
8. What is the significance of the phrase "released on one's own recognizance"?

LOCAL PROCEDURE

1. Within what period of time must the initial appearance take place?
2. May an accused enter a plea at the initial appearance?
3. May a defendant be denied bail for protective detention?
4. Can a defendant be prosecuted for failure to appear after posting bail?

ENDNOTES

1. 318 U.S. 332 (1943).
2. 354 U.S. 449 (1957).
3. *Kinney v. County of Contra Costa,* 87 Cal Rptr 638 (1970).
4. 342 U.S. 1 (1951).
5. 342 U.S. 524 (1952).
6. 95 L. Ed 2d 697 (1987).

Pretrial Proceedings

CHAPTER 5

ARRAIGNMENT

During the arraignment, the defendant is given an opportunity to enter a plea to
the charge alleged in the complaint. The defendant may either enter the plea at that
time or request time to consider the plea to be entered. Depending upon the jurisdiction, the defendant may enter any one or more of the following pleas: (1) guilty,
(2) not guilty, (3) nolo contendere, (4) not guilty by reason of insanity, (5) former
jeopardy, or (6) former judgment of acquittal or conviction. Generally, the law provides that if a defendant does not plead "not guilty by reason of insanity," he or she
shall be conclusively presumed to have been sane at the time the crime was committed.

Guilty Plea

At one time in our history, defendants were not permitted to enter guilty pleas,
since it was thought that the only way justice could be accomplished was by a trial.
A plea of guilty is an admission of every element of the offense charged, and no
proof of the crime needs to be presented.[1] A plea of guilty is more than a confession that admits that the accused did various acts; it is itself a conviction; nothing
remains but to give judgment and determine punishment. Thus the plea of guilty
cannot be accepted lightly by a judge.

Generally, in felony cases, a plea of guilty must be made by the defendant in
open court either orally or in writing. The purpose behind the requirement that the

defendant personally enter the plea is to ensure that it is his or her own plea. Most states provide that a judge may not accept a plea of guilty, particularly in felony cases, unless the defendant is informed of his or her right to the assistance of counsel. If the defendant understands this right to counsel and waives the right, the judge may then accept the plea of guilty. However, some states will not permit a judge to accept a guilty plea to a capital offense charge, or one in which the punishment is life imprisonment, without the possibility of parole, unless the defendant is represented by counsel. A few states will not permit a defendant to enter a guilty plea to a capital offense even with the assistance of counsel. In lesser offenses (misdemeanors and infractions), most states allow counsel to enter guilty pleas on behalf of their clients.

In accordance with the U.S. Supreme Court's *Boykin* v. *Alabama* decision, before a judge may accept a guilty plea to any charge, misdemeanor or felony, the judge must inform the defendant of the significance of the guilty plea. The defendant must be informed that by pleading guilty, he or she waives all right against self-incrimination, the right to a jury trial, and all right to be confronted by his or her accusers. Even though the defendant is represented by counsel at the time of the guilty plea, the records of the case in felony cases must reflect that the judge advised the defendant of the guarantees that would be waived by the plea of guilty. The laws of some states provide that before the judge may accept a guilty plea, an inquiry must be made to make certain that the accused has actually committed a crime serious enough to justify the guilty plea. The extent of the inquiry will depend largely upon the facts of each case. The judge may confine the inquiry to the facts in the transcript of the preliminary hearing or of the grand jury. Or the judge may use whatever procedure is best under the circumstances, including interrogating the attorneys involved in the case. The accused does not have to admit guilt expressly at the time of the guilty plea. In some states, a guilty plea may be accepted even though accompanied by a claim of innocence.[2] A judge does not have to accept a guilty plea, particularly if the judge feels that the defendant does not understand the significance of the plea or if there is some question about the plea being voluntarily given. Most jurisdictions hold that defendants who are not citizens of the United States must be advised that if they plead guilty, they may be subject to deportation.

After a plea of guilty is accepted, the next step is to sentence the defendant. If the charge is a misdemeanor, the judge of the inferior court has the authority to mete out the sentence, but if the charge is a felony, the case must be transferred to the superior court for sentencing. A judge of an inferior court has the authority to accept a guilty plea to a felony charge in most jurisdictions, and the plea will have the same effect as if it had been entered in the superior court. A few jurisdictions do not permit a defendant to enter a plea to a felony charge in the inferior court, and the case must be transferred to the superior court for both the acceptance of the plea and the sentencing.

Withdrawal of Guilty Plea

In most jurisdictions, a defendant, upon showing a good cause, may withdraw a guilty plea and enter a not guilty plea or one of the other pleas at any time before the pronouncement of sentence. A few jurisdictions hold that if the defendant was not represented by counsel at the time the guilty plea was entered, the judge must permit the defendant to withdraw the guilty plea upon showing good cause. For this reason, most judges are reluctant to accept a plea of guilty if the defendant was not represented by counsel, particularly in felony cases. The request of a defendant to withdraw a guilty plea is not taken lightly. If the withdrawal is permitted, then the defendant is entitled to a trial on one of the other pleas that may have been entered. This action could inconvenience witnesses, crowd court calendars, and cause additional expense. But if the defendant can show sufficiently good cause, the withdrawal should be permitted by the trial judge; otherwise, the denial of the withdrawal may be overturned by an appellate court. The problem created by this procedure is determining what would be considered good cause. It has been held that if the defendant did not understand the meaning or significance of the guilty plea, this allegation is sufficient showing of good cause. In *Henderson* v. *Morgan*,[3] the U.S. Supreme Court permitted the withdrawal of a guilty plea nine years after it was originally entered upon the grounds that the plea had been involuntarily given. In that case, the trial court accepted a guilty plea to a charge of second degree murder. The defendant later attempted to withdraw the guilty plea on the grounds that he did not know that "intent" was a necessary element of second degree murder and, further, that he had not been sufficiently informed of the sentence he would receive if he pleaded guilty. The appellate courts of New York upheld the judge's denial of the withdrawal, and the case was appealed to the U.S. Supreme Court upon the grounds that the defendant had been denied due process of law. The Supreme Court held that since the defendant had not been advised by either the judge or the attorneys involved that intent was a necessary element of the crime of second degree murder, his plea of guilty was "as a matter of law involuntary and must be set aside." It was stated that a plea could not have been voluntarily given unless the defendant had "received real notice of the true nature of the charge against him, the first and most universally recognized requirement of due process." But it was felt that the defendant had been sufficiently informed of the sentence that he might receive if the guilty plea was received. In most jurisdictions, there is no requirement that a defendant be advised in advance of the sentence that may be imposed if a guilty plea is accepted. The acceptance of a guilty plea upon the basis of the sentence that may be imposed is discussed in Chapter 9, under the heading "Plea Negotiation."

An additional reason some states require a judge to make an inquiry concerning the facts surrounding a guilty plea is to prevent a defendant from later challenging the plea as being a free and voluntary act, as was successfully done by Morgan some nine years after his guilty plea in the *Henderson* v. *Morgan* case. The dissenting justices in that case felt that the withdrawal of the guilty plea should have been denied. It was their opinion that the trial judge had held a factual inquiry and that the inquiry revealed that the defendant had sufficient knowledge of the elements of the crime. Thus, these justices believed that the guilty plea had been voluntarily given. The facts in *Parker* v. *North Carolina*[4] present an interesting attempt to withdraw a guilty plea. The defendant argued that his guilty plea was the product of a coerced confession. The court stated that even on the assumption that the confession had been coerced, the court could not believe that the alleged police conduct during the interrogation period was of such nature or had such enduring effect as to make involuntary a plea of guilty entered over a month later. According to the appellate court, the trial judge was within his rights to refuse the request for withdrawal of the guilty plea.

Not Guilty Plea

When a plea of not guilty is entered by the defendant, a trial will be held. If the plea is to a misdemeanor charge, the case may be set immediately for trial, which, in most instances, will take place in the minor court. If the not guilty plea is to a felony charge, further proceedings must take place either by a grand jury hearing or by a preliminary hearing before the case can be set for trial in the superior or district court. This procedure protects the accused from being held for trial without sufficient cause. The grand jury and preliminary hearings will be discussed later. Most jurisdictions permit a defendant to withdraw a not guilty plea and to enter a plea of guilty at any time during the trial. This possibility eliminates much trial time, particularly if the change of plea takes place early in the trial proceedings.

Occasionally, a defendant will refuse to enter any plea and stands mute before the court. History reveals that when this behavior occurred in early common law, the defendant was returned to the prison from which he or she had been brought and made to lie naked on his on her back on the floor. Great weights of iron were placed on the defendant who was fed only three "morsels of the worst bread" the first day, and three sips of stagnant water the next, with this diet alternating daily until the prisoner died or entered a plea. In later years, a more humane procedure was followed. When the defendant stood mute before the court, the silence was treated as a guilty plea. Today, if the defendant refuses to plead, a plea of not guilty is entered for him or her, followed by a trial. By entering a plea of guilty, the defendant admits that he or she is the person named in the indictment or information.

Nolo Contendere Plea

A plea of nolo contendere, meaning "I will not contest it," or "no contest," is essentially equivalent to a plea of guilty. In some states, the nolo contendere plea is known as "non volt contendere" and is sometimes abbreviated as "non volt." As with the plea of guilty, the judge must inform the defendant of those rights that he or she is entitled to and of those that he or she waives by such a plea. The most significant effect of the nolo contendere plea is that it may not be used against the defendant in a civil matter because the defendant has not admitted guilt. As pointed out, a plea of guilty is a formal type of confession of the act charged. Not all states permit a nolo contendere plea to be entered by a defendant. In those states in which the plea has been adopted, there is a variance in who must agree to accept the plea. In some states, only the judge must agree to accept the plea; in others, the prosecuting attorney also must agree before the nolo contendere plea may be accepted.

This plea has been adopted to satisfy the thinking of two types of defendants charged with a violation. Some defendants will admit to committing a particular act but will refuse to admit that the act was a crime, so they enter the "no contest" plea of nolo contendere. For example, a person may be charged with speeding on a freeway. She may admit to excessive speed but allege that, since no one was injured or endangered, no crime was committed. Thus, she merely enters the plea of nolo contendere.

Other defendants have committed acts that may subject them to civil suits for damages or restitution as well as to criminal prosecution. They feel that the evidence against them is so great that it would be useless to contest the criminal charges, but they do not want to permit the guilty plea to be introduced against them in a civil trial. Under these circumstances, they may wish to enter the nolo contendere plea. As an example, this plea is frequently entered by a defendant who has been arrested for driving under the influence of alcohol after being involved in a serious accident in which persons were injured or killed. The defendant may know that the evidence against him is strong enough that a trial would result in a conviction. To save the expense of a trial and to prevent the conviction from being used against him in a civil suit, the defendant will attempt to enter a plea of nolo contendere. In this instance, the judge may refuse to allow the defendant to enter the nolo contendere plea, since it could be an injustice to the victims of the accident. A defendant may not plead nolo contendere as a matter of right but must have the consent of the judge, its acceptance being entirely a matter of grace.

Not Guilty by Reason of Insanity Plea

By entering a plea of not guilty by reason of insanity, the defendant is admitting the commission of the act for which he or she is charged, but the defendant alleges that he or she cannot be held responsible for the crime because he or she was not sane at the time the act was committed. The whole issue of the ensuing trial is whether the defendant was sane or insane at the time the crime was committed. The defendant's present sanity is not at stake because he or she cannot be tried if he or she is not sane at the time of the trial.

Most states provide that if the defendant enters this plea, he or she has the burden of proving that he or she was insane at the time the offense was committed, and the prosecution may endeavor to meet that allegation by introducing evidence to prove that the defendant was sane at the time of the offense. A few states hold that the burden of proving beyond a reasonable doubt that the defendant was sane at the time he or she committed the act still rests with the prosecution. The defendant has only to meet the prosecution's case by creating a doubt of his or her sanity. If the defendant is found to have been sane at the time he or she committed the crime, the only procedure to follow is sentencing the defendant because he or she has already admitted guilt by the plea of not guilty by reason of insanity. If the defendant is found to have been insane at the time the offense was committed, then technically he or she is entitled to be set free because his or her present sanity is not in question. However, most jurisdictions provide that the judge hearing the case may demand that the defendant be confined for a period, usually not less than ninety days, for observation to determine that the defendant is not a danger to society. If, after the confinement period, it is determined that the defendant is not a danger, he or she must be released from custody.

A few states permit a defendant to enter dual pleas. He or she may enter a plea of not guilty and at the same time enter a plea of not guilty by reason of insanity. This procedure has been criticized, since the pleas are actually inconsistent pleas. Upon entering the plea of not guilty, the defendant is denying his or her guilt. In the second plea, the defendant is confessing guilt but alleging that he or she cannot be held responsible for the offense because of his or her insanity at the time. Where this procedure is permitted, the trial on the not guilty plea takes place first. If the defendant is found not guilty, he or she is entitled to be released without further action being taken. If the defendant is found to be guilty, the trial on the plea of not guilty by reason of insanity must follow. If the defendant is found to be sane at the time of committing the act, the sentencing procedure will take place. But if the defendant is found to have been insane at the time he or she committed the offense, the same procedure for release or observation will be set in motion as was previously described.

Not all states permit a plea of not guilty by reason of insanity to be entered, but insanity may be raised as a defense to the crime charged. Appendix B consists of an actual psychological report entered in trial at a case involving the issue of not guilty by reason of insanity.

Plea of Once in Jeopardy

The guarantee against being placed twice in jeopardy, also referred to as the *right against double jeopardy,* is of ancient origin, having been found in procedures of early Greek and Roman jurisprudence. It was established in the common law of England and brought to this country by the colonists. The guarantee is embodied in the Fifth Amendment to the U.S. Constitution and the laws of all the states. Basically, the guarantee provides that no person shall be placed in jeopardy of his or her life or liberty more than once for the same offense. It prohibits undue harassment and oppression by those in authority. If it were not for this guarantee against double jeopardy, an accused could be tried and retried until found guilty. Likewise, he or she might be retried if it were felt that the sentence resulting from the first trial was not severe enough.

If an accused is charged with a crime and believes that he or she has been previously placed in jeopardy by court action on that same charge, the accused may enter the plea of "once in jeopardy." But many ramifications are involved in this plea, such as what composes jeopardy and under what conditions an accused may be placed twice in jeopardy. Many persons are under the impression that an accused cannot be tried twice for the same offense. This is not always the case. There are situations in which a defendant may be tried two or more times for the same offense. Generally, if a defendant is acquitted of a crime, he or she cannot be tried again for that particular offense. But if a defendant is convicted, he or she may appeal the conviction to an appellate court. If the conviction is reversed upon appeal, the case may be retried. Upon appealing the conviction, the defendant is in a sense waiving his or her guarantee against double jeopardy. In the same manner, if the defendant requests a new trial after being convicted, he or she is waiving the double jeopardy guarantee. Furthermore, it has been held that if the jury cannot arrive at a verdict, the case may be retried by a different jury without the second trial's being a violation of the double jeopardy right.

The determination of when an accused has been placed in jeopardy is not without its complications. The Fifth Amendment guarantee against double jeopardy is of little assistance, since it merely provides that an accused shall not "be subject for the same offense to be twice put in jeopardy of life or limb." As the courts began to grant the guarantee against double jeopardy, it became necessary to determine when jeopardy attaches. In making this determination, the courts looked to the common law of England. The common law rule at the time that the Fifth Amendment was adopted was comparatively simple, merely providing that a defendant had been placed in jeopardy only when there had been a conviction or an acquittal after a complete trial. Early English history of jurisprudence reveals that, once commenced, most trials were completed. It is stated that the traditional practice was to keep the jury together unfed and without drink until they could deliver a unanimous verdict. As late as 1866, an English Court stated that the rule seemed to command the confinement of the jury until death if it did not agree on a verdict. At the time of the enactment of the Fifth Amendment, most criminal prosecutions in this country proceeded until a verdict was reached. At that time, neither the defendant nor the prosecution had any right to appeal an adverse verdict. The verdict in such a case was unquestionably final and barred further prosecution for the same offense.

But as time passed, this strict rule was relaxed through U.S. Supreme Court decisions. One of the first relaxations was the right granted to one convicted of a crime to be able to appeal the conviction if some error was committed during the trial. If the conviction was reversed upon appeal because of some error during the trial, the prosecution could retry the case. As stated, the appeal by the defendant amounted to a waiver of the right against double jeopardy. However, the U.S. Supreme Court in *Burks* v. *United States*[5] held that once a jury's verdict of acquittal is returned, that acquittal is a bar against further prosecutive action against the accused for the offense charged. The Court stated that the acquittal is an absolute bar "no matter how erroneous its [the jury's] decision" may be. In the past, some states have held that if the jury returned an erroneous verdict of acquittal, the defendant could be retried because jeopardy did not set in until a just verdict had been rendered. The *Burks* decision has eliminated such a contention.

Since it was believed that jeopardy did not set in until the verdict stage was reached, many trials were commenced but did not reach the verdict state. A judge often would stop a trial if he or she believed that the defendant was guilty and that the jury selected would not return a guilty verdict. The judge would dismiss that particular jury and have the trial started over with a new jury. This procedure could be repeated until the judge and prosecution felt that the jury selected would return a guilty verdict. Since this procedure resulted in injustices, to prevent such injustices, rules were established that held if a jury was dismissed without sufficient cause after the trial began, the defendant would have been placed in jeopardy and could not be retried.

The reason behind this rule was expressed by the U.S. Supreme Court in the *Burks* v. *United States* decision. The Court stated as follows:

> The Double Jeopardy Clause forbids a second trial for the purpose of affording the prosecution another opportunity to supply evidence which it failed to muster in the first proceeding. This is central to the objective of the prohibition against successive trials. The Clause does not allow the state to make repeated attempts to convict an individual for an alleged offense since the constitutional prohibition against double jeopardy was designed to protect an individual from being subjected to the hazards of trial and possible conviction more than once for an alleged offense.

The Court further stated in the case of *Crist* v. *Bretz:*[6]

> The basic reason for holding that a defendant is put in jeopardy even though the criminal proceeding against him terminated before verdict was perhaps best stated in *Green* v. *United States,* 355 US 184: "the underlying idea, one that is deeply ingrained in at least the Anglo-American system of jurisprudence, is that the State with all its resources and power should not be allowed to make repeated attempts to convict an individual for an alleged offense, thereby subject-

ing him to embarrassment, expense and ordeal and compelling him to live in a continuing state of anxiety and insecurity, as well as enhancing the possibility that even though innocent he may be found guilty."

The ruling that held that a defendant had been placed in jeopardy once the jury trial began created the problem of determining at what point the jury trial commenced. The legislatures and courts of the various states tried to establish guidelines to solve this problem, but there was no uniformity among the states. Some states held that a jury trial began once the jury was selected and sworn to do its duty in arriving at a verdict. Other states held that a jury trial did not commence until after the jury was selected and the first witness was sworn. The U.S. Supreme Court settled the problem in *Crist* v. *Bretz* by holding that a jury trial commences once the jury is selected and sworn. The Court stated as follows:

> ...the federal rule that jeopardy attaches when the jury is empaneled and sworn is an integral part of the constitutional guarantee against double jeopardy. .... The reason for holding that jeopardy attaches when the jury is empaneled and sworn lies in the need to protect the interest of an accused in retaining a chosen jury. That right was described in *Wade* v. *Hunter* as a defendant's valued right to have his trial completed by a particular tribunal. It is an interest with roots deep in the historic development of trial by jury in the Anglo-American system of criminal justice. Throughout that history there ran a strong tradition that once banded together a jury should not be discharged until it had completed its solemn task of announcing a verdict.

The rule provides that the defendant will have been placed in jeopardy if, once the trial begins, the jury is dismissed without sufficient cause before the verdict stage is reached.

There is no clear criterion concerning what is considered sufficient cause for a trial not to continue to the verdict stage. A sufficient cause may result from a mistrial having been declared by a judge. Often during a trial, a situation such as misconduct by a juror or some improper remark by a witness while testifying may cause a judge to believe that the defendant could not receive a fair trial if the trial was allowed to proceed. Even when a mistrial is declared primarily for the benefit of the defendant, the defendant usually must agree to the mistrial's being declared; otherwise, an appellate court may conclude that jeopardy had set in and the defendant could not be retried.

The U.S. Supreme Court in *Crist* v. *Bretz* indicated that a court trial (that is, a trial by the judge without a jury) begins when the first witness is sworn. Unless the trial is continued to the verdict stage, the defendant will be placed in jeopardy. Remember that the defendant may be retried if the trial is discontinued for good cause.

Plea of Former Judgment of Conviction or Acquittal

The plea "former conviction" or "former acquittal" is not included in the statutes of all states. However, it has been held by some states that a defendant is not properly protected by the plea of double jeopardy in some instances. When a defendant commits an act and breaks both state and federal criminal laws, the defendant could be prosecuted by either the state or the federal government. The question arises, May the defendant be prosecuted by both without a violation of the double jeopardy guarantee? This question was answered by the U.S. Supreme Court in the case of *United States* v. *Lanza*[7] and reiterated in *Abbate* v. *United States*,[8] in which cases the Court concluded that a defendant could be tried by *both* federal and state governments. The Court based its decisions upon the fact that a citizen of this nation owes a duty to both the federal and the state governments. In committing an act that violates the laws of both sovereignties, both may prosecute. About half the states have statutory provisions that hold that if a defendant is prosecuted by one government, prosecution by the local courts in that state for the same act is prohibited. The plea of former judgment of conviction or acquittal would be the proper plea under the circumstances.

This plea would be proper also if a defendant were acquitted of one charge and retried on a lesser charge arising out of the same act. However, most states hold that the plea of once in jeopardy covers this situation and have not included the former judgment of conviction or acquittal plea in their statutes.

THE GRAND JURY

A grand jury is a group of persons representing a cross section of a community, usually a county, whose primary purpose is to hear certain types of criminal accusations in order to determine whether there are sufficient facts to hold the accused for trial. As was stated by the U.S. Supreme Court case of *Wood* v. *Georgia:*[9]

> Historically, this body (the grand jury) has been regarded as a primary security to the innocent against hasty, malicious and oppressive persecution; it serves the invaluable function in our society of standing between the accuser and the accused, whether the latter be an individual, minority group, or other, to determine whether a charge is founded upon reason or was dictated by an intimidating power or by malice and personal ill will.

The grand jury procedure came into being early in the common law of England. The Magna Charta provided that no freeman was to be seized and imprisoned except by judgment of his or her peers. This provision established the procedure that before a person could be held for trial on a serious charge, the accusation had to be presented to a council comprising the accused's peers to determine whether the charge was well founded. The council later became known as a grand jury, as opposed to the petit or trial jury. The grand jury consisted of no fewer than sixteen persons and no more than twenty-three. There is really no logical reason for these numbers having been selected, except that it was thought that since a person was accused of a serious crime, a reasonable number of his or her peers should hear the accusation and determine whether the accused should be held for trial. Also, to prevent the body from becoming too large and unwieldy, a maximum of twenty-three was selected.

The grand jury was created as a safeguard for the accused. It prevented the accused from being held on a serious charge without sufficient cause or justification. The idea of the grand jury was brought to this country from England, and it was embodied in the Fifth Amendment of the U.S. Constitution. This amendment provides that "no person shall be held to answer for a capital or otherwise infamous crime, unless on presentment or indictment of a grand jury." A capital offense is one punishable by death; an infamous crime has been defined as one punishable by hard labor or imprisonment for more than one year. For all practical purposes, an infamous crime is any felony. This amendment was applicable only to federal charges, and the states were free to establish their own safeguards. Approximately one-half of the states hold that all felonies, and in some instances serious misdemeanors, must be presented to a grand jury. The remaining states provide that the accusation may be presented to a judge or magistrate in the form of a preliminary hearing in lieu of grand jury action.

Selection and Qualification of Grand Jurors

The selection of grand jurors varies greatly from state to state. In some states, they are selected at random, often using the list of voters for the territorial jurisdiction. The clerk of the court will cut the names from the list and place them in a box from which the required number of names will be drawn. In other states, the trial judge, or judges, of the county will furnish to the clerk of the court the names of prospective jurors. These names will be placed in a box from which the required number will be drawn. In some areas, the grand jury comprises persons who volunteer their services because it is considered to be a position of honor to serve on a grand jury.

Following the common law tradition, grand juries in this country vary from sixteen to twenty-three persons, but most grand juries consist of nineteen persons. They are usually selected at the beginning of the calendar year and generally serve for one year. The qualifications necessary to serve on the grand jury are very similar to those of a petit jury. Those qualifications demand that the individual be eighteen years of age or over, a citizen of the United States, a resident of the jurisdiction for at least one year, and have sufficient knowledge of the English language to properly communicate. After the grand jurors have been selected, they are given an oath in which they promise to do their duty and to keep their proceedings secret and confidential. The oath is generally administered by a superior court judge. At this time, the grand jury is considered to be impaneled. After the grand jury is impaneled, the judge either will appoint a member of the grand jury to act as foreperson or may instruct the grand jury to select one of their members to act as foreperson. When the appointment of a foreperson is completed, the grand jury is authorized to hear criminal charges to determine whether an accused should be held for trial.

The Indictment

Prior to the grand jury hearings, the prosecuting attorney will prepare a formal document setting forth the charge against the accused. This document is known as an indictment. It is also referred to as a "bill of indictment" in some jurisdictions. At one time in our history, the indictment was a very technically worded document, and any failure to word it properly would give a judge the right to dismiss the charge. In fact, the wording became ridiculously technical. For example, if the charge was for murder and if the indictment did not particularly designate the deceased as a human being, the indictment was considered faulty. Or if the initials A.D. did not accompany the date, it was held that the indictment did not reflect that the charge had not been outlawed by a passage of time. Today, the indictment is a comparatively simply worded instrument. It is very similar in form to the complaint. The indictment sets forth the name of the accused, the crime that is alleged to have been committed, the date and place of the alleged crime, and a few pertinent facts about the crime.

The indictment serves several purposes. First, it informs the grand jury of the charge about which they will receive evidence during the hearing. Second, if the required number of grand jurors votes in favor of holding the accused for trial, they will so designate that fact by having the foreperson sign the indictment, or as it is known, "endorsing the indictment." In some states, the grand jury in upholding the indictment find it a "true bill of indictment." The indictment is then filed with the court in which the trial will take place. Third, if the accused is not in custody when the indictment is endorsed and filed with the court, the indictment will enable the judge to issue a warrant of arrest. The indictment is also an accusatory pleading and is the document that sets the trial in motion in the superior court. Finally, the indictment informs the defendant of the charge against which he or she must defend himself or herself. If the accused is charged with more than one crime, these additional crimes may be included in the same indictment, and they are referred to as counts.

Grand Jury Hearings

The frequency with which the grand jury meets depends upon the number of criminal charges that must be heard. In highly populated areas, the grand jury may meet daily, Monday through Friday. In other areas, it may meet only when there is an occasion to do so, which could be only once a month or less frequently. Although the grand jury may call a hearing on its own, the members usually meet at the request of the prosecuting attorney. The grand jury meets in closed hearings, and the procedure is secret. In determining whether an accused should be held for trial, jury members will question witnesses and receive the evidence that is deemed pertinent by the prosecuting attorney. Before testifying, each witness takes an oath to tell the truth and not to reveal the proceedings that take place during his or her presence before the grand jury. During the examination of the witnesses, the prosecuting attorney is usually present to assist in questioning. A court reporter who records the testimony of the witnesses is also usually present.

After hearing all the witnesses and receiving the evidence of the case, the grand jurors will deliberate on the facts of the matter among themselves. After deliberating on the facts, they will vote to determine whether in their minds there are sufficient facts to believe that a crime has been committed and whether the accused committed it. Their belief does not have to be to a point beyond a reasonable doubt as to guilt, but only sufficient probable cause to believe that the accused is guilty of the act. Only the grand jurors may be present during the deliberation and voting. Jurisdictions vary somewhat on the number that must vote to hold the accused for trial, or "vote for the indictment." If the grand jury comprises nineteen members, some states require only twelve to vote in favor of the indictment, whereas other states require fourteen. If the grand jury comprises twenty-three persons, some states require fourteen to vote in favor of the indictment, and others require sixteen. If the required number vote in favor of holding the accused for trial, the foreperson of the grand jury will endorse the indictment indicating that the grand jury believes in the truthfulness of the charge. Thus, we get the true bill as a name for an indictment that is returned by the grand jury holding an accused for trial. In some states, if a grand jury investigates a criminal charge that was not referred to them by the prosecuting attorney, the accusatory pleading is known as a presentment rather than an indictment.

If the required number does not vote in favor of holding the accused for trial, the foreperson will so designate on the indictment. At one time in our history, the

LAW IN PRACTICE

[The following grand jury indictment was taken from a case in Texas. The defendant was indicted for capital murder. He was charged with committing murder in a state prison while serving a sentence for another murder. Note that he is charged in two separate counts with the same murder. After the evidence is admitted, the State will generally move to dismiss one count depending on how the evidence is developed at trial. Also note that at the end of the indictment, the crime is alleged as "against the peace and dignity of the state." Most states require that all crimes be against the peace and dignity of the state. This case ended with a plea bargain for a guilty plea to Count 1 and an agreed sentence of 35 years to be served at the end of his present prison term of 30 years.]

The State of Texas v. *Eric Roberto Acosta*
Charge: Capital Murder, Penal Code
19.03(a)(6)(A)

In the Name and by Authority of the State of Texas:

The Grand Jury, for the County of Bee, State of Texas, duly selected, impaneled, sworn, charged, and organized as such at the July Term A.D., 1999, of the 156th Judicial District Court for said County, upon their oaths present in and to said court at said term that:

Eric Roberto Acosta

Count 1

Hereinafter styled Defendant, on or about the 13th day of July A.D., 1996, and before the presentment of this indictment, in the County and State aforesaid, Eric Roberto Acosta while in a penal institution to-wit: The Garza East Unit of the Texas Department of Criminal Justice, Institutional Division and serving a sentence for the offense of Murder; did then and there intentionally and knowingly cause the death of another, Daniel Vela, by kicking the said Daniel Vela on or about the head and facial area with Eric Roberto Acosta's shoe clad feet;

Count 2

And hereinafter styled Defendant, on or about the 13th day of July, A.D., 1996, and before the presentment of this indictment, in the County and State aforesaid, Eric Roberto Acosta while in a penal institution to-wit: The Garza East Unit of the Texas Department of Criminal Justice, Institutional Division and serving a sentence for the offense of Murder, did then and there, intending to cause serious bodily injury to an individual, Daniel Vela, commit an act clearly dangerous to human life, to-wit: by kicking the said Daniel Vela on or about the head and facial area with Eric Roberto Acosta's shoe clad feet thereby causing the death of said Daniel Vela, against the peace and dignity of the state.

[Signed by Presiding Grand
Juror chairperson]

foreperson would write the word *ignoramus* on the indictment, indicating that the grand jury ignored the indictment. Today, the foreperson will usually write on the indictment that the grand jury does not believe in the charge, or in other words, that there is no bill of indictment forthcoming, or a *no bill.*

The defendant is not entitled to be present during a grand jury hearing, and there is some doubt whether the defendant may demand to present evidence in his or her own behalf. If the grand jurors feel that other witnesses besides those presented by the prosecution would be helpful in determining the truth of the indictment, the grand jurors have the authority to call additional witnesses, including the accused. The accused does not have to answer any questions that might subject him or her to punishment.

If a grand jury fails to hold the accused for trial, the question arises whether the facts may be presented to a new grand jury. The answer to the question varies from state to state. Most states permit the indictment to be submitted to a different grand jury. Some states have statutory regulations prohibiting presenting the case to another grand jury. Other states are silent on the matter, thereby indicating that there is no bar to presenting the case again, since a grand jury hearing is not an action in which jeopardy will attach.

Secret Indictment

If the defendant is not in custody at the time the indictment is returned, a warrant of arrest will be issued on the basis of this indictment. Under these circumstances, no public record is made of the indictment and warrant in order that the defendant will not be alerted to the fact that he or she is wanted, thereby making his or her location and apprehension more difficult. The indictment in this case is referred to as a secret indictment or sealed indictment.

Open Hearings

Frequently, a grand jury is called on to investigate and hold hearings concerning alleged acts of misconduct by public officials. In these situations, most jurisdictions permit the hearing to be open to the public when it is believed to be in the best interest of justice. To hold an open hearing usually requires that a request be made to the presiding judge by the prosecuting attorney and by the foreperson of the grand jury.

Dismissal of Indictment

Prosecution does not necessarily follow even though an indictment has been returned by a grand jury. The indictment may be dismissed. In many jurisdictions, the prosecuting attorney is permitted to dismiss the indictment. This procedure is referred to as a nolle prosequi action, a formal entry on the record of the case stating that no further prosecutive action will be taken in the matter. Other jurisdictions hold that only the presiding judge may dismiss the indictment. The presiding judge may dismiss the indictment on his or her own if he or she does not believe that the facts will support a conviction, or the judge may dismiss the indictment upon the recommendation of the prosecuting attorney. It may seem to be somewhat paradoxical for the prosecuting attorney to seek an indictment and then dismiss it. But the prosecuting attorney may take this action because a material witness has become unavailable or if facts have been developed that, in the best interest of justice, indicate that the case should not go to trial.

Additional Functions of the Grand Jury

In many states, the sole function of the grand jury is to hold hearings on criminal charges to determine whether a crime has been committed and whether the accused should be held for trial. But in a few states, the grand jury performs other functions, such as investigating public expenditures. It may also inspect jails, prisons, and mental institutions within its territorial jurisdiction to determine whether these facilities are complying with safety and health regulations.

Criticism of the Grand Jury System

Many legal scholars have severely criticized the grand jury system. It has been alleged that the grand jury is not a safeguard of the accused but that it is merely a rubber stamp of the prosecuting attorney. Another allegation is that the grand jury is not representative of the peers of the accused, as was indicated to be necessary by the Magna Charta. The term *peers* seems to weave its way into the legal language of criminal procedure, but the term is seldom found in the qualifications necessary for being a member of either a petit or a grand jury. The dictionary definition of "peers" reflects that they are one's equals or associates. Under this definition, a grand jury of one's peers could result in the impaneling of an odd group of persons, particularly if the accused had spent much of his or her life in prison. Generally, it is held that if the grand jury is a representative group of citizens from throughout the county, or a cross section of the county, it is the equivalent of one's peers, and such a group will fulfill the due process of law provision. However, greater emphasis is being placed on what determines a representative group when a member of a minority society is the accused. The cross section of the county provision has also been challenged by younger defendants, particularly since the age qualification for service on juries has been changed from twenty-one to eighteen.

As valid as the argument is that the grand jury does not represent a cross section of society, it is most difficult to obtain a truly representative group. Most grand jurors receive little or no compensation for their services. In those areas in which the grand jury holds frequent hearings, most persons cannot afford to serve on a grand jury. This circumstance results in many grand jurors who are retired or wealthy individuals who can afford to give their services. It has also been alleged that the grand jury is a cumbersome system because it cannot do anything that a magistrate could not do more efficiently at less cost. Those advocating the retention of the grand jury system in lieu of a preliminary hearing by a magistrate often quote Justice Harlan's dissenting opinion in the case of *Hurtado* v. *California*.[10] Justice Harlan stated the following:

> . . . nothing stands between the citizen and prosecution for his life, except the judgment of a justice of the peace [in a preliminary hearing]. Anglo-Saxon liberty would, perhaps, have perished long before the adoption of our Constitution, had it been in the power of government to put the subject on trial for his life whenever a justice of the peace, holding his office at the will of the crown, should certify that he had committed a capital crime. That such officers are, in some of the States, elected by the people, does not add to the protection of the citizen; for, one of the peculiar benefits of the grand jury system, as it exists in this country and England [the grand jury system has since been abolished in England] is that it is composed, as a general rule, of a body of private persons, who do not hold office at the will of the government, or at the will of voters. In many if not in all of the States civil officers are disqualified to sit on grand juries. In the secrecy of the investigations by grand juries, the weak and helpless—proscribed perhaps, because of their race, or pursued by an unreasoning public clamor—have found, and will continue to find, security against official oppression, the cruelty of mobs, the machination of falsehood, and the malevolence of

private persons who would use the machinery of the law to bring ruin upon their personal enemies.

Thus, we find the grand jury system continuing to function in many states; however, as time passes, it is highly possible that more states will adopt the preliminary hearing procedure.

THE PRELIMINARY HEARING

To speed up the justice process, about half the states have adopted another form of safeguard, in lieu of the grand jury hearing, for one accused of a serious crime. That safeguard is the preliminary hearing, also referred to as the preliminary examination. The preliminary hearing is very much like a junior trial. It is conducted before a magistrate. A magistrate has been described as any officer of the court who has the power to issue a warrant of arrest. From a practical standpoint, the magistrate is a judge of the inferior court who acts in the capacity of a magistrate as well as a trial judge.

During the preliminary hearing, the magistrate sits without a jury, and the prosecuting attorney presents the evidence against the accused. This evidence will consist of the testimony of witnesses and such physical evidence as the prosecuting attorney may deem pertinent. The defendant must be present and may be represented by an attorney. There must be an opportunity for the defendant or his or her attorney to cross-examine the witnesses of the prosecution.

As previously pointed out, the Fifth Amendment of the U.S. Constitution, among other provisions, provides that all capital or otherwise infamous crimes be presented to a grand jury. Most of the provisions of the Fifth Amendment have been made applicable to the states through the Due Process Clause of the Fourteenth Amendment of the Constitution. When the preliminary hearing procedure was first adopted, there was some doubt whether this procedure would fulfill the Due Process Clause, but this doubt was resolved by the *Hurtado* case, in which the U.S. Supreme Court upheld the preliminary hearing procedure. The Court stated that the preliminary hearing "carefully considers and guards the substantial interest of the prisoner. It is merely a preliminary proceeding, and can result in no final judgment, except as the consequence of a regular judicial trial, conducted precisely as in the cases of indictments." Therefore, the safeguard of the preliminary hearing is as great as a grand jury action and fulfills the Due Process Clause of the Fourteenth Amendment.

Even though the preliminary hearing procedure has been adopted by a number of states, the grand jury system has not been eliminated in most of those states. Instances may arise in which the prosecuting attorney will prefer presenting a charge to the grand jury to holding a preliminary hearing. It is the prerogative of the prosecuting attorney to decide whether a preliminary hearing will be held or whether the case will be presented to a grand jury. When the defendant is in custody and the felony charge is of a routine nature, a preliminary hearing will be held in most instances. If the defendant is not in custody and if a secret indictment is desired, the charge will be presented to a grand jury.

Before a preliminary hearing may be held, the defendant must have been arrested and a complaint filed charging him or her with a felony or, in some jurisdictions, either a felony or a serious misdemeanor. If the defendant enters a plea of not guilty, the judge will set a date for the preliminary hearing, which is usually only a few days after the plea. The hearing is open to the public unless the defendant requests that the hearing be closed, which the defendant has the right to do in most jurisdictions. Even if the hearing is not closed, the witnesses, at the request of either the prosecution or the defense, may be excluded from the courtroom until after they have testified. The judge may also exclude the witnesses on his or her own motion. During the hearing, the prosecution must present enough evidence to convince the judge that there is sufficient cause to believe that a crime has been committed and that the defendant committed it, in order to hold the defendant for trial in the superior court. This is the same degree of proof that must be presented to the grand jury.

After the prosecution has presented its evidence, the defendant may enter evidence in his or her own behalf, in an effort to convince the judge that he or she should not be held for trial. If the judge is under the belief that a crime has been committed and if there is sufficient probable cause to believe that the defendant committed it, the judge will hold the defendant to answer for trial in the superior court. This process is sometimes termed being "bound over for trial." If the judge is not convinced that a crime has been committed or that the defendant committed it, he or she will dismiss the charge, and the defendant is entitled to be released. Unless there is some statutory regulation against further presentation of the matter, the case could be presented to a grand jury to determine whether an indictment was forthcoming, but usually the prosecuting attorney will not go this far to seek prosecution.

If the judge holds the defendant to answer for trial, the prosecuting attorney must prepare a legal document setting forth the charge against the defendant. This document is known as an *information*. It is very similar in form to the indictment returned by the grand jury, and the information serves the same purposes as the indictment. It is the accusatory pleading that sets the trial in motion in the superior court. The information must be filed in the superior court within a few days, usually fifteen, after the defendant is held to answer for trial. Failure to comply with this time regulation could be grounds for dismissal of the charge.

In some jurisdictions, the complaint that is filed with the magistrate before the initial appearance is known as an information. If the defendant is held to answer for trial, the information will be filed with the clerk in the court where the trial will be heard.

Waiver of Preliminary Hearing

Although the preliminary hearing is a safeguard established for the benefit of the defendant, he or she may waive it if he or she so desires. However, in most jurisdictions, the waiver must be agreed to by the prosecuting attorney and the judge. There are advantages and disadvantages to both the defendant and the prosecution in the waiver of the preliminary hearing. If the defendant is unable to make bail, a waiver of the hearing results in an earlier trial date being set. On the other hand, by demanding a preliminary hearing, a defendant might bring about a dismissal of the charge and his or her release from custody. The judge might conclude as a result of the hearing that there was insufficient cause to hold the defendant for trial. Another advantage to the defendant in having a preliminary hearing is that he or she may discover evidence held by the prosecution as it is unfolded during the hearing. This outcome is particularly true in those jurisdictions where the right of the defendant to examine the evidence held by the prosecution before the trial is not recognized. This right is known as the "right of discovery" or the "right of inspection." It is granted to defendants in order that they may better prepare their defense.

As it relates to the prosecution, there may be advantages in holding a preliminary hearing because it gives the prosecuting attorney an opportunity to obtain the testimony of the witnesses on an official record or transcript at a time when the facts are fresh in their memories and they are less likely to falsify. This record can be used during the trial should a witness become unavailable. In those states in which the right of discovery is not recognized, the prosecuting attorney may agree with the waiver so that he or she will not have to reveal evidence to the defense. The waiver will also eliminate a dilemma for the prosecuting attorney. In a preliminary hearing, the prosecuting attorney must present enough evidence to convince the judge that the accused should be held for trial, but the prosecuting attorney does not want to reveal any more evidence than is necessary in order to prevent the defense from endeavoring to obtain perjured testimony to meet the prosecution's case.

Although the grand jury system was established to safeguard the accused, this system has been under attack by defendants. It has been alleged that the preliminary hearing more nearly fulfills the Due Process Clause of the Fourteenth Amendment. The reasoning behind this allegation is the fact that the grand jury meets in secret, and the defendant is not permitted to be present, nor can the defendant demand to present evidence in his or her own behalf. Generally, the courts have held that either the grand jury hearing or the preliminary hearing system may be adopted by the states, as they see fit, and both satisfy the due process of law requirement. As was stated by the Court in the *Hurtado* decision:

> It is said by the court [the U.S. Supreme Court] that the Constitution of the United States was made for an undefined and expanding future, and that its requirement of due process of law in proceedings involving life, liberty and property, must be interpreted as not to deny to the law the capacity of progress and improvement; that the greatest security for the fundamental principles of justice resides in the right of the people to make their own laws and alter them at pleasure.

As stated, the courts in most jurisdictions have held that an accused is protected from unwarranted prosecution by either a grand jury indictment or a preliminary hearing. The supreme court of one state recently held, however, that even though an accused had been indicted, he was still entitled to a preliminary hearing. The court held that only by granting the accused a postindictment preliminary hearing was his fundamental right of due process of law protected. These rights include the right of counsel, the right of confrontation, the right of cross-examination, and the right to present evidence in one's own behalf.

This decision has been criticized by many legal scholars as being unnecessary to protect an accused as well as imposing an additional burden upon the prosecution. Whether other state courts will follow this precedent in granting an accused the right to a postindictment preliminary hearing, only time will tell.

The Arraignment

When an indictment is returned or an information is filed with the trial court, the accused will be arraigned upon that accusatory pleading. At the arraignment, the accused will be permitted to enter a plea to the charge set forth in that accusatory pleading. If a plea of not guilty or not guilty by reason of insanity is entered, a trial must take place. If the accused was not arrested before the indictment was returned, this arraignment may be the initial appearance for the accused. At the arraignment, the accused will again be advised of his or her constitutional rights. Even though the accused may have been taken before a magistrate after a complaint was filed, the accused is still entitled to be arraigned after the filing of the indictment or information. In a sense, the indictment or information is a separate formal charge. The arraignment under these circumstances is not to be confused with the initial appearance even though, in some areas, the initial appearance is referred to as an arraignment.

GRANTS OF IMMUNITY FOR WITNESSES

The government may compel the testimony of a witness if he or she has been granted immunity. When immunity is granted, the witness's testimony is not self-incriminating. There are two types of immunity: (1) transactional and (2) use and derivative use. If a person receives transactional immunity, he or she cannot be prosecuted for the transaction about which the witness was compelled to testify. It is the broadest type of immunity and gives the witnesses greater protection than is constitutionally required.

Use and derivative use immunity restricts the government from using the testimony or any other information obtained directly or indirectly from the testimony. For example, the government may still prosecute a person who has use and derivative use immunity as long as the government establishes that the evidence it offers at trial was derived from a legitimate independent source. In *Kastigar* v. *United States,* 406 U.S. 441 (1972), the Supreme Court held that use and derivative use immunity was sufficient to compel a person to testify regarding an event. The Court noted that the burden was on the government to establish that the evidence used to convict the defendant was not obtained as a result of the compelled testimony. In *United States* v. *North,* 920 F.2d. 940 (D.C. Cir. 1990), a court of appeals held that the government did not fulfill its burden of showing that the evidence was free from the taint of immunized testimony where the government witnesses used at trial had seen Oliver North's immunized testimony on national television.

THE MEDICAL EXAMINER

A coroner should go to the place where any person is slain or suddenly dead or wounded . . . summon a jury out of four or five neighboring towns to make inquiry upon view of the body; and the coroner should inquire into the manner of the killing. [Jarvis on Coroners, 1829]

From a sequential standpoint in the study of the administration of justice, the next procedure to be considered includes the various ramifications of the trial. Before entering that phase of the procedure, however, it is well to consider the medical examiner or county coroner and the important part he or she plays in the judicial process. The primary function of the coroner is to investigate the cause of certain deaths that take place within the county. In most jurisdictions, a medical examiner has replaced the coroner.

The coroner came into being in England shortly after the Norman Conquest, with the coroner's existence being traced as far back as A.D. 1194. The coroner was a direct representative of the king, or the crown or corona—thus coroner. The coroners were elected by the king's judges as they rode through the countryside. In the beginning, each county had four coroners. Their responsibility was to keep records on all that went on in the county as it concerned the administration of justice and to guard the revenues that might come to the king if justice was done. In the early history of England, as previously pointed out, if a person was convicted of a felony, his or her property was confiscated by the king, thereby resulting in a sizable revenue for the king. It was to the king's interest to see that those accused of felonies were brought to trial and that their property was not dissipated before conviction. Thus, the office of the coroner was created. Around the beginning of the thirteenth century, the coroners began to investigate all sudden deaths that took place in their jurisdiction to determine whether they were brought about by criminal means. Although this investigation was primarily the duty of the sheriff, it was thought that since the sheriff was responsible only to the people of the county, the sheriff might be hesitant to bring the offender to trial. The sheriff knew that, if convicted, the accused would undoubtedly be put to death or banished from the county and his property confiscated.

Duties of the Medical Examiner or Coroner

As time passed and the king was no longer able to confiscate the property of a felon, the coroner should have disappeared from the judicial picture. But by that time, the coroner had become so entrenched in the judicial process that the coroner remained a public official, and the office was carried from England to the United States. The coroner is a part of most county governments throughout the United States, and his or her present duties deviate greatly from those first performed in this position.

The duties and power vary somewhat among the states, but the primary function is quite uniform among all the states. It is the duty and right of the coroner to inquire into and determine the circumstances, manner, and cause of all violent, sudden, and unusual deaths. In general, these would be deaths believed to have been the result of hanging, suicide, burns, poisoning, cutting, stabbing, drowning, vehicular accidents, industrial accidents, explosion, gunshot, electrical shock, alcoholism, drug addiction, strangulation, suffocation, criminal means, illegal abortion, starvation, or contagious disease. In most jurisdictions, the coroner will also inquire into the cause of a death that occurs when no one else is present, when in a penal institution, when a physician has not been in attendance for ten days or some similar number of days depending upon the jurisdiction, or when the attending physician is unable to state the cause. It is the duty of any law enforcement officer, physician, funeral director, or other person knowing of such an aforementioned death to report it to the medical examiner or coroner.

Upon receiving such a report, the coroner's inquiry may be very informal if he or she determines that the death was the result of natural causes, or that no negligence by another or by criminal means was involved. If the cause of death cannot be readily determined, the coroner has the authority to take possession of the deceased body and to have an autopsy performed and to conduct such other investigation as may be necessary to assist him or her in determining the cause of death. The coroner also may hold an inquest as a further aid. Most jurisdictions permit the coroner, at his or her discretion, to hold the inquest sitting alone or before a coroner's jury. During the inquest, witnesses who have some knowledge concerning the cause and manner of the death will be questioned. Physical evidence, including the body of the deceased, may be viewed if deemed pertinent. If the coroner decides to use a jury, the members of the jury will be selected from persons in the community who could qualify as petit jurors. The number selected varies among the states, but between nine and fifteen people will usually be called, from which at least six or more will serve on the jury.

The purpose of the inquest is to determine what the name of the deceased is; what were the time and place that the death took place; what was the medical cause of the death; and whether the death was by natural causes, suicide, accident, or at the hands of another. Some jurisdictions require that during the inquest, it not only be determined whether the death was at the hands of another, but, if so, at whose hands and whether by criminal means. In those jurisdictions following this latter procedure, some permit the coroner to issue a warrant of arrest for the accused if it is determined that the death was caused by criminal means. Other jurisdictions hold that the inquest merely determines whether the death was brought about by the hands of another. Any arrest or prosecution that may follow will be at the discretion of the prosecuting attorney. Jurisdictions vary as to the admissibility of the information developed by the inquest.

Selection and Qualifications of the Medical Examiner or Coroner

In some jurisdictions, the medical examiner or coroner is appointed by the county governing body, and in other places, he or she is elected by the people of the county. Generally, no prescribed qualifications are set forth. Even though the coroner's responsibility is to determine the medical cause of death, in most jurisdictions, there is no requirement that the coroner be medically trained. When not, the coroner will have to rely upon a physician to perform the autopsies. In some jurisdictions, the sheriff is permitted to act in the capacity of coroner as well as that of sheriff. By legislative action, other jurisdictions have authorized county governments to replace the coroner with a medical examiner. The law sometimes provides that the coroner will act as the sheriff, should the sheriff become incapacitated or unable to perform his or her duties. In those jurisdictions where the sheriff and the coroner are the same individual, this dual capacity creates an awkward situation if the sheriff is unable to act. Most jurisdictions, however, provide that if the sheriff becomes incapacitated, the undersheriff, or the next in line, will act until the sheriff can be replaced. Even though the coroner may not function as a sheriff, the coroner does have the status of a peace officer in many states.

The medical examiner or coroner is often required, in addition to his or her other duties, to take custody of the personal property in the immediate possession of the deceased. This usually includes the property on the person of the deceased, but it may also include taking the necessary precautions to see that the property in a residence is secured if no relative or other responsible person is available. The property is then released to the legal representative of the deceased when that person is determined.

CAPSTONE CASE

North Carolina v. *Alford*
400 U.S. 25, 91 S.Ct. 160, 27 L.Ed.2d 162 (1970)

Justice White delivered the opinion of the Court.

[*Note:* Alford was indicted for the capital crime of first-degree murder. At that time, North Carolina law provided for the penalty of life imprisonment when a plea of guilty was accepted to a capital crime and the punishment for second-degree murder was imprisonment from 2 to 30 years. Alford's attorney, because of the strong evidence against him, recommended that he plead guilty. The prosecutor agreed to accept a plea to second-degree murder. The trial court heard damaging evidence from certain witnesses before accepting a plea. Appellee pleaded guilty, although disclaiming guilt, because of the threat of the death penalty, and was sentenced to 30 years' imprisonment. The Court of Appeals, on an appeal from a denial of a writ of habeas corpus, found that appellee's guilty plea was involuntary because it was motivated principally by fear of the death penalty.]

We held in *Brady* v. *United States,* 397 U.S. 742 (1970), that a plea of guilty which would not have been entered except for the defendant's desire to avoid a possible death penalty and to limit the maximum penalty to life imprisonment or a term of years was not for that reason compelled within the meaning of the Fifth Amendment. . . . The standard was and remains whether the plea represents a voluntary and intelligent choice among the alternative courses of action open to the defendant. . . . That he would not have pleaded except for the opportunity to limit the possible penalty does not necessarily demonstrate that the plea of guilty was not the product of a free and rational choice, especially where the defendant was represented by competent counsel whose advice was that the plea would be to the defendant's advantage. The standard fashioned and applied by the Court of Appeals was therefore erroneous and we would, without more, vacate and remand the case for further proceedings with respect to any other claims of Alford which are properly before that court, if it were not for other circumstances appearing in the record which might seem to warrant an affirmance of the Court of Appeals.

As previously recounted after Alford's plea of guilty was offered and the State's case was placed before the judge, Alford denied that he had committed the murder but reaffirmed his desire to plead guilty to avoid a possible death sentence and to limit the penalty to the 30-year maximum provided for second-degree murder. Ordinarily, a judgment of conviction resting on a plea of guilty is justified by the defendant's admission that he committed the crime charged against him and his consent that judgment be entered without a trial of any kind. The plea usually subsumes both elements, and justifiably so, even though there is no separate, express admission by the defendant that he committed the particular acts claimed to constitute the crime charged in the indictment. Here Alford entered his plea but accompanied it with the statement that he had not shot the victim.

If Alford's statements were to be credited as sincere assertions of his innocence, there obviously existed a factual and legal dispute between him and the State. Without more, it might be argued that the conviction entered on his guilty plea was invalid, since his assertion of innocence negatived any admission of guilt, which, as we observed last Term in Brady, is normally "central to the plea and the foundation for entering judgment against the defendant. . . ."

In addition to Alford's statement, however, the court had heard an account of the events on the night of the murder, including information from Alford's acquaintances that he had departed from his home with his gun stating his intention to kill and that he had later declared that he had carried out his intention. Nor had Alford wavered in his desire to have trial court determine his guilt without a jury trial. Although denying the charge against him, he nevertheless preferred the dispute between him and the State to be settled by the judge in the context of a guilty plea proceeding rather than by a formal trial. Thereupon, with the State's telling evidence and Alford's denial before it, the trial court proceeded to convict and sentence Alford for second-degree murder.

State and lower federal courts are divided upon whether a guilty plea can be accepted when it is accompanied by protestations of innocence and hence contains only a waiver of trial but no admission of guilt. Some courts, giving expression to the principle that "[o]ur law only authorizes a conviction where guilt is shown," require that trial judges reject such pleas. But others have concluded that they should not "force any defense on a defendant in a criminal case," particularly when advancement of the defense might "end in disaster. . . ." They have argued that, since "guilt, or the degree of guilt, is at times uncertain and elusive," "an accused, though believing in or entertaining doubts respecting his innocence, might reasonably conclude a jury would be convinced of his guilt and that he would fare better in the sentence by pleading guilty. . . ."

This Court has not confronted this precise issue, but prior decisions do yield relevant principles. In *Lynch* v. *Overholser*, 369 U.S. 705 (1962), Lynch, who had been charged in the Municipal Court of the District of Columbia with drawing and negotiating bad checks, a misdemeanor punishable by a maximum of one year in jail, sought to enter a plea of guilty, but the trial judge refused to accept the plea since a psychiatric report in the judge's possession indicated that Lynch had been suffering from "a manic depressive psychosis, at the time of the crime charged," and hence might have been not guilty by reason of insanity. Although at the subsequent trial Lynch did not rely on the insanity defense, he was found not guilty by reason of insanity and committed for an indeterminate period to a mental institution. On habeas corpus, the Court ordered his release, construing the congressional legislation seemingly authorizing the commitment as not reaching a case where the accused preferred a guilty plea to a plea of insanity. The Court expressly refused to rule that Lynch had an absolute right to have his guilty plea accepted, but implied that there would have been no constitutional error had his plea been accepted even though evidence before the judge indicated that there was a valid defense.

The issue in *Hudson* v. *United States*, 272 U.S. 451 (1926), was whether a federal court has power to impose a prison sentence after accepting a plea of nolo contendere, a plea by which a defendant does not expressly admit his guilt, but nonetheless waives his right to a trial and authorizes the court for purposes of the case to treat him as if he were guilty. The Court held that a trial court does have such power, and except for the cases which were rejected in Hudson, the federal courts have uniformly followed this rule, even in cases involving moral turpitude. Implicit in the nolo contendere cases is a recognition that the Constitution does not bar imposition of a prison sentence upon an accused who is unwilling expressly to admit his guilt but who, faced with grim alternatives, is willing to waive his trial and accept the sentence.

These cases would be directly in point if Alford had simply insisted on his plea but refused to admit the crime. The fact that his plea was denominated a plea of guilty rather than a plea of nolo contendere is of no constitutional significance with respect to the issue now before us, for the Constitution is concerned with the practical consequences, not the formal categorizations, of state law. Thus, while most pleas of guilty consist of both a waiver of trial and an express admission of guilt, the latter element is not a constitutional requisite to the imposition of criminal penalty. An individual accused of crime may voluntarily, knowingly, and understandingly consent to the imposition of a prison sentence even if he is unwilling or unable to admit his participation in the acts constituting the crime.

Nor can we perceive any material difference between a plea that refuses to admit commission of the criminal act and a plea containing a protestation of innocence when, as in the instant case, a defendant intelligently concludes that his interests require entry of a guilty plea and the record before the judge contains strong evidence of actual guilt. Here the State had a strong case of first-degree murder against Alford. Whether he realized or disbelieved his guilt, he insisted on his plea because in his view he had absolutely nothing to gain by a trial and much to gain by pleading. Because of the overwhelming evidence against him, a trial was precisely what neither Alford nor his attorney desired. Confronted with the choice between a trial for first-degree murder, on the one hand, and a plea of guilty to second-degree murder, on the other, Alford quite reasonably chose the latter and thereby limited the maximum penalty to a 30-year term. When his plea is viewed in light of the evidence against him, which substantially negated his claim of innocence and which further provided a means by which the judge could test whether the plea was being intelligently entered, its validity cannot be seriously questioned. In view of the strong factual basis for the plea demonstrated by the State and Alford's clearly expressed desire to enter it despite his professed belief in his innocence, we hold that the trial judge did not commit constitutional error in accepting it. . . .

Justice Black . . . concurs in the judgment and in substantially all of the opinion in this case. Justice Brennan, with whom Justice Douglas and Justice Marshall join, dissenting.

It is sufficient in my view to state that the facts set out in the majority opinion demonstrate that Alford was "so gripped by fear of the death penalty" that his decision to plead guilty was not voluntary but was "the product of duress as much so as choice reflecting physical constraint."

[*Note:* Footnote 11 to the court's opinion stated: "Our holding does not mean that a trial judge must accept every constitutionally valid guilty plea merely because a defendant wishes so to plead. A criminal defendant does not have an absolute right under the Constitution to have his guilty plea accepted by the court, although the States may by statute or otherwise confer such a right. Likewise, the States may bar their courts from accepting guilty pleas from any defendants who assert their innocence. . . ."]

REVIEW QUESTIONS

1. What is a guilty plea?
2. Before a guilty plea may be accepted, of what must the defendant be advised?
3. What is the next procedural step after the acceptance of a guilty plea?
4. What is the significance of a nolo contendere plea?
5. Define double jeopardy.

6. What is a grand jury?
7. List the qualifications for being a grand juror.
8. What is an indictment?
9. Who may be present during a grand jury's deliberation on an indictment?
10. What is a no bill?
11. What is a secret indictment?
12. Explain a nolle prosequi action.
13. What criticisms have been made of the grand jury system?
14. What is the purpose of the preliminary hearing?
15. What is an information?
16. Describe the primary function of the coroner.

LOCAL PROCEDURE

1. What pleas may a defendant enter in your jurisdiction?
2. May a defendant enter a plea of guilty to a capital punishment charge? If so, under what circumstances?
3. How many members compose a grand jury in your state?
4. May a defendant be brought to trial on a felony charge by an information, or must he or she be indicted?
5. How are the grand jurors selected?
6. May the prosecuting attorney enter a nolle prosequi?
7. In your state, is the accused entitled to a preliminary hearing even though indicted?

ENDNOTES

1. *Boykin* v. *Alabama,* 395 U.S. 238 (1969).
2. *North Carolina* v. *Alford,* 400 U.S. 25 (1970).
3. 426 U.S. 637 (1976).
4. 397 U.S. 790 (1970).
5. 437 U.S. 1 (1978).
6. 437 U.S. 28 (1978).
7. 260 U.S. 377 (1922).
8. 359 U.S. 187 (1959).
9. 370 U.S. 375 (1962).
10. 110 U.S. 516 (1884).

CHAPTER 6

Place and Time of the Trial

> In all criminal prosecutions, the accused shall enjoy the right to a speedy and public trial, by an impartial jury of the State and district wherein the crime shall have been committed. . . .
> —U.S. Constitution, Amendment VI

PRETRIAL ACTION

Before the trial phase of the administration of justice begins, many decisions must be made. It must be determined when and where the trial will take place, whether the trial will be by the judge alone or by a jury, whether the defendant will represent himself or herself or be assisted by counsel, what witnesses will be called, what physical evidence will be presented, and whether a pretrial hearing will be held. In view of the importance of each of these processes, we will discuss each in some detail. These decisions and the trial procedure are largely the same whether the charge involved is a felony or a misdemeanor.

PLACE OF THE TRIAL

Venue

The Sixth Amendment to the U.S. Constitution guarantees to an accused the right to a "speedy and public trial by an impartial jury of the State and district wherein the crime shall have been committed." This guarantee was placed in the Sixth Amendment as a result of the colonists' having been dragged from their homes to some secret place, often to England, and tried away from their peers. This guarantee applies to the states through the Due Process Clause of the Fourteenth Amendment. Thus, the place of the trial, or *venue*, lies within the judicial district in which the crime occurred. The term *venue* is derived from the French word *visne* meaning "neighborhood." If the charge is a felony, the judicial district is the county; if it is a misdemeanor, the judicial district would be that specific area of the county so designated and established by law. The burden is on the prosecution to present evidence during the trial to prove that the crime was committed within the judicial district in which the trial is being held. Proving venue may be accomplished merely by an investigating officer's testifying on the specific location where the crime was committed within the county. If venue is not established by the prosecution, a conviction may be reversed on appeal because it is the right of the defendant to have the jury chosen from the judicial district in which the crime was committed.

Motion to Change Venue.   Although the defendant is entitled to have the trial in the district where the crime occurred, that right may be waived and a request made that the trial be held in some other district. This outcome is particularly true in felony cases. The defendant often believes that a fair and impartial trial cannot be had in the county in which the crime was committed. This viewpoint is usually based on a belief that adverse publicity, the nature of the crime, or community hostility makes it impossible for the defendant to obtain an impartial jury. Under these circumstances, the defendant will file with the trial court a written request, known as a "motion to change venue." The trial judge will hold a hearing on this request, at which time the defendant will present evidence in an effort to convince the judge that a change of venue should be granted. It may be alleged that, because the defendant is an outsider and the victim of the crime was popular, there is adverse feeling toward the accused. Or it may be alleged that because of the widespread publicity given to the crime, most persons in the county already believe in the defendant's guilt. In most instances, the prosecuting attorney will oppose the change of venue because of the inconvenience to witnesses and staff and because of the cost involved. However, the cost is not to be considered by the judge in granting or denying a change of venue because the accused is entitled to a fair and an impartial trial, regardless of cost. The prosecuting attorney will oppose the change of venue on grounds other than cost in most instances. Also, the prosecuting attorney may contend that even though many persons have formed opinions unfavorable to the defendant as a result of what was published, it does not follow that persons without such views could not be found within the county to act as jurors or that those who had adverse opinions could not set those opinions aside and try the case in a fair and an impartial manner on the basis of the evidence. Or the prosecuting attorney may contend that because of the widespread publicity given to the crime, it would be equally difficult to obtain an impartial jury in another county. Another contention may be that the emotional involvement with the crime has subsided sufficiently by trial time so that an impartial jury could be selected.

If, from the evidence presented during the hearing, the judge feels that a change of venue should be granted, the trial will be held in a county in which it is believed that a fair trial can be had. In most instances, the trial will be moved to an adjoining county. The cost of the trial will be borne by the county where the crime occurred. If the rule were otherwise, a county could impose on an adjoining county a terrific cost burden for trials of crimes not taking place within that adjoining county. If the judge does not grant a change of venue and the defendant is convicted, the refusal to grant a change of venue may be grounds for appeal. If the appellate court concludes that a change of venue should have been granted, the conviction will be reversed.

Time of Request for Change of Venue.   Generally, a request for change of venue must take place before the date set for the commencement of the trial. A change may be made after the commencement date if the jury panel is exhausted without a jury's being selected or if there is danger of violence taking place within the district.

TIME OF THE TRIAL

The Sixth Amendment to the U.S. Constitution provides that the "accused shall enjoy the right to a speedy trial." This same guarantee is embodied in the laws of all the states. The right to a speedy trial is a fundamental right of an accused; otherwise, many injustices may be suffered. The people, or society, also have an interest in the guarantee that an accused be brought to trial without unnecessary delay. This is the only way that society can be properly protected from the offender. These guarantees provide few guidelines on exactly when a trial must be held in order to comply with the speedy trial regulation. So the decision of when to hold a trial becomes a troublesome and difficult one to make. The right to a speedy trial does not permit the defendant to demand that a trial be held the same day as the arrest because the prosecution has the right to prepare its case against the defendant. But the prosecution may not take an indefinite time in its preparation. In setting the trial date, many factors must be considered, such as what is a reasonable length of time to permit each side to prepare its case and whether the accused is in jail or has posted bail. Further, the rules of procedure of most states require that criminal trials be set for those in jail ahead of those who have posted bail when other factors are equal. Even if a trial date is set, the trial may not necessarily begin on that date, since continuances may be granted that will cause delay.

Continuances

Although the right to a speedy trial is designed primarily for the benefit of the accused, this right, like others rights, may be waived by the defendant, and often is. Defendants make frequent requests for continuances in bringing the case to trial. Often months pass between the time that an arrest is made and when the defendant is brought to trial, particularly in felony cases. Regardless of the hardships that may be suffered in not having a speedy trial, the defendant often will delay the trial date as long as possible. Delay often works to the advantage of the accused because, with the passage of time, witnesses for the prosecution are more likely to become unavailable and their memories are more likely to dull. In addition, physical evidence becomes difficult to identify and is likely to become lost or contaminated.

Although the defendant may suffer from continuances, others also suffer, particularly witnesses who must return to court many times only to find that the case has been continued. These witnesses usually receive no notice that a continuance will be granted. A continuance often is not granted until the case is called for trial, so notice is not possible. As a result, many witnesses must take time off from work, thus losing pay and experiencing the expense and inconvenience of traveling to and from court many times. It is understandable that people become reluctant to admit witnessing a crime. Delays also cause overcrowding of the court calendar, and other trials must be delayed, particularly civil trials.

Although the statutes of most states provide that a continuance may be granted only upon sufficient grounds and with sufficient notice, in most instances, no specific grounds or time for the notice is stated. The most frequent ground alleged for a continuance is adequate time to prepare the case. Other grounds include obtaining witnesses or physical evidence, securing adequate and effective counsel for the defense, and ensuring the sound physical condition of the defendant. There is no set procedure to be followed in making a request for a continuance. It may be made orally in open court or by written request in advance of the trial date. Whether a continuance will be granted is at the discretion of the trial judge.

The U.S. Supreme Court, in the case of *Barker* v. *Wingo*,[1] discussed many of the ramifications of a speedy trial and the effect of delays on both the accused and the people. The Court also discussed some of the factors to be considered in determining whether the guarantee to a speedy trial had been violated. In view of the enlightening language of this decision, it is set forth in some detail for review by the reader. The facts of this case reflect that on July 20, 1958, in Christian County, Kentucky, an elderly couple was beaten to death by intruders wielding an iron tire tool. Two suspects, Silas Manning and Willie Barker, the petitioner, were arrested shortly thereafter. The grand jury indicted them on September 15. Counsel was appointed on September 17, and Barker's trial was set for October 21. The Commonwealth had a stronger case against Manning, and it believed that Barker could not be convicted unless Manning testified against him. Manning was naturally unwilling to incriminate himself. Accordingly, on October 23, the day Silas Manning was brought to trial, the Commonwealth sought and obtained the first of what was to be a series of 16 continuances of Barker's trial. Barker made no objection. By first convicting Manning, the Commonwealth would remove possible problems of self-incrimination and would be able to assure his testimony against Barker.

The Commonwealth encountered more than a few difficulties in its prosecution of Manning. The first trial ended in a hung jury. A second trial resulted in a conviction, but the Kentucky Court of Appeals reversed because of the admission of evidence obtained by an illegal search. At his third trial, Manning was again convicted, and the Court of Appeals again reversed because the trial court had not granted a change of venue. A fourth trial resulted in a hung jury. Finally, after five trials, Manning was convicted, in March 1962, of murdering one victim, and after a sixth trial in December 1962, he was convicted of murdering the other.

The Christian County Circuit Court holds three terms each year—in February, June, and September. Barker's initial trial was to take place in the September term of 1958. The first continuance postponed it until the February 1959 term. The second continuance was granted for one month only. Every term thereafter, for as long as the Manning prosecutions were in process, the Commonwealth routinely moved to continue Barker's case to the next term. When the case was continued from the June 1959 term until the following September, Barker, having spent 10 months in jail, obtained his release by posting a $5,000 bond. He thereafter remained free in the community until his trial. Barker made no objection, through his counsel, to the first 11 continuances.

When on February 12, 1962, the Commonwealth moved for the twelfth time to continue the case until the following term, Barker's counsel filed a motion to dismiss the indictment. The motion to dismiss was denied two weeks later, and the State's motion for a continuance was granted. The State was granted further continuances in June 1962 and September 1962, to which Barker did not object. In February 1963, the first term of court following Manning's final conviction, the Commonwealth moved to set Barker's trial for March 19. But on the day scheduled for trial, the Commonwealth again moved for a continuance until the June term. It gave as its reason the illness of the ex-sheriff who was the chief investigating officer in the case. To this continuance, Barker objected unsuccessfully.

The witness was still unable to testify in June, and the trial, which had been set for June 19, was continued again until the September term, again over Barker's objection. This time the court announced that the case would be dismissed for lack of prosecution if it were not tried during the next term. The final trial date was set for October 9, 1963. On that date, Barker again moved to dismiss the indictment, and this time specified that his right to a speedy trial had been violated. The motion was denied; the trial commenced with Manning as the chief prosecution witness; Barker was convicted and given a life sentence.

Barker appealed his conviction through the Kentucky Court of Appeals and the U.S. District Court of Appeals. Both affirmed the conviction. The case was then appealed to the U.S. Supreme Court on the grounds that the Due Process Clause of the Fourteenth Amendment of the Constitution had been violated because the defendant had been denied a speedy trial as provided by the Sixth Amendment now made applicable to the states through U.S. Supreme Court decisions.

In studying the case, the U.S. Supreme Court stated the following:

> The right to a speedy trial is generically different from any of the other rights enshrined in the Constitution for the protection of the accused. In addition to the general concern that all accused persons be treated according to decent and fair procedures, there is a societal interest in providing a speedy trial which exists separate from and at times in opposition to the interests of the accused. The inability of courts to provide a prompt trial has contributed to a large backlog of cases in urban courts which, among other things, enables defendants to negotiate more effectively for pleas of guilty to lesser offenses and otherwise manipulate the system. In addition, persons released on bond for lengthy periods awaiting trial have an opportunity to commit other crimes. It must be of little comfort to the residents of Christian County, Kentucky, to know that Barker was at large on bail for over four years while accused of a vicious and brutal murder of which he was ultimately convicted. Moreover, the longer an accused is free awaiting trial, the more tempting becomes his opportunity to jump bail and escape. Finally, delay between arrest and punishment may have a detrimental effect on rehabilitation.
>
> If an accused cannot make bail, he is generally confined, as was Barker for 10 months, in a local jail. This contributes to the overcrowding and generally deplorable state of those institutions. Lengthy exposure to these conditions has a destructive effect on human character and makes the rehabilitation of the individual offender much more difficult. At times the result may even be violent rioting. Finally, lengthy pretrial detention is costly. The cost of maintaining a prisoner in jail varies from $3 to $9 per day, and this amounts to millions across the Nation. In addition, society loses wages which might have been earned, and it must often support families of incarcerated breadwinners.
>
> A second difference between the right to speedy trial and the accused's other constitutional rights is that deprivation of the right may work to the accused's advantage. Delay is not an uncommon defense tactic. As the time between the commission of the crime and trial lengthens, witnesses may become

unavailable or their memories may fade. If the witnesses support the prosecution, its case will be weakened, sometimes seriously so. And it is the prosecution which carries the burden of proof. Thus, unlike the right to counsel or the right to be free from compelled self-incrimination, deprivation of the right to speedy trial does not per se prejudice the accused's ability to defend himself.

Finally, and perhaps most importantly, the right to speedy trial is a more vague concept than other procedural rights. It is, for example, impossible to determine with precision when the right has been denied. We cannot definitely say how long is too long in a system where justice is supposed to be swift but deliberate. As a consequence, there is no fixed point in the criminal process when the State can put the defendant to the choice of either exercising or waiving the right to a speedy trial. If, for example, the State moves for a 60-day continuance, granting that continuance is not a violation of the right to speedy trial unless the circumstances of the case are such that further delay would endanger the values the right protects. It is impossible to do more than generalize about when those circumstances exist.

The nature of the speedy-trial right does make it impossible to pinpoint a precise time in the process when the right must be asserted or waived, but that fact does not argue for placing the burden of protecting the right solely on defendants. A defendant has no duty to bring himself to trial; the State has that duty as well as the duty of ensuring that the trial is consistent with due process. Moreover, for the reasons earlier expressed, society has particular interest in bringing swift prosecutions, and society's representatives are the ones who should protect that interest.

The Court stated, however, that the defendant had some responsibility to assert his right to a speedy trial. The approach that the Court accepted was a balancing test in which the conduct of both the prosecution and the defendant was to be weighed. The Court continued by stating as follows:

A balancing test necessarily compels courts to approach speedy-trial cases on an ad hoc basis. We can do little more than identify some of the factors which courts should assess in determining whether a particular defendant has been deprived of his right. Though some might express them in different ways, we identify four such factors: length of delay, the reason for the delay, the defendant's assertion of his right, and prejudice to the defendant.

We have discussed previously the societal disadvantages of lengthy pretrial incarceration, but obviously the disadvantages for the accused who cannot obtain his release are even more serious. The time spent in jail awaiting trial has a detrimental impact on the individual. It often means loss of a job; it disrupts family life; and it enforces idleness. Most jails offer little or no recreational or rehabilitative programs. The time spent in jail is simply dead time. Moreover, if a defendant is locked up, he is hindered in his ability to gather evidence, contact witnesses, and otherwise prepare his defense. Imposing those consequences on anyone who has not yet been convicted is serious. It is especially unfortunate to impose them on those persons who are ultimately found to be innocent. Finally, even if an accused is not incarcerated prior to trial, he is still disadvantaged by restraints on his liberty and by living under a cloud of anxiety, suspicion, and often hostility. . . .

The difficulty of the task of balancing these factors is illustrated by this case, which we consider to be close. It is clear that the length of delay between arrest and trial—well over five years—was extraordinary. Only seven months of that period can be attributed to a strong excuse, the illness of the ex-sheriff who was in charge of the investigation. Perhaps some delay would have been permissible under ordinary circumstances, so that Manning could be utilized as a witness in Barker's trial, but more than four years was too long a period, particularly since a good part of the period was attributable to the Commonwealth's failure or inability to try Manning under circumstances that comported with due process.

Two counter-balancing factors, however, outweigh these deficiencies. The first is that prejudice was minimal. Of course, Barker was prejudiced to some extent by living for over four years under a cloud of suspicion and anxiety. Moreover, although he was released on bond for most of the period, he did spend 10 months in jail before the trial. But there is no claim that any of Barker's witnesses died or otherwise became unavailable owing to the delay. The trial transcript indicates only two very minor lapses of memory on the part of prosecution witnesses which were in no way significant to the outcome.

More important than the absence of serious prejudice, is the fact that Barker did not want a speedy trial.... The probable reason for Barker's attitude was that he was gambling on Manning's acquittal. The evidence was not terribly strong against Manning, as the reversals and hung juries suggest, and Barker undoubtedly thought that if Manning were acquitted, he would never be tried.

We hold, therefore, that Barker was not deprived of his due process right to a speedy trial.

Out-of-State Incarceration

In the past, an acceptable ground for delay in bringing a case to trial was the incarceration of the defendant in another state. Under these circumstances, it was assumed that the prosecution had no obligation to bring a defendant to trial if he or she was unavailable because of imprisonment beyond the jurisdiction of the court in which he or she was charged with a crime. This viewpoint was changed by the U.S. Supreme Court in the case of *Smith* v. *Hooey*.[2] The Court held that a defendant was entitled to a speedy trial even while serving time in another state, particularly if the defendant demanded to be brought to trial. The facts of the *Smith* case reflect that in 1960 the defendant was indicted in Harris County, Texas, upon a charge of theft. The defendant was then, and still was when the decision was handed down in 1969, a prisoner in the federal penitentiary at Leavenworth, Kansas. Shortly after the Texas charge was filed, the defendant mailed a letter to the Texas trial court requesting a speedy trial. The reply stated that a trial would commence within two weeks of any date the defendant could be present. For the next six years, the defendant made periodic efforts to be brought to trial. Texas authorities made no effort to obtain the defendant's appearance in the Harris County trial court. The defendant appealed the case to the U.S. Supreme Court on due process of law grounds in that a speedy trial had been denied.

In agreeing with the contention of the defendant the Court stated:

At first blush it might appear that a man already in prison under a lawful sentence is hardly in a position to suffer from "undue and oppressive incarceration prior to trial." But the fact is that delay in bringing such a person to trial on a pending charge may ultimately result in as much oppression as is suffered by one who is jailed without bail upon an untried charge. First, the possibility that the defendant already in prison might receive a sentence at least partially concurrent with the one he is serving may be forever lost if trial of the pending charge is postponed. Secondly, under procedures now widely practiced, the duration of his present imprisonment may be increased, and the conditions under which he must serve his sentence greatly worsened, by the pendency of another criminal charge outstanding against him.

And while it might be argued that a person already in prison would be less likely than others to be affected by "anxiety and concern accompanying public accusation," there is reason to believe that an outstanding untried charge (of which even a convict may, of course, be innocent) can have fully as depressive an effect upon a prisoner as upon a person who is at large. In the opinion of the former Director of the Federal Bureau of Prisons: "It is in their effect upon the prisoner and our attempts to rehabilitate him that detainees are most corrosive. The strain of having to serve a sentence with the uncertain prospect of being taken into the custody of another state at the conclusion interferes with the prisoner's ability to take maximum advantage of his institutional opportunities. His anxiety and depression may leave him with little inclination towards self-improvement."

Finally, it is self-evident that the possibilities that long delay will impair the ability of an accused to defend himself are markedly increased when the accused is incarcerated in another jurisdiction. Confined in a prison, perhaps far from the place where the offense covered by the outstanding charge allegedly took place, his ability to confer with potential defense witnesses, or even to keep track of their whereabouts, is obviously impaired. And, while evidence and witnesses disappear, memories fade, and events lose their perspective, a man isolated in prison is powerless to exert his own investigative efforts to mitigate these erosive effects of the passage of time.

The *Smith* case did not resolve the question as to the action that must be taken, if any, when a defendant does not demand to be brought to trial, and the *Barker* decision was of little assistance. The Court in the *Barker* case stated that the prosecution is responsible for bringing the defendant to trial. However, the Court did not absolve the defendant of all responsibility in bringing about the trial. At first glance, it would appear that if the prosecution learns that a defendant is incarcerated in another state that some action should be taken by the prosecution to return the defendant for a speedy trial before the expiration date of the sentence in the other state. Otherwise, it could be held that the defendant was denied the right to due process of law. On the other hand, if a defendant knows that he or she is wanted in another place for a crime committed, the failure to demand to be brought to trial could be interpreted as a waiver of the right to a speedy trial.

Statutory Regulations

To assist those involved in the administration of justice, most states have enacted statutes setting forth guidelines on when a trial should take place, but even these guidelines have much flexibility. For example, many states have passed statutes similar to the following:

> The welfare of the people requires that all proceedings in criminal cases shall be set for trial and heard and determined at the earliest possible time, and it shall be the duty of all courts and judicial officers and of all prosecuting attorneys to expedite such proceedings to the greatest degree that is consistent with the ends of justice. In accordance with this policy, criminal cases shall be given precedence over, and set for trial and heard prior to any civil matters. Also no contin-

uance of a criminal trial shall be granted except upon sufficient cause shown in open court, and upon reasonable notice to the opposition. It is held also that cases of those accused of a crime who are in custody are to take precedence over those who have been released on bail.

In addition, most states have provisions stating that unless an accused is brought to trial within a set number of days after the filing of the appropriate accusatory pleading, the charge shall be dismissed, and, if in custody, the defendant shall be released or bail be exonerated. The period of time is usually 30 days if the charge is a misdemeanor, or within a period of 60 to 120 days, depending upon the jurisdiction, if the charge is a felony. This period may be waived by the defendant. In most instances, if a misdemeanor charge is dismissed, further prosecution will be barred on that particular offense, but states vary in the effect of a dismissal of a felony charge. Some states hold that further prosecution is barred. Other states hold that the defendant must be released after the dismissal but may be rearrested upon the filing of a new accusatory document, and the time period begins to run again. How many times such procedures could take place before it would be considered a violation of the speedy trial guarantee is uncertain. If it can be proved that the refiling was for harassment purposes, even one refiling would undoubtedly be considered a denial of due process.

It has also been held that unless reasonable efforts are made to execute a warrant of arrest after it has been issued, the accused may have been denied the right to a speedy trial. In one case, for example, a felony warrant of arrest was issued for an accused, but no efforts were made to execute the warrant of arrest even though the accused had resided at the address listed on the warrant for nearly six months after the warrant was issued. The accused left the area for a few months but returned and again lived at the address listed on the warrant for several months before being arrested on a minor charge. After the conviction on the felony charge, the appellate court held that because of the delay in executing the warrant of arrest, the accused had been denied a speedy trial. However, if a reasonable effort is made to execute a warrant of arrest and the accused cannot be located, the delay in the execution of the warrant will not be interpreted as a denial of a speedy trial. It has been held that if there is a good reason for not serving the warrant of arrest immediately after it is issued, the defendant's right to a speedy trial is not denied. In one case, there was a delay of five months between the time that the warrant of arrest was issued and the time of service. The court held that since the delay was for the purpose of identifying other members of a narcotic ring and that this undertaking would have been hampered by an immediate arrest, the delay was justified. Similarly, it has been held that if there is a good cause for a delay in having a warrant of arrest issued after a crime is committed, the defendant has not been denied the right to a speedy trial.

Statute of Limitations

To further assure that one accused of committing a crime is afforded a speedy trial, a statute of limitations is incorporated into the laws of all the states. This has been termed a humanitarian statute, since it provides that some prosecutive action must be commenced against an accused within a reasonable time after the crime is committed. The statute prevents the state or society from holding the threat of prosecutive action for an indefinite period over the head of an offender. The statute has also been described as an act of grace, since there is a surrendering by the sovereignty of its right to prosecute.

The statute forces society to take some action from two aspects. It gives law enforcement the responsibility of taking immediate and continuous action upon a reported crime in order to identify the perpetrator so that he or she may be afforded a speedy trial. The statute also gives the prosecutive officials the burden of commencing prosecution within a specified time after the identity of an offender is established. There are occasions when a crime is committed and the law enforcement agency involved is unsuccessful in identifying the perpetrators of that crime until after the time stated in the statute of limitations has lapsed. Under those circumstances, the perpetrators may not be brought to trial even if later identified. In most states, the statute of limitations is considered to be a jurisdictional matter and may not be waived. If the perpetrators of a crime are identified before the statutory period runs out and their whereabouts are unknown, some prosecutive action, such as filing a complaint or indictment, must still be commenced before the statutory time expires, or future prosecutive action will be barred.

There was no statute of limitations, as we know it today, at common law in England. If a crime was committed at common law, it was a crime against the king, and it was presumed that prosecution might occur at any time. It was particularly true in murder cases. This background may be the reason that even today, in the United States, the statute of limitations never lapses on a murder charge. With most other crimes, there is a specified time within which prosecutive action must commence. The time varies among states. On a felony charge, the statute of limitations varies from three years to six years depending upon the state. On a misdemeanor charge, the period is between six months and one year. A few states list other felonies besides murder, such as the embezzlement of public funds or falsification of public records, for which there are not statutory periods. If, during the investigation of a case, it is determined that the perpetrator of the crime has left the state in which the crime was committed, the statute of limitations is suspended, or *tolled*, while the perpetrator is out of state.

CAPSTONE CASE

Doggett v. *United States*
112 S.Ct. 2686, 120 L.Ed.2d 520 (1992)

Justice Souter delivered the opinion of the Court.

On February 22, 1980, petitioner Marc Doggett was indicted for conspiring with several others to import and distribute cocaine. Douglas Driver, the Drug Enforcement Administration's principal agent investigating the conspiracy, told the United States Marshal's Service that the DEA would oversee the apprehension of Doggett and his confederates. On March 18, 1980, two police officers set out under Driver's orders to arrest Doggett at his parents' house in Raleigh, North Carolina, only to find that he was not there. His mother told the officers that he had left for Colombia four days earlier.

To catch Doggett on his return to the United States, Driver sent word of his outstanding arrest warrant to all United States Customs stations and to a number of law enforcement organizations. He also placed Doggett's name in the Treasury Enforcement Communication System (TECS), a computer network that helps Customs agents screen people entering the country, and in the National Crime Information Center computer system, which serves similar ends. The TECS entry expired that September, however, and Doggett's name vanished from the system.

In September 1981, Driver found out that Doggett was under arrest on drug charges in Panama and, thinking that a formal extradition request would be futile, simply asked Panama to "expel" Doggett to the United States. Although the Panamanian authorities promised to comply when their own proceedings had run their course, they freed Doggett the following July and let him go to Colombia, where he stayed with an aunt for several months. On September 25, 1982, he passed unhindered through Customs in New York City and settled down in Virginia. Since his return to the United States, he has married, earned a college degree, found a steady job as a computer operations manager, lived openly under his own name, and stayed within the law.

Doggett's travels abroad had not wholly escaped the Government's notice, however. In 1982, the American Embassy in Panama told the State Department of his departure to Colombia, but that information, for whatever reason, eluded the DEA, and Agent Driver assumed for several years that his quarry was still serving time in a Panamanian prison. Driver never asked DEA officials in Panama to check into Doggett's status, and only after his own fortuitous assignment to that country in 1985 did he discover Doggett's departure for Colombia. Driver then simply assumed Doggett had settled there, and he made no effort to find out for sure or to track Doggett down, either abroad or in the United States. Thus Doggett remained lost to the American criminal justice system until September 1988, when the Marshal's Service ran a simple credit check on several thousand people subject to outstanding arrest warrants and, within minutes, found out where Doggett lived and worked. On September 5, 1988, nearly 6 years after his return to the United States and 8½ years after his indictment, Doggett was arrested.

He naturally moved to dismiss the indictment, arguing that the Government's failure to prosecute him earlier violated his Sixth Amendment right to a speedy trial. The Federal Magistrate hearing his motion found, however, that Doggett had made no affirmative showing that the delay had impaired his ability to mount a successful defense or had otherwise prejudiced him. In his recommendation to the District Court, the Magistrate contended that this failure to demonstrate particular prejudice sufficed to defeat Doggett's speedy trial claim.

The District Court took the recommendation and denied Doggett's motion. A split panel of the Court of Appeals affirmed.

The Sixth Amendment guarantees that, "in all criminal prosecutions, the accused shall enjoy the right to a speedy trial." On its face, the Speedy Trial Clause is written with such breadth that, taken literally, it would forbid the government to delay the trial of an "accused" for any reason at all. Our cases, however, have qualified the literal sweep of the provision by specifically recognizing the relevance of four separate enquiries: whether delay before trial was uncommonly long, whether the government or the criminal defendant is more to blame for that delay, whether, in due course, the defendant asserted his right to a speedy trial, and whether he suffered prejudice as the delay's result.

The first of these is actually a double inquiry. Simply to trigger a speedy trial analysis, an accused must allege that the interval between accusation and trial has crossed the threshold dividing ordinary from "presumptively prejudicial" delay, since, by definition, he cannot complain that the government has denied him a "speedy" trial if it has, in fact, prosecuted his case with customary promptness. If the accused makes this showing, the court must then consider, as one factor among several, the extent to which the delay stretches beyond the bare minimum needed to trigger judicial examination of the claim. This latter enquiry is significant to the speedy trial analysis because, as we discuss below, the presumption that pretrial delay has prejudiced the accused intensifies over time. In this case, the extraordinary 8½-year lag between Doggett's indictment and arrest clearly suffices to trigger the speedy trial enquiry; its further significance within that enquiry will be dealt with later.

As for Barker's second criterion, the Government claims to have sought Doggett with diligence. The findings of the courts below are to the contrary, however, and we review trial court determinations of negligence with considerable deference. The Government gives us nothing to gainsay the findings that have come up to us, and we see nothing fatal to them in the record. For six years, the Government's investigators made no serious effort to test their progressively more questionable assumption that Doggett was living abroad, and, had they done so, they could have found him within minutes. While the Government's lethargy may have reflected no more than Doggett's relative unimportance in the world of drug trafficking, it was still findable negligence, and the finding stands.

The Government goes against the record again in suggesting that Doggett knew of his indictment years before he was arrested. Were this true, Barker's third factor, concerning invocation of the right to a speedy trial, would be weighed heavily against him. But here again, the Government is trying to revisit the facts. At the hearing on Doggett's speedy trial motion, it introduced no evidence challenging the testimony of Doggett's wife, who said that she did not know of the charges until his arrest, and of his mother, who claimed not to have told him or anyone else that the police had come looking for him. . . . The Government is left, then, with its principal contention: that Doggett fails to make out a successful speedy trial claim because he has not shown precisely how he was prejudiced by the delay between his indictment and trial.

We have observed in prior cases that unreasonable delay between formal accusation and trial threatens to produce more than one sort of harm, including "oppressive pretrial incarceration . . . anxiety and concern of the accused," and "the possibility that the defense will be impaired" by dimming memories and loss of exculpatory evidence. Of these forms of prejudice, "the most serious is the last, because the inability of a defendant adequately to prepare his case skews the fairness of the entire system." Doggett claims this kind of prejudice, and there is probably no other kind that he can claim, since he was subjected neither to pretrial detention nor, he has successfully contended, to awareness of unresolved charges against him.

The Government answers Doggett's claim by citing language in three cases, *United States* v. *Marion*, 404 U.S. 307 (1971), *United States* v. *MacDonald*, 456 U.S. 1 (1982), and *United States* v. *Loud Hawk*, 474 U.S. 302 (1986), for the proposition that the Speedy Trial Clause does not significantly protect a criminal defendant's interest in fair adjudication. In so arguing, the Government asks us, in effect, to read part of Barker right out of the law, and that we will not do. In context, the cited passages support nothing beyond the principle, which we have independently based on textual and historical grounds, that the Sixth Amendment right of the accused to a speedy trial has no application beyond the confines of a formal criminal prosecution. Once triggered by arrest, indictment, or other official accusation, however, the speedy trial enquiry must weigh the effect of delay on the accused's defense just as it has to weigh any other form of prejudice that Barker recognized.

As an alternative to limiting Barker, the Government claims Doggett has failed to make any affirmative showing that the delay weakened his ability to raise specific defenses, elicit specific testimony, or produce specific items of evidence. Though Doggett did indeed come up short in this respect, the Government's argument takes it only so far: consideration of prejudice is not limited to the specifically demonstrable, and, as it concedes, affirmative proof of particularized prejudice is not essential to every speedy trial claim. Barker explicitly recognized that impairment of one's defense is the most difficult form of speedy trial prejudice to prove because time's erosion of exculpatory evidence and testimony "can rarely be shown." And though time can tilt the case against either side, one cannot generally be sure which of them it has prejudiced more severely. Thus, we generally have to recognize that excessive delay presumptively compromises the reliability of a trial in ways that neither party can prove or, for that matter, identify. While such presumptive prejudice cannot alone carry a Sixth Amendment claim without regard to the other Barker criteria, it is part of the mix of relevant facts, and its importance increases with the length of delay.

This brings us to an enquiry into the role that presumptive prejudice should play in the disposition of Doggett's speedy trial claim. We begin with hypothetical and somewhat easier cases and work our way to this one.

Our speedy trial standards recognize that pretrial delay is often both inevitable and wholly justifiable. The government may need time to collect witnesses against the accused, oppose his pretrial motions, or, if he goes into hiding, track him down. We attach great weight to such considerations when balancing them against the costs of going forward with a trial whose probative accuracy the passage of time has begun by degrees to throw into question. Thus, in this case, if the Government had pursued Doggett with reasonable diligence from his indictment to his arrest, his speedy trial claim would fail. Indeed, that conclusion would generally follow as a matter of course however great the delay, so long as Doggett could not show specific prejudice to his defense.

The Government concedes, on the other hand, that Doggett would prevail if he could show that the Government had intentionally held back in its prosecution of him to gain some impermissible advantage at trial. That we cannot doubt. Barker stressed that official bad faith in causing delay will be weighed heavily against the government, and a bad-faith delay the length of this negligent one would present an overwhelming case for dismissal.

Between diligent prosecution and bad-faith delay, official negligence in bringing an accused to trial occupies the middle ground. While not compelling relief in every case where bad-faith delay would make relief virtually automatic, neither is negligence automatically tolerable simply because the accused cannot demonstrate exactly how it has prejudiced him. It was on this point that the Court of Appeals erred, and on the facts before us, it was reversible error.

Barker made it clear that "different weights are assigned to different reasons" for delay. Although negligence is obviously to be weighed more lightly than a deliberate intent to harm the accused's defense, it still falls on the wrong side of the divide between acceptable and unacceptable reasons for delaying a criminal prosecution once it has begun. And such is the nature of the prejudice presumed that the weight we assign to official negligence compounds over time as the presumption of evidentiary prejudice grows. Thus, our toleration of such negligence varies inversely with its protractedness, and its consequent threat to the fairness of the accused's trial. Condoning prolonged and unjustifiable delays in prosecution would both penalize many defendants for the state's fault and simply encourage the government to gamble with the interests of criminal suspects assigned a low prosecutorial priority. The Government, indeed, can hardly complain too loudly, for persistent neglect in concluding a criminal prosecution indicates an uncommonly feeble interest in bringing an accused to justice; the more weight the Government attaches to securing a conviction, the harder it will try to get it.

To be sure, to warrant granting relief, negligence unaccompanied by particularized trial prejudice must have lasted longer than negligence demonstrably causing such prejudice. But even so, the Government's egregious persistence in failing to prosecute Doggett is clearly sufficient. The lag between Doggett's indictment and arrest was 8½ years, and he would have faced trial 6 years earlier than he did but for the Government's inexcusable oversights. The portion of the delay attributable to the Government's negligence far exceeds the threshold needed to state a speedy trial claim; indeed, we have called shorter delays "extraordinary." When the Government's negligence thus causes delay six times as long as that generally sufficient to trigger judicial review, and when the presumption of prejudice, albeit unspecified, is neither extenuated, as by the defendant's acquiescence, nor persuasively rebutted, the defendant is entitled to relief.

[Dissenting and concurring opinions omitted.]

REVIEW QUESTIONS

1. Where must a criminal trial take place?

2. What is meant by a change of venue?

3. What is meant by a speedy trial?

4. List four factors that the U.S. Supreme Court set forth in the *Barker* v. *Wingo* decision that should be taken into account in determining whether a defendant has been denied a speedy trial.

5. List three societal disadvantages of lengthy pretrial incarceration.

6. Why should granting continuances be discouraged?

7. What effect, if any, does out-of-state incarceration have on a speedy trial?

8. What is the statute of limitations?

LOCAL PROCEDURE

1. In your home state, what is the statute of limitations for the following:
   a. Misdemeanors?
   b. Felonies?

2. In your home state, if a felony is dismissed for the failure to bring the defendant to trial within statutory limitations, may the charge be refiled?

ENDNOTES

1. 407 U.S. 514 (1972).
2. 393 U.S. 374 (1969).

CHAPTER 7

The Trial

The majestic equality of the law forbids the rich as well as the poor to sleep under bridges, to beg in the streets, and to steal bread.

—Anatole France

BENCH TRIAL VERSUS JURY TRIAL

By the beginning of the eighteenth century, the accused was being confronted by the witnesses against him or her, and hearsay evidence was eliminated. Witnesses were placed under oath to relate facts of their own knowledge. Juries rendered their verdicts upon the testimony of witnesses given in open court and not from what the jurors had learned about an accusation outside court. Rules of evidence were being formulated. The trial by jury as it is known today was rapidly becoming part of the judicial system in Great Britain and was adopted by the colonists. The colonists had deep reverence for trial by jury, and they strongly resented interference by the king of Great Britain in his efforts to subdue them. This resentment was manifested by the colonists in the Declaration of Independence. Among other provisions, they included in this declaration the following: "The history of the present King of Great Britain is a history of repeated injuries. To prove this, let facts be submitted to a candid world. . . . For his [the King] depriving us in many cases, of benefits of trial by jury."

Accused's Right Jury Trial

After the colonists gained their independence from Great Britain, a new government was established. To prevent possible future interference with the right to a trial by jury in this newly formed government, the Sixth Amendment to the U.S. Constitution contained the provision that all persons accused of a crime had the right to be tried by an impartial jury. The Sixth Amendment right to trial by jury is made binding on the states through the "due process of law" clause of the Fourteenth Amendment, as is the right to a speedy trial. These rights are also contained in all state constitutions or statutes. Although the Sixth Amendment did not mention the number of persons required to constitute a jury, it was generally accepted that the common law rule of twelve persons would prevail. So strongly was it felt that a jury must consist of twelve persons in a criminal case that a trial by jury consisting of fewer than twelve would be a denial of due process of law. The idea of an accused's being permitted to waive a jury and having the case held by a judge alone was practically unthought of. It was not until 1930 in the case of *Patton* v. *United States*[1] that the U.S. Supreme Court held that a verdict rendered by a jury comprising fewer than twelve members was not a violation of an accused's constitutional right to a trial by jury. In the *Patton* case, the trial started with a jury comprising twelve persons, but during the trial one of the jurors became incapacitated. The defendant agreed to continue the trial with only eleven jurors. He was convicted, and the case was taken to the U.S. Supreme Court to determine whether a defendant has the right to waive a jury trial. The defendant did not waive the entire jury in the *Patton* case, but even the waiver of one juror and continuing with only eleven was so foreign to the common law procedure that the U.S. Supreme Court felt that the matter was worth their consideration. The Court in the *Patton* case stated that, after an examination of Article III, Section 2, and the Sixth Amendment of the U.S. Constitution, they had come to the conclusion that a jury trial was a right that the accused might "forego at his election" and that the right to a trial by jury was a privilege and not an "imperative right." As such, the defendant could waive a jury comprising fewer than twelve persons. This decision gave an implied permission to waive the jury entirely and have the case heard by a judge sitting alone.

Even though the Court in the *Patton* case sanctioned the right of an accused to waive his or her right to a jury, it did emphasize the necessity of preserving the jury trial system. The Court stated as follows:

> Not only must the right of the accused to a trial by a constitutional jury be jealously preserved, but the maintenance of the jury as a fact-finding body in criminal cases is of such importance and has such a place in our traditions that, before any waiver can become effective, the consent of government counsel and the sanction of the court must be had, in addition to the express and intelligent consent of the defendant.

The U.S. Supreme Court further emphasized the importance of the right of an accused to a trial by jury in the case of *Duncan* v. *Louisiana*.[2] The Court in that decision stated the following:

> Providing an accused with the right to be tried by a jury of his peers gave him an inestimable safeguard against the corrupt or overzealous prosecutor and against the compliant, biased, or eccentric judge. If the defendant preferred the common sense judgment of a jury to the more tutored but perhaps less sympathetic reaction of the single judge, he was to have it. Beyond this, the jury trial provisions in the Federal and State Constitutions reflect a fundamental decision about the exercise of official power—a reluctance to entrust plenary powers over the life and liberty of the citizens to one judge or to a group of judges. Fear of unchecked power, so typical of our State and Federal Governments in other respects, found expression in the criminal law in this insistence upon community participation in

the determination of guilt or innocence. The deep commitment of the Nation to the right of jury trial in serious criminal cases as a defense against arbitrary law enforcement qualities for protection under the Due Process Clause of the Fourteenth Amendment, and must therefore be respected by the States.

Trial by Judge Alone

Further advantages of a jury trial over a trial by a judge sitting alone, also referred to as a court trial, include the belief that a jury of twelve persons, representing a cross section of society, may be better able to evaluate the demeanor of witnesses than a judge sitting alone; that the group judgment of a jury is better than that of a single person, the judge; that there is a value in community participation in the administration of justice; and that the jury injects the common law test into the legal system instead of the legalistic viewpoint.

With all these listed advantages to a trial by jury, why would a defendant wish to waive a jury and be tried by a judge sitting alone? Situations arise in which it may be advantageous to the accused to waive his or her right to a jury trial in favor of a court trial. The crime of which the defendant is accused may be a heinous one. The emotional involvement of the people within the community may make the selection of an impartial jury very difficult. The defendant's general appearance may be such that a jury may become prejudiced. There may be a serious past criminal record subjecting the defendant to possible impeachment should the witness stand be taken as a defense, and the probability of the jury's convicting the defendant on past record rather than on the evidence contended in the present charge is great. Or the defendant may be a part of an organized criminal syndicate or of a minority group that local feeling is against, and the jury may convict the accused by association rather than on the facts of the case. A judge is considered less inclined to be affected by any of these situations than would a jury.

Procedure in the Waiver of a Jury.   Prior to the *Patton* decision, only a few states had considered allowing a defendant to waive a trial by jury. However, after the *Patton* decision, a large majority of the states began permitting the defendant to waive his or her right to a trial by jury. States differ considerably regarding the conditions and the procedure to be followed in permitting a waiver of a jury trial. A few states still do not permit the defendant to waive a jury trial. Others permit the waiver in misdemeanor cases but not on felony charges. Still others permit the jury to be waived in all cases except those with a maximum penalty of death. One state permits the defendant to waive the jury in capital cases and be tried by a panel of three judges. A few states permit the jury to be waived in any type of charge, including capital cases.

States differ also in the procedure to be followed regarding who must give the consent and how the consent is given. Some states provide that the waiver is solely the right of the defendant, whereas others hold that the waiver must be consented to by the prosecution as well as the defendant. A few states require that the defendant, the prosecution, and the judge all must agree to the waiver of the jury, and a few others provide that the defendant and the judge agree to the waiver, but the consent of the prosecution is not required. This latter position has been criticized, since it is believed that the prosecution should be permitted to disagree with the waiver. The reasoning is that a judge may be known to be sympathetic to the defendant or that the judge may be under political pressure making him or her feel forced to render a verdict in favor of the defendant. In most instances, the prosecution will agree with the waiver of the jury, since the waiver expedites the trial by eliminating the time-consuming selection of the jury. Time is also saved by not having to stop during a jury trial to explain the law of the case to the jury.

The form in which the waiver of the jury takes place also varies among states. In some states, the defendant must waive the jury in open court by an express statement to that effect. Other states require the defendant to consent to the waiver in writing before the date of the trial. Some states hold that unless the defendant demands a jury trial at the time that he or she enters the plea of not guilty, a jury trial is automatically waived. If the waiver of a jury takes place, it is usually before the jury is selected, but a few states permit the defendant to waive the jury anytime before the verdict is rendered.

A question that sometimes arises is, After consent to a waiver of the jury, may the defendant later demand to be tried by a jury? Generally, unless there is sufficient evidence of a miscarriage of justice, the defendant may not demand a jury trial, particularly if the trial has begun. The reason is that a jury would have to be selected and the trial would have to start over. Once the trial has begun, the waiver of a jury creates no particular difficulty, since the judge will have heard all the evidence during the trial's progress and will be in a position to render the verdict. Whether the defendant is permitted to withdraw the waiver of the jury is within the discretion of the trial judge. In making the decision, the judge may consider such matters as the timeliness of the motion to withdraw the waiver, the reason for the requested withdrawal, and the possibility of undue delay of the trial or inconvenience to witnesses that would result from granting the withdrawal of the waiver.

May the Defendant Demand a Bench Trial?   As previously pointed out, there are times when a defendant may wish to be tried by a judge sitting alone. Under these circumstances, may the defendant waive the jury and demand a bench trial, also known as a court trial? This question was answered by the U.S. Supreme Court in the case of *Singer* v. *United States*.[3] In that decision, the Court held that although a defendant could waive the right to a jury trial, there is no correlative right to a bench trial. The Court in the Singer decision stated the following:

> The ability to waive a constitutional right does not ordinarily carry with it the right to insist upon the opposite of that right. For example, although a defendant can, under some circumstances, waive his constitutional right to a public trial, he has no absolute right to compel a private trial. Although he can waive his right to be tried in the State and district where the crime was committed, he cannot in all cases compel transfer of the case to another district, and although he can waive his right to be confronted by the witnesses against him, it has never been seriously suggested that he can thereby compel the Government to try the case by stipulation. . . .

Trial by jury has been established by the Constitution as the "normal and . . . preferable mode of disposing of issues of fact in a criminal case."

In light of the Constitution's emphasis on jury trial, we find it difficult to understand how the petitioner can submit the bald proposition that to compel a defendant in a criminal case to undergo a jury trial against his or her will is contrary to his or her right to a fair trial or to due process. A defendant's only constitutional right concerning the method of trial is to an impartial trial by jury. We find no constitutional impediment in conditioning a waiver of this right on the consent of the prosecuting attorney and the trial judge when, if either refuses to consent, the result is simply that the defendant is subject to an impartial trial by jury—the very thing that the Constitution guarantees him or her.

The Court concluded that it was not a violation of any constitutional right of an accused by forcing a jury trial even though the defendant might feel that it was advantageous to have a court trial. In this regard, many states permit the judge to refuse to consent to a court trial in lieu of a trial by jury. Those states adopting this policy feel that protection against community criticism should be provided when the judge might have to render an unpopular verdict.

Denial of a Jury Trial: Petty Offenses

Although the right to a trial by jury is an established guarantee to one accused of a crime, it is not an absolute right in all instances. As early as 1937, the U.S. Supreme Court in the case of *District of Columbia* v. *Clawans*[4] sanctioned a nonjury trial to one accused of a petty offense. This same sanction has been reiterated from time to time by the U.S. Supreme Court.[5]

In the *Duncan* v. *Louisiana* decision, the Court stated the following:

> So-called petty offenses were tried without juries both in England and in the Colonies and have always been held to be exempt from the otherwise comprehensive language of the Sixth Amendment's jury trial provisions. There is no substantial evidence that the Framers intended to depart from this established common-law practice, and the possible consequences to defendants from convictions for petty offenses have been thought insufficient to outweigh the benefits to efficient law enforcement and simplified judicial administration resulting from the availability of speedy and inexpensive non-jury adjudications. These same considerations compel the same result under the Fourteenth Amendment. Of course the boundaries of the petty offense category have always been ill defined, if not ambulatory.

Determining Petty Offenses.   In determining whether an offense is a "petty" one, the courts have had to turn to some criteria upon which to work. Although the statutes of some states have designated certain offenses as petty ones, this designation is not conclusive, and the courts may render different interpretations of petty offenses.

As stated by the U.S. Supreme Court in the *Frank* decision, to determine whether a particular offense could be classified as petty, the Court sought objective indications of the seriousness with which society regarded the offense. The Court stated that the most relevant indication of the seriousness of an offense was the severity of the penalty that could be imposed for the commission of the offense. The severity of the penalty being that authorized by law, and not the penalty actually imposed by the judge, was to be the criterion.

In the *Frank* case, the Supreme Court implied that they were relying upon the criterion set forth in the *Cheff* decision for a definition of petty offense. The *Cheff* decision adopted the definition of a petty offense found in 18 U.S. Code, Section 1, where it is described as any misdemeanor, the penalty for which does not exceed imprisonment for a period of six months or a fine of $500.

It would appear from these U.S. Supreme Court decisions that the states could pass statutes denying an accused the right to a trial by a jury for the commission of an offense for which the penalty would not exceed six months' imprisonment or a fine of not more than $500, and the accused would not be denied due process of law. A few states grant a defendant the right to a jury trial in all misdemeanor charges irrespective of the penalty but deny him or her the right to a jury trial on infractions—violations for which no imprisonment may be imposed.

Juries Comprising Fewer than Twelve

In line with the common-law tradition, the laws of the United States, as well as of most of the states, require that a criminal trial jury consist of twelve persons. There are a few states where the law provides that in misdemeanor violations, the jury may comprise any number fewer than twelve, agreed upon in open court by the defendant and the prosecution. How many fewer than twelve is not indicated, but the U.S. Supreme Court has not approved the use of a jury with fewer than six members. As in the Patton case, in some states, it is held that a felony trial must commence with twelve persons in the jury, but if one should become incapacitated and unable to act as a juror, the trial may continue with fewer than twelve if agreed to by the defendant, his or her attorney, and the prosecution. If it is not agreed to, the judge must declare a mistrial, and the case will have to be heard again with a new jury.

A few states have broken with the traditional number of twelve in a jury, even in felony cases, and have passed laws providing that a jury may comprise fewer than twelve both in misdemeanor and in felony cases. The problem that arises is whether trial by a jury comprising fewer than twelve when not consented to, particularly by the defendant, is a denial of the right to trial by jury. This question was answered in the case of *Williams* v. *Florida,*[6] in which the U.S. Supreme Court held that a jury comprising fewer than twelve persons, in accordance with the laws of the state involved, did not violate the Due Process Clause of the Fourteenth Amendment. The facts in the *Williams* case reflect that Williams was charged with robbery in the state of Florida. Williams, referred to as the petitioner by the Court, filed a pretrial motion to impanel a twelve-person jury instead of the six-person jury provided by Florida law in all but capital cases. The motion was denied, and Williams was convicted and sentenced to life imprisonment. He appealed his case to the U.S. Supreme Court upon the grounds that his right to a jury trial as provided in the Sixth Amendment to the U.S. Constitution, made applicable to the states by the Fourteenth Amendment, had been violated by requiring him to submit to a trial by a jury comprising only six persons. The Court stated as follows:

> The question in this case is whether the constitutional guarantee of a trial by "jury" necessarily requires trial by exactly 12 persons, rather than some lesser number, in this case six. We hold that the 12-man panel is not a necessary ingredient of "trial by jury," and that respondent's [state's] refusal to impanel more than six members provided for by Florida law did not violate petitioner's Sixth Amendment rights as applied to the States through the Fourteenth.
>
> We had occasion in *Duncan* v. *Louisiana* to review briefly the oft-told history of the development of trial by jury in criminal cases. That history revealed a long tradition attaching great importance to the concept of relying on a body of one's peers to determine guilt or innocence as a safeguard against arbitrary law enforcement. That same history, however, affords little insight into the considerations which gradually led the size of that body to be generally fixed at 12. Some have suggested that the number 12 was fixed upon simply because that was the

number of the presentment jury from the hundred, from which the petty jury developed. Other, less circular, but more fanciful reasons for the number 12 have been given, "but they were all brought forward after the number was fixed," and rest on little more than mystical or superstitious insights into the significance of "12." Lord Coke's explanation that the "number twelve is much respected in holy writ, as 12 apostles, 12 stones, 12 tribes, etc." is typical. In short, while sometime in the 14th century the size of the jury at common law came to be fixed generally at 12, that particular feature of the jury system appears to have been an historical accident, unrelated to the great purposes which gave rise to the jury in the first place. The question before us is whether this accidental feature of the jury has been immutably codified into our Constitution. . . .

It might be suggested that the 12-man jury gives a defendant a greater advantage since he has more "chances" of finding a juror who will insist on acquittal and thus prevent conviction. But the advantage might just as easily belong to the State, which also needs only one juror out of twelve insisting on guilt to prevent acquittal. What few experiments have occurred—usually in the civil area—indicate that there is no discernible difference between the results reached by the two different sized juries. In short, neither currently available evidence nor theory suggests that the 12-man jury is necessarily more advantageous to the defendant than a jury composed of fewer members.

Similarly, while in theory the number of viewpoints represented on a randomly selected jury ought to increase as the size of the jury increases, in practice the difference between the 12-man and the 6-man jury in terms of the cross section of the community represented seems likely to be negligible. Even the 12-man jury cannot ensure representation of every distinct voice in the community, particularly given the use of the peremptory challenge. As long as arbitrary exclusions of a particular class from the jury rolls are forbidden, the concern that the cross section will be significantly diminished if the jury is decreased in size from 12 to 6 seems an unrealistic one.

We conclude, in short, as we began: the fact that the jury at common law was composed of precisely 12 is an historical accident, unnecessary to effect the purposes of the jury system and wholly without significance "except to mystics."

Since the *Williams* decision has been handed down by the U.S. Supreme Court, it is highly possible that more and more states will enact laws permitting juries to comprise fewer than twelve members in all but capital cases. However, the U.S. Supreme Court, in *Ballew* v. *Georgia*,[7] held that a jury may not comprise fewer than six persons. Ballew was convicted of a misdemeanor charge by a jury of five persons, as provided by a Georgia statute. The conviction was upheld by the Georgia appellate courts. Ballew appealed his case to the U.S. Supreme Court on the grounds that his constitutional guarantee of a trial by jury had been denied, thereby denying him due process of law. The U.S. Supreme Court stated that a jury of six persons had been upheld in the *Williams* case and the "line between five and six member juries is not difficult to justify, but a line has to be drawn somewhere if the substance of the jury trial is to be preserved." The Court further stated that assembled research data

raise substantial doubt about the reliability and appropriate representation of panels smaller than six. Because of the fundamental importance of the jury trial to the American system of criminal justice, any further reduction that promotes inaccurate and possibly biased decision making, that causes untoward differences in verdicts, and that prevents juries from truly representing their communities, attains constitutional significance . . . and such reduction from six-member to five-member juries is not to be permitted.

PUBLIC TRIAL

Not only does the Sixth Amendment to the U.S Constitution, as well as the laws of all the states, provide that an accused person is entitled to a trial by jury, but also it further provides that he or she is guaranteed a public trial. The purpose of this guarantee is to ensure that the accused is dealt with fairly and not unjustly convicted. As was stated by the U.S. Supreme Court in the case of *Estes* v. *Texas:*[8]

> History has proven that secret tribunals were effective instruments of oppression. As our Brother Black so well said in *In re Oliver*, 333 US 257 (1948): the traditional Anglo-American distrust for secret trials has been variously ascribed to the notorious use of this practice by the Spanish Inquisition, to the excesses of the English Court of Star Chamber, and to the French monarchy's abuse of the lettre de cachet. Whatever other benefits the guarantee to an accused that his trial be conducted in public may confer upon our society, the guarantee has always been recognized as a safeguard against any attempt to employ our courts as instruments of persecution.
>
> Clearly the openness of the proceedings (the trial) provides other benefits as well (as a safeguard against oppression): it arguably improves the quality of testimony, it may induce unknown witnesses to come forward with relevant testimony, it may move all the trial participants to perform their duties conscientiously, and it gives the public the opportunity to observe the courts in the performance of their duties and to determine whether they are performing adequately.

What Makes a Trial "Public"?

Although an accused's guarantee to a public trial appears on the surface to be a clear and explicit right, it is not without complications. Just what constitutes a public trial is not defined either by the Sixth Amendment or by any of the laws of the states. The problems that arise are the following: What is a public trial? Who constitutes the public? How many persons must be in attendance to make a trial a public one? And since the right to a public trial is basically a right of the accused, may the right be waived, resulting in a private trial? Over time, partial answers to these questions have come from court decisions, but the answers to some questions have not been unanimous.

It is clear that a public trial is one that is not secret. The commonsense interpretation of public trial is one that the general public is free to attend. The doors of the courtroom are expected to be kept open. However, if no member of the public is in attendance, there is no requirement that a trial be stopped in order to satisfy the guarantee of a public trial. Under ordinary circumstances, the public includes persons of all classes, races, sexes, and ages.

There are times when it may not be necessary to permit every person to attend trial proceedings in order for a trial to be a public trial. It has been held that to satisfy the constitutional guarantee to a public trial, it is not necessary to provide a stadium large enough to accommodate all who might want to attend a particular trial. Yet a courtroom should be large enough to permit a reasonable number of the public to observe the trial proceedings. It also has been held that a judge may limit the number of persons attending a trial to the seating capacity of the courtroom facilities without violating the right of a public trial. A judge may eject any spectator or member of the public who becomes unruly and disrupts the trial proceedings. The judge may even clear the courtroom of all spectators if they become disruptive. However, that action does not permit locking the courtroom doors and prohibiting other members of the public who conduct themselves properly from attending the trial.

Public Right to Attend

The courts were far from unanimous in answering the question of public exclusion from the courtroom. The issue is whether or not the public may be excluded in any situation without violating the guarantee to a public trial. The question usually surfaced when a trial involved salacious testimony. Two cases that addressed the exclusion of the public from trial were *Richmond Newspapers, Inc.* v. *Virginia*[9] and *Globe Newspapers Co.* v. *Superior Court for the County of Norfolk.*[10]

Closing the Entire Trial.   The Court in the *Richmond Newspapers, Inc.* case recognized that the press and public right to access to criminal trials was based on the First Amendment of the U.S. Constitution and not on the Sixth Amendment right of a defendant to a public trial. The defendant was charged with murder and had been brought to trial on three prior occasions, each time ending in a mistrial. At the time of the fourth trial, the defense attorney requested that the trial be closed to the public because of prior interferences by spectators. The prosecution voiced no objection to a closed trial, and the judge granted the defense request to close the courtroom to the press and the public. This right was granted to judges by the Virginia statutes. Richmond Newspapers, Inc., filed an objection to being barred from the courtroom, and a hearing was held on the objection. The Virginia Appellate Court upheld the judge's ruling to close the courtroom. The case was appealed to the U.S. Supreme Court on the grounds that the First Amendment right to freedom of the press had been violated by barring the press from the trial. Since the defendant had requested that the trial be closed, the U.S. Supreme Court could not consider the case on the Sixth Amendment right to a public trial. Consideration of the case was then based on First Amendment rights. The Court pointed out that the First Amendment does not mention the right of public access to a criminal trial explicitly but held that the First Amendment is broad enough in scope to encompass certain rights not specifically mentioned, including the right of access to criminal trials. The Court stated the following:

> Underlying the First Amendment right of access to criminal trials [by the public] is the common understanding that a major purpose of that Amendment was to protect the free discussion of governmental affairs. By offering such protection, the First Amendment serves to ensure that the individual citizen can effectively participate in and contribute to our republican system of self-government. . . . Thus to the extent that the First Amendment embraces a right of access to crim-

inal trials, it is to ensure that this constitutionally protected discussion of governmental affairs is an informed one.

Closing a Portion of a Trial. *The Richmond Newspapers, Inc.* decision pertained to the closing of the entire trial to the press and public, which the Court held was in violation of the First Amendment. That decision still left the question of whether the press and public could be excluded from a portion of the trial when it may be in the best interest of fairness to make such an exclusion. The U.S. Supreme Court discussed this issue in the *Globe Newspapers Co.* case. In *Globe,* the Court stated the following:

> Although the right of access to criminal trials is of constitutional stature, it is not absolute. But circumstances under which the press and public can be barred from a criminal trial are limited; the State's justification in denying access must be a weighty one. Where, as in the present case, the State attempts to deny the right of access in order to inhibit the disclosure of sensitive information, it must be shown that the denial is necessitated by a compelling governmental interest, and is narrowly tailored to serve that interest.

In the *Globe Newspapers Co.* case, the defendant was charged with the rape of three teenage girls. The law of the state of Massachusetts required that under all circumstances, the press and public must be excluded during the testimony of a minor victim in a sex offense trial. In *Globe,* the Supreme Court focused on the reasons behind the mandatory exclusion. By passing this law, the state of Massachusetts tried to protect minor victims of sex crimes from further trauma and embarrassment and to encourage such victims to come forward and testify in a truthful and credible manner. The Court stated that it agreed with the state of Massachusetts's interest in safeguarding the physical and psychological well-being of a minor but that this interest did not justify a mandatory exclusion rule for all cases. The Court felt that the trial judge could determine case by case whether a closure is necessary to protect the welfare of a minor victim. Among factors to be weighed by the judge are the minor victim's age, psychological maturity and understanding, the nature of the crime, the desires of the victim, and the interests of the parents and relatives.

The Court further stated in the *Globe Newspapers Co.* case that the victims were already a matter of public record and that there was no showing that they would not testify in the presence of the public and press. Additionally, there was no showing that a closure of a trial during the testimony of a minor victim would result in others' coming forth and reporting such crimes. For these reasons, the Court held that the mandatory exclusion of the press and public in all such matters violated the First Amendment to the U.S. Constitution. The Globe decision would appear to allow a trial judge to exclude the press and public during the giving of testimony by a witness when it would be in the best interest of fairness to make that exclusion. The burden of showing that such an exclusion was in the best interest of all would be on the trial judge.

In a state court case, the trial judge's exclusion of the press and public during the testimony of the prosecution's principal witness, a sixteen-year-old pregnant girl, was upheld by the state appellate court. The exclusion order was based partly on concern for the welfare of the young expectant mother and her unborn child and partly on her own subjective fear of reprisal if she testified in public. In another state case, the exclusion of the press and public by the trial judge was upheld by the state appellate court during the testimony of an undercover police officer whose safety might have been endangered if his identity had been publicly exposed.

Public Exclusion from Pretrial Hearings.   The *Richmond Newspaper, Inc.* and the *Globe Newspapers Co.* cases are not to be confused with the case of *Gannett Co.* v. *DePasquale.*[11] In *Gannett,* the U.S. Supreme Court held that the press and public may be excluded from pretrial hearings, such as a pretrial hearing on the suppression of evidence or a preliminary hearing. *Gannett* upheld the exclusion of the press and public from pretrial hearings on the grounds that adverse prepublicity given to such hearings could pose a risk to the defendant and prevent a fair trial. The Court pointed out that there is a difference between the trial itself and pretrial hearings. The Court in the *Gannett* case stated the following:

> Publicity concerning pretrial suppression hearings such as the one involved in the present case poses special risks of unfairness. The whole purpose of such hearings is to screen out unreliable or illegally obtained evidence and ensure that this evidence does not become known to the jury. Publicity concerning the proceedings at a pretrial hearing, however, could influence the public opinion against a defendant and inform potential jurors of inculpatory information wholly inadmissible at the actual trial. This Court has long recognized that adverse publicity can endanger the ability of a defendant to receive a fair trial.

The *Gannett* decision does not demand that all pretrial hearings be closed to the press and public, but be done so only on request made to the trial judge or on the judge's own discretion.

Fair Trial versus Freedom of the Press

From our foregoing discussion, it may be concluded that the public is entitled to know that justice is taking place during a criminal trial. Therefore, the public, with some reservations, is permitted to attend trial proceedings. Since not all the public who may have an interest in a particular trial may be able to attend, the news media have assumed the responsibility of informing the public about what takes place during certain trials. The problem that arises is just how far the news media may go in obtaining information and reporting it to the public. The courts and the news media are often in conflict over the answer to this question. The news media rely upon the First Amendment to the U.S. Constitution for support in the uninhibited right to exercise their power in getting the news. This amendment provides, among other provisions, that "Congress shall make no law . . . abridging the freedom of speech, or of the press. . . .

When the courts attempt to curtail the media in obtaining news, the media allege violation of their rights under the First Amendment. The courts, on the other hand, hold that an accused is entitled to a fair trial by an impartial jury, and when the right is interfered with by the news media, they have exceeded their prerogative. Because of the right of the public to be informed of what takes place during criminal trials, the courts generally have permitted reporters to be present during criminal trials; and in many instances, special areas in courtrooms are set aside for reporters in order that they may have a vantage point to assist them in obtaining the news. With the advent of the camera, radio, and television, conflicts have arisen over whether this type of equipment should be permitted in the courtroom. It is conceded by the courts that when the gathering of news during trial proceedings becomes too disruptive or otherwise denies the defendant a fair trial by an impartial jury, some control must be exercised.

This viewpoint was emphasized by the U.S. Supreme Court in the *Estes* case. Estes was convicted in the state court in Texas on an extensive swindling charge. His case was taken to the U.S. Supreme Court on the grounds that, because of massive pretrial and trial publicity, he had been denied the right of due process of law as provided by the Fourteenth Amendment to the U.S. Constitution. The Supreme Court concluded that the defendant had been denied a fair trial because of the live radio and television coverage, and so the conviction was reversed. The Court set forth some pertinent arguments against permitting live news coverage of criminal trials; these arguments are still being presented by those opposing live coverage.

At the time the *Estes* case was heard by the U.S. Supreme Court, the attorneys representing the state of Texas contended that the television portions of the trial did not constitute a denial of due process, since there was no showing of prejudice of *Estes* resulting from the television coverage. The state also argued that the public has a right to know what goes on in the courts and that televising criminal trials would be enlightening to the public and promote greater respect for the courts. To this argument, the Court stated the following:

> It is true that the public has a right to be informed as to what occurs in its courts, but reporters of all media, including television, are always present if they wish to be and are plainly free to report whatever occurs in open court through their respective media. . . .
>
> As has been said, the chief function of our judicial machinery is to ascertain the truth. The use of television, however, cannot be said to contribute materially to this objective. Rather its use amounts to the injection of an irrelevant factor into court proceedings. In addition experience teaches that there are numerous situations in which it might cause actual unfairness, some so subtle as to defy detection by the accused or control by the judge. We enumerate some in summary:
>
> 1. The potential impact of television on the jurors is perhaps of the greatest significance. They are the nerve center of the fact-finding process. . . . From the moment the trial judge announces that a case will be televised it becomes *cause celebre.* The whole community, including prospective jurors, becomes interested in all the morbid details surrounding it. The approaching trial immediately assumes an important status in the public press and the accused is highly publicized, along with the offense with which he is charged. Every juror carries with him into the jury box these solemn facts and thus increase the chance of prejudice that is present in every criminal case. And we must remember that realistically it is only the notorious trial which will be broadcast, because of the necessity for paid sponsorship. The conscious or unconscious effect on the juror's judgment cannot be evaluated, but experience indicates that it is not only possible but highly probable that it will have a direct bearing on his vote as to guilt or innocence. Where pretrial publicity of all kinds has created intense public feeling which is aggravated by the telecasting or picturing of the trial, the televised jurors can not help but feel the pressures of knowing that friends and neighbors have their eyes upon them. If the community is hostile to an accused, a televised

juror, realizing that he must return to neighbors who saw the trial themselves, may well be led "not to hold the balance nice, clear, and true between the State and the accused. . . ."

2. The quality of the testimony in criminal trials will often be impaired. The impact upon a witness of the knowledge that he is being viewed by a vast audience is simply incalculable. Some may be demoralized and frightened, some cocky and given to overstatement; memories may falter, as with anyone speaking publicly, and accuracy of statement may be severely undermined. Embarrassment may impede the search for the truth, as may a natural tendency toward overdramatization. Furthermore, inquisitive strangers and "cranks" might approach witnesses on the street with jibes, advice or demands for explanation of testimony. There is little wonder that the defendant cannot "prove" the existence of such factors. Yet we all know from experience that they exist.

3. A major aspect of the problem is the additional responsibilities the presence of television places on the trial judge. His job is to make certain that the accused receives a fair trial. This most difficult task requires his undivided attention. Still, when television comes into the courtroom he must also supervise it. . . . In addition, laying physical interruptions aside, there is the ever-present distraction that the mere awareness of television's presence prompts. Judges are human beings also and are subject to the same psychological reactions as laymen. Telecasting is particularly bad where the judge is elected, as is the case in all save a half dozen of our States. The distractions inherent in broadcasting divert his attention from the task at hand—the fair trial of the accused.

But this is not all. There is the initial decision that must be made as to whether the use of television will be permitted. This is perhaps an even more crucial consideration. Our judges are high-minded men and women. But it is difficult to remain oblivious to the pressures that the news media can bring to bear on them both directly and through the shaping of public opinion. Moreover, where one judge in a district or even in a State permits telecasting, the requirement that the others do the same is almost mandatory. Especially is this true where the judge is selected at the ballot box.

Finally, we cannot ignore the impact of courtroom television on the defendant. Its presence is a form of mental—if not physical—harassment. . . . A defendant on trial for a specific crime is entitled to his day in court, not in a stadium, or a city or nationwide arena. The heightened public clamor resulting from radio and television coverage will inevitably result in prejudice.

After the *Estes* decision, courts for a time generally prohibited live coverage of criminal trials. But the news media eventually renewed their pressure to permit live coverage of trials. Many judges and attorneys have resisted this pressure principally on the grounds presented in the *Estes* decision. Regardless of these strong arguments against live coverage, more and more courts are permitting live coverage of trials. In 1996, the nation watched the televised trial of O. J. Simpson. As in the results of coverage of that trial, there is a serious concern of many in the justice system about the effects of this type of coverage, not only from the standpoint of the defendant but also concerning the safety of witnesses. Great strides have been made to protect the victims of rape cases from embarrassment during trials, in order to encourage victims to come forth and report such offenses. It is believed that with live coverage of trials, many victims of all types of crimes will refuse to report offenses rather than face embarrassment and possible harm from testifying before television cameras.

Gag Orders

Courts throughout the nation are aware that the news media are entitled to report events occurring during a trial as well as crimes taking place, and no effort is made to suppress this type of reporting. However, the courts have periodically issued orders limiting the information that may be given to the press. Referred to as gag orders, they are issued to prevent extensive pretrial or trial publicity that could deny a defendant a fair trial because of the resulting difficulty in selecting and maintaining an impartial jury. But the news media have strongly protested the issuance of gag orders on the grounds that such orders violate the First Amendment. Thus, balancing the right of a defendant to a fair trial with the right of the freedom of the press has continually plagued the courts. In *Sheppard* v. *Maxwell*,[12] the U.S. Supreme Court criticized the trial judge for the failure to restrain pretrial publicity. The facts of that case reveal that Dr. Sheppard was accused of killing his wife. Prior to the trial, there were numerous newspaper stories concerning the questioning of the accused as well as articles about his personal life and love affairs. The jury list was published, and many of the prospective jurors received telephone calls concerning the case. Inaccurate news releases were given to the press by the police. The judge, who was coming up for election, permitted extensive live news coverage of the trial. Sheppard was convicted and eventually appealed the case to the U.S. Supreme Court on the grounds that due process of law had been denied during the trial. The U.S. Supreme Court reversed the conviction because it felt that pretrial publicity and extensive live coverage of the trial had kept the defendant from receiving a fair trial. The Court stated

> [that the trial judge] should have made some effort to control the release of leads, information, and gossip to the press by police officers, witnesses, and the counsel for both sides. . . . The courts must take steps by law and regulation that will protect their processes from prejudicial outside interference. Neither prosecutors, counsel for defense, the accused, witnesses, court staff nor enforcement officers coming under the jurisdiction of the court should be permitted to frustrate its function.

Although the Court in the *Sheppard* case stated that trial judges "have the duty of so insulating the trial from publicity as to insure its fairness," the Court did not set down any fixed rules to guide the trial judges and others on what could and could not be printed. But acting upon the suggestion of the *Sheppard* case, trial judges have occasionally issued gag orders. In *Nebraska Press Association* v. *Stewart*,[13] the U.S. Supreme Court discouraged, but did not rule out, the use of gag orders. The Court stated, "This Court has frequently denied that the First Amendment rights are absolute and has consistently rejected the proposition that a prior restraint can never be employed." The Court indicated that such prior restraint should be used only when absolutely necessary to assure a fair trial. As stated by one of the justices, before a prior restraint is to be used there must be "a showing that (i) there is a clear threat to the fairness of trial, (ii) such a threat is posed by the actual publicity to be restrained, and (iii) no less restrictive alternatives are available."

The U.S. Supreme Court in this case felt that the trial judge had overstepped his rights in issuing the gag order. He prohibited the publication of information brought out in an open preliminary hearing that the public was free to attend. The Court did not rule out the possible use of a gag order to prevent pretrial publicity concerning information not otherwise known that would prevent a fair trial from being obtained when other less restrictive measures were unavailable. But the Court did not indicate what less restrictive measures might be substituted for the gag order.

One less restrictive measure suggested for use instead of issuing a gag order was the granting of a change in venue. But many crimes committed receive such extensive publicity that a change in venue would accomplish little. Under these circumstances, judges may still issue gag orders to prevent undue pretrial publicity and will undoubtedly receive the sanction of the U.S. Supreme Court.

Even before the *Sheppard* decision, law enforcement officers and prosecuting attorneys restricted the release of certain information to the news media. This restrictive action, taken even without a gag order, was the result of criticism directed at law enforcement officers in *Rideau* v. *Louisiana.*[14] The U.S. Supreme Court in that case was critical of the law enforcement agencies involved in permitting the televising of a confession while it was being given by the defendant. The facts of the case reveal the following: Some two months before petitioner's (Rideau's) trial began and some two weeks before he was arraigned on charges of robbery, kidnapping, and murder, a local TV station broadcast three different times in the space of two days a twenty-minute film of petitioner, flanked by the sheriff and two state troopers, admitting in detail the commission of the various offenses in response to leading questions by the sheriff.

Rideau was convicted of the charges against him, and his case was taken to the U.S. Supreme Court on the grounds that he had been denied due process of law when a change of venue request was denied by the trial judge. The Supreme Court reversed the conviction, stating the following:

> . . . we hold that it was a denial of due process of law to refuse the request for a change of venue, after the people of the Parish had been exposed repeatedly and in depth to the spectacle of Rideau personally confessing in detail to the crimes with which he was later to be charged. For anyone who has ever watched television the conclusion cannot be avoided that this spectacle, to the tens of thousands of people who saw and heard it, in a very real sense was Rideau's trial—at which he pleaded guilty to murder. Any subsequent court proceedings in a community so pervasively exposed to such a spectacle could be but a hollow formality.

After the *Rideau* decision, many law enforcement officers and prosecuting attorneys decided it was generally best not to reveal to the press whether an accused person has confessed or to comment on the results of any tests that may have been given. Some officers will not reveal any criminal record of an accused. However, not all are in agreement with this viewpoint, since some contend that if an accused has been previously convicted, the court record of the conviction is a public record, and that the news media should be able to obtain this information. But self-imposed restrictions by officers and prosecutors may help ensure a fair trial. Judges often impose further restrictions during a trial to prevent jurors from being influenced by comments made in the news media.

Capstone Case ———————————————————

J.E.B. v. *EX REL. T.B.*
114 S.Ct. 1419, 128 L.Ed.2d 89 (1994)

Justice Blackmun delivered the opinion of the Court.

On behalf of relator T.B., the mother of a minor child, respondent State of Alabama filed a complaint for paternity and child support against petitioner J.E.B. in the District Court of Jackson County, Alabama. On October 21, 1991, the matter was called for trial and jury selection began. The trial court assembled a panel of 36 potential jurors, 12 males and 24 females. After the court excused three jurors for cause, only 10 of the remaining 33 jurors were male. The State then used 9 of its 10 peremptory strikes to remove male jurors; petitioner used all but one of his strikes to remove female jurors. As a result, all the selected jurors were female.

Before the jury was empaneled, petitioner objected to the State's peremptory challenges on the ground that they were exercised against male jurors solely on the basis of gender, in violation of the Equal Protection Clause of the Fourteenth Amendment. . . . The court rejected petitioner's claim and empaneled the all female jury. The jury found petitioner to be the father of the child and the court entered an order directing him to pay child support. On post-judgment motion, the court reaffirmed its ruling that Batson does not extend to gender-based peremptory challenges.

We granted certiorari to resolve a question that has created a conflict of authority—whether the Equal Protection Clause forbids peremptory challenges on the basis of gender as well as on the basis of race. Today we reaffirm what, by now, should be axiomatic: Intentional discrimination on the basis of gender by state actors violates the Equal Protection Clause, particularly where, as here, the discrimination serves to ratify and perpetuate invidious, archaic, and overbroad stereotypes about the relative abilities of men and women.

Discrimination on the basis of gender in the exercise of peremptory challenges is a relatively recent phenomenon. Gender-based peremptory strikes were hardly practicable for most of our country's existence, since, until the 19th century, women were completely excluded from jury service. So well-entrenched was this exclusion of women that in 1880 this Court, while finding that the exclusion of African-American men from juries violated the Fourteenth Amendment, expressed no doubt that a State "may confine the selection of jurors to males." *Strauder* v. *West Virginia*, 100 U.S. 303.

Many States continued to exclude women from jury service well into the present century, despite the fact that women attained suffrage upon ratification of the Nineteenth Amendment in 1920. States that did permit women to serve on juries often erected other barriers, such as registration requirements and automatic exemptions, designed to deter women from exercising their right to jury service. The prohibition of women on juries was derived from the English common law which, according to Blackstone, rightfully excluded women from juries under "the doctrine of propter defectum sexus, literally, the 'defect of sex.'" In this country, supporters of the exclusion of women from juries tended to couch their objections in terms of the ostensible need to protect women from the ugliness and depravity of trials. Women were thought to be too fragile and virginal to withstand the polluted courtroom atmosphere. . . .

Taylor v. *Louisiana* . . . relied on Sixth Amendment principles, but the opinion's approach is consistent with the heightened equal protection scrutiny afforded gender-based classifications. Since *Reed* v. *Reed*, 404 U.S. 71(1971), this Court consistently has subjected gender-based classifications to heightened scrutiny in recognition of the real danger that government policies that professedly are based on reasonable considerations in fact may be reflective of "archaic and over broad" generalizations about gender, or based on "outdated misconceptions concerning the role of females in the home rather than in the 'marketplace and world of ideas.'"

Despite the heightened scrutiny afforded distinctions based on gender, respondent argues that gender discrimination in the selection of the petit jury should be permitted, though discrimination on the basis of race is not. Respondent suggests that "gender discrimination in this country . . . has never reached the level of discrimination" against African-Americans, and therefore gender discrimination, unlike racial discrimination, is tolerable in the courtroom. While the prejudicial attitudes toward women in this country have not been identical to those held toward racial minorities, the similarities between the experiences of racial minorities and women, in some contexts, "overpower those differences." As a plurality of this Court observed in *Frontiero* v. *Richardson*, 411 U.S. 677 (1973):

> Throughout much of the 19th century the position of women in our society was, in many respects, comparable to that of blacks under the pre-Civil War slave codes. Neither slaves nor women could hold office, serve on juries, or bring suit in their own names, and married women traditionally were denied the legal capacity to hold or convey property or to serve as legal guardians of their own children. . . . And although blacks were guaranteed the right to vote in 1870, women were denied even that right—which is itself preservative of other basic civil and political rights—until adoption of the Nineteenth Amendment half a century later.

Certainly, with respect to jury service, African-Americans and women share a history of total exclusion, a history which came to an end for women many years after the embarrassing chapter in our history came to an end for African-Americans.

We need not determine, however, whether women or racial minorities have suffered more at the hands of discriminatory state actors during the decades of our Nation's history. It is necessary only to acknowledge that "our Nation has had a long and unfortunate history of sex discrimination," a history which warrants the heightened scrutiny we afford all gender-based classifications today. Under our equal protection jurisprudence, gender-based classifications require an exceedingly persuasive justification" in order to survive constitutional scrutiny. Thus, the only question is whether discrimination on the basis of gender in jury selection substantially furthers the State's legitimate interest in achieving a fair and impartial trial. In making this assessment, we do not weigh the value of peremptory challenges as an institution against our asserted commitment to eradicate invidious discrimination from the courtroom. Instead, we consider whether peremptory challenges based on gender stereotypes provide substantial aid to a litigant's effort to secure a fair and impartial jury. Far from proffering an exceptionally persuasive justification for its gender-based peremptory challenges, respondent maintains that its decision to strike virtually all the males from the jury in this case "may reasonably have been based upon the perception, supported by history, that men otherwise totally qualified to serve upon a jury might be more sympathetic and receptive to the arguments of a man alleged in a paternity action to be the father of an out-of-wedlock child, while women equally qualified to serve upon a jury might be more sympathetic and receptive to the arguments of the complaining witness who bore the child."

We shall not accept as a defense to gender-based peremptory challenges "the very stereotype the law condemns." Respondent's rationale, not unlike those regularly expressed for gender-based strikes, is reminiscent of the arguments advanced to justify the total exclusion of women from juries. Respondent offers virtually no support for the conclusion that gender alone is an accurate predictor of juror's attitudes; yet it urges this Court to condone the same stereotypes that have justified the wholesale exclusion of women from juries and the ballot box. Respondent seems to assume that gross generalizations that would be deemed impermissible if made on the basis of race are somehow permissible when made on the basis of gender.

Discrimination in jury selection, whether based on race or on gender, causes harm to the litigants, the community, and the individual jurors who are wrongfully excluded from participation in the judicial process. The litigants are harmed by the risk that the prejudice which motivated the discriminatory selection of the jury will infect the entire proceedings. The community is harmed by the State's participation in the perpetuation of invidious group stereotypes and the inevitable loss of confidence in our judicial system that state-sanctioned discrimination in the courtroom engenders. When state actors exercise peremptory challenges in reliance on gender stereotypes, they ratify and reinforce prejudicial views of the relative abilities of men and women. Because these stereotypes have wreaked injustice in so many other spheres of our country's public life, active discrimination by litigants on the basis of gender during jury selection "invites cynicism respecting the jury's neutrality and its obligation to adhere to the law." The potential for cynicism is particularly acute in cases where gender-related issues are prominent, such as cases involving rape, sexual harassment, or paternity. Discriminatory use of peremptory challenges may create the impression that the judicial system has acquiesced in suppressing full participation by one gender or that the "deck has been stacked" in favor of one side.

In recent cases we have emphasized that individual jurors themselves have a right to nondiscriminatory jury selection procedures. Contrary to respondent's suggestion, this right extends to both men and women. All persons, when granted the opportunity to serve on a jury, have the right not to be excluded summarily because of discriminatory and stereotypical presumptions that reflect and reinforce patterns of historical discrimination. Striking individual jurors on the assumption that they hold particular views simply because of their gender is "practically a brand upon them, affixed by law, an assertion of their inferiority." It denigrates the dignity of the excluded juror; and, for a woman, reinvokes a history of exclusion from political participation. The message it sends to all those in the courtroom, and all those who may later learn of the discriminatory act, is that certain individuals, for no reason other than gender, are presumed unqualified by state actors to decide important questions upon which reasonable persons could disagree.

Our conclusion that litigants may not strike potential jurors solely on the basis of gender does not imply the elimination of all peremptory challenges. Neither does it conflict with a State's legitimate interest in using such challenges in its effort to secure a fair and impartial jury. Parties still may remove jurors whom they feel might be less acceptable than others on the panel; gender simply may not serve as a proxy for bias. Parties may also exercise their peremptory challenges to remove from the venire any group or class of individuals normally subject to "rational basis" review. Even strikes based on characteristics that are disproportionately associated with one gender could be appropriate, absent a showing of pretext. . . .

Failing to provide jurors the same protection against gender discrimination as race discrimination could frustrate the purpose of Batson itself. Because gender and race are overlapping categories, gender can be used as a pretext for racial discrimination. Allowing parties to remove racial minorities from the jury not because of their race, but because of their gender, contravenes well-established equal protection principles and could insulate effectively racial discrimination from judicial scrutiny.

Justice O'Connor, concurring.

I agree with the Court that the Equal Protection Clause prohibits the government from excluding a person from jury service on account of that person's gender. . . . I therefore join the Court's opinion in this case. But today's important blow against gender discrimination is not costless. I write separately to discuss some of these costs, and to express my belief that today's holding should be limited to the government's use of gender-based peremptory strikes.

Batson v. *Kentucky* itself was a significant intrusion into the jury selection process. Batson mini-hearings are now routine in state and federal trial courts, and Batson appeals have proliferated as well. Demographics indicate that today's holding may have an even greater impact than did Batson itself. In further constitutionalizing jury selection procedures, the Court increases the number of cases in which jury selection—once a sideshow—will become part of the main event.

. . . Our belief that experienced lawyers will often correctly intuit which jurors are likely to be the least sympathetic, and our understanding that the lawyer will often be unable to explain the intuition, are the very reason we cherish the peremptory challenge. But, as we add, layer by layer, additional constitutional restraints on the use of the peremptory, we force lawyers to articulate what we know is often inarticulable.

In so doing we make the peremptory challenge less discretionary and more like a challenge for cause. We also increase the possibility that biased jurors will be allowed onto the jury, because sometimes a lawyer will be unable to provide an acceptable gender-neutral explanation even though the lawyer is in fact correct that the juror is unsympathetic. Similarly, in jurisdictions where lawyers exercise their strikes in open court, lawyers may be deterred from using their peremptories, out of the fear that if they are unable to justify the strike the court will seat a juror who knows that the striking party thought him unfit. Because I believe the peremptory remains an important litigator's tool and a fundamental part of the process of selecting impartial juries, our increasing limitation of it gives me pause.

Nor is the value of the peremptory challenge to the litigant diminished when the peremptory is exercised in a gender-based manner. We know that like race, gender matters. A plethora of studies make clear that in rape cases, for example, female jurors are somewhat more likely to vote to convict than male jurors. Moreover, though there have been no similarly definitive studies regarding, for example, sexual harassment, child custody, or spousal or child abuse, one need not be a sexist to share the intuition that in certain cases a person's gender and resulting life experience will be relevant to his or her view of the case.

Today's decision severely limits a litigant's ability to act on this intuition, for the import of our holding is that any correlation between a juror's gender and attitudes is irrelevant as a matter of constitutional law. But to say that gender makes no difference as a matter of law is not to say that gender makes no difference as a matter of fact. . . . In extending Batson to gender we have added an additional burden to the state and federal trial process, taken a step closer to eliminating the peremptory challenge, and diminished the ability of litigants to act on sometimes accurate gender-based assumptions about juror attitudes. . . .

Accordingly, I adhere to my position that the Equal Protection Clause does not limit the exercise of peremptory challenges by private civil litigants and criminal defendants. This case itself presents no state action dilemma, for here the State of Alabama itself filed the paternity suit on behalf of petitioner. But what of the next case? Will we, in the name of fighting gender discrimination, hold that the battered wife—on trial for wounding her abusive husband—is a state actor? Will we preclude her from using her peremptory challenges to ensure that the jury of her peers contains as many women members as possible? I assume we will, but I hope we will not.

Chief Justice Rehnquist, dissenting.

Unlike the Court, I think the State has shown that jury strikes on the basis of gender "substantially further" the State's legitimate interest in achieving a fair and impartial trial through the venerable practice of peremptory challenges. The two sexes differ, both biologically and, to a diminishing extent, in experience. It is not merely "stereotyping" to say that these differences may produce a difference in outlook which is brought to the jury room. Accordingly, use of peremptory challenges on the basis of sex is generally not the sort of derogatory and invidious act which peremptory challenges directed at black jurors may be.

Justice Scalia, with whom the Chief Justice and Justice Thomas join, dissenting.

The core of the Court's reasoning is that peremptory challenges on the basis of any group characteristic subject to heightened scrutiny are inconsistent with the guarantee of the Equal Protection Clause. That conclusion can be reached only by focusing unrealistically upon individual exercises of the peremptory challenge, and ignoring the totality of the practice. Since all groups are subject to the peremptory challenge (and will be made the object of it, depending upon the nature of the particular case) it is hard to see how any group is denied equal protection. That explains why peremptory challenges coexisted with the Equal Protection Clause for 120 years. This case is a perfect example of how the system as a whole is even-handed. While the only claim before the Court is petitioner's complaint that the prosecutor struck male jurors, for every man struck by the government, petitioner's own lawyer struck a woman. To say that men were singled out for discriminatory treatment in this process is preposterous.

The situation would be different if both sides systematically struck individuals of one group, so that the strikes evinced group-based animus and served as a proxy for segregated venire lists. The pattern here, however, displays not a systemic sex-based animus but each side's desire to get a jury favorably disposed to its case. That is why the Court's characterization of respondent's argument as "reminiscent of the arguments advanced to justify the total exclusion of women from juries" is patently false. Women were categorically excluded from juries because of doubt that they were competent; women are stricken from juries by peremptory challenge because of doubt that they were well disposed to the striking party's case. . . .

Even if the line of our later cases guaranteed by today's decision limits the theoretically boundless Batson principle to race, sex, and perhaps other classifications subject to heightened scrutiny (which presumably would include religious belief), much damage has been done. It has been done, first and foremost, to the peremptory challenge system, which loses its whole character when (in order to defend against "impermissible stereotyping" claims) "reasons" for strikes must be given. And make no mistake about it: there really is no substitute for the peremptory. Voir dire (though it can be expected to expand as a consequence of today's decision) cannot fill the gap. The biases that go along with group characteristics tend to be biases that the juror himself does not perceive, so that it is no use asking about them. It is fruitless to inquire of a male juror whether he harbors any subliminal prejudice in favor of unwed fathers. . . .

REVIEW QUESTIONS

1. What amendment of the U.S. Constitution embodies the right to trial by jury?
2. List three advantages to an accused of a trial by jury over a court trial.
3. Why would an accused waive a trial by jury?
4. What reasons has the U.S. Supreme Court set forth in prohibiting the accused from demanding and receiving a court trial?
5. Some jurisdictions hold that an accused may be denied a jury trial on petty offenses. What criteria has the U.S. Supreme Court set forth in determining what qualifies as a petty offense?
6. What U.S. Supreme Court decision upheld that a trial by a jury comprising fewer than twelve persons was not a denial of the Due Process Clause of the Fourteenth Amendment?
7. What is considered a public trial?
8. Why is the accused guaranteed a public trial?
9. Must a demand by an accused for a private trial be granted?
10. Why did the *Richmond* case base the public right to access to criminal trials on the First Amendment of the U.S. Constitution instead of the Sixth Amendment?
11. In what way may a fair trial and the freedom of the press be in conflict?
12. What is meant by a gag order, and why may one be placed in effect?

LOCAL PROCEDURE

1. May a defendant waive a jury trial in your state? If so, are there any restrictions on the type of offense for which the jury trial may be waived?
2. If a jury trial may be waived, who must give consent to the waiver?
3. Can a jury comprise fewer than twelve persons in your state?
4. May a petty offense charge be tried without a jury in your state?

ENDNOTES

1. 281 U.S. 276.
2. 391 U.S. 145 (1968).

3. 380 U.S. 24 (1965).
4. 300 U.S. 617 (1937).
5. See *Duncan* v. *Louisiana,* 391 U.S. 145 (1968); *Cheff* v. *Schnackenberg,* 384 U.S. 373 (1966); and *Frank* v. *United States,* 395 U.S. 147 (1969).
6. 399 U.S. 78 (1970).
7. 55 L.Ed. 2d. 234 (1978).
8. 381 U.S. 532 (1965).
9. 448 U.S. 555 (1980).
10. 457 U.S. 596 (1982).
11. 443 U.S. 368 (1979).
12. 384 U.S. 333 (1966).
13. 427 U.S. 539 (1976).
14. 373 U.S. 723 (1963).

CHAPTER 8

Confrontation and Assistance of Counsel

> Once I decide to take a case, I have only one agenda: I want to win. I will try, by every fair and legal means, to get my client off—without regards to the consequences.
>
> —Alan Dershowitz, *The Best Defense*

THE PRESENCE OF THE DEFENDANT AT A TRIAL

In some countries, an accused person may be tried and convicted of a crime without being present and without knowing that a trial has taken place. This procedure is referred to as *conviction in absentia.* To prevent such action from taking place in the United States, the Sixth Amendment of the U.S. Constitution, as well as the laws of all the states, includes a provision entitling an accused to be confronted with the witnesses for the prosecution. This guarantee has a dual purpose. It guarantees that witnesses against a defendant must appear in person in court to present their facts, and it provides a defendant with the right to be present during every phase of trial proceedings.

For many years, the interpretation of the right of an accused to be present during a trial was so rigid that, if a defendant was not present, a trial had to be halted until he or she was in attendance. Knowing the court's rigid interpretation of this right, defendants occasionally took advantage by being so disruptive that the trial could not continue with their presence or by failing to appear in court while out on bail, thus preventing the trial from taking place. Many states included provisions in their statutes stating that in felony cases, the defendant had to be present during all phases of the trial. But as time passed, some courts relaxed the rule requiring the defendant's presence when he or she voluntarily was absent.

Law in Practice   **Motion Not to Be Tried in Jail Clothes or Restraints**

To the Honorable judge of Said Court:

NOW COMES the Defendant in the above-entitled and numbered cause by and through his attorney of record and files this Motion not to be tried before the Jury in jail clothes and restraints and in support thereof would show the following:

I.

On Defendant's being placed in confinement, his regular civilian type clothing was taken from him and he has been compelled to be dressed in identifiable prison clothing. When Defendant is brought from the Prison to Court, he will be handcuffed and shackled or be required to wear other such restraints.

II.

Compelling the Defendant to be tried before a jury in such distinctive, identifiable attire and restraints will affect the jury's judgment and violates the Defendant's constitutional right of presumption of innocence.

WHEREFORE, PREMISES CONSIDERED, Defendant prays that the Court order the Sheriff or Warden not to bring the Defendant to the courtroom for the purpose of trial or into the presence of any member of the jury panel attired in a prison uniform or in restraints of any kind. Respectfully submitted,

Respectfully submitted,
STATE COUNSEL FOR OFFENDERS

_____

Attorney for Defendant

Disruption of the Trial

A separate issue is raised when the defendant is present and demands to remain present but becomes so disruptive that the trial cannot take place. This question was answered in the case of *Illinois* v. *Allen*,[1] in which the U.S. Supreme Court held that a defendant had waived his right to be present at his trial by his own disruptive action.

The facts of the *Allen* case state that Allen was convicted of armed robbery by an Illinois jury and was sentenced to serve ten to thirty years in the Illinois State Penitentiary. During the trial, Allen insisted upon acting as his own attorney, and when the judge appointed an attorney for him, Allen began to argue with the judge in an abusive and a disrespectful manner. The judge ordered Allen to remain silent and to let his attorney speak for him. Despite this admonition, the defendant continued to talk and argue with the judge, proclaiming that the appointed attorney was not going to act for him. Allen also informed the judge that "when I go out for lunchtime, you're going to be a corpse here." At the same time, Allen tore up his attorney's file and threw the pieces on the floor. The judge informed Allen that he would be removed from the courtroom if another disruption occurred. This warning had no effect upon Allen, and the judge had him removed from the courtroom. The jury was selected in his absence. Later in the day, Allen was permitted to return to the courtroom but became disruptive again, forcing the judge to remove him a second time. Allen remained out of the courtroom during most of the prosecution's presentation of the case but, on promising that he would conduct himself properly, was permitted to return and remain in the courtroom during the presentation by his attorney.

The *Allen* conviction was upheld by the Illinois appellate courts but was reversed by the U.S. District Court of Appeals. This court held that Allen's removal from the courtroom was a denial of his guarantee of confrontation as provided by the Sixth Amendment to the U.S. Constitution. The court stated that Allen could have been bound and gagged to prevent him from being disruptive and that the judge erred in removing Allen from the courtroom.

The case was then taken to the U.S. Supreme Court to determine whether Allen was denied due process of law because his Sixth Amendment guarantee of confrontation had been violated. The Supreme Court upheld the conviction and stated that the Sixth Amendment guarantee of confrontation could be "lost by consent or at times even by misconduct." The Court further stated the following:

> Although mindful that courts must indulge every reasonable presumption against the loss of constitutional rights . . . we explicitly hold today that a defendant can lose his right to be present at trial if, after he had been warned by the judge that he will be removed if he continues his disruptive behavior, he nevertheless insists on conducting himself in a manner so disorderly, disruptive, and disrespectful of the court that his trial cannot be carried on with him in the courtroom. Once lost, the right to be present can, of course, be reclaimed as soon as the defendant is willing to conduct himself consistently with the decorum and respect inherent in the concept of courts and judicial proceedings.
>
> It is essential to the proper administration of criminal justice that dignity, order, and decorum be the hallmarks of all court proceedings in our country. The flagrant disregard in the courtroom of elementary standards of proper conduct should not and cannot be tolerated. We believe trial judges confronted with disruptive, contumacious, stubbornly defiant defendants must be given sufficient discretion to meet the circumstances of each case. No one formula for maintaining the appropriate courtroom atmosphere will be best in all situations. We think there are at least three constitutionally permissible ways for a trial judge to handle an obstreperous defendant like Allen: (1) bind and gag him, thereby keeping him present; (2) cite him for contempt; (3) take him out of the courtroom until he promises to conduct himself property.
>
> Trying a defendant for a crime while he sits bound and gagged before the judge and jury would to an extent comply with that part of the Sixth Amendment's purposes that accords the defendant an opportunity to confront the witnesses at the trial. But even to contemplate such a technique, much less see it, arouses a feeling that no person should be tried while shackled and gagged except as a last resort. Not only is it possible that the sight of shackles and gags might have a significant effect on the jury's feelings about the defendant, but the use of this technique is itself something of an affront to the very dignity and decorum of judicial proceedings that the judge is seeking to uphold. . . . However, in some situations which we need not attempt to foresee, binding and gagging might possibly be the fairest and most reasonable way to handle a defendant who acts as Allen did here.

In citing the unruly defendant for contempt of court, the Court in the Allen case stated:

> It is true that citing or threatening to cite a contumacious defendant for criminal contempt might in itself be sufficient to make a defendant stop interrupting a trial. If so, the problem would be solved easily, and the defendant could remain

in the courtroom. Of course, if the defendant is determined to prevent any trial, then a court in attempting to try the defendant for contempt is still confronted with the identical dilemma that the Illinois court faced in this case. Any criminal contempt has obvious limitations as a sanction when the defendant is charged with a crime so serious that a very severe sentence such as death or life imprisonment is likely to be imposed. In such a case the defendant might not be affected by a mere contempt sentence when he ultimately faces a far more serious sanction. Nevertheless, the contempt remedy should be borne in mind by a judge in the circumstances of this case.

Another aspect of the contempt remedy is the judge's power, when exercised consistently with state and federal law, to imprison an unruly defendant such as Allen for civil contempt and discontinue the trial until such time as the defendant promises to behave himself. This procedure is consistent with the defendant's right to be present at trial, and yet it avoids the serious shortcomings of the use of shackles and gags. It must be recognized, however, that a defendant might conceivably, as a matter of calculated strategy, elect to spend a prolonged period in confinement for contempt in the hope that adverse witnesses might be unavailable after a lapse of time. A court must guard against allowing a defendant to profit from his own wrong in this way.

The trial court in this case decided under the circumstances to remove the defendant from the courtroom and to continue his trial in his absence until and unless he promised to conduct himself in a manner befitting an American courtroom. As we said earlier, we find nothing unconstitutional about this procedure. Allen's behavior was clearly of such an extreme and aggravated nature as to justify either his removal from the courtroom or his total physical restraint. Prior to his removal he was repeatedly warned by the trial judge that he would be removed from the courtroom if he persisted in his unruly conduct, and, as Judge Hastings observed in his dissenting opinion, the record demonstrates that Allen would not have been at all dissuaded by the trial judge's use of his criminal contempt powers. Allen was constantly informed that he could return to the trial when he would agree to conduct himself in an orderly manner. Under these circumstances we hold that Allen lost his right guaranteed by the Sixth and Fourteenth Amendments to be present throughout his trial.

It is not pleasant to hold that the respondent Allen was properly banished from the court for a part of his own trial. But our courts, palladiums of liberty as they are, cannot be treated disrespectfully with impunity. Nor can the accused be permitted by his disruptive conduct indefinitely to avoid being tried on the charges brought against him. It would degrade our country and our judicial system to permit our courts to be bullied, insulted, and humiliated and their orderly progress thwarted and obstructed by defendants brought before them charged with crimes.

Voluntary Absence from Trial

The *Allen* decision definitely established that a trial could take place in the absence of a defendant when he or she was so disruptive that his or her removal from the courtroom became necessary. This decision also provided that a defendant who voluntarily absented himself or herself waived all right to be present. Even before the *Allen* decision, the courts were beginning to accept that if a defendant was voluntarily absent from his or her trial, the trial could proceed in his or her absence. This viewpoint was expressed in the case of *Cureton* v. *United States*.[2] The Court concluded that "if a defendant at liberty remains away during his trial the court may proceed provided it is clearly established that his absence is voluntary. He must be aware of the processes taking place, of his right and of his obligation to be present, and he must have no sound reason for remaining away." This viewpoint is sometimes referred to as the *Cureton* test. In other words, the defendant must have "knowingly and voluntarily absented himself."

As a result of the *Allen* decision and the viewpoint expressed in the *Cureton* case, many states have passed provisions similar to that of the *Federal Rules of Criminal Procedure,* which provides that "in prosecutions for offenses, not punishable by death, the defendant's voluntary absence after the trial has been commenced in his presence shall not prevent continuing the trial to and including the return of the verdict." The federal rule, as well as the provisions of many states, holds that the trial may continue in the absence of the defendant if the trial was commenced in his or her presence. Under these circumstances, the trial cannot commence unless the defendant is present. After the trial date is set, a defendant out on bail could keep the trial from taking place merely by not showing up for the trial. Of course, the judge could issue a bench warrant for the defendant's arrest, but it could take time to locate the defendant, thus delaying the trial. To overcome this problem, several states have provisions stating that a trial may commence when the defendant, knowing that the case is set for trial, voluntarily fails to appear on that date.

In those states requiring a trial to begin in the defendant's presence, for it to continue if the accused is voluntarily absent, the court must establish that the trial actually began while the defendant was present. Remember that a jury trial begins once the jury is sworn, and a court trial begins when the first witness is sworn. In one case, the defendant was present during the selection of eleven jurors before court was adjourned for the day. The following day the defendant failed to appear for the trial. The judge concluded that the defendant had voluntarily absented himself. Over the objections of the defense attorney, the judge permitted a twelfth juror to be selected, and the trial continued to the verdict stage in the absence of the defendant. The defendant was convicted, and he appealed his conviction on the grounds that he had been denied due process. The conviction was reversed since the law of the particular state provided that a trial could continue only if commenced in the presence of the defendant. Since the jury had not been selected and sworn in the presence of the defendant, the trial had not begun.

Even in those states that hold that a trial may continue only if it began in the presence of the defendant, this rule usually refers to felony charges. In a misdemeanor case, most states provide that if a defendant voluntarily fails to appear at the time the case is set for trial or is voluntarily absent during the course of the trial, the judge may proceed when the defendant has full knowledge that the trial was to be held. In most jurisdictions, whether the charge is a felony or misdemeanor, it is not necessary to advise the defendant that this action will take place in the event of voluntary absence.

The problem created by these rules is establishing that the defendant knowingly and voluntarily absented himself or herself from the trial. Establishing this could take time, and the judge would have to delay the progress of the trial until this could be determined. The delay might be only a few hours, but it could take several days. If the court cannot determine satisfactorily whether the defendant was absent knowingly and voluntarily, the judge must declare a mistrial or delay the present trial until the defendant can be located and arrested on a bench warrant. If it cannot be determined that the defendant was absent without cause and if a conviction results, a new trial must be granted unless a satisfactory reason for absence is given. Thus, the courts are cautious in continuing a trial in the absence of a defendant.

The Sixth Amendment provision that "an accused shall enjoy the right . . . to be confronted with the witnesses against him" has been interpreted to mean not only the right to be present during the trial against him or her but the right of a face-to-face confrontation with the witnesses as held by the U.S. Supreme Court in the case of *Coy* v. *Iowa*.[3] The facts of the case reflect that the accused was charged with the sexual assault of two thirteen-year-old girls. In accordance with an Iowa State statute, a screen was placed between the accused and the girls during their testimony. The purpose of the statute was to protect young victims of sexual assault from the "fear and trauma of testifying in front of the accused" by placing a screen between the victim and the accused. The screen in this case was placed in such a way that the girls could be observed by the judge and the jury during their testimony. They could also be dimly seen by the accused, but the girls could not see the accused.

The accused was convicted of the assault, and he appealed his conviction to the U.S. Supreme Court on the grounds that his Sixth Amendment right of confrontation had been violated, since he had not been allowed the right to a face-to-face confrontation with the witnesses against him. The Court agreed with this contention, stating that:

> There is something deep in human nature that regards face-to-face confrontation between accused and accuser as essential to a fair trial in a criminal prosecution. . . . It is more difficult to tell a lie about a person to his face than behind his back. . . . The screen issue [in this case] was specifically designed to enable the witnesses to avoid viewing the appellant [the accused] as they gave their testimony. . . . It is difficult to imagine a more obvious or damaging violation of the defendant's right to a face-to-face encounter.

Thus, the conviction was reversed.

THE RIGHT TO COUNSEL

Under the common law of England, a person on trial for a felony was not entitled to the assistance of counsel. If the charge was a misdemeanor, however, the defendant had the right of counsel. Various reasons have been given for this paradoxical situation. In felony cases, it was thought that the judge would be sympathetic to the defendant because if the defendant were convicted, he would be subjected to severe punishment and might have his property confiscated by the king. In misdemeanor cases, the judge would have less interest in protecting the accused. Another theory is that because the property of a felon could be confiscated, the king knew that the chances for the defendant's conviction would be greater if the assistance of counsel was not allowed. Thus, the king did not permit the assistance of counsel in a felony trial.

The denial of the assistance of counsel in felony cases was rejected by the colonists, and in most of the colonies, the right of counsel became a part of their due process of law. The right to counsel had become such an accepted practice that when the Bill of Rights was formulated, the following provision was included in the Sixth Amendment of the U.S. Constitution: "In all criminal prosecutions, the accused shall . . . have the assistance of counsel for his defense." This guarantee pertained only to federal prosecutions, but the states included similar provisions in their constitutions or statutes upon admittance to the Union. These provisions are usually worded similar to that of the following: "In criminal prosecutions the accused shall have the right to appear and defend, and in person and with counsel."

For many generations, this right to the assistance of counsel was interpreted as meaning if an accused appeared in court with an attorney, the accused could not be denied the assistance of the attorney. If, however, defendants were unable to afford an attorney to assist in their defense, it was their misfortune. Little thought was given to providing counsel for the accused. Neither was assistance of counsel considered essential for the accused prior to the time of the trial. But as time passed, new interpretations were placed upon the Sixth Amendment guarantee of counsel, particularly by the U.S. Supreme Court.

Providing the Accused with Counsel

One of the earliest decisions in which the U.S. Supreme Court held that in certain instances, an accused must be provided with an attorney, if he or she cannot afford one, was the case of *Powell* v. *Alabama*.[4] The facts of this case reflect that ignorant and friendless black youths, strangers in the community without means to obtain counsel, were hurried to trial in an Alabama state court for capital offense without appointment of counsel. The youths were convicted, and their case was taken to the U.S. Supreme Court on the grounds that the defendants had been denied due process of law. The U.S. Supreme Court agreed that the defendants had been denied due process of law in that they had not been provided with counsel to assist them in their defense. The Court stated as follows:

> All that is necessary now to decide, as we do decide, is that in a capital case, where the defendant is unable to employ counsel, and is incapable adequately of making his own defense because of ignorance, feeblemindedness, illiteracy, or the like, it is the duty of the court, whether requested or not, to assign counsel for him as a necessary requisite of due process of law. . . .

In the *Powell* case, the charge was a capital offense, and the Court held that in capital offenses, the judge must appoint an attorney when the accused is unable to obtain counsel. This decision was in effect until the case of *Gideon* v. *Wainwright*,[5] when the U.S. Supreme Court held that counsel must be provided for any defendant brought to trial irrespective of the charge. The facts of the *Gideon* case reveal that Gideon (the petitioner) was charged in a Florida state court with breaking and entering into a poolroom with intent to commit a misdemeanor. This offense is a felony under Florida law. Appearing in court without funds and without a lawyer, the petitioner asked the court to appoint counsel, but the judge informed the petitioner that under the laws of the state of Florida, the only time that the court could appoint counsel to represent a defendant is when that person is charged with a capital offense. Gideon attempted to conduct his own defense by making an opening statement, cross-examining prosecution witnesses, and presenting witnesses in his own behalf. Gideon was convicted and sentenced to five years in the state prison. The case was taken to the U.S. Supreme Court on the grounds that he had been denied due process of law in that his Sixth Amendment guarantee to the assistance of counsel had been denied. The U.S. Supreme Court agreed with this contention and reversed the conviction. The Court, in its decision, stated that:

... reason and reflection require us to recognize that in our adversary system of criminal justice, any person hauled into court, who is too poor to hire a lawyer, cannot be assured a fair trial unless counsel is provided for him. This seems to us to be an obvious truth. Governments, both state and federal, quite properly spend vast sums of money to establish machinery to try defendants accused of crime. Lawyers to prosecute are everywhere deemed essential to protect the public's interest in an orderly society. Similarly, there are few defendants charged with crime, few indeed, who fail to hire the best lawyers they can get to prepare and present their defenses. That government hires lawyers to prosecute and defendants who have the money hire lawyers to defend are the strongest indications of the widespread belief that lawyers in criminal courts are necessities, not luxuries. The right of one charged with crime to counsel may not be deemed fundamental and essential to fair trials in some countries, but it is in ours. From the very beginning, our state and national constitutions and laws have laid great emphasis on procedural and substantive safeguards designed to assure fair trials before impartial tribunals in which every defendant stands equal before the law. This noble ideal cannot be realized if the poor man charged with crime has to face his accusers without a lawyer to assist him. A defendant's need for a lawyer is nowhere better stated that in the moving words of Mr. Justice Sutherland in *Powell* v. *Alabama:* "The right to be heard would be, in many cases, of little avail if it did not comprehend the right to be heard by counsel. Even the intelligent and educated layman has small and sometimes no skill in the science of law. If charged with crime, he is incapable, generally, of determining for himself whether the indictment is good or bad. He is unfamiliar with the rules of evidence. Left without the aid of counsel he may be put on trial without a proper charge, and convicted upon incompetent evidence, or evidence irrelevant to the issue or otherwise inadmissible. He lacks both the skill and knowledge adequately to prepare his defense, even though he has a perfect one. He requires the guiding hand of counsel at every step in the proceedings against him. Without it, though he be not guilty, he faces the danger of conviction because he does not know how to establish his innocence."

Right to Counsel in Petty Cases

Although the Court in the *Gideon* case held that any person haled into court who is too poor to hire a lawyer cannot be assured a fair trial unless counsel is provided for him or her, the charge in the *Gideon* case was a felony. Thus, there remained some question whether counsel must be appointed for one brought to trial on a petty charge. This doubt was resolved in the case of *Argersinger* v. *Hamlin,*[6] in which the U.S. Supreme Court held that no person may be imprisoned for any offense, petty or otherwise, unless he or she is represented by counsel. The facts of the case show that Argersinger was charged in Florida with carrying a concealed weapon, an offense punishable by imprisonment up to six months. Argersinger was tried before a judge and was not represented by counsel, since he could not afford such, and the state contended that since the charge was a petty one, counsel did not have to be appointed for the defendant. Argersinger was convicted and sentenced to jail for ninety days. The conviction was upheld by the Florida Supreme Court, and the case was taken to the U.S. Supreme Court on the grounds that the defendant had been denied the right to counsel. The Court stated the following:

> ... The Sixth Amendment, which in enumerated situations has been made applicable to the States by reason of the Fourteenth Amendment ... provides specified standards for all criminal prosecutions.

Major U.S. Supreme Court Cases Granting the Right to Counsel

Case	Stage and Ruling
Moore v. *Michigan,* 355 U.S. 155 (1957)	The defendant has the right to counsel when submitting a guilty plea to the court.
Brady v. *United States,* 397 U.S. 742 (1970)	Counsel is required during the plea bargaining process.
Powell v. *Alabama,* 287 U.S. 45 (1932)	Defendants have the right to counsel at their trial in a state capital case.
Hamilton v. *Alabama,* 368 U.S. 52 (1961)	The arraignment is a critical stage in the criminal process, so that denial of the right to counsel is a violation of due process of law.
Coleman v. *Alabama,* 399 U.S. 1 (1970)	The preliminary hearing is a critical stage in a criminal prosecution requiring the state to provide the indigent defendant with counsel.
United States v. *Wade,* 388 U.S. 218 (1967)	A defendant in a pretrial, postindictment lineup for identification purposes has the right to assistance of counsel.
Gideon v. *Wainwright,* 372 U.S. 335 (1963)	An indigent defendant charged in a state court with a noncapital felony has the right to the assistance of free counsel at trial under the due process clause of the Fourteenth Amendment.
Argersinger v. *Hamlin,* 407 U.S. 25 (1972)	A defendant has the right to counsel at trial whenever he or she may be imprisoned, even for one day, for any offense, whether classified as a misdemeanor or a felony.
Faretta v. *California,* 422 U.S. 806 (1975)	The defendant has a constitutional right to defend herself or himself if her or his waiver of the right to counsel is knowing and intelligent.
Escobedo v. *Illinois,* 378 U.S. 478 (1964)	The defendant has the right to counsel during the course of any police interrogation.
Miranda v. *Arizona,* 384 U.S. 436 (1966)	Procedural safeguards, including the right to counsel, must be followed at custodial interrogation to secure the privilege against self-incrimination.
Massiah v. *United States,* 377 U.S. 201 (1964)	The defendant has the right to counsel during post-indictment interrogation.
In re Gault, 387 U.S. 1 (1967)	Procedural due process, including the right to counsel, applies to juvenile delinquency adjudication that may lead to a child's commitment to a state institution.
Townsend v. *Burke,* 334 U.S. 736 (1948)	A convicted offender has a right to counsel at the time of sentencing.
Douglas v. *California,* 372 U.S. 353 (1963)	An indigent defendant granted a first appeal from a criminal conviction has the right to be represented by counsel on appeal.
Mempa v. *Rhay,* 389 U.S. 128 (1967)	A convicted offender has the right to assistance of counsel at probation revocation hearings where the sentence has been deferred.
Morrissey v. *Brewer,* 408 U.S. 471 (1972)	The defendant has the right to counsel in the court's discretion at parole revocation hearings.
Gagnon v. *Scarpelli,* 411 U.S. 778 (1973)	The defendant has a right to counsel in the court's discretion at probation revocation hearings.

One is the requirement of a public trial . . . the right to a public trial was applicable to a state proceeding even though only a 60-day sentence was involved.

Another guarantee is the right to be informed of the nature and cause of the accusation. Still another, the right of confrontation. And another, compulsory process for obtaining witnesses in one's favor. We have never limited these rights to felonies nor to lesser but serious offenses. . . .

While there is historical support for limiting the deep commitment to trial by jury to serious criminal cases, there is no such support for a similar limitation on the right to assistance of counsel. . . .

The assistance of counsel is often a requisite to the very existence of a fair trial. . . .

The requirement of counsel may well be necessary for a fair trial even in a petty offense prosecution. We are by no means convinced that legal and constitutional questions involved in a case that actually leads to imprisonment even for a brief period are any less complex than when a person can be sent off for six months or more.

The trial of vagrancy cases is illustrative. While only brief sentences of imprisonment may be imposed, the cases often bristle with thorny constitutional questions.

Beyond the problem of trials and appeals is that of the guilty plea, a problem which looms large in misdemeanor as well as in felony cases. Counsel is needed so that the accused may know precisely what he is doing, so that he is fully aware of the prospect of going to jail or prison, and so that he is treated fairly by the prosecution.

We hold, therefore, that absent a knowing and intelligent waiver, no person may be imprisoned for any offense, whether classified as petty, misdemeanor, or felony, unless he was represented by counsel at his trial.

Waiver of Counsel

Although the Sixth Amendment guarantees the right to counsel, may this constitutional guarantee, like most others, be waived, or is it mandatory that the defendant be represented by counsel? This question was answered in *Adams* v. *United States,*[7] in which the U.S. Supreme Court held that a capable defendant could waive the right to the assistance of counsel. But it must be determined first that the accused is capable of defense without counsel's assistance.

The right of a defendant to represent himself or herself was carried one step further by the U.S. Supreme Court in *Faretta* v. *California,*[8] where the Court held that when a defendant "knowingly and intelligently" waives the right to the assistance of counsel, the defendant has the constitutional right to self-representation. The facts reveal that Faretta was charged with grand theft. At the arraignment, the judge appointed a public defender to represent Faretta, but before the trial, Faretta requested that he be permitted to represent himself. In an effort to determine whether Faretta was capable of representing himself, the judge questioned Faretta and learned that he had represented himself in a prior criminal prosecution, that he had a high school education, and that he did not want to be represented by the public defender. After further questioning by the judge at a later time, the judge concluded that Faretta had not intelligently waived his right to the assistance of counsel. The judge also ruled that Faretta did not have a constitutional right to self-representation. Faretta was represented by a public defender, and he was convicted and sentenced to prison. He appealed his case to the U.S. Supreme Court, which agreed to hear the case to settle the question of whether an accused has a Sixth Amendment right to decline counsel. The Court ruled that there is such a constitutional right. The Court pointed out that in early common law, those accused of serious crimes had to represent themselves and that only later was an accused given the choice of receiving the assistance of counsel. This was the practice at the time that the colonists came to America and at the time that the Sixth Amendment was written. The Court stated that it recognized the advantages of an accused's having the assistance of counsel but was unable to find an instance where a colonial court required an accused to accept an unwanted attorney as his or her representative. The Court felt that when the framers of the Sixth Amendment included the right of an accused to have the assistance of counsel, they were not denying the accused the right of self-representation. The Court stated the following:

> . . . in most criminal prosecutions defendants could better defend with counsel's guidance than by their own unskilled efforts. But where the defendant will not voluntarily accept representation by counsel, the potential advantage of a lawyer's training and experience can be realized, if at all, only imperfectly. To force a lawyer on a defendant can only lead him to believe that the law contrives against him. Moreover, it is not inconceivable that in some rare instances, the defendant might in fact present his case more effectively by conducting his own defense. Personal liberties are not rooted in the law of averages. The right to defend is personal. The defendant, and not his lawyer or the State, will bear the personal consequences of a conviction. It is the defendant, therefore, who must be free personally to decide whether in his particular case counsel is to his advantage. And although he may conduct his own defense ultimately to his own detriment, his choice must be honored out of that respect for the individual which is the lifeblood of the law. When an accused manages his own defense, he relinquishes, as a purely factual matter, many of the traditional benefits associated with the right to counsel. For this reason, in order to represent himself, the accused must "knowingly and intelligently" forego those relinquished benefits. Although a defendant need not himself have the skill and experience of a lawyer in order competently and intelligently to choose self-representation, he should be made aware of the dangers and disadvantages of self-representation, so that the record will establish that "he knows what he is doing and his choice is made with eyes open." Here, weeks before trial, Faretta clearly and unequivocally declared to the trial judge that he wanted to represent himself and did not want counsel. The record affirmatively shows that Faretta was literate, competent, and understanding, and that he was voluntarily exercising his informed free will.

Knowing and Intelligent Waiver.   The Court in the *Faretta* case stated that "in order to represent himself the accused must knowingly and intelligently" waive the right to the assistance of counsel. This statement placed a serious burden on trial judges in determining whether a defendant is capable of knowingly and intelligently waiving the right to the assistance of counsel. The problem created by this decision is that if a trial judge concludes that the defendant is capable of self-representation and the defendant is convicted, the defendant may appeal, and the appellate court may hold that the defendant was not capable of making an intelligent waiver of the right to counsel. On the other hand, as in *Faretta*'s case, if the judge concludes that the defendant was incapable of intelligently waiving the right to the assistance of counsel and is convicted, the appellate court may decide that the defendant had been denied the right of self-representation. The dissenting Justices in the *Faretta* case pointed out that the majority of justices had created a problem that undoubtedly would cause confusion for trial courts, since no guidelines were set forth for the trial courts to follow in their efforts to determine when an accused was capable of self-representation.

Since the U.S. Supreme Court has held that an accused has the constitutional right of self-representation when the right to the assistance of counsel is knowingly and intelligently waived, a trial court must make a careful evaluation of the accused's ability to make the waiver. When an accused requests permission for self-representation, it is usually necessary for the trial judge to hold a hearing to determine the capability of the accused to make the waiver. This hearing has been referred to as a "*Faretta* hearing." The time required to conduct this hearing varies with the circumstances of each case. It may become obvious to the judge after a short questioning of the accused that he or she has a limited educational background or knowledge of court procedure. The judge will conclude quickly that such an accused is not capable of making a knowing and intelligent waiver and will require representation by counsel. Other defendants who have some educational background and some knowledge of court procedures may insist on self-representation, and the hearing can be lengthy. The appellate courts have held that a "perfunctory hearing is improper. The record must show that the defendant made a knowing and intelligent election" to waive assistance of counsel. Further, "the actual conducting of a *Faretta* hearing may be difficult, time-consuming and trying of the patience of the trial judge, particularly if the defendant is eccentric, or prone to causing exasperation in others, or engages in the playing of games, or harassing the establishment. However the judge should not be misled by a confusion of the issue to be determined, that is, whether the defendant is capable of making the waiver."

Judges are inclined to conclude that a defendant is not capable of intelligently waiving the right to the assistance of counsel because of the many problems encountered by an untrained defendant attempting self-representation. The untrained defendant causes the trial to last longer, tries to introduce inadmissible evidence, makes improper objections to questions, and often argues with the judge over rulings. Deciding whether assistance should be provided by the trial judge for the self-represented defendant becomes a further issue. Many judges believe that with all the other duties to be performed during the trial, it is dangerous to try to assist the defendant because of the possibility of mistaken or misunderstood assistance. Yet, some appellate courts have stated that one of the major functions of the trial judge is to make certain that the "innocence or guilt of those accused of a crime is based upon the merits of the trial and not upon their inability to understand legal procedure." Therefore, the trial judge should render that assistance necessary for a fair trial.

The dissenting justices in the *Faretta* case recognized that these problems would be encountered by trial judges and believed that the majority justices had read into the Sixth Amendment something not intended by its framers.

Standby Counsel.   The majority justices in the *Faretta* case did indicate that a trial judge, even over the objections of the defendant, could appoint a "standby counsel" to aid the defendant, if and when the defendant requests help, and to be available to represent the defendant in the event that termination of the defendant's self-representation should become necessary. The appointment of a standby attorney is not a practical solution, however, since trial judges may appoint standby attorneys in most instances, tying up the services of an attorney and increasing court costs.

In *McKaskle* v. *Wiggins*,[9] the U.S. Supreme Court reaffirmed the *Faretta* ruling that a trial judge may appoint a standby attorney over the objections of the defendant. The Court stated as follows:

> A defendant's Sixth Amendment rights are not violated when a trial judge appoints standby counsel even over the defendant's objection—to relieve the judge of the need to explain and enforce basic rules of courtroom protocol or to assist the defendant in overcoming routine obstacles that stand in the way of the defendant's achievement of his own clearly indicated goals.

The Court further stated the following:

> A defendant does not have a constitutional right to receive personal instruction from the trial judge on courtroom procedure. Nor does the Constitution require judges to take over chores for a *pro se* defendant [one representing himself] that would normally be attended to by trained counsel as a matter of course. The right of self-representation is not a license to abuse the dignity of the courtroom. Neither is it a license not to comply with relevant rules of procedure and substantive law.

Although the *McKaskle* decision reaffirmed a trial judge's right to appoint standby counsel over the defendant's objections, the decision did not solve all the problems connected with the appointment of a standby attorney. The trial judge is still faced with deciding how far a standby attorney may proceed over the defendant's objections without the assistance being a violation of the defendant's right to self-representation. The Court in the *McKaskle* case gave few guidelines in this respect but stated that a defendant's rights to self-representation

> . . . are not infringed upon when standby counsel assists the defendant in overcoming routine procedural or evidentiary obstacles to the completion of some specific task, such as the introducing evidence or objecting to testimony, that the defendant has clearly shown he wishes to complete. Nor are they infringed when counsel merely helps to ensure the defendant's compliance with basic rules of courtroom protocol and procedure. In neither case is there any significant interference with the defendant's actual control over the presentation of his defense.

Why an Accused Chooses Self-Representation

With the advantages to an accused in having the assistance of counsel and with the disadvantages of self-representation, one might ask why a defendant would insist upon self-representation rather than having the assistance of counsel. The saying is that an attorney who chooses self-representation has a fool for a client. Yet many defendants either do not trust attorneys or question their capabilities. One defendant, for example, conceded that an attorney had "more on the ball" than he himself did, but he also stated that there are certain questions "the attorney might not ask certain witnesses that are very potent, important, in regard to the case itself." Some defendants feel that attorneys do not have their client's best interests at stake or that attorneys are in collusion with the prosecuting attorney, with the result that the defendants will be railroaded into prison. Other defendants receive a certain gratification from representing themselves. Some are aware that by representing themselves they are entitled to confer with codefendants and witnesses in private, enabling them to conspire against the prosecution.

A defendant who represents himself or herself is referred to as appearing in propria persona ("in one's own proper person"), or in person. This circumstance is sometimes referred to by the courts as pro per.

When the Right to Counsel Begins

For many years, the Sixth Amendment guarantee to the assistance of counsel was interpreted as meaning assistance at the time of trial. The *Gideon* decision did not materially change that interpretation, since that decision referred to the fact that "any person hauled into court, who is too poor to hire a lawyer, cannot be assured a fair trial unless counsel is provided for him." It was generally accepted that counsel need not be provided for the indigent defendant until the time of trial. However, later U.S. Supreme Court decisions established a new interpretation of when the right to counsel began and when counsel had to be provided for the indigent defendant.

In the case of *Escobedo* v. *Illinois,*[10] the U.S. Supreme Court held that the right to the assistance of counsel begins long before the time of the trial and may occur even before an arrest is made. The Court stated that when the investigation of a crime "shifts from the investigatory to accusatory," the accused is entitled to the assistance of counsel and that such assistance could be very hollow if denied until the time of trial.

The facts of the *Escobedo* case reflect that Escobedo was arrested on a charge of murder. He was taken to a Chicago police station for interrogation. En route, Escobedo requested the right to consult with his attorney. Shortly after Escobedo arrived at the police station, his attorney arrived and requested permission to talk to Escobedo. Both were advised by the police that they could confer after the interrogation was completed. During the interrogation, Escobedo made certain admissions that implicated him in the murder charge. These admissions were used against him during the trial. Escobedo was convicted of murder, and his conviction was upheld by the Illinois Supreme Court. The case was taken to the U.S. Supreme Court upon the grounds that Escobedo was denied the assistance of counsel in violation of the Sixth Amendment guarantee. The attorneys for the State of Illinois argued that the right to counsel was not operative until the indictment stage of proceedings. To this argument, the Court stated that:

> . . . in *Gideon* v. *Wainwright* we held that every person accused of a crime, whether state or federal, is entitled to a lawyer at trial. The rule sought by the State here, however, would make the trial no more than an appeal from the interrogation; and the "right to use counsel at the formal trial (would be) a very hollow thing if, for all practical purposes, the conviction is already assured by pretrial examination." *In re Groban,* 352 US 330 (1957) (Black, J., dissenting): One can imagine a cynical prosecutor saying: "Let them have the most illustrious counsel, now. They can't escape the noose. There is nothing that counsel can do for them at a trial."
>
> It is argued that if the right to counsel is afforded prior to indictment, the number of confessions obtained by the police will diminish significantly, because most confessions are obtained during the period between arrest and indictment,

and "any lawyer worth his salt will tell the suspect in no uncertain terms to make no statement to police under any circumstances." This argument, of course, cuts two ways. The fact that many confessions are obtained during this period points up its critical nature as a "stage when legal aid and advice" are surely needed. The right to counsel would indeed be hollow if it began at a period when few confessions were obtained. There is necessarily a direct relationship between the police in their quest for a confession and the criticalness of that stage to the accused in his need for legal advice. Our Constitution, unlike some others, strikes the balance in favor of the right of the accused to be advised by his lawyer of his privilege against self-incrimination.

We hold, therefore, that where, as here, the investigation is no longer a general inquiry into an unsolved crime but has begun to focus on a particular suspect, the suspect has been taken into police custody, the police carry out a process of interrogations that lends itself to eliciting incriminating statements, the suspect has requested and been denied an opportunity to consult with his lawyer, and the police have not effectively warned him of his absolute constitutional right to remain silent, the accused has been denied "the assistance of Counsel" in violation of the Sixth Amendment to the Constitution as "made obligatory upon the States by the Fourteenth Amendment," *Gideon* v. *Wainwright*, and that no statement elicited by the police be used against him at a criminal trial. . . .

Nothing we have said today affects the powers of the police to investigate "an unsolved crime" by gathering information from witnesses and by other "proper investigative efforts." We hold only that when the process shifts from investigatory to accusatory—when its purpose is to elicit a confession—our adversary system begins to operate, and, under the circumstances here, to consult with his lawyer.

The Escobedo decision provided that once suspicion is focused upon a particular suspect, he or she is entitled to consult with an attorney, but nothing was said about having to furnish the accused with an attorney. In the *Miranda* case, as previously stated, the Court held that before an accused could be interrogated, he or she must be advised of the right to the assistance of counsel. The accused must be advised of the right to remain silent and of the right to the assistance of counsel during the interrogation; and if the accused cannot afford an attorney, then one will be provided free.

Although both the *Escobedo* and *Miranda* decisions are more related to the field of evidence and the admissibility of confessions than to procedure, these decisions emphasized the importance of the assistance of counsel and set forth guidelines on when that right to assistance begins.

Effective Counsel

A defendant is entitled not only to the assistance of counsel but also to effective counsel. An effective counsel is one who has knowledge of the defendant's rights and who is capable of presenting the defenses to which the accused is entitled. Establishing the effectiveness of counsel is not easy. A counsel may be knowledgeable in one field but unfamiliar with crucial problems in another. If counsel does not effectively represent a defendant, whether through lack of knowledge or interest, or because of mere carelessness, a conviction could be overruled upon appeal because of the denial of assistance of counsel.

Farce or Sham Test.   In determining whether a conviction should be reversed because of ineffective counsel, many state appellate courts have stated that it must appear that counsel's lack of diligence or competence reduced the trial to a "farce or sham." Today's courts have rejected the traditional farce or sham test and have adopted a less stringent criterion for determining competency of counsel. Counsel is considered ineffective if in representing the defendant, the counsel fails to meet the standard of competence expected of criminal case attorneys. Counsel is held as ineffective when not exercising the customary skills and diligence that a reasonably competent attorney would have performed under similar circumstances. Effective counsel has the duty to investigate carefully all defenses of fact and law of a case. If counsel's failure to do so results in the failure to present crucial defense during the trial, the defendant has been denied proper assistance of counsel. Further, mere allegations by the defendant indicating a lack of preparation by or general incompetence of counsel is not enough to show ineffectiveness. The defendant must show acts or omissions resulting in a failure to present a crucial defense. Counsel does not have to interview or call every witness with knowledge of the case, since many witnesses may be of little assistance to the defense.

Crucial Error by Counsel.   The effectiveness of counsel is usually raised when the court appoints an attorney to represent the defendant who cannot afford to choose an attorney. There are times when a defendant will complain about the effectiveness of chosen counsel (retained counsel). If an attorney selected by the accused is so ineffective that the defendant was denied a fair trial, the conviction will be reversed on appeal. For a time, courts were inclined to require a lesser degree of competence from an attorney of the defendant's own choosing. Today, it is accepted that whether an attorney is appointed for the defendant or the attorney is one of the defendant's own choosing, competence will be measured by the same degree. As stated by the U.S. Supreme Court in *Strickland* v. *Washington*,[11] "An accused is entitled to be assisted by an attorney, whether retained or appointed, who plays the role necessary to ensure that the trial is fair." A defendant may not expect an error-free attorney, but if an error is crucial to the defense, effective counsel has been denied. Determining whether an error was crucial has been a major problem for appellate courts. Defendants who have been convicted have successfully appealed their convictions on the allegation that effective counsel had been denied. Since no guidelines were set forth to measure effectiveness of counsel, many convictions were reversed. In *Strickland,* the Court endeavored to correct this situation by providing some criteria to measure effectiveness. The Court stated that "when a convicted defendant complains of the ineffectiveness of counsel's assistance, the defendant must show that counsel's representation fell below an objective standard of reasonableness. More specific guidelines are not appropriate."

Burden of Proof.   *Strickland* points out that the burden of proving ineffective assistance of counsel is on the defendant. When a convicted defendant claims that counsel's assistance was so defective as to require a reversal of a conviction or a death sentence, the defendant must prove two things. First, the defendant must show that counsel's performance was deficient. The defendant is thus required to show that errors made were so serious that counsel did not function as a reasonably competent attorney. Second, the defendant must show that the deficient performance prejudiced the defense. Counsel's errors must be so serious as to deprive the defendant of a fair trial.

A defendant may allege ineffectiveness of counsel when there may have been acts or omissions such as the failure of counsel to enter a proper plea when applicable (such as a plea of not guilty by reason of insanity); the failure to raise the defense of diminished capacity; the failure to cross-examine prosecution witnesses; or the failure to object to the introduction of evidence improperly obtained. In one case, an appellate court overruled a conviction when the defense attorney's request for a continuance was denied, and the attorney thereafter refused to assist in the selection of the jury. The appellate court held that the defense counsel had reduced the trial to a sham.

The Public Defender and Appointed Counsel

As has been stated, an accused is entitled to the assistance of counsel when that assistance is requested. If the accused is not in a position to employ private counsel, the court must appoint effective counsel. It is not always easy for a judge to obtain effective counsel to represent one accused of a crime. If effective counsel cannot be readily obtained, all prosecutive action must be suspended. To overcome this problem, many counties have established the public defender, whose function is representing those defendants who cannot afford an attorney of their own. These defendants are referred to as indigent persons or indigent defendants. The public defender, like the prosecuting attorney, is paid out of public funds. Many do not understand the use of public funds to employ a prosecuting attorney to prosecute offenders and, at the same time, to pay a public defender to defend the accused. But until the indigent defendant is furnished with the assistance of counsel, no prosecutive action can be taken. This delay can be expensive in time and money. If there is no public defender in a particular jurisdiction, the court must draw local attorneys from private practice. This necessity creates a problem, since most of these attorneys practice civil law and have little knowledge of the intricacies of a criminal trial; furthermore, in case of a conviction, the question of whether there was effective assistance of counsel could arise.

Before an accused may have the assistance of the public defender or an appointed private attorney, it must be established that the defendant is an indigent person, and this is sometimes a difficult problem. Approximately 85 percent of all those arrested on felony charges are without question unable to afford an attorney. Determining which of the others can afford an attorney is difficult. Some courts have held that if the defendant can post bail, he or she is not indigent. Others have adopted the test that counsel is to be provided for any defendant who is unable to obtain counsel without serious financial hardship. The mere fact that friends or relatives have posted bail is not sufficient ground for denying the defendant free counsel. Another test is whether or not a private attorney would be interested in representing the defendant in his or her present economic circumstances. Undoubtedly, there have been defendants who have taken advantage of these tests to obtain free counsel, but with the large number of defendants who claim indigency, a thorough inquiry into each case is impossible. Judges who doubt the indigency status of a defendant have required the defendant to file a financial statement under oath. If it is determined later that the defendant was not indigent, prosecution for perjury as well as civil charges may be filed for the cost of the appointed counsel.

CAPSTONE CASE ————————————————————————

Faretta v. California
422 U.S. 806, 95 S.Ct. 2525, 45 L.Ed.2d 562 (1975)

Justice Stewart delivered the opinion of the Court.

The Sixth and Fourteenth Amendments of our Constitution guarantee that a person brought to trial in any state or federal court must be afforded the right to the assistance of counsel before he can be validly convicted and punished by imprisonment. This clear constitutional rule has emerged from a series of cases decided here over the last 50 years. The question before us now is whether a defendant in a state criminal trial has a constitutional right to proceed without counsel when he voluntarily and intelligently elects to do so. Stated another way, the question is whether a State may constitutionally hale a person into its criminal courts and there force a lawyer upon him, even when he insists that he wants to conduct his own defense. It is not an easy question, but we have concluded that a State may not constitutionally do so.

Anthony Faretta was charged with grand theft in . . . the Superior Court of Los Angeles County, California. At the arraignment, the Superior Court Judge assigned to preside at the trial appointed the public defender to represent Faretta. Well before the date of trial, however, Faretta requested that he be permitted to represent himself. Questioning by the judge revealed that Faretta had once represented himself in a criminal prosecution, that he had a high school education, and that he did not want to be represented by the public defender because he believed that that office was "very loaded down with . . . a heavy case load." The judge responded that he believed Faretta was "making a mistake" and emphasized that in further proceedings Faretta would receive no special favors. Nevertheless . . . the judge, in a "preliminary ruling," accepted Faretta's waiver of the assistance of counsel. The judge indicated, however, that he might reverse this ruling if it later appeared that Faretta was unable adequately to represent himself.

Several weeks thereafter, but still prior to trial, the judge sua ponte held a hearing to inquire into Faretta's ability to conduct his own defense, and questioned him specifically about both the hearsay rule and the state law governing the challenge of potential jurors. After consideration of Faretta's answers, and observation of his demeanor, the judge ruled that Faretta had not made an intelligent and knowing waiver of his right to the assistance of counsel, and also ruled that Faretta had no constitutional right to conduct his own defense. The judge, accordingly, reversed his earlier ruling permitting self-representation and again appointed the public defender to represent Faretta. Faretta's subsequent request for leave to act as cocounsel was rejected, as were his efforts to make certain motions on his own behalf. Throughout the subsequent trial, the judge required that Faretta's defense be conducted only through the appointed lawyer from the public defender's office. At the conclusion of the trial, the jury found Faretta guilty as charged, and the judge sentenced him to prison. The California Court of Appeal affirmed the trial judge's ruling that Faretta had no federal or state constitutional right to represent himself, and the California Supreme Court denied review.

In the federal courts, the right of self-representation has been protected by statute since the beginnings of our Nation. Section 35 of the Judiciary Act of 1789, 1 Stat. 73, 92, enacted by the First Congress and signed by President Washington one day before the Sixth Amendment was proposed, provided that "in all the courts of the

United States, the parties may plead and manage their own causes personally or by the assistance of . . . counsel . . ." . . . With few exceptions, each of the several States also accords a defendant the right to represent himself in any criminal case. The Constitutions of 36 States explicitly confer that right. Moreover, many state courts have expressed the view that the right is also supported by the Constitution of the United States. This Court has more than once indicated the same view. . . . [And] the United States Courts of Appeals have repeatedly held that the right of self-representation is protected by the Bill of Rights.

This Court's past recognition of the right of self-representation, the federal court authority holding the right to be of constitutional dimension, and the state constitutions pointing to the right's fundamental nature form a consensus not easily ignored. "The mere fact that a path is a beaten one," Mr. Justice Jackson once observed, "is a persuasive reason for following it." We confront here a nearly universal conviction, on the part of our people as well as our courts, that forcing a lawyer upon an unwilling defendant is contrary to his basic right to defend himself if he truly wants to do so. This consensus is soundly premised. The right of self-representation finds support in the structure of the Sixth Amendment, as well as in the English and colonial jurisprudence from which the Amendment emerged.

The Sixth Amendment includes a compact statement of the rights necessary to a full defense. . . . The rights to notice, confrontation, and compulsory process, when taken together, guarantee that a criminal charge may be answered in a manner now considered fundamental to the fair administration of American justice through the calling and interrogation of favorable witnesses, the cross-examination of adverse witnesses, and the orderly introduction of evidence. In short, the Amendment constitutionalizes the right in an adversary criminal trial to make a defense as we know it.

The Sixth Amendment does not provide merely that a defense shall be made for the accused; it grants to the secured personally the right to make his defense. It is the accused, not counsel, who must be "informed of the nature and cause of the accusation," who must be "confronted with the witnesses against him," and who must be accorded "compulsory process for obtaining witnesses in his favor." Although not stated in the Amendment in so many words, the right to self representation—to make one's own defense—is thus necessarily implied by the structure of the Amendment. The right to defend is given directly to the accused; for it is he who suffers the consequences if the defense fails.

The counsel provision supplements this design. It speaks of the "assistance" of counsel, and an assistant, however expert, is still an assistant. The language and spirit of the Sixth Amendment contemplate that counsel, like the other defense tools guaranteed by the Amendment, shall be an aid to a willing defendant—not an organ of the State interposed between an unwilling defendant and his right to defend himself personally. To thrust counsel upon the accused, against his considered wish, thus violates the logic of the Amendment. In such a case, counsel is not an assistant, but a master; and the right to make a defense is stripped of the personal character upon which the Amendment insists. It is true that when a defendant chooses to have a lawyer manage and present his case, law and tradition may allocate to the counsel the power to make binding decisions of trial strategy in many areas. This allocation can only be justified, however, by the defendant's consent, at the outset, to accept counsel as his representative. An unwanted counsel "represents" the defendant only through a tenuous and unacceptable legal fiction. Unless the accused has acquiesced in such representation, the defense presented is not the defense guaranteed him by the Constitution, for, in a very real sense, it is not his defense.

The Sixth Amendment, when naturally read, thus implies a right of self-representation. This reading is reinforced by the Amendment's roots in English legal history. In the long history of British criminal jurisprudence, there was only one tribunal that ever adopted a practice of forcing counsel upon an unwilling defendant in a criminal proceeding. The tribunal was the Star Chamber. That curious institution, which flourished in the late 16th and early 17th centuries, was of mixed executive and judicial character, and characteristically departed from common-law traditions. For those reasons, and because it specialized in trying "political" offenses, the Star Chamber has for centuries symbolized disregard of basic individual rights. . . .

In the American Colonies the insistence upon a right of self-representation was, if anything, more fervent than in England. The colonists brought with them an appreciation of the virtues of self-reliance and a traditional distrust of lawyers. When the Colonies were first settled, "the lawyer was synonymous with the cringing Attorneys-General and Solicitors-General of the Crown and the arbitrary justices of the King's Court, all bent on the conviction of those who opposed the King's prerogatives, and twisting the law to secure convictions." This prejudice gained strength in the Colonies where "distrust of lawyers became an institution." . . .

This is not to say that the Colonies were slow to recognize the value of counsel in criminal cases. Colonial judges soon departed from ancient English practice and allowed accused felons the aid of counsel for their defense. At the same time, however, the basic right of self-representation was never questioned. We have found no instance where a colonial court required a defendant in a criminal case to accept as his representative an unwanted lawyer. Indeed, even where counsel was permitted, the general practice continued to be self-representation. . . . After the Declaration of Independence, the right of self-representation, along with other rights basic to the making of a defense, entered the new state constitutions in wholesale fashion. The right to counsel was clearly thought to supplement the primary right of the accused to defend himself, utilizing his personal rights to notice, confrontation, and compulsory process. . . . At the time James Madison drafted the Sixth Amendment, some state constitutions guaranteed an accused the right to be heard "by himself" and by counsel; others provided that an accused was to be "allowed" counsel. The various state proposals for the Bill of Rights had similar variations in terminology. In each case, however, the counsel provision was embedded in a package of defense rights granted personally to the accused. There is no indication that the differences in phrasing about "counsel" reflected any differences of principle about self-representation. . . .

There can be no blinking the fact that the right of an accused to conduct his own defense seems to cut against the grain of this Court's decisions holding that the Constitution requires that no accused can be convicted and imprisoned unless he has been accorded the right to the assistance of counsel. See *Powell* v. *Alabama, Johnson* v. *Zerbst, Gideon* v. *Wainwright*, and *Argersinger* v. *Hamlin*. For it is surely true that the basic thesis of those decisions is that the help of a lawyer is essential to assure the defendant a fair trial. And a strong argument can surely be made that the whole thrust of those decisions must inevitably lead to the conclusion that a State may constitutionally impose a lawyer upon even an unwilling defendant.

But it is one thing to hold that every defendant, rich or poor, has the right to the assistance of counsel, and quite another to say that a State may compel a defendant to accept a lawyer he does not want. The value of state-appointed counsel was not unappreciated by the Founders, yet the notion of compulsory counsel was utterly foreign to them. And whatever else may be said of those who wrote the Bill of Rights, surely there can be no doubt that they understood the inestimable worth of free choice. It is undeniable that in most criminal prosecutions defendants could better defend with counsel's guidance than by their own unskilled efforts. But where the defendant will not voluntarily accept representation by counsel, the potential advantage of a lawyer's training and experience can be realized, if at all, only imperfectly. To force a lawyer on a defendant can only lead him to believe that the law contrives against him. Moreover, it is not inconceivable that in some rare instances, the defendant might in fact present his case more effectively by conducting his own defense. Personal liberties are not rooted in the law of averages. The right to defend is personal. The defendant, and not his lawyer or the State, will bear the personal consequences of a conviction. It is the defendant, therefore, who must be free personally to decide whether in his particular case counsel is to his advantage. And although he may conduct his own defense ultimately to his own detriment, his choice must be honored out of "that respect for the individual which is the lifeblood of the law."

When an accused manages his own defense, he relinquishes, as a purely factual matter, many of the traditional benefits associated with the right to counsel. For this reason, in order to represent himself, the accused must "knowingly and intelligently" forgo those relinquished benefits. Although a defendant need not himself have the skill and experience of a lawyer in order competently and intelligently to choose self-representation, he should be made aware of the dangers and disadvantages of self-representation, so that the record will establish that "he knows what he is doing and his choice is made with eyes open."

Here, weeks before trial, Faretta clearly and unequivocally declared to the trial judge that he wanted to represent himself and did not want counsel. The record affirmatively shows that Faretta was literate, competent, and understanding, and that he was voluntarily exercising his informed free will. The trial judge had warned Faretta that he thought it was a mistake not to accept the assistance of counsel, and that Faretta would be required to follow all the "ground rules" of trial procedure. We need make no assessment of how well or poorly Faretta had mastered the intricacies of the hearsay rule and the California code provisions that govern challenges of potential jurors on voir dire. For his technical legal knowledge, as such, was not relevant to an assessment of his knowing exercise of the right to defend himself.

In forcing Faretta, under these circumstances, to accept against his will a state-appointed public defender, the California courts deprived him of his constitutional right to conduct his own defense. . . .

Chief Justice Burger, with whom Justice Blackmun and Justice Rehnquist join, dissenting.

. . . The most striking feature of the Court's opinion is that it devotes so little discussion to the matter which it concedes is the core of the decision, that is, discerning an independent basis in the Constitution for the supposed right to represent oneself in a criminal trial. Its ultimate assertion that such a right is tucked between the lines of the Sixth Amendment is contradicted by the Amendment's language and its consistent judicial interpretation.

The conclusion that the rights guaranteed by the Sixth Amendment are "personal" to an accused reflects nothing more than the obvious fact that it is he who is on trial and therefore has need of a defense. . . . [No. 1 proposition nor the language of the Amendment, which speaks in uniformly mandatory terms, leads to the further conclusion that the right to counsel is merely supplementary and may be dispensed with at the whim of the accused. Rather, this Court's decisions have consistently included the right to counsel as an integral part of the bundle making up the larger "right to a defense as we know it." [The] reason for this hardly requires explanation. The fact of the matter is that in all but an extraordinarily small number of cases an accused will lose whatever defense he may have if he undertakes to conduct the trial himself.

[Nor] is it accurate to suggest, as the Court seems to later in its opinion, that the quality of his representation at trial is a matter with which only the accused is legitimately concerned. Although we have adopted an adversary system of criminal justice, the prosecution is more than an ordinary litigant, and the trial judge is not simply an automaton who ensures that technical rules are adhered to. Both are charged with the duty of ensuring that justice, in the broadest sense of that term, is achieved in every criminal trial. That goal is ill-served, and the integrity of and public confidence in the system are undermined, when an easy conviction is obtained due to the defendant's ill-advised decision to waive counsel. The damage thus inflicted is not mitigated by the lame explanation that the defendant simply availed himself of the "freedom" to go to jail under his own banner. The system of criminal justice should not be available as an instrument of self-destruction.

. . . True freedom of choice and society's interest in seeing that justice is achieved can be vindicated only if the trial court retains discretion to reject any attempted waiver of counsel and insist that the accused be tried according to the Constitution. This discretion is as critical an element of basic fairness as a trial judge's discretion to decline to accept a plea of guilty. . . .

[The Court] attempts to use history to take it where legal analysis cannot. Piecing together shreds of English legal history and early state constitutional and statutory provisions, without a full elaboration of the context in which they occurred or any evidence that they were relied upon by the drafters of our Federal Constitution, creates more questions than it answers and hardly provides the firm foundation upon which the creation of new constitutional rights should rest. We are well reminded that this Court once employed an exhaustive analysis of English and colonial practices regarding the right to counsel to justify the conclusion that it was fundamental to a fair trial and, less than 10 years later, used essentially the same material to conclude that it was not. . . . It can hardly be suggested that the Members of the Congress of 1789, then few in number, were unfamiliar with the Amendment's carefully structured language, which had been under discussion since the 1787 Constitutional Convention. And it would be most remarkable to suggest, had the right to conduct one's own defense been considered so critical as to require constitutional protection, that it would have been left to implication. Rather, under traditional canons of construction, inclusion of the right in the Judiciary Act and its omission from the constitutional amendment drafted at the same time by many of the same men, supports the conclusion that the omission was intentional. . . .

In this case, therefore, history ought to lead judges to conclude that the Constitution leaves to the judgment of legislatures, and the flexible process of statutory amendment, the question whether criminal defendants should be permitted to conduct their trials pro se. (See *Betts* v. *Brady*) And the fact that we have not hinted at a contrary view for 185 years is surely entitled to some weight in the scales. . . . Society has the right to expect that, when courts find new rights implied in the Constitution, their potential effect upon the resources of our criminal justice system will be considered. However, such considerations are conspicuously absent from the Court's opinion in this case. [The] Court blandly assumes that once an accused has elected to defend himself he will be bound by his choice and not be heard to complain of it later. This assumption ignores the role of appellate review, for the reported cases are replete with instances of a convicted defendant being relieved of a deliberate decision even when made with the advice of counsel. It is totally unrealistic, therefore, to suggest that an accused will always be held to the consequences of a decision to conduct his own defense. Unless, as may be the case, most persons accused of crime have more wit than to insist upon the dubious benefit that the Court confers today, we can expect that many expensive and goodfaith prosecutions will be nullified on appeal for reasons that trial courts are now deprived of the power to prevent.

Justice Blackmun, with whom the Chief Justice, and Justice Rehnquist join, dissenting.

I fear that the right to self-representation constitutionalized today frequently will cause procedural confusion without advancing any significant strategic interest of the defendant. [Although] the Court indicates that a pro se defendant necessarily waives any claim he might otherwise make of ineffective assistance of counsel, the opinion leaves open a host of other procedural questions. Must every defendant be advised of his right to proceed pro se? If so, when must that notice be given? Since the right to assistance of counsel and the right to self-representation are mutually exclusive, how is the waiver of each right to be measured? If a defendant has elected to exercise his right to proceed pro se, does he still have a constitutional right to assistance of standby counsel? How soon in the criminal proceeding must a defendant decide between proceeding by counsel or pro se? Must he be allowed to switch in mid-trial? May a violation of the right to self-representation ever be harmless error? Must the trial court treat the pro se defendant differently than it would professional counsel? I assume that many of these questions will be answered with finality in due course. Many of them, however, such as the standards of waiver and the treatment of the pro se defendant, will haunt the trial of every defendant who elects to exercise his right to self-representation. The procedural problems spawned by an absolute right to self-representation will far outweigh whatever tactical advantage the defendant may feel he has gained by electing to represent himself.

If there is any truth to the old proverb that "one who is his own lawyer has a fool for a client," the Court by its opinion today now bestows a constitutional right on one to make a fool of himself.

REVIEW QUESTIONS

1. What is the significance of the constitutional guarantee that an accused be confronted with the witnesses against him or her?

2. May a trial ever be conducted in the absence of the defendant? If so, under what circumstances?

3. What procedure, suggested by the U.S. Supreme Court, might be taken against an unruly defendant during trial proceedings, and in what decision was the procedure suggested?

4. In what amendment to the U.S. Constitution is the right to the assistance of counsel embodied?

5. What was the significance of the *Gideon* v. *Wainwright* decision in reference to the assistance of counsel?

6. In the *Argersinger* v. *Hamlin* decision, what arguments were presented by the Court in granting the accused the assistance of counsel in the trial of a petty charge?

7. Under what circumstances, if any, may an accused waive the assistance of counsel and represent himself or herself during a trial?

8. When does the accused's right to counsel begin?

9. What is the significance of the term "effective assistance of counsel"?

10. What is the function of a public defender?

ENDNOTES

1. 397 U.S. 337 (1970).
2. 130 U.S. App. DC 22 (1968).
3. 101 L.Ed. 2d 857 (1988).
4. 287 U.S. 45 (1932).
5. 372 U.S. 335 (1963).
6. 407 U.S. 25 (1972).
7. 317 U.S. 269 (1942).
8. 422 U.S. 806 (1975).
9. 79 L.Ed. 2d 122 (1984).
10. 378 U.S. 478 (1964).
11. 466 U.S. 668 (1984).

Pretrial Motions, Hearings, and Plea Negotiations

> If criminals wanted to grind justice to a halt, they could do it by banding together and all pleading not guilty. It's only because we have plea-bargaining that our criminal justice system is still in motion.
>
> —Dorothy Wright Wilson, former dean, Southern California Law Center, 1974

Prior to a trial, the prosecution and defense each may request that the trial judge take some action on a particular matter. These requests are usually referred to as *motions*. The motion may be made orally to the judge, but in most instances, it will be in written form and filed with the appropriate court. Accompanying the motion will be an affidavit setting forth the reasons the judge should take the action requested. A copy of the motion will be furnished to the opposing side, and generally, the judge will hold a hearing on the motion during which each side may present arguments for and against it; however, not all motions are opposed. It is not mandatory that the defendant be present at these hearings in every instance, but many judges demand that the defendant be present at all proceedings. More motions are filed by the defense than by the prosecution, since more matters affect the rights of a defendant than the prosecution. A few more prevalent motions will be discussed, but they are in no way inclusive of all motions that may be filed either before or during a trial. The sequence of the motions discussed here is not necessarily in the same order that will he taken at trial. One of the earliest motions that may be filed is for pretrial discovery.

PRETRIAL RIGHT OF DISCOVERY

The right of discovery, or inspection, is more closely related to the subject of evidence than to the procedures in the justice system. However, one of the responsibilities of the attorneys for both the prosecution and the defense is to exercise the right of discovery. The right of pretrial discovery in criminal matters is of comparatively recent origin. It was unknown at common law and still is not recognized in criminal matters in some states. As stated in Chapter 5, the right of discovery is the pretrial right of the adversary to inspect, review, and copy certain materials held by the opposition that are anticipated to be introduced as evidence during the trial.

The Defendant's Right of Discovery

The right of pretrial discovery was created primarily for the benefit of the defendant. The theory was that the right would assist the defendant in case preparation and aid in getting a fair trial. The right would also enable the defense attorney to better cross-examine the witnesses for the prosecution and assist in impeaching witnesses who have questionable credibility. The purpose of a trial is to determine the truth of what happened in a particular case. The parties involved in a trial are not to play games or create surprises. As expressed in *People* v. *Riser:*[1]

> Absent some governmental requirement that information be kept confidential for the purposes of effective law enforcement, the state has no interest in denying the accused to all evidence that can throw light on issues in the case, and in particular it has no interest in convicting on the testimony of witnesses who have not been as rigorously cross-examined and as thoroughly impeached as the evidence permits.

The right of pretrial discovery may come into being either by legislative action or by appellate court decisions and may be exercised in two ways. The defense may make an oral request to the prosecuting attorney or to the law enforcement agency involved, for permission to examine the material held in the case. The alternative method consists of a written request by the defendant's attorney in the form of a motion to produce the evidence held by the prosecution. This motion is presented to the appropriate trial judge, who will issue an order to produce the material for examination by the defense.

What the Defendant May Inspect

Even in those states in which the right of discovery is recognized, the material and the information that the defendant may examine vary. Some states and the federal government are quite liberal in the matters that may be examined. Rule 16 of the Federal Rules of Criminal Procedure is typical of the broader right of discovery by a defendant. This rule provides the following:

> . . . Upon request of the defendant the government shall permit the defendant to inspect and copy or photograph books, papers, documents, photographs, tangible objects, buildings or places, or copies or portions thereof, which are in the possession, custody or control of the government, and which are material to the preparation of his defense or are intended for use by the government as evidence in chief at the trial, or were obtained from or belong to the defendant.

The defendant is entitled to the names and addresses of witnesses whom the government intends to call in the case preparation, as well as any record of prior felony convictions of such witnesses. The defendant is also permitted to inspect and copy any statements made to officers of the government as well as his or her prior criminal record.

Decisions Affirming the Defendant's Constitutional Rights at Trial

Constitutional Right	Decision
Confrontation of witnesses	*Coy* v. *Iowa*
Jury trial	*Duncan* v. *Louisiana*
Right to counsel	*Gideon* v. *Wainwright*
Self-representation	*Faretta* v. *California*
Speedy trial	*Klopfer* v. *North Carolina*
Fair trial/free press	*Nebraska Press Association* v. *Stuart*
Public trial	*Richmond Newspapers, Inc.* v. *Commonwealth of Virginia*

Appendix C contains a copy of a motion for the production and inspection of evidence.

Denial of the Right of Discovery

A few states have not granted the right of pretrial discovery to a defendant in criminal matters. Those states allege that this right is a one-way street created for the defendant. It is also alleged that the defendant already has the balance of advantages in his or her favor in a criminal trial because the prosecution must prove the defendant guilty beyond a reasonable doubt, and in most jurisdictions, the verdict must be unanimous. The right of discovery would be an additional advantage. Further, permitting the defendant the right of pretrial discovery would enable him or her to secure perjured testimony and to fabricate evidence to meet the prosecution's case. The chance of witnesses for the prosecution being intimidated is increased if the defendant learns prior to the trial the names and addresses of witnesses and the nature of their testimony.

In states where the right of pretrial discovery is not recognized, the defendant must rely on the preliminary hearing, when applicable, for any assistance received in case preparation. In these instances, the defendant will probably demand a preliminary hearing even though the defendant knows that he or she will be held for trial.

Those arguing against permitting a defendant the right of discovery often quote a statement made by Judge Learned Hand, in the case of *United States* v. *Garison*,[2] in which he stated the following:

> Under our criminal procedure the accused has every advantage. While the prosecution is held rigidly to the charge, he (the defendant) need not disclose the barest outline of his defense. He is immune from question or comment on his silence; he cannot be convicted when there is the least fair doubt in the minds of any one of the twelve. Why in addition he should in advance have the whole evidence against him to pick over at his leisure, and make his defense, fairly or foully, I have never been able to see. . . . Our dangers do not lie in the too little tenderness to the accused. Our procedure has been always haunted by the ghost of the innocent man convicted. It is an unreal dream. What we need to fear is the

archaic formalism and the watery sentiment that obstructs, delays, and defeats the prosecution of crime.

Prosecution's Right of Pretrial Discovery

Even those states recognizing the right to pretrial discovery have granted little pretrial right of discovery to the prosecution. This trend supports the contention that the right of pretrial discovery is a one-way street. The most convincing argument against allowing pretrial discovery by the prosecution is that the right would compel the defendant to be a witness against himself or herself. Many legal scholars are at a loss to understand how furnishing the names and addresses of witnesses, or the defense to be used—such as an alibi or insanity defense—would be self-incrimination, but there are state courts that have prohibited the prosecution from exercising the right of pretrial discovery upon the self-incrimination claim.

In addition to the self-incrimination allegation, the supreme court of one state has held that it is the burden of the prosecution to prove the defendant guilty beyond a reasonable doubt and that any discovery by the prosecution that would lessen that burden is not permissible. It is almost impossible to imagine any discovery that would not in some respect lessen the burden of the prosecution. This holding by that court has been highly criticized in legal circles as being too restrictive and without merit.

Rule 16 of the Federal Rules of Criminal Procedure grants to the government (the prosecution) almost the identical rights of pretrial discovery that are granted to the defendant. More states in the future may follow the precedent set by the federal government in granting the right of pretrial discovery to the prosecution. Several states and the federal government have adopted the requirement that a defendant advise the prosecution in advance of the trial that an alibi defense is to be used. In an alibi defense, the claim is that the accused was in another location at the time the crime was allegedly committed. This type of defense is most difficult to refute, since it usually comes late during the trial, catching the prosecution by surprise. The requirement that this information be furnished to the prosecution upon demand has received the sanction of the U.S. Supreme Court in the case of *Williams* v. *Florida*.[3] The facts of the *Williams* case reflect that, prior to his trial for robbery, Williams filed a motion with the trial court to he excused from the requirements of the Florida Rules of Criminal Procedure. This rule requires a defendant, on written demand of the prosecuting attorney, to give notice in advance of the trial if the defendant intends to claim an alibi and to furnish the prosecuting attorney with information on the place he or she claims to have been and with the names and addresses of the alibi witnesses. Williams, referred to as the petitioner, claimed that this rule compelled him to witness against himself in violation of the Fifth and Fourteenth Amendment rights. The motion was denied, and Williams was convicted and sentenced to life imprisonment. He took his case to the U.S. Supreme Court on the grounds that his Constitutional rights had been violated. The Supreme Court upheld the conviction and stated the following:

> Florida law provides for liberal discovery by the defendant against the State, and the notice-of-alibi rule is itself carefully hedged with reciprocal duties requiring state disclosure to the defendant. Given the ease with which an alibi can be fabricated, the State's interest in protecting itself against an eleventh hour defense is both obvious and legitimate. Reflecting this interest, notice-of-alibi

provisions, dating at least from 1927, are now in existence in a substantial number of States. The adversary system of trial is hardly an end to itself; it is not yet a poker game in which players enjoy an absolute right always to conceal their cards until played. We find ample room in that system, at least as far as "due process" is concerned, for the instant Florida rule, which is designed to enhance the search for truth in the criminal trial by insuring both the defendant and the State ample opportunity to investigate certain facts crucial to the determination of guilt or innocence.

Petitioner's major contention is that he was "compelled to be a witness against himself" contrary to the commands of the Fifth and Fourteenth Amendments because the notice-of-alibi rule required him to give the State the name and address of Mrs. Scotty in advance of trial and thus to furnish the State with information useful in convicting him. No pretrial statement of petitioner was introduced at trial; but armed with Mrs. Scotty's name and address and the knowledge that she was to be petitioner's alibi witness, the State was able to take her deposition in advance of trial and to find rebuttal testimony. Also, requiring him to reveal the elements of his defense is claimed to have interfered with his right to wait until after the State had presented its case to decide how to defend against it. We conclude, however, as has apparently every other court which has considered the issue, that the privilege against self-incrimination is not violated by a requirement that the defendant give notice of an alibi defense and disclose his alibi witnesses.

The defendant in a criminal trial is frequently forced to testify himself and to call other witnesses in an effort to reduce the risk of conviction. When he presents his witnesses, he must reveal their identity and submit them to cross-examination which in itself may prove incriminating or which may furnish the State with leads to incriminating rebuttal evidence. That the defendant faces such a dilemma demanding a choice between complete silence and presenting a defense has never been thought an invasion of the privilege against compelled self-incrimination. The pressures generated by the State's evidence may be severe but they do not vitiate the defendant's choice to present an alibi defense and witnesses to prove it, even though the attempted defense ends in catastrophe for the defendant. However "testimonial" and "incriminating" the alibi defense proves to be, it cannot be considered "compelled" within the meaning of the Fifth and Fourteenth Amendments.

Despite the *Williams* decision, a number of states have not passed legislation requiring a defendant to notify the prosecution that he or she plans an alibi defense. Some state courts still contend that if furnishing the names and addresses of witnesses will incriminate the defendant, it is not necessary to provide them to the prosecution. Thus, the right of pretrial discovery by the prosecution is seriously curtailed.

THE MOTION TO SUPPRESS EVIDENCE

At common law, it was held that any evidence that would assist in determining the truth of what happened in a particular case was admissible during a trial. The same policy was followed in this country for a number of years in spite of the constitutional guarantee contained in the Fourth Amendment of the U.S. Constitution against unreasonable searches and seizures. In the early 1920s, a few states, either by legislation or court decisions, began to hold that unlawfully obtained evidence was not admissible during a trial in attempting to prove a defendant guilty. The inadmissibility of unlawfully obtained evidence is known as the *exclusionary rule*. In 1961, the landmark case of *Mapp* v. *Ohio*[4] placed the exclusionary rule in effect for all the states. Since that decision, much use has been made of the *motion to suppress evidence*.

Either as a result of pretrial discovery or through the preliminary hearing, the defense may learn that the prosecution plans to introduce evidence during the trial that, in the opinion of the defense, was unlawfully acquired. This evidence may be material that the defense alleges was obtained through an unlawful search or seizure, or it may be a confession that the defense states was improperly obtained. When this occurs, the defense counsel will usually file a motion to suppress evidence with the appropriate trial court. A hearing will be held on this motion, and the prosecution will present facts and testimony in an effort to prove that the material or confession was lawfully obtained. The defense may present evidence in an effort to prove that the evidence should be suppressed or not be introduced because of illegality.

Hearing to Suppress

The hearing to suppress evidence must be held prior to the trial time in some jurisdictions, and the hearing is held before a judge alone and not before a jury. If the judge concludes that the evidence was illegally obtained, he or she will suppress it or hold that it is not admissible during the trial. If the judge believes that the material was lawfully obtained, it may be introduced against the defendant during the trial, and the jury will give the evidence the weight to which they feel it is entitled.

The reason that the hearing on the motion must be made prior to the trial in some jurisdictions is that it is felt that the trial judge should not be required to stop in midtrial to determine whether evidence presented by the prosecution was lawfully obtained. If the evidence is ruled inadmissible, the prosecuting attorney may decide to dismiss the charge if a conviction would not be possible without the suppressed evidence. Thus, the time and expense of a trial would be saved.

Some jurisdictions permit the defense to object to the introduction of the evidence again at the trial, and the judge may consider at that time whether the evidence is admissible. A few jurisdictions require that the motion to suppress be made prior to trial, holding that unless the motion is made prior to the trial, the defendant waives the constitutional right to object to the method of obtaining evidence. In these instances, courts have held that there is no waiver if the defendant could not have reasonably made the motion prior to the trial. A reasonable cause may be that the defendant was unaware of the allegedly illegal search or seizure, or did not have reasonable time to make the motion before the trial. Other states hold that a pretrial motion to suppress evidence is premature and that the objection should take place during the trial. Pretrial motions and hearings to suppress evidence unnecessarily delay setting the case for trial, and, since an objection to the introduction of the evidence may be made again in most jurisdictions during the trial, it is a duplication of effort.

In jurisdictions where the pretrial motion to suppress is not mandatory, many defense attorneys will not file a pretrial motion. They will wait and object to the introduction of the evidence at the preliminary hearings. It is the prosecution's responsibility to present testimony in an effort to prove that the evidence was lawfully obtained. Through cross-examination by the defense and the testimony of witnesses, efforts will be made to prove that the offered evidence was unlawfully obtained. If the judge holds that the evidence was illegally obtained, the defendant will be released unless other evidence causes the judge to reasonably believe that the defendant should be held for trial. If the evidence is lawfully obtained and the defendant is held for trial, a second objection to the introduction of the evidence may be made during the trial.

Grounds for Evidence Suppression

Obtaining confessions and unreasonable searches and seizures are two areas that include numerous grounds for challenging the introduction of evidence. A confession obtained through the psychological pressure of threats or promises would be suppressed. Search warrants may be improperly issued, or permission for consent searches involuntarily may be given. An officer exceeding the permissible area on a search incident to arrest provides grounds for a motion to suppress. A sample document for a typical motion to suppress evidence appears in the accompanying illustration.

THE MOTION TO DISMISS CHARGES

After a complaint, an information, or an indictment has been filed against a defendant, facts are sometimes revealed that, in the interest of justice, demand the charge be dismissed. In some jurisdictions, this action may be taken by the prosecuting attorney and is known as entering a nolle prosequi. Other jurisdictions do not grant the prosecuting attorney nolle prosequi authority. In these jurisdictions, a charge may be dismissed only by a judge, by judicial motion, or upon recommendation of the prosecuting attorney.

There are many reasons a prosecuting attorney may recommend that a charge be dismissed after it is filed. The original allegation may be unfounded; the evidence to be introduced may have been unlawfully obtained, making a conviction impossible; or a material witness may no longer be available to testify. Dismissals have also been granted to a defendant to allow testimony against codefendants. The defense may file a motion to dismiss on the grounds that the indictment or information was seriously defective or that a case was not brought to trial within the prescribed time.

A dismissal by a judge on judicial or defense motion is not always a bar to further prosecutive action on the matter, particularly if the charge is a felony. The prosecuting attorney may refile the charge. How many times this action may take place is not firmly established, but the right to a speedy trial prevents too many dismissals and refilings from taking place.

THE MOTION FOR CONTINUANCE

Criminal cases are to be heard as soon as reasonably possible, and they are to be given precedence over civil matters. Most state codes provide that no continuance of a criminal trial shall be granted except where the ends of justice require a continuance. The codes also provide that the continuance shall not be for a period longer

(TITLE OF COURT)

Notice of Motion and Motion to Suppress Evidence

In the Matter of Property   Cr. No. _____

Seized from (<u>names of persons from whom the property was seized</u>)

To (<u>Names of all police officers known to have participated in the seizure of the property</u>)

PLEASE TAKE NOTICE that on _____, 20 _____ at _____.m., or as soon thereafter as the matter can be heard, at the courtroom of the Criminal District Court, Parish of Orleans at _____, City of New Orleans, State of Louisiana; Defendant Jon Notguilty will move the Court for an order directing various levying officers, including the above-named, to return to the movants forthwith certain personal property, _____ a schedule of which is attached to this motion, and which on _____ 19_____, at the premises known as _____, was unlawfully seized and taken from the movants by those levying officers, and directing that the property seized be suppressed as evidence against _____ in any criminal proceeding.

This motion is made on the grounds that:

1. _____.
2. _____.

This motion is based on this notice, the pleadings, records, and files in this proceeding, the attached memorandum of points and authorities and the attached supporting declaration of _____.

Dated: _____

_____ (signed)

Attorney for Defendant

than justice requires. Despite these provisions, perhaps no motion is made with greater frequency than the motion for a continuance, particularly by the defense. What is within the "ends of justice" and how long "justice" requires the continuance to be are primarily within the discretion of the trial judge.

Grounds for a Continuance

There are no specified grounds on which the continuance may be based. Justice requires that a continuance be granted to obtain a material witness. But before a continuance to obtain such a witness will be granted, the side making the request must present further evidence on why the witness is material, what effort has been made to locate the witness, and how the testimony of this witness is not available through any other witness. Continuances have been granted to defendants that they may obtain effective counsel, and they often take advantage of this opportunity. Defendants have employed counsel and then at trial time, they have discharged counsel and requested a continuance to obtain new counsel. There are cases in which this request was made as many as ten to thirteen times. Occasionally, the defendant will have employed new counsel just prior to the trial date, and the defense counsel will make a motion for continuance on the grounds that additional time is needed to prepare the defense. Continuances have been granted when a defendant is not physically able to attend trial or when the defense attorney is ill or engaged in another trial. The length of time a trial may be delayed because of these reasons is undetermined. If the defendant is not feigning illness, the court has no alternative but to grant continuance until the defendant recovers. But how long may defense counsel delay a trial? It has been held that unless a defense counsel is available for trial within a reasonable time, the defendant must obtain substitute counsel.

A continuance will not usually be granted for longer than thirty to sixty days. At the end of that period, a new request may be made, and frequently it is granted. As a result, many criminal trials are not heard for more than a year after the crime has been committed.

When a motion for a continuance is to be made, reasonable notice must be given to the trial judge and the opposing side. Reasonable notice is difficult to determine. Unfortunately, the notice may be given on the trial date. If a continuance is granted at that time, it works a hardship on everyone involved in the trial proceeding. It may be particularly inconvenient for witnesses who have taken time off from work and have traveled great distances to appear in court. The witnesses will have to reappear on the new date set for the trial. The defense makes these frequent requests for continuances because they usually work to the advantage of the defendant. The possibilities of prosecution witnesses' becoming unavailable and memories dulling increase with the passage of time.

THE MOTION FOR SEVERANCE OF OFFENSES

Criminals often commit a series of crimes in a relatively short period. For example, a burglar may commit a number of burglaries within a few days or weeks. If the burglar is caught and charged, it is logical to try the offender on all the charges at one time. Consolidating several charges into one trial saves time and expense by eliminating separate trials for each crime. Most state laws permit a series of crimes committed in one jurisdiction to be combined into one accusatory pleading. Each of the crimes charged in the accusatory pleading is referred to as a *count*. Crimes must be of the same general nature to be consolidated. If the crimes are all similar offenses, such as all burglaries or all robberies, there is no doubt about consolidating them into one accusatory pleading. It has also been held that if the crimes are of a different nature but are part of the same transaction, scheme, or plan, they may be consolidated. For example, if an offender should commit a burglary and then commit arson to hide the burglary, these two offenses could be consolidated, since they are a part of the same transaction or plan. However, a crime of robbery and a crime of burglary could not be consolidated without being parts of the same transaction.

A defendant having a series of crimes consolidated into one trial has the advantage of avoiding defense in separate trials. Yet there are times when a defendant will make a motion for a severance of offenses. This motion is based upon the premise that being tried on several counts during the same trial is prejudicial to the defendant. As stated in the case of *Cross* v. *United States:*[5]

> Prejudice may develop when an accused wishes to testify on one but not the other of two joined offenses which are clearly distinct in time, place and evidence. His decision whether to testify will reflect a balancing of several factors with respect to each count: the evidence against him, the availability of defense evidence other than his testimony, the plausibility and substantiality of his testimony, the possible effects of demeanor, impeachment, and cross-examination. But if the two charges are joined for trial, it is not possible for him to weigh these factors separately as to each count. If he testifies on one count, he runs the risk that any adverse effects will influence the jury's consideration of the other count. Thus he runs the risk on both counts, although he may benefit on only one. Moreover, a defendant's silence on one count would be damaging in the face of his express denial of the other. Thus he may be coerced into testifying on the count upon which he wished to remain silent.

Also in *Drew* v. *United States,*[6] the Court stated the following:

> The justification for a liberal rule on joinder of offenses appears to be the economy of a single trial. The argument against joinder is that the defendant may be prejudiced for one or more of the following reasons: (1) he may become embarrassed or confounded in presenting separate defenses; (2) the jury, may use the evidence of one of the crimes charged to infer a criminal disposition on the part of the defendant from which is found his guilt of the other crime or crimes charged; or (3) the jury may cumulate the evidence of the various crimes charged and find guilt when, if considered separately, it would not so find. A less tangible, but perhaps equally persuasive, element of prejudice may reside in a latent feeling of hostility engendered by the charging of several crimes as distinct from only one. Thus, in any given case the court must weigh prejudice to the defendant caused by the joinder against the obviously important consideration of economy and expedition in judicial administration.

THE MOTION FOR SEVERANCE

The laws of most states hold that when two or more defendants are jointly charged with the same offense, they must be tried jointly unless the judge feels that in the best interest of justice separate trials should be granted. Jointly trying codefendants promotes economy and efficiency, and avoids multiplicity of trials. But defendants often file a motion for severance to avoid the possibility of prejudice. The prejudice may stem from the fact that evidence against one defendant is not applicable to others, and a jury may have difficulty in separating the evidence. One defendant may have a particularly bad reputation, and a codefendant could be convicted by association. A defendant may have given a confession implicating other codefendants, and this confession is to be introduced during the trial. Under such circumstances, unless the identifying data concerning codefendants cannot be adequately deleted from the confession, they are not admissible. Otherwise, separate trials must be granted. The jury would then be expected to perform the overwhelming task of considering a confession in determining the guilt or innocence of the confessor and then ignoring the confession in determining the guilt or innocence of codefendants.[7]

Since the concern with joint trials stems principally from the fact that the jury might be prejudiced against the defendant, should a severance be granted if a jury is waived in favor of a court trial? Jurisdictions are divided on the answer to this question. Some hold that a judge is competent to separate evidence between co-defendants, whether it be a confession, testimonial, or physical evidence. Therefore, a severance of codefendants may be denied. Other jurisdictions hold that upon an allegation of prejudice, a defendant has an absolute right to a severance whether the trial is a court trial or a jury trial.

THE MOTION TO DETERMINE COMPETENCY

If the present mental state of the defendant is in question at any time prior to or during a trial, the defense counsel should make a motion for a hearing on competency. Insanity refers to the accused's mental state at the time of the act. Competency refers to the accused's mental state at trial time. A hearing may be ordered on the competency question if the actions of the defendant would cause doubt in the judge's mind. Competency of the defendant must be determined because a person cannot be tried, sentenced, or punished while insane. The procedure of determining competency is referred to as both a hearing and a trial. Usually the hearing is conducted before a judge sitting alone, unless the defense demands that a jury trial be held. In some states, like Texas, the accused has a right to a jury trial on the issue of competency.

The competency hearing should not be confused with a trial on a plea of not guilty by reason of insanity, as discussed later in the text. The hearing to determine the competency of the defendant has nothing to do with guilt or innocence; it ascertains the defendant's *present* mental capabilities. The test of competency determines the defendant's present ability to understand the nature and purpose of the proceedings, and it measures the capacity to assist in the defense in a rational manner. If the defendant is unable to understand the charge and possible defenses and is also unable properly to confer with counsel in regard to the conduct of the trial, the trial should not take place. The test to determine competency is not the same as that used in a trial on a plea of not guilty by reason of insanity.

Once the competency of the defendant is questioned, all prosecutive proceedings must be halted until the issue of competency can be determined. The next step is the competency hearing or trial. Prior to the hearing, the defendant will normally be examined by psychologists or psychiatrists appointed by the court and by those selected by the defense, if desired. During the hearing, these specialists and any other witnesses able to shed light on the defendant's competency may be called to testify. If the prosecution thinks that the defendant is presently able to defend himself or herself, evidence may be offered in an effort to prove that the defendant is competent. If determined incompetent, the defendant may be confined to a mental hospital until recovery. There is no formal procedure to determine that the defendant has recovered his or her competency other than certification to that effect by the hospital superintendent. After the defendant has recovered, he or she will be brought back for trial unless the recovery period is extensive and the charge has been dismissed in the interest of justice.

If the competency hearing determines that the defendant is presently sane, the prosecutive proceedings will commence again from the point where they stopped. This is the case unless the trial on guilt or innocence was in progress and the trial judge dismissed the jury and declared a mistrial. Under those circumstances, the trial would be resumed from the beginning with a new jury. Various other motions will be discussed as the trial proceedings unfold.

PRETRIAL CONFERENCE

Pretrial conferences in civil matters have been effectively used for years. These conferences are informal meetings, usually in the judge's chambers, between both attorneys and the judge. The strong and weak points of the case are discussed in an effort to arrive at a settlement without going to trial. With court calendars becoming more and more crowded, greater use is being made of the pretrial conference in criminal matters. As the trial date approaches, the trial judge will often call for a pretrial conference. During these conferences, the judge will determine whether both sides will be ready for trial on the date set or if a continuance will be requested. The judge will also try to ascertain the approximate number of days each side anticipates taking to present its case. By gathering this information, the judge will be better able to set other cases for trial and decide whether alternate jurors should be selected.

The attorneys may try to arrive at some sequence in calling witnesses, particularly professional persons or expert witnesses. The attorneys will attempt to agree, or to stipulate, to certain testimony. There are advantages to each side in stipulating to certain facts that a witness may present if called to testify. The stipulation may concern some uncontroversial matter when the presentation of proof during the trial would be of little consequence—thus saving trial time. The stipulation of some fact that the prosecution can prove convincingly may be to the advantage of the defense because it eliminates a witness from going into great detail to the detriment of the defendant. Those facts having a stipulation are brought to the attention of the jury at the appropriate time, and the jury considers those facts as though they had been presented in testimony during the trial. The presentation of facts by stipulation does not violate the defendant's right of confrontation, since the defendant has waived his or her right of confrontation of that particular witness, or witnesses, by agreeing to the facts.

PLEA NEGOTIATION

Plea negotiating, or *plea bargaining* as it is more commonly known, is nothing more than agreement between the prosecuting attorney and the defense to reduce a charge to a lesser crime, to drop certain charges, or to receive a lessened sentence in return for a guilty or nolo contendere plea. Plea negotiating usually takes place shortly after the initial appearance or the arraignment of a defendant. In most jurisdictions, the negotiating can continue to the time that the verdict is rendered. Plea negotiating is often discussed during the pretrial conference. Although it has been held that the judge should not be a part of the negotiation, he or she should be made aware of it, and in many instances must, by law, accept the conditions of the plea bargaining before the guilty or nolo contendere plea is acceptable.

Plea bargaining has been both praised and criticized. Some allege that plea bargaining is important in the administration of criminal law, is advantageous to the state by saving time and money, and increases efficiency and flexibility in the criminal process. The advantage to the defendant is reduced punishment. Plea bargaining has been criticized, particularly by some law enforcement officers, because it allows a criminal to take advantage of the justice system by not being convicted and sentenced for the crime actually committed. The result is a much lighter penalty.

Benefits of Plea Bargaining

Although the practice of accepting negotiated pleas has been criticized, many prosecuting attorneys state that the acceptance of a negotiated plea often is for more justifiable reasons than lightening caseloads and clearing crowded court calendars. Sometimes an offender is initially charged on a *more serious* crime than is warranted by the evidence. Or an offender may be charged with a more serious crime so that a higher bail will be set. Reducing the number of charges in exchange for a negotiated plea may be justified on the grounds that many judges tend to give concurrent sentences. There would be little advantage in going to trial on a larger number of charges over accepting a plea on a reduced number. As to accepting a negotiated plea on the promise of a lighter sentence, prosecutors point out that they have little or no control over the sentence that may be given one convicted of a crime. Even if the accused were convicted as a result of a trial, the sentence could be the same as that agreed to in the negotiated plea.

In the past, plea bargaining was not discussed openly since it was considered to be unethical, if not illegal. Judges seldom were aware of any agreements made by plea bargaining because, to be valid, a guilty or nolo contendere plea had to be freely and voluntarily given. If the plea was induced upon some promise of leniency, there was a question of its being freely and voluntarily given. The secrecy of plea bargaining was eliminated by legislative action and court decisions, and today plea bargaining is openly engaged in as a part of the justice system.

Supreme Court and Plea Bargaining

Much of the change in viewpoint was brought about by the case of *Brady* v. *United States,*[8] in which the U.S. Supreme Court gave sanction to plea bargaining. The facts of the case show that Brady was charged with a kidnaping violation and faced a maximum penalty of death if the verdict of the jury should so recommend. Brady entered a plea of guilty to the charge and was sentenced to 30 years' imprisonment. The case was taken to the U.S. Supreme Court upon the grounds that the plea was not freely and voluntarily given because of representations of a reduction of sentence and clemency. Brady alleged that this inducement was compelling him to be a witness against himself in violation of the Fifth Amendment to the U.S. Constitution. The Supreme Court concluded that the guilty plea "was voluntarily and knowingly made" even though it may have been induced by representations with respect to reduction of sentence and clemency, and, as such, Brady's guarantee against self-incrimination had not been violated.

The Court in this decision stated the following:

> ...That a guilty plea is a grave and so solemn act to be accepted only with care and discernment has long been recognized. Central to the plea and the foundation for entering judgment against the defendant is the defendant's admission in open court that he committed the acts charged in the indictment. He thus stands as a witness against himself and he is shielded by the Fifth Amendment from being compelled to do so, hence the minimum requirement that his plea be the voluntary expression of his own choice.

The voluntariness of Brady's plea can be determined only by considering all of the relevant circumstances surrounding it. One of these circumstances was the possibility of a heavier sentence following a guilty verdict after a trial. It may be that Brady, faced with a strong case against him and recognizing that his chances for acquittal were slight, preferred to plead guilty and thus limit the penalty to life imprisonment rather than to elect a jury trial, which could result in a death penalty.

The State to some degree encourages pleas of guilty at every important step in the criminal process. For some people, their breach of a State's law is alone sufficient reason for surrendering themselves and accepting punishment. For others, apprehension and charge, both threatening acts by the Government, jar them into admitting their guilt. In still other cases, the postindictment accumulation of evidence may convince the defendant and his counsel that a trial is not worth the agony and expense to the defendant and his or her family. All these pleas of guilty are valid in spite of the State's responsibility for some of the factors motivating the pleas; the pleas are no more improperly compelled than is the decision by a defendant at the close of the State's evidence at trial that he or she must take the stand or face certain conviction.

Of course, the agents of the State may not produce a plea by actual or threatened physical harm or by mental coercion overbearing the will of the defendant. But nothing of the sort is claimed in this case; nor is there evidence that Brady was so gripped by fear of the death penalty or hope of leniency that he did not or could not, with the help of counsel, rationally weigh the advantages of going to trial against the advantages of pleading guilty.

The issue we deal with is inherent in the criminal law and its administration, because guilty pleas are not constitutionally forbidden, because the criminal law characteristically extends to judge or jury a range of choice in setting the sentence in individual cases, and because both the State and the defendant often find it advantageous to preclude the possibility of the maximum penalty authorized by law. For a defendant who sees slight possibility of acquittal, the advantages of pleading guilty and limiting the probable penalty are obvious—his or her exposure is reduced, the correctional processes can begin immediately, and the practical burdens of a trial are eliminated. For the State, there are advantages: the more promptly imposed punishment after an admission of guilt may more effectively attain the objectives of punishment; and with the avoidance of trial, scarce judicial and prosecutorial resources are conserved for those cases in which there is a substantial issue of the defendant's guilt or in which there is substantial doubt that the State can sustain its burden of proof. It is this mutuality of advantage that perhaps explains the fact that at present, well over three-fourths of the criminal convictions in this country rest on pleas of guilty, a great many of them no doubt motivated at least in part by the hope or assurance of a lesser penalty than might be imposed if there were a guilty verdict after a trial to judge or jury.

Of course, that the prevalence of guilty pleas is explainable does not necessarily validate those pleas or the system that produces them. But we cannot hold that it is unconstitutional for the State to extend a benefit to a defendant who in turn extends a substantial benefit to the State and who demonstrates by his or her plea that the defendant is ready and willing to admit his or her crime and to enter the correctional system in a frame of mind that affords hope for success in rehabilitation over a shorter period of time than might otherwise be necessary.

The Court further stated that even if a guilty plea were entered through some inducement of leniency, that plea could not be withdrawn at a later date if the plea had been freely and voluntarily given. The standard of voluntariness of a guilty plea was set forth in the *Brady* decision, which is as follows:

> A plea of guilty entered by one fully aware of the direct consequences, including the actual value of any commitments made to him by the court, prosecutor, or his own counsel, must stand unless induced by threats or promises to discontinue improper harassment, misrepresentation including unfulfilled or unfulfillable promises, or perhaps by promises that are by their nature improper as having no proper relationship to the prosecutor's business (e.g., bribes).

Generally, before a negotiated plea is accepted, the judge and the prosecuting attorney must agree on the terms involved. Some judges have held that they may accept a negotiated plea without the concurrence of the prosecution and can even accept such a plea over the objections of the prosecutor. This contention is based on the fact that a judge may accept an *unnegotiated plea* without the consent or concurrence of the prosecutor; therefore, it is believed that the judge may accept a *negotiated plea* without the consent of the prosecutor.

Pleas to Be Related to the Offense Charged

It has been held that a negotiated plea should be related to the crime charged in the accusatory pleading, but the plea does not have to be confined to the one in the accusatory pleading. The negotiated plea may be to an offense of a lesser degree than the one in the accusatory pleading. For example, a defendant may be charged in the pleading with the crime of murder but may be permitted to plead guilty to voluntary manslaughter. The plea to the offense of voluntary manslaughter would be a plea to a related crime of murder. It is also held that if the negotiated plea is to a crime committed in the course of conduct that leads to the charge in the accusatory pleading, this plea would be to a related crime. For example, during the course of a robbery, the defendant may take the victim from his or her home to his or her place of business to open a safe. The defendant may be charged in the accusatory pleading with kidnaping but may be permitted to plead guilty to robbery. This would be a related crime, since the robbery offense was in the course of conduct that led to the kidnaping charge. It is important that the negotiated plea be to a related crime so that the plea will more nearly reflect the true criminal history of the crime for which the defendant was arrested. Often if the accused is awaiting trial on two or more separate unrelated indictments, the plea bargain will include an agreement to dismiss the other indictments.

Notable U.S. Supreme Court Cases on the Regulation of Plea Bargaining

Case	Decision
Boykin v. *Alabama* (1969)	The defendant must make an affirmative statement that the plea is voluntary before the judge can accept it.
Brady v. *United States* (1970)	Avoiding the possibility of the death penalty is not grounds to invalidate a guilty plea.
North Carolina v. *Alford* (1970)	Accepting a guilty plea from a defendant who maintains his or her innocence is valid.
Santobello v. *New York* (1971)	The promise of a prosecutor that rests on a guilty plea must be kept in a plea bargaining agreement.
Bordenkircher v. *Hayes* (1978)	A defendant's constitutional rights are not violated when a prosecutor threatens to reindict the accused on more serious charges if he or she is not willing to plead guilty to the original offense.
Hill v. *Lockhart* (1985)	To prove ineffectiveness of defense counsel, the defendant needs to show a reasonable probability that, except for counsel's errors, the defendant would not have pleaded guilty.
Ricketts v. *Admason* (1987)	The defendant is required to keep his or her side of the bargain to receive the promised offer of leniency, because plea bargaining rests on an agreement between the parties.
United States v. *Mezzanatto* (1995)	A defendant who wants to plea bargain in federal court can be required to agree that, if he or she testifies at trial, his or her statements during the plea bargain negotiations can be used against him or her.

Withdrawal of the Negotiated Plea

A guilty plea may be withdrawn if the bargain is not complied with by either the judge or the prosecuting attorney. The statutes of those states where negotiated pleas have been enacted usually provide that a negotiated plea of guilty or nolo contendere must be approved by both the judge and the prosecuting attorney. If the approval is not forthcoming, the defendant is permitted to withdraw the plea of guilty or nolo contendere and to enter another plea. Once the approval is given, the bargain must be complied with, or the defendant may also withdraw the guilty or nolo contendere plea. This is true even though the defendant may not have been entirely honest in dealing with the court. In *People* v. *Johnson,*[9] for a negotiated plea of guilty, the judge promised the defendant that the matter would be handled as a misdemeanor rather than as a felony and that the defendant would be given probation. After discovering that the defendant had concealed his true identity and past criminal record, the judge sentenced the defendant to the state prison.

Upon appeal, the judgment was reversed, and the trial court was directed to permit the defendant to withdraw the guilty plea and enter a new plea. The appellate court relied upon the state statute providing that "where such plea [negotiated plea] is accepted by the prosecuting attorney in open court and is approved by the court, the defendant . . . cannot be sentenced on such plea to a punishment more severe than that specified in the plea." The statute further provided that if the court approves the plea, the defendant, before accepting it, must be informed that the court might withdraw the approval in light of other consideration of the matter. In such case, the defendant shall have the right to withdraw the plea if so desired.

In the *Johnson* case, the judge failed to inform the defendant of his right to withdraw the plea. During the argument before the state supreme court in this case, Johnson's attorney requested that, since the trial judge erred, the Supreme Court should give Johnson the alternative of enforcing the original bargain or of withdrawing his plea. The Court held that since there was a serious misrepresentation by Johnson, it was reluctant to create a right, for a defendant, to a specific performance of an original plea bargain rather than permit a withdrawal of the plea of guilty.

CAPSTONE CASE

United States v. *Benchimol*
471 U.S. 453, 105 S.Ct. 2103, 85 L.Ed.2d 462 (1985)
Per Curiam.

[Respondent pleaded guilty to an information charging him with one count of mail fraud pursuant to a plea bargain whereby the Government agreed to recommend probation on condition that restitution be made. The District Court disregarded the recommendation and sentenced respondent to six years of treatment and supervision under the Youth Corrections Act. He filed a motion to withdraw his guilty plea or, in the alternative, to have his sentence vacated and be resentenced to the time already served, claiming that the Government had failed to comply with its part of the plea bargain.]

The District Court that had received the guilty plea also heard respondent's application for collateral relief, and denied it. The Court of Appeals had this view of the Benchimol agreement to plead guilty. "The government concedes that in exchange for the guilty plea it promised to recommend probation with restitution." However, at the sentencing hearing, the presentence report incorrectly stated that the government would stand silent. Benchimol's counsel informed the court that the government instead recommended probation with restitution. The Assistant United States Attorney then stated: "That is an accurate representation."

The Court of Appeals concluded that the Government had breached its plea bargain because, although the Assistant United States Attorney concurred with defense counsel's statement that the Government recommended probation with restitution, it "made no effort to explain its reasons for agreeing to recommend a lenient sentence but rather left an impression with the court of less-than-enthusiastic support for leniency."

We think this holding misconceives the effect of the relevant rules and of the applicable case law. Federal Rule of Criminal Procedure 11(e) provides an elaborate formula for the negotiation of plea bargains, which allows the attorney for the Government to agree to move for dismissal of other charges and to agree that a specific sentence is the appropriate disposition of the case. It also authorizes the Government attorney to make a recommendation for a particular sentence, or agree not to oppose the defendant's request for such a sentence, with the understanding that such recommendation or request shall not be binding upon the court.

It may well be that the Government in a particular case might commit itself to "enthusiastically" make a particular recommendation to the Court, and it may be that the Government in a particular case might agree to explain to the Court the reasons for the Government's making a particular recommendation. But respondent does not contend, nor did the Court of Appeals find, that the Government had in fact undertaken to do either of these things here. The Court of Appeals simply held that as a matter of law such an undertaking was to be implied from the Government's agreement to recommend a particular sentence. But our view of Rule 11(e) is that it speaks in terms of what the parties in fact agree to, and does not suggest that such implied-in-law terms as were read into this agreement by the Court of Appeals have any place under the Rule.

The Court of Appeals relied on [certain] cases for the conclusion it reached with respect to the requirement of "enthusiasm," but it appears to us that in each of these cases the Government attorney appearing personally in court at the time of the plea bargain expressed personal reservations about the agreement to which the Government had committed itself. This is quite a different proposition than an appellate determination from a transcript of the record made many years earlier that the Government attorney had "left an impression with the court of less-than-enthusiastic support for leniency." When the Government agrees pursuant to Rule 11(e) to make a recommendation with respect to sentence, it must carry out its part of the bargain by making the promised recommendation; but even if Rule 11(a) allows bargaining about degrees of enthusiasm, there appears to have been none here.

Rule 11(e) may well contemplate agreement by the Government in a particular case to state to the court its reasons for making the recommendation which it agrees to make. The Government suggests that spreading on the record its reasons for agreement to a plea bargain in a particular case, for example, that it did not wish to devote scarce resources to a trial of a particular defendant, or that it wished to avoid calling the victim as a witness would frequently harm, rather than help, the defendant's quest for leniency. These may well be reasons why the defendant would not wish to exact such a commitment from the Government, but for purposes of this case it is enough that no such agreement was made in fact. Since Rule 11(e) speaks generally of the plea bargains that the parties make, it was error for the Court of Appeals to imply as a matter of law a term which the parties themselves did not agree upon. For these reasons, we conclude that there was simply no default on the part of the Government in this case. Reversed.

Justice Stevens, concurring in the judgment.

. . . If the Government erred in failing to recommend affirmatively the proper sentence, the time to object was at the sentencing hearing or on direct appeal. . . .

Justice Brennan, with whom Justice Marshall joins, dissenting.

The Court today continues its unsettling practice of summarily reversing decisions rendered in favor of criminal defendants, based not on broad principle but on idiosyncratic facts and without full briefing or oral argument. . . . Because I find this one-sided practice of summary error correction inappropriate, I would vote merely to deny this petition for certiorari. Accordingly, I respectfully dissent.

Law in Practice

Set forth here is an actual copy of a psychological report entered into evidence by a defense counsel in an attempt to establish that the defendant lacked competency to stand trial. [*Note:* Jury found a lack of competency in this case. *Note:* TDC referred to in the report is the Texas Department of Corrections.]

July 18, 2001

Competency to Stand Trial
NAME: Richard Cole Masters
DOB: 12/10/58
DATE OF EVALUATION: 06/29/2001
CAUSE NO.: 12,943

Presenting Problem

Richard was referred for competency and sanity evaluations in connection with an alleged aggravated assault on another inmate which occurred on 3/31/01 and which ultimately led to the death of the victim. The assault occurred in a day room at Skyview and was witnessed by numerous staff and inmates. Richard has a very extensive history of mental health and disciplinary problems while in TDC, including serious assaultiveness. He has been evaluated extensively and given many courses of psychiatric treatment, including treatment with antipsychotic, anti-seizure, and antidepressant medications. His TDC record documents extensive refusal of treatment. Aside from obvious antisocial personality symptoms, Richard's most common diagnosis has been paranoid schizophrenia; and his TDC medical record is replete with references to psychotic functioning. His TDC record includes frequent observations of his having played with feces, but there have also been incidents in which he uses feces or urine as an aggressive instrument—as when on 10-5-00 he set up a cup of urine to fall on a guard's head when the guard came to give medication.

Evaluation Methods

Richard's TDC medical record was reviewed prior to the evaluation and he was given a mental status exam on 6/26/01. It was intended to do cognitive and personality testing but the interview was ended prematurely by the inmate. The Internal Affairs Division offense report with multiple witness statements was reviewed.

Prior to any interviewing, Richard's Miranda rights were reviewed as well as my connection to Inmate Legal Services and the disposition of a report of the evaluation. Richard did agree to proceed with the evaluation but focused his attention very aggressively and in a suspicious manner on the examiner's role; and Richard could never be worked out of this stance so that the cognitive and personality testing could proceed.

The total time spent face to face with the inmate was 35 minutes.

Findings

Richard is viewed as clearly not competent to stand trial on the charges against him. His mental status is so extremely poor that he cannot relate to someone who is even on his side of things. He is consistently aggressive and intrusive to the point where this completely disrupts even a superficial relationship. His behavior is viewed as quite unmanageable. His view of his involvement in the charged offense is highly distorted and shows little relationship to the witness statements, in so far as Richard was even able to comment on that event. He stated, "I believe someone is making a big issue out of nothing." He stated he has not been appointed a lawyer, and when the incident was raised with him for discussion he said, "They have not a witness."

Richard was incapable of understanding the role of the examiner in this evaluation and it is likely he will be confused and highly suspicious about a relationship with his defense attorney. He seemed unconcerned with the seriousness of the charges against him. He is so hyper-vigilant it is unlikely he would disclose all relevant material to his attorney. He is viewed as not capable of testifying effectively for his defense in his own behalf.

continued

Law in Practice   *Continued*

His actions were clearly and consistently self-protective and self-justifying but were completely self-defeating in nature because of his extreme aggressiveness and distortion. These distortions are not viewed as psychotic but as merely very self-serving. Richard's presentation at this evaluation is consistent with his presentation when visited by his attorney who noted the following: that Richard had to be manipulated with food even to agree to see the attorney, that Richard said the attorney had no right to talk to him, and that Richard refused to talk with him. After review of his TDC record it is likely he will become competent for a reasonable period of time only if he is consistently on psychotropic medication.

(signed)

Robert J. Martin, Ph.D

REVIEW QUESTIONS

1. What is the right of discovery?
2. What is the theory behind the right of discovery as it relates to the defendant?
3. In general, what may the defendant expect by exercising his or her right of discovery?
4. What reasons have been presented by some states in denying the defendant the right of discovery?
5. What is the chief argument against permitting the prosecution the right of discovery?
6. In relation to the right of discovery by the prosecution, what was the significance of the *Williams* v. *Florida* decision?
7. In general, what is the chief argument presented by the defense in support of a motion to suppress evidence?
8. Explain the significance of the exclusionary rule on the admissibility of evidence.
9. List two reasons for granting a trial continuance.
10. List the advantages and disadvantages of granting a motion to separate offenses.
11. What is the primary purpose of a motion to determine the present sanity of an accused?
12. What is the purpose of the pretrial conference?
13. What is a negotiated plea?
14. What are some of the advantages and disadvantages in plea bargaining?

LOCAL PROCEDURE

1. Is the defendant granted the right of discovery in your home state?
2. Is the prosecution afforded any right of discovery? If so, to what extent?
3. At what point must the motion to suppress evidence be made during a criminal proceeding?

ENDNOTES

1. 47 Cal.2d 566 (1956).
2. 291 F. 646 (1923).
3. 399 U.S. 78 (1970).
4. 367 U.S. 643 (1961).
5. 335 F.2d. 987 (1964).
6. 331 F.2d 85 (1964).
7. *Burton* v. *United States,* 391 U.S. 123 (1968).
8. 397 U.S. 742 (1970).
9. 12 CalRptr. 556 (1974).

The Trial: Roles of Major Participants

CHAPTER 10

Injustice anywhere is a threat to justice everywhere.

—Martin Luther King Jr. [in a letter written from his jail cell
in Birmingham, Alabama, published in *Atlantic Monthly*, August, 1963.]

THE ADVERSARY SYSTEM

Before discussing the actual trial proceedings, the roles of the other major participants in a criminal trial, in addition to the defendant, should be examined. These include the judge, prosecuting attorney, defense counsel, clerk of the court, bailiff, and court reporter. All are considered officers of the court. An examination of the function of the jury and the witnesses will be made later. By the trial time, the law enforcement officer will have completed his or her major role in the administration of justice. The investigation will be finished, and the final duty will be serving as a witness and testifying in a truthful, convincing manner.

The criminal trial procedure varies little—whether the charge is a felony or misdemeanor or whether the trial is a court trial or jury trial. The defendant is entitled to a fair trial before an impartial judge and an honest jury, and in an atmosphere of judicial calm.

Our justice system is an adversary system, meaning that it has two sides. In a criminal trial, these are the prosecution and the defense. Each is permitted to present evidence in its own behalf. Theoretically, both sides come into the trial on an equal basis. But Justice White of the United States Supreme Court, in *United States* v. *Wade,* pointed out that our system is not a true adversary system with both sides entering the trial on an equal footing. He stated the following:[1]

Law enforcement officers (and prosecuting attorneys) have the obligation to convict the guilty and to make sure they do not convict the innocent. They must

THE STEPS IN A JURY TRIAL

be dedicated to making the criminal trial a procedure for the ascertainment of the true facts surrounding the commission of the crime. To this extent, our so-called adversary system is not adversary at all: nor should it be. But defense counsel has no comparable obligation to ascertain or present the truth. Our system assigns him a different mission. He must be and is interested in not convicting the innocent, but absent a voluntary plea of guilty, we also insist that he defend his client whether he is innocent or guilty. The State has the obligation to present the evidence. Defense counsel need present nothing, even if he knows what the truth is. He need furnish no witnesses to the police, reveal any confidences of his client, nor furnish any other information to help the prosecution's case. If he can confuse a witness, even a truthful one, or make him appear at a disadvantage, unsure or indecisive, that will be his normal course. Our interest in not convicting the innocent permits counsel to put the State to its proof, to put the State's case in the worst possible light, regardless of what he thinks or knows to be the truth. Undoubtedly there are some limits which defense counsel must observe but more often than not, defense counsel will cross-examine a prosecution witness, and impeach him if he can, even if he thinks the witness is telling the truth, just as he will attempt to destroy a witness who he thinks is lying. In this respect, as part of our modified adversary system and as part of the duty imposed on the most honorable defense counsel, we countenance or require conduct which in many instances has little, if any, relation to the search for truth.

THE JUDGE

Although the terms *judge* and *the court* are used interchangeably, they should be distinguished. The judge presides over the trial proceedings and exercises those duties and power imposed by law. The court is a judicial proceeding presided over by a judge. The judge plays a very important role both before and during the trial. There is a great deal of power and authority, and many decisions are solely at the judge's discretion. Since unscrupulous acts could seriously affect the administration of justice, the judge's actions are subject to review by appellate courts. This scrutiny avoids any abuse of power or authority by the judge. Fortunately, most are honest individuals who endeavor to do a conscientious job.

Superior or District Court Judges

In most states, the judges of the superior or district court, or its equivalent, are elected by the people of the judicial district where they serve. This district is often the county. These judges are attorneys with past experience in the practice of law. One might wonder why an attorney with a number of years in law practice would wish to become a judge. Probably the most prevalent reason is the prestige that the office holds. Judges are generally held in high esteem within a community. One might be fearful that a judge, being an elected official, would have political obligations interfering with the ability to carry out functions impartially. As practicing attorneys, most candidates for a judgeship are fairly well known to the people of the community. The campaigning is primarily through personal contacts and the assistance of friends and does not place the victorious judge in a position where he or she is bound to grant political favors. This situation does not mean that members of organized crime have not tried to influence elections, as well as judges, in some areas. But the great majority of judges have proven to be above this corrupt influence.

Inferior Court Judges

As in the case of the superior or district court judges, inferior court judges are elected in most states. They are elected by the people of the judicial district where they serve, but this district is only a portion of a county. The qualifications for this position vary greatly among states. In many outlying rural areas, there is not enough court business to justify a full-time judge, so the judge may be a local practicing attorney elected to act as the judge when court business is required. The judge may also be the operator of a local market or a service station, or may be a retired person who needs a part-time job, as usually there is no requirement that the judge of these courts be trained in law. The fact that these judges are often poorly paid encourages bribery. Some judges work on a commission, receiving a percentage of fines levied, often creating the temptation to fine excessively, particularly in traffic violation cases. The brand of justice meted out in such courts some-times leaves a great deal to be desired. But again, like superior court judges, most of the judges are honest individuals elected because of the community's faith in their honesty and integrity. However, some inferior courts, like municipal courts in some districts, require the judge be an attorney before acting in the capacity of judge, and the judges of these courts are capable of handling the responsibilities imposed on them.

The Function of the Trial Judge

As pointed out in previous chapters, many duties have already been performed by the judge prior to the trial. With the judge sitting as magistrate, arraignments and preliminary hearings will have been held. Further, decisions will have been made on motions presented, appointments of counsel for indigent defendants will be completed, and the right to a speedy and fair trial will have been preserved. Though a fair trial is essential, a perfect trial is not expected.

During the trial, the judge has the primary responsibility for seeing that justice is carried out. The judge has a duty not only to protect the interests of the defendant but also to protect the interests of the public, ensuring that the guilty are convicted. The judge controls all proceedings during the trial and limits the introduction of evidence and arguments of counsel to relevant and material matters, with a view to the expeditious and effective ascertainment of the truth. The judge must control the conduct of the defendant and the spectators; determine the competency of witnesses and the admissibility of evidence; rule on objections made to questions asked by the attorneys; protect witnesses from harassment during cross-examination; interpret for the jury the laws involved in the particular case; and in some jurisdictions, comment on the weight of the evidence presented and the credibility of witnesses. In many jurisdictions, the judge sentences the defendant after conviction. If the trial is a court trial, the judge renders a verdict of guilt or innocence. Additional duties during the trial will be enumerated as the discussion of the trial progresses.

Contempt of Court.   A trial is to be conducted in a calm, dignified atmosphere. It is the responsibility of the judge to maintain such an atmosphere. Assisting in this regard is the authority to punish one who interrupts this atmosphere by declaring the offender in contempt of court. Contempt is an act that is disrespectful to the court or adversely affects the administration of justice. Any act that embarrasses, hinders, or obstructs the court in the administration of justice may be declared by the judge as contempt of court. Typical acts falling within this category include contemptuous or insulting remarks made to the judge and counsel's persistent arguments with the judge after an admonition to desist has been given. A judge may not go so far as to hold a defense counsel in contempt when counsel is merely defending his client vigorously. Disorderly conduct by a defendant or by the spectators may cause the judge to exercise the right of contempt. A witness who refuses to be sworn in and testify could be held in contempt of court. These acts generally take place within the presence of the judge and are known as direct contempt. The judge may punish the offender summarily—that is, there and then—without any hearing or other procedure taking place. The punishment may be imprisonment and/or a fine.

Not only are insulting remarks made toward a judge possible contemptuous acts, but such remarks between the prosecuting attorney and the defense counsel may also be contempt. In *People* v. *Fusaro,* one case in which the two attorneys had exchanged a series of acrimonious remarks, the judge held both in contempt of court. The defense counsel accused the prosecuting attorney of "indulging in crap," to which the prosecuting attorney, according to the judge, "sank to the occasion by voicing an epithet denoting fecal matter of a male bovine."[2] On another occasion, a prosecuting attorney was held in contempt upon using an old southern colloquialism implying that the defendant was the incestuous son of a canine mother.

An interesting development arose out of the *Fusaro* case. The defense counsel was held in contempt and was imprisoned in the middle of the trial. The facts of the case reflect the following: "The record reveals an acrimonious five day trial in which the attorneys mistook bickering and side remarks for vigorous advocacy. The prosecutor . . . was guilty of at least one act of misconduct," and the defense attorney

> . . . in his turn cluttered and interrupted the trial with frivolous objections. He aroused the trial judge's ire by permitting a witness to remain in the courtroom despite an exclusion order. He was twice late in returning to the trial after a recess.
>
> On the afternoon of the third day he was 15 minutes late, apologized and explained that the judge of another court had detained him. Outside the jury's presence the trial court held him in contempt for tardiness and imposed a one-day suspended jail sentence.

This exchange of remarks between the prosecuting attorney and defense counsel "indulging in crap" took place thereafter:

> At that point the judge recessed the trial, rebuked the attorneys, indicated that he wanted to consider their behavior and put the matter over to the next morning.
>
> The next morning, outside the jury's presence, the court found both attorneys in contempt.

The prosecuting attorney apologized, and the judge fined him $50. The defense counsel endeavored to justify the language. The judge

> . . . imposed a 24-hour jail sentence on defense counsel, refused to stay the execution and committed him to jail immediately. In view of the jailing, defendant's trial was recessed until the following morning.

The defendant was convicted on four narcotics charges. The conviction was appealed on the grounds that the judge had abused discretion in holding the defense counsel in contempt and immediately imposing a jail sentence. The defendant alleged that the jailing of the counsel prejudiced the defendant in the eyes of the jury and that a speedy trial was denied because of the interruption. Although the Appellate Court upheld the conviction, the Court took a dim view of jailing a defense counsel in the middle of a trial. The Court stated the following:

A trial court has inherent statutory power to exercise reasonable control over the trial in order to insure the orderly administration of justice and to maintain the dignity and authority of the court; it has power to punish summarily for contempts committed in its immediate view and presence. In accordance with the code of the State as punishment for contempt a court may impose a fine not exceeding $500 or up to five days imprisonment or both.

Attorneys as well as others may be held in contempt more than once during a trial and may be punished for each time they are so held. Offenders have been known to receive sentences running into years if the sentences are made to run consecutively. The United States Supreme Court has held that under these circumstances, the offender is entitled to a trial on the contempt charge. The Court stated that criminal contempt is a crime and that the offender is entitled to the same trial procedure as in any other crime. If total sentences exceed six months, the offender is entitled to a trial by jury. If the sentence is not more than six months, the offender may be tried by a judge sitting without a jury, but the Court stated that the trial should be conducted by a judge other than the one holding the offender in contempt because of the possible emotional involvement in the matter.[3] Some states grant a person accused of a crime a jury trial for all violations. The offender would then be entitled to a jury trial even though the sentence would not exceed six months.

The United States Supreme Court has considerably restricted the right of a trial judge to take summary contempt action and confused the action that may be taken. But the Court apparently did not eliminate the right entirely. The wording of the Court indicated that if it is necessary to preserve the calm atmosphere and dignity of the court, a judge may exercise the contempt action right at the time of the misconduct and may even sentence the person involved. But if the judge waits until the conclusion of the trial to take the contempt action, the offender is entitled to a trial on the contempt charge.

Defense counsels are held in contempt more frequently than prosecuting attorneys. If a prosecuting attorney indulges in misconduct, the misconduct may be considered prejudicial error, and a conviction may be reversed on appeal.

In addition, acts not performed in the presence of the judge may also be declared as contempt. These acts are known as indirect, or constructive, contempt, and they are usually the results of failures to abide by court orders. For example, jurors may discuss the facts of the case during a recess—in violation of the judge's order not to discuss the case, a juror may refuse to appear in court without sufficient good reason after receiving a summons to appear, or a witness may not appear as directed. Since indirect contempt does not occur in the presence of the judge, a hearing is held to determine whether the alleged offender should be held in contempt. Prior to the hearing, the judge will issue an order requesting the offender to show cause why he or she should not be held in contempt of court. Witnesses both for and against will be questioned at the hearing to assist in determining whether the accused should be held in contempt. If the judge determines that the person should be held in contempt, it would appear that the offender is entitled to a trial on the contempt charge, since the act was not committed in the presence of the judge.

The right of contempt is a powerful weapon, and it is meant to be. It permits a judge to prohibit court proceedings from getting out of hand because of misconduct. It also protects those involved in the court proceedings. If a judge should abuse his or her power of contempt, appeals may be made to a higher court for review and possible remedy.

THE VICTIM AND THE PERPETRATOR

The Victim

The victim of any crime is often the forgotten party in the criminal justice system. For many years, victims were perceived as simply another witness to the crime.[4] The prevailing attitude was that the real victim was the "People of the State" in which the crime was committed. Families of murder victims could not obtain information regarding the case and were often ignored by overworked and understaffed criminal justice personnel. Within the last twenty years, this attitude has begun to change as we become more aware of the needs and desires of crime victims.

Law enforcement professionals dealing with crime victims must understand that these victims may be suffering emotional and/or physical trauma as a result of the offense.[5] Care must be taken to ensure that victims understand how the process works and what their rights are. It is also important to realize that there are individuals other than the original victim who have an interest in the process. These parties include the victim's family and friends, and in some situations, the victim's employer. All the appropriate parties should be notified of every significant event within the criminal justice process. Law enforcement professionals must also respect and protect the victim's right to privacy if that is the victim's desire.

Victims of crime will normally have a number of questions and concerns regarding the court system and their involvement in it. One of the most frustrating aspects of this process is the fact that victims oftentimes perceive that the defendant has more rights and faster access to the courts than they do.

The Perpetrator

The perpetrator of a crime is guaranteed certain rights within our form of government. Many aspects of the criminal procedure process are controlled by the U.S. Constitution, specifically the Bill of Rights (the original ten amendments to the Constitution). These federal constitutional protections concerning individual rights are, for the most part, binding on state courts.[6]

These rights attach to the perpetrator early in the criminal procedure process, and violation of these rights may result in the case's being dismissed. For example, if the perpetrator confesses to the crime of murder and if that confession is obtained in violation of his or her constitutional rights, it may be suppressed.[7] If the confession is the only link connecting the defendant to the crime, the case may have to be dismissed. When these types of incidents occur, it is very difficult for the victim to understand why the defendant goes free when there has been a confession.

THE PROSECUTOR

The prosecuting attorney is known by a variety of names. In some places, he or she is known as the district attorney, or the D.A., and in other areas as the county attorney. In the federal system, the title is the United States Attorney. The "public official" role of the prosecuting attorney is comparatively recent. For many years, it was the responsibility of the victim or relatives to prosecute when a crime was committed. Attorneys were employed by these persons to assist in the prosecution. As time passed, it was deemed advisable to have a full-time public prosecutor, since the offense was actually committed against society, and therefore the office of the prosecuting attorney was established.

In most states, the prosecuting attorney is an elected official of the county. In large urban areas, it is a sought-after position, since it holds prestige, it pays well, and the prosecuting attorney has a number of deputies for assistance. In many places, there may be no staff, and in sparsely settled counties, the position may be only a part-time job. When not engaged in handling official duties, the prosecuting attorney in such counties may have a private law practice. A few states have permitted several counties to form a judicial district and employ a single prosecuting attorney to handle the duties. Many attorneys have no interest in running for the position of prosecuting attorney, since their private practices are more lucrative. Others shun the idea of running as a candidate in an election. As a result, in many counties, the office of the prosecuting attorney is a training ground for younger attorneys willing to run for the office to gain experience and to tide them over financially while building a private practice. In most counties, the prosecuting attorney is a capable and reputable local attorney who has a sincere interest in making certain that justice is done.

Responsibilities of the Prosecuting Attorney

The prosecuting attorney has a great deal of power, irrespective of personal capabilities or jurisdiction of service. The prosecuting attorney is charged with grave responsibilities to the public that demand integrity, zeal, and conscientious effort in the administration of justice. As stated by the Court in the *Gideon* decision, prosecuting attorneys "are everywhere deemed essential to protect the public's interest in an orderly society." The public prosecutor institutes proceedings before magistrates for the arrest of persons charged with or reasonably suspected of committing a public offense. In addition to acting as prosecutor, in most instances, he or she represents the county on all civil matters.

The prosecuting attorney enters the justice procedural picture early in the prosecutive process. A great number of arrests are made by law enforcement officers on their own determination that there is reasonable cause to believe a crime has been committed. Unless the alleged offender is released by the arresting agency without further action being taken, the prosecuting attorney must be consulted to determine whether prosecutive action will be taken against the arrested person. The prosecuting attorney evaluates the weight of evidence against the accused and the nature of the charge in making the decision whether to prosecute. If the prosecuting attorney decides against prosecution, the accused will be released. If it is decided that prosecutive action should be taken, a complaint will be prepared by the prosecuting attorney and filed with the appropriate court. The accused is then taken before a committing magistrate for the initial appearance, or arraignment as it is referred to in some jurisdictions. Often law enforcement agencies conduct an investigation of alleged violations before making an arrest. In these instances, the prosecuting attorney is usually consulted to determine whether there is sufficient evidence against the accused to justify

---

The National District Attorneys Association states that it is the fundamental duty of prosecutors to seek truth and justice, not merely convictions. If you were the prosecutor, how would you handle the following situations?

You are assigned to prosecute a robbery case. The victim has identified the perpetrator in a photographic lineup and at the beginning of the trial. A detective has testified that the defendant has confessed to the crime. During a break in the trial, the victim tells you he is not sure whether the defendant was the person who robbed him.

During cross-examination of a rape defendant, you start to doubt the testimony of the victim and begin to believe that the act may have been consensual in nature.

You are in charge of issuing cases, and you are screening one involving a terrorist who was found with explosives and plans to detonate an explosive devise on a cruise ship. You discover that the arrest was invalid, and therefore, if you do not issue a complaint, he will go free. If you issue the case, the investigating officer assures you that he can find other crimes to charge the terrorist with and keep him in confinement.

---

prosecutive action, whether a complaint should be filed, and whether a warrant of arrest should be obtained. As pointed out in Chapter 5, the prosecuting attorney may prefer to present the charge to the grand jury to determine whether prosecutive action should be taken or whether a secret indictment should be sought. This procedure is followed in felony charges. If the crime for which the arrest was made is a less serious misdemeanor, the prosecutive decision may be left to the discretion of the law enforcement agency involved. Even the preparation of the complaint and the prosecution during the trial may be handled by the officer, and the prosecuting attorney may not even appear on the scene unless some special problem should arise. In the more serious misdemeanor cases and on felony charges, the prosecuting attorney will be involved from the time of arrest through the appeal.

If the charge is a serious one and the prosecuting attorney decides to prosecute, there are many decisions and duties to perform. The first decision is to determine what charge or charges the evidence will support so that the appropriate accusatory pleading may be filed. The prosecuting attorney must decide whether the charges, when more than one, are to be separated into different trials or consolidated into one. In some jurisdictions, if the charge is a felony, it must be decided whether the facts are to be presented in a preliminary hearing or to a grand jury. The information or the indictment must be prepared depending on the type of hearing conducted. Where appropriate, the granting of motions requested by the defense must be disputed.

At the time of the trial, another responsibility is to present enough evidence to prove the defendant guilty beyond a reasonable doubt. The prosecuting attorney must also assist in the selection of the jury, decide what witnesses to call, and determine what physical evidence should be introduced. It is not necessary that every person who has some knowledge of the facts in the case be called, nor is it necessary that all physical evidence collected by the law enforcement officers during an investigation be presented during a trial. The prosecuting attorney must present enough witnesses and physical evidence to ensure the defendant a fair trial, and may not withhold any evidence that would be advantageous to the defendant. If the defense presents witnesses in its behalf, the prosecuting attorney must cross-examine them. The responsibilities of making recommendations to the judge on the severity of the sentence and of assisting the state attorney general with appeals also fall to the prosecuting attorney.

THE STATE ATTORNEY GENERAL

In most states, the attorney general has broad authority to coordinate local prosecutions. This authority includes the right to prosecute on his or her own and to supervise, assist, and consult local prosecuting attorneys. If a local prosecuting attorney needs assistance or fails to perform his or her duties, the attorney general is free to act. Unless called on by the local prosecutor or unless the local prosecutor fails to prosecute when the facts warrant it, the state attorney general does not ordinarily intervene. There are a few states where the attorney general has no authority over local prosecutions. If there should be a malfeasance in office by the local prosecuting attorney in those states, the governor could be called to appoint a special prosecutor to perform the duties of the local prosecutor. When a case is appealed, in most jurisdictions it is the responsibility of the state attorney general to present the case to the appellate court. The attorney general will be assisted by the prosecuting attorney of the county in which the trial took place.

THE DEFENSE COUNSEL

The defense attorney represents the rights and interests of the perpetrator. Unlike the prosecutor, who is concerned with justice and fairness, the defense attorney's obligation as established by the American Bar Association's General Standards of Conduct is to use all of his or her courage, devotion, and skills to protect the rights of the accused. Many defense attorneys interpret this obligation as requiring that they do everything possible to obtain an acquittal even if they know that the defendant in fact committed the offense.

The Sixth Amendment to the U.S. Constitution requires that those who are accused of crimes have a right to be represented by an attorney. The Supreme Court in the landmark case of *Gideon* v. *Wainwright* established the principle that all defendants have a right to counsel in all felony cases even if they could not afford to hire their own attorney.[8] The court extended this concept to misdemeanor cases in *Argersinger* v. *Hamilin,* holding that absent a waiver no person may be imprisoned for any offense, either misdemeanor or felony, unless he or she has been represented by an attorney.[9]

There are basically four types of defense attorneys: public defenders, contract defense services, assigned defense counsel, and private defense counsel. Public defenders are hired and paid for by the government and are appointed to represent those persons charged with crimes who cannot afford to hire an attorney to represent them. Many counties have public defenders' offices that are staffed by very able, aggressive attorneys. However, there are instances, when for a variety of reasons, the public defenders office has a conflict of interest in a case. For example, this conflict might occur if there were two defendants in one case. In this situation, the court might appoint an attorney from the contract defense services to represent one of the two defendants. Contract defense services normally comprise a group of attorneys who have entered into an agreement with the county to represent indigent defendants for a specified amount of money. Assigned defense counsel exist in the majority of the counties in the United States.[10] Many of these counties are small and cannot afford the cost of maintaining a public defenders office. Under the assigned defense counsel format, the court maintains a list of attorneys who are willing to be appointed to represent indigent criminal defendants. When a defendant appears in court, the judge appoints the next attorney on the list to represent the perpetrator. The last form of defense attorney is the private defense counsel. These attorneys usually represent those defendants who are capable of paying for their services. Well-known examples of private defense counsel include attorneys such as Johnny Cochran, F. Lee Bailey, and Alan Dershowitz of the "Dream Team" who represented O. J. Simpson.

Not only do perpetrators have a right to an attorney, the courts have held that the attorney must be competent.[11] Although the Constitution requires competent counsel who will vigorously defend the perpetrator, there is no requirement or right to have an attorney who will knowingly present perjured testimony. In *Nix* v. *Whiteside,* the defense attorney, upon learning that his client was going to take the stand and commit perjury, informed the client that he could not permit such testimony and that if the client insisted upon going forward and giving this testimony, the attorney would disclose the perjury and withdraw from the case. The perpetrator testified and did not commit perjury; however, he did file an appeal claiming ineffective counsel. The court disagreed, holding that attorneys who follow their state's rules of professional (ethical) conduct do not violate the Sixth Amendment right to counsel.[12]

The Right to Represent Oneself

The Supreme Court has held that the Sixth Amendment right to counsel allows a defendant to proceed pro se or to represent himself or herself without counsel.[13] The rationale is that the right to counsel guaranteed by the Sixth Amendment is a personal right of the accused, not a right bestowed upon an attorney representing the accused. The defendant who desires to proceed pro se must make a knowing and an intelligent waiver of his or her right to an appointed counsel. The right to represent oneself does not mean that the defendant can engage in disrespectful or disruptive conduct in court. Additionally, the courts have stated that when a defendant knowingly waives the right to counsel, he or she cannot later raise the issue of ineffective representation; in essence, the accused has waived any appeal on this issue.

Privileged Communication

Defense counsels are often placed in a most awkward position because of the age-old relationship of privileged communication between attorney and client. This relationship provides that information furnished to an attorney in confidence by his or her client may not be revealed without the permission of the client. Law enforcement agencies may be unaware of crimes discussed by a client. In one instance, a client told his attorney about two murders that he had committed and where the bodies were buried. The problem created by receiving this information is whether the attorney should furnish it to the appropriate law enforcement agency or keep it in strictest confidence. The answer to this question has been debated by many legal scholars with no concrete answer forthcoming. It would appear that the better view would be to furnish the information to the appropriate law enforcement agency in order that the bodies be recovered and relatives notified. Society, as well as the criminal, is entitled to some consideration and justice. In most instances, prosecutive action could not be taken, since the exclusionary rule would prohibit the use of the information as evidence.

If the facts of a case are such that an attorney absolutely cannot accept the responsibility of effectively defending a client, the case should be refused. Once the case is accepted, it is the attorney's duty to remain until it has been brought to a logical conclusion. The defense attorney has many functions to perform, both before and during the trial. A conference with the accused should be held as soon as practically possible. This conference should be private and unobserved even though the accused is in jail at the time. If there are codefendants, the defense counsel must decide whether all can be effectively represented without a conflict of interest. If either counsel or one of the defendants feels that being represented by just one counsel would result in prejudice, each defendant is entitled to and must be provided with individual counsel.

The defense counsel will advise the defendant on the plea that should be entered at the arraignment, and counsel will be present for the purpose of cross-examining witnesses at the preliminary hearing. Counsel also has a right to be present during an identification lineup procedure if the defendant has been formally charged; however, the attorney has no right to interfere with the lineup or to prohibit the defendant from participating. The counsel will file those motions that are in the best interest of the defendant. The defendant is entitled to sit with counsel at the counsel table during the trial so that they may confer on the defense. This assistance is another reason why a defendant is entitled to be present during a trial. Defense counsel will cross-examine prosecution witnesses when appropriate and will present such evidence on behalf of the defendant deemed necessary under the circumstances. Further duties of the defense counsel will be pointed out in the discussion of trial procedures.

THE CLERK OF THE COURT

With the judge, the prosecuting attorney, and the defense counsel all playing dramatic roles during a criminal trial, one could easily overlook the clerk of the court, or county clerk, as the position is also known. This official also has a most important function in the justice system not only during the trial but before and after as well. The main function of the court clerk is to maintain all records of a particular case. These records include items such as copies of all the accusatory pleadings and motions that have been filed. The clerk also issues subpoenas, and, in many jurisdictions, prepares the jury panel. He or she attends trials to swear in witnesses, marks exhibits, and maintains the evidence that is introduced. The clerk also keeps copies of the court transcripts, judgments rendered, and motions for appeals.

THE BAILIFF

The court bailiff may be a permanent member of the justice system or an individual appointed to assist in a particular trial. In some jurisdictions, the bailiff is a member of the county government and carries the title of marshal. The bailiff assists the judge in maintaining order in the court and calls the witnesses to testify. If the defendant has not been released from custody, it is the duty of the bailiff to guard the defendant in the courtroom. When the jury is sequestered, it is the responsibility of the bailiff to make certain that the jurors are free from all contact with the public; the bailiff will return the jury to the courtroom after they have reached a verdict. In many jurisdictions, the bailiff serves court orders and other court papers.

THE COURT REPORTER

The responsibility of recording everything said during the trial proceeding belongs to the court reporter. This includes the testimony of all the witnesses, objections made to the attorney's questions, rulings made by the judge, and conferences between the attorneys and the judge. If the case is taken up on appeal, the recorded notes must be transcribed.

The court reporter must be highly skilled to record transactions as they take place, often at a rapid pace. The reporter may record the proceedings in shorthand or with a stenotype machine. When first used in the courtroom, tape recorders were not very reliable. However, today many jurisdictions are using audiotapes to record the trial proceedings. These recorders have improved in both their reliability and the quality of recording.

THE COURT COMMISSIONER

In many judicial districts, court commissioners are appointed to assist trial judges. In most instances, they must possess the same qualifications as the judge, and a commissioner may substitute for a judge in an emergency situation. Otherwise, the commissioners hold hearings on motions filed, set and accept bail, and perform other duties as may be imposed on them by law.

CAPSTONE CASE ————————————————————————

Strickler v. *Greene*
527 U.S. 263; 119 S.Ct. (1999); 144 L.Ed. 2d 286 (1999)

The District Court for the Eastern District of Virginia granted petitioner's application for a writ of habeas corpus and vacated his capital murder conviction and death sentence on the grounds that the Commonwealth had failed to disclose important exculpatory evidence and that petitioner had not, in consequence, received a fair trial. The Court of Appeals for the Fourth Circuit reversed because petitioner had not raised his constitutional claim at his trial or in state collateral proceedings. In addition, the Fourth Circuit concluded that petitioner's claim was, "in any event, without merit." Finding the legal question presented by this case considerably more difficult than the Fourth Circuit, we granted certiorari, to consider (1) whether the State violated *Brady* v. *Maryland*, 373 U.S. 83, 10 L.Ed. 2d 215, 83 S.Ct. 1194 (1963), and its progeny. . . .

In the early evening of January 5, 1990, Leanne Whitlock, an African-American sophomore at James Madison University, was abducted from a local shopping center and robbed and murdered. In separate trials, both petitioner and Ronald Henderson were convicted of all three offenses. Henderson was convicted of first-degree murder, a non-capital offense, whereas petitioner was convicted of capital murder and sentenced to death.

At both trials, a woman named Anne Stoltzfus testified in vivid detail about Whitlock's abduction. The exculpatory material that petitioner claims should have been disclosed before trial includes documents prepared by Stoltzfus, and notes of interviews with her, that impeach significant portions of her testimony. We begin, however, by noting that, even without the Stoltzfus testimony, the evidence in the record was sufficient to establish petitioner's guilt on the murder charge. Whether petitioner would have been convicted of capital murder and received the death sentence if she had not testified, or if she had been sufficiently impeached, is less clear. To put the question in context, we review the trial testimony at some length.

THE TESTIMONY AT TRIAL

At about 4:30 P.M. on January 5, 1990, Whitlock borrowed a 1986 blue Mercury Lynx from her boyfriend, John Dean, who worked in the Valley Shopping Mall in Harrisonburg, Virginia. At about 6:30 or 6:45 P.M., she left her apartment, intending to return the car to Dean at the mall. She did not return the car and was not again seen alive by any of her friends or family.

Petitioner's mother testified that she had driven petitioner and Henderson to Harrisonburg on January 5. She also testified that petitioner always carried a hunting knife that had belonged to his father. Two witnesses, a friend of Henderson's and a security guard, saw petitioner and Henderson at the mall that afternoon. The security guard was informed around 3:30 P.M. that two men, one of whom she identified at trial as petitioner, were attempting to steal a car in the parking lot. She had them under observation during the remainder of the afternoon but lost sight of them at about 6:45.

At approximately 7:30 P.M., a witness named Kurt Massie saw the blue Lynx at a location in Augusta County about 25 miles from Harrisonburg and a short distance from the cornfield where Whitlock's body was later found. Massie identified petitioner as the driver of the vehicle; he also saw a white woman in the front seat and another man in the back. Massie noticed that the car was muddy, and that it turned off Route 340 onto a dirt road.

At about 4:30 or 5 A.M. on January 6, petitioner drove Henderson to Kenneth Workman's apartment in Timberville. Henderson went inside to get something, and petitioner and Tudor drove off without waiting for him. Workman testified that Henderson had blood on his pants and stated he had killed a black person.

Petitioner and Tudor then drove to a motel in Blue Ridge. A day or two later they went to Virginia Beach, where they spent the rest of the week. Petitioner gave Tudor pearl earrings that Whitlock had been wearing when she was last seen. Tudor saw Whitlock's driver's license and bank card in the glove compartment of the car. Tudor testified that petitioner unsuccessfully attempted to use Whitlock's bank card when they were in Virginia Beach.

When petitioner and Tudor returned to Augusta County, they abandoned the blue Lynx. On January 11, the police identified the car as Dean's, and found petitioner's and Tudor's fingerprints on both the inside and the outside of the car. They also found shoe impressions that matched the soles of shoes belonging to petitioner. Inside the car, they retrieved a jacket that contained identification papers belonging to Henderson.

The police also recovered a bag at petitioner's mother's house that Tudor testified she and petitioner had left when they returned from Virginia Beach. The bag contained, among other items, three identification cards belonging to Whitlock and a black "tank top" shirt that was later found to have human blood and semen stains on it.

On January 13, a farmer called the police to advise them that he had found Henderson's wallet; a search of the area led to the discovery of Whitlock's frozen, nude, and battered body. A 69-pound rock, spotted with blood, lay nearby. Forensic evidence indicated that Whitlock's death was caused by "multiple blunt force injuries to the head." The location of the rock and the human blood on the rock suggested that it had been used to inflict these injuries. Based on the contents of Whitlock's stomach, the medical examiner determined that she died fewer than six hours after she had last eaten.

A number of Caucasian hair samples were found at the scene, three of which were probably petitioner's. Given the weight of the rock, the prosecution argued that one of the killers must have held the victim down while the other struck her with the murder weapon.

ANNE STOLTZFUS' TESTIMONY

Anne Stoltzfus testified that on two occasions on January 5 she saw petitioner, Henderson, and a blonde girl inside the Harrisonburg mall, and that she later witnessed their abduction of Whitlock in the parking lot. She did not call the police, but a week and a half after the incident she discussed it with classmates at James Madison University, where both she and Whitlock were students. One of them called the police. The next night a detective visited her, and the following morning she went to the police station and told her story to Detective Claytor, a member of the Harrisonburg City Police Department. Detective Claytor showed her photographs of possible suspects, and she identified petitioner and Henderson "with absolute certainty" but stated that she had a slight reservation about her identification of the blonde woman.

At trial, Stoltzfus testified that, at about 6 P.M. on January 5, she and her 14-year-old daughter were in the Music Land store in the mall looking for a compact disc. She further testified to seeing the petitioner several times at the mall.

At trial Stoltzfus identified Whitlock from a picture as the driver of the car and pointed to petitioner. "When asked if pretrial publicity about the murder had influenced her identification, Stoltzfus replied "absolutely not." She explained:

> First of all, I have an exceptionally good memory. I had very close contact with [petitioner] and he made an emotional impression with me because of his behavior. He caught my attention and I paid attention. So I have absolutely no doubt of my identification of him.

The Commonwealth did not produce any other witnesses to the abduction. Stoltzfus' daughter did not testify.

THE STOLTZFUS DOCUMENTS

The materials that provide the basis of petitioner's Brady claim consist of notes taken by Detective Claytor during his interviews with Stoltzfus, and letters written by Stoltzfus to Claytor. They cast serious doubt on Stoltzfus' confident assertion of her "exceptionally good memory." Because the content of the documents is critical to petitioner's procedural and substantive claims, we summarize their content.

> Exhibit 1 is a handwritten note prepared by Detective Claytor after his first interview with Stoltzfus on January 19, 1990, just two weeks after the crime. The note indicates that she could not identify the black female victim. The only person Stoltzfus apparently could identify at this time was the white female.

> Exhibit 2 is a document prepared by Detective Claytor some time after Febrary 1. It contains a summary of his interviews with Stoltzfus conducted on January 19 and January 20, 1990. At that time "she was not sure whether she could identify the white males but felt sure she could identify the white female."

> Exhibit 3 is entitled "Observations" and includes a summary of the abduction.

> Exhibit 4 is a letter written by Stoltzfus to Claytor three days after their first interview "to clarify some of my confusion for you." The letter states that she had not remembered being at the mall, but that her daughter had helped jog her memory. Her description of the abduction includes the comment: "I have a very vague memory that I'm not sure of. It seems as if the wild guy that I saw had come running through the door and up to a bus as the bus was pulling off. . . . Then the guy I saw came running up to the black girl's window. Were those 2 memories the same person?" In a postscript she noted that her daughter "doesn't remember seeing the 3 people get into the black girl's car. . . ."

> Exhibit 5 is a note to Claytor captioned "My Impressions of 'The Car,' " which contains three paragraphs describing the size of the car and comparing it with Stoltzfus' Volkswagen Rabbit, but not mentioning the license plate number that she vividly recalled at the trial.

> Exhibit 6 is a brief note from Stoltzfus to Claytor dated January 25, 1990, stating that after spending several hours with John Dean, Whitlock's boyfriend, "looking at current photos," she had identified Whitlock "beyond a shadow of a doubt." The District Court noted that by the time of trial her identification had been expanded to include a description of her clothing and her appearance as a college kid who was "singing" and "happy."

> Exhibit 7 is a letter from Stoltzfus to Detective Claytor, dated January 16, 1990, in which she thanks him for his "patience with my sometimes muddled memories." She states that if the student at school had not called the police, "I never would have made any of the associations that you helped me make."

> In Exhibit 8, which is undated and summarizes the events described in her trial testimony, Stoltzfus commented:

So where is the 3 × 4 card? . . . It would have been very nice if I could have remembered all this at the time and had simply gone to the police with the information. But I totally wrote this off as a trivial episode of college kids carrying on and proceeded with my own full-time college load at JMU. . . . Monday, January 15th. I was cleaning out my car and found the 3 × 4 card. I tore it into little pieces and put it in the bottom of a trash bag.

There is a dispute between the parties over whether petitioner's counsel saw Exhibits 2, 7, and 8 before trial. The prosecuting attorney conceded that he himself never saw Exhibits 1, 3, 4, 5, and 6 until long after petitioner's trial, and they were not in the file he made available to petitioner. For purposes of this case, therefore, we assume that petitioner proceeded to trial without having seen Exhibits 1, 3, 4, 5, and 6.

STATE PROCEEDINGS

Petitioner was tried in Augusta County, where Whitlock's body was found, on charges of capital murder, robbery, and abduction. Because the prosecutor maintained an open file policy, which gave petitioner's counsel access to all of the evidence in the Augusta County prosecutor's files, petitioner's counsel did not file a pretrial motion for discovery of possible exculpatory evidence. In closing argument, petitioner's lawyer effectively conceded that the evidence was sufficient to support the robbery and abduction charges, as well as the lesser offense of first-degree murder, but argued that the evidence was insufficient to prove that petitioner was guilty of capital murder.

The judge instructed the jury that petitioner could be found guilty of the capital charge if the evidence established beyond a reasonable doubt that he "jointly participated in the fatal beating" and "was an active and immediate participant in the act or acts that caused the victim's death." The jury found petitioner guilty of abduction, robbery, and capital murder. After listening to testimony and arguments presented during the sentencing phase, the jury made findings of "vileness" and "future dangerousness," and unanimously recommended the death sentence that the judge later imposed.

The Virginia Supreme Court affirmed the conviction and sentence. It held that the trial court had properly instructed the jury on the "joint perpetrator" theory of capital murder and that the evidence, viewed most favorably in support of the verdict, amply supported the prosecution's theory that both petitioner and Henderson were active participants in the actual killing.

FEDERAL HABEAS CORPUS PROCEEDINGS

In March 1996, petitioner filed a federal habeas corpus petition in the Eastern District of Virginia. The District Court entered a sealed, ex parte order granting petitioner's counsel the right to examine and to copy all of the police and prosecution files in the case. That order led to petitioner's counsel's first examination of the Stoltzfus materials, described above. Based on the discovery of those exhibits, petitioner for the first time raised a direct claim that his conviction was invalid because the prosecution had failed to comply with the rule of *Brady* v. *Maryland*. The District Court granted the Commonwealth's motion to dismiss all claims except for petitioner's contention that the Commonwealth violated *Brady*, that he received ineffective assistance of counsel, and that he was denied due process of law under the Fifth and Fourteenth Amendments. In its order denying the Commonwealth's motion to dismiss, the District Court found that petitioner had "demonstrated cause for his failure to raise this claim earlier [because] defense counsel had no independent access to this material and the Commonwealth repeatedly withheld it throughout Petitioner's state habeas proceeding."

After reviewing the Stoltzfus materials, and making the assumption that the three disputed exhibits had been available to the defense, the District Court concluded that the failure to disclose the other five was sufficiently prejudicial to undermine confidence in the jury's verdict. It granted summary judgment to petitioner and granted the writ.

The Court of Appeals vacated in part and remanded. It held that petitioner's *Brady* claim was procedurally defaulted because the factual basis for the claim was available to him at the time he filed his state habeas petition. Given that he knew that Stoltzfus had been interviewed by Harrisonburg police officers, the court opined that "reasonably competent counsel would have sought discovery in state court" of the police files, and that in response to this "simple request, it is likely the state court would have ordered the production of the files." Therefore, the Court of Appeals reasoned, it could not address the *Brady* claim unless petitioner could demonstrate both cause and actual prejudice.

The first question that our order granting certiorari directed the parties to address is whether the State violated the *Brady* rule. We begin our analysis by identifying the essential components of a *Brady* violation.

In *Brady* this Court held "that the suppression by the prosecution of evidence favorable to an accused upon request violates due process where the evidence is material either to guilt or to punishment, irrespective of the good faith or bad faith of the prosecution." Such evidence is material "if there is a reasonable probability that, had the evidence been disclosed to the defense, the result of the proceeding would have been different."

These cases, together with earlier cases condemning the knowing use of perjured testimony, illustrate the special role played by the American prosecutor in the search for truth in criminal trials. Within the federal system, for example, we have said that the United States Attorney is "the representative not of an ordinary party to a controversy, but of a sovereignty whose obligation to govern impartially is as compelling as its obligation to govern at all; and whose interest, therefore, in a criminal prosecution is not that it shall win a case, but that justice shall be done."

This special status explains both the basis for the prosecution's broad duty of disclosure and our conclusion that not every violation of that duty necessarily establishes that the outcome was unjust. Thus the term "*Brady* violation" is sometimes used to refer to any breach of the broad obligation to disclose exculpatory evidence—that is, to any suppression of so-called "*Brady* material"—although, strictly speaking, there is never a real "Brady violation" unless the nondisclosure was so serious that there is a reasonable probability that the suppressed evidence would have produced a different verdict. There are three components of a true *Brady* violation: The evidence at issue must be favorable to the accused, either because it is exculpatory, or because it is impeaching; that evidence must have been suppressed by the State, either willfully or inadvertently; and prejudice must have ensued.

Two of those components are unquestionably established by the record in this case. The contrast between (a) the terrifying incident that Stoltzfus confidently described in her testimony and (b) her initial perception of that event "as a trivial episode of college kids carrying on" that her daughter did not even notice, suffices to establish the impeaching character of the undisclosed documents. Moreover, with respect to at least five of those documents, there is no dispute about the fact that they were known to the State but not disclosed to trial counsel. It is the third component—whether petitioner has established the prejudice necessary to satisfy the "materiality" inquiry—that is the most difficult element of the claimed *Brady* violation in this case.

Because petitioner acknowledges that his *Brady* claim is procedurally defaulted, we must first decide whether that default is excused by an adequate showing of cause and prejudice. In this case, cause and prejudice parallel two of the three components of the alleged Brady violation itself. The suppression of the Stoltzfus documents constitutes one of the causes for the failure to assert a *Brady* claim in the state courts, and unless those documents were "material" for *Brady* purposes, their suppression did not give rise to sufficient prejudice to overcome the procedural default.

Although it is true that petitioner's lawyers—both at trial and in post-trial proceedings—must have known that Stoltzfus had had multiple interviews with the police, it by no means follows that they would have known that records pertaining to those interviews, or that the notes that Stoltzfus sent to the detective, existed and had been suppressed. Indeed, if the Commonwealth is correct that Exhibits 2, 7, and 8 were in the prosecutor's "open file," it is especially unlikely that counsel would have suspected that additional impeaching evidence was being withheld. The prosecutor must have known about the newspaper articles and Stoltzfus' meetings with Claytor, yet he did not believe that his prosecution file was incomplete.

There is no suggestion that tactical considerations played any role in petitioner's failure to raise his *Brady* claim in state court. Moreover, under *Brady* an inadvertent nondisclosure has the same impact on the fairness of the proceedings as deliberate concealment. "If the suppression of evidence results in constitutional error, it is because of the character of the evidence, not the character of the prosecutor."

In summary, petitioner has established cause for failing to raise a *Brady* claim prior to federal habeas because (a) the prosecution withheld exculpatory evidence; (b) petitioner reasonably relied on the prosecution's open file policy as fulfilling the prosecution's duty to disclose such evidence; and (c) the Commonwealth confirmed petitioner's reliance on the open file policy by asserting during state habeas proceedings that petitioner had already received "everything known to the government." We need not decide in this case whether any one or two of these factors would be sufficient to constitute cause, since the combination of all three surely suffices.

The differing judgments of the District Court and the Court of Appeals attest to the difficulty of resolving the issue of prejudice. Unlike the Fourth Circuit, we do not believe that "the Stolzfus [sic] materials would have provided little or no help to Strickler in either the guilt or sentencing phases of the trial." Without a doubt, Stoltzfus' testimony was prejudicial in the sense that it made petitioner's conviction more likely than if she had not testified, and discrediting her testimony might have changed the outcome of the trial.

That, however, is not the standard that petitioner must satisfy in order to obtain relief. He must convince us that "there is a reasonable probability" that the result of the trial would have been different if the suppressed documents had been disclosed to the defense. [T]he question is whether "the favorable evidence could reasonably be taken to put the whole case in such a different light as to undermine confidence in the verdict."

Even if Stoltzfus and her testimony had been entirely discredited, the jury might still have concluded that petitioner was the leader of the criminal enterprise because he was the one seen driving the car by Kurt Massie near the location of the murder and the one who kept the car for the following week. In addition, Tudor testified that petitioner threatened Henderson with a knife later in the evening.

More importantly, however, petitioner's guilt of capital murder did not depend on proof that he was the dominant partner: Proof that he was an equal participant with Henderson was sufficient under the judge's instructions. Accordingly, the strong evidence that Henderson was a killer is entirely consistent with the conclusion that petitioner was also an actual participant in the killing. Furthermore, there was considerable forensic and other physical evidence linking petitioner to the crime. The weight and size of the rock, and the character of the fatal injuries to the victim, are powerful evidence supporting the conclusion that two people acted jointly to commit a brutal murder.

We recognize the importance of eyewitness testimony; Stoltzfus provided the only disinterested, narrative account of what transpired on January 5, 1990. However, Stoltzfus' vivid description of the events at the mall was not the only evidence that the jury had before it. The record provides strong support for the conclusion that petitioner would have been convicted of capital murder and sentenced to death, even if Stoltzfus had been severely impeached. The jury was instructed on two predicates for capital murder: robbery with a deadly weapon and abduction with intent to defile.

Accordingly, the judgment of the Court of Appeals is Affirmed.

REVIEW QUESTIONS

1. What is the primary function of the judge?
2. List four duties of the judge during trial proceedings.
3. What is contempt of court?
4. Name three types of misconduct that might cause one to be held in contempt of court.
5. List five duties and/or responsibilities of the prosecuting attorney.
6. What are some of the problems that a defense attorney encounters with a client?
7. List four duties of a defense counsel.
8. Describe the functions of the following:
    a. the clerk of court
    b. the bailiff
    c. the court reporter

LOCAL PROCEDURE

1. Does the state attorney general have the authority to assist local prosecuting attorneys in handling prosecutions?

ENDNOTES

1. 388 US 218 (1967).
2. See *People* v. *Fusaro,* 18 Cal App 3rd 877 (1971).
3. See *Taylor* v. *Hayes,* 418 US 488; and *Codispoti* v. *Pennsylvania,* 418 US 506 (1974).
4. This section has been adapted from H. Wallace, *Victimology: Legal, Psychological and Social Perspectives* (Allyn & Bacon, Boston), 1996.
5. M. Randell & L. Haskell, "Sexual Violence in Women's Lives," 1/1 *Violence Against Women* 6 (1995).
6. The Fifth Amendment's right to grand jury indictment and the Eighth Amendment's right regarding excessive bail have not been applied to the states. See *Hurtado* v. *California,* 110 U.S. 516 (1884).

7. If the confession was obtained by coercion, it may not be admitted even for impeachment purposes. See *Mincey* v. *Arizona,* 437 U.S. 385 (1978).
8. 372 U.S. 335 (1963).
9. 407 U.S. 25 (1972). See also *Scott* v. *Illinois,* 440 U.S. 367 (1979) where the U.S. Supreme Court held that the right to counsel only applies where imprisonment is actually imposed rather than merely authorized by statute.
10. Bureau of Justice Statistics Bulletin, *Criminal Defense Systems* Washington, D.C: U.S. Department of Justice, (August 1984), p. 6.
11. *Strickland* v. *Washington,* 466 U.S. 668 (1984).
12. 475 U.S. 157 (1986).
13. *Faretta* v. *California,* 422 U.S. 806 (1975).

CHAPTER 11 # The Jury

Gentlemen, a court is no better than each man of you sitting before me on this jury. A court is only as sound as its jury, and a jury is only as sound as the men who make it up.

—Harper Lee, *To Kill a Mockingbird,* 1960

INTRODUCTION

Once the trial date has arrived and the prosecution and defense indicate their readiness, the next step is the selection of the jury. However, before entering this phase of the trial proceedings, a few questions need to be answered. First, who are these persons who serve on a jury, and where do they come from? Further, what qualities must they possess to qualify as jurors? A defendant is entitled to be tried in the judicial district in which the crime was committed and to have an impartial jury selected from that district. A criminal would not pick a particular judicial district in which to commit a crime because of greater faith in a jury from that district. This right to be tried within the judicial district in which the crime was committed is included in the Sixth Amendment of the U.S. Constitution. It was included because of experiences that the colonists suffered from being "hauled away" to Great Britain for trials of crimes allegedly committed in the colonies. The jurors were thus picked in Great Britain. Therefore, unless a change of venue is granted because an impartial jury cannot be selected within that district, one committing a crime rests his or her fate with those in the judicial district where the crime was committed.

A JURY OF ONE'S PEERS

The only jury qualification set forth in the Sixth Amendment is that it be an "impartial jury" chosen from the judicial district in which the crime was committed. Similar provisions are included in the constitutions or statutes of the states. Any additional qualifications believed necessary for service as a juror come from suppositions of legislative action. Though not specifically provided for in most state statutes, it is generally conceded that the jury is to comprise the accused's peers. This concept stems from a provision in the Magna Charta that provides that no freeman shall be seized and imprisoned except by judgment of "his peers." This provision did not pertain to a trial jury but to an accusatory jury. The Magna Charta, which was prepared by noblemen for their own benefit, was intended to prohibit the king from seizing and imprisoning a nobleman merely on a whim. Seizure and imprisonment were to be made only after an accusation was determined to be well-founded by the judgment of fellow noblemen. Although the Magna Charta was designed primarily for the benefit of noblemen, the lower classes of persons in Great Britain at the time also received benefit from this provision, and it became a part of the due process of law of Great Britain.

Trial by One's Peers

As the trial jury was created, it was assumed that it would comprise one's peers. This concept was brought to America by the colonists. Yet few states have directly indicated that a trial jury must consist of one's peers. More and more, this concept of trial by peers is directing the selection of juries. In the past, if the jury comprised twelve persons "good and true" picked from the community where the trial was to be held, the nebulous "peers" qualification had been satisfied. In recent years, a closer look has been taken at the term *one's peers,* and whether the requirement, though not specifically and formally set forth in the statutes, is met. The dictionary defines *peers* as one's equals, or those of equal status; one's friends; or associates. To take this definition too literally in composing a jury would imply that a medical doctor could be tried only by a jury comprising other doctors, a farmer by other farmers, a former convict by other convicts, or a sixteen-year-old defendant by only other sixteen-year-olds. Such juries would undoubtedly fulfill the "peers" qualification but would be most difficult to find in some jurisdictions. If such a jury were possible, the chances for jury impartiality would be low. Fortunately, courts have not gone this far in selecting juries. As long as the jury is made up of persons representing a cross section of the community in which the trial takes place, it is regarded as comprising one's peers.

At one time, only white males were qualified to serve as jurors. In fact, most states did not permit women to serve on juries until they were granted the right to vote with the passage of the Nineteenth Amendment to the U.S. Constitution in 1920. Persons of certain races, religions, and national origins were excluded, if not by statutory provision, then by those making the jury panel selection. These exclusions were justified by those responsible for the jury panel, since they were to select only persons who were males, over twenty-one years of age, honest, intelligent, and of good character and sound judgment. It was alleged that members of minority groups did not meet these qualifications. To overcome this practice, the federal government passed legislation stating that no citizen shall be excluded from service on a federal grand jury or a federal petit jury because of race, color, religion, sex, national origin, or economic status, and that persons are to be selected at random from a fair cross section of the community.[1]

Cross Section of the Community Standard

Many states have adopted the cross section of the community standard to meet the peer group regulation, particularly in view of U.S. Supreme Court decisions. In *Glasser* v. *United States,*[2] the Court stated, "The American tradition of trial by jury, considered in connection with either criminal or civil proceedings, necessarily contemplates an impartial jury drawn from a cross section of the community." The Court has also stated that it is part of the established tradition in the use of juries as instruments of public justice that the jury be a body truly representative of the community. However, what is a truly representative body? Does it pertain only to races, education, age, sex, religion, economic status, or philosophical thinking, or must *all* of these matters be considered when composing a jury panel? These questions were partially answered by the U.S. Supreme Court in *Fay* v. *New York,*[3] when the Court stated the following:

> There is no constitutional right to a jury drawn from a group of uneducated and unintelligent persons. Nor is there any right to a jury chosen solely from those at the lower end of the economic and social scale. But there is a constitutional right to a jury drawn from a group which represents a cross section of the community. And a cross section of the community includes persons with varying degrees of training and intelligence and with varying economic and social positions. Under our Constitution, the jury is not to be made the representative of the most intelligent, the most wealthy or the most successful, nor of the least intelligent, the least wealthy or the least successful. It is a democratic institution, representative of all qualified classes of people.

Only by being able to select a jury from persons who truly represent a cross section of a community can the accused be assured of an impartial jury.

In order to have a truly representative cross section of a community on a jury panel, more and more jurisdictions are conducting surveys to determine the percentage of persons of minority races and different national origins within the community. In this way, a like percentage can be included on jury panels. Younger people make up a larger percentage of those selected to serve on jury panels. In the past, juries frequently comprised older persons, since they were less likely to suffer financially by serving on juries. As idealistic as it may be to have a truly representative cross section of the community, juries often are not truly representative because many classes of persons suffer financial hardships by serving and are thus excused. However, as long as there is no systematic exclusion of any class of persons, the cross-section requirement is fulfilled. As pointed out by the courts, it is not necessary that a jury include one of each class of persons to be truly representative of a cross section of a community.

When the courts use the term *community,* they generally mean the judicial district in which the crime was committed. In most instances, the judicial district is the county, but in the case of inferior courts, the judicial district may be only a portion of a county.

When a jury is challenged as not being a true representation of a cross section of a community, the challenge usually is made by a defendant who fails to find one of his or her particular sex, race, or group among those from whom the jury may be chosen. But in *Taylor* v. *Louisiana,*[4] the U.S. Supreme Court held that a defendant may object to the exclusion of a class of persons from the jury panel even though the defendant was not one of the excluded class. In that case, a male defendant objected to the exclusion of women from the jury unless they volunteered for jury duty. The Court pointed out that although 53 percent of persons eligible for jury duty in the judicial district were female, only 10 percent of these had volunteered, and thus there was not a true representation of the cross section of the community. The defendant had a right to object to the exclusion of women from his jury even though he was not a member of the excluded class.

THE JURY PANEL OR JURY LIST

The procedure of jury selection varies somewhat among states and even among districts within a state. In some larger metropolitan districts, a jury commissioner is often appointed, whose duty it is to select persons within his or her district to be available for jury duty. This group of persons is referred to as a jury panel or jury list. In other districts, the selection of the panel may fall to the court clerk. In most jurisdictions, the selection of a jury panel is made annually, usually at the beginning of the calendar year. Generally, no guidelines are set forth for selection. As noted, the federal government provided that no person was to be excluded from serving on a jury because of race, religion, and so forth, and that the persons were to be a community cross section picked "at random." No procedure was set forth for how those persons were to be randomly selected. This regulation did provide that each federal judicial district devise and place into operation a written plan for how the jurors were to be selected—whether from voter registration lists or some other source. In this way, the courts would have some record to verify that no class of persons had been systematically excluded.

The official making the selection has almost complete power over the selection of names to be placed on the jury panel, and in most districts, the sources from which he or she obtains the names are solely at his or her discretion. Whatever list is used, the names will be individually placed in a box from which the official will randomly pull those to be placed on the jury panel. As a matter of convenience, officials often use the voter registration list, but it is generally not required that a juror be a registered voter. However, this list is often utilized with greater frequency than any other list for two reasons. First, the list is more likely to be representative of a cross section of the community than other lists. Second, the qualifications for voting more nearly coincide with those that a juror must possess. However, the supreme courts of some states have held that the use of only voter registration is too restrictive since many members of minority groups do not register to vote. These courts have suggested that other sources in addition to voter registration lists be utilized to get a better cross section of a community. Tax assessors' lists have been used, but this source has been criticized since it has been held that property owners are more likely to be "convicting" juries than nonproperty owners. Church membership lists have also been used, but with such lists, religious conflicts ensue. Some officials have selected names randomly from telephone books in the area, or they select every tenth name or some similar numerical sequence. In sparsely settled districts, the officials have made selections through personal contact or by selecting names furnished by acquaintances. On one occasion, an official used the membership list of the area League of Women Voters to get a representative number of women on the panel. The use of this list was criticized as being too restrictive in the class of women selected and not a cross section of the women of the community (see *Glasser* v. *United States*). To assure that the jury panel is truly representative of a cross section of a community, some courts have held that the selection be made from two lists, such as a voter registration list and a driver's license list.

Juror Qualifications

Although individual juror qualifications may vary somewhat among states, the general qualifications are the same. The person must be a citizen of the United States, eighteen years of age or over, and a resident of the judicial district for a specified time, usually one year. This latter qualification has been criticized by some as being too restrictive and not representative of a community, because many residents of a community move more frequently than once a year. In view of this contention, the legislatures of some states have changed the residence requirement from one year to one month. Those upholding the one-year requirement contend that it takes at least a year for a person to learn the thinking and moral standards of a community. For this reason, many states still use the one-year residence requirement.

The person must be in possession of his or her natural faculties, meaning that the person must be able to see, hear, talk, feel, smell, and be comparatively mobile. Some states have passed legislation that a person is not disqualified as a juror because of loss of sight, hearing, or other disabilities that substantially interfere with mobility. This legislation is criticized as being unrealistic by many within the justice system. The belief is that the amount of physical evidence presented during a trial prevents a blind person from adequately functioning as a juror. Similarly, since most evidence presented during a trial is through testimony of witnesses, a person unable to hear the testimony would be unable to perform duties as a juror. A person with limited or impaired mobility may be in a better position to act as a juror, unless that impairment prevents the person from sitting where the sights and sounds of the trial are adequate. The proponents of this legislation argue that such persons should not be deprived of performing their civic duty merely because of an impairment. They allege that if there is a reason that the impaired person could not perform in a particular case, a challenge for cause could be made. This challenge, however, is not without its complications, as we will see later.

Some states hold that a decrepit person may not qualify as a juror. Although the law does not specify the characteristics that make a person decrepit, it appears to be aimed at someone who is of advanced age, cannot move about freely, and may be senile. Determining when one has reached this condition is difficult.

A person must also be of "ordinary" intelligence to qualify as a juror in most states. This is another nebulous term. What might be considered ordinary intelligence by some might not be considered ordinary by others. And by what standards is intelligence to be measured? This qualification has led to the exclusion of competent persons from the jury panel. To establish whether a prospective juror is of ordinary intelligence, many conscientious efforts have been made to devise tests to assist in making the determination. These tests have been challenged by many defendants. They maintain that words unfamiliar to many ethnic groups are included in the tests, thus preventing a jury from being truly representative of the community. Because of these challenges, most such tests have been eliminated. The prospective juror must have sufficient knowledge of the English language to communicate properly and to understand the trial proceedings. Not all persons on voter lists understand English, nor do all have the full use of their natural faculties. Thus, registered voters are not necessarily qualified as jurors. Aliens, those convicted of malfeasance in office, of any felony, or of other high crime are excluded by most jurisdictions from jury duty. However, even this exclusion has been challenged as excluding a cross section of society.

Some jurisdictions exclude persons who have served as jurors during the preceding year. This is to discourage the "professional jurors" who continually hang around courthouses attempting to serve on juries because they have little else to do. Whether there is anything wrong with the professional juror is subject to debate.

Obtaining Jurors

Because of the number of persons in a community who do not qualify as jurors, are exempt, or are excused, obtaining a sufficient number of persons who are available for jury duty is not always easy. In one large metropolitan area, the jury commissioner selected 300,000 names in order to maintain a panel of 15,000 persons—the estimated need for the coming year in that district. Generally, it is the responsibility of the official in charge of the jury panel to determine whether the persons selected are qualified to serve or are exempt. To facilitate this determination, many officials will mail a questionnaire to the selected person, requesting certain information. A sample questionnaire may be seen in the accompanying illustration.

The procedure of mailing questionnaires to prospective jurors also has been challenged by defendants. They contend that many members of minority groups do not respond to the questionnaires and thus do not become eligible to be placed on the jury panel. Regardless of these challenges, many jurisdictions still send out questionnaires to assist in obtaining competent persons to act as jurors. The courts recognize that though there is no ideal way to select prospective jurors, the system used is acceptable if no groups of people are eliminated.

When the selection of prospective jurors is completed, those persons found to be competent are placed on the jury panel. As each trial date is set, a number of these persons will be notified to appear in court on that date. The notice is usually by legal document, referred to as a *summons,* served on the prospective juror by the sheriff, marshal, or other official of the district involved. If the person does not appear as directed after being personally served with the summons, a contempt charge may result unless good cause is shown for not appearing. For example, a prospective juror with a serious illness could not be expected to appear. From this group that appears in court, the trial jury is selected.

The number of persons called to appear in court varies with the type of crime charged and the amount of pretrial publicity that may have been given the case. Usually, not fewer that twenty-five persons will be summoned to appear in court, and if the charge is murder and the case has received wide publicity, as many as one hundred persons may be summoned. There have been times when even with this number, a trial jury could not be picked, and additional persons from the panel had to be called to appear in court. The first twelve names called by the clerk at the time of the trial may not be those of the ones who will serve on the jury.

In some districts, the official will not establish a jury panel very far in advance of a trial. As juries are needed, the official will have a number of persons sum-

---

Typical Jury Questionnaire

Name _____ Address _____

1. Occupation _____ Employed by _____
   If retired, state former occupation _____

2. Do you own your own business? _____ (Yes or No) Firm name _____
   How many employees? _____

3. Age _____ Condition of hearing _____ Eyesight _____

4. Do you have any physical or mental disability that would interfere with or prevent you from serving as a juror? _____ (Yes or No) If so, describe fully.
   Doctor's name _____

5. Can you read and understand English? _____ (Yes or No)

6. Have you ever been convicted of any felony in a State or Federal Court? _____
   (Yes or No) If your answer is yes, have your civil rights been restored by pardon
   or amnesty? _____ (Yes or No)

7. Have you been a resident of this County and State for one year immediately before this date? _____ (Yes or No)

8. Have you served as a juror in this State within the last two years? _____ (Yes or
   No) If yes, when? _____

9. Do you have minor children? _____ Ages: _____

10. Do you have dependents who require your personal constant care? _____
    If yes, please explain: _____

11. If you are entitled to legal exemption or have legal grounds for excuse from jury
    duty, do you claim it? _____ (Yes or No) If so, explain fully the ground for your
    claim.

I certify (or declare) under penalty of perjury that the answers to the
foregoing questions are true and correct.

Executed in _____ County, State of _____, on the _____ day of
_____, 20____.

Signature _____

---

moned to appear in court on a particular day. At this time, it will be determined
whether those summoned are qualified to serve on a jury. The difficulty with this
procedure is that many of those summoned may not qualify for jury duty, and more
will have to be notified to appear in order that a trial jury may be selected.

When it is established that those persons appearing in court qualify for jury
duty, their names will individually be written on slips of paper and placed in a box.
When the trial jury is selected, the clerk will pick, at random, twelve individuals (or
fewer, depending upon the jurisdiction) who are to act as the trial jurors. They will
take seats in an area provided for them, commonly known as the jury box. The
prosecuting attorney and the defense counsel very closely scrutinize the jurors to
determine whether this is the group with which they wish to rest their case. If not,
the attorneys may decide to replace all or a few of the jurors.

EXEMPTION FROM JURY DUTY

Many persons have the qualifications to be a juror but are exempt from jury duty because of their occupations. It is believed that the functions they perform within a community outweigh their responsibility to serve on a jury. Included among those most often exempted from jury duty are members of legislative bodies; members of the armed services on active duty; attorneys and their staffs; ministers and priests; teachers; physicians; correctional officers; law enforcement officers; mail carriers; and most public officers of the county, state, or federal government. However, those persons exempt from jury duty do not have to claim the exemption and are free to serve as jurors if they so choose. Some state statutes do not designate any class of persons who are exempt from jury duty but do include a provision that the court has the authority to excuse a person upon finding that jury service would entail undue hardship on the person or on the public. However, since it is a citizen's civic duty to serve on juries when called, a person may not be excused for a trivial cause or because of mere inconvenience. The courts are considerate of those for whom jury duty would create a real hardship. This group includes persons operating one-person businesses requiring individual attention, students in the midst of a school year, mothers with small children, and persons caring for sick dependents. Since jury duty is an inconvenience if not an actual hardship for most persons, many districts will excuse a person from further jury duty during the year if he or she has served as many as twenty days, or some other predetermined number, as a juror. This does not mean that a juror may be excused in the middle of a trial after serving twenty days. The juror must continue serving until that particular trial is completed, even if it takes several more weeks.

CHALLENGING THE JURORS FOR CAUSE

In most instances, by the time the jurors reach the jury box, it will have been determined that each possesses the qualifications necessary to act as a juror. If this has not been determined, the judge or prosecuting attorney will read to the jurors the qualifications necessary, and if anyone seated in the jury box does not possess those qualifications, that juror will be excused, and another name will be pulled from the box to replace the excused juror. There have been instances where a person selected to act as a juror did not qualify yet refused to acknowledge the lack of qualification. If either the prosecuting attorney or defense attorney knows that the juror is not qualified, that attorney may challenge the juror's right to serve. For example, it may be known that one of the jurors has been convicted of a felony. That person could be challenged. These challenges are referred to as *challenges for cause.* In other words, there may be some cause why a person should not serve on the jury. There are a number of other reasons why a juror may be challenged for cause besides not being qualified. After viewing the jury, the defense counsel may conclude that it does not represent a cross section of the community because there is no member of the same race, national origin, or age level as the defendant. The defense counsel may then challenge the entire jury panel. If this challenge is made and the judge knows that there was no systematic exclusion of any class of persons, the judge will deny the challenge, and the trial activities will proceed. If any other challenges are forthcoming, they will have to be made on other grounds. If the judge should question the possibility of certain classes of persons being excluded, a recess may be declared until doubt is resolved by determining the method used to select the panel.

Preconceived Ideas of Guilt or Innocence

One of the grounds for challenging a juror for cause is preconceived ideas about the guilt or innocence of the defendant. A juror is often asked how much he or she has heard or read about the case through newspapers, radio, and television. In many instances, the juror, or all jurors, may admit hearing or reading about the case. The juror will then be asked if he or she has an opinion formed regarding the guilt or innocence of the defendant. If the juror has, he or she will be challenged for cause, and the judge will undoubtedly excuse that juror unless there is an indication that the opinion could be changed as a result of evidence presented during the trial. The problem is whether a juror can in reality throw off an opinion of guilt or innocence already formed irrespective of how strong the evidence may be on either side. The questioning of a prospective juror on a challenge for cause is often referred to as a voir dire examination.

In almost all instances, the prospective juror who has formed an opinion about guilt or innocence prior to a trial has formed that opinion as a result of pretrial publicity given to the case. This circumstance creates a continuing battle between the freedom of the press and the defendant's right to a fair trial by an impartial jury. Publicity is given to many cases, particularly murder charges, and it is next to impossible for prospective jurors not to have learned something about the case. As stated by U.S. Supreme Court Justice Clark in the case of *Irvin* v. *Dowd*:[5]

> It is not required . . . that the jurors be totally ignorant of the facts and issues involved (in a case). In these days of swift, widespread and diverse methods of communication, an important case can be expected to arouse the interest of the public in the vicinity, and scarcely any of those best qualified to serve as jurors will not have formed some impression or opinion as to the merits of the case. This is particularly true in criminal cases. To hold that the mere existence of any preconceived notion as to the guilt or innocence of an accused, without more, is sufficient to rebut the presumption of a prospective juror's impartiality would establish an impossible standard. It is sufficient if the juror can lay aside his impression or opinion and render a verdict based upon the evidence presented in court.

In the *Irvin* case, pretrial newspaper stories described the defendant as a confessed slayer of six and a parole violator. Because of deep-seated preconceived opinions of the guilt of the defendant by members of the jury, the Court felt that the defendant had been denied a fair trial by an impartial jury.

Returning again to the *Sheppard* v. *Maxwell* case discussed in Chapter 7, the U.S. Supreme Court held that the defendant had been denied a fair trial, as in the *Irvin* case. In the *Sheppard* decision, extensive pretrial publicity accusing the defendant of the crime was given to the case even though he had not been arrested or charged with the crime. Headlines such as "Why Don't Police Quiz Top Suspect?" appeared, with a demand that Sheppard be taken to the police headquarters for questioning. One newspaper described Sheppard in the following language:

"now proved under oath to be a liar . . . still free to go about his business shielded by his family, . . . protected by a smart lawyer who has made monkeys of the police and authorities, . . . carrying a gun part of the time, . . . left free to do whatever he pleases." After the arrest of the defendant, the publicity intensified and continued throughout the trial. The Court felt that if the prospective jurors did not have a preconceived opinion of the guilt of the defendant, they reached that opinion during the trial primarily from the publicity given the case and not from the evidence presented.

Although the trial judge in the *Sheppard* case endeavored to keep the jurors from being exposed to publicity, the effort was apparently not successful. At the beginning of the trial, the judge stated the following: "I would suggest to you and caution you that you do not read any newspapers during the progress of this trial, that you do not listen to radio comments nor watch or listen to television comments, insofar as this case is concerned. . . . After it is all over, you can read it all to your heart's content." At intervals during the trial, the judge repeated his suggestions. But the "jurors were thrust into the role of celebrities by the judge's failure to insulate them from reporters and photographers. The numerous pictures of the jurors, with their addresses, which appeared in the newspaper before and during the trial itself exposed them to expressions of opinion from both cranks and friends."

As a result of these U.S. Supreme Court decisions, local courts have been encouraged to control information released to the news media. This control does not interfere with the freedom of the press but assists in picking jurors without preconceived opinions on the guilt or innocence of the defendant because of pretrial publicity. The control is designed to prevent the jury from being influenced during the trial by extensive publicity, some of which may be inaccurate. Because of the freedom of the press in this country, much pretrial and during-the-trial publicity is given many cases, despite "gag order" controls. Because of pretrial publicity, extensive questioning of prospective jurors takes place to determine whether the prospective juror has a deep-seated opinion of guilt or innocence that cannot be overcome by the evidence presented during the trial. In some of the more notorious cases, it has taken several weeks just to select a jury.

Challenging the Jurors for Bias

A preconceived idea on guilt or innocence is not the only grounds for challenging a juror for cause. Another ground is bias, either implied or actual.

Implied bias is set by law and disqualifies a juror from serving. Implied bias may include consanguinity or affinity (that is, kinship or relationship) to within the fourth degree to the victim of the crime or to the defendant. Other examples of implied bias are having a relationship of employer and employee, or landlord and tenant, to either the victim of the crime or to the defendant, or having served on a jury that tried another person for the offense charged. Actual bias is prejudice that a juror may admit to having because of a dislike for a particular race, religion, national origin, or class of persons. For example, the juror may admit to a bias against law enforcement officers that would create prejudice against the prosecution.

Since some states do not disqualify prospective jurors because of blindness, an attorney might challenge a blind person for cause if there will be evidence presented during the trial requiring visual examination. However, because of the general sympathy for blind people, an attorney should be cautious in excusing a blind person for cause under these circumstances. That same sympathy might be given a prospective deaf juror, causing other jurors to become prejudiced against the attorney. Even though a challenge is made, complications in executing the challenge can occur, as in the following instance. A hearing-impaired person was challenged in a criminal case because of his inability to hear the testimony. The excluded person countered the challenge for cause, alleging an inherent right to be a juror. He stated that it was the court's responsibility to supply an interpreter capable of using sign language to translate the testimony to the hearing-impaired juror. The judge concluded that persons could be challenged for cause on other grounds permitted by law and that there was no inherent right to be a juror in all circumstances. The judge further pointed out that even if an interpreter was a practical solution to the challenge, there was always the danger of misinterpretation of the testimony by the interpreter or misconception in the translation by the juror. To further complicate the matter, at the final deliberation, only jurors could be present. The judge's position was further supported by the fact that a person without a sense of smell or feeling could be excused for cause if these faculties were important to the examination of evidence.

Prospective Jurors Opposed to the Death Penalty

Prior to the U.S. Supreme Court decision in *Witherspoon* v. *Illinois*,[6] if a juror was against the death penalty, a challenge for cause could be made in cases carrying a maximum penalty of death. The facts of the *Witherspoon* case show that Witherspoon, the petitioner, was brought to trial in Cook County, Illinois, on a charge of murder. The jury found him guilty and fixed the penalty at death. At the time of trial, an Illinois statute provided the following: "In trials for murder it shall be a cause for challenge of any juror who shall, being examined, state that he has conscientious scruples against capital punishment or that he is opposed to the same."

During the trial, the prosecution eliminated approximately half the jury panel on a challenge for cause when prospective jurors expressed any qualms about capital punishment. Those persons chosen for the trial jury were ones with no conscientious scruples against the death penalty. Witherspoon took the case to the U.S. Supreme Court on the grounds that a fair trial by an impartial jury representative of the cross section of the community had been denied. Witherspoon maintained that persons who were not against the death penalty were more likely to be convicting jurors. Since many persons were against the death penalty, eliminating those persons from a jury resulted in a jury that was not representative of the community. The Supreme Court agreed with Witherspoon and held that merely having conscientious scruples against capital punishment was not a sufficient cause to disqualify a person from serving on a jury. The Court did state that if a prospective juror advised that under no circumstances could he or she vote to convict a defendant if the death penalty was the sentence, that person could be excused on a challenge for cause.

In those states in which the death penalty may be imposed upon conviction of certain crimes, the prosecuting attorney may ask whether a prospective juror is opposed to the death penalty. If the juror indicates opposition, the prosecuting attorney may then ask whether the juror could vote for conviction knowing that the death penalty could be imposed. A prospective juror who states that he or she could vote for conviction may not be challenged for cause. The problem created by the *Witherspoon* decision is just what action may be taken against the prospective juror who merely indicates some reservations about being able to vote for conviction. Some appellate courts have held that the prospective juror must state positively that he or she could not consider a guilty verdict, if the penalty is death, in order to have the person challenged for cause. There were three dissenting justices in the *Witherspoon* decision who felt that permissible questioning of prospective jurors on the death penalty would not result in a different kind of jury and that prosecutors would be put to a great deal of trouble for nothing.

The *Witherspoon* decision has caused great complication in the voir dire examination of prospective jurors in capital punishment cases. Some appellate courts have adopted the view that the *Witherspoon* decision holds that to constitutionally excuse a prospective juror for cause due to opposition to the death penalty, the juror must make it unmistakably clear that, first, the juror would automatically vote against the death penalty without regard to evidence presented, or that, second, this attitude toward the death penalty would prevent the prospective juror from making an impartial decision on the defendant's guilt.

Prosecuting attorneys and judges have attempted to abide by the *Witherspoon* decision, but just how positive must the feeling be against the death penalty before a prospective juror is excused? In one case, a prospective juror stated on voir dire examination that she was against the death penalty. The judge asked, "Are you so against the death penalty that you would just automatically vote against the death penalty?" To this the prospective juror stated, "I think there might be a hypothetical case in which so heinous a crime was committed that I would consider the death penalty. But I have not been able to think of a hypothetical case that heinous." With this statement, the judge excused the prospective juror for cause. The defendant in that case was convicted, and the case was automatically appealed to the state supreme court, which reversed the death penalty on the grounds that the prospective juror had been improperly excused as not stating that she would automatically vote against the death penalty. There was a dissenting justice in that case who felt that the juror had been properly excused. The case indicates the difficulty facing the courts in determining when a prospective juror was properly excused for cause in being against the death penalty.[7]

In another state case, a prospective juror was asked whether any personal feelings might prevent participation in the deliberation of a case carrying a possible death sentence. The prospective juror replied that he was a born-again Christian and did not think that he could have any part of sitting in on a case that would send anyone to the electric chair. With this reply, the judge excused the man. After the defendant was convicted and given the death penalty, the state supreme court in that case reversed the death penalty on the grounds that the prospective juror was improperly excused since it was not made unmistakably clear that the juror's participation in the deliberation of the case was not possible because of the penalty. The dissenting justice in that case felt that the court was only seeking a way to reverse death penalties. Justices who have personal feelings against the death penalty have been able to effectively overrule death penalty sentences by holding that a prospective juror was improperly excused in violation of the *Witherspoon* decision. This treatment has brought about criticism of those justices for not upholding the will of the people.

In the case of *Wainright* v. *Witt*,[8] the U.S. Supreme Court somewhat relaxed the strict rule of the *Witherspoon* decision. In this case, the Court set forth a new standard for determining when a prospective juror may be excused for cause because of his or her views on capital punishment: "That standard is whether the juror's views would prevent or substantially impair the performance of his duties as a juror in accordance with his instructions and his oath. . . . We [the Supreme Court] note that, in addition to dispensing with Witherspoon's reference to 'automatic' decision making, this standard likewise does not require that a juror's bias be proved with 'unmistakable clarity.' " Remember that state appellate courts have the power to make rules for their own trial courts. These may be more restrictive than the ones set forth by the U.S. Supreme Court and, as such, may still adhere to the strict rule set forth in the *Witherspoon* decision.

The voir dire examination of prospective jurors can be extensive in any type of case. To limit this examination, some states have passed legislation permitting the trial judge to conduct the voir dire examination. In other states, the trial judge will often call into the courtroom all the jury panel selected to appear for the particular trial, and the judge will conduct a portion of the voir dire examination. The panel will be asked whether they have any preconceived opinions on guilt or innocence as a result of pretrial publicity given to the case. The judge may also go into other phases of possible bias. Even though this procedure is followed, the prosecuting attorney and particularly the defense counsel are permitted a reasonable voir dire examination opportunity. Some judges conduct no voir dire examinations, since they believe that selecting the jury is the prerogative of the attorneys involved and that any interference with it is a denial of their rights. Most attorneys enjoy the privilege of conducting voir dire examinations in challenging for cause, since it gives them an opportunity to become better acquainted with the jurors who are finally selected. Some courts frown on this reason for voir dire examinations as having no place in the justice system. These courts hold that voir dire examinations by the attorneys are for determining whether a juror should be disqualified by a challenge for cause. In these courts, the attorneys are limited to questions pertinent to the cause for which they may be attempting to disqualify the juror. Other courts permit a certain freedom when questioning a prospective juror. This aids the attorneys in determining whether a peremptory challenge should be exercised when an undesired juror cannot be disqualified for cause. As long as the attorneys' questions relate to a challenge for cause, the questioning can be almost limitless, particularly when the cause is for bias. For this reason, some judges try to limit the questioning to matters directly relating to the particular case involved. If a judge should be too restrictive in permitting the questioning by the defense counsel, a conviction could be reversed on appeal through the allegation that the jury was not impartial.

PEREMPTORY CHALLENGE

After the prosecution and defense have exhausted their challenges for cause, there is one more opportunity to remove an undesired juror or jurors. Each attorney is given the right to excuse a juror whom he or she may not want on the jury. The right to excuse a juror under these circumstances is known as a *peremptory challenge*. Both the prosecution and the defense have a certain number of peremptory challenges that permit either attorney to excuse a juror without stating a reason. The challenges are granted upon the theory that they assist the attorneys in more nearly selecting an impartial jury. A prosecuting attorney, for example, may exercise the right of peremptory challenge to excuse a juror who, during challenge for cause, indicated reservations against the death penalty but could vote for a conviction if the evidence against the defendant was strong enough. Even though this is the real reason the juror was excused, the attorney does not have to give the reason. A defense attorney may excuse a juror who stated during challenge for cause that there was a feeling that the defendant was guilty but that it could be controlled with the juror guided by the evidence of the case.

Prohibiting the Peremptory Challenge

Generally, the trial judge has no authority to prohibit a juror from being excused on a peremptory challenge. However, the U.S. Supreme Court in *Batson* v. *Kentucky*[9] held that an attorney may not use peremptory challenges to exclude persons from a jury solely on the basis of race. Batson was of the black race, and during the jury selection, the prosecuting attorney excluded all persons of the black race from the jury by the use of his peremptory challenges. The Supreme Court stated the following:

> Although a prosecutor ordinarily is entitled to exercise permitted peremptory challenges for any reason at all as long as that reason is related to the outcome of the case to be tried ... the Equal Protection Clause [of the 14th Amendment of the U.S. Constitution] forbids the prosecutor to challenge potential jurors solely on account of their race or on the presumption that black jurors as a group will be unable impartially to consider the State's case against a black defendant.

The supreme court of one state held that "peremptory challenges may not be used to remove prospective jurors solely on the basis of presumed group bias. We define group bias as a presumption that certain jurors are biased merely because they are members of an identifiable group distinguished on racial, religious, ethnic, or similar grounds."[10]

The Court in the *Batson* case based its decision primarily on the violation of the Equal Protection clause of the U.S. Constitution. But some state courts have limited the use of peremptory challenges to exclude persons of a certain group on the theory that a defendant is entitled to be tried by an impartial jury representative of a cross section of the community. The exclusion of members of a defined group by the use of peremptory challenges denies the defendant that right. The prosecution has the same right to question the use of peremptory challenges by the defense in the exclusion of certain classes of persons. The prosecution is also entitled to have the case tried by a jury representative of a cross section of the community.

The *Batson* decision did not eliminate all use of peremptory challenges to exclude from a jury persons of a defined group. But when it becomes apparent that such an attempted exclusion is taking place, the opposing side may question the procedure. The trial judge has the responsibility to determine whether there is a justification for the exclusions. If the offending attorney can establish a bonafide justification for the exclusions, the peremptory challenges will stand. The justification is generally based on some attitude displayed by the excluded juror, such as being unduly friendly toward the defendant or his attorney or displaying an unwholesome attitude toward law enforcement.

As in the case of the challenge for cause, when a juror is excused by the peremptory challenge, the court clerk will pick another name from the jury panel box, and that prospective juror will take the seat of the excused juror in the jury box. That juror and any others who may replace excused jurors may be questioned to determine whether they should be challenged for cause. Thus, another time-consuming procedure occurs in the selection of the jury. The number of peremptory challenges for the prosecution and the defense varies among states. Some states grant the prosecution and defense an equal number of peremptory challenges, usually ten each. Other states grant the defense ten challenges and the prosecution only five. Some jurisdictions grant more peremptory challenges for felony trials than for misdemeanor trials. Where the maximum penalty is death, most jurisdictions permit twice as many peremptory challenges as in noncapital cases.

Holding Challenges in Reserve

Both the prosecuting attorney and the defense attorney will hold one or two of their peremptory challenges in reserve. The reason is that a person who is most unsatisfactory to one side or the other may have his or her name drawn from the panel, leaving no way to disqualify this person for cause. If all the peremptory challenges have been exhausted, there is no way of preventing that person from being a

---

U.S. Supreme Court Decisions Regarding the Peremptory Challenge

Case	*Decision*
Batson v. *Kentucky* (1986)	Under the Fourteenth Amendment, the Supreme Court ruled that prosecutors were barred from using peremptory challenges to remove black jurors because of their race.
Powers v. *Ohio* (1991)	The Supreme Court concluded that a defendant has the standing to object to race-based exclusion of jurors by the use of peremptory challenges on the grounds of equal protection, even if the defendant is not of the same race as the challenged jurors.
Edmonson v. *Leesville Concrete Co.* (1991)	The Court held that the *Batson* ruling applies to attorneys in civil lawsuits. A private party in a civil action may not use peremptory challenges to exclude jurors on the basis of race.
Georgia v. *McCollum* (1992)	On the basis of *Batson,* the Court prohibited the exercise of race-based peremptory challenges by defense attorneys in criminal cases.
J.E.B. v. *Alabama* (1994)	The Supreme Court held that the equal protection clause of the Fourteenth Amendment bars discrimination in jury selection on the basis of sex. Discrimination in jury selection, whether based on race or gender, causes harm to the litigants, the community, and the individual jurors who are wrongfully excluded from participation in the judicial process.

juror. The person may have a history of never having voted for conviction or having a known dislike for a particular race or religion, yet this dislike cannot be established in questioning for cause. Defense attorneys generally do not like to have law enforcement officers, either active or retired, on a jury, since such a person tends to assume guilt from the mere arrest and formal charging of the defendant. This type of tendency may be impossible to establish in order to excuse the officer on cause, but no cause is needed in the peremptory challenge. Both prosecuting attorneys and defense attorneys will question prospective jurors for cause as extensively as the court will permit. This questioning enables them to get a better idea of how a particular prospective juror may think or react in reaching a verdict. The attorneys may then utilize their peremptory challenges more effectively.

Who Make the Best Jurors?

All attorneys engaged in the trial of cases, whether civil or criminal, constantly try to analyze persons in an effort to determine who make the best jurors. There is no way to predict how a person will react in each instance, but attorneys feel that certain groups or classes of persons tend to react in more definite patterns than others. For example, defense attorneys feel that minority groups who have encountered hardships and discrimination tend to be more tolerant of defendants than members of the white Anglo groups of medium or higher income. Younger persons are alleged to be more permissive and forgiving in their attitudes toward a defendant, particularly if the defendant is also a younger person. For that reason, defense attorneys try to have more persons between the ages of eighteen and twenty-one on jury panels as well as more members of minority groups. But obtaining these classes of people for jury duty is not easy. Many younger persons attending school are excused so that their school year will not be interrupted. If not in school, many are married and are in a lower-income bracket, as are many in minority groups who are excused from jury duty because of the extreme financial hardship that might be suffered. In most jurisdictions, the compensation for jury duty is meager, since it is considered to be a civic duty to serve on a criminal trial jury. Jurors in some areas receive only $5 a day plus a small mileage fee. It has been recommended that the compensation be increased in order that younger persons and those of minority groups in lower-income brackets may afford to serve on the jury. But court costs are already extremely high, and each increase in jury fees makes the court costs that much greater, another burden on the taxpayer. A few jurisdictions have increased the jurors' compensation to ease the financial hardship suffered by those who serve, as well as to obtain a wider selection of persons.

Many attorneys feel that the most satisfactory juror is one who takes pride in serving on a jury, takes the duty seriously, endeavors to conscientiously evaluate the evidence presented during the trial, and attempts to arrive at a just verdict. The financial burden upon the juror should not be great, and they should not have to worry about children or day-care issues.

After the prosecution and defense have exhausted their challenges for cause, have no desire to further exercise their right of peremptory challenges, and indicate to the judge that they are satisfied with the jury selected, the jury will then be sworn to perform their duty. The oath administered to the jurors will in substance be that each of them will endeavor to reach a true and just verdict based on the evidence of the case. After the jurors have been sworn in, the trial begins. Some jurisdictions still swear jurors individually, but most jurisdictions will administer the oath to the jury as a group once they have been selected and accepted by both sides and by the judge.

ALTERNATE JURORS

Records reveal that often during a lengthy trial, one or more jurors become incapacitated and cannot continue. If this possibility happens and the defendant does not agree to continue the trial with those jurors remaining, the judge must declare a mistrial, and the trial must be restarted. If several weeks have elapsed before the juror becomes incapacitated, having to start the trial over is frustrating as well as expensive. To avoid the possibility of having to start a new trial, most states have statutes providing that alternate jurors may be selected at the discretion of the trial judge. Determining the approximate time that the prosecution and defense plan to take in presenting their sides of the case enables the judge to decide whether and how many alternate jurors should be selected.

Alternate jurors are selected in the same manner as regular jurors. The alternates may be challenged for cause, and usually one additional peremptory challenge is granted for each alternate selected. The judge may decide that only one alternate will be necessary, or he or she may decide on more if the trial is to be extremely lengthy. Usually not more than four alternates are selected. If there is more than one alternate and one of the regular jurors becomes incapacitated, the clerk will draw the name of the alternate who will be substituted for the incapacitated juror. Some states permit an alternate to be substituted for the incapacitated juror up to the time that the case is given to the jury for deliberation. Other states permit an alternate to be substituted anytime before the verdict is reached. The alternate jurors must be situated in the courtroom where they can observe all the proceedings and can hear all that takes place. Usually, an area next to the jury box is reserved for alternate jurors to facilitate their being able to see and hear. After selection, the alternate jurors are given the same oath as the regular jury.

The use of the alternate juror system has been criticized by some legal scholars. They allege that the alternate juror creates a jury of thirteen instead of twelve, particularly if the alternate is substituted during the deliberation. It has been alleged that permitting a substitution during the deliberation handicaps the alternate juror, since he or she has not had the benefit of the group dynamics during the preceding deliberation. Because of these criticisms, some states do not permit substitution after the deliberation begins, and once the case is given to the jury for a verdict, the alternate juror or jurors are discharged. The problem created by discharging alternate jurors at the time of deliberation is that, after a lengthy trial, the deliberation could take several days and a juror could possibly become incapacitated during that time. If this possibility happens, the jury would have to be dismissed and the trial started over, thus defeating the purpose of the alternate juror system. Those jurisdictions permitting a substitution of an alternate during deliberation believe that there is no reason the alternate could not be thoroughly briefed on the deliberation up to the time of the substitution, thus enabling the alternate to cast an intelligent vote for the verdict.

The alternate jury system has also been criticized as unfair to the defendant, because the alternate juror, knowing that chances of substitution are slight, may not take much interest in the case and be unable to properly evaluate the evidence during deliberation if substituted. To overcome this possibility, it has been proposed that, if alternate jurors are to be selected, the entire jury—including alternates—be selected at one time. At the time the case is given to the jury for deliberation, the court clerk would draw twelve names from the jury selection box. In this way, none of the jurors would know who were regulars and alternates until all the evidence of the case had been presented, and all would have an equal interest in the presentation.

Although the alternate juror system has been criticized by some as being unfair to the defendant, these criticisms seem shallow compared with the benefits gained by having a juror who can replace one who may become incapacitated. It must be remembered that the alternate juror system was established because, in most instances, a defendant will not agree to continue a trial with less than a full jury should one of the jurors become incapacitated. The refusal to continue with the trial is usually based on the belief that delays in a trial work to the defendant's advantage. In addition, it is impossible to make every situation arising in the justice system idealistic for the defendant. In fact, many in the justice system feel that the system is already balanced heavily in favor of the defendant.

SEQUESTERING THE JURY

Once the jury has been selected and sworn in, the judge must decide whether it is to be sequestered, or "locked up." When a jury is sequestered, it is segregated from all outside contact. The primary reason for the sequestering of the jury is to protect its members from possible outside influence in arriving at their verdict. When not in the courtroom, the jurors are kept together as a body at all times under the guard of a bailiff or some other court officer. They eat together and are housed in a hotel, motel, or some other convenient place until the trial is concluded. Even the newspapers that they may be permitted to read or the news broadcasts that they may listen to must be monitored to ensure that nothing that might affect their verdict is brought to their attention. As was pointed out in the *Sheppard* case, the jury was aware of the extensive news media publicity throughout the entire trial. According to the U.S. Supreme Court, the publicity influenced the jury in their opinion on guilt, and the Court reversed the conviction. The Court suggested that the judge should have had greater control over the news releases or should have sequestered the jury during the trial to prevent undue influence. Generally, it is held that when a jury is not sequestered, the judge has the authority to forbid the jurors from reading any newspapers or listening to any broadcasts about the case, and if they should inadvertently read about or listen to something about the case, they are to disregard it.

In a few states, the jury must be sequestered during a trial on certain charges, but otherwise sequestering is at the discretion of the judge. The jury may be sequestered at any time during the trial proceedings. The jury may be sequestered on the judge's own decision or at the request of either the prosecution or the defense. If the jury is not sequestered during the presentation of the evidence, it will usually be sequestered during the deliberation when the trial pertains to a serious charge. In a few jurisdictions, the jury must be sequestered during the deliberation. If the jury is sequestered, the alternate jurors are sequestered—so, but are generally sequestered separately from the regular jury. In those jurisdictions where it is at the judge's discretion to sequester the jury prior to the time of deliberation, most judges hesitate to sequester the jury because of the hardship imposed. The jurors lose all contact with their families and friends during the period of sequestration. Most of the jurors are unacquainted with one another before the trial begins, yet they must be housed together. Often personality clashes occur, affecting their judgment during the deliberation. From the standpoint of the taxpayer, sequestering a jury is expensive because taxes pay for housing and feeding the jury during this period. Most jurors dislike being sequestered, and when that possibility is apparent, prospective jurors will do everything possible to be excused from that particular trial. Thus, in addition to the hardships experienced by the jurors themselves, selecting a jury becomes even more difficult than usual. When a jury is sequestered during a trial at the request of the prosecution or defense, it is the policy of the judge not to inform the jury which side made the request, in order to avoid any prejudice by the jurors toward that side. Whether the jury is sequestered or not, each time the court is adjourned, the judge must advise the jurors against discussing the facts of the case among themselves or with others, and against forming any opinions about the case until the time of deliberation.

THE FUTURE OF THE JURY SYSTEM

Interviews with persons who have accepted their duty to serve on criminal juries reveal that many become disenchanted with the jury system. The most common complaint is the time spent by prospective jurors waiting to be called for duty on a particular case. Many wait hours in the uncomfortable surroundings of the courthouse halls. Some even wait all day without being called, only to be ordered to return the next day to suffer a similar experience. This waiting usually stems from last-minute requests for continuances, hearings on other motions presented, or plea bargaining.

Many persons believe that average jurors are neither able to cope with the facts of the more complex trials nor able to understand and abide by the instructions given them by the judge. There are those who feel that too many jurors permit emotions and personality conflicts to interfere with judgment in arriving at a verdict. In those states where the unanimous verdict must be returned, one juror may prevent such a verdict from being rendered just because of an emotional or a personality conflict, thereby hampering the justice system. Many persons believe that our justice system would not come to a sudden halt if the jury system were abolished and verdicts were decided by a body of three or more judges. Irrespective of what persons may think or believe, as long as the Sixth Amendment guarantee to a trial by jury is in effect, the jury system will not be eliminated.

CAPSTONE CASE

Batson v. *Kentucky*
476 U.S. 79, 106 S.Ct. 1712, 90 L.Ed.2d 69 (1986)

Justice Powell delivered the opinion of the Court.

This case requires us to reexamine that portion of *Swain* v. *Alabama,* 380 U.S. 202 (1965), concerning the evidentiary burden placed on a criminal defendant. Accordingly,

The rules below were provided to the jury in the murder trial of the former football star, O. J. Simpson. Realizing that the O. J. Simpson case was provoking unusual interest, Judge Lance Ito, with suggestion from the attorneys on both sides, drew up the following document:

Date: 23 September 1994
Department 103
HON. LANCE A. ITO, Judge
D. ROBERTSON, Deputy Clerk

Superior Court of the State of California in and for the County of Los Angeles
People vs. *Orenthal James Simpson*
Case #BA097211

Court Order
   Each juror and alternate juror selected to serve in this matter is ordered and directed to:

1. Not to read or listen to or watch any accounts or discussions of this case reported by newspapers, television, radio, or any other news media.

2. Not to visit or view the premises or place where the offense or offenses charged were allegedly committed or any premises or place involved in this case unless directed by the court to do so.

3. Not to converse with other jurors or with anyone else upon any subject connected with the trial unless and until permitted to do so by the court.

4. Not to request, accept, agree to accept, or discuss with any person receiving or accepting, any payment or benefit in consideration for supplying any information concerning this trial for a period of 180 days from the return of a verdict or the termination of the case, whichever is earlier.

5. Promptly to report to the court any incident within their knowledge involving an attempt by any person improperly to influence any member of the jury.

Dated: _____, 19_____

_____
Hon. Lance A. Ito

I agree to the above order and understand that if I violate the provisions of this order that I can be ordered to pay a sanction to the court of up to $1,500 for each violation pursuant to Code of Civil Procedure Section 177.5, to reimburse or make payment to the County of Los Angeles for costs caused by a violation pursuant to California Rules of Court, Rule 227, or punished by a fine or imprisonment for contempt pursuant to Code of Civil Procedure Section 1218.

Dated: _____, 19_____

_____
Juror

Additional Instructions
After about six weeks the attorneys and the judge decided that the first set of rules were not strong enough, so the following regulations were devised:

Date: 12 December 1994
Department 103
HON. LANCE A. ITO, Judge
D. ROBERTSON, Deputy Clerk

Superior Court of the State of California in and for the County of Los Angeles
People vs. *Orenthal James Simpson*
Case #BA097211

Court Order
   During the course of this trial, and until further order of this court, the trial jurors and alternates in this case shall NOT read any newspaper article or other written account including magazines or books or watch any television programs dealing with this case, the defendant or his family, the victims or their families, the attorneys or any other matter concerning this case. The court will distribute to the jurors and alternates the local daily newspaper of their choice, edited to remove any coverage of this case. Jurors and alternates shall NOT listen to any radio programming. Each juror and alternate may listen to audio tapes and compact disks, including books on

Continued

LAW IN PRACTICE　　*Rules for the Jurors in the O. J. Simpson Trial (Continued)*

tape that do not concern this case. Jurors and alternates who need current weather and traffic information may get this information by dialing (213) 962-3279.

Jurors and alternates shall NOT watch:

1. <u>ANY</u> television news program or news break.

2. <u>ANY</u> television "*tabloid*" program such as Hard Copy, A Current Affair, Inside Edition, American Journal, or Premiere Story.

3. <u>ANY</u> television talk show such as Marilu, Leeza, Jenny Jones, Sally Jessy Raphael, Oprah, Donahue, Good Morning America, Today, CBS This Morning, The Montel Williams Show, The Maury Povich Show, Ricki Lake, Rolonda, Rush Limbaugh and Geraldo.

4. <u>ANY</u> television news magazine program such as 60 Minutes, 20/20, Dateline, Eye to Eye, 48 Hours, or Primetime Live.

5. <u>ANY</u> entertainment news magazine such as Entertainment Tonight and EXTRA.

6. CNN, CNN Headline News, CNBC, The E! Channel, Sports Center on ESPN, Press Box on Prime Ticket, The News on MTV, any news or talk show on BET and Dennis Miller Live on HBO.

7. The Tonight Show (Jay Leno) and The Late Show with David Letterman.

Jurors and alternates <u>MAY</u> watch:

1. Normal television entertainment programming, including sports and home shopping channels, not excluding above, <u>however. Jurors are strongly cautioned to avoid watching advertisements for upcoming news broadcasts known as "teasers."</u>

2. Cable or satellite television channels: American Movie Classics, Showtime, Cinemax, The Disney Channel, The Movie Channel, The Shopping Channel, The Family Channel, The Cartoon Channel, Turner Classic Movies, MTV, Discovery Channel, Arts and Entertainment (A&E), Bravo, Lifetime, Nashville, Nickelodeon and Home Box Office.

3. Movies and other programming on video tape that do not involve this case, the defendant or his family, the victims or their families, or the attorneys and their families.

Any questions regarding this order shall be directed to the Clerk of the Court.

<u>IT IS SO ORDERED</u>.

---

the component of the jury selection process at issue here, the State's privilege to strike individual jurors through peremptory challenges, is subject to the commands of the "Equal Protection Clause." Although a prosecutor ordinarily is entitled to exercise permitted peremptory challenges "for any reason at all, as long as that reason is related to his view concerning the outcome" of the case to be tried, the Equal Protection Clause forbids the prosecutor to challenge potential jurors solely on account of their race or on the assumption that black jurors as a group will be unable impartially to consider the State's case against a black defendant. . . .

Swain required the Court to decide, among other issues, whether a black defendant was denied equal protection by the State's exercise of peremptory challenges to exclude members of his race from the petit jury. The record in Swain showed that the prosecutor had used the State's peremptory challenges to strike the six black persons included on the petit jury venire. While rejecting the defendant's claim for failure to prove purposeful discrimination, the Court nonetheless indicated that the Equal Protection Clause placed some limits on the State's exercise of peremptory challenges.

The Court sought to accommodate the prosecutor's historical privilege of peremptory challenge free of judicial control, and the constitutional prohibition on exclusion of persons from jury service on account of race. While the Constitution does not confer a right to peremptory challenges, those challenges traditionally have been viewed as one means of assuring the selection of a qualified and unbiased jury. To preserve the peremptory nature of the prosecutor's challenge, the Court in Swain declined to scrutinize his actions in a particular case by relying on a presumption that he properly exercised the State's challenges.

The Court went on to observe, however, that a state may not exercise its challenges in contravention of the Equal Protection Clause. It was impermissible for a prosecutor to use his challenges to exclude blacks from the jury "for reasons wholly unrelated to the outcome of the particular case on trial" or to deny to blacks "the same right and opportunity to participate in the administration of justice enjoyed by the white population." Accordingly, a black defendant could make out a prima facie case of purposeful discrimination on proof that the peremptory challenge system was "being perverted" in that manner.

In this case, petitioner made a timely objection to the prosecutor's removal of all black persons on the venire. Because the trial court flatly rejected the objection without requiring the prosecutor to give an explanation for his action, we remand this case for further proceedings. If the trial court decides that the facts establish, prima facie, purposeful discrimination and the prosecutor does not come forward with a neutral explanation for his action, our precedents require that petitioner's conviction be reversed.

Justice Marshall, concurring.

I wholeheartedly concur in the Court's conclusion that use of the peremptory challenge to remove blacks from juries, on the basis of their race, violates the Equal Protection Clause. I would go further, however, in fashioning a remedy adequate to eliminate that discrimination. Merely allowing defendants the opportunity to challenge the racially discriminatory use of peremptory challenges in individual cases will not end the illegitimate use of the peremptory challenge.

Evidentiary analysis similar to that set out by the Court has been adopted as a matter of state law in States including Massachusetts and California. Cases from those jurisdictions illustrate the limitations of the approach. First, defendants cannot attack the discriminatory use of peremptory challenges at all unless the challenges are so flagrant as to establish a prima facie case. This means, in those States, that where only one or two black jurors survive the challenges for cause, the prosecutor need have no compunction about striking them from the jury because of their race. Prosecutors are left free to discriminate against blacks in jury selection provided that they hold that discrimination to an "acceptable" level.

Second, when a defendant can establish a prima facie case, trial courts face the difficult burden of assessing prosecutors' motives. Any prosecutor can easily assert facially neutral reasons for striking a juror, and trial courts are ill equipped to second-guess those reasons. How is the court to treat a prosecutor's statement that he struck a juror because the juror had a son about the same age as defendant, or seemed "uncommunicative," or "never cracked a smile" and, therefore "did not possess the sensitivities necessary to realistically look at the issues and decide the facts in this case?" If such easily generated explanations are sufficient to discharge the prosecutor's obligation to justify his strikes on nonracial grounds, then the protection erected by the Court today may be illusory.

Nor is outright prevarication by prosecutors the only danger here. "[I]t is even possible that an attorney may lie to himself in an effort to convince himself that his motives are legal." A prosecutor's own conscious or unconscious racism may lead him easily to the conclusion that a prospective black juror is "sullen," or "distant," a characterization that would not have come to his mind if a white juror had acted identically. A judge's own conscious or unconscious racism may lead him to accept such an explanation as well supported. . . .

The inherent potential of peremptory challenges to distort the jury process by permitting the exclusion of jurors on racial grounds should ideally lead the Court to ban them entirely from the criminal justice system. . . .

Chief Justice Burger, joined by Justice Rehnquist, dissenting.

The Court acknowledges, albeit in a footnote, the "very old credentials" of the peremptory challenge and "the widely held belief that peremptory challenge is a necessary part of trial by jury." But proper resolution of this case requires more than a nodding reference to the purpose of the challenge. . . . The Court's opinion, in addition to ignoring the teachings of history, also contrasts with Swain in its failure to even discuss the rationale of the peremptory challenge. Swain observed: "The function of the challenge is not only to eliminate extremes of partiality on both sides, but to assure the parties that the jurors before whom they try the case will decide on the basis of the evidence placed for them, and not otherwise. In this way the peremptory satisfies the rule that 'to perform its high function in the best way, justice must satisfy the appearance of justice.'"

Permitting unexplained peremptories has long been regarded as a means to strengthen our jury system in other ways as well. One commentator has recognized:

> The peremptory, made without giving any reason, avoids trafficking in the core of truth in most common stereotypes. . . . Common human experience, common sense, psychosociological studies, and public opinion polls tell us that it is likely that certain classes of people statistically have predispositions that would make them inappropriate jurors for particular kinds of cases. But to allow this knowledge to be expressed in the evaluative terms necessary for challenges for cause would undercut our desire for a society in which all people are judged as individuals and in which each is held reasonable and open to compromise . . . though experience reveals that black males as a class can he biased against young alienated blacks who have not tried to join the middle class, to enunciate this in the concrete expression required of a challenge for cause is societally divisive. Instead we have evolved in the peremptory challenge a system that allows the covert expression of what we dare not say but know is true more often than not.

For reasons such as these, this Court concluded in Swain that "the peremptory challenge is one of the most important of the rights" in our justice system. For close to a century, then, it has been settled that "the denial or impairment of the right is reversible error without a showing of prejudice." The Court also invokes general equal protection principles in support of its holding. But peremptory challenges are often lodged, of necessity, for reasons "normally thought irrelevant to legal proceedings or official action, namely, the race, religion, nationality, occupation or affiliations of people summoned for jury duty." Moreover, in making peremptory challenges, both the prosecutor and defense attorney necessarily act on only limited information or hunch. The process can not be indicted on the sole basis that such decisions are made on the basis of "assumption" or "intuitive judgment." As a result, unadulterated equal protection analysis is simply inapplicable to peremptory challenges exercised in any particular case. A clause that requires a minimum "rationality" in government actions has no application to "an arbitrary and capricious right"; a constitutional principle that may invalidate state action on the basis of "stereotypic notions" does not explain the breadth of a procedure exercised on the "sudden impressions and unaccountable prejudices we are apt to conceive upon the bare looks and gestures of another."

That the Court is not applying conventional equal protection analysis is shown by its limitation of its new rule to allegations of impermissible challenge on the basis of race; the Court's opinion clearly contains such a limitation. . . . But if conventional equal protection principles apply, then presumably defendants could object to exclusions on the basis of not only race, but also sex, age, religious or political affiliation, mental capacity, number of children, living arrangements, and employment in a particular industry or profession.

In short, it is quite probable that every peremptory challenge could be objected to on the basis that, because it excluded a venireman who had some characteristic not shared by the remaining members of the venire, it constituted a "classification" subject to equal protection scrutiny. Compounding the difficulties, under conventional equal protection principles some uses of peremptories would be reviewed under "strict scrutiny and . . . sustained only if . . . suitably tailored to serve a compelling state interest," others would be reviewed to determine if they were "substantially related to a sufficiently important government interest," and still others would be reviewed to determine whether they were "a rational means to serve a legitimate end."

The Court never applies this conventional equal protection framework to the claims at hand, perhaps to avoid acknowledging that the state interest involved here has historically been regarded by this Court as substantial, if not compelling.

The Court also purports to express "no views on whether the Constitution imposes any limit on the exercise of peremptory challenges by defense counsel." But the clear and inescapable import of this novel holding will inevitably be to limit the use of this valuable tool to both prosecutors and defense attorneys alike. Once the Court has held that prosecutors are limited in their use of peremptory challenges, could we rationally hold that defendants are not? . . . Confronted with the dilemma it created, the Court today attempts to decree a middle ground. To rebut a prima facie case, the Court requires a "neutral explanation" for the challenge, but is at pains to "emphasize" that the "explanation need not rise to the level justifying exercise of a challenge for cause." I am at a loss to discern the governing principles here. A "clear and reasonably specific" explanation of "legitimate reasons for exercising the challenge will be difficult to distinguish from a challenge for cause. Anything short of a challenge for cause may well be seen as an "arbitrary and capricious" challenge, to use Blackstone's characterization of the peremptory. Apparently the Court envisions permissible challenges short of a challenge for cause that are just a little bit arbitrary but not too much. While our trial judges are "experienced in supervising voir dire," they have no experience in administering rules like this.

An example will quickly demonstrate how today's holding, while purporting to "further the ends of justice," will not have that effect. Assume an Asian defendant, on trial for the capital murder of a white victim, asks prospective jury members, most of whom are white, whether they harbor racial prejudice against Asians. The basis for such a question is to flush out any juror who believes that [Asians] are violence-prone or morally inferior. . . . Assume further that all white jurors deny harboring racial prejudice but that the defendant, on trial for his life, remains unconvinced by these protestations. Instead, he continues to harbor a hunch, an "assumption" or "intuitive judgment," that these white jurors will be prejudiced against him, presumably based in part on race. The time-honored rule before today was that peremptory challenges could be exercised on such a basis. . . . The effect of the Court's decision, however, will be to force the defendant to come forward and "articulate a neutral explanation," for his peremptory challenge, a burden he probably cannot meet. This example demonstrates that today's holding will produce juries that the parties do not believe are truly impartial. This will surely do more than "disconcert" litigants; it will diminish confidence in the jury system. . . .

Today we mark the return of racial differentiation as the Court accepts a positive evil for a perceived one. Prosecutors and defense attorneys alike will build records in support of their claims that peremptory challenges have been exercised in a racially discriminatory fashion by asking jurors to state their racial background and national origin for the record, despite the fact that "Such questions may be offensive to some jurors and thus are not ordinarily asked on voir dire." This process is sure to tax even the most capable counsel and judges since determining whether a prima facie case has been established will "require a continued monitoring and recording of the group composition of the panel present and prospective. . . ."

REVIEW QUESTIONS

1. Who are one's peers as the term relates to a jury?
2. In what amendment is found the right to trial by an impartial jury?
3. What is a jury panel or jury list?
4. List four qualifications for being a juror.
5. What persons may be exempt from jury duty, and why is the exemption granted?
6. What is meant by challenging a juror for cause?
7. List three possible challenges for cause.
8. What is the purpose of permitting a challenge for cause?
9. What is a peremptory challenge?
10. Who are alternate jurors, and why are they selected?
11. What is meant by sequestering the jury?
12. Explain the purpose of sequestering a jury.

LOCAL PROCEDURE

1. What are the qualifications for a juror?
2. If a juror becomes incapacitated, may he or she be replaced by an alternate during the deliberation?
3. Must the jury be sequestered? If so, at what point during the trial?
4. How many peremptory challenges are permitted to the prosecution and the defense?

ENDNOTES

1. See 18 U.S. Code, section 1861.
2. 328 U.S. 128 (1942).
3. 332 U.S. 261 (1947).
4. 419 U.S. 522 (1975).
5. 366 U.S. 717 (1961).
6. 391 U.S. 510 (1968).
7. *People* v. *Velasquez,* 26 Cal.3d 425 (1980).
8. 83 L.Ed. 2d 841(1985).
9. 476 U.S. 79 (1986).
10. *People* v. *Johnson,* 47 Cal.3rd 1194 (1989).

CHAPTER 12 Trial Procedure

Whatever disagreement there may be as to the scope of the phrase "due process of law" there can be no doubt that it embraces the fundamental conception of a fair trial, with the opportunity to be heard.

—Oliver Wendell Holmes, in *Frank v. Mangum,* 237 U.S. 309 (1915)

OPENING STATEMENTS

In order that the jury may be informed of both the charge against the defendant and the plea entered, it is the policy of most courts to have the accusatory pleading read to the jury. If the charge is a felony, the accusatory pleading will be an information or an indictment, depending on the circumstances. If the charge is a misdemeanor, the accusatory pleading is usually a complaint that may or may not be read, depending upon the custom of the jurisdiction.

Prosecuting Attorney Opening Statement

After the jury have been sworn in and the charge read to them, the prosecution is the first to present its evidence. Prior to calling the first witness, the judge will ask the prosecuting attorney whether he or she wishes to make an opening statement. An opening statement will be made in most instances, since it provides an opportunity to explain further the charge against the defendant. By making an opening statement, the prosecuting attorney is able to outline the evidence planned for the trial, thereby allowing the jury more intelligently to follow the presentation of the prosecution's side of the case. The opening statement is probably more important in jury trials than in court trials because it orients the jury toward what is to follow and prepares them for the evidence.

The prosecuting attorney has considerable latitude in referring to the evidence that he or she plans to introduce during the trial, but the statements are not considered facts of the case. If for some reason the evidence is not admitted, the jury may not consider the attorney's statements as evidence of the case. It has been held to be *prejudicial error* for a prosecuting attorney to mention evidence known to be inadmissible. Prejudicial error may result from a statement or an act of misconduct by a prosecuting attorney or a witness that will prevent the defendant from getting a fair trial or that is so prejudicial that either a mistrial will be declared or a conviction will be reversed on appeal. It is also prejudicial error for a prosecuting attorney to refer to the defendant as an ex-convict, or to imply that he or she has committed prior crimes. A defendant is entitled to be tried on the facts stated in the accusatory pleading; any reference to other crimes or prior convictions is considered to be so prejudicial against the defendant that the judge may declare a mistrial at that time. If the judge does not declare a mistrial and the defendant is convicted, the conviction may be reversed on appeal.

Defense Counsel Opening Statement

After the prosecuting attorney has completed the opening statement, the judge will often ask whether the defense attorney wishes to make an opening statement. In some jurisdictions, the judge may delay the defense attorney's opening statement until after the prosecution has presented its side of the case. Many defense attorneys believe that it is a mistake to make an opening statement before the prosecution has completed its side of the presentation of the evidence, since the defense strategy may change. If an opening statement is made before the prosecution presents its side of the evidence, statements may be made that will not conform with the defense strategy, and the jury may be confused about what happened or may question the innocence of the defendant. In making an opening statement immediately after the prosecuting attorney has made his or her opening statement, the defense attorney may alert the prosecution to an anticipated defense, most defense attorneys try to avoid this. Many defense attorneys waive the right of making an opening statement at any time, since they feel that the disadvantages of making one outweigh the advantages. Often defense witnesses do not measure up to expectation or do not appear at all. If their testimony has been previously outlined, the jury may question the validity of the defense.

On the other hand, some defense attorneys believe that it is a mistake not to make an opening statement immediately following the opening statement of the prosecuting attorney. They theorize that the prosecuting attorney will have made a favorable impression on the jury and that it is dangerous not to challenge those statements immediately. These defense attorneys state that it is not necessary to go into any detail of the defense at that time. They can merely inform the jury that the defense plans to present evidence to prove that the facts of the case are not as alleged by the prosecuting attorney. These defense attorneys will request the jury to keep an open mind until the defense has the opportunity to present contrary evidence.

REASONABLE DOUBT

In our system of justice, the defendant in a criminal case is presumed to be innocent until proved otherwise. It is the burden of the prosecution to prove the defendant guilty beyond a reasonable doubt. The U.S. Supreme Court has held in a number of cases that proof of a criminal charge *beyond a reasonable doubt* is constitutionally

Proof and Criminal Justice Activities

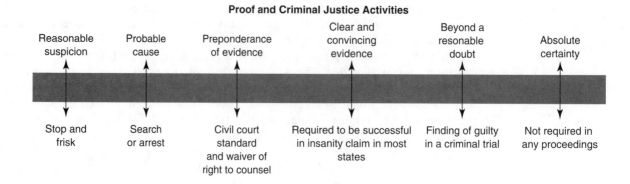

required though not included in the Bill of Rights. This Court stated the following in the case of *In re Winship:*

> . . . it is the duty of the Government to establish guilt beyond a reasonable doubt. This notion—basic in our law and rightly one of the boasts of a free society—is a requirement and safeguard of due process of law in the historic, procedural content of due process . . . that guilt in a criminal case must be proved beyond a reasonable doubt and by evidence confined to that which long experience in the common law tradition, to some extent embodied in the Constitution, has crystallized into rules of evidence consistent with that standard. These rules are historically grounded rights of our system, developed to safeguard men from dubious and unjust convictions, with resulting forfeitures of life, liberty and property. . . .
>
> The requirement of proof beyond a reasonable doubt has this vital role in our criminal procedure for cogent reasons. The accused during a criminal prosecution has at stake interests of immense importance, both because of the possibility that he may lose his liberty upon conviction and because of the certainty that he would be stigmatized by the conviction. Accordingly, a society that values the good name and freedom of every individual should not condemn a man for commission of a crime when there is reasonable doubt about his guilt. . . .
>
> Moreover, use of the reasonable doubt standard is indispensable to command the respect and confidence of the community in application of the criminal law. It is critical that the moral force of the criminal law not be diluted by a standard of proof which leaves people in doubt whether innocent men are being condemned. It is also important in our free society that every individual going about his ordinary affairs have confidence that his government cannot adjudge him guilty of a criminal offense without convincing a proper factfinder of his guilt with utmost certainty.[1]

The term *reasonable doubt* is familiar to all. Yet many jurors are confused about the real meaning of the term and when it has been reached. They desire some explanation, but the more one tries to interpret the meaning of reasonable doubt, the more confusing it becomes. To further confuse the issue, some courts and statutes have provided that the defendant must be proved guilty beyond a reasonable doubt and to a moral certainty. A statute of one state defines reasonable doubt as follows:

It is not a mere possible doubt, because everything relating to human affairs, and depending upon moral evidence, is open to some possible or imaginary doubt. It is that state of the case, which, after the entire comparison and consideration of all the evidence, leaves the minds of jurors in that condition that they cannot say they feel an abiding conviction, to a moral certainty, of the truth of the charge.

After reading this definition, there is some question whether the jury would have any better understanding of the meaning of reasonable doubt than before. To state it in a simpler form, it is that doubt that a juror may have after weighing all the evidence of the case and is still not satisfied that the defendant is guilty of the crime charged.

WITNESSES

The defendant is entitled to be confronted by the witnesses against him or her. As stated by the U.S. Supreme Court in *California* v. *Green,* this confrontation

> . . . (1) insures that the witness will give his statements under oath thus impressing him with the seriousness of the matter and guarding against the lie by the possibility of a penalty for perjury; (2) forces the witness to submit to cross examination, the "greatest legal engine ever invented for the discovery of the truth"; (3) permits the jury that is to decide the defendant's fate to observe the demeanor of the witness in making his statement, thus aiding the jury in assessing his credibility.[2]

Since the defendant has the right to be confronted by opposing witnesses, most of the prosecution's evidence attempting to prove guilt beyond a reasonable doubt will be presented through the testimony of witnesses. As indicated earlier, the U.S. Constitution has been interpreted to require that a defendant has a right to confront and cross-examine all witnesses against him or her. However, this right is not absolute.[3] For example, hearsay statements of another person may be admitted against the defendant even though he or she does not have the opportunity to cross-examine the person making those statements. The U.S. Supreme Court also examined another aspect of this constitutional right when it addressed the issue of the use of closed-circuit television in child abuse cases in *Maryland* v. *Craig.*[4]

In October 1986, a Howard County grand jury charged Sandra Ann Craig with a number of child abuse offenses. The victim, Brooke, was a six-year-old girl who from August 1984 to June 1986 attended a kindergarten and prekindergarten center owned and operated by Craig. In March of 1987, before the case went to trial, the state sought to invoke a Maryland statute that allowed the judge and jury to view the victim via closed-circuit television. The victim was to be located in a separate room outside the presence of the defendant. Although the defendant and her attorney could view the television and ask questions, they would not be allowed to physically confront the victim.

In support of its motion, the state presented expert testimony that Brooke, as well as a number of other children who were alleged to have been abused, would suffer serious emotional distress such that they could not reasonably communicate if required to testify in the courtroom and face the defendant. Another expert testified that Brooke would probably stop talking and would withdraw and curl up into a ball if she were in the same room as the defendant. The trial court ruled that because of the possible distress that the victims would suffer in seeing the suspect, the closed-circuit television would be authorized.

In upholding such a procedure, the U.S. Supreme Court held that a strict reading of the Confrontation Clause would do away with every hearsay exception and that this was too extreme a result. Therefore, the court held that the Confrontation Clause reflects a preference for face-to-face confrontations at trial but that preference must occasionally give way to considerations of public policy and the necessities of the case. Thus, the holding in *Maryland* v. *Craig* allows the use of closed-circuit television under certain circumstances in child-abuse cases. Specifically, there must be a state statute that authorizes such a procedure, and the state must establish that the child is unable to face his or her accused molester in person.

There are two kinds of witnesses, the *lay,* or ordinary, witness and the *expert* witness. The lay witness is an individual who has some personal knowledge of the facts of the case derived from personal perceptions, that is, from what was seen, heard, or felt. An expert witness is an individual who has knowledge and skill in a particular field that is beyond the knowledge of the average person on the street. The expert witness gives the judge and the jury the benefit of acquired knowledge, often in the form of an opinion, to assist them in arriving at the truth of a matter. The jury may either accept the opinion of the expert or reject it, as they see fit. Before an expert witness may testify, the side calling this witness must qualify him or her as an expert. By training, experience, or education, the expert witness must prove knowledge or skill in a particular field above that of the average person on the street. This expertise is established by questioning the witness about his or her ability in a particular field. The judge must then declare the witness to be qualified as an expert before testimony or an opinion on the facts of the case may be given. Establishing the qualifications of the expert witness is referred to as a voir dire examination.

It is not necessary for the prosecution to call every person who has some knowledge about the facts of the case to be a witness. The prosecuting attorney must call enough witnesses to prove the defendant guilty beyond a reasonable doubt. It is difficult to determine how many witnesses this step will take in any given case. At first glance, it may appear that the prosecuting attorney should not gamble on how many witnesses should be called but should call all that may know something about the case. However, to accept testimony from every person who may have some personal knowledge about the case could be time-consuming and could cause the jury to become weary and lose interest in the prosecution's presentation. But the prosecution will call all the witnesses necessary to completely relate the story of what happened in the case. In addition, a few witnesses will probably be called to corroborate the testimony of other witnesses. The prosecution will have to present those witnesses necessary to establish that a crime was committed—that is, it will have to prove the elements of the crime. This process of proving that a crime was committed is known as establishing the corpus delicti.

The sequence in which the witnesses are called to testify may not result in the events being related in the same sequence in which they occurred. The prosecuting attorney will decide the sequence in accordance with how the facts can best be presented in a logical, understandable manner.

THE SUBPOENA

Persons are officially notified to appear in court as witnesses by a legal document known as a subpoena. Subpoenas will be issued for the attendance of both prosecution and defense witnesses. Depending upon the jurisdiction, a subpoena may be issued by a judge, prosecuting attorney, clerk of the court, or public defender.

Occasionally, a witness will be commanded to bring books, papers, documents, or other physical evidence with him or her. If so, a subpoena duces tecum will be issued to the witness. The subpoena duces tecum follows the same general form as the subpoena, but it includes a description of the material that the witness is to produce in court.

Generally, a subpoena or subpoena duces tecum may be served by anyone, but most frequently it will be served by an officer of the court. Service is made by personally delivering a copy of the subpoena to the witness. After the service is made, the person serving the subpoena will make a written return on a copy of the subpoena stating the date, time, and place that the service was made.

It has been held that a person owes a duty to society to appear and testify as a witness in criminal cases when subpoenaed to do so. Because of this duty, witnesses generally are not compensated when appearing to testify. Yet it is recognized that a witness should not suffer undue financial hardship in performing duty as a witness. Since a subpoena is valid anyplace within the state in which it is issued, most jurisdictions provide for the payment of reasonable travel expenses to a witness who must travel a great distance to testify.

Before a witness can be compensated in some jurisdictions, the judge involved in the trial must endorse the subpoena with a statement that the witness is a material witness and that this attendance is absolutely necessary.

Witnesses Failing to Appear

The failure of a witness to appear as commanded in a subpoena can bring about contempt of court charges unless good cause for not appearing can be shown. In addition to being held in contempt, the witness, if subpoenaed by the defense, can in some states be civilly sued by the defendant for failure to appear. It is not necessary for a person to be served with a subpoena to be a witness. The witness may orally agree to appear but cannot be held in contempt for failing to be present at the trial.

In the past, since a subpoena was good only within the state in which it was issued, there was no way to command the appearance of a witness who was out of the state. Today, most states have adopted the "Uniform Act to Secure the Attendance of Witnesses from without the State in Criminal Cases." This act enables a court to command the appearance of a material witness beyond the jurisdiction of the court because the witness resides in another state. The court in which the witness is needed to appear will issue a certificate naming this person as a material witness, the date and place that he or she is to appear, and the approximate number of days that the person will be needed as a witness. This certificate is transmitted to the appropriate court in the state where the needed witness resides. The court in that state will order the witness to come before it for a hearing to determine whether the person is a necessary and material witness and whether any undue hardship will be caused by the person's appearing in the other state as a witness. If the judge concludes that the person is a necessary and material witness and that no hardship will be suffered, the person will be tendered expense money and ordered to appear in the demanding court as a witness. Should the person fail to appear as commanded, contempt of court charges may be filed in the state where the material witness resides. The witness is immune from arrest on any prior crimes committed in the demanding state while in the state to testify.

Excluding Witnesses

Prior to the time that any of the witnesses testify, the judge must decide whether the witnesses may remain in the courtroom or be excluded until after they have testified. This decision may be made on the judge's own motion or on the request of either the prosecution or the defense. The primary purpose for excluding witnesses from the courtroom is to prevent them from trying to corroborate the testimony of other witnesses. The effort to corroborate another witness's testimony is not always done with an intent to falsify. It may be done because one witness may be uncertain of some of the facts. Although witnesses are excluded from the courtroom, it is almost impossible to keep them from conversing about their testimony even though the judge admonishes them against such action.

EXAMINATION OF WITNESSES

The Oath

Before being permitted to testify, an oath must be administered in which the witness promises to tell the truth. Throughout the history of trial by jury, witnesses have given an oath that their allegations are true. In the past, these oaths have involved a call to the deity to assist the oath giver in substantiating the truthfulness of the statements made, as well as a call for assistance in telling the truth. It was the general belief that, after giving such an oath, should one falsely testify, divine punishment would result. So strong was the belief in divine punishment at common law that if one did not believe in God, the person was considered incompetent to testify.

Although most jurisdictions presently do not prescribe wording for the oath administered to a witness, generally a call to the deity to assist the witness in telling the truth is still included. Oaths that are administered to witnesses today are substantially as follows: "Do you hereby solemnly swear to tell the truth, and nothing but the truth, in the matter now pending before this court, so help you God?" At one time, while this oath was being administered, the witness was required to raise the right hand and lay the left hand on a Bible. Most jurisdictions have dispensed with the use of the Bible in administering the oath, but the witness is still required to raise his or her right hand during administration of the oath.

Affirmation.   Although there is no requirement that the word *God* be mentioned in the oath, it usually is included. Some persons consider it objectionable to "swear to God" to tell the truth. They feel this way either because they believe that the use of the word *God* under the circumstances is sacrilegious or because they do not believe in a God and object to swearing to something in which they have no belief. To accommodate these individuals, courts permit them to *affirm* to tell the truth. When either the court clerk or other court officer administers the oath, or *swears in* the witness as the procedure is known, the witness is asked to stand and be sworn. If the oath is found objectionable, the witness will advise the officer that the truth will be affirmed. The officer will then require the witness to raise the right hand, and the officer will state words to this effect: "Do you hereby solemnly affirm to tell the truth and nothing but the truth in the matter now pending before this court?" This procedure has been referred to as an *affirmation*. Whether a witness swears to tell the truth or affirms to tell the truth, both procedures are technically known as the "oath."

A few legal scholars argue that administering the oath is a useless procedure and a waste of time, since it does not guarantee that the witness will testify truthfully. But the great majority of persons engaged in the trial of cases believe that administering the oath to the witness gives a certain legal solemnity to the occasion and may cause the witness to reflect upon the necessity to tell the truth. As is stated in the federal procedure, the wording of the oath may be of any nature that will awaken the witness to the necessity of telling the truth.

Even though the oath may not guarantee that the truth will be told, the witness may be prosecuted for perjury if testimony is intentionally falsified after the oath is administered. This threat may be enough to encourage some to testify truthfully, when they might not otherwise do so.

Refusal to Be Sworn. If a witness refuses to be sworn, a contempt of court charge can be filed against the witness. The only exception to the administration of the oath to a witness is in the case of a small child or a mentally retarded person who may not understand the meaning of the oath. Under these circumstances, before the child or mentally retarded person is allowed to testify, the judge will conduct a voir dire examination to determine whether the prospective witness knows that it is wrong to tell a falsehood and that it is necessary to tell the truth. If this can be established by the judge through the questioning of the prospective witness, the oath will be eliminated.

Direct Examination

After the oath has been administered to the witness, the witness will begin his or her testimony, that is, facts will be related within the witness's knowledge of the case. Prior to making any statements about the case, the witness will be required to state his or her name, address, and, in some instances, occupation for identification purposes. Because of threats that have been made to law enforcement officers and their families, some jurisdictions permit the officers to give their headquarters address instead of their home address. After the identification data are furnished by the prosecution witness, the prosecuting attorney will start the examination. The questioning of the witness by the side that calls him or her is known as *direct examination*. The prosecuting attorney may approach the direct examination in one of two ways or in a combination of both. The prosecuting attorney may request the witness to relate in his or her own words the facts about the case. This procedure is sometimes referred to as the *narrative* approach. The prosecuting attorney may also use the *short question and answer approach.* Both procedures have their advantages and disadvantages. The narrative approach permits the witness to tell the story in a more logical form so that the jury may be better able to follow the testimony. But unless the witness is familiar with the rules of evidence, irrelevant material and hearsay evidence may be included, or facts may be related that the prosecuting attorney wishes to avoid. By asking the witness short, direct questions, the prosecuting attorney has greater control over the facts to be related and can limit the testimony to relevant facts. The short-question-and-answer form of examination is frequently time-consuming, and sometimes this type of testimony becomes boring to the jury. If a witness is shy or perhaps somewhat reluctant to testify, it may be necessary to revert to the short-question-and-answer procedure.

During the direct examination, the attorney may not ask the witness leading questions. A leading question is one that indicates the desired answer to the witness. For example, the attorney may ask the witness, "You did see the defendant threaten the victim with a knife, didn't you?" Clearly, the attorney wants a yes answer. But by rephrasing the question, the witness may be asked, "Did you see the defendant threaten the victim with a knife?" Although the attorney may still desire a yes answer, that wish has not been indicated to the witness, and the witness is free to give either a yes or no answer. The mere fact that a question calls for a yes or no answer does not make it a leading one, but if phrased to indicate the answer desired, it is a leading question. The reason these questions are not generally permitted during direct examination is that the witness is usually favorable to the side that calls the witness, and thus there may be a tendency to assist that side irrespective of the truth, if a desired answer is indicated.

Occasionally, a witness called by the prosecution will display hostility toward the prosecution, making the expected testimony difficult to obtain. Under these circumstances, the prosecuting attorney may request the judge to declare for the record that the witness is a *hostile witness.* If the witness is declared to be hostile, the prosecuting attorney may then ask leading questions. This type of questioning is permitted because it is assumed that the witness will answer truthfully, because of the displayed hostility, even though a desired answer is indicated. Although a hostile witness may be asked leading questions during direct examination, using that method does not mean that obtaining the desired testimony from the witness will become any less difficult. To be declared a hostile witness, a person must display hostility and uncooperativeness. The mere fact that a witness does not meet expectations or is reluctant to furnish information will not be sufficient grounds for the judge to declare the witness hostile.

A limited use of leading questions is permitted in the examination of children, senior citizens, and mentally retarded persons, in order to assist them in telling their stories. Leading questions may also be asked concerning identifying matters, such as name, address, and place of employment, pertaining to the witness, since these matters are usually not in controversy. Occasionally, a leading question may be permitted to assist in refreshing the memory of a witness.

Objections to Questions

During the direct examination by the prosecuting attorney, the defense attorney may object to some of the questions asked. If so, the objection will be indicated to the judge, who must rule upon the objection. After an objection is made, the witness should not answer the question until the judge has ruled on it. If the judge believes that the objection is well founded, he or she will *sustain* the objection, meaning that the witness may not answer the question. If the judge does not agree with the objection, he will *overrule* the objection, whereupon the witness must answer. There is any number of reasons the defense attorney may object to a question. The question may call for an answer that would be hearsay information; it may be leading; or it may require the witness to state an opinion about some matter. If the prosecution asks an improper question or one that calls for information that is not admissible, unless the defense attorney objects, the answer is permitted to go into the record of the case and generally is not grounds for appeal should the defendant be convicted. For this reason, defense attorneys make frequent objections during the trial. From a psychological standpoint, defense attorneys may also inject objections from time to time in an effort to lessen the impact of the testimony of the prosecution's witnesses.

Occasionally, a witness will become overzealous in answering the prosecuting attorney's questions and will answer a question to which an objection is made before the judge is able to rule on it. If the objection is overruled, no serious consequences result, other than the judge's becoming irritated because the witness did not wait for the ruling. However, if the objection is sustained, the answer has been improperly given, and therefore it must be stricken from the record with the jury's being advised to disregard the answer. But the problem is, can a jury completely forget such a statement? Knowing the difficulty of disregarding some statements, especially if the answer is highly prejudicial against the defendant, the judge may declare a mistrial, and the case will have to be restarted with a different jury. In addition, the witness could be held in contempt of court, particularly if previously admonished against answering before the judge could rule on an objection.

Cross-Examination

After the prosecuting attorney has concluded questioning the witness on direct examination, the defense attorney is permitted to cross-examine the witness. The primary purpose of cross-examination is to assist in arriving at the truth. Cross-examination enables the opposition or adversary to challenge the witness's veracity, accuracy, and prejudices. One of the basic reasons that the accused is entitled to confront adverse witnesses is to enable cross-examination. This right was made mandatory on the states by the case of *Pointer* v. *Texas*.[5] The U.S. Supreme Court stated the following in the *Pointer* decision:

> . . . We hold today that the Sixth Amendment's right of an accused to confront the witnesses against him is likewise a fundamental right and is made obligatory on the States by the Fourteenth Amendment.
>
> It cannot seriously be doubted at this late date that the right of cross-examination is included in the right of an accused in a criminal case to confront the witnesses against him. And probably no one, certainly no one experienced in the trial of lawsuits, would deny the value of cross-examination in exposing falsehood and bringing out the truth in a trial of a criminal case . . . the right of cross-examination is one of the safeguards essential to a fair trial.

If the defense attorney believes that the witness told the truth during the direct examination and nothing is to be gained by cross-examining the witness, the right to cross-examine that particular witness may be waived. Cross-examination is at best a dangerous procedure for a defense attorney. Before deciding whether to cross-examine a witness, the defense counsel must carefully weigh whether there is more to be lost than gained by the cross-examination. If a witness was telling the truth during direct examination, the cross-examination may merely result in the witness's being able to reemphasize the story to the jury. There is also the possibility that the witness may become emotionally upset by vigorous cross-examination, thus often receiving the sympathy of the jury.

Impeachment.   On the other hand, if a witness testified falsely during direct examination, has made prior inconsistent statements, or has colored the testimony because of some prejudice, these facts may be disclosed to the jury only through cross-examination. Cross-examination under these circumstances is necessary in order that the jury may disregard the testimony or give it the proper weight. This devaluation of the testimony by cross-examination is referred to as *impeachment* in the field of evidence.

Generally, cross-examination is an unpleasant experience for both the witness and the attorney. As we pointed out, if the witness told the truth during direct examination and cannot be upset by cross-examination, the defense attorney may suffer the unpleasantness of the witness's retelling the story to the jury. Many times a defense attorney does not receive the answer anticipated during cross-examination but is usually bound by the answer and thus often is powerless to overcome the damage the answer may cause. If a witness testifies truthfully during direct examination, there is usually little to fear from cross-examination. However, a few attorneys feel that the only way to properly represent the defendant in a criminal case is to vigorously cross-examine all witnesses. If the witness has given testimony particularly damaging to the defense, the defense attorney may endeavor to devaluate the testimony by belittling or embarrassing the witness during cross-examination. Although having the responsibility of protecting a witness from overzealous cross-examination, the judge may not unduly restrict the defense attorney from vigorous cross-examination. Occasionally, a witness may have been indiscreet in some action or statement made that may be brought out during cross-examination, and the judge would be powerless to prevent this embarrassment. If the witness, and particularly the law enforcement officer, has testified discreetly in conduct and content, any attempt at embarrassment by the defense attorney may result in the officer's favor. Juries often react unfavorably to this cross-examination tactic.

Although leading questions may not generally be asked during direct examination, they are permitted on cross-examination if the attorney feels that utilizing them is an advantage. Leading questions are frequently asked during vigorous cross-examination. The reason that these questions are permitted during cross-examination is that usually the witness who is being cross-examined is not favorable to the side doing the cross-examining, and the witness will not give a desired answer even though it is indicated, unless it is the truth.

Limited Cross-Examination.   States differ in the extent of the cross-examination. A majority of the states limit the cross-examination to the facts brought out during direct examination. This procedure is referred to as *limited* or *restricted cross-examination*. Other states permit the witness to be cross-examined about any pertinent facts in the case that may be within the knowledge of the witness. This procedure is known as *unlimited* or *unrestricted cross-examination*. Those favoring the restricted cross-examination allege that attorneys are able to control the material that is presented by a witness and may prepare the presentation in a more logical manner.

This method enables the jury to follow more closely the facts as they unfold. Those who advocate the unrestricted cross-examination allege that the unrestricted procedure saves time, in that a witness may be examined extensively while on the stand rather than being recalled at a later time. Also, the procedure eliminates objections by the opposing side that the questions asked during cross-examination did not pertain to matters brought out during direct examination. In those states following the restricted cross-examination procedure, witnesses are usually cautioned to confine their answers to questions asked during direct examination and not to volunteer additional information, since they may subject themselves to unnecessary and extensive cross-examination. This outcome is one of the dangers of permitting the story to be told in the witness's own words, since facts may be included that could be used to devaluate the testimony during cross-examination. Whether the restricted or unrestricted procedure is followed, witnesses are seldom permitted to give the facts in their own way during cross-examination. The cross-examiner desires to control the testimony and can better do so by confining the questions to ones that require short answers, often only a yes or no.

Redirect Examination and Recross-Examination.   After the defense attorney has completed his or her cross-examination, the judge will permit the prosecuting attorney to further question the witness. This questioning is known as *redirect examination*. The questioning must be confined to clarifying facts brought out during cross-examination. Sometimes the defense attorney will require that the witness answer a question with only a yes or no, but the answer does not reflect the true situation without further explanation. When the prosecuting attorney further questions the witness after cross-examination, the answers can be explained more fully by the witness. Seldom will a judge permit any new material to be brought forth during the redirect examination. To do so would start the whole questioning process again and could encourage sloppy practice by attorneys by not properly preparing the direct examination. Unless the prosecuting attorney believes that redirect examination will be beneficial, it may be waived.

If the prosecuting attorney further questions the witness on redirect examination, at the conclusion of this questioning, the defense attorney is entitled to recross-examine the witness on facts stated on redirect examination. After this series takes place, the witness is excused, and the next witness is called. The same sequence of examinations may take place with each prosecution and defense witness that is called, or the sequence could stop after the direct examination. When the whole series is repeated with each witness, criminal trials can become very lengthy.

Refusal to Answer Questions

The witness must answer all questions asked throughout the entire examination. The only exception is that if the answer to a question will incriminate the witness, the witness may refuse to answer the question. An incriminating answer is one that would subject the witness to prosecution. The Fifth Amendment to the U.S. Constitution provides that one may not be compelled to witness against oneself. But all other questions must be answered even though the answer may be embarrassing or life-endangering to the witness or his or her family. The degrading or endangering questions must be pertinent to the case, however, and not asked merely to embarrass the witness. Otherwise, the judge may not permit the question to be answered. Refusal to answer questions occurs more frequently during cross-examination than during direct examination. It is during cross-examination that the witness is questioned by the adversary, and it is then that questions may be asked that the witness would be hesitant to answer. If a witness persists in refusing to answer a question that is not incriminating, the entire testimony may be stricken from the record and the jury advised to disregard it. It is held that a witness may not testify to those facts that may be favorable and refuse to testify to matters that may be unfavorable. In addition to having the testimony stricken from the record, the witness could be held in contempt of court until the questions were answered.

There are times during a trial when arriving at the truth of what happened is more important than the prosecution of some witness incriminated by answering a question. Under these circumstances, the witness may be granted immunity from prosecution by the judge. If immunity is granted, the witness must answer all questions.

Examination by the Judge and Jury

Although it is the primary responsibility of the prosecution and defense to call and examine the witnesses that they believe necessary, witnesses may also be called by the trial judge if deemed necessary in the interest of justice. Most jurisdictions permit the judge to question prosecution and defense witnesses if such questioning may furnish information not brought forth by the prosecutor or defense counsel. Occasionally, a juror may wish to question a witness in order that some point may be clarified. Most judges will permit a limited amount of questioning by a juror if it is felt that the questioning is in good faith, but such questioning could very easily get out of hand, since some jurors may desire to get into the "act" and become counsels. The questioning of witnesses by jurors is generally not encouraged. When a juror wishes to ask a witness a question, the judge usually will require the juror to write the question on a slip of paper and have it handed to the judge, who will ask the question for the juror. This precaution keeps a juror from trying to become one of the questioning attorneys.

Introduction of Physical Evidence

During the investigation of a crime, officers will usually discover physical evidence, or material objects, that are pertinent to the crime. These objects, such as a latent fingerprint developed at a crime scene and identified as that of the defendant, often assist in connecting the defendant to the crime. Physical evidence may include objects taken during a robbery or burglary that were found in the possession of the defendant. These objects may be described by the officer who found them, and it is not necessary that they be presented in court. But in almost all instances, the prosecuting attorney will introduce these objects as evidence in order to substantiate the officer's testimony and to emphasize the facts of the case. These physical objects must be introduced by some witnesses who can connect the objects with the crime charged. The witness will have to describe where the object was found, when, and under what circumstances. Who can forget the controversy surrounding the bloody glove in the O. J. Simpson murder trial? Once the object is introduced into evidence, the jury may examine it and consider it part of the facts of the case.

Viewing the Crime Scene

There are times when a judge may feel that a jury can better follow the testimony of the witnesses if they view the area in which the crime was committed. Under these circumstances, the judge will order the jury, as a body, to be taken to the crime scene by an officer of the court. Since viewing the crime scene is, in a sense, receiving facts of the case, the viewing in some jurisdictions is considered as evidence of the case. For that reason, the prosecuting attorney, defense attorney, defendant, and judge must accompany the jury. It has been established as improper for a jury, either as individuals or as a group, to view the crime scene without authorization from the judge.

In making the decision, the judge must consider several factors. If photographs of the crime scene are displayed to the jury, will that display accomplish as much as the actual viewing? Have material changes taken place in the crime scene that may cause more confusion than clarification?

Prosecution Rests

After presentation of all the prosecution witnesses and physical evidence that the prosecuting attorney believes is necessary, the prosecuting attorney will usually state, "The prosecution rests, your honor. . . ." This statement is an indication to all those involved in the trial that the prosecution has presented the evidence that it believes is sufficient to convince the jury that the defendant is guilty beyond a reasonable doubt. In other words, the prosecution rests its side of the case in the hands of the jury with the hope of getting a favorable verdict.

Judgment of Acquittal

After the prosecution rests, the defense may present evidence in its own behalf. Before doing so, however, the usual procedure is for the defense counsel to request permission from the judge to *approach the bench*—that is, permission to speak to the judge. Permission is usually granted, and the defense attorney then will request that the jury be excused so that a motion can be made for a judgment of acquittal.

If the judge permits the motion to be argued, the defense attorney will endeavor to convince the judge that the prosecution failed to establish that a crime was committed or that the defendant committed it. Or the defense attorney may contend that the prosecution failed to present enough evidence to substantiate, or uphold, a conviction on appeal. If the judge agrees with the defense attorney, the judge has the authority to take the case out of the hands of the jury and enter a judgment of acquittal, which is a bar to any further action against the defendant on the crime charged. This procedure is also commonly referred to as a motion for a *directed verdict.* However, the directed verdict has another meaning in some states. In such states, if a motion for a directed verdict is granted, the judge instructs the jury to return a verdict of not guilty. The jury is not bound by this direction in some states. The jury may disregard the motion and return a verdict of guilty. A few states contend that a judge does not have the right to enter either a motion of acquittal or a directed verdict, since the procedure takes the case out of the hands of the jury, who are the exclusive judge of the facts of the case.

The reason that a defense attorney will request the jury to be excused during the time the motion is made for a judgment of acquittal is that if the motion is not granted, the jury may be convinced that the judge believes the defendant guilty. This belief could affect their verdict. The motion for a judgment of acquittal or a directed verdict does not always have to be argued. The judge may be convinced that the evidence presented by the prosecution does not support a conviction. The judge may then make a motion to enter a judgment of an acquittal or may direct a verdict of acquittal.

However, even though convinced at the time the prosecution rests that the defendant is guilty beyond a reasonable doubt, the judge may neither enter a judgment of conviction nor direct a verdict of conviction. Such action would be denying the defendant the right to a trial by jury.

DEFENSE PRESENTATION

If the judge does not agree to enter a judgment of acquittal or to direct a verdict of acquittal, the defense attorney must make a decision. It must be decided whether to allow the case to go to the jury at that time with the hope that they have some doubt about the guilt of the defendant or whether evidence should be presented in behalf of the defendant in an effort to create such a doubt. Generally, if there is any defense that can be presented, the defendant's attorney will present evidence rather than take a chance on the jury's returning a guilty verdict. If the defendant has admitted guilt to counsel but refuses to enter a plea of guilty, presenting a defense may be a difficult task for the defense attorney.

Defense Approaches

If the charge is homicide or aggravated assault, the defense may attempt to prove that the defendant committed the act in self-defense. In the case of a forceful rape, the defense may allege that the victim consented to the act of intercourse with the defendant. One of the more prevalent defenses is the alibi defense. Also, a defense attorney will occasionally endeavor to prove that the defendant is of such good character that a crime as charged in the accusatory pleading could not have been committed. This is not always an easy defense to present, particularly if the defendant has a criminal record. The moment that the defendant endeavors to prove reputable character through witnesses, the prosecution can discredit the testimony by showing the defendant's criminal record. This is one of the few times that the past record of a defendant may be introduced in evidence.

Should the Defendant Testify

While planning the defense, an attorney must decide whether the defendant should be permitted to testify. Often it is not an easy decision to make, since many factors must be considered. The attorney must consider the impression that the defendant may make on the jury while testifying. If the defendant has a criminal record, and particularly a conviction on a felony, this may be brought out during cross-examination. On the stand, the defendant is treated the same as any other witness in most jurisdictions, and witnesses may be impeached by revealing certain past convictions. Being aware of the defendant's past record of convictions could affect the jury's verdict. If the defendant does take the stand, what will be the jury's reaction to this failure to testify and to explain personal knowledge of the facts?

In the past, if the defendant did not take the stand in his or her own defense, the failure to do so could be commented on by the prosecuting attorney and the judge as the case was being summarized to the jury. But in the case of *Griffin* v. *California,* the U.S. Supreme Court held that such comments were improper, since they tend to force the defendant to be a witness against oneself in violation of the Fifth Amendment of the U.S. Constitution.[6] The facts of the *Griffin* case reflect that the defendant was convicted of murder in a jury trial. The defendant did not testify at the trial on the issue of guilt, and the trial court instructed the jury that a defendant has a constitutional right not to testify. But it told the jury the following: "As to any evidence or facts within his knowledge, if he does not testify or if, though he does testify, he fails to deny or explain such evidence, the jury may take that failure into consideration as tending to indicate the truth of such evidence and as indicating that among the inferences that may be reasonably drawn therefrom those unfavorable to the defendant are the most probable."

The petitioner (the defendant) had been seen with the deceased the evening of her death, the evidence placing him with her in the alley where her body was found. The prosecutor made much of the failure of petitioner to testify (and made the following statements to the jury):

> The defendant certainly knows whether Essie Mae (the deceased) had this beat up appearance at the time he left her apartment and went down the alley with her.
>
> What kind of a man is it that would want to have sex with a woman that he beat up if she was beat up at the time he left?
>
> He would know that. He would know how she got down the alley. He would know how the blood got on the bottom concrete steps . . . .
>
> These things he has not seen fit to take the stand and deny or explain. And in the whole world, if anybody would know, this defendant would know. Essie Mae is dead, she can't tell you her side of the story. The defendant won't.

The case was taken to the U.S. Supreme Court on a writ of certiorari to consider whether comment on the failure to testify violated the self-incrimination clause of the Fifth Amendment made applicable to the states by the Fourteenth Amendment. The Supreme Court pointed out that a defendant has a constitutional right to remain silent and not testify, and permitting the prosecuting attorney and judge to comment on the defendant's failure to testify was

> . . . a penalty imposed by the courts for exercising a constitutional privilege. It cut down on the privilege by making its assertion costly. It is said, however, that the inference of guilt for failure to testify as to facts peculiarly within the accused's knowledge is in any event natural and irresistible, and that comment on the failure does not magnify that inference into a penalty for asserting a constitutional privilege. What the jury may infer, given no help from the court, is one thing. What it may infer when the court solemnizes the silence of the accused into evidence against him is quite another.

The defendant's Fifth Amendment right against self-incrimination and the fact that the exercise of that right may not be called to the attention of the jury were both clearly illustrated by the *Griffin* case. However, in most jurisdictions, if the defendant does take the stand and fails to explain certain facts that logically should have been explained, that failure may be commented on by the judge and prosecuting attorney. The theory behind this permitted comment is that it is held that a defendant should not be able to testify on only those matters that are beneficial but fail to explain other facts that may be unfavorable. Another problem created for a defense attorney arises when the client insists on taking the stand, and the attorney does not believe such action to be wise. Does a defendant have a right to testify in his or her own behalf over the objections of counsel? This question has not been answered in all jurisdictions, but a few have held that a defendant does have a right to present evidence in one's own behalf, even to testifying over the objections of counsel. The court of one state made this comment concerning the right of a defendant to testify:

> We are satisfied that the right to testify in one's own behalf is of such fundamental importance that a defendant whose timely demands to take the stand contrary to the advice given by his counsel has the right to give an exposition of his defense before a jury. The defendant's insistence upon testifying may in the final analysis be harmful to his case, but the right is of such importance that every defendant should have it in a criminal case. Although normally the decision whether a defendant should testify is within the competence of the trial attorney where, as here, a defendant insists that he wants to testify, he cannot be deprived of that opportunity.[7]

However, the defendant does not have a right to have his or her attorney present perjured testimony. The courts have stated that there is no Sixth Amendment right to an attorney who will knowingly present perjured testimony. In one case, the defendant told his attorney that although he never saw a gun in the victim's hand, he was going to take the stand and raise the issue of self-defense. His attorney told him that conduct would be perjury, and if the defendant attempted to testify in that manner, the attorney would disclose the perjury and withdraw from the case. The defendant testified but did not raise the self-defense issue. He was convicted and appealed, claiming he was denied effective counsel since the attorney's refusal to allow him to testify in the way he wanted violated his right to counsel. The U.S. Supreme Court held that it was not a violation of the defendant's Sixth Amendment right for his counsel to act in accordance with state laws governing professional conduct.[8]

REBUTTAL BY THE PROSECUTION

After the defense has presented its side of the case and rests, the prosecution may present additional evidence to meet or rebut that presented by the defense. The presentation of rebuttal evidence is permitted because, in most instances, the prosecution will have no advance knowledge of the approach that the defense may take in an effort to prove the defendant not guilty. Although after resting, the prosecuting attorney may have felt that the defendant was proved guilty beyond a reasonable doubt, the defense may have created some new doubt by presenting its evidence. The evidence presented by the defense may not have been based upon true facts. For example, the defense may have tried to prove that the defendant was at some place other than where the crime was committed, creating a doubt in the minds of the jury about the guilt of the defendant. This alibi evidence may have been attempted through perjured testimony. To allow this testimony to stand unchallenged by the prosecution would be an injustice to society. The only way that this testimony can be effectively challenged, except through cross-examination, is for the prosecution to present further testimony to prove that the defendant was at the scene of the crime.

Generally, no new evidence pertaining to the guilt of the defendant may be presented during the rebuttal. This is the case because permitting new evidence would cause the whole sequence of the trial examination procedure to take place again. The only time that additional evidence may be introduced is when new material evidence has been discovered. The prosecution must be in a position to convince the judge that the newly discovered evidence was not available when the prosecution first presented its side of the case and that its discovery was not due to carelessness, inadequate investigation, or poor preparation. In the interest of justice, the judge may permit the newly discovered evidence to be introduced, but the defense may again present evidence in an effort to overcome that presented by the prosecution. This presentation is sometimes referred to as the *rejoinder* in some jurisdictions, and in others it is known as the *defense rebuttal.*

After the prosecution has finished the rebuttal, the defense may again make a motion for a judgment of acquittal to be entered. If this motion is denied by the judge, the next procedure, depending upon the procedure of the jurisdiction, is either presentation of closing arguments by the prosecution and the defense or instruction to the jury on the law of the case.

Depositions

Sometimes during a trial, a witness for one side or the other is unable to attend court to testify, yet the testimony of that witness is material to the case. Rather than continuing the trial until the witness is able to appear in court, an out-of-court written statement, or *deposition,* given under oath, will be taken from the witness. Before a deposition may be taken, the opposing side must be notified that a deposition is to be taken at a particular time, date, and place. This notice is necessary so that the opposing side may be present to cross-examine the witness. The deposition is usually in a question-and-answer form much as the testimony would be given in court. The deposition will be read to the jury at the appropriate time during the trial, and the information will become part of the facts of the case. Because of the right of the defendant to be presented with the witnesses against him or her, some states do not permit the prosecution to introduce depositions in evidence.

NOT GUILTY BY REASON OF INSANITY

Because the procedure on the defense of not guilty by reason of insanity differs among states, a discussion of that defense is in order at this time. Not all states permit a separate plea of not guilty by reason of insanity. In those states where this plea is not permitted, the insanity defense is alleged by the defense after the prosecution rests, in the same manner as other defenses that the defendant may utilize, such as the alibi or self-defense. Under these circumstances, the prosecution will present its evidence to prove the defendant guilty beyond a reasonable doubt.

After the presentation of this evidence, the defendant alleges that he or she cannot be held criminally liable for the crime, since he or she was insane at the time of committing the act. The defendant then presents evidence in his or her behalf in an endeavor to prove that he or she was insane at the time. This type of defense can catch the prosecution by surprise, and obtaining rebuttal evidence may be difficult. Further, with this type of defense being alleged, the prosecution has a double burden. Not knowing of the insanity defense in advance, the prosecution usually must present much evidence to prove that the defendant committed the crime, but by claiming the insanity defense, the defendant is in a sense admitting the act but alleging that there is no criminal liability. To rebut this allegation, the prosecution must prove that the defendant was sane at the time the crime was committed. Because of the element of surprise to the prosecution by the insanity defense and the double burden imposed upon the prosecutor, efforts have been made to have this defense included in the right of discovery by the prosecution. In those jurisdictions permitting a separate plea of not guilty by reason of insanity, the prosecuting attorney is not surprised and usually has ample opportunity to prepare the case to meet the allegation.

In those states where a separate plea of not guilty by reason of insanity is permitted, unless the defendant enters that plea, sanity is presumed at the time that the crime was committed, and no defense of insanity may be entered. As pointed out in Chapter 5, a few states permit the defendant to enter dual pleas. The defendant may enter a plea of "not guilty" and at the same time enter a plea of "not guilty by reason of insanity." When the dual pleas are entered, the trial on the not guilty plea will be tried first. If the defendant is found not guilty, no further action may take place. But if the defendant is found guilty, a second trial takes place to determine the sanity of the defendant at the time the crime was committed. These trials may be heard by the same jury or different juries depending on the wishes of the defendant or the procedure of the jurisdiction involved. In some states, the two trials are consolidated into one.

The Burden of Proof

States differ in their approach regarding the burden of proof on the insanity issue. Some states contend that, by entering the plea of not guilty by reason of insanity, the defendant has admitted guilt. Having admitted guilt, the defendant is not entitled to the presumption of innocence, and the prosecution has no burden of proof on the guilt issue. Since it is presumed that all persons are sane unless, and until, proved otherwise, in some states the defendant has the burden of proving insanity at the time the crime was committed. Having this burden, the defense will open the trial proceedings by presenting the defendant's evidence first, followed by the prosecution. In the effort to prove insanity, the defendant may produce expert witnesses in the field of psychology, who, after examining the defendant, may express their opinions on the defendant's mental state at the time the crime occurred. The defense counsel may call witnesses acquainted with the defendant to express their opinions on the defendant's sanity for corroboration with the opinions of the experts. The amount of proof that the defendant must present differs among states. Some states require the defendant to prove insanity by a preponderance of evidence; other states require that insanity be proved to the satisfaction of the jury. The line of demarcation between these proofs is very fine, but it is conceded that the defendant does not have to prove beyond a reasonable doubt that the crime was committed while insane.

After the defendant has presented evidence to prove insanity, the prosecution has the responsibility of going forward with the evidence and proving that the defendant was sane at the time of the act. How much evidence must the prosecution present to prove sanity? Merely going forward with the evidence generally implies meeting the evidence of the opposition. The consensus is that the prosecution must do more than meet the evidence. There must be more than a doubt about the sanity of the defendant before the jury may conclude that the defendant was sane at the time the crime occurred. Most jurisdictions contend that the prosecution still has the burden of proving the defendant sane beyond a reasonable doubt. In fact, in some jurisdictions, if the defendant enters the plea of guilty by reason of insanity, the prosecution opens the trial and presents evidence to prove the defendant sane beyond a reasonable doubt, and the defense may meet that evidence by merely creating a doubt about sanity at the time the act was committed.

The Test for Sanity

Determining sanity is not easy. Whatever procedure is followed, the ultimate determination to be made is whether the defendant was in such a state of mind at the time the crime was committed that he or she cannot be held legally responsible. Some acceptable test must be applied. The problem becomes more complicated because it is not the defendant's present state of mind that is at issue. As has been previously pointed out, unless a defendant is mentally capable of defending himself or herself, the trial cannot take place. Since the case is going to trial, it has been ad-

Various Insanity Defense Standards

Test	Legal Standard of Mental Illness	Final Burden of Proof	Who Bears Burden of Proof
M'Naghten	"Didn't know what he was doing or didn't know it was wrong."	Balance of probabilities	Defense
Irresistible impulse	"Could not control his conduct."	Beyond reasonable doubt	Prosecutor
Durham	"The criminal act was caused by his mental illness."	Beyond reasonable doubt	Prosecutor
Substantial capacity	"Lacks substantial capacity to appreciate the wrongfulness of his conduct or to control it."	Beyond reasonable doubt	Prosecutor
Present federal law	"Lacks capacity to appreciate the wrongfulness of his conduct."	Clear and convincing evidence	Defense

judged that the defendant is presently sane. It is necessary then to go back in time in attempting to establish the sanity of the defendant. Even the most knowledgeable experts in the field of psychology can give only an opinion of the mental condition at the time of the crime, unless the defendant was under a doctor's treatment.

Devising a test that will accurately establish a defendant's mental condition months before has been very difficult. For many years in England, the "wild beast test" was used. This test has also been referred to as the "good and evil" test. It was held that if an accused did not know any more than a wild beast would when the crime was committed, then no criminal responsibility could result from the act. In other words, if the accused had no more conception of good and evil than a wild beast while committing the crime, he could not be held responsible. The good and evil test was used until it was replaced by the *right and wrong* test in 1843.[9] In that case, Daniel M'Naghten was indicted for the murder of Edward Drummond, private secretary to Sir Robert Peel, Prime Minister of England. M'Naghten mistook Drummond for Peel, whom M'Naghten felt was persecuting him. M'Naghten was found not guilty by reason of insanity. The acquittal generated so much public indignation in London, including that of the Queen, that the judges were called before the House of Lords and requested to explain the test that was used to determine the sanity of M'Naghten. The judges answered the House of Lords inquiry with the following test, which the jury was to consider in determining the sanity of one accused of crime. The judges stated that

> . . . the jurors ought to be told in all cases that every man is to be presumed to be sane, and possess a sufficient degree of reason to be responsible for his crimes, until the contrary be proved to their satisfaction; and that to establish a defense on the ground of insanity, it must be clearly proved that, at the time of the committing of the act, the party accused was laboring under such a defect of reason, from disease of mind, as not to know the nature of the act he was doing; or, if he did know it, that he did not know he was doing what was wrong. The mode of putting the latter part of the question to the jury on these occasions has generally been whether the accused at the time of doing the act knew the difference between right and wrong.

The test has been referred to as the *M'Naghten test.* It has since been followed in England and has been adopted by a majority of the states in this country. Although the test has been criticized by some legal scholars and psychologists, it has been replaced in only a few states. The M'Naghten test continues to have acceptance because it is generally felt that no better test has been devised and that the jury is better able to understand it than other tests that have been suggested.

Because of the confusion surrounding the M'Naghten test, in 1887 some jurisdictions adopted the Irresistible Impulse test. The landmark case in this area was *Parsons* v. *State,* where an Alabama court set forth the modern version of the Irresistible Impulse test.[10] This test holds that a person will be considered insane if as a result of a disease of the mind, he or she was unable to control his or her behavior. Just as the name of this test implies, if the defendant could prove that he or she was suffering from a disease of the mind so that there was an impulse to commit criminal acts that he or she could not control, then the defendant would be considered insane.

This test also was controversial, and in 1954, the U.S. Court of Appeals in Washington, D.C., decided the case of *Durham* v. *United States*.[11] Although this decision was also controversial, some jurisdictions adopted its rationale as their test for insanity. The court stated that the "rule" to be followed in determining criminal responsibility is as follows:

> It is simply that an accused is not criminally responsible if his unlawful act was the product of mental disease or mental defect . . . .
>
> Whenever there is some evidence that the accused suffered from a diseased or defective mental condition at the time the unlawful act was committed, the trial court must provide the jury with guides for determining whether the accused can be held criminally responsible. We do not, and indeed could not, formulate an instruction which would be either appropriate or binding in all cases. But under the rule now announced, any instruction should in some way convey to the jury the sense and substance of the following: If you the jury believe beyond a reasonable doubt that the accused was not suffering from a diseased or defective mental condition at the time he committed the criminal act charged, you may find him guilty.

The same problems inherent in the M'Naghten test regarding mental disease or defect were present in the *Durham* case. The Durham test has been severely criticized in the case of *United States* v. *Currens*, where the court said it is too vague and indefinite to be workable in the determination of criminal responsibility.[12] The Durham test does not give the jury any real guidelines to determine whether an unlawful act was the product of a mental disease or mental defect.

The other major test used is the American Law Institute's "substantial capacity" test (also known as the ALI test). The Model Penal Code uses the ALI test. Also, it is being used in a growing number of states. The test is found in Section 4.01 of the Model Penal Code and is as follows:

1. A person is not responsible for criminal conduct if at the time of such conduct as a result of mental disease or defect he lacks substantial capacity either to appreciate the criminality (wrongfulness) of his conduct or to conform his conduct to the requirements of the law.
2. As used in the Article, the terms mental disease or defect do not include abnormally manifested only by repeated criminal or otherwise antisocial conduct.

The primary difference between the M'Naghten and the ALI tests is that the M'Naghten test requires the defendant to show total mental impairment, whereas the ALI test requires that the defendant show only that he lacked the "substantial capacity" to conform his or her conduct to the requirements of law, that is, lack of self-control.

A number of states now use the "guilty, but mentally ill" procedure for handling the insanity issue. Under this procedure, when an insanity defense is raised, the court, if the evidence permits, may find the defendant guilty but mentally ill. In most states, when the defense is raised, the case is tried without regard to the insanity defense. If a finding of guilty results, the jury is asked to determine whether the defendant is insane.

Syndromes

Starting in the 1980s, a range of "syndromes" that affect the mental state of the defendant have been presented to excuse or justify the conduct of the defendant. One of the most famous is the "Twinkie defense." When considering nutrition and criminal behavior, consider that Americans buy 700 million "Twinkies" a year—80 percent of them on impulse. Over 50 billion Twinkies have been sold in the past sixty years.

On May 22, 1979, Dan White, a former San Francisco, California, County Supervisor, was convicted of voluntary manslaughter for the November 1978 killing of San Francisco Mayor George Moscone and Supervisor Harvey Milk. White was originally charged with first degree murder (a capital offense). The prosecutor argued to the jury that White was guilty of cold-blooded murder. It was established that White had gone to city hall to talk to the mayor. He had entered through a window to avoid the metal detector at the main entrance. At the time, he was carrying a snub-nosed revolver. He shot Mayor Moscone and Supervisor Milk nine times with the weapon, killing both of them. White readily admitted killing both the mayor and the supervisor, the latter being his most vocal opponent on the San Francisco Board of Supervisors.

White's defense attorney, Douglas Schmidt, presented evidence to establish that White had suffered from "diminished capacity" caused by a "biochemical change" in his brain. According to the defense's theory of the case, White was incapable of the premeditation, deliberation, and malice required to obtain a murder conviction. Evidence at the trial indicated that White was a manic depressive with a high degree of stress caused by financial and other personal problems. A defense medical expert testified that White suffered from a "genetically caused melancholia," and at the time, he was "discombobulated." Defense witnesses, who comprised family members, friends and experts, testified about White's moods and his diet. One defense psychiatrist testified that White's compulsive diet of candy bars, Twinkies, and cokes was evidence of a deep depression and resulted in excessive sugar intake, which either caused or aggravated a chemical imbalance in his brain. The Twinkie defense or syndrome apparently has not been successfully used since the Dan White trial.

XYY Syndrome.   Some efforts have been made by defense attorneys to utilize the alleged effects of the XYY syndrome as an insanity defense. This defense is based upon the theory that individuals with an abnormal complement of chromosomes are legally insane and as such cannot be held criminally responsible for their acts. Generally, courts have been rejecting this defense, primarily because the geneticists, in studying the extra Y chromosomes, differ in their opinions on the effects. It is generally conceded that not all individuals with an abnormal complement of chromosomes are, by nature, involuntary aggressive. Also, these experts hold that it cannot be stated with certainty that a criminal act is the result of an abnormal complement of chromosomes.

PMS Syndrome.   Another widely discussed defense is the premenstrual stress syndrome (PMS). The problems with the PMS defense are first, that the defense must establish that PMS is a disease; second, that the defendant suffers from PMS; and third, that the PMS must cause the mental impairment that excuses the conduct. Premenstrual syndrome, or premenstrual tension (PMT), is believed to affect approximately 40 percent of American women between the ages of twenty and forty.[13] Normally, the symptoms begin ten to fourteen days prior to the onset of the menstrual period and become progressively worse until the onset of menstruation. In some women, it continues for several days after the onset. Common symptoms include irritability, anxiety, mood swings, depression, migraine headaches, fainting, dizziness, and allergies.

As one woman stated, "There is a pervasive sense of things always falling apart." Susan Lark, in her book *Premenstrual Syndrome Self-Help Book,* states that severely afflicted women are most vulnerable to extreme behavior during this period.[14] Katherine Dalton, an English physician, reports an increase in the likelihood of accidents, alcohol abuse, suicide attempts, and crimes committed by some women suffering from premenstrual tension. In "Menstruation and Tensions," she states that in many cases, the affected women have Dr. Jekyll and Mr. Hyde personality splits; that is, they are "mean," "witchy," and "irritable" during the PMT period. They often yell at their children, pick fights with their husbands, and snap at friends and coworkers. After the symptoms leave, they often spend the rest of the month trying to repair the damage done to the relationships.[15] There is a lot of skepticism regarding the PMS/PMT defense, which has generally not been successful.

Battered Spouse Syndrome. In recent years, wives who have killed their abusing spouses have attempted to use the battered spouse defense. In the 1980s, *The Burning Bed,* a popular film that was based on a real-life case, depicted a woman who killed her husband while he slept. The husband had apparently abused and threatened her. When he went to sleep, she set fire to the bed, killing him. Traditionally, self-defense is not available in these cases because at the time of the killings, the spouses were not in imminent danger. As one court stated, a battered woman cannot reasonably fear imminent life-threatening danger from her sleeping spouse. For the most part, courts have rejected the battered spouse syndrome as a defense to spousal killings. A growing minority of courts have, however, held that the fact that the other spouse was sleeping does not preclude self-defense. When courts allow persons who have been abused to use self-defense as a shield to liability, this practice is known as the "imperfect self-defense plea."

The use of the imperfect self-defense plea received national attention when two sons claimed they had been sexually abused since childhood and therefore found it necessary to kill their mother and father. Eric and Lyle Menendez, along with a series of family violence experts, testified that, as a result of the continued sexual abuse, they believed that they were in imminent danger of death or great bodily injury.

More and more courts are accepting the use of the imperfect self-defense plea in battered women cases. There is a gradual acceptance that some women can be trapped emotionally in an abusive relationship and honestly believe that they must kill their abusers to survive.[16] However, a number of courts still do not recognize this syndrome. In *State* v. *Stewart,* evidence at trial indicated that Mike Stewart had abused Peggy Stewart during their marriage and had sexually abused her two daughters by an earlier marriage. On one occasion, he shot one of Peggy's cats and then held the gun to Peggy's head and threatened to pull the trigger.

Peggy left Mike and moved to Oklahoma. Because Peggy was suicidal, she was committed to a hospital. Mike came to the hospital, checked her out, and took her back home. As they drove back home to Kansas, Mike told Peggy that it was all in her head, that from now on, he would decide what was right for her. When they arrived home, Mike forced her to have oral sex, and then he went to bed. Later that day, as Mike slept, Peggy heard voices in her head repeating over and over, "kill or be killed." She then took a gun that she had hidden in the house and killed him with it. The court ruled that the facts do not constitute self-defense and that the state does not recognize the battered spouse syndrome. To excuse a killing under these circumstances would be the same as permitting capital punishment to be used for spousal abuse.[17]

Irrespective of the sanity test or defense that is applied, if the jury finds the defendant to have been sane at the time the crime occurred, the only procedure left is sentencing. On the other hand, if the jury finds that the defendant was insane when the crime was committed, the accused is theoretically entitled to be released. As pointed out in Chapter 5, if the defendant was found to have been insane when committing the crime, in most jurisdictions, confinement will be in a mental hospital under a civil commitment to make certain that there is no threat to society. One court went so far as to hold that "an accused person who is acquitted by reason of insanity is presumed to be insane and may be committed for an indefinite period to a hospital for the insane."[18] In another decision, it was stated that "even where there has been a specific finding that the accused was competent to stand trial and assist in his own defense, the court would be well advised to invoke the code provision so that the accused may be confined as long as the public safety and his welfare require."[19]

CLOSING ARGUMENTS

After both sides have presented their evidence, the next procedure in most jurisdictions is the closing arguments by the prosecuting attorney and the defense attorney. Closing arguments are merely a summarization of the evidence presented during the trial. Attorneys have mixed emotions regarding the value of closing arguments. Some attorneys allege that the closing arguments have no effect on the jury and that the arguments are a waste of time. Other attorneys feel that a closing argument may be the difference between losing a case and winning it. Irrespective of viewpoints, in most criminal trials, both the prosecution and the defense will give closing arguments. There is no limit on the length of time of a closing argument. The attorneys may take only a few minutes, or they may take several days, depending on the length of the trial. The judge does have the right to limit the time involved, but he or she may not be too restrictive. With the possible exception of an insanity trial, the usual procedure is for the prosecuting attorney to give the closing argument first, followed by the defense. After the defense has completed its closing argument, the prosecuting attorney may give a rebuttal argument. Some jurisdictions reverse this procedure and permit the defense attorney to present the closing argument first, followed by the prosecution.

It is considered improper for the attorneys to appeal to the sympathy or emotions of the jurors, but frequently the closing arguments are a dramatic performance that results in an appeal to the emotions. In fact, during the questioning of the jurors for cause, attorneys may inject questions designed to later enable them to weave the personal lives of some of the jurors into the closing arguments. At this point in the trial, each side is endeavoring to sell the jury on the fact that its side is entitled to the verdict.

Closing Argument by the Prosecution

During the closing argument, the prosecuting attorney will summarize the evidence presented, emphasizing the strong points that indicate guilt. To substantiate the closing statements, the physical evidence already introduced may be displayed again. The prosecuting attorney may state that the evidence clearly proves that the defendant is guilty of the crime charged. It is held to be prejudicial error, however, for the prosecuting attorney to state that from personal knowledge, the defendant is known to be guilty, implying that information not brought forth during the trial is in his or her possession. The courts have stated that the right to discuss the merits of a case, both regarding the law and the facts, is very wide and that the prosecuting attorney has the right to state what the evidence shows and what conclusions are to be drawn. The adverse party cannot complain if the reasoning is faulty and the deductions illogical, since such matters are ultimately for the consideration of the jury. It has been held that the prosecuting attorney should be circumspect in remarks concerning the defendant and counsel, but the use of derogatory epithets does not necessarily represent misconduct.

In the case of *People* v. *Jones*,[20] the prosecuting attorney referred to the defendant's behavior as consistent with animalistic and felonious tendencies, and also implied that there was a strange, twisted reason for the actions of the accused. The Court in that case stated the following:

> We recognize that prosecutors, like all others who have responsible roles in the trial of a criminal case, are human; as humans they may be affected by the tensions of a trial to the point of error and, on occasion, even to misconduct. We recognize, too, that the great increase in crime and the corresponding increase in the number of prosecutions in recent years has placed a heavy burden on district attorneys, who frequently must rely on inexperienced deputies to try cases. Be that as it may, prosecutors should be ever aware that in all they do and say they are representatives of the government of whom the public, including those who are prosecuted, are entitled to expect a high degree of ethical conduct.
>
>   . . . while some of the references to the appellant (defendant), more particularly, "animalistic tendencies" and "felonious tendencies" were quite strong, we hold that, under the facts of this case, they were within the bounds of legitimate argument and did not constitute misconduct.

Following such arguments by the prosecuting attorney, the judge will often instruct the jury that the closing arguments are not to be considered as evidence in the case and that the jury is to disregard any statements not based on the evidence. If a prosecuting attorney does indulge in misconduct during the closing argument, the misconduct could lead to a mistrial being declared at the time or to a reversal of a conviction on appeal.

Closing Argument by the Defense

Technically, the same rules of conduct that apply to the prosecuting attorney also apply to the defense attorney. Since defense counsel misconduct is not appealable if the defendant should be acquitted, the defense attorney often engages in considerable freedom in arguing the case to the jury. An appeal will often be made to the sympathy of the jury. It may be pointed out that in rendering a guilty verdict, the jury will deprive the defendant of freedom and companionship with family. In one case, the defendant appeared in court wearing long hair and a shaggy beard. In the defense attorney's argument to the jury, counsel stated that in looking over the jury, no member representative of the defendant's peer group could be seen. The defense attorney recalled a trial some two thousand years before at which the defendant also was wearing a beard, had long hair, and was tried without peer group representation. Keeping that fact in mind, the defense attorney felt that the appearance of the defendant would not deter the jury from rendering a verdict in favor of acquittal. Although the defense attorney may be dramatic in appealing to a jury, there are times when the jury may resent what they feel to be an insult to their intelligence in defense counsel arguments.

Even though represented by an attorney, occasionally a defendant will insist upon making a closing argument in addition to the one given by the attorney. It is at the judge's discretion whether the defendant may make a closing argument. If the defendant is self-represented, a closing argument is always permitted.

Rebuttal Closing Argument

After the defense attorney has concluded the closing argument for the accused, the prosecuting attorney is entitled to make a rebuttal closing argument. Statements and challenges presented during the defense attorney's closing argument can be met. At this time, the prosecuting attorney's final remarks must be circumspect to avoid making statements amounting to misconduct in response to challenges presented by the defense.

CAPSTONE CASE

Rock v. *Arkansas*
483 U.S. 44, 107 S.Ct 2704, 97 L.Ed.2d 37 (1987)

Justice Blackmun delivered the opinion of the Court.

The issue presented in this case is whether Arkansas' evidentiary rule prohibiting the admission of hypnotically refreshed testimony violated petitioner's constitutional right to testify on her own behalf as a defendant in a criminal case.

Petitioner Vickie Lorene Rock was charged with manslaughter in the death of her husband, Frank Rock, on July 2, 1983. A dispute had been simmering about Frank's wish to move from the couple's small apartment adjacent to Vickie's beauty parlor to a trailer she owned outside town. That night a fight erupted when Frank refused to let petitioner eat some pizza and prevented her from leaving the apartment to get something else to eat. When police arrived on the scene they found Frank on the floor with a bullet wound in his chest. Petitioner urged the officers to help her husband, and cried to a sergeant who took her in charge, "please save him" and "don't let him die." The police removed her from the building because she was upset and because she interfered with their investigation by her repeated attempts to use the telephone to call her husband's parents. According to the testimony of one of the investigating officers, petitioner told him that "she stood up to leave the room and [her husband] grabbed her by the throat and choked her and threw her against the wall and . . . at that time she walked over and picked up the weapon and pointed it toward the floor and he hit her again and she shot him." Because petitioner could not remember the precise details of the shooting, her attorney suggested that she submit to hypnosis in order to refresh her memory. Petitioner was hypnotized twice by Doctor Betty Back, a licensed neuropsychologist with training in the field of hypnosis. Doctor Back interviewed petitioner for an hour prior to the first hypnosis session, taking notes on petitioner's general history and her recollections of the shooting. Both hypnosis sessions were recorded on tape. Petitioner did not relate any new information during either of the sessions, but, after the hypnosis, she was able to remember that at the time of the incident she had her thumb on the hammer of the gun, but had not held her finger on the trigger. She also recalled that the gun had discharged when her husband grabbed her arm during the scuffle. As a result of the details that petitioner was able to remember about the shooting, her counsel arranged for a gun expert to examine the handgun, a single action Hawes .22 Deputy Marshal. That inspection revealed that the gun was defective and prone to fire, when hit or dropped, without the trigger's being pulled.

When the prosecutor learned of the hypnosis sessions, he filed a motion to exclude petitioner's testimony. The trial judge held a pretrial hearing on the motion and concluded that no hypnotically refreshed testimony would be admitted. The court issued an order limiting petitioner's testimony to "matters remembered and stated to the examiner prior to being placed under hypnosis." At trial, petitioner introduced testimony by the gun expert, but the court limited petitioner's own description of the events on the day of the shooting to a reiteration of the sketchy information in Doctor Back's notes. The jury convicted petitioner on the manslaughter charge and she was sentenced to 10 years' imprisonment and a $10,000 fine.

On appeal, the Supreme Court of Arkansas rejected petitioner's claim that the limitations on her testimony violated her right to present her defense. The court concluded that "the dangers of admitting this kind of testimony outweigh whatever probative value it may have," and decided to follow the approach of States that have held hypnotically refreshed testimony of witnesses inadmissible per se. . . . It ruled that the exclusion of petitioner's testimony did not violate her constitutional rights. Any "prejudice or deprivation" she suffered "was minimal and resulted from her own actions and not by any erroneous ruling of the court."

Petitioner's claim that her testimony was impermissibly excluded is bottomed on her constitutional right to testify in her own defense. At this point in the development of our adversary system, it cannot be doubted that a defendant in a criminal case has the right to take the witness stand and to testify in his or her own defense. This, of course, is a change from the historic common-law view, which was that all parties to litigation, including criminal defendants, were disqualified from testifying because of their interest in the outcome of the trial. The principal rationale for this rule was the possible untrustworthiness of a party's testimony. Under the common law, the practice did develop of permitting criminal defendants to tell their side of the story, but they were limited to making an unsworn statement that could not be elicited through direct examination by counsel and was not subject to cross-examination.

This Court in *Ferguson* v. *Georgia,* 365 U.S. 570 (1961), detailed the history of the transition from a rule of a defendant's incompetency to a rule of competency. As the Court there recounted, it came to be recognized that permitting a defendant to testify advances both the "detection of guilt" and "the protection of innocence," and by the end of the second half of the 19th century, all States except Georgia had enacted statutes that declared criminal defendants competent to testify.

The right to testify on one's own behalf at a criminal trial has sources in several provisions of the Constitution. It is one of the rights that "are essential to due process of law in a fair adversary process." *Faretta* v. *California.* The necessary ingredients of the Fourteenth Amendment's guarantee that no one shall be deprived of liberty without due process of law include a right to be heard and to offer testimony. . . .

The right to testify is also found in the Compulsory Process Clause of the Sixth Amendment, which grants a defendant the right to call "witnesses in his favor." . . . Logically included in the accused's right to call witnesses whose testimony is "material and favorable to his defense," *United States* v. *Valenzuela-Bernai,* 458 U.S. 858 (1982), is a right to testify himself, should he decide it is in his favor to do so. In fact, the most important witness for the defense in many criminal cases is the defendant himself. There is no justification today for a rule that denies an accused the opportunity to offer his own testimony. Like the truthfulness of other witnesses, the defendant's veracity, which was the concern behind the original common-law rule, can be tested adequately by cross-examination.

Moreover, in *Faretta* v. *California,* the Court recognized that the Sixth Amendment "grants to the accused personally the right to make his defense." Even more fundamental to a personal defense than the right of self representation, which was found to be "necessarily implied by the structure of the Amendment," *Faretta,* is an accused's right to present his own version of events in his own words. A defendant's opportunity to conduct his own defense by calling witnesses is incomplete if he may not present himself as a witness.

The opportunity to testify is also a necessary corollary to the Fifth Amendment's guarantee against compelled testimony. In *Harris* v. *New York,* 401 U.S. 222 (1971), the Court stated: "Every criminal defendant is privileged to testify in his own defense, or to refuse to do so." Three of the dissenting Justices in that case agreed that the Fifth Amendment encompasses this right: "[privilege against self-incrimination] is fulfilled only when an accused is guaranteed the right to remain silent unless he chooses to speak in the unfettered exercise of his own will. . . . The choice of whether to testify in one's own defense. . . . is an exercise of the constitutional privilege."

The question now before the Court is whether a criminal defendant's right to testify may be restricted by a state rule that excludes her post-hypnosis testimony. This is not the first time this Court has faced a constitutional challenge to a state rule, designed to ensure trustworthy evidence, that interfered with the ability of a defendant to offer testimony. In *Washington* v. *Texas,* 388 U.S. 14 (1967), the Court [struck down] . . . a state statute that prevented persons charged as principals, accomplices, or accessories in the same crime from being introduced as witnesses for one another. . . . By preventing the defendant from having the benefit of his accomplice's testimony, "the State arbitrarily denied him the right to put on the stand a witness who was physically and mentally capable of testifying to events that he had personally observed, and whose testimony would have been relevant and material to the defense." . . . Just as a State may not apply an arbitrary rule of competence to exclude a material defense witness from taking the stand, it also may not apply a rule of evidence that permits a witness to take the stand, but arbitrarily excludes material portions of his testimony. In *Chambers* v. *Mississippi,* the Court invalidated a State's hearsay rule on the ground that it abridged the defendant's right to "present witnesses in his own defense."

Of course, the right to present relevant testimony is not without limitation. The right "may, in appropriate cases, bow to accommodate other legitimate interests in the criminal trial process." Chambers . . . . But restrictions of a defendant's right to testify may not be arbitrary or disproportionate to the purposes they are designed to serve. In applying its evidentiary rules a State must evaluate whether the interests served by a rule justify the limitation imposed on the defendant's constitutional right to testify.

The Arkansas rule enunciated by the state courts does not allow a trial court to consider whether posthypnosis testimony may be admissible in a particular case; it is a per se rule prohibiting the admission at trial of any defendant's hypnotically refreshed testimony on the ground that such testimony is always unreliable. Thus, in Arkansas, an accused's testimony is limited to matters that he or she can prove were remembered before hypnosis. This rule operates to the detriment of any defendant who undergoes hypnosis, without regard to the reasons for it, the circumstances under which it took place, or any independent verification of the information it produced.

In this case, the application of that rule had a significant adverse effect on petitioner's ability to testify. It virtually prevented her from describing any of the events that occurred on the day of the shooting, despite corroboration of many of those events by other witnesses. Even more importantly, under the court's rule petitioner was not permitted to describe the actual shooting except in the words contained in Doctor Back's notes. The expert's description of the gun's tendency to misfire would have taken on greater significance if the jury had heard petitioner testify that she did not have her finger on the trigger and that the gun went off when her husband hit her arm.

In establishing its per se rule, the Arkansas Supreme Court simply followed the approach taken by a number of States that have decided that hypnotically enhanced testimony should be excluded at trial on the ground that it tends to be unreliable. Other States that have adopted an exclusionary rule, however, have done so for the testimony of witnesses, not for the testimony of a defendant. The Arkansas Supreme Court failed to perform the constitutional analysis that is necessary when a defendant's right to testify is at stake.

Although the Arkansas court concluded that any testimony that cannot be proved to be the product of pre-hypnosis memory is unreliable, many courts have eschewed a per se rule and permit the admission of hypnotically refreshed testimony. Hypnosis by trained physicians or psychologists has been recognized as a valid therapeutic technique since 1958, although there is no generally accepted theory to explain the phenomenon, or even a consensus on a single definition of hypnosis. The use of hypnosis in criminal investigations, however, is controversial, and the current medical and legal view of its appropriate role is unsettled.

Responses of individuals to hypnosis vary greatly. The popular belief that hypnosis guarantees the accuracy of recall is as yet without established foundation and, in fact, hypnosis often has no effect at all on memory. The most common response to hypnosis, however, appears to be an increase in both correct and incorrect recollections. Three general characteristics of hypnosis may lead to the introduction of inaccurate memories: the subject becomes "suggestible" and may try to please the hypnotist with answers the subject thinks will be met with approval; the subject is likely to "confabulate," that is, to fill in details from the imagination in order to make an answer more coherent and complete; and, the subject experiences "memory hardening," which gives him great confidence in both true and false memories, making effective cross-examination more difficult. See generally M. Orne, et al., Hypnotically Induced Testimony. . . . Despite the unreliability that hypnosis conceivably may introduce, however, the procedure has been credited as instrumental in obtaining investigative leads or identifications that were later confirmed by independent evidence.

The inaccuracies the process introduces can be reduced, although perhaps not eliminated, by the use of procedural safeguards. One set of suggested guidelines calls for hypnosis to be performed only by a psychologist or psychiatrist with special training in its use and who is independent of the investigation. See Orne, The Use and Misuse of Hypnosis in Court. . . . These procedures reduce the possibility that biases will be communicated to the hypersuggestive subject by the hypnotist. Suggestion will be less likely also if the hypnosis is conducted in a neutral setting with no one present but the hypnotist and the subject. Tape or video recording of all interrogations, before, during, and after hypnosis, can help reveal if leading questions were asked. Such guidelines do not guarantee the accuracy of the testimony, because they cannot control the subject's own motivations or any tendency to confabulate, but they do provide a means of controlling overt suggestions.

The more traditional means of assessing accuracy of testimony also remain applicable in the case of a previously hypnotized defendant. Certain information recalled as a result of hypnosis may be verified as highly accurate by corroborating evidence. Cross-examination, even in the face of a confident defendant, is an effective tool for revealing inconsistencies. Moreover, a jury can be educated to the risks of hypnosis through expert testimony and cautionary instructions. Indeed, it is probably to a defendant's advantage to establish carefully the extent of his memory prior to hypnosis, in order to minimize the decrease in credibility the procedure might introduce.

We are not now prepared to endorse without qualifications the use of hypnosis as an investigative tool; scientific understanding of the phenomenon and of the means to control the effects of hypnosis is still in its infancy. Arkansas, however, has not justified the exclusion of all of a defendant's testimony that the defendant is unable to prove to be the product of prehypnosis memory. A State's legitimate interest in barring unreliable evidence does not extend to per se exclusions that may be reliable in an individual case. Wholesale inadmissibility of a defendant's testimony is an arbitrary restriction on the right to testify in the absence of clear evidence by the State repudiating the validity of all posthypnosis recollections. The State would be well within its powers if it established guidelines to aid trial courts in the evaluation of posthypnosis testimony and it may be able to show that testimony in a particular case is so unreliable that exclusion is justified. But it has not shown that hypnotically enhanced testimony is always so untrustworthy and so immune to the traditional means of evaluating credibility that it should disable a defendant from presenting her version of the events for which she is on trial.

In this case, the defective condition of the gun corroborated the details petitioner remembered about the shooting. The tape recordings provided some means to evaluate the hypnosis and the trial judge concluded that Doctor Back did not suggest responses with leading questions. Those circumstances present an argument for admissibility of petitioner's testimony in this particular case, an argument that must be considered by the trial court. Arkansas' per se rule excluding all posthypnosis testimony infringes impermissibly on the right of a defendant to testify on his or her own behalf. The judgment of the Supreme Court of Arkansas is vacated and the case is remanded to that court for further proceedings not inconsistent with this opinion.

Chief Justice Rehnquist, with whom Justice White, Justice O'Connor, and Justice Scalia join, dissenting.

In deciding that petitioner Rock's testimony was properly limited at her trial, the Arkansas Supreme Court cited several factors that undermine the reliability of hypnotically induced testimony. Like the Court today, the Arkansas Supreme Court observed that a hypnotized individual becomes subject to suggestion, is likely to confabulate, and experiences artificially increased confidence in both true and false memories following hypnosis. No known set of procedures, both courts agree, can insure against the inherently unreliable nature of such testimony. Having acceded to the factual premises of the Arkansas Supreme Court, the Court nevertheless concludes that a state trial court must attempt to make its own scientific assessment of reliability in each case where it is confronted with a request for the admission of hypnotically induced testimony. I find no justification in the Constitution for such a ruling. In the Court's words, the decision today is "bottomed" on recognition of Rock's "constitutional right to testify in her own defense." While it is true that this Court, in dictum, has recognized the existence of such a right, the principles identified by the Court as underlying this right provide little support for invalidating the evidentiary rule applied by the Arkansas Supreme Court.

As a general matter, the Court first recites, a defendant's right to testify facilitates the truth-seeking function of a criminal trial by advancing both the "detection of guilt" and "the protection of innocence." Quoting *Ferguson* v. *Georgia*. Such reasoning is hardly controlling here, where advancement of the truth-seeking function of Rock's trial was the sole motivation behind limiting her testimony. The Court also posits, however, that "a rule that denies an accused the opportunity to offer his own testimony" cannot be upheld because, "Like the truthfulness of other witnesses, the defendant's veracity . . . can be tested adequately by cross-examination." But the Court candidly admits that the increased confidence inspired by hypnotism makes "cross-examination more difficult," thereby diminishing an adverse party's ability to test the truthfulness of defendants such as Rock. . . .

This Court has traditionally accorded the States "respect for establishment and implementation of their own criminal trial rules and procedures." Chambers. . . . One would think that this deference would be at its highest in an area such as this, where, as the Court concedes, "scientific understanding is still in its infancy." . . . The Supreme Court of Arkansas' decision was an entirely permissible response to a novel and difficult question. M. Orne et al., Hypnotically Refreshed Testimony. . . . As an original proposition, the solution this Court imposes upon Arkansas may be equally sensible, though requiring the matter to be considered res nova by every single trial judge in every single case might seem to some to pose serious administrative difficulties. But until there is a much more general consensus on the use of hypnosis than there is now, the Constitution does not warrant this Court's mandating its own view of how to deal with the issue.

REVIEW QUESTIONS

1. What is the purpose of the opening statement?
2. Define reasonable doubt.
3. What amendment guarantees a defendant the right to be confronted with the witnesses against him or her?
4. What is the purpose of a subpoena?
5. In what way does the oath differ from the affirmation?
6. Why was the affirmation adopted?
7. What is direct examination?

8. Define a leading question.

9. What is the primary purpose of cross-examination?

10. Must the defendant present evidence in his or her own behalf?

11. What is the purpose of rebuttal by the prosecution?

12. State the purpose of the M'Naghten test.

13. What purpose do closing arguments serve?

LOCAL PROCEDURE

1. In your home state, may a defendant enter a plea of not guilty by reason of insanity, or is insanity raised only as a defense?

2. Is the M'Naghten or some other test for insanity followed in your home state?

ENDNOTES

1. 397 U.S. 358 (1970).
2. 399 U.S. 149 (1970).
3. Portions of this section dealing with the use of closed-circuit television have been adapted from H. Wallace, *Family Violence: Legal, Medical, and Social Perspectives* (Allyn & Bacon, Boston), 1996.
4. 110 S.Ct. 3157 (1990).
5. 380 U.S. 400 (1965).
6. 380 U.S. 609 (1965).
7. See *People* v. *Robles,* 85 Cal.Rptr. 166 (1970).
8. *Nix* v. *Whiteside,* 475 U.S. 157 (1986).
9. 8 Eng. Reprint 718 (1843).
10. 81 Ala. 577, 2 So. 854 (1887). It should be noted that the Irresistible Impulse test actually predated the M'Naghten test. For an excellent historical discussion of the evolution of these early insanity rules, see Keedy, "Irresistible Impulse as a Defense in Criminal Law," 100 *Univ. of Penn. Law Review,* 1952, pp. 956–961.
11. 214 F.2d 862 (D.C. Cir. 1954).
12. 290 E. 2d 751 (1961).
13. Susan Lark, *Premenstrual Syndrome Self-Help Book* (Forman, Los Angeles), 1984:19.
14. Katherine Dalton, "Menstruation and Crime," *British Medical Journal* No. 3, 1961, p. 1752.
15. J. H. Morton et al., "A Clinical Study of Premenstrual Tension," *Amer. J. of Obstetrics and Gynecology,* No. 65, 1953, pp. 1182–1191.
16. H. Wallace, "Battered Women Syndrome: Self-Defense and Duress as Mandatory Defenses? The History and Acceptance of the Battered Women Syndrome in American Courts," *The Police Journal,* London, England, 1994.
17. *State* v. *Stewart,* 763 P.2d 572 (Kansas, 1988).
18. See *Orencia* v. *Overholser,* 82 U.S. App. D.C. 285 (1947).
19. See *Barry* v. *White,* 62 U.S. App. D.C. 69 (1933).
20. 86 Cal.Rptr 516 (1970).

CHAPTER 13

Instructions and Deliberation of the Jury

A jury verdict is a quotient of the prejudices of twelve people. . . .

—Kenneth Grub, attorney

INSTRUCTIONS TO THE JURY

On completion of the closing arguments, in most jurisdictions, the judge instructs the jury on the law applicable to the case. Instructing the jury is also known as *charging the jury* or as the *charge to the jury*. In a few states, the judge may instruct the jury prior to the closing arguments in order that the attorneys involved may include comments on the instructions during their closing arguments. Although the procedure of instructing the jury follows the presentation of the evidence, the judge has the responsibility of explaining the law to the jury as the trial progresses for their guidance in following the evidence. During the charge to the jury, the judge will summarize the points of law explained to them during the trial and instruct them on their function as jurors. Also, the judge will instruct the jury on any additional laws applicable that were not explained as the trial progressed.

Defense and Prosecution Recommendations

As a general rule, the prosecuting attorney and defense attorney prepare written instructions that they desire to be given to the jury. These instructions will be furnished to the judge prior to the closing arguments. After reviewing these instructions, the judge selects those that appear to be applicable. Other instructions not suggested by the attorneys may also be given. The judge has the responsibility of instructing the jury on the laws applicable whether requested to do so or not.

The defendant is entitled to instructions being given on all pertinent evidence regardless of its importance. The failure to give an instruction concerning pertinent evidence, whether requested or not by the defense, could be grounds for the reversal of a conviction on appeal. However, a judge does not have to give instructions that are repetitive or that include some statement of fact in the form of evidence in the case.

The judge also has the responsibility of instructing the jury in clear and understandable language. Too often the instructions are lengthy, complicated, and difficult for the jury to understand. For example, an instruction on the meaning of reasonable doubt may be confusing to the jury, but the defendant is entitled to an instruction on the presumption of innocence. The judge will read to the jury the definition of reasonable doubt as set forth in Chapter 12. The jury will be informed that a defendant in a criminal action is presumed innocent until the contrary is proved, and that if there is a reasonable doubt of guilt, the defendant is entitled to an acquittal. The effect of this presumption places on the state the burden of proving guilt beyond a reasonable doubt.

The following are samples of additional instructions generally given to a jury. The jury will be informed that it is the function of the judge to interpret the law but that the jury is the exclusive judge of the facts. The jury must determine those facts only from the evidence presented in court, and it must conscientiously consider and weigh the evidence during the trial. It must also carefully determine the credibility of each witness. In measuring the credibility of a witness, the jury may consider the demeanor of the witness as he or she testifies; the opportunity of the witness to have gained the facts about which he or she testifies; and the witness's ability to observe, retain, and communicate the matters. The jury will be informed that it must not consider as evidence any statement made by the attorneys involved, nor is the jury to speculate on what an answer to a question may have been when an objection to the question was sustained. Neither may the jury consider in its deliberation on the verdict any statement that was stricken from the record. The jurors will be advised that they must not be governed by mere sentiment, sympathy, passion, or prejudice in arriving at a verdict and that they must reach a just verdict regardless of the consequences of that verdict. The jurors will also be informed that it is their duty to consult one another and to deliberate on a just verdict but that the verdict is to express the individual opinion of each juror. The jury will then be advised of the previously mentioned presumption of innocence and reasonable doubt instructions.

The foregoing instructions are applicable in all criminal trials but are not all-inclusive of those that may be given in a trial proceeding. In addition to these general instructions, more specific instructions applicable to the particular case will be included. Instructions may be given on the meaning of direct and circumstantial evidence. The jury will be informed that direct evidence directly proves the fact in issue, whereas circumstantial evidence proves a fact by an inference drawn from another set of facts having been proved. At this point in the instructions, the jury is often again hopelessly lost in the explanation. The right of an expert witness to give an opinion on controversial questions is explained. It will be explained that the jury may consider the qualifications of the expert and must give the testimony the proper weight. The meaning of intent and motive may be explained. If an alibi defense was alleged, the judge will inform the jury that if they have reasonable doubt about the defendant's being present at the scene of the crime, an acquittal should result. The meaning of *consciousness of guilt* will be explained, as well as those acts that may fall within that category, such as a suspect's running from a crime scene.

The jury will be informed that the defendant has a right not to testify and that no inference of guilt is to be drawn from the failure to testify. Since most jurisdictions permit a jury to return a verdict to a lesser degree of crime than that charged in the accusatory pleading, the jury will be given an instruction to this effect. Most jurisdictions permit the jury to take the written instructions given by the judge with them during deliberations.

Comments by the Judge

States differ materially in permitting a judge to comment on the evidence of a case and the credibility of witnesses. About half the states prohibit comments by the judge on the evidence and credibility of the witnesses, since it is believed that such comments are an invasion of the function of the jury. A few states and federal courts grant considerable freedom to a judge to comment on the evidence and credibility of the witnesses. It has been stated that the judge should be a real factor in the administration of justice and not a mere referee of the adversary system. The judge must summarize the evidence in an impartial and instructive manner, but he or she may point out weaknesses in the evidence of the prosecution and defense or may question the credibility of witnesses. However, the judge's right to comment on the evidence and witnesses is not unlimited. Courts have stated that the judge must be "fair, objective and impartial and must not ignore evidence favorable to the defendant." It has been held improper for the judge to directly state the belief that the defendant is guilty. Comments in one case were considered improper when the judge indicated to the jury that in viewing the evidence in its most favorable light to the defendant, one was still left with the conclusion that the defendant was guilty. The judge further stated that if he were deciding the case, the accused would be found guilty.

Comments to the jury may be made before or after the instructions, at the judge's discretion. Except in states where the judge gives the instructions to the jury prior to the closing arguments, the jury begins its deliberations once the instructions are given.

DELIBERATIONS

If the jury has not been sequestered prior to the case's being given to the jury, the judge must decide whether or not to do so during deliberations. As we pointed out earlier, in some states, the jury must be sequestered during the deliberations. In other states, it is at the discretion of the judge. The jury may decide on the verdict in the courtroom, but in most instances, they will retire to some private and convenient place for deliberations. This place is generally referred to as the jury room.

Inside the Jury Room

While deliberating, the jurors will be under the guard of an officer of the court. The court officer will have been sworn to keep the jurors together, not permit any person to speak to them, and not speak to them himself or herself except on orders of the court. During the deliberation, no one—not even the officer in charge of the jury—may be present in the jury room except the jurors. On one occasion, an alternate juror was inadvertently given permission by the officer in charge of the jury to sit in the jury room merely to observe during the deliberation. On learning of the presence of the alternate juror during the deliberation, the judge declared a mistrial although the alternate juror did not in any way engage in the deliberation. The courts of a few states, however, have permitted an alternate juror to be sequestered with the other jurors during the deliberation, but only after the judge has instructed the alternate juror not to participate in the deliberation.

In one case, the officer in charge of the jury was also a material witness for the prosecution. He and other officers transported the jury back and forth to their hotel while the jury was being sequestered, and these officers also ate at the same table with the jurors and conversed with them. Although it was alleged that there was no conversation about the facts of the case during these associations, the U.S. Supreme Court held that the presence of the officer interfered with the defendant's right to be tried by an impartial jury. The presence of the officer, according to the Court, may have established a favorable rapport with the jury that may have affected their verdict of guilty.[1]

In reference to only jurors' being present during the deliberation, we return to the problem encountered by the hearing-impaired person who becomes a juror. By necessity, this juror's interpreter must be present during the deliberation to interpret the communication that takes place among the jurors as they attempt to arrive at a verdict. How may it be determined that the deliberation was accurately interpreted, or was that juror somehow influenced by the interpretation? Would it be held that the interpreter was an extra juror present during the deliberation? If the defendant was convicted, could the defense challenge on appeal the presence of the interpreter during deliberation, or would this challenge have been waived by the lack of challenge for cause during jury selection? Only future cases will decide the answers to these questions.

Prior to beginning the deliberation, the jury will select one of their members to act as the foreperson—their leader and spokesperson. If, during the deliberation, the jury desires further instructions on the law or information concerning the case, the foreperson will advise the officer in charge, who in turn will notify the judge of the request. The judge, in most instances, will require that the jury be returned to the courtroom for the requested information. It is considered improper for the officer in charge to act as a messenger carrying information from the judge to the jury.

Materials Inside the Jury Room

On entering deliberation, the jury may take with them any and all documents introduced during the trial. However, in many jurisdictions, the jury may not take any depositions with them. The reason for this prohibition is that to permit the jury to take the depositions would possibly allow them to give greater weight to the testimony of a witness not present over one who was present. The rules of evidence in most states provide that the jury may take any document introduced and also permit the jury to take any exhibits or physical evidence, such as a gun, plaster-of-paris cast, or fingerprint, that may have been introduced. Courts in some jurisdictions have held that the jury should be permitted to take with them all evidence introduced, including depositions, any prepared transcript or recorded testimony, and personal notes as long as the defendant is not unduly prejudiced and the jury is not likely to use the evidence improperly.

A great majority of the states permit jurors to take notes at the discretion of the judge. Judges differ in their attitudes toward note-taking. Some judges argue that most jurors are not trained in the art of taking notes. Not being trained, they may take down trivial matters and overlook important facts, or they may try to take down everything and get hopelessly lost in the process, missing material testimony as it is presented. It is argued also that the better note-takers will tend to dominate the deliberation or that jurors will quarrel over whose notes are a correct record of the testimony. Those arguing in favor of note-taking by jurors allege that it is asking too much of a juror to remember all the testimony during a lengthy trial and that permitting notes to be taken enables the jurors to refresh their memory during the deliberation. Usually, the reporter's transcript is not available at the time of the deliberation, and unless the jurors have their notes, the only way that testimony may be recalled in some instances is to have the jury returned to the courtroom and the reporter's notes read to the jury. This procedure is time-consuming, and judges often frown on this activity when engaged in too frequently by a jury. It is argued that the benefits derived from a juror's taking notes during a trial far exceed any detriment that may be suffered.

Length of Deliberation

How long the jury may deliberate on a case before reaching a verdict will depend largely on the length of the trial and on how convincing the evidence may have been. The jury may decide on a verdict after conferring for a few minutes, or they may take days to decide on a verdict. In many instances, they cannot agree at all. When the jury cannot agree on a verdict, it is referred to as a *hung* jury. When this situation occurs, the jury is discharged, and a mistrial may be declared by the judge. The trial will have to be restarted with a new jury. It is not unusual for a trial to end with a hung jury. As we previously pointed out, most juries in a criminal case consist of twelve persons. In a great majority of the states, the verdict must be unanimous: that is, all the jurors must agree on either guilt or innocence. To get twelve people to agree on the guilt or innocence of an accused is often difficult.

Judges would rather permit a reasonable amount of time for deliberation than have to start the case over with a new jury, since this step is both time-consuming and expensive. Most judges will do their utmost to encourage a jury to reach a verdict. A judge may call the jury back into the courtroom from time to time to determine whether the foreperson believes that a verdict can be reached. The judge may even inquire about how the jury is numerically split in reaching a verdict, but it is considered improper for the judge to ask how they are split on guilt or innocence. If the foreperson should inadvertently state how the jury is split on guilt or innocence, it is not generally considered to be a reversible error. The judge must be circumspect in urging the jury to reach a verdict. He or she must not do or say anything that may be interpreted as a threat to the jury or as forcing a verdict on the jury. Any statement or instruction to the jury at this point that could be interpreted as coercive is considered improper and could result in the reversal of a conviction on appeal. An instruction has been held to be coercive when a judge emphasizes that a verdict must be reached because of the simplicity of the evidence or when a judge threatens to lock up the jury until the verdict is agreed on. In one case, a jury had been deliberating from Monday until Wednesday afternoon before Thanksgiving. Late Wednesday afternoon, the judge called the jurors in and indicated that it would be wise for them to agree on a verdict soon so that it would not be necessary to sequester them over the Thanksgiving holidays. After deliberating for a few more hours, the jury returned a guilty verdict. The conviction was reversed on appeal because of the threat by the judge to the jury.

After a judge has made an inquiry about the possibility of the jurors' reaching a verdict, the judge will undoubtedly discharge the jury if the foreperson feels that the jury is hopelessly deadlocked and cannot agree on a verdict. If possible, the judge will avoid this action. The jury may be asked to further consider the matter, particularly if the majority is for a verdict, with only one or two persons disagreeing. In some states, the judge may read to the jury what is referred to as the *Allen charge,* or *Allen instruction.* This instruction has been called the "dynamite charge," since its purpose is to blast the jury into action so that they will arrive at a verdict. This charge was originally approved by the U.S. Supreme Court in the case of *Allen* v. *United States.*[2] The Allen instruction is substantially as follows:

> Ladies and gentlemen of the jury, in a large proportion of cases and perhaps strictly speaking, in all cases, absolute certainty cannot be attained or expected. Although the verdict to which a juror agrees must, of course, be his own verdict, the result of his own convictions and not a mere acquiescence in the conclusion of his or her fellows, yet in order to bring twelve minds to a unanimous result, you must examine the questions submitted to you with candor and with a proper regard and deference to the opinions of each other. You should consider that the case must at some time be decided, that you are selected in the same manner and from the same source from which any future jury must be selected, and there is no reason to suppose the case will ever be submitted to twelve men or women more intelligent, more impartial or more competent to decide it, or that more or clearer evidence will be produced on the one side or the other. And with this view, it is your duty to decide the case, if you can conscientiously do so.
>
> In order to make a decision more practicable, the law imposes the burden of proof on one party or the other in all cases. In the present case, the burden of proof is on the prosecution to establish every part of it beyond a reasonable doubt. And if in any part of it you are left in doubt, the defendant is entitled to the benefit of the doubt and must be acquitted. But in conferring together, you ought to pay proper respect to each other's opinions and listen with a disposition to be convinced to each other's arguments.
>
> And on the other hand, if much the larger of your panel are for a conviction, a dissenting juror should consider whether a doubt in his or her own mind is a reasonable one, which makes no impression upon the minds of so many men or women equally honest, equally intelligent with himself or herself and to have heard the same evidence with the same attention and with an equal desire to arrive at the truth and under the sanction of the same oath.
>
> And on the other hand, if a majority are for acquittal, the minority ought seriously to ask themselves whether they may not reasonably and ought not to doubt the correctness of a judgment, which is not concurred in by most of those with whom they are associated, and distrust the weight or sufficiency of that evidence which fails to carry conviction to the minds of their fellows.
>
> That is given to you as a suggestion of the theory and rationale behind jurors coming to a decision one way or the other. So the Court is going to ask you to retire and continue in your deliberations.

The courts in some states are opposed to the reading of the Allen instruction to a jury. These courts are of the opinion that the jury may interpret the instructions as commanding them to reach a verdict. Yet many courts consider the Allen instruction to be a proper reminder to the jurors of their obligation to attempt to arrive at a just verdict and not allow personal pride, prejudice, or personalities to interfere with their judgment. As was stated by Justice Burger in the case of *Fuiwood* v. *United States:*[3]

> The Allen charge is a carefully balanced method of reminding jurors of their elementary obligations, which they lose sight of during protracted deliberations. It is perfectly valid to remind them that they should give some thought to the views of others and should reconsider their position in light of those views. The charge as given here did not require the jury to reach a verdict but only reminded them of their duty to attempt an accommodation. While it suggests to the minority that they reconsider their position in light of a majority having a different view, it reminds them that they should not acquiesce in a verdict which does not represent their own convictions.

Instead of using the Allen instruction to encourage jurors to arrive at a verdict, the courts of some states have adopted the instruction recommended by the American Bar Association, which is in substance the following:

> It is your duty, as jurors, to consult with one another and to deliberate with a view to reaching an agreement, if you can do so without violence to individual judgment. Each of you must decide the case for yourself, but do so only after an impartial consideration of the evidence with your fellow jurors. In the course of your deliberations, do not hesitate to reexamine your own views and change your opinion if convinced it is erroneous. But do not surrender your honest conviction as to the weight or effect of evidence solely because of the opinion of your fellow jurors, or for the mere purpose of returning a verdict.

Even if the Allen instruction or a similar instruction is read to the jury, they still may be unable to reach a verdict. Some persons may have sincere doubts about the guilt or innocence of a defendant and so will not retract that doubt regardless of the urging of the majority of the jurors. Unfortunately, there are also persons who, for reasons of their own, take a delight in opposing the majority on any issue. When these individuals are on juries, reaching a verdict is next to impossible. As the old story goes, when the judge inquired of a jury foreperson regarding the possibility of reaching a verdict, the foreperson replied that the jury were still attempting to arrive at an agreement but that doing so would take time. The foreperson then suggested that the judge order eleven dinners and one bale of hay in order that they might eat before further deliberations.

Less-than-Unanimous Verdicts

To avoid hung juries caused by one or two jury members, some states have broken with the traditional unanimous verdict rule in criminal trials. Legislation has been passed in these states permitting less-than-unanimous verdicts to be reached in certain criminal cases. All states require that the verdict be unanimous in cases in which the maximum penalty may be death but vary somewhat in the number required to arrive at a verdict. Some states require an eleven-to-one verdict, and some a nine-to-three verdict. The less-than-unanimous verdict has received the sanction of the U.S. Supreme Court in two companion cases decided in 1972.[4] In the

Johnson case, the defendant was convicted of robbery by a nine-to-three verdict in the Criminal District Court of the Parish of Orleans. In the *Apodaca* case, the facts reveal that Robert Apodaca, Henry Morgan Cooper, Jr., and James Arnold Madden were convicted, respectively, of assault with a deadly weapon, burglary in a dwelling, and grand larceny, before separate Oregon juries, all of which returned less-than-unanimous verdicts. The vote in the case of Cooper was ten to two, the minimum requisite vote under Oregon law for sustaining a conviction. Johnson as well as the defendants in the Apodaca case took their convictions to the U.S. Supreme Court on the ground that they had been denied their guarantee of a trial by jury as provided by the Sixth Amendment and made applicable to the states by the Fourteenth Amendment. These defendants contended that permitting the conviction of a less-than-unanimous verdict did not constitute a trial by jury.

Johnson alleged that when a jury rendered such a verdict, the prosecution had failed to prove the defendant guilty beyond a reasonable doubt, thus violating the right to due process of law. The Court did not agree with this contention and stated the following:

> We conclude that as to the nine jurors who voted to convict, the State satisfied its burden of proving guilt beyond a reasonable doubt. The remaining question under the Due Process Clause is whether the vote of three jurors for acquittal can be said to impeach the verdict of the other nine and to demonstrate that guilt was not in fact proved beyond such doubt. We hold that it cannot.
>
> Of course, the State's proof could be regarded as more certain if it had convinced all 12 jurors instead of only nine; it would have been even more compelling if it had been required to convince and had, in fact, convinced 24 or 36 jurors. But the fact remains that nine jurors—a substantial majority of the jury—were convinced by the evidence. In our view disagreement of three jurors does not alone establish reasonable doubt, particularly when such a heavy majority of the jury, after having considered the dissenters' views, remains convinced of guilt. That rational men disagree is not in itself equivalent to a failure of proof by the State, nor does it indicate infidelity to the reasonable doubt standard. Jury verdicts finding guilt beyond a reasonable doubt are regularly sustained even though the evidence was such that the jury would have been justified in having a reasonable doubt; even though the trial judge might not have reached the same conclusion as the jury; and even though appellate judges are closely divided on the issue whether there was sufficient evidence to support a conviction.

In the *Apodaca* decision, the Supreme Court further discusses the reasonable doubt argument as well as upholding the rights of the states to permit a less-than-unanimous verdict and still be within the Due Process Clause. In the *Apodaca* decision, the Court stated the following:

> In *Williams* v. *Florida,* we had occasion to consider a related issue: whether the Sixth Amendment's right to trial by jury requires that all juries consist of 12 men. After considering the history of the 12-man requirement and the functions it performs in contemporary society, we concluded that it was not of constitutional stature. We reach the same conclusion today with regard to the requirement of unanimity.

> Like the requirement that juries consist of 12 men, the requirement of unanimity rose during the Middle Ages and had become an accepted feature of the common-law jury by the 18th century.

Our inquiry must focus upon the function served by the jury in contemporary society. As we said in *Duncan,* the purpose of trial by jury is to prevent oppression by the Government by providing a safeguard against the corrupt or overzealous prosecutor and against the compliant, biased, or eccentric judge. Given this purpose, the essential feature of a jury obviously lies in the interposition between the accused and his accuser of the common sense judgment of a group of laymen. A requirement of unanimity, however, does not materially contribute to the exercise of this common sense judgment. As we said in *Williams,* a jury will come to such a judgment as long as it consists of a group of laymen representative of a cross section of the community who have the duty and the opportunity to deliberate, free from outside attempts at intimidation, on the question of a defendant's guilt. In terms of this function we perceive no difference between juries required to act unanimously and those permitted to convict or acquit by votes of 10 to two or 11 to one. Requiring unanimity would obviously produce hung juries in some situations where nonunanimous juries will convict or acquit. But in either case, the interest of the defendant in having the judgment of his peers interposed between himself and the officers of the State who prosecute and judge him is equally well served.

The defendants in the *Apodaca* case contended, as did Johnson, that a unanimous verdict was necessary in order to comply with the beyond-a-reasonable-doubt requirement for guilt, but the Court stated as follows:

We are quite sure that the Sixth Amendment itself has never been held to require proof beyond a reasonable doubt in criminal cases. The reasonable doubt standard developed separately from both the jury trial and the unanimous verdict. As the Court noted in the *Winship* case, the rule requiring proof of crime beyond a reasonable doubt did not crystallize in this country until after the Constitution was adopted. And in that case, which held such a burden of proof to be constitutionally required, the Court purported to draw no support from the Sixth Amendment.

Defendant's argument that the Sixth Amendment requires jury unanimity in order to give effect to the reasonable doubt standard thus founders on the fact that the Sixth Amendment does not require proof beyond a reasonable doubt at all. The reasonable doubt argument is rooted, in effect, in due process and has been rejected in *Johnson* v. *Louisiana.*

Mr. Justice Powell in his concurring opinion made some comments worthy of noting in upholding the less-than-unanimous verdict. Among other comments, he stated that

. . . There is no reason to believe, on the basis of experience in Oregon or elsewhere, that a unanimous decision of 12 jurors is more likely to serve the high purpose of jury trial, or is entitled to greater respect in the community, than the same decision joined in the 10 members of a jury of 12. The standard of due process assured by the Oregon Constitution provides a sufficient guarantee that the government will not be permitted to impose its judgment on an accused without first meeting the full burden of its prosecutorial duty. . . .

Removal of the unanimity requirement could well minimize the potential for hung juries occasioned either by bribery or juror irrationality. Furthermore, the rule that juries must speak with a single voice often leads, not to full agreement among the 12 but to agreement by none and compromise by all, despite the frequent absence of a rational basis for such compromise. . . .

The petitioners (defendants) contended that their right to a jury comprising a cross section of a community was interfered with by the less-than-unanimous verdict. Their petitions alleged that unless unanimity is required, the viewpoint of a minority of the jurors representing minority groups is excluded from discussion during the deliberation. They also alleged that whether the verdict is conviction or acquittal, it may be the unjust product of racism, bigotry, or an emotionally inflamed trial. To this contention, Mr. Justice Powell stated the following:

> Such fears materialize only when the jury's majority, responding to these extraneous pressures, ignores the evidence and the instructions of the court as well as the rational arguments of the minority. The risk, however, that a jury in a particular case will fail to meet its high responsibility is inherent in any system which commits decisions of guilt or innocence to untrained laymen drawn at random from the community. In part, at least, the majority-verdict rule must rely on the same principle which underlies our historic dedication to jury trial; both systems are premised on the conviction that each juror will faithfully perform his assigned duty. . . . Even before the jury is sworn substantial protection against the selection of a representative but wilfully irresponsible jury is assured by the wide availability of peremptory challenges and challenges for cause. The likelihood of miscarriage of justice is further diminished by the judges' use of full jury instructions, detailing the applicable burdens of proof, informing the jurors of their duty to weigh the views of fellow jurors, and reminding them of the solemn responsibility imposed by their oaths. Trial judges also retain the power to direct acquittals in cases in which the evidence of guilt is lacking, or to set aside verdicts once rendered when the evidence is insufficient to support a conviction. Furthermore, in cases in which public emotion runs high or pretrial publicity threatens a fair trial, judges possess broad power to grant changes of venue, and to impose restrictions on the extent of press coverage.
>
> In light of such protections it is unlikely that the Oregon "ten-of-twelve" rule will account for an increase in the number of cases in which injustice will be occasioned by a biased or prejudiced jury. It may be wise to recall Mr. Justice White's admonition in *Murphy* v. *Waterfront Comm'n,* that the Constitution "protects against real dangers, not remote and speculative possibilities."

Since the U.S. Supreme Court has given sanction to less-than-unanimous verdicts, it is highly possible that other states in the future will adopt this verdict requirement.

It has been argued that there is no sound reason, other than tradition, for the requirement of the unanimous verdict. The origin of the unanimous verdict is unclear. By the latter part of the fourteenth century, the unanimous verdict was required, but it was not the jury verdict as we know it today. As pointed out in the history of the jury trial, in the fourteenth century, convicted persons were often subject to cruel and unusual punishment. It has been alleged that one of the reasons for the unanimous verdict at that time was to avoid such punishment as often as possible. Those who are for the less-than-unanimous verdict allege that since the convicted person is not subjected to cruel and unusual punishment today, there is no need for the unanimous verdict. The less-than-unanimous verdict would also eliminate many hung juries, resulting in fewer retrials and saving court costs.

The arguments of those who oppose the less-than-unanimous verdict are just as strong. It is stated that abolishing the unanimous verdict in order to prevent hung juries is a shallow argument and not sufficient reason for such an action.

Some argue, as did Mr. Justice Douglas in his dissent in the *Johnson* case, that the less-than-unanimous verdict prohibits the minority members of the jury from presenting their arguments, which might prevent a conviction when the minority have a real doubt of guilt. It is also argued that if this verdict is permitted, the next step may be eliminating the presumption of innocence or proving the defendant guilty beyond a reasonable doubt. It should be pointed out that the Bill of Rights says nothing about a specific number of twelve persons being required to compose a jury, a verdict's being unanimous, proving the defendant guilty beyond a reasonable doubt, or presuming innocence. These rights of the accused have been established by tradition but allegedly have a constitutional standard, and any break with this standard will weaken our justice system.

The U.S. Supreme Court, however, in *Burch* v. *Louisiana*,[5] held that the verdict of a jury comprising only six persons must be unanimous for "nonpetty offenses." The court stated that "to hold anything less than a unanimous verdict by a jury of only six persons would be a threat to the constitutional guarantee of a trial by an impartial jury."

REVIEW QUESTIONS

1. What is the purpose of the charge to the jury?
2. List five points of law that a judge may explain to the jury before it goes into deliberation.
3. What is the purpose of the deliberation?
4. What may the jury take with it during the deliberation?
5. Define a hung jury.
6. What is the purpose of the Allen instruction?

LOCAL PROCEDURE

1. In your home state, may the judge comment on the weight of the evidence and the credibility of the witnesses?
2. May the Allen instruction be read to the jury?
3. Must the jury reach a unanimous verdict?
4. May an alternate juror be sequestered with the jury during deliberations?

ENDNOTES

1. *Turner* v. *Louisiana,* 379 U.S. 466 (1965).
2. 164 U.S. 492 (1896).
3. 125 U.S. App. D.C. 183 (1967).
4. *Johnson* v. *Louisiana* 406 U.S. 356 (1972); and *Apodaca* v. *Oregon,* 406 U.S. 404 (1972).
5. 60 L.Ed.2d 96 (1979).

CHAPTER 14

The Verdict and Appeals

In this court dissents have gradually become majority opinions.
—Supreme Court Justice Felix Frankfurter in *Graves* v. *New York*, 360 U.S. 466, 1939

A murder trial is the most solemn proceeding known to the law. . . . Such trials are invariably dignified and deliberate so far as the conduct of the legal side of the case is concerned. No judge, however unqualified for the bench; no prosecutor, however light-minded; no lawyer, however callous, fails to feel the serious nature of the transaction or to be affected strongly by the fact that he is dealing with life and death. A prosecutor who openly laughed or sneered at a prisoner charged with murder would severely injure his case. The Jury, naturally, is overwhelmed with the gravity of the occasion and the responsibility resting upon them.
—New York Prosecutor Arthur Train, 1909

THE VERDICT

Derived from the Latin word *verdictum,* the word *verdict* means "a true declaration." In a court trial, the verdict is the decision of the judge. In a criminal trial, the verdict is the decision of the jury. Once the verdict in a criminal trial has been agreed on, the foreperson will so advise the bailiff, the officer who is in charge of the jury. The bailiff will then inform the judge, who will reconvene court in order that the verdict may be received. Since the deliberation often takes considerable time, the judge usually will adjourn court on the case while the jury are deliberating. This action permits the judge to perform other duties while being available at all times to furnish further instructions or information that the jury may request while deliberating. After the court is reconvened, the judge will instruct the bailiff to return the jury to the courtroom. On their arrival, the judge may request that their names be called to make certain that all the jurors are present. If a juror should be missing, the judge may have to declare a mistrial unless the juror's whereabouts can be determined and his or her presence can be immediately obtained. After all the jurors are accounted for, the judge will ask the foreperson whether the jury have agreed on a verdict. If the foreperson answers in the affirmative, the judge may ask him or her to announce the verdict, or if the verdict is in writing, the judge may request that it be given to the clerk of the court to read. Not all jurisdictions require that the verdict be in writing and signed by the foreperson. Whether required to be in writing or not, most jurisdictions furnish forms to the jury on which they may record their verdict. The defendant must be present at the time the verdict is announced in open court unless his or her whereabouts cannot be determined. In that case, the verdict may be announced in the absence of the accused.

After the verdict is announced, the prosecution or the defense may request that the jurors be polled individually to determine how each voted on the verdict. When the verdict must be unanimous, if one or more jurors allege that the verdict does not express all the jurors' opinions, the judge may instruct the jury to return to the jury room for further deliberation. If the facts should warrant such action, the judge may discharge the jury and declare a mistrial.

If the jury finds the verdict to be not guilty, the defendant is entitled to immediate release if in custody. If the defendant is out on bail, the security will be returned to the person who posted it, since it will have served its purpose. In either event, the defendant is free from further prosecution on the crime charged.

If the defendant is found guilty, the next procedural step is sentencing. A few other matters should be considered before the discussion of the sentencing. The jury may have found the defendant guilty as charged in the accusatory pleading, or the jury may have found the defendant guilty of a lesser degree. It is possible that the jury found the defendant guilty on some of the charges stated in the accusatory pleading and not guilty on others. In addition to finding the defendant guilty, the jury may be called upon to determine whether the defendant was armed at the time that a crime was committed. All these matters may affect the sentence imposed. Once the verdict is announced in open court, it will be recorded in the record of the case. At this point, the jury is entitled to be discharged unless they are involved in the sentencing procedure. If it is a court trial, the judge has the responsibility of rendering the verdict.

Even though the jury returns a verdict of guilty, most jurisdictions permit the judge to modify the verdict. If the judge believes that the evidence shows the defendant was not guilty to the degree that the jury found him or her guilty, the judge may modify the verdict by finding the defendant guilty of a lesser degree or lesser crime included in the criminal act. A few states permit the judge to go one step further. The guilty verdict of a jury may be set aside and a judgment of acquittal entered, or the judge may set aside the verdict and dismiss the charge. In either event, the judge's action in this regard is usually a bar to any further prosecutive action against the defendant. The right of a judge to set aside the entire verdict is very powerful. But such action is permitted on the grounds that if the evidence is insufficient to establish the defendant guilty beyond a reasonable doubt, the judge must set aside the verdict in the interest of justice. However, a judge may not set aside a verdict of not guilty, since this action would deny the defendant the right of a trial by jury.

New Trial and Mistrial

If a judge believes that the prosecution has failed to prove the defendant guilty beyond a reasonable doubt, the judge may enter a judgment of acquittal in some jurisdictions. This action occurs before the case is turned over to the jury for deliberation and takes the case out of their hands. But by permitting the judge to set aside the jury's guilty verdict, the case is taken from the jury after it has fulfilled its function. This action often draws criticism from jurors, since it voids their function. To avoid this criticism, judges will grant a motion for a new trial rather than enter the judgment of acquittal or set aside the verdict.

After a jury has returned a verdict of guilty, the defense may request that a new trial be granted. Generally, a new trial may be granted only on the motion, or request, of the defendant, and not on the judge's own motion. If a new trial is granted, the case will therefore be heard again from the beginning, usually before the same judge but with a new jury. The grounds for granting a new trial are specifically set forth in the codes of most states. These grounds usually include such matters as the jury's receiving evidence of the case out of court; the jurors separating without permission of the court after being sequestered; the verdict's being decided on by lot or by means other than a fair expression of opinion; misconduct of the jurors, preventing the defendant from receiving a fair trial; or a guilty verdict's being returned that was not supported by the evidence. Although it has been stated that a new trial may be granted only on statutory grounds, courts have held that new trials should be granted on nonstatutory grounds when a failure to do so would result in a denial of a fair trial to the defendant. In one case, the judge stated in comments to the jury that, in all his experience as a lawyer and judge, he had never seen so many defense witnesses, including the defendant himself, whose truthfulness was in doubt. Even though the judge informed the jurors that it was their duty to weigh the credibility of the witnesses, he felt that, after a guilty verdict was returned by the jury, a new trial should be granted in the interest of justice. In this way, the judge was correcting his own remarks that bordered on directing the jury to return a verdict of guilty.

One of the more frequent grounds used for granting a new trial is newly discovered evidence by the defense. In order for a defendant to avail oneself of this ground, the defense must be in a position to prove to the satisfaction of the judge that the newly discovered evidence was material and that the evidence could not with due diligent search have been discovered by the time of the first trial. It has been held by some courts that the newly discovered evidence must be of sufficient importance to indicate a probable acquittal in a new trial. This evidence must be more than just a repetition of the evidence presented by the defense during the first trial unless the repetitive evidence would materially strengthen previously presented evidence.

The prosecution has the right to argue against the granting of a new trial. It may endeavor to prove that there was not due diligent search before the first trial to justify a new trial or may argue against other grounds presented by the defense. It is not always necessary for the prosecution to argue against the motion for a new trial. The judge may deny the motion without any argument's being presented.

Granting a new trial is not to be confused with declaring a mistrial. The motion for a new trial may not be made until a verdict of guilty has been rendered. A mistrial may be declared anytime during the trial proceedings, on the judge's own motion or at the request of the defense. The right of the prosecution to request a mistrial is somewhat restricted and not permitted in all jurisdictions. A mistrial may be declared at any time that there is misconduct that is so prejudicial that the defense would be denied a fair trial. The misconduct may occur early in the trial proceedings. For example, if during the opening statement by the prosecuting attorney, he or she should refer to the defendant as an "excon" or otherwise imply a past criminal record, the judge may decide that the remarks were so prejudicial that the defendant could not get a fair trial. The judge may at that time declare a mistrial. If the mistrial is declared at that point in the proceedings, not too much trial time is lost; but if the misconduct comes late in the trial, such as just before deliberation, much time, energy, and money will have been wasted.

Sometimes, rather than declare a mistrial, the judge will instruct the jury to disregard the misconduct and inform them that it is not to affect them in rendering a verdict. This admonition is not always effective, since jurors cannot always erase something that they have heard. If the defendant is convicted, the failure to declare a mistrial may be grounds for reversal on appeal. As stated, a judge may declare a mistrial when the jury cannot agree on a verdict. Defendants have argued that the inability of a jury to agree on a verdict indicates both that the prosecution has not proved the defendant guilty beyond a reasonable doubt and that the defendant is entitled to a judgment of acquittal. This argument has been rejected by the U.S. Supreme Court. The Court has held that the defendant may be retried under these circumstances. The Court stated that it recognizes "society's interest in giving the prosecution one complete opportunity to convict those who have violated its laws."[1] However, before a mistrial may be declared when a jury cannot agree on a verdict, the judge must weigh the situation carefully. Courts have held that if a judge declares a mistrial too quickly when further deliberation would have resulted in a verdict, the defendant has been deprived of the "valued right to have his trial completed by a particular tribunal." But if the judge fails to declare a mistrial when the jury cannot agree on a verdict after lengthy deliberation, there is a risk that a verdict may result from pressure by some jurors on others that would deny the jurors an opportunity for individual expression.

If a mistrial is declared at the request of the defense, generally, the case can be tried again at the discretion of the prosecuting attorney. The retrial is not considered a violation of the double jeopardy guarantee, since the defendant, in requesting a mistrial, waives the guarantee against double jeopardy. However, some jurisdictions hold that unless there is sufficient cause to declare a mistrial or unless the defendant agrees to the mistrial, jeopardy may have set in, and the defendant cannot be retried. If the misconduct prejudicial to the prosecution was committed by defense counsel or by the accused, the prosecution may have little or no remedy.

However, in *Arizona* v. *Washington,* the U.S. Supreme Court did uphold the action of the trial judge in declaring a mistrial at the request of the prosecution when a defense attorney made improper statements to the jury during the opening argument. The trial judge concluded that the remarks were so prejudicial that the prosecution would be denied the right to have the case tried before an impartial jury. The Supreme Court stated that before a trial judge could declare a mistrial over the objections of the defense, it must be established that there was a "manifest necessity" for such action. In other words, there must be sufficient evidence to prove that such action should be taken. The Court stated the following:

> Because of the variety of circumstances that may make it necessary to discharge a jury before a trial is concluded, and because those circumstances do not invariably create unfairness to the accused, his valued right to have the trial concluded by a particular tribunal is sometimes subordinate to the public interest in affording the prosecutor one full and fair opportunity to present his evidence to an im-

partial jury. Yet in view of the importance of the right, and the fact that it is frustrated by any mistrial, the prosecutor must shoulder the burden of justifying the mistrial if he is to avoid the double jeopardy bar. His burden is a heavy one. The prosecutor must demonstrate "manifest necessity" for any mistrial over the objections of the defendant.

Yet in *Carsey* v. *United States*,[2] the U.S. Court of Appeals held that the improper remarks made by the defense attorney to the jury during the closing argument could have been corrected if the judge had instructed the jury to disregard the improper remarks of the defense attorney. The court held that declaring a mistrial was improper and that the defendant had been placed in jeopardy and could not be retried.

In a dissenting opinion in the *Carsey* case, Justice Tamm took the opposite view from that of the majority, stating as follows:

> When appellant's (defendant's) trial counsel, in his closing plea to the jury, advised the jury of two prior mistrials he did it deliberately for the purpose of creating doubt of the defendant's guilt in the minds of the jurors who, understandably, would ask themselves whether a reasonable doubt of guilt had not been established when two prior juries, upon the same evidence, had been unable to reach a verdict. If the prosecutor had made the same statement to the jury for the purpose of injecting into their thinking a fact completely outside of the evidence before them, we would label it as both a "foul blow" and an "improper method calculated to produce a wrongful convictions." I am unwilling and unable to agree that the questioned statement herein was proper when made by defense counsel when it so obviously would have been improper if made by Government counsel. The statement would have been adequate and proper basis for the granting of a mistrial if the prosecutor had made it, and I must conclude that it was proper and adequate for the trial judge's action when it was made by defense counsel. Defense counsel's initial statement created and triggered the factual situation resulting in the mistrial, despite the majority's feeble attempt to transfer the responsibility to the prosecuting attorney.
>
> The majority opinion places a premium on chicanery and invites the defense counsel to engage in it by its "you cannot lose" result. If this opinion is to prevail, defense counsel may resort to trickery in the court room secure in the knowledge that if he gets by with it he will have the benefit of his misconduct, and if he does not a mistrial will be declared and thereby he reaps an even greater reward for his unethical behavior.

The facts of another case reflect that during the trial recess, the defendant, who was out on bail, approached a drinking fountain in the courthouse hall and drew a cup of water and handed it to one of the women jurors, at the same time carrying on a conversation with her. Thereafter, the defendant proceeded to give other members of the jury drinks of water. This conduct was observed by an officer, who informed the judge. After court reconvened, the judge questioned the officer on the stand about the incident, and the judge declared a mistrial. The defense attorney endeavored to place the defendant on the stand to prove that no conversation pertaining to the facts of the case took place. The defense attorney also tried to accept the blame for the misconduct of the defendant by stating that he had failed to admonish the defendant against having any contact with the jury. The judge's opinion was that the defendant was endeavoring to make a favorable impression on the jury, and a mistrial was declared. In addition, the defendant was held in contempt of court. On retrial, the defendant entered a plea of once in jeopardy that the judge refused to accept, and the defendant was found guilty on the original charge of attempted robbery. The defendant appealed the conviction on the grounds that the guarantee against double jeopardy had been violated by the retrial. The appellate court agreed with the defendant. The court stated the following:

> Once a jury has been impaneled and sworn to try a defendant, jeopardy attaches, and its subsequent discharge when not authorized by law or by defendant's consent, is equivalent to an acquittal and constitutes former jeopardy barring retrial.
>
> As to what constitutes sufficient cause to authorize the discharge of a jury, the courts have required a showing that there exists some legal necessity resulting from physical causes beyond the control of the court.
>
> The determination as to whether the required legal necessity exists is a matter left to the discretion of the trial court. However, "the power of the Court to discharge a jury without the consent of the prisoner is not an absolute, uncontrolled discretionary power. It must be exercised in accordance with established legal rules and a sound legal discretion in the application of such rules to the facts and circumstances of each particular case, and in this State is subject to review by an appellate court."
>
> The trial court's action in summarily declaring a mistrial solely on the basis of the officer's testimony that he had observed defendant talking with two of the jurors during the recess on their way back to the court room from the water cooler was unjustified and constituted an abuse of discretion. Before the matter was ruled on defendant should have been given a reasonable opportunity to present his version of the incident and with proper participation by his counsel.[3]

This decision has been criticized by many legal scholars on the basis that the judge did have sufficient cause to declare a mistrial. It is alleged that the misconduct by the defendant in contacts with the jury could not help creating some favorable impression to the detriment of the prosecution. It is further alleged that if a material witness for the prosecution had made this contact with the jury, the judge undoubtedly would have declared a mistrial, since the defendant could not have received a fair trial from an impartial jury.

Arrest of Judgment and Pronouncement of Judgment

If a new trial is not granted after the verdict is rendered, the next procedure is the pronouncement of judgment by the judge. Pronouncement of judgment is usually thought of as the oral sentencing of the defendant by the judge. But technically, pronouncement of judgment entails more than the oral statement of what the sentence will be. The pronouncement of judgment will be reduced to a written document generally known as the judgment. This judgment will set forth the plea entered, the verdict, and if guilty, will reflect the sentence or other disposition of the case—all of which are entered in the case record. Technically, the pronouncement of judgment is made whether there is an acquittal or a conviction, but in many jurisdictions, it is synonymous with the pronouncement of the sentence. In misdemeanor cases, most jurisdictions permit the pronouncement of judgment in the absence of the defendant. In a felony conviction, the presence of the defendant is required unless the accused cannot be located after due diligent search; in this case, pronouncement of judgment may be made in his or her absence.

Jurisdictions vary somewhat in the time within which the pronouncement of judgment must take place after a guilty plea is entered or a guilty verdict is returned. In misdemeanor convictions in some jurisdictions, the pronouncement may be made immediately; if not, it must be pronounced within a few days. Other jurisdictions provide that the pronouncement of judgment may not occur in fewer than six hours and not more than five days. The six-hour limit allows time for the convicted defendant to arrange personal affairs before serving time. In felony convictions, there is usually a considerable delay permitted in the pronouncement of judgment. The delay permits time for a presentence investigation, conducted in order that a more equitable sentence may be imposed. The delay is usually not longer than one month. It is to the advantage of both society and the convicted defendant to have sentence pronounced without unnecessary delay. The defendant is entitled to know the sentence as soon as possible in order that the term may begin. As for society's interest, there is little comfort in having a felon free on bail who may be in a position to commit other crimes while awaiting the pronouncement of sentence.

Prior to the pronouncement of judgment, the defendant may file a motion in the arrest of judgment, or in most jurisdictions, the judge may enter the motion. In many jurisdictions, the law provides that at the time the convicted defendant is brought before the judge for pronouncement of judgment, the judge must inquire of the defendant, "Is there any legal reason why judgment should not be pronounced?" It is at this time that the defendant will show legal cause for the arrest of judgment. Some jurisdictions hold that making the inquiry of the defendant is a useless procedure, and the defendant is entitled to make a motion at any time after the verdict is rendered.

The motion for the arrest of judgment is made on statutory grounds. These grounds include such matters as present insanity of the defendant. If it is determined that the defendant is insane at the time of the pronouncement of judgment, it must be postponed until sanity has been restored, since a defendant may not be sentenced while insane. The motion may be on the grounds that there was some defect in the accusatory pleading that had not been successfully challenged previously, such as the failure to state that a crime had been committed. If the motion for arrest of judgment is denied or none is entered, the next procedure is the pronouncement of the sentence. In most jurisdictions, before the sentence is pronounced, the defendant is entitled to make a statement in his or her own behalf. This statement is generally a plea for leniency or consideration in the sentencing. If a judge fails to grant the defendant an opportunity to make a statement, the sentence may be set aside on appeal. The case does not have to be retried under the circumstances, but the sentence will be set aside and the case will be sent back to the trial court for resentencing after the defendant has been given an opportunity to speak. After the defendant has made a plea, if any, to the judge or jury, he or she will be sentenced. Before entering into the sentencing procedure, the appeals that may be taken by the defendant or the prosecution should be discussed. The outcome of the appeal could determine whether a defendant serves a sentence.

APPEALS

Appeal by the Defendant

If convicted, a defendant will usually appeal the conviction to the appropriate appellate court if there is any basis at all for the appeal. The defendant's appeal may be well founded, since some error may have been committed during the trial that was prejudicial. Or the defendant may attempt to appeal the case merely to delay serving the imposed sentence.

Freedom Pending Appeal.   Generally, the defendant must file a notice of appeal within a few days after the pronouncement of judgment. Whether the defendant remains free on bail pending the outcome of appeal is largely within the discretion of the judge. There is no inherent right to remain free from custody once convicted, since the presumption of innocence is lost. In determining whether a defendant should be free pending the appeal, the judge may consider whether the efforts to appeal were based on frivolous grounds; whether the appeal was merely a delaying tactic to avoid serving the sentence; whether there may be a temptation to flee the jurisdiction of the court pending the appeal; or whether the defendant may be a threat to the community if free on bail.

Whether the defendant remains free on bail or is incarcerated, the judge in most instances will have sentenced the defendant. If remaining free on bail, no time will be served until the outcome of the appeal is determined. If the conviction is reversed, the defendant will not have served any time. But if the defendant is incarcerated pending the appeal, the sentence will have begun to be served. If the conviction is reversed and the defendant is not retried or cannot be retried, little can be done to compensate for the time spent other than to clear the name of the accused. But if the conviction is affirmed or if the defendant is retried after a reversal, credit will be given for the time spent in incarceration pending the appeal. Not all appeals are made immediately after a conviction. An appeal may not be taken until several years of a sentence have been served. These appeals are usually based on the result of some U.S. Supreme Court decision that changes the justice procedure in some manner and is made retroactive; that is, the decision is applicable to all convictions irrespective of when the case was tried. If the decision is not made retroactive, it is applicable only to those defendants whose cases have not been decided previous to the U.S. Supreme Court's decision.

Not all efforts by a defendant to appeal a conviction to an appellate court are successful. Sufficient grounds must be alleged in order for the appellate court to hear the appeal. The grounds on which a defendant may appeal a case are numerous. Whatever grounds are alleged, it must be shown that the error committed during the trial was sufficiently prejudicial that the defendant was denied a fair trial or that there was a miscarriage of justice. Some of the grounds most frequently alleged on appeal are as follows: There was insufficient probable cause to make a lawful arrest; a confession that was improperly obtained was admitted as evidence; physical evidence was introduced that was unlawfully seized; a failure was made to grant a change of venue; there was insufficient representation of competent counsel; a failure to give pertinent instructions to the jury existed; a denial of a new trial was made; or there was a failure to declare a mistrial when there was prejudicial misconduct.

Method of Appeal.   Upon appealing the case, the defendant, through counsel or on his or her own, will submit to the appropriate appellate court a brief that sets forth the alleged error committed during the trial with citations of appellate court decisions upholding the contended error. A transcript of the trial proceedings will accompany the brief. The prosecution will submit a brief in an effort to show why the conviction should be affirmed and not reversed. The appellate court will review the briefs and the transcript. After doing so, it may conclude that there is no ground for appeal, and the court will deny a hearing on the matter. A hearing date will be set if the appellate court feels that the appeal is worthy of a hearing. At the hearing, the defense attorney and the prosecution's representative, usually the state attorney general, assisted by the prosecuting attorney who was responsible for the conviction, will be present to argue their sides of the case. The defendant is usually not present, since it is not an inherent right to be present at an appeal hearing. After the hearing, the appellate court justices will consider the matter and conclude whether the conviction should be affirmed or reversed. In making its determination, the appellate court will consider whether there was error or conduct that was so prejudicial that the defendant was denied a fair trial. Sometimes the appellate court will hold that there was error or misconduct during the trial but that this was not serious enough to deny the defendant a fair trial. Under these circumstances, the error is referred to as "harmless error."

If the appellate court denies the defendant a hearing on the appeal, there is little the defendant can do about the decision. The appellate court may be called the court of "last resort"; its decision is usually final unless the defendant can prove that one of the constitutional guarantees was violated, and then the defendant may eventually appeal to the U.S. Supreme Court. The Supreme Court may or may not grant a hearing, depending upon the validity of the alleged violation. It may grant a hearing in an effort to determine whether there was a violation; if there was, the Supreme Court will reverse the conviction. If the Supreme Court denies the hearing or affirms the conviction, no further appeal can be taken by the defendant.

Retrial after Reversal.   If a conviction is reversed by either the state appellate court or the U.S. Supreme Court, the states differ on whether the defendant may be retried. If the reversal is based on the fact that a law is unconstitutional, that jeopardy had attached, or that a law is too vague in wording to indicate the violation, there cannot be a retrial. But if the reversal is based on the introduction of illegally seized evidence or an improperly obtained confession, in many states, the defendant may be retried, and the improperly introduced evidence will not be admissible during the retrial. The prosecuting attorney has to determine whether the other evidence was sufficient in obtaining a conviction. If not, the charge will undoubtedly be dismissed. A few states do not permit a retrial on reversal of a conviction, since it would be a violation of the guarantee against double jeopardy. Other states hold that on appealing a conviction, the defendant waives the double jeopardy guarantee. If a defendant is successful in getting a conviction reversed on appeal and is retried and convicted, may the judge impose an increased sentence after the new trial? This question was answered by the U.S. Supreme Court in the case of *North Carolina* v. *Pearce*.[4] The Court in that decision held that if identifiable misconduct by the defendant took place after the first trial, the judge might impose an increased sentence, but the increase should not be based on the fact that the defendant has appealed his or her case. The Court stated the following:

Due process of law requires that vindictiveness against a defendant for having successfully attacked his first conviction must play no part in the sentence he receives after a new trial. And since the fear of such vindictiveness may unconstitutionally deter a defendant's exercise of the right to appeal or collaterally attack his first conviction, due process also requires that a defendant be freed of apprehension of such a retaliatory motivation on the part of the sentencing judge.

In order to assure the absence of such a motivation, we have concluded that whenever a judge imposes a more severe sentence upon a defendant after a new trial, the reasons for his doing so must affirmatively appear. Those reasons must be based upon objective information concerning identifiable conduct on the part of the defendant occurring after the time of the original sentencing proceedings. And the factual data upon which the increased sentence is based must be made part of the record, so that the constitutional legitimacy of the increased sentence may be fully reviewed on appeal.

Justice White, who concurred in part with the majority opinion, stated that in his opinion, he would "authorize an increased sentence on retrial based on any objective, identifiable factual data not known to the trial judge at the time of the original sentencing proceeding." Only future decisions will tell whether the Court would sanction this reason for an increased sentence, rather than the majority's limited reason of "identifiable conduct" by the defendant after the original sentence. The Court did conclude that on an increased sentence after a new trial, the defendant must be given credit for the time served on the original sentence.

Appeal by Prosecution

States vary considerably concerning the prosecution's right of appeal. A few states deny the prosecution any right to appeal, since it would result in a violation of the guarantee against double jeopardy. Some permit a limited right of appeal by the prosecution when the appeal does not involve the double jeopardy guarantee. Generally, an appeal may be taken by the prosecution on a judge's order setting aside or dismissing an accusatory pleading. But the appeal may be taken only when the setting aside or dismissal was before the trial began; otherwise, jeopardy will have set in. An appeal may also be taken on a grant of a new trial, an arrest of judgment, or a modification of a verdict or punishment imposed. In most states, there is no right by the prosecution to appeal a case when an acquittal verdict has been rendered. As stated in *Washington* v. *Arizona,* a judgment of acquittal is final regardless of how erroneously it may have been arrived at. However, a few states do allow an appeal by the prosecution after a verdict of acquittal has been returned. The appeal is followed when the prosecution alleges that a serious error was made by the judge on a ruling of law or procedure. The appeal is permitted so that guidelines may be established for future cases, but the appellate court has no authority to reverse the acquittal.

An increasing number of states allow the prosecution to appeal a judge's order suppressing evidence. It is generally held that where such an appeal is permissible, the appeal may be taken only on an order suppressing evidence that was made before the trial began and may not be taken during the trial. Some states do not permit an appeal of an order suppressing evidence that was made even before the trial. The courts of these states hold that the prosecution is no more disadvantaged by an erroneous ruling before the trial than one during the trial when such ruling leads to an acquittal.

Appeal Involving a Guilty Plea

As we previously discussed, since a plea of guilty is equal to a conviction, this fact must be explained to the defendant before the plea may be accepted. Therefore, it is paradoxical to permit a defendant to appeal a conviction resulting from a voluntary plea of guilty, but some states do permit a defendant to appeal a guilty plea. The grounds for the appeal are based upon some alleged constitutional, jurisdictional, or other grounds concerning the legality of the proceedings. For example, the defendant may allege that the judge failed to explain the significance of the guilty plea as required by *Boykin* v. *Alabama,* that the judge denied the defendant the right to withdraw the guilty plea, or that there was a violation of the agreement pertaining to the plea bargain. There have been times when a defendant was denied a request for suppression of evidence and thereafter entered a plea of guilty, knowing that the trial would result in conviction. Under these circumstances, the defendant may appeal the guilty plea in an effort to determine whether the evidence should have been suppressed.

APPELLATE COURT CITATIONS

Judges of the appellate courts are generally referred to as justices. The number of justices composing an appellate court varies from one state to another as well as from one appellate court to another. Many states have only a single appellate court, which is generally referred to as the Supreme Court. Other states have a bilateral appellate court system in which there is an appellate court and a supreme court. Usually only three justices will compose an appellate court, whereas the supreme court varies usually from five to nine justices. Not all justices must agree on the decision, only a majority. Once the decision is made, one of the justices agreeing with the majority will put the decision in writing, stating whether the conviction was upheld or reversed, and the reasoning behind the decision. A dissenting justice, if any, may or may not decide to write a dissenting opinion, setting forth the reasons for disagreement with the majority.

Recording Court Decisions

The decisions handed down by the appellate courts are recorded in official publications so that they may act as guidelines for future cases. Each decision is given a citation number in order that the decision may be filed, indexed, and located by attorneys, judges, and others having occasion to refer to a particular decision. The citation will include the name, or title, of the case; the name of the official record book; the volume and page number; and the year in which the decision was handed down by the appellate court.

The following is a typical example of an appellate court citation: *State* v. *Tison,* 142 Ariz. 446 (1999). *State* v. *Tison* is the title of the decision; 142 refers to the volume number of the official record; Ariz. is an abbreviation for the state of Arizona, indicating that the decision is that of the Arizona Supreme Court; 446 is the page number where the decision begins; 1999 is the date or year in which the decision was handed down by the Arizona Supreme Court. Sometimes the date will precede the volume and page number. The way that the titles of the decisions refer to persons involved varies among the states. Instead of the title being *State* v. *Tison,* the title may be *Tison* v. *State,* depending on the manner in which the appeal was taken. In some states, the word *People* or *Commonwealth* is substituted for *State.*

In addition to the appellate decision's being published in official publications, the decisions, particularly those of the Supreme Court, are included in the publications of private companies. A different citation is reflected for these publications. In order that a particular decision may be more readily located by a judge or an attorney, both the official citation and the citation of private companies are included when a case decision is referred to. For example, the West Publishing Company, St. Paul, Minnesota, publishes the decisions of the supreme courts of the various states. These decisions are reported by geographic areas. This reporting system is known as the National Reporter System. The supreme court decisions of the states of Iowa, Michigan, Minnesota, Nebraska, North Dakota, South Dakota, and Wisconsin are published in the *North Western Reporter,* and the citation carries the abbreviation of NW. Returning to the case of *State* v. *Tison,* 142 Ariz. 446, there may be the additional citation of 690 P.2d 747 (1999). The P. indicates that the decision can be located in the *Pacific Reporter* of the National Reporter System. The 2d indicates the second series of the *Pacific Reporter* volumes. The supreme court decisions of the states of Connecticut, Delaware, Maine, Maryland, New Hampshire, New Jersey, Pennsylvania, Rhode Island, and Vermont are published in the *Atlantic Reporter,* abbreviated as A. The supreme court decisions of the states of Illinois, Indiana, Massachusetts, New York, and Ohio are published in the *North Eastern Reporter.* The decisions of the supreme courts of the states of Alaska, Arizona, California, Colorado, Hawaii, Idaho, Kansas, Montana, Nevada, New Mexico, Oklahoma, Oregon, Utah, Washington, and Wyoming are published in the *Pacific Reporter.* The *South Eastern Reporter* includes the supreme court decisions of the states of Georgia, South Carolina, Virginia, and West Virginia. The *Southern Reporter* publishes the decisions of the supreme courts of the states of Alabama, Florida, Louisiana, and Mississippi. The *South Western Reporter* publishes the decisions of the supreme courts of the states of Arkansas, Missouri, Kentucky, Tennessee, and Texas. If a decision is handed down by the U.S. Supreme Court on an alleged violation of a constitutional guarantee, the following is an example of the official citation that would be used: *Batson* v. *Kentucky,* 476 U.S. 79 (1986). The U.S. Supreme Court decisions are also published by the West Publishing Company in a publication known as the *Supreme Court Reporter,* abbreviated as S.Ct. The Batson decision would be cited as 106 S.Ct. 1712. The Lawyers Cooperative Publishing Company also publishes the U.S. Supreme Court decisions in a publication known as the *Supreme Court Reporter* Lawyer's Edition, abbreviated as L.Ed. Thus the Batson decision may be cited as 90 L.Ed.2d 69. Or a decision may carry all three citations as follows: *Batson* v. *Kentucky,* 476 U.S. 79, 106 S.Ct. 1712, 90 L.Ed.2d 69 (1986).

In those states in which there is an appellate court below the supreme court, the decisions of these appellate courts are also published in an official publication. These decisions can usually be distinguished from the decisions of the supreme court by the abbreviation App. appearing after the abbreviation of the state.

Capstone Case

United States v. *Scott*
437 U.S. 82, 98 S.Ct. 2187, 57 L.Ed.2d 65 (1978)

Justice Rehnquist delivered the opinion of the Court.

On March 5, 1975, respondent, a member of the police force in Muskegon, Mich., was charged . . . with distribution of various narcotics. Both before his trial in the United States District Court and twice during the trial, respondent moved to dismiss the two counts of the indictment which concerned transactions that took place during the preceding September, on the ground that his defense had been prejudiced by preindictment delay. At the close of all the evidence, the court granted respondent's motion. . . .

The Government sought to appeal the dismissals of the first two Counts to the United States Court of Appeals for the Sixth Circuit. That court, relying on our opinion in *United States* v. *Jenkins,* 420 U.S. 358 (1975), concluded that any further prosecution of respondent was barred by the Double Jeopardy Clause of the Fifth Amendment, and therefore dismissed the appeal. . . . We granted certiorari to give further consideration to the applicability of the Double Jeopardy Clause to Government appeals from orders granting defense motions to terminate a trial before verdict. We now reverse. . . .

A detailed canvass of the history of the double jeopardy principles in *United States* v. *Wilson,* 420 U.S. 332 (1975), led us to conclude that the Double Jeopardy Clause was primarily "directed at the threat of multiple prosecutions," and posed no bar to Government appeals "where those appeals would not require a new trial." We accordingly held in Jenkins, that, whether or not a dismissal of an indictment after jeopardy had attached amounted to an acquittal on the merits, the Government had no right to appeal, because "further proceedings of some sort, devoted to the resolution of factual issues going to the elements of the offense charged, would have been required upon reversal and remand." If Jenkins is a correct statement of the law, the judgment of the Court of Appeals would in all likelihood have to be affirmed. Yet, though our assessment of the history and meaning of the Double Jeopardy Clause in *Wilson, Jenkins, and Serfass* v. *United States,* 420 U.S. 377 (1975), occurred only three Terms ago, our vastly increased exposure to the various facets of the Double Jeopardy Clause has now convinced us that Jenkins was wrongly decided. It placed an unwarrantedly great emphasis on the defendant's right to have his guilt decided by the first jury empaneled to try him so as to include those cases where the defendant himself seeks to terminate the trial before verdict on grounds unrelated to factual guilt or innocence. We have therefore decided to overrule Jenkins, and thus to reverse the judgment of the Court of Appeals in this case.

. . . At the time the Fifth Amendment was adopted, its principles were easily applied, since most criminal prosecutions proceeded to final judgment, and neither the United States nor the defendant had any right to appeal an adverse verdict. The verdict in such a case was unquestionably final, and could be raised as a bar against any further prosecution for the same offense.

It was not until 1889 that Congress permitted criminal defendants to seek a writ of error in this Court, and then only in capital cases. Only then did it become necessary for this Court to deal with the issues presented by the challenge of verdicts on appeal. And, in the very first case presenting the issues, *Ball* v. *United States,* 163 U.S. 662 (1896), the Court established principles that have been adhered to ever since. Three persons had been tried together for murder: two were convicted, the other acquitted. This Court reversed the convictions, finding the indictment fatally defective, whereupon all three defendants were tried again. This time all three were convicted and they again sought review here. This Court held that the Double Jeopardy Clause precluded further prosecution of the defendant who had been acquitted at the original trial but that it posed no such bar to the prosecution of those defendants who had been convicted in the earlier proceeding.

. . . These then, at least, are two venerable principles of double jeopardy jurisprudence. The successful appeal of a judgment of conviction, on any ground other than the insufficiency of the evidence to support the verdict, *Burks* v. *United States,* poses no bar to further prosecution on the same charge. A judgment of acquittal, whether based on a jury verdict of not guilty or on a ruling by the court that the evidence is insufficient to convict, may not be appealed and terminates the prosecution when a second trial would be necessitated by a reversal. What may seem superficially to be a disparity in rules governing a defendant's liability to be tried again is explainable by reference to the underlying purposes of the Double Jeopardy Clause. . . . The law attaches particular significance to an acquittal. To permit a second trial after an acquittal, however mistaken the acquittal may have been, would present an unacceptably high risk that the Government, with its vastly superior resources, might wear down the defendant so that even though innocent, he may be found guilty. (*Green* v. *United States,* 355 U.S. 184, 1957). On the other hand, to require a criminal defendant to stand trial again after he has successfully invoked a statutory right of appeal to upset his first conviction is not an act of governmental oppression of the sort against which the Double Jeopardy Clause was intended to protect. . . .

Although the primary purpose of the Double Jeopardy Clause was to protect the integrity of a final judgment, this Court has also developed a body of law guarding the separate but related interest of a defendant in avoiding multiple prosecutions even where no final determination of guilt or innocence has been made. Such interests may be involved in two different situations: the first, in which the trial judge declares a mistrial; the second, in which the trial judge terminates the proceedings favorably to the defendant on a basis not related to factual guilt or innocence. . . .

We turn now to the relationship between the Double Jeopardy Clause and reprosecution of a defendant who has successfully obtained not a mistrial, but a termination of the trial in his favor before any determination of factual guilt or innocence. Unlike the typical mistrial, the granting of a motion such as this obviously contemplates that the proceedings will terminate then and there in favor of the defendant. The prosecution, if it wishes to reinstate the proceedings in the face of such a ruling, ordinarily must seek reversal of the decision of the trial court. . . .

It is quite true that the Government with all its resources and power should not be allowed to make repeated attempts to convict an individual for an alleged offense. This truth is expressed in the three common-law pleas of autrefois acquit, autrefois convict and pardon, which lie at the core of the area protected by the Double Jeopardy Clause. As we have recognized in cases from *Ball* to *Sanabria* v. *United States,* 437 U.S. 54 (1978), a defendant once acquitted may not be again subjected to trial without violating the Double Jeopardy Clause.

But that situation is obviously a far cry from the present case, where the Government was quite willing to continue with its production of evidence to show the defendant guilty before the jury first empaneled to try him, but the defendant elected to seek termination of the trial on grounds unrelated to guilt or innocence. This is scarcely a picture of an all-powerful state relentlessly pursuing a defendant who had either been found not guilty or who had at least insisted on having the issue of guilt submitted to the first trier of fact. It is instead a picture of a defendant who chooses to avoid conviction and imprisonment, not because of his assertion that the Government has failed to make out a case against him, but because of a legal claim that the Government's case against him must fail even though it might satisfy the trier of fact that he was guilty beyond a reasonable doubt.

We have previously noted that "the trial judge's characterization of his own action cannot control the classification of the action." . . . [A defendant is acquitted only when "the ruling of the judge," whatever its label, actually represents a resolution in the defendant's favor, correct or not, of some or all of the factual elements of the offense charged. Where the court, before the jury returns a verdict, enters a judgment of acquittal pursuant to Fed. Rule Crim. Proc. 29, appeal will be barred only when "it is plain that the District Court . . . evaluated the Government's evidence and determined that it was legally insufficient to support a conviction." *United States* v. *Martin Linen Supply Company*, 430 U.S. 564 (1977).

Our opinion in Burks necessarily holds that there has been a "failure of proof" requiring an acquittal when the Government does not submit sufficient evidence to rebut a defendant's essentially factual defense of insanity, though it may otherwise be entitled to have its case submitted to the jury. The defense of insanity, like the defense of entrapment, arises from "the notion that Congress could not have intended criminal punishment for a defendant who has committed all the elements of a proscribed offense," *United States* v. *Russell,* where other facts established to the satisfaction of the trier of fact provide a legally adequate justification for otherwise criminal acts. Such a factual finding does "necessarily establish the criminal defendant's lack of criminal culpability," post (Brennan, J., dissenting), under the existing law; the fact that "the acquittal may result from erroneous evidentiary rulings or erroneous interpretations of governing legal principles," ibid., affects the accuracy of that determination, but it does not alter its essential character. By contrast, the dismissal of an indictment for preindictment delay represents a legal judgment that a defendant, although criminally culpable, may not be punished because of a supposed constitutional violation. . . .

[I]n the present case, [defendant] successfully avoided a submission of [a part] of the indictment [to the jury] by persuading the trial court to dismiss it on a basis which did not depend on guilt or innocence. He was thus neither acquitted nor convicted, because he himself successfully undertook to persuade the trial court not to submit the issue of guilt or innocence to the jury which had been empaneled to try him. . . . [Defendant] has not been "deprived" of his valued right to go to the first jury; only the public has been deprived of its valued right to "one complete opportunity to convict those who have violated its laws." *Arizona* v. *Washington*. No interest protected by the Double Jeopardy Clause is invaded when the Government is allowed to appeal and seek reversal of such a mid-trial termination of the proceedings in a manner favorable to the defendant.

Justice Brennan, with whom Justice White, Justice Marshall, and Justice Stevens join, dissenting.

. . . While the Double Jeopardy Clause often has the effect of protecting the accused's interest in the finality of particular favorable determinations, this is not its objective. For the Clause often permits Government appeals from final judgments favorable to the accused. See *United States* v. *Wilson* (whether or not final judgment was an acquittal, Government may appeal if reversal would not necessitate a retrial). The purpose of the

Clause, which the Court today fails sufficiently to appreciate, is to protect the accused against the agony and risks attendant upon undergoing more than one criminal trial for any single offense. . . . Society's "willingness to limit the Government to a single criminal proceeding to vindicate its very vital interest in enforcement of criminal laws" bespeaks society's recognition of the gross unfairness of requiring the accused to undergo the strain and agony of more than one trial for any single offense. *United States* v. *Jorn,* 400 U.S. 470 (1971). Accordingly, the policies of the Double Jeopardy Clause mandate that the Government be afforded but one complete opportunity to convict an accused and that when the first proceeding terminates in a final judgment favorable to the defendant any retrial be barred. The rule as to acquittals can only be understood as simply an application of this larger principle.

Judgments of acquittal normally result from jury or bench verdicts of not guilty. In such cases, the acquittal represents the factfinder's conclusion that, under the controlling legal principles, the evidence does not establish that the defendant can be convicted of the offense charged in the indictment. But the judgment does not necessarily establish the criminal defendant's lack of criminal culpability; the acquittal may result from erroneous evidentiary rulings or erroneous interpretations of governing legal principles induced by the defense. Yet the Double Jeopardy Clause bars a second trial. . . . The reason is not that the first trial established the defendant's factual innocence, but rather that the second trial would present all the untoward consequences the Clause was designed to prevent. Government would be allowed to seek to persuade a second trier of fact of the defendant's guilt, to strengthen any weaknesses in its first presentation, and to subject the defendant to the expense and anxiety of a second trial.

The whole premise for today's . . . decision . . . is the Court's new theory that a criminal defendant who seeks to avoid conviction on a "ground unrelated to factual innocence" somehow stands on a different constitutional footing than a defendant whose participation in his criminal trial creates a situation in which a judgment of acquittal has to be entered. This premise is simply untenable. . . . [T]he reasons that bar a retrial following an acquittal are equally applicable to a final judgment entered on a ground "Unrelated to factual innocence." The heavy personal strain of the second trial is the same in either case. So too is the risk that, though innocent, the defendant may be found guilty at a second trial. If the appeal is allowed in either situation, the Government will, following any reversal, not only obtain the benefit of the favorable appellate ruling but also be permitted to shore up any other weak points of its case and obtain all the other advantages at the second trial that the Double Jeopardy Clause was designed to forbid.

Moreover, the Government's interest in retrying a defendant simply cannot vary depending on the ground of the final termination in the accused's favor. I reject as plainly erroneous the Court's suggestion that final judgments not based on innocence deprive the public of "its valued right to one complete opportunity to convict those who have violated its laws," quoting *Arizona* v. *Washington,* and therefore differ from "true acquittals." The Government has the same "complete opportunity" in either situation by virtue of its participation as an adversary at the criminal trial.

Equally significant, the distinction between the two is at best purely formal. Many acquittals are the consequence of rulings of law made on the accused's motion that are not related to the question of his factual guilt or innocence: e.g., a ruling on the law respecting the scope of the offense or excluding reliable evidence. . . .

. . . A critical feature of today's holding appears to be the Court's definition of acquittal as "a resolution [in the defendant's favor], correct or not, of some or all of the factual elements of the offense charged." . . . The language quoted from Martin Linen Supply Co. was tied to the particular issue in that case and was never intended to serve as an all encompassing definition of acquittal for all purposes. Rather, Martin Linen Supply referred generally to "acquittal" as "a legal determination on the basis of facts adduced at trial relating to the general issue of the case," and this is the accepted definition.

This . . . traditional definition of "acquittal" obviously is responsive to the values protected by the Double Jeopardy Clause. . . .

REVIEW QUESTIONS

1. What is a verdict?
2. Where is the verdict announced?
3. Must the defendant be present when the verdict is announced?
4. In what way are a mistrial and a new trial alike? In what way do they differ?
5. What is meant by an arrest of judgment?
6. What does the term pronouncement of judgment mean?
7. List three grounds on which the defendant may appeal a conviction.
8. Why is the prosecution limited in its right to appeal a verdict of acquittal in most jurisdictions?
9. What is the purpose of an appellate citation?
10. Explain the meaning of the following citation: *Batson* v. *Kentucky*, 476 U.S. 79 (1986).

LOCAL PROCEDURE

1. In your home state, may the prosecution appeal a verdict of acquittal?
2. If an appellate court reverses a conviction, may the defendant be retried?

ENDNOTES

1. *Arizona* v. *Washington*, 54 L.Ed. 2d 717 (1978).
2. 392 F. 2d (1967).
3. *People* v. *Huff*, 63 Cal.Rptr. 317 (1967).
4. 397 U.S. 711 (1969).

CHAPTER 15

Sentencing

You have so many options when you sentence. You can put a defendant on probation, order him to be put on work-release and go to a half-way house, or send him to an institution. But what it comes right down to is that there is no alternative that's any good. I guess you could call it a judge's dilemma.

—Charles Halleck, Judge, Superior Court of the District of Columbia

HISTORY OF PUNISHMENT

In order to more fully understand the history of punishment and its severity, we begin by discussing early societies. The social world of early mankind comprised separate isolated groups, referred to as clans. These clans were an aggregate of families. Each family was a unit within the clan. The eldest male was the ruler in these ancient societies. If harm was done to some member of the clan by another member of the clan, it was the ruler's responsibility to right the wrong. If he was unable to right the wrong, other clan members were pressed into service for assistance. If the wrong was committed by a neighboring clan member, it was a religious duty of each wronged clan member to avenge the wrong. The belief was that an injury to any clan member was an injury to the entire clan. This philosophy of revenge usually ended with the clan's waging war on the offender. If the offender could not be located, the revenge could be inflicted on any other member of the neighboring clan.

The Blood Feud

As time passed, avenging the wrong became more of a family responsibility. The offended family member had the first and foremost responsibility to avenge the wrong. If the victim should be killed by the offender or die before the crime had been avenged, other family members had the responsibility to avenge the wrong. Again, if the offender could not be located, then the revenge would be inflicted on other family members. This procedure resulted in what was known as the blood feud. Retaliation during a blood feud was often brutal and usually ended in the death of the offender.

In ancient days when the vengeance took the form of the blood feud, there was little that the offender could do to escape. Even the members of the offender's own family would provide little protection, since they would become the victims of the blood feud if the offender were not found. When time passed without a crime's being avenged, family members often became disenchanted with carrying on the blood feud, particularly when they were not personally offended. Consequently, members of the offended family became willing to accept money or property in return for not inflicting physical retaliation on the offender or on his or her relations. This procedure became known as atonement. By the twelfth century, atonement had grown in popularity, and the blood feud had been all but abolished. In the beginning, atonement was primarily a family affair. But as families and clans were taken over by kingdoms, atonement was a source of revenue for kings or the church, depending on the crime. By this time, the church had begun to take a dominant part in the affairs of mankind and thus sought sources of revenue. Not all crimes could be atoned for, so the offender was required to stand trial. Trial could be by ordeal, battle, or compurgation. If found guilty by trial, the offender was subjected to the punishment prescribed for that particular crime. In many instances, the punishment was death. If the death penalty were not imposed, the convicted offender would often be subjected to another form of severe physical punishment such as having a hand or ear amputated, or an eye gouged out. On display in the Marksburg Castle in Germany is a hinged metal, helmet-type face mask that was heated red hot and applied to the head of anyone convicted of treason. If a person bearing the scars of such punishment were later seen in public, anyone could kill that person without recourse being taken against the slayer.

As late as the middle of the twentieth century, certain primitive societies inflicted forms of unusual punishment on offenders. In New Guinea, for example, an unusual form of punishment was meted out to men caught in the act of adultery. The offended husband was permitted to shoot an arrow at the groin of the offender, who stood fifty paces away. If the wife got pregnant, the husband was permitted to chop off the offender's head. This method of avenging the wrong was probably a carryover from ancient societies. Adultery was considered to be the worst offense that could be committed among clan members. It was thought that adultery disrupted the family unit more than murder and threatened the foundation of the tribal religion.

Protection Within a Church

A study of early judicial procedure reveals that offenders in England were also subjected to many forms of severe punishment. Often to escape punishment, an offender entered a church for sanctuary from pursuers who were attempting to inflict punishment. The offender was safe as long as he or she remained inside the church. Sometimes the pursuers surrounded the church and remained there for days to prevent escape. Often the pursuers would try to have the priests or clergy starve the offender into submission. Usually, the priests would not have anything to do with matters that interfered with the holiness of the sanctuary. This practice was the beginning of what became known as the benefit of clergy. Generally, whatever punishment was imposed for conviction of a particular crime was a mandatory sentence carried out regardless of severity.

Imprisonment as Punishment

Imprisonment as a form of punishment was not used at that time. In fact, under Roman law, imprisonment as punishment was illegal. In early English history, imprisonment was a means of holding the offender for trial and sentencing, but not for punishment. The imprisonment of convicted offenders was, and still is, a troublesome and an expensive form of punishment.

Thus, we find that in earlier times, swifter and less expensive forms of punishment were inflicted. Some use of imprisonment as a form of punishment was used at common law in England for a few minor offenses, such as vagrancy. The ecclesiastical courts also imposed imprisonment on convicted clergymen in some instances. But the death penalty, mutilation, and banishment were still the most frequently imposed forms of punishment. When a convicted person was banished from England, not only was the offender required to leave home, family, and friends, but his property was also confiscated by the king or the church. Banishment became another source of revenue for both king and church. It is alleged that as many as 100,000 persons were banished to the American colonies from England before the colonies received independence. As late as the early 1800s, England had more than 200 violations carrying a possible death penalty. But shortly thereafter, imprisonment and banishment to Australia were substituted for the death penalty as a form of punishment.

Punishment in Early America

As the colonies were being settled, the colonists brought with them much of the criminal procedure that they had known in England. At that time, retribution, or vengeance, was still the philosophy behind punishment. This philosophy was also brought to the colonies; consequently, the royal colonial governors continued to inflict cruel and unusual punishment on offenders in the colonies. The death penalty was frequently inflicted, and the manner in which it was carried out was many times as inhumane as it had been in England. Other forms of cruel and unusual punishment, such as mutilation, were also practiced. Much corporal punishment was inflicted—particularly whipping—and the pillory, stocks, and public cage were also used. It is little wonder that, with such practices existing, the framers of the U.S. Constitution included the Eighth Amendment guarantee against "cruel and unusual punishment." However, after a time, the colonists began substituting imprisonment for the death penalty, allegedly as a more humane form of punishment. But early imprisonment, in most instances, was far from humane, and most imprisoned offenders would probably have preferred other forms of punishment, even death, at that period in history. Since retribution was still the primary force behind punishment, little consideration was given to the imprisoned offender. The food that was furnished, if any, was meager; no thought was given to providing any comforts of warmth, lighting, ventilation, or sanitation. Prisoners often died of neglect. Each small community was responsible for providing places of confinement, which in many instances were abandoned stockades or fortresses.

William Penn, himself a prisoner for nine months in the Tower of London, is given credit for the first improvement in prison conditions, as well as for reforms in the types of punishment imposed. In 1681, Penn received the charter to a large tract of land, known as Pennsylvania, in payment of a debt owed to his father. Shortly thereafter, Penn moved to a new city that he named Philadelphia and established a government along the lines of republicanism and religious freedom. The death penalty was abolished for all offenses except murder. Around 1683, a jail was erected to replace the fort that had been used to confine offenders. Since this jail was nothing more than a boxlike room that soon became inadequate, other houses were erected to confine convicted offenders. Penn had further reforms in mind, but he died in 1718 before they could be completed. Almost immediately thereafter, Queen Anne reinstituted some of the harsh penalties. The death penalty was imposed as the punishment for thirteen different crimes. Whipping and mutilation were again inflicted for a number of offenses.

Penalty reforms for convicted offenders were begun after the colonies achieved independence from England. Improvements were also made in the conditions of confinement. In 1786, an act was passed that provided for imprisonment at hard labor for many crimes that previously carried the death penalty or corporal punishment. Although the act was an improvement, much reform was still needed. Places of confinement soon became overcrowded. There was little supervision. There was no segregation according to sex, age, or offense committed. Liquor was freely sold to inmates, and prostitution was practiced. In 1790, a block of cells was added to the Walnut Street jail in Philadelphia. It was to house the more hardened criminals and was referred to as the "penitentiary house." Inmates began to be separated according to sex, age, and offense committed, and they were sent to this jail from other parts of the state. It became a focal point of study by persons interested in prison reform.

Present Sentencing Procedure

Each rule of conduct written throughout history has required that a punishment be established for convicted violators. Usually, the more serious the crime, the more severe the punishment. But which punishments should be inflicted for each particular crime has plagued society for centuries. Even today, the sentencing of a convicted offender may be the most complex part of the judicial process. Convicting the offender may be easier than deciding what should be done after the conviction. In primitive times, retaliation was the philosophy behind punishment, and the victim inflicted any punishment he or she desired. As more organized societies were developed, those in the judicial process began to make an effort to fit the penalty to the crime committed. Nevertheless, vengeance or retaliation against the offender was still prevalent in the thoughts of those trying to establish appropriate punishments. The problem became what penalty the offender should be subjected to in order to satisfy society's desire for vengeance and still have the penalty fit the crime. Thus, in the early sentencing process, a thief might have a hand cut off, a perjurer might have the tongue cut out, and the male adulterer might be castrated. The punishment continued to be cruel and severe.

As time passed, imprisonment became the generally accepted way of punishing an offender, and society turned from the retaliatory approach to the isolation philosophy of punishment. Instead of trying to get even with the offender, society attempted to protect itself by imprisonment. As long as the offender was confined, society would be free of recurrent harm. As a result, when penitentiaries were first built in the United States, they were built with the idea of confining the offenders in maximum security to isolate them from society for the prescribed length of the sentence. The offenders became known as inmates. These penitentiaries were fortresslike structures. There were high walls with gun towers surrounding the buildings and cell blocks. Inmates spent much time locked in their cells. They were required to wear a distinctive uniform; for a long time, the uniform was made of black-and-white-striped material. Many of the penitentiaries built in the late 1800s and early 1900s are still in use.

Isolation as Punishment

With punishment based on the isolation theory, the problem was how long an offender should be isolated for society's protection. Early in our history, the sentencing of an offender to imprisonment was solely the responsibility of the trial judge. In most instances, there were no guidelines to assist in determining how long an offender should be confined. As a result, there was a great discrepancy among judges in the sentence imposed for the same offense. Much depended on the judge's attitude and personal philosophy. When legislators began to establish appropriate penalties for each crime, they concentrated on the felony. There is considerable difference between states on the sentences that may be imposed. In some states, legislation has been passed providing a minimum and maximum number of years that an offender must serve for the conviction of a particular crime. For example, an offender convicted of burglary may receive a sentence of not less than one year in prison and not more than ten years. In other states, the law sets forth the maximum length of imprisonment that may be imposed. The law may provide that an offender may not be sentenced for a term longer than ten years. Under this system, an offender could be sentenced to a single hour in confinement, and this outcome has happened in a few instances. As will be seen, under both systems, the trial judge has great leeway in the sentence to be imposed. As legislators considered the penalties for felonies, misdemeanors were also considered. As with felonies, the length of time to be imposed was usually left to the trial judge, with the maximum set forth in the state statutes.

Other Possible Penalties

Although imprisonment became one form of punishment, it is not the only penalty that may be imposed on a convicted offender. The types of sentences possible for criminal offenders are set forth in the codes of the various states. Penalty is still referred to as punishment in most codes. A penalty may be one or a combination of the following: imprisonment; fine; probation; suspended sentence; and in some states, the death penalty. Removal from public office and the disqualification to hold public office are also listed as forms of punishment in some states.

In a few jurisdictions, the terms *punishment* and *sentence* imply imprisonment. Therefore, probation is not considered to be a sentence but rather a disposition of the case. However, in most jurisdictions, the term sentence is the judgment of the court after conviction. The "sentence" is the final disposition of the trial, whether by imprisonment, suspended sentence, probation, or fine. But punishment is sometimes more closely associated with imprisonment than are other forms of sentence. Technically, punishment means any unpleasantness that the convicted offender may suffer. Any restrictions placed upon the offender, whether by imprisonment, suspended sentence, or probation, are forms of unpleasantness, as is the financial hardship imposed by a fine.

Deterrence

As reformists in the justice system continued to study punishment, its purpose shifted from isolation theory to deterrence. The movement to rehabilitate the offender followed. As our study will emphasize, the isolation approach has not been entirely abandoned, since there are inmates from whom society is safe only during their confinement. Neither deterrence nor rehabilitation is applicable to some hardened criminals.

Whatever sentence is imposed, its primary purpose is for the protection of society. The protection may be a result of isolating the offender from society or deterring the offender from committing future crimes, thus serving as an example to others inclined to commit crimes. The protection may also be through rehabilitation so that the offender will refrain from committing future crimes.

TYPES OF SENTENCING AND SENTENCES

To better understand the deterrence and rehabilitation theories of sentencing, we should discuss the type of sentence to be imposed. Perhaps in no other area of the justice system is there a greater variance between states than in the sentencing phase of the justice proceedings.

Misdemeanor Sentencing

Upon conviction of a misdemeanor charge, the statutes of most states provide that the penalty imposed shall not exceed one year imprisonment and/or a $1,000 fine. As stated, in most jurisdictions, the sentence is imposed by the trial judge, and if imprisonment is imposed, the time is generally served in a county or city jail. Most jurisdictions permit the judge to suspend the sentence and place the offender on probation; to grant probation with the provision that a certain amount of time must be spent in imprisonment; or merely to impose a fine.

Although the laws of most states provide that an offender convicted on a misdemeanor charge may not be sentenced for a period of more than one year, it is possible for him or her to serve more than a single year. This possibility results when the offender is convicted on more than one misdemeanor charge. The judge may impose a sentence for one year on each charge and have the sentence run consecutively. A consecutive sentence is one that must be served before the next begins. A consecutive sentence for minor convictions is the exception; in most instances, if the offender is convicted on more than one charge, the judge will provide that the sentences are to be served concurrently, that is, at the same time.

Felony Sentencing

In a majority of the states, it is still the prerogative of the trial judge to impose the sentence. But in some states, the jury will impose the sentence, and in a few states, a jury must be impaneled to impose the sentence even though a jury trial has been waived. If the convicted offender is imprisoned, in some states, the length of time that must be served is determined by a board or committee appointed for that purpose. Generally, depending upon the jurisdiction, the types of imprisonment or sentence that may be imposed are the definite sentence, the indefinite sentence, or the indeterminate sentence. Although the sentences are classified as such, confusion has arisen because a "definite sentence" in one state may be known as an "indefinite sentence" in another state. Irrespective of their names, we will discuss each classification in order that the reader will have some insight into the sentencing procedures followed in the various states.

The Definite Sentence

As imprisonment began to be substituted for other forms of punishment, there were few guidelines to assist judges in deciding the number of years to be imposed. Since retribution, or social retaliation, was still the primary purpose behind punishment, lengthy sentences were often imposed. Some judges became arbitrary and discriminatory in imposing sentences. To overcome this practice, legislation was passed in most states setting forth a prescribed sentence, or a definite mandatory sentence, to be required of one convicted of a particular offense. The theory behind the definite sentence was that it would be applied equally to all, irrespective of race, religion, or social or economic status. The judges no longer had any control over the length of time to be served. On conviction, the mandatory sentence was imposed, and the offender was required to serve that period of time. After serving the prescribed period of time, the offender was released back into society, but never was the offender released prior to that time. The first major change in the definite sentencing procedure came with the introduction of the conditional release. A few states passed legislation permitting the governing board of the penal system to grant time off from the definite sentence for good behavior. If, as an inmate, the convicted offender's behavior was proper, the sentence was reduced by a few days each month. Good behavior principally consisted of complying with prison rules.

The definite sentence was severely criticized by reformists as being inflexible and rigid. The definite sentence did not permit any aggravating or mitigating factors, such as age of the offender, prior criminal record, or other circumstances surrounding the commission of the crime to be taken into consideration. Since the definite, or mandatory, sentencing procedure was inflexible, judges often would dismiss a charge against an offender rather than impose a severe definite sentence when there were mitigating circumstances. An offender would then be permitted to go unpunished. Because of the inflexibility of the definite sentence, it has all but disappeared from the justice system.

The Indefinite Sentence

As the definite sentence lost favor, it was replaced by the indefinite sentence. In some states, the indefinite sentence is referred to as the indeterminate sentence or as the determinate sentence. Technically, there is a difference in the application of the indefinite, or determinate, sentence and the indeterminate sentence. With the appearance of the indefinite sentence, legislative bodies passed statutes prescribing the maximum penalty that could be imposed on the convicted offender. For example, if an offender were convicted of armed robbery, the statute might read that the offender "shall not be imprisoned for a period of more than thirty-five years." Under the indefinite sentencing procedure, the imposition of the sentence was returned to the judge in most states. A few states provided for the jury to impose the sentence.

The theory behind the indefinite sentence was that it enabled the sentence to fit the offender and not the crime. The sentencing body would weigh the situation and impose the number of years deemed to be just under the circumstances. Since sentencing is far from an exact science, determining the number of years to be served was, and still is, a difficult problem. The problem is magnified because an individual's future conduct is difficult, if not impossible, to predict. Society's reaction to imposed sentences is also unpredictable. There are persons who would lead us to believe that vengeance plays no part in the sentencing procedure of our civilized society. However, realistically, society's vengeance may still be felt in a community when an atrocious crime is committed. Thus, in imposing a sentence, it must be of sufficient length to satisfy the desire for social retaliation but not so long as to discourage the offender from wanting to reform. In most instances, when legislation was passed prescribing the maximum sentence to be imposed, that time was long enough that the most vengeful individual could not take exception. It was the duty of the sentencing body to impose the exact length of a sentence. Since there were no guidelines on the length of an equitable sentence, it often reflected the judge's or the jury's feelings and philosophy. There were wide discrepancies between judges and juries in the sentences imposed for the same offenses. Also, some judges became very lenient in the sentences they imposed.

To overcome this leniency and to assist in establishing some sentencing guidelines, the legislatures of several states passed statutes that prescribed both a minimum and maximum sentence. For example, on a conviction of armed robbery, the penalty prescribed may state that the offender "shall not serve less than five years and not more than thirty-five years imprisonment." It became the responsibility of the judge or jury to decide on an appropriate number of years between the minimum and the maximum allowed.

Presentence Investigations.   To assist judges in attempting to arrive at an equitable sentence and to more nearly make the sentence fit the offender, many judges require a presentence investigation. The presentence investigation is usually conducted by a staff member of the probation department. The investigation generally includes such matters as the offender's family status, educational background, work experience, and prior criminal record. It also includes circumstances surrounding the commission of the crime. Whether it was a crime of passion, a thrill, or an emotional involvement may have an impact on the sentence to be prescribed. The offender's attitude toward the crime will be reported. The investigation will also show whether the offender is remorseful over having committed the crime or is only unhappy about being caught. Even with the assistance of the information contained in a presentence report, the sentence to be imposed still involves a difficult decision for the judge. Not all judges have staffs available to them to make presentence investigations, so in most instances, they must rely solely on their contact with the offender during the trial and their own insight regarding what sentence should be imposed. The judge may consider the mental state of the offender at the time the crime was committed. Was the offender in a state of diminished capacity? Was the mental condition so diminished by intoxication or drugs that the offender could not have formulated an intent, created a motive, or entertained malice toward the victim? If so, the judge may impose a lesser penalty. Some states have permitted diminished capacity to be pleaded as a defense to a criminal charge, but currently this use has been abolished in most states and may be considered only by the judge at the time of sentencing.

Juries Imposing Sentences.   Juries generally do not have access to any presentence investigative material. When the jury imposes the sentence, it is too often nothing more than a calculated guess on what is appropriate. Often juries will be either extremely harsh or very lenient in sentencing, because of deep emotional involvement with a crime committed in their community. The sentence of the jury is many times the result of a compromise brought about by bargaining over the verdict. Attempting to get a jury to arrive at what may be an equitable sentence is often more difficult than reaching a unanimous verdict. One may wonder why juries are permitted to impose the sentence in some states in view of the problems involved. This practice is a carryover from colonial days. The colonists frequently had unpleasant experiences with the royal judges, as well as some postindependence judges, as being too arbitrary and discriminatory in the imposition of sentences. To overcome this practice, a few state legislatures provided that the imposition of the sentence was to be the prerogative of the jury.

Whether a sentence is imposed by a judge or a jury, it will stipulate the exact number of years to be served. At first glance, it would appear that this sentencing procedure is of the definite type. The definite and indefinite sentences differ in that with the definite sentence, the law prescribes a definite mandatory number of years that must be served by all offenders on conviction of a particular crime. With the indefinite sentence, the law prescribes either a maximum amount of time that may be imposed or a minimum and a maximum, and from this indefinite period of time, the judge or jury will decide upon a definite amount of time for the sentence.

With the passing of time and the growing interest in rehabilitation, the indefinite sentence has become even more indefinite because, after serving a portion of the sentence, the inmate may become eligible for parole, thereby shortening the time to be served. Parole will be discussed more fully later in the chapter. Because the exact number of years that must be served is indefinite, or indeterminate, and because of the possibility of parole, this sentencing procedure is referred to as the indeterminate sentence in some states.

The Indeterminate Sentence

The true indeterminate sentence removes the sentencing of a prescribed number of years from the hands of a judge or a jury. The length of sentence is determined by a board or committee appointed for that purpose sometime after the imprisonment has been pronounced. The primary purpose of the indeterminate sentence is to permit the sentence to more nearly fit the offender and to assist in the rehabilitation process. But this was not the original purpose of the indeterminate sentence. On the continent of Europe during the seventeenth and eighteenth centuries, the indeterminate sentence was used to lengthen the sentences of dangerous criminals for protective detention after they had served their original sentences. This procedure eventually died out in Europe. The indeterminate sentence was adopted in this country, but for a different reason. This sentence permitted a mitigation of the sentence that might otherwise have been imposed with the view that the indeterminate sentence would assist the offender in reforming. When this sentence was first adopted in this country, the offender was imprisoned for an indeterminate time in order to accomplish physical, emotional, and mental rehabilitation so that his or her renewed freedom would no longer endanger the welfare of society. Once the offender arrived at this status as decided by a board of managers of the penal system, the inmate was entitled to be released. Thus, the inmate could be held for an indeterminate period, even for an entire lifetime—until reaching that point of physical, emotional, and mental rehabilitation where there was no threat to society on his or her release.

Very few states have adopted the true indeterminate sentencing procedure. Under this procedure, the legislature prescribes both the minimum and the maximum terms for each offense punishable by imprisonment in the state prison. Upon conviction of such an offense, and if neither a new trial nor probation is granted, the trial judge does not specify the length of imprisonment but merely sentences the defendant as "prescribed by law." A board appointed by the governor then determines, within statutory limits, the length of time that the offender will actually be required to serve. This board is frequently referred to as the parole board.

The indeterminate sentence has been interpreted to mean that on being sentenced as prescribed by law, the offender has been sentenced to the maximum time prescribed by the statutes for the particular offense. But the indeterminate sentence process permits the shortening of the offender's sentence on a showing of rehabilitation. The theory behind the indeterminate sentence is to place before the inmate a great incentive to reform in order that the sentence be reduced in length from the maximum prescribed.

When Is an Offender Rehabilitated?

Determining when an offender has been rehabilitated to a point where there is no longer a threat to society on release is an almost impossible task. Some never reach that point and have to serve the maximum time. However, each inmate is entitled eventually to have the length of his or her sentence determined by the board. In making the determination, the board will take many things into consideration. Each penal institution maintains a file or cumulative folder on each inmate. The board will study these files and hold a hearing at which the inmate may appear to plead the case. Generally, the hearing will not be held until the inmate has served six months to one year of the maximum time prescribed. By holding the hearing after the inmate has started serving a portion of the sentence, the board has an opportunity to study the inmate's reaction to incarceration, since these data, as well as much other information, will be included in the cumulative file. The file will contain the name and age of the inmate, the place and time of conviction, the charge for which the inmate was convicted, and the minimum and maximum sentence prescribed by the statutes. The presentence investigative report will be included in order that the board may have background knowledge on the inmate. Also included may be the results of tests given to the inmate upon incarceration, as well as a record of the inmate's efforts to improve academically by attempting to learn some salable work skill. The board will consider the general attitude of the inmate toward society, law, and authority as expressed by the inmate in the appearance before the board.

After a review of the entire matter, the board will endeavor to arrive at some equitable length of time to be served. The board may conclude that the inmate should serve six years on a sentence prescribed by law to be not less than one year and not more than ten years. The board may conclude further that the inmate should serve four of those years in actual confinement and the other two years on parole. After the time has been set, if the inmate should demonstrate an inability to conform to prison regulations or that no attempt to reform has been made, the board has the authority to reset the length of the sentence, even as much as requiring the inmate to serve the maximum time. For this reason, it has been interpreted that an offender sentenced under the indeterminate sentence procedure is sentenced to the maximum prescribed, and any time less than the maximum is based on the rehabilitation of the inmate. It has been held that the indeterminate sentence grants the inmate no vested right to a permanently fixed length of sentence at any time.

Advantages and Disadvantages of the Indeterminate Sentence

The indeterminate sentence has been attacked by inmates on the allegation that it violates the due process of law because of its uncertainness, and as such, is cruel and unusual punishment. However, to date, these attacks have been unsuccessful, since the courts have interpreted that the sentence is fixed at the maximum and that it is the inmate's reformation that permits the maximum to be reduced. The courts have held that as long as a minimum and maximum sentence prescribed by the legislature is not disproportionate to the offense committed, the sentence is not cruel and unusual. It has been stated that whether a particular punishment is disproportionate to the offense is a question of degree. Courts have described a disproportionate punishment as one in which the length of the sentence is so disproportionate as to shock the moral sense of all reasonable people or so disproportionate as to shock the moral sense of the community.

The proponents of the true indeterminate sentencing procedure allege that a board is in a better position than a judge to determine the sentence that should be imposed. The board comes in contact with all convicted offenders who are imprisoned, whereas judges are in contact with only those convicted in their particular court. The board therefore is able to view the inmates' progress in an overview as one large unit and can follow this progress during confinement as well as parole. As such, the board can weigh what sentence is more likely to be equitable. The board also has personal contact with the inmate during confinement and, before determining the sentence, can study responses to treatment over a period of months. The judge must make a sentence determination at the end of a trial—without any guidelines on a defendant's reaction to the rehabilitation processes. As previously stated, judges under both the indeterminate and the indefinite sentencing procedures are able to retain jurisdiction over a defendant by granting probation in lieu of imposing a sentence of imprisonment.

The Suspended Sentence and Probation

The right of benefit of clergy was carried a step further in England during the thirteenth and fourteenth centuries. The right of benefit of clergy may be called the forerunner of the suspended sentence. Under certain circumstances, an accused was permitted to have a trial transferred from the king's court to the ecclesiastical court. By so doing, the offender was able to avoid the death penalty but still might be imprisoned for life. However, in most instances, the offender was only mutilated in some minor way and released back into society. The philosophy of the right of benefit of clergy was brought to America by the colonists. Instead of a transfer of courts being possible, either there was a substitution of some other punishment for the death penalty, or the judge might suspend carrying out the death penalty for the lifetime of the offender, depending on good behavior.

The suspended sentence is recognized in our system of justice today, but in most instances, it is coupled with a period of probation. In many jurisdictions, there cannot be a suspended sentence without probation being imposed for a prescribed period. In those jurisdictions where the suspended sentence is permitted without probation, the judge merely suspends imposing a sentence. The offender is free to return into society. Generally, no restrictions are placed on the offender other than good behavior during the period of the suspended sentence. If the offender breaks the law again, the judge may impose a sentence on the original charge as well as the new charge, if convicted.

Probation, like the suspended sentence, permits the convicted offender to remain free from custody, but by being placed on probation, the offender is under the supervision of some person who assists him or her in leading a law-abiding life. The person is usually a public officer known as a probation officer. The primary purpose of the suspended sentence and probation is for the rehabilitation of the offender. By granting the convicted offender a suspended sentence or probation, it is assumed that there is no threat to society by the offender's remaining free from custody.

Origins of Probation.   Probation, primarily of American origin, is an outgrowth of the suspended sentence and is the newest form of correctional treatment for the offender. Probation is believed to have begun in America when a cobbler, John Augustus, attended a police court in Boston, Massachusetts, in August 1841. He decided to post bail for a man charged with being a common drunkard. The judge permitted Augustus to post the bail and ordered the defendant to return in three weeks for sentencing. When the man returned, the judge noted an improvement in the defendant's attitude. Instead of sentencing the defendant to imprisonment, the judge fined the defendant one cent and court costs. Encouraged by his first experience, Augustus posted bail for other first offenders who seemed worthy of consideration. In each case, Augustus agreed to supervise the activities of the offenders and to report to the judge on their progress. Augustus continued this work until his death in 1859. His work was continued by Rufus R. Cook, a chaplain of a county jail. In 1878, Massachusetts passed a law providing for the appointment of a paid probation officer for the courts in Boston. At the same time, experiments were being made in the use of probation in England. Although probation made its appearance in America in the mid-1800s, it was not until well into the twentieth century that probation as a form of sentencing came into extensive use.

Probation is a form of clemency, and an offender has no inherent right to demand to be placed on probation. In most states, there are certain violations for which probation may not be granted. Otherwise, in most jurisdictions, the judge has wide discretionary power to grant probation. In most instances, the judge's decision is final. Prior to granting probation, the judge may, or in some cases must, have a probation or presentence investigation conducted to determine whether the offender could benefit from probation. This investigation is generally conducted by a probation officer who may or may not give a recommendation on whether probation should be granted. In most states, the recommendation is not binding upon the judge, and probation may be granted even though not recommended by the probation officers, or vice versa. Probation is often granted as a result of plea bargaining.

But the mere fact that an offender enters a guilty plea is no assurance that there will be benefits from probation or that society is better protected by the granting of probation.

One of two procedures is usually followed in granting probation. On conviction, the judge merely suspends pronouncing any sentence and places the offender on probation for a prescribed time. Or the judge may impose a sentence such as a prescribed period of imprisonment, but the execution of the sentence will be suspended, and the offender will be placed on probation for a prescribed time. The time that the offender may be placed on probation is generally at the discretion of the judge, but in most instances, it is not for a period longer than the maximum time of imprisonment for the particular crime.

Conditions of Probation.   The general condition imposed on the offender, when placed on probation, is that he or she be a law-abiding individual during the period of probation. Many other restrictions may also be imposed at this time. For example, the judge may restrict the offender's area of travel and associates, or the offender may be prohibited from patronizing bars. Restitution for damages or injuries caused while violating the law may be required. In some instances, as a condition of probation, the offender must agree to having his or her person or home searched without a warrant at any time by either a probation officer or a law enforcement officer. When these conditions are imposed, however, it is generally held that the search may not be a harassment procedure but that it is to be made only when there is probable cause to believe that the offender has violated probation. Whenever restrictions are placed on an offender, it has been stated that the restrictions should have some connection with the crime committed. For example, in one case, the defendant was convicted of grand theft. Prior to the conviction, the defendant had given birth to three illegitimate children fathered by different men. As a condition of probation, the judge advised the defendant that she was not to become pregnant out of wedlock again during the probation period. She did become pregnant out of wedlock, and the judge then revoked her probation and sentenced her to prison. She appealed the sentence as constituting cruel and unusual punishment. The appellate court agreed with her and reversed the case, sending it back to the judge for further consideration. The appellate court stated that the trial judge might be commended for the attempt to prevent illegitimacy but that the attempt should have been made in a different manner, since the restriction on pregnancy had no connection with the crime committed. However, judges frequently require a person placed on probation to do work for charity organizations, a requirement that appears to have no connection with the crime committed. There are times when a judge may grant probation with the stipulation that a short time be spent in imprisonment. Some reformists have criticized the use of imprisonment for one placed on probation as being a handicap to the rehabilitation process. Others justify the imprisonment as being a means of awakening the offender to the realization of what could happen if probation is violated.

There is a difference among states on the question of whether a convicted offender may refuse probation. In some states, it is held that the offender does not have to give consent to being placed on probation; therefore, there is no right to refuse to accept probation. In other states, it is held that the convicted offender must give consent to be placed on probation. Although probation is generally preferable to imprisonment, a judge, in granting probation, may impose certain restrictions that the offender may feel are intolerable. In this case, the offender may prefer a limited time of imprisonment. Since probation is not considered a form of punishment, but a rehabilitation process, it is believed that the convicted offender should be willing to be placed on probation. Otherwise, the rehabilitative effect of probation is lost. There are a few states in which an offender may be placed on probation prior to conviction. On a complaint's being filed, an offender can be placed on probation, thereby avoiding a conviction. It is felt that the consent of the offender is necessary under these circumstances. In some states, this procedure is known as diversion.

Revocation of Probation.   If during the period of probation, the offender, known as a probationer, violates the law or fails to abide by other restrictions that may have been imposed, the probation may be revoked and the probationer sentenced to imprisonment. Whether or not probation is revoked is at the discretion of the trial judge. In *Gagnon* v. *Scarpelli,* the U.S. Supreme Court held that before probation may be revoked, the probationer is entitled to a hearing, stating the following:

> Probation revocation, like parole revocation, is not a stage of a criminal prosecution, but does result in a loss of liberty. Accordingly, we hold that a probationer, like a parolee, is entitled to a preliminary and final revocation hearing, under the conditions specified in *Morrissey* v. *Brewer.* . . .

Criticism of Probation.   Generally, one would not quarrel with the primary purpose of probation, which is rehabilitating the offender. But many persons both in and out of the justice system believe that judges grant probation too often. Probation has been granted to prevent overcrowding of prisons. It has also been granted to offenders who have no incentive to mend their ways. In one case, for example, an offender was convicted of burglary and placed on three years' probation. While on probation, the offender was convicted on another burglary charge, and the same judge again placed the offender on probation, to run concurrently with the probationary period of the prior conviction. It is for this reason that some states have passed legislation that prohibits an offender from being placed on probation after conviction for certain crimes or for using a gun while committing crimes. In spite of the efforts to curb the use of probation, it is still extensively utilized. At any given time, more than two million persons are on probation in the United States.

DEATH PENALTY

The toughest part of this job is sentencing. I've lost all kinds of sleep over sentences. I find it dreadful.

—Malcolm Muir, Judge, U.S. District Court

I think a judge's education is very imperfect when it comes to the sentencing process.

—Edward Davis, former Chief of Police, Los Angeles

Heated arguments have taken place over the years concerning the merits of the death penalty. Those who oppose the death penalty do so principally on the grounds that it has no place in a civilized society. They hold that the death penalty is a form of cruel and unusual punishment, and further allege that the death penalty does not act as a deterrent. An equal number contend that the death penalty is a deterrent and as such should be retained. But they concede that the deterrent effect does not function effectively, because, as previously pointed out, for any deterrent to be effective, the punishment must be swift and sure. Certainly, the days between the imposition of the death penalty and the execution make the death penalty anything but swift in coming and sure in being carried out.

Cruel and Unusual Punishment

The question of whether or not the death penalty is cruel and unusual punishment in violation of the Eighth Amendment was placed before the U.S. Supreme Court in the case of *Furman* v. *Georgia*.[1] The Court held in that case that the death penalty as such was not cruel and unusual punishment but that the indiscriminatory manner in which it was applied made the death penalty cruel and unusual punishment in violation of the Eighth Amendment.

The Court in the Furman decision indicated that perhaps, if the death sentence was to be made mandatory on all of equal guilt, the sentence would not be discriminatory and thus would not violate the cruel and unusual punishment provision of the Eighth Amendment. As a result, many state legislatures passed statutes making the death penalty mandatory on conviction for certain crimes. This mandatory sentence took from the jury or judge the right to determine the sentence to be imposed on conviction for crimes previously carrying the alternate sentence of life imprisonment or death.

However, the U.S. Supreme Court, in *Woodson* v. *North Carolina*,[2] overruled as cruel and unusual punishment a North Carolina statute making the death penalty mandatory. The Court held that such a statute did not allow any consideration to be given to the character and record of the offender. The Court stated, "Consideration of both the offender and the offense in order to arrive at a just and appropriate sentence has been viewed as a progressive and humanizing development."

Consequently, those state statutes making the death penalty mandatory had to be revised to conform with the *Woodson* decision. Statutes were then passed allowing the jury or judge to take into consideration aggravating or mitigating circumstances in imposing the alternate sentence of life imprisonment or death. A Georgia statute of this nature was upheld by the U.S. Supreme Court in *Gregg* v. *Georgia*.[3] In reaffirming that the death penalty was not in violation of the Eighth Amendment guarantee against cruel and unusual punishment, the Court stated the following:

> The imposition of the death penalty for the Crime of murder has a long history of acceptance both in the United States and in England. The common-law rule imposed a mandatory death sentence on all convicted murderers. And the penalty continued to be used into the 20th century by most American States, although the breadth of the common-law rule was diminished, initially by narrowing the class of murders to be punished by death and subsequently by widespread adoption of laws expressly granting juries the discretion to recommend mercy.
>
> It is apparent from the text of the Constitution itself that the existence of capital punishment was accepted by the Framers. At the time the Eighth Amendment was ratified, capital punishment was a common sanction in every

State. Indeed, the First Congress of the United States enacted legislation providing death as the penalty for specified crimes. The Fifth Amendment, adopted at the same time as the Eighth, contemplated the continued existence of the capital sanction by imposing certain limits on the prosecution of capital cases: "No person shall be held to answer for a capital, or otherwise infamous, crime unless on a presentment or indictment of a Grand Jury . . .; nor shall any person be subject for the same offense to be twice put in jeopardy of life or limb; . . . nor be deprived of life, liberty, or property, without due process of law . . .." And the Fourteenth Amendment, adopted over three-quarters of a century later, similarly contemplates the existence of the capital sanction in providing that no State shall deprive any person of "life, liberty, or property" without due process of law.

For nearly two centuries, this Court, repeatedly and often expressly, has recognized that capital punishment is not invalid per se.

In holding that the death penalty is not a violation of the guarantee against cruel and unusual punishment, the dissenting justices in the *Furman* case stated as follows:

> Punishments are cruel when they involve torture or a lingering death; but the punishment of death is not cruel, within the meaning of that word as used in the Constitution. It implies there something inhuman and barbarous, something more than the mere extinguishment of life. . . .
>
> The traditional humanity of modem Anglo-American law forbids the infliction of unnecessary pain in the execution of the death sentence. . . . The cruelty against which the Constitution protects a convicted man is cruelty in the method of punishment, not the necessary suffering involved in any method employed to extinguish life humanely.

The gas chamber, electric chair, hanging, lethal injection, and firing squad have all been sanctioned by the court as humane means of carrying out the death penalty.

In the *Gregg* decision, the Court made some interesting comments on the death penalty as a deterrent as well as a necessary form of punishment to satisfy society's demand for justice. The Court stated the following:

> The death penalty is said to serve two principal social purposes: retribution and deterrence of capital crimes by prospective offenders.
>
> In part, capital punishment is an expression of society's moral outrage at particularly offensive conduct. This function may be unappealing to many, but it is essential in an ordered society that asks its citizens to rely on legal processes rather than self-help to vindicate their wrongs. "The instinct for retribution is part of the nature of man and channeling that instinct in the administration of criminal justice serves an important purpose in promoting the stability of a society governed by law. When people begin to believe that organized society is unwilling or unable to impose upon criminal offenders the punishment they deserve, then there are sown the seeds of anarchy—of self-help, vigilante justice, and lynch law." Retribution is no longer the dominant objective of the criminal law, but neither is it a forbidden objective nor one inconsistent with our respect for the dignity of men. Indeed, the decision that capital punishment may be the appropriate sanction in extreme cases is an expression of the community's belief that certain crimes are themselves so grievous an affront to humanity that the only adequate response may be the penalty of death.

Statistical attempts to evaluate the worth of the death penalty as a deterrent to crimes by potential offenders have occasioned a great deal of debate. The results simply have been inconclusive. Although some of the studies suggest that the death penalty may not function as a significantly greater deterrent than lesser penalties, there is no convincing empirical evidence either supporting or refuting this view. We may nevertheless assume safely that there are murderers, such as those who act in passion, for whom the threat of death has little or no deterrent effect. But for many others the death penalty undoubtedly is a significant deterrent.

The Alternate Sentencing Procedure

Since the *Woodson* decision held that the alternate sentencing procedure must be followed, it is important to discuss the procedure's development. For many years, the death penalty was made mandatory upon the conviction of certain specified crimes in most states. Jurors aware of this situation knew that on voting for a guilty verdict, they were voting for the execution of a human being. Many jurors had reservations about the death penalty. When it came time to vote on the verdict, they could not bring themselves to vote guilty irrespective of the strength of the evidence of guilt. This inability to vote for a guilty verdict caused many trials to end with hung juries. In an effort to overcome this problem, the legislatures of many states enacted statutes setting forth alternate sentences of life imprisonment or death on conviction of certain crimes. The statutes further provided that the jury in the jury trial was to make the decision about which penalty was to be imposed. Under these circumstances, the juror with reservations about the death penalty could still vote for a guilty verdict but be in a position to vote for life imprisonment after the conviction. In 2002, the U.S. Supreme Court held that the factual determination about the existence of "aggravating factors" that make a convicted murder eligible for the death penalty must be made by the jury and not the judge.

When the alternate sentence was made possible, one of two procedures was generally followed. In some states, a trial was first held to determine the guilt or innocence of the accused. If the accused was found guilty, a second trial was held to determine whether the death penalty was to be imposed or whether the sentence was to be life imprisonment. In other states, only one trial was held. The jury would deliberate first on the guilt or innocence of the accused, and, if the jury voted a guilty verdict, then they would then deliberate on the penalty to be imposed. Both procedures have received the sanction of the U.S. Supreme Court. Under both procedures, the juror with reservations about imposition of the death penalty could still vote for a guilty verdict without voting for the death of the defendant.

During the trial or sentence determination hearing, the jury must consider both aggravating and mitigating circumstances, and weigh them against each other. The *Gregg* decision listed such aggravating circumstances as a murder committed by a convict under a sentence of imprisonment; a murder committed by one previously convicted of murder or a felony involving violence; a murder committed at the time the defendant committed another murder; a murder committed while committing or attempting to commit robbery, rape, arson, burglary, or kidnapping; a murder committed for the purpose of avoiding arrest; and a murder committed in an especially cruel or atrocious manner. As to mitigating circumstances, the Court suggested that it be taken into consideration whether the defendant had no significant prior criminal record; whether the murder was committed while the defendant was under some emotional stress; whether the defendant was an accomplice of another person who actually did the murder and whether the defendant's participation in the homicidal act was relatively minor; whether at the time of the murder the defendant was acting under a diminished capacity; and whether the defendant was of youthful age.

In most jurisdictions, when the death penalty is imposed, the case is automatically appealed to the highest appellate court within the jurisdiction. The court will review the facts of the case to determine whether the conviction should be affirmed and whether the death penalty is justified from the evidence presented. The appellate court may affirm both the conviction and the death penalty, or it may affirm the conviction but hold that the death penalty is not justified under the circumstances. In this instance, either the case will be returned to the trial court for revision of the sentence, or depending on the court, the life sentence may be imposed automatically. If the appellate court reverses the conviction, the penalty phase will not be considered.

The death penalty may be imposed in approximately two-thirds of the states and within the federal system, yet opponents undoubtedly will continue to attempt to have the death penalty abolished as being cruel and unusual punishment. In fact, in their dissenting opinions in the *Gregg* decision, Justices Marshall and Brennan were adamant in their contention that the death penalty is cruel and unusual punishment and thus a violation of the Eighth Amendment guarantee.

Death Penalty as Excessive Punishment for the Crime of Rape

Appellate courts have from time to time held that a particular sentence was excessive and disproportionate to the crime committed, and thus the sentence was cruel and unusual punishment. In such an instance, the sentence will be set aside and the case referred to the trial court for resentencing. What is considered excessive punishment is not easily determined and often rests largely upon the personal viewpoints of the justices involved. In *Coker* v. *Georgia,*[4] the U.S. Supreme Court held that the death penalty for the rape of an adult woman was excessive and disproportionate to the crime. The Court stated the following:

> We do not discount the seriousness of rape as a crime. It is highly reprehensible, both in a moral sense and in its almost total contempt for the personal integrity and autonomy of the female victim and for the latter's privilege of choosing those with whom intimate relationships are to be established. Short of homicide, it is the "ultimate violation of self." It is also a violent crime because it normally involves force, or the threat of force or intimidation, to overcome the will and the capacity of the victim to resist. Rape is very often accompanied by physical injury to the female and can also inflict mental and psychological damage. Because it undermines the community's sense of security, there is public injury as well.
>
> Rape is without doubt deserving of serious punishment; but in terms of moral depravity and of the injury to the person and to the public, it does not compare with murder, which does involve the unjustified taking of human life. Although it may be accompanied by another crime, rape by definition does not include the death or even the serious injury to another person. The murderer kills; the rapist, if no more than that, does not. Life is over for the victim of the murderers; for the rape victim, life may not be nearly so happy as it was, but it is not over and normally is not beyond repair. We have the abiding conviction that

the death penalty, which "is unique in its severity and irrevocability," is an excessive penalty for the rapist, who, as such, does not take human life.

Justice Powell, who voted with the majority in the *Coker* decision, dissented in one respect. He felt that the majority went beyond what was necessary in that decision when it held

> . . . that capital punishment always—regardless of the circumstances—is a disproportionate penalty for the crime of rape. . . .
>
> The plurality (the majority) draws a bright line between murder and all rapes regardless of the degree of brutality of the rape or the effect upon the victim. I dissent because I am not persuaded that such a bright line is appropriate. There is extreme variation in the degree of culpability of rapists. The deliberate viciousness of the rapist may be greater than that of the murderer. Rape is never an act committed accidentally. Rarely can it be said to be unpremeditated. There is also wide variation in the effect on the victim. The plurality opinion says that "life is over for the victim of the murderer; for the rape victim, life may not be nearly so happy as it was, but it is not over and normally is not beyond repair." But there is indeed extreme variation in the crime of rape. Some victims are so grievously injured physically or psychologically that life is beyond repair.
>
> Thus it may be that the death penalty is not disproportionate punishment for the crime of aggravated rape. Final resolution of the questions must await careful inquiry into objective indicators of society's "evolving standards of decency, particularly legislative enactments and the responses of juries in capital cases. The plurality properly examines these indicia, which do support the conclusion that society finds the death penalty unacceptable for the crime of rape in the absence of excessive brutality or severe injury. But it has not been shown that society finds the penalty disproportionate for all rapists. In a proper case a more discriminating inquiry than the plurality undertakes well might discover that both juries and legislatures have reserved the ultimate penalty for the case of an outrageous rape resulting in serious, lasting harm to the victim. I would not prejudge the issue.

This statement indicates that if legislation were passed making it possible to impose the death penalty in aggravated rape cases, such a penalty might not be declared excessive. However, the *Coker* decision, in which four justices declared the death penalty excessive in all instances except where murder was involved, may make the passage of such legislation difficult. And even if such legislation were passed, there is no assurance that the U.S. Supreme Court would not hold the death penalty excessive.

Chief Justice Burger and Justice Rehnquist expressed concern in the *Coker* case over the majority's decision in holding the death penalty as excessive. These justices pointed out the following facts:

> On December 5, 1971, Coker raped and then stabbed to death a young woman. Less than eight months later Coker kidnapped and raped a second young woman. After twice raping this 16-year-old victim, he stripped her, severely beat her with a club, and dragged her into a wooded area where he left her for dead. He was apprehended and pleaded guilty to offenses stemming from these incidents. He was sentenced by three separate courts to three life terms, two 20-year terms, and one eight-year term of imprisonment. Each judgment specified that

the sentences it imposed were to run consecutively rather than concurrently. Approximately one and one-half years later, on September 2, 1974, petitioner escaped from the state prison where he was serving these sentences. He promptly raped another 16-year-old woman in the presence of her husband, abducted her from her home, and threatened her with death and serious bodily harm. It is this crime for which the sentence now under review was imposed.

The Court today holds that the State of Georgia may not impose the death penalty on Coker. In so doing, it prevents the State from imposing any effective punishment upon Coker for his latest rape. The Court's holding, moreover, bars Georgia from guaranteeing its citizens that they will suffer no further attacks by this habitual rapist. In fact, given the lengthy sentences Coker must serve for the crimes he has already committed, the Court's holding assures that petitioner (Coker) and others in his position will henceforth feel no compunction whatsoever about committing further rapes as frequently as he may be able to escape from confinement and indeed even within the walls of the prison itself. To what extent we have left States "elbow room" to protect innocent persons from depraved human beings like Coker remains in doubt.

These two dissenting justices were also concerned over the Coker decision because there was an indication that the majority would declare the death penalty excessive for any crime in which there was not a murder involved. These justices stated the following:

> Since the Court (the majority) now invalidates the death penalty as a sanction for all rapes of adults at all times for all circumstances, I reluctantly turn to what I see as the broader issues raised by this holding.
>
> The plurality acknowledges the gross nature of the crime of rape. A rapist not only violates a victim's privacy and personal integrity, but inevitably causes serious psychological as well as physical harm in the process. The long-range effect upon the victim's life and health is likely to be irreparable; it is impossible to measure the harm which results. Volumes have been written by victims, physicians and psychiatric specialists on the lasting injury suffered by rape victims. Rape is not a mere physical attack, it is destructive of the human personality. The remainder of the victim's life may be gravely affected, and this in turn may have a serious detrimental effect upon her husband and any children she may have. I therefore wholly agree with Mr. Justice White's conclusion as far as it goes that short of homicide, rape is the "ultimate violation of the self." Victims may recover from the physical damage of knife or bullet wounds, or a beating with fists or a club, but recovery from such a gross assault on the human personality is not healed by medicine or surgery. To speak blandly, as the plurality does, of rape victims who are "unharmed," or, as the concurrence, to classify the human outrage of rape in terms of "excessively brutal," versus "moderately brutal," takes too little account of the profound suffering the crime imposes upon the victims and their loved ones.

Despite its strong condemnation of rape, the Court reaches the inexplicable conclusion that the "death penalty is an excessive penalty" for the perpetrator (Coker) of this heinous offense. As pointed out by one of the dissenting justices in the *Coker* decision, Chief Justice Warren Burger, the result of the case is that the death penalty may be imposed only on the conviction of murder. Burger also pointed out that the Court's conclusion in that case was very disturbing. He stated that

> the clear implication of today's holding appears to be that the death penalty may he properly imposed only as to crimes resulting in death of the victim. This case casts serious doubt upon the unconstitutional validity of statutes imposing the death penalty for a variety of conduct which, though dangerous, may not necessarily result in any immediate death, e.g., treason, airplane hijacking and kidnaping. In that respect, today's holding does even more harm than is initially apparent. We cannot avoid judicial notice that crimes such as airplane hijacking and mass terrorist activity can constitute a serious and increasing danger to the safety of the public. It would be unfortunate indeed if the effect of today's holding were to inhibit States and the Federal Government from experimenting with various remedies—including possibly imposition of the death penalty—to prevent and deter such crimes.

Burger further stated that some of the justices of the U.S. Supreme Court are inclined to interject their own feelings against the death penalty by restricting its implementation through strict imitations of its use. This same attitude has been manifested by some state supreme court justices in the strict interpretation of the *Witherspoon* case. As previously mentioned, *Witherspoon* dealt with the alleged undue exclusion of prospective jurors and the question of whether the facts of a particular case fell within the special circumstances permitting the death penalty to be imposed.

Subsequent Death Penalty Legislation

Since the Coker decision was handed down, the U.S. Supreme Court has invalidated the death penalty in two other landmark cases, establishing new approaches to death penalty limitations. In the case of *Godfrey* v. *Georgia,*[5] the U.S. Supreme Court held that the sentence of death amounted to cruel and unusual punishment when pronounced on the defendant Godfrey, even though two murders had been committed. The Court quoted the Georgia statute providing that the death penalty could be invoked when the offense of murder was "outrageously or wantonly vile, horrible or inhuman." The Court held that to fall within that category, the evidence must demonstrate that the offender committed the murder through torture, depravity of mind or an aggravated battery before killing the victim. In the Godfrey case, the facts reflect that the defendant shot both victims in the head with a shotgun and that they died instantly. There was no evidence of serious suffering by the victims that would justify the death penalty under the Georgia statute. There were dissenting justices in that case that felt that the killings by the defendant did fall within the statute as being outrageously or wantonly vile, horrible, and inhuman. In the case of *Enmund* v. *Florida,*[6] the facts reveal that Enmund and two other defendants entered into a conspiracy to rob a victim of money. The three went to the home of the victim Kersey, and two of the robbers approached Kersey to commit the crime. Kersey resisted and called for help. His wife came to the rescue and wounded one of the robbers. In retaliation, the robbers killed both Kersey and his wife. During this time, Enmund was sitting in the getaway car. After the killing, the three left the scene of the crime but were later identified, arrested, and tried on a charge of first degree murder. In accordance with the Florida statute providing that "the killing of a human being while engaged in the perpetration of or in the attempt to perpetrate the offense of robbery is murder in the first degree even though there is no intent to kill, and for which upon conviction the death penalty may be imposed," all three defendants were convicted of first degree murder and sentenced to death.

Enmund appealed the death sentence on the grounds that the death penalty under the circumstances was in violation of the cruel and unusual punishment clause of the Eighth Amendment of the U.S. Constitution. Enmund alleged that he did not participate in the actual killing and had no intent to kill during the robbery, and as such the death penalty as applied was disproportionate to the crime he committed. The U.S. Supreme Court agreed with Enmund that the death penalty in his instance was cruel and unusual punishment. The Court stated the following:

> We have no doubt that robbery is a serious crime deserving serious punishment. It is not, however, a crime so grievous an affront to humanity that the only adequate response may be the penalty of death. It does not compare with murder, which does involve the unjustified taking of human life. Although it may be accompanied by another crime, robbery by definition does not include the death of another person. The murderer kills; the robber if no more than that, does not. Life is over for the victim of the murderer; for the robbery victim, life is not beyond repair. As we said of the crime of rape in the *Coker* case, we have the abiding conviction that the death penalty, which is unique in its severity and irrevocability, is an excessive penalty for the robber who, as such, does not take human life.

The dissenting justices in the *Enmund* case felt that the death penalty was not disproportionate to the crime of felony murder even though Enmund did not actually kill or intend to kill the victims. They pointed out that Enmund planned the robbery and assisted in carrying it out by going with the other two defendants to the victim's home and sat in the getaway car to aid in the escape after the robbery. As such, he was as guilty of murder as the other two defendants.

The majority of the justices in the *Enmund* case did not rule out all death penalty sentences in which a coconspirator did not actually do the killing, but as stated by one of the dissenting justices, to invoke the death penalty in such instances there must be proving of intent at the time that the robbery was planned. This requirement could be most difficult, since intent is a state of mind, and proving the state of mind when a robbery was planned is troublesome. Imposing the intent phase in such cases does preclude the death penalty's being imposed in most instances.

The U.S. Supreme Court in *Tison* v. *Arizona*[7] modified the intent ruling set forth in the Enmund decision. The Court in the *Tison* case stated that although the defendants had no specific intent to kill the victims of their crime, their mental state was one of such "reckless disregard for human life" that the death penalty was not cruel and unusual punishment under the circumstances.

The facts of the *Tison* case reflect that Gary Tison was serving a life sentence for the murder of a guard in an attempted escape. After serving a number of years in prison, Gary Tison's wife and his three sons, Raymond, Donald, and Ricky, conspired to assist him in escaping. In furtherance of the conspiracy, they assembled an arsenal of weapons, which the Tison brothers smuggled into the Arizona State Prison where Gary Tison was serving time. The brothers armed Gary Tison and his cellmate, Randy Greenwalt, who also was serving a life sentence for murder. The five were able to overpower the guards and forced them and the visitors who were present at the time into a closet. The five fled the prison grounds in the Tisons' Ford and proceeded to a house nearby where the brothers had secreted a Lincoln automobile.

The five abandoned the Ford and proceeded in the Lincoln toward Flagstaff, going by way of back desert roads. On the way, a tire blew out on the Lincoln, so they decided to flag down a motorist and steal his car. Raymond stood in front of the Lincoln to flag a car while the others hid beside the road.

One car passed; then a Mazda automobile containing John Lyons, his wife, his two-year-old son, and John's fifteen-year-old niece stopped to render aid. As Raymond showed John Lyons the flat tire, the others emerged and, at gunpoint, forced the Lyons family into the back seat of the Lincoln. Raymond and Donald Tison drove the Lincoln down a dirt road further into the desert, followed by Gary, Ricky Tison, and Greenwalt in the Mazda. After traveling a short distance, both cars stopped, and Gary Tison blasted the radiator of the Lincoln with a shotgun, presumedly to further disable it. The Lyons family were made to stand in front of the Lincoln, where John Lyons pleaded with the group to spare his family's life and requested that they be given water so that they could survive in the desert. He asked as well for the five to take the Mazda and go on their way. Gary Tison ordered his sons to get some water from the Mazda. The sons did not know why their father gave them that order except that he seemed to be confused about what to do because of the baby. As the boys were returning with the water, they saw Gary Tison and Randy Greenwalt brutally murder the entire Lyons family, including the baby, with blasts from shotguns. The five men then got into the Mazda and drove away. Several days later, the group encountered a police roadblock. During a shootout, Donald Tison was killed. Gary Tison escaped but died of exposure from the desert heat. Greenwalt, Ricky Tison, and Raymond Tison were captured, tried, convicted of murder, and given the death penalty.

Ricky and Raymond Tison appealed their death penalty sentence to the U.S. Supreme Court on the grounds set forth in the *Enmund* decision, alleging that their death penalty was cruel and unusual punishment, since they had no intent to murder the victims of the crime. The Court rejected their contention. The Court pointed out that the Tison brothers were major participants in a long series of events leading up to the murder of the four victims and that, after the killing, the brothers further assisted in the escape. The Court maintained that they should have anticipated that serious injury or death would occur as a result of their activities. The Court also held that the whole mental attitude of the Tison brothers was one of "reckless indifference to the value of human life" and that this reckless disregard of human life was every bit as shocking to the moral sense as an intent to kill. As such it was sufficient to justify the death penalty and was not in violation of the Eighth Amendment guarantee against cruel and unusual punishment.

Attention is called to the fact that even though an appellate court reverses the death penalty, the offender is not necessarily set free. In most instances, the sentence will be reduced from the death penalty to life imprisonment without the possibility of parole or to life imprisonment only, depending on the statutes of the particular state. A life sentence without the possibility of parole may also be changed to life imprisonment by a governor at any time. Under a life sentence, most offenders are eligible for parole after serving a term of approximately twelve years. That possibility does not mean that the offender will be paroled after that period, but an offender sentenced for life usually does not serve until his or her death.

Retarded Defendants

In 2002, the U.S. Supreme Court held by a six to three decision that the Constitution's ban on "cruel and unusual punishment" bars the execution of mentally retarded people. The decision was a turnaround for the Court that 13 years prior had found no reason to bar the execution of the mentally retarded. The *Atkins* v. *Virginia* case involved Daryl Atkins, who had an I.Q. of 59. He had been sentenced to death for a murder and a robbery committed when he was 18 years old. The majority decision of the Court noted that the tide of public opinion had turned and that now most states either prohibit capital punishment altogether or ban its use against the mentally retarded. Also, they noted that public opinion polls have demonstrated a steadily dwindling public enthusiasm for capital punishment in general. At the time of the decision, about 20 states allowed the execution of retarded persons. The decision failed to provide guidance to the states on what constitutes "mental retardation" for the purposes of the capital punishment prohibition.

FINES

The origin of the fine as a form of punishment is lost in history. Its early use as a form of punishment served a dual purpose. Money or property was taken from the wrongdoer and paid to the victim of the crime or to relatives. The fine was also a source of revenue to the king or church, depending on the law that was broken. As other means of reimbursing the victim of a crime became available, such as civil suits, the fine was no longer used for that purpose, but fines were levied as a source of revenue for government. The fine is still employed as a form of punishment for minor crimes.

The use of the fine as punishment in serious cases has dwindled considerably since the decision of *Williams* v. *Illinois* was handed down by the U.S. Supreme Court.[8] The statutes of most states provide for a penalty of imprisonment plus a specific amount of money that can be imposed in the form of a fine. This provision is applicable to most felonies as well as misdemeanors. As a result, judges, in the past, were able to impose a maximum time of imprisonment plus a fine. If unable to pay the fine, the convicted offender was imprisoned and "worked out" the fine by being given credit in a prescribed daily amount. In the *Williams* case, the U.S. Supreme Court held that imprisoning one who was indigent and unable to pay the fine beyond the maximum amount of imprisonment prescribed by law was in violation of the Equal Protection Clause of the Fourteenth Amendment. The facts of the *Williams* case show that Williams was convicted of petty theft and received the maximum sentence provided by law, which was one year imprisonment and a $500 fine. Williams was also taxed $5 court costs. "The judgment directed, as permitted by statute, that if Williams was in default of payment of the fine and court costs at the expiration of the one-year sentence, he should remain in jail pursuant to the Illinois Criminal Code to 'work off' the monetary obligations at the rate of $5 per day." The Court in that case stated the following:

> . . . Thus, whereas the maximum term of imprisonment for petty theft was one year, the effect of the sentence imposed here required appellant (Williams) to be confined for 101 days beyond the maximum period of confinement fixed by the statute since he could not pay the fine and costs of $505. . . .
>
> We conclude that when the aggregate imprisonment exceeds the maximum period fixed by the statute and results directly from an involuntary non-payment of a fine or court costs we are confronted with an impermissible discrimination which rests on ability to pay, and accordingly, we reverse.
>
> Nothing in today's decision curtails the sentencing prerogative of a judge because, as noted previously, the sovereign's purpose in confining an indigent beyond the statutory maximum is to provide a coercive means of collecting or "working out" a fine. After having taken into consideration the wide range of factors underlying the exercise of his sentencing function, nothing we now hold precludes a judge from imposing on an indigent, as on any defendant, the maximum penalty prescribed by law.
>
> It bears emphasis that our holding does not deal with a judgment of confinement for nonpayment of a fine in the familiar pattern of alternative sentence of "$30 or 30 days." We hold only that a state may not constitutionally imprison beyond the maximum duration fixed by statute a defendant who is financially unable to pay a fine. A statute permitting a sentence of both imprisonment and fine cannot be parlayed into a longer term of imprisonment than is fixed by the statute since to do so would be to accomplish indirectly as to an indigent that which cannot be done directly. We have no occasion to reach the question whether a State is precluded in any other circumstances from holding an indigent accountable for a fine by use of penal sanction. We hold only that the Equal Protection Clause of the Fourteenth Amendment requires that the statutory ceiling placed on imprisonment for any substantive offense be the same for all defendants irrespective of their economic status.

Although the U.S. Supreme Court did not rule out the alternative penalties, such as thirty days in jail or a $30 fine, some appellate courts contend that application of such alternative penalties necessarily results in different treatment for the rich offender and the poor one. The nature of the penalty actually inflicted by the thirty days in jail or $30 fine depends on the offender's financial ability and personal choice. If the offender chooses and is able to pay the fine, imprisonment may be avoided. If he or she chooses imprisonment, the fine may be avoided. If unable to pay the fine, imprisonment cannot be avoided. Thus, the indigent offender has no choice, and the alternative penalties work as a violation of the Equal Protection Clause. However, to date, the alternative penalty procedure has not disappeared from the justice system, and fines will continue to be imposed as a form of penalty for some time to come.

Capstone Case

United States v. *Grayson*
438 U.S. 41, 98 S.Ct. 2610, 57 L.Ed.2d 582 (1978)

Chief Justice Burger delivered the opinion of the Court.

We granted certiorari to review a holding of the Court of Appeals that it was improper for a sentencing judge, in fixing the sentence within the statutory limits, to give consideration to the defendant's false testimony observed by the judge during the trial.

In August 1975, respondent Grayson was confined in a federal prison camp under a conviction for distributing a controlled substance. In October, he escaped but was apprehended two days later by FBI agents in New York City. He was indicted for prison escape in violation of 18 U.S.C. § 751(a). During its case in chief, the United States proved the essential elements of the crime, including his lawful confinement and the unlawful escape. In addition, it presented the testimony of the arresting FBI agents that Grayson, upon being apprehended, denied his true identity.

Grayson testified in his own defense. He admitted leaving the camp but asserted that he did so out of fear: "I had just been threatened with a large stick with a nail protruding through it by an inmate that was serving time at Allenwood, and I was scared, and I just ran." He testified that the threat was made in the presence of many inmates by prisoner Barnes, who sought to enforce collection of a gambling debt and followed other threats and physical assaults made for the same purpose. Grayson called one inmate, who testified: "I heard [Barnes] talk to Grayson in a loud voice one day, but that's all. I never seen no harm, no hands or no shuffling whatsoever."

Grayson's version of the facts was contradicted by the Government's rebuttal evidence and by cross-examination on crucial aspects of his story. For example, Grayson stated that after crossing the prison fence he left his prison jacket by the side of the road. On recross, he stated that he also left his prison shirt but not his trousers. Government testimony showed that on the morning after the escape, a shirt marked with Grayson's number, a jacket, and a pair of prison trousers were found outside a hole in the prison fence. Grayson also testified on cross-examination: "I do believe that I phrased the rhetorical question to Captain Kurd, who was in charge of [the prison], and I think I said something if an inmate was being threatened by somebody, what would he do? First of all he said he would want to know who it was." On further cross-examination, however, Grayson modified his description of the conversation. Captain Kurd testified that Grayson had never mentioned in any fashion threats from other inmates. Finally, the alleged assailant, Barnes, by then no longer an inmate, testified that Grayson had never owed him any money and that he had never threatened or physically assaulted Grayson.

The jury returned a guilty verdict, whereupon the District judge ordered the United States Probation Office to prepare a presentence report. At the sentencing hearing, the judge stated:

> I'm going to give my reasons for sentencing in this case with clarity, because one of the reasons may well be considered by a Court of Appeals to be impermissible; and although I could come into this Court Room and sentence this Defendant to a five-year prison term without any explanation at all, I think it is fair that I give the reasons so that if the Court of Appeals feels that one of the reasons which I am about to enun-

ciate is an improper consideration for a trial judge, then the Court will be in a position to reverse this Court and send the case back for re-sentencing.

In my view a prison sentence is indicated, and the sentence that the Court is going to impose is to deter you, Mr. Grayson, and others who are similarly situated. Secondly, it is my view that your defense was a complete fabrication without the slightest merit whatsoever. I feel it is proper for me to consider that fact in the sentencing, and I will do so.

He then sentenced Grayson to a term of two years' imprisonment, consecutive to his unexpired sentence.

On appeal, a divided panel of the Court of Appeals for the Third Circuit directed that Grayson's sentence be vacated and that he be resentenced by the District Court without consideration of false testimony. . . . We reverse.

In *Williams* v. *New York,* 337 U.S. 241 (1949), Mr. Justice Black observed that the "prevalent modern philosophy of penology [is] that the punishment should fit the offender and not merely the crime, and that, accordingly, sentences should be determined with an eye toward the preformation and rehabilitation of offenders." But it has not always been so. In the early days of the Republic, . . . the period of incarceration was generally prescribed with specificity by the legislature. Each crime had its defined punishment. . . .

Approximately a century ago, a reform movement asserting that the purpose of incarceration, and therefore the guiding consideration in sentencing, should be rehabilitation of the offender, dramatically altered the approach to sentencing. A fundamental proposal of this movement was a flexible sentencing system permitting judges and correctional personnel, particularly the latter, to set the release date of prisoners according to informed judgments concerning their potential for, or actual, rehabilitation and their likely recidivism. . . . Indeterminate sentencing under the rehabilitation model presented sentencing judges with a serious practical problem: how rationally to make the required predictions so as to avoid capricious and arbitrary sentences, which the newly conferred and broad discretion placed within the realm of possibility. An obvious, although only partial, solution was to provide the judge with as much information as reasonably practical concerning the defendant's "character and propensities . . . his present purposes and tendencies," and, indeed, "every aspect of life." *Williams* v. *New York.* Thus, most jurisdictions provided trained probation officers to conduct presentence investigations of the defendant's life and, on that basis, prepare a presentence report for the sentencing judge.

Constitutional challenges were leveled at judicial reliance on such information, however. In *Williams* v. *New York,* a jury convicted the defendant of murder but recommended a life sentence. The sentencing judge, partly on the basis of information not known to the jury but contained in a presentence report, imposed the death penalty. The defendant argued that this procedure deprived him of his federal constitutional right to confront and cross-examine those supplying information to the probation officer and, through him, to the sentencing judge. The Court rejected this argument. It noted that traditionally "a sentencing judge could exercise a wide discretion in the sources and types of evidence used to assist him in determining the kind and extent of punishment to be imposed within limits fixed by law, . . . And modern concepts individualizing punishment have made it all the more necessary that a sentencing judge not be denied an opportunity to obtain pertinent information," indeed, "to deprive sentencing judges of this kind of information would undermine modern pedagogical procedural policies that have been cautiously adopted throughout the nation after careful consideration and experimentation." Accordingly, the sentencing judge was held not to have acted unconstitutionally in considering either the defendant's participation in criminal conduct for which he had not been convicted or information secured by the probation investigator that the defendant was a "menace to society."

Of course, a sentencing judge is not limited to the often far-ranging material compiled in a presentence report. "[B]efore making [the sentencing] determination, a judge may appropriately conduct an inquiry broad in scope, largely unlimited either as to the kind of information he may consider, or the source from which it may come." *United States* v. *Tucker,* 404 U.S. 443 (1972). Congress recently reaffirmed this fundamental sentencing principle by enacting 18 U.S.C. § 3577:

> No limitation shall be placed on the information concerning the background, character, and conduct of a person convicted of an offense which a court of the United States may receive and consider for the purpose of imposing an appropriate sentence.

Thus, we have acknowledged that a sentencing authority may legitimately consider the evidence heard during trial, as well as the demeanor of the accused. *Chaffin* v. *Stynchcombe,* 412 U.S. 17 (1973). More to the point presented in this case, one serious study has concluded that the trial judge's "opportunity to observe the defendant, particularly if he chose to take the stand in his defense, can often provide useful insights into an appropriate disposition." ABA Sentencing Alternatives and Procedures § 5.1 (App.Draft 1968).

A defendant's truthfulness or mendacity while testifying on his own behalf, almost without exception, has been deemed probative of his attitudes toward society and prospects for rehabilitation and hence relevant to sentencing. Soon after *Williams* was decided, the Tenth Circuit concluded that "the attitude of a convicted defendant with respect to his willingness to commit a serious crime [perjury] is a proper matter to consider in determining what sentence shall be imposed within the limitations fixed by statute." *Humes* v. *United States,* 186 F.2d 875 (1951). The Second, Fourth, Fifth, Sixth, Seventh, Eighth, and Ninth Circuits have since agreed. Only one Circuit has directly rejected the probative value of the defendant's false testimony in his own defense. In *Scott* v. *United States,* 135 U.S.App. D.C. 377 (1969), the court argued that the peculiar pressures placed upon a defendant threatened with jail and the stigma of conviction make his willingness to deny the crime an unpromising test of his prospects for rehabilitation if guilty. It is indeed unlikely that many men who commit serious offenses would balk on principle from lying in their own defense. The guilty man may quite sincerely repent his crime but yet, driven by the urge to remain free, may protest his innocence in a court of law.

The Scott rationale rests not only on the realism of the psychological pressures on a defendant in the dock—which we can grant—but also on a deterministic view of human conduct that is inconsistent with the underlying precepts of our criminal justice system. A "universal and persistent" foundation stone in our system of law, and particularly in our approach to punishment, sentencing, and incarceration, is the "belief in freedom of the human will and a consequent ability and duty of the normal individual to choose between good and evil." Given that long-accepted view of the "ability and duty of the normal individual to choose," we must conclude that the defendant's readiness to lie under oath—especially when, as here, the trial court finds the lie to be flagrant—may be deemed probative of his prospects for rehabilitation.

Against this background we evaluate Grayson's constitutional argument that the District Court's sentence constitutes punishment for the crime of perjury for which he has not been indicted, tried, or convicted by due process. A second argument is that permitting consideration of perjury will "chill" defendants from exercising their right to testify on their own behalf.

In his due process argument, Grayson does not contend directly that the District Court had an impermissible purpose in considering his perjury and selecting the sentence. Rather, he argues that this Court, in order to preserve due process rights, not only must prohibit the impermissible sentencing practice of incarcerating for the purpose of saving the Government the burden of bringing a separate and subsequent perjury prosecution but also must prohibit the otherwise permissible practice of considering a defendant's untruthfulness for the purpose of illuminating his need for rehabilitation and society's need for protection. He presents two interrelated reasons. The effect of both permissible and impermissible sentencing practices may be the same: additional time in prison. Further, it is virtually impossible, he contends, to identify and establish the impermissible practice. We find these reasons insufficient justification for prohibiting what the Court and the Congress have declared appropriate judicial conduct.

First, the evolutionary history of sentencing, set out [above] . . . demonstrates that it is proper—indeed, even necessary for the rational exercise of discretion—to consider the defendant's whole person and personality, as manifested by his conduct at trial and his testimony under oath, for whatever light those may shed on the sentencing decision . . . . Second, in our view, Williams fully supports consideration of such conduct in sentencing. There the Court permitted the sentencing judge to consider the offender's history of prior antisocial conduct, including burglaries for which he had not been duly convicted . . . . Third, the efficacy of Grayson's suggested "exclusionary rule" is open to serious doubt. No rule of law, even one garbed in constitutional terms, can prevent improper use of firsthand observations of perjury. The integrity of the judges, and their fidelity to their oaths of office, necessarily provide the only, and in our view adequate, assurance against that.

Grayson's argument that judicial consideration of his conduct at trial impermissibly "chills" a defendant's statutory right, 18 U.S.C. § 3481, and perhaps a constitutional right, to testify on his own behalf is without basis. The right guaranteed by law to a defendant is narrowly the right to testify truthfully in accordance with the oath—unless we are to say that the oath is mere ritual without meaning. This view of the right involved is confirmed by the unquestioned constitutionality of perjury statutes, which punish those who willfully give false testimony. Further support for this is found in an important limitation on a defendant's right to the assistance of counsel: Counsel ethically cannot assist his client in presenting what the attorney has reason to believe is false testimony. Assuming, arguendo, that the sentencing judge's consideration of defendant's untruthfulness in testifying has any chilling effect on a defendant's decision to testify falsely, that effect is entirely permissible. There is no protected right to commit perjury.

Grayson's further argument that the sentencing practice challenged here will inhibit exercise of the right to testify truthfully is entirely frivolous. That argument misapprehends the nature and scope of the practice we find permissible. Nothing we say today requires a sentencing judge to enhance, in some wooden or reflex fashion, the sentences of all defendants whose testimony is deemed false. Rather, we are reaffirming the authority of a sentencing judge to evaluate carefully a defendant's testimony on the stand, determine—with a consciousness of the frailty of human judgment—whether that testimony contained willful and material falsehoods, and, if so, assess in light of all the other knowledge gained about the defendant the meaning of that conduct with respect to his prospects for rehabilitation and restoration to a useful place in society. Awareness of such a process realistically cannot be deemed to affect the decision of an accused but unconvicted defendant to testify truthfully in his own behalf.

Justice Stewart, with whom Justice Brennan and Justice Marshall join, dissenting.

The Court begins its consideration of this case with the assumption that the respondent gave false testimony at his trial. But there has been no determination that his testimony was false. This respondent was given a greater sentence than he would otherwise have received—how much greater we have no way of knowing—solely because a single judge thought that he had not testified truthfully. In essence, the Court holds today that whenever a defendant testifies in his own behalf and is found guilty, he opens himself to the possibility of an enhanced sentence. Such a sentence is nothing more or less than a penalty imposed on the defendant's exercise of his constitutional and statutory rights to plead not guilty and to testify in his own behalf.

It does not change matters to say that the enhanced sentence merely reflects the defendant's "prospects for rehabilitation" rather than an additional punishment for testifying falsely. The fact remains that all defendants who choose to testify, and only those who do so, face the very real prospect of a greater sentence based upon the trial judge's unreviewable perception that the testimony was untruthful. The Court prescribes no limitations or safeguards to minimize a defendant's rational fear that his truthful testimony will be perceived as false. Indeed, encumbrance of the sentencing process with the collateral inquiries necessary to provide such assurance would be both pragmatically unworkable and theoretically inconsistent with the assumption that the trial judge is merely considering one more piece of information in his overall evaluation of the defendant's prospects for rehabilitation. But without such safeguards I fail to see how the Court can dismiss as "frivolous" the argument that this sentencing practice will "inhibit exercise of the right to testify truthfully."

The minimal contribution that the defendant's possibly untruthful testimony might make to an overall assessment of his potential for rehabilitation . . . cannot justify imposing this additional burden on his right to testify in his own behalf. I do not believe that a sentencing judge's discretion to consider a wide range of information in arriving at an appropriate sentence, *Williams* v. *New York,* allows him to mete out additional punishment to the defendant simply because of his personal belief that the defendant did not testify truthfully at the trial. Accordingly, I would affirm the judgment of the Court of Appeals.

REVIEW QUESTIONS

1. What amendment includes the guarantee against cruel and unusual punishment?
2. Why was imprisonment not used as a form of punishment in early criminal procedures?
3. What contribution did William Penn make to the sentencing procedure?
4. What is the primary purpose behind sentencing an offender?

5. List the different forms of punishment that may presently be imposed upon a convicted offender.
6. Explain the significance of each of the following types of sentences:
   a. The definite sentence
   b. The indefinite sentence
   c. The indeterminate sentence

7. What is the primary purpose of granting probation?
8. Why has the alternative sentence of a fine of $30 or thirty days in jail been criticized?

LOCAL PROCEDURE

1. Which type of sentence is imposed—the indefinite or indeterminate—in your home state?
2. Who sentences the defendant—the judge, the jury, or some other body?

ENDNOTES

1. 408 U.S. 238 (1972).
2. 428 U.S. 280 (1976).
3. 428 U.S. 153 (1976).
4. 433 U.S. 584 (1977).
5. 446 U.S. 420 (1980).
6. 458 U.S. 782 (1982).
7. 95 L.Ed. 2d 127 (1987).
8. 339 U.S. 235 (1970).

Collateral Proceedings

What we seek is the reign of law, based upon the consent of the governed and sustained by the organized opinion of mankind.
—Woodrow Wilson, on the League of Nations, in a speech at Mount Vernon, July 4, 1918.

In this chapter, we will examine the two collateral proceedings that are essential to the judicial process. "Collateral proceedings" refer to those proceedings that are not part of the normal judicial process involved in the conviction and sentencing or the acquittal of a defendant, but that are a necessary part of the criminal justice system. The collateral proceedings discussed in this chapter are extradition and writs.

EXTRADITION

From a sequential standpoint, extradition should have been included in the discussion on arrest, but in view of the technicalities involved in this subject, we believe that its discussion will be more understandable if delayed until this time. Extradition is the procedure followed in returning an accused from one state or foreign country to the state where the crime was committed, for the purposes of prosecution. The extradition proceedings may be international or interstate. Interstate extradition is referred to by some legal writers as rendition.

Interstate Extradition

Interstate extradition is based upon Article IV, Section 2, of the U.S. Constitution. This section provides that "A person charged in any state with treason, felony, or other crime, who shall flee from justice, and be found in another state, shall on demand of the executive authority of the state from which he fled, be delivered up, to be removed to the state having jurisdiction over the crime." Because of certain deficiencies of this provision in covering all phases of extradition, most states have adopted the Uniform Criminal Extradition Act. Prior to the Act's adoption, it was necessary to prove that an accused had actually fled from the state in which the crime was committed to avoid prosecution. The Act makes it unnecessary to prove that the accused fled from justice. The mere presence of the accused in another state is all that is necessary. Prior to the adoption of the Act, an accused who was found in another state to which he or she had not voluntarily gone could not be extradited. For example, in one case, a fugitive was wanted for robbery in Utah but fled to Oklahoma. While in Oklahoma, the offender committed a bank robbery and was sentenced to serve a federal sentence in the penitentiary in Leavenworth, Kansas. Utah attempted to extradite the fugitive from Kansas after the completion of the bank robbery sentence. It was held that since the fugitive did not voluntarily flee to Kansas, he could not be extradited. The adoption of the act permits extradition from any state even though the accused did not voluntarily go to that state. An accused may be extradited on either a misdemeanor or a felony charge. However, because of the expense and procedure involved, fugitives are seldom extradited on a misdemeanor charge.

Requirements for Extradition.   In order to extradite an accused, there must be a warrant of arrest outstanding against that individual, based on an accusatory pleading filed in the county in which the crime took place. After determining that the accused is in another state, the prosecuting attorney of the county in which the crime was committed will make an application to the governor of his or her state. The application is a request for the governor to make a demand on the governor of the state where the accused is presently located for the return of the fugitive to the demanding state for prosecution. The application must reflect the name of the fugitive, the crime charged, the approximate time and date of the offense, the circumstances surrounding the commission of the crime, and the state and location where it is believed that the fugitive is located. It must also be alleged that the fugitive was in the demanding state at the time that the crime was committed. The application, along with copies of the accusatory pleading and a warrant, will be submitted to the governor of the demanding state. On approval of the application for extradition, the governor of the demanding state will appoint an officer to deliver the extradition papers to the governor of the state in which the fugitive is located, with a demand that the fugitive be returned to the demanding state for prosecution. The state in which the fugitive is located is generally referred to as the asylum state.

Acting on the Extradition Request.   On receipt of the papers, the governor will review them in an effort to determine whether the fugitive should be surrendered to the demanding state. The governor may request the attorney general, or any prosecuting attorney of his or her state, to conduct an investigation to assist in making the determination. The investigation may include an inquiry to determine that the person sought is actually the one charged in the demanding state, and the offender's identity must be certainly established. An inquiry may be made by the asylum state to make certain that the accused has been substantially charged in the demanding state. This is a determination of whether or not a complaint has been filed or an indictment returned and a warrant of arrest issued. The governor of the asylum state may wish to be satisfied that the accused sought was in the demanding state at the time the crime was committed and that he or she then left the demanding state. If the investigation concludes that the fugitive should be surrendered, the governor will issue a governor's warrant of arrest directing some officer to place the fugitive under arrest. After the arrest is made, the fugitive will be taken before a local magistrate, who will set a date for an extradition hearing. If the offense for which the fugitive is being extradited is a bailable offense in the demanding state, the local magistrate may set bail in order that the fugitive may post bail and be free from custody pending the extradition hearing. The hearing is usually set within a few days after the arrest. During the hearing, two major facts will be considered. First, is the fugitive in custody the person named in the accusatory pleading of the demanding state? Second, was the fugitive in the demanding state at the time the crime was committed? If the magistrate has any reservations about either of these items, a request may be made that the demanding state present further evidence to prove the identity and whereabouts of the fugitive. The fugitive is entitled to the assistance of counsel at the hearing and to present evidence in his or her own behalf. If the magistrate is satisfied that the fugitive at the hearing is the one named in the accusatory pleading and was in the demanding state at the time that the crime was committed, the fugitive will be turned over to the custody of an officer of the demanding state for return to that state. Evidence of the fugitive's guilt or innocence is not pertinent at the hearing and will not be presented. After returning to the demanding state, the fugitive may be prosecuted on any charge, not just the one named in the extradition proceedings. In fact, the fugitive does not even have to be prosecuted on that charge if the prosecuting attorney wishes to substitute a different charge.

The Fugitive Already Arrested.   Not all fugitives wanted in another state are first arrested on a governor's warrant. Frequently, an individual is arrested on a minor local charge, after which it will be determined that there is an outstanding warrant of arrest for that individual in another state. The laws of most states permit a temporary detention of the arrested person until extradition proceedings can be instituted. Many times, extradition proceedings are waived under these circumstances. If the person in custody waives the right to extradition proceedings, the waiver will eliminate the application to the governor of the demanding state and the other extradition formalities previously described. Upon agreeing to waive extradition, the arrested person is taken before a local magistrate, from whom consent to be returned to the demanding state will be given. Usually, the consent is given in writing. The magistrate will then order the arrested person's return to the demanding state.

Refusal to Extradite.   Although the U.S. Constitution provides that a person charged with a crime who has fled a state shall, upon demand, be "delivered up" to the demanding state, there have been times when a governor of an asylum state has refused to honor this constitutional provision. Both the U.S. Supreme Court and many state courts have held that the governor of an asylum state has the duty to abide by the demand, but there is no authority that can compel the governor to extradite a person wanted for prosecution. It has been held, however, that the governor of the asylum state must, within a reasonable time, either abide by the demand or refuse to extradite. The action cannot just be postponed indefinitely. The demanding state is entitled to know whether the fugitive is to be returned or not.[1] It has also been held that the asylum state has no right to question the merits or motives of the demanding state. The guilt or innocence of the offender is the sole responsibility of the demanding state.

In one case, the supreme court of an asylum state ordered a local court to investigate the conditions of the prison in the demanding state from which the offender escaped before the asylum state would authorize the extradition of the offender. However, the U.S. Supreme Court held in the case of *Pacileo* v. *Walker*[2] that the state supreme court had exceeded its authority. The facts of the *Pacileo* case reflect that Walker, the defendant, escaped from an Arkansas prison and was later apprehended in California. The governor of Arkansas requested that Walker be extradited to Arkansas to serve the remainder of his sentence. The governor of California signed the extradition papers, but the California Supreme Court ordered a local court to investigate the conditions of the Arkansas prison system to determine whether conditions in the Arkansas prison system violated the Cruel and Unusual Punishment Clause of the Eighth Amendment to the U.S. Constitution. The local sheriff who was charged with the responsibility of making the investigation contended that the courts of the asylum state did not have the authority to investigate the prison conditions of the demanding state. The sheriff's contention was appealed to the U.S. Supreme Court, which held that once the governor of the asylum state signs the extradition papers, the courts of that state may consider only whether or not the extradition documents of the demanding state and asylum state are in order. Any further inquiry is beyond the local court's authority. The U.S. Supreme Court held that this issue had been previously decided in other cases.

Federal Law against Unlawful Flight

Interstate extradition proceedings are not to be confused with the procedure followed under the federal Unlawful Flight to Avoid Prosecution Statute. In the 1930s, gangsters began to plague local law enforcement officers by going into a community and committing a series of serious crimes and then immediately fleeing to parts unknown. These officers were often handicapped in their efforts to locate the gangsters, because many times they would flee to another state. Because of the seriousness of the situation, Congress passed the Unlawful Flight to Avoid Prosecution Statute. This Statue permits the federal government, through the Federal Bureau of Investigation (FBI), to assist in locating and arresting badly wanted fugitives. When a fugitive is identified as having left the state where a crime was committed, the local prosecuting attorney can have a local warrant of arrest issued. The U.S. Attorney for that district is then requested to file a complaint charging the fugitive with the violation of the Unlawful Flight Statute. A warrant is issued on the federal complaint giving the FBI the authority to locate and arrest the fugitive. In most instances, the local prosecuting attorney must agree to handle extradition proceedings, since the Statute was passed to assist in locating and arresting the fugitive and not for return to the demanding state. Originally, the Statute permitted assistance in only a few major crimes; however, the Statute now permits assistance to be given for any felony violation.

International Extradition

International extradition is based entirely on treaties with certain countries; these treaties specify the crimes for which an accused may be extradited. In most instances, political crimes are excluded. If a fugitive is extradited from a foreign country, he or she may be prosecuted only on the extradition charge. This safeguard prevents countries from extraditing a political fugitive under the pretext of a specified crime and then instigating prosecution for an alleged attempt to overthrow a government or for another political or unspecified crime. International extradition is handled in the United States through the Department of State. Instead of the governor of the demanding state directly contacting the officials in the asylum country, the governor will forward the demand for extradition to the secretary of state. The secretary of state will submit the demand to the officials of the asylum country, requesting that the fugitive be surrendered to officials of the United States in order that he or she be returned to this country for prosecution. If those officials decide that extradition is in order, the fugitive will be surrendered to this country. As in the case of the governor who does not honor the constitutional provision on interstate extradition, little can be done to compel a foreign country to extradite a person wanted in this country, with the exceptions of registering a protest or breaking a treaty. In most instances, however; the asylum country honors the demand. Treaties differ somewhat between countries. Some treaties provide that any person may be extradited for the specified crimes; other treaties exempt citizens of that particular country. This provision could hamper extradition, since many countries recognize dual citizenship. The lack of a treaty between two countries does not prevent one of them from surrendering a wanted fugitive to the other. Under these circumstances, the fugitive may be prosecuted for any crime unless the two countries agree otherwise.

WRITS

A writ defies simple definition. Legally, a writ is defined as a mandatory precept, under seal, issued by a court, and commanding the person to whom it is addressed to do or not to do some act. One might think of a writ as a written order issued by a court directing some other court officer to do or not to do a particular act. A number of writs may be issued by a court, but only the more frequently encountered writs will be discussed here.

Writ of Habeas Corpus

The writ of habeas corpus has been termed the great writ because its purpose is to obtain the prompt release of one who is being unlawfully detained. The right to this writ is embodied in the Constitution of the United States and in the laws of all the states. The statutes of the states read similarly to the following: Every person unlawfully imprisoned or restrained of liberty, under any pretense whatever, may request a writ of habeas corpus to inquire into the cause of the imprisonment or restraint. The person who believes that he or she is being unlawfully imprisoned, or someone in that person's behalf, may petition the appropriate court to have a writ of habeas corpus issued. Generally, a writ of habeas corpus may be issued by a judge of the superior court or its equivalent, or by a justice of an appellate court. In most states, the judge of the inferior court has no authority to issue a writ of habeas corpus.

The petition must state the place of confinement, the officer or person doing the confining, and the facts as to why the petitioner feels unlawfully imprisoned. If the reason is valid, the writ will be issued and served on the person holding the prisoner, commanding that the prisoner be brought before the issuing court for a hearing to determine whether there is sufficient cause to confine the prisoner. A copy of the writ is furnished to the local prosecuting attorney in order that evidence may be presented endeavoring to prove the legality of the imprisonment. But the burden of proof is on the imprisoned person to prove by a preponderance of evidence that the imprisonment is unlawful. If the offense for which the person is imprisoned is a bailable one, the person is entitled to post bail pending the habeas corpus hearing.

If, after hearing the evidence presented by the prisoner and the prosecuting attorney, the judge concludes that the prisoner is being unlawfully detained, an order for the prisoner to be set free will be issued. The prisoner may not be charged further on that offense unless additional evidence is developed showing reasonable cause for an arrest and commitment by a legal process. If the judge concludes that the imprisonment was lawful, the prisoner will remain in custody to await the appropriate judicial processes.

The early use of the writ of habeas corpus was limited to obtaining the immediate release of one unlawfully restrained. But in recent years, the use of this writ has been broadened materially to make it applicable in a number of situations. For example, if an offender believes that the bail set for release is excessive, a writ of habeas corpus may be filed in an effort to get a reduction in bail. Further, if a convicted person believes that the sentence is excessive, this writ may be filed to have a determination made on the sentence's being excessive. This writ has also been used to determine the effectiveness of counsel. One of the more extensive uses made of the writ in recent years has resulted from some appellate court decisions, particularly those of the U.S. Supreme Court, that affect the rights of one convicted. For example, the *Witherspoon* decision held that a prospective juror could not be challenged for cause just because the juror had reservations against the death penalty. This decision caused writs of habeas corpus to be filed by all those convicted and given the death penalty in trials in which prospective jurors had been excused for cause as being against the death penalty. These writs of habeas corpus requested that the sentence of death be reduced to life imprisonment. This action was possible, since the U.S. Supreme Court made the *Witherspoon* decision retroactive. When a decision is made retroactive, it is effective even though a trial is completed and the appeal period has passed. If a decision is not made retroactive, only those offenders whose trial or appeal has not been completed may take advantage of the decision.

The writ is also the way that the death penalty from state criminal trials is traditionally attacked in federal court. In the past, convictions have been voided years after the defendants were found guilty. The process has also been used to delay the imposition of the death penalty. To eliminate this possibility, in 1996, the U.S. Congress passed the Antiterrorism and Effective Death Penalty Act. This act establishes limitation periods for the bringing of habeas actions and requires that federal courts generally defer to state courts' determinations. Under the act, a habeas petitioner will normally have one year in which to seek relief. If the claim has been adjudicated in state court, relief will not be available unless the state court's adjudication resulted in a decision that is either contrary to, or involved an unreasonable application of, clearly established federal law as determined by the U.S. Supreme Court, or was based on an unreasonable determination of the facts in light of the evidence presented in the state court proceedings. The presumption of correctness accorded state courts' factual findings was also strengthened. Second or successive habeas actions presenting new claims must be dismissed unless the claim is shown to rely on a new, previously unavailable rule of constitutional law or unless the factual predicate for the claim could not have been discovered previously through due diligence and the new facts would be sufficient to establish by clear and convincing evidence that, except for the error, no reasonable fact finder would have convicted.[3]

Writ of Certiorari

This writ is issued by an appellate court to permit the review of a decision or judgment by a lower court. This writ is often issued when other means of appeal are not possible. The writ of certiorari is often granted by a state supreme court to review a lower court's decision in order to establish guidelines to be followed in future cases by either trial judges or lower appellate courts. This is particularly the case if there is some doubt concerning a law or procedure. This writ is automatically issued in most jurisdictions to review a case when the death penalty is imposed to determine whether the facts warrant a conviction and the imposition of the death penalty. The U.S. Supreme Court frequently issues this writ to review the decision of a state appellate court when there may be a possible denial of a U.S. constitutional guarantee. The *Coker* decision is a good example. As stated, Coker was convicted of forceful rape and sentenced to death in a trial court in Georgia. The Georgia Supreme Court affirmed both the conviction and the death penalty. The U.S. Supreme Court granted Coker a writ of certiorari in order to determine whether the death penalty was excessive for the conviction of rape and, thus, a violation of the Eighth Amendment.

REVIEW QUESTIONS

1. What is extradition?
2. Upon what is international extradition based?
3. Upon what is interstate extradition based?
4. In relation to prosecution, how do international and interstate extradition differ?
5. In what way did the Uniform Criminal Extradition Act correct certain weaknesses in the extradition procedure?
6. Briefly outline the procedure that must be followed in extraditing an offender.
7. What is the purpose of each of the following writs:
   a. Habeas corpus?
   b. Certiorari?

LOCAL PROCEDURE

1. Has your state adopted the Uniform Criminal Extradition Act?
2. Does your state have statutory procedures for handling writs?

ENDNOTES

1. *State of South Dakota* v. *Brown*, 144 Cal.Rptr. 758 (1978).
2. 449 U.S. 86 (1981).
3. 18 U.S. Code 3663A.

CHAPTER 17

Victims' Rights

Rape is the only crime in which the victim becomes the accused and, in reality, it is she who must prove her good reputation, her mental soundness, and her impeccable propriety.

—Freda Adler, 1975

THE HISTORICAL PERSPECTIVE

The majority of this text has focused on the criminal justice system and the offender. Understanding how we responded to offenders is an important part of the criminal justice process; however, we must also understand how the victim of a crime fits within this system. This chapter will examine a newly emerging trend in the United States, that of victim interaction in the criminal justice system.[1] During the late 1960s, victims of crime began volunteering to serve within various victim assistance programs. As these crime victims continued to speak out about their treatment in the criminal justice system, the states and the federal government reacted by establishing commissions to study crime and its consequences.

The federal government responded by establishing the Law Enforcement Assistance Administration (LEAA). This agency provides funds to law enforcement agencies for a variety of purposes, including the establishment of victim and witness programs.[2] In 1975, the LEAA called a meeting in Washington, D.C., of various victim advocates to discuss methods of increasing victims' rights. One of the consequences of this meeting was the formation of the National Organization for Victim Assistance (NOVA). Today, NOVA is considered by many to be one of the leading victim rights organizations in the world.

Gains and Losses

During the late 1970s and early 1980s, the movement foundered. Lack of funding by the federal government caused many community-based victim organizations and service providers to cease operations. Additionally, within the movement, issues such as professionalism and training caused increasing divisiveness. The movement began to splinter into specialized groups that focused on specific issues. Several sexual assault and domestic violence organizations, such as the National Coalition Against Sexual Assault, were established to address the specific needs of those victims.[3] Although there was tension between various service providers because of diminishing funding and disagreement regarding specific goals, there was also progress in other areas of the victims' movement during this period. Parents of Murdered Children (POMC) was founded by Robert and Charlotte Hullinger in 1978, and Mothers Against Drunk Driving (MADD) was founded by Candy Lighter in 1980. Both of these organizations continue to have an impact on victims' rights and the victims' movement.

Increased Public Awareness

From 1982 through 1986, victims' organizations began to use the media to increase public awareness of crime victim issues. President Ronald Reagan and Congress responded to this heightened awareness with actions that would eventually have long-term consequences for the victims' movement. In 1982, President Reagan appointed a Task Force on Victims of Crime. This task force published a report that has since become a platform for victims' rights.[4]

Question: "How important do you think it is for the judicial system to provide victims and their families with each of the following?"

	Very Important	Somewhat Important	Not too Important	Not at all Important	Not Sure
Right to be notified about dates and places of trials and related hearings	84%	13%	1%	1%	1%
Right to be physically present at trials and related hearings	82	15	1	0	1
Opportunity to discuss case with prosecutor during plea bargaining	72	18	3	3	4
Opportunity to discuss case with prosecutor during trial	57	28	6	4	4
Opportunity to make statement prior to sentencing about how crime affected them	72	20	5	2	2
Right to be paid for stolen or damaged property or injuries received in crime	81	15	2	1	1

*Percents may not add to 100 because of rounding.
Source: Kathisen Maguire and Ann L. Pastore (eds.), Sourcebook of Criminal Justice Statistics 1992. *U.S. Department of Justice Statistics (Washington: GPO, 1993). p. 199, Table 2.49.*

In 1984, another key event took place when Congress passed the Victims of Crime Act (VOCA).[5] The Office for Victims of Crime (OVC) was created in the Department of Justice to implement the task force's recommendations. OVC provides grants to states for programs with direct services for victims of all crimes. VOCA also established the Crime Victims Fund to provide money to local victim assistance programs and state victim compensation programs. The fund receives money from federal criminal fines, penalties, and bond forfeitures.

Increased Professionalism

From 1984 to the present, the victims' movement has been characterized by an increase in the professionalism of its advocates and providers. In previous times, the victims' movement was highlighted by strong dynamic leaders with vision and determination. At present, the movement has expanded beyond the ability of any one person's being able to influence its direction. It is now a national movement with a tremendous influence on local, state, and national politics.

Universities are expanding their victim-related courses. Organizations such as NOVA are offering increased training opportunities, and in 1995, the U.S. Department of Justice sponsored the first National Victim Assistance Academy in Washington, D.C. This academy was repeated in 1996 using distance-learning technology to link three universities in a joint academic effort. It continues to be offered on various college campus across the nation.

The public awareness of victim issues continues to grow, and victim advocates have become an acknowledged force in modern-day politics. Victim service providers are realizing that their profession requires multidisciplinary training. There is a growing awareness that to be accepted by other professionals requires continuing education, certifications, or other acknowledged credentials. This increased professionalism should translate into more sophisticated interventions and a faster rate of progress within the victims' movement.

Additional Laws

Increased professionalism also means increased knowledge and insight into the problems of victims. Congress has acknowledged the plight of victims by passing a Victims' Bill of Rights. By 1990, two-thirds of the states had enacted similar types of laws protecting victims. In 1994, Congress enacted the Violent Crime Control and Law Enforcement Act. Title IV of that law is the Violence Against Women Act (VAWA). Congress mandated that various professions form partnerships and work together to respond to all forms of violence against women.

The attorney general is required to report to Congress annually on the grants that are awarded under the act and to ensure that research examining violence against women is encouraged. The report must include the number of grants, funds distributed, and other statistical information. Additionally, the report must assess the effectiveness of any programs that are funded under VAWA.

The Act provides funding for a variety of research-based studies. It also requires that federal agencies engage in research regarding violence against women. For example, the National Institute of Justice is mandated to conduct four important projects: (1) the development of a research agenda that will address violence with particular emphasis on underserved populations; (2) the assessment of establishing state databases to record the number of sexual and domestic violence inci-

The Concept of a "Victim" under Alaska Law.

Alaska Statutes

Section 12.55.185. Definitions. In this chapter, unless the context requires otherwise, "victim" means:

    A. a person against whom an offense has been perpetrated;

    B. one of the following, not the perpetrator, if the person specified in (A) of this paragraph is a minor, incompetent, or incapacitated:

        i. an individual living in a spousal relationship with the person specified in (A) of this paragraph; or

        ii. a parent, adult child, guardian, or custodian of the person;

    C. one of the following, not the perpetrator, if the person specified in (A) of this paragraph is dead:

        i. a person living in a spousal relationship with the deceased before the deceased died;

        ii. an adult child, parent, brother, sister, grandparent, or grandchild of the deceased; or

        iii. any other interested person, as may be designated by a person having authority in law to do so.

Source: Alaska State Legislature.

dents; (3) a study to determine how abusive partners obtain addresses of their victims; and (4) an examination with other agencies of the battered woman syndrome.[6]

In 2000, Congress passed the Victims of Trafficking and Violence Prevention Act. In Division A, the act addresses the issue of trafficking of persons into the sex trade, slavery, and slavery-like conditions through prosecution of traffickers and assistance for victims of trafficking. This act increases penalties for slavery and trafficking crimes and provides for restitution for trafficking victims. Division B of the act expands the Violence Against Women Act and expands the definition of a victim of terrorism to include a person who is a national of the United States or an officer or employer of the U.S. government who is injured or killed as a result of a terrorist act or mass violence outside the United States.

There were several laws that were added to aid victims of September 11, 2001. Title IV of the Air Transportation Safety and System Stabilization Act of 2001 established the September 11th Victim Compensation Fund of 2001 to address the economic and noneconomic losses of victims of this specific act of terrorism. (The final rules regarding this act were published March 6, 2002.) The USA Patriot Act of 2001 addresses the needs and concerns of victims of terrorist acts, including immigrant victims of the attacks on September 11, 2001. The Victims of Terrorism Tax Relief Act of 2001 exempts from income taxes any individual who dies as a result of wounds or injury incurred from the terrorist attacks against the United States on September 11, 2001.

In what may become one of the most critical dates in the history of victims' rights, on June 25, 1996, President Clinton proposed a Victims' Rights Constitutional Amendment to the U.S. Constitution. In a speech made in the Rose Garden announcing the Victims' Rights Constitutional Amendment, President Clinton stated that after studying all the alternatives, he was convinced that the only way to fully safeguard the rights of victims was to amend the Constitution to guarantee victims certain rights.[7]

The Victims' Rights Constitutional Amendment faces a long and complex process before it becomes law. It must be approved by Congress and then adopted by three-quarters of the states to become part of the Constitution. It is not something that will happen in a few weeks or months, and there are those who already claim that the proposed amendment is too detailed and should be made broader. No matter what the outcome, the simple fact that such an amendment has actually been proposed is a significant acknowledgment of the plight of victims of crimes.

RESTITUTION

Introduction

The 1982 *Final Report of the President's Task Force on Victims of Crime* included several key points regarding restitution.[8] The report recommended that legislation be enacted requiring judges to order restitution for property loss and personal injury in all cases unless the judge explicitly finds that restitution is not appropriate. However, the report went on to point out that although restitution is a proper goal to be pursued, it has limitations. The report noted that restitution cannot be ordered unless the perpetrator is caught and convicted. Even if it is ordered, the offender often has no resources with which to make any payments. Finally, those perpetrators who can make payments may take many years to finally pay off the balance. In the interim, the victim is left to bear the cost of the crime.[9]

As a result of this report and other factors influencing the victim's movement over the last decade, a number of laws have been enacted addressing the issue of restitution. Hillenbrand reports that one of the reasons that these laws have been enacted may be the change in perception regarding restitution. She states that society began to view restitution not as a way to punish or rehabilitate the offender, but as a method of bringing justice to victims.[10] Other authorities argue that laws mandating restitution have been passed as "politically correct" with little or no thought given to their effect. This situation has resulted in a system that does not deliver its promise of making victims whole. Consequently, victims become more disillusioned with the criminal justice system when they learn that the court order mandating the offender to pay restitution carries no weight or authority.[11]

Even the definition of restitution causes conflict. It represents many things to many people. The victim may view restitution as a way to regain financial loss and punish the offender, whereas the court may see it as a method of instilling responsibility in the offender. The agency charged with collecting restitution may view it as simply one more task for an already overburdened department. Traditionally, restitution is a court-ordered sanction that involves payment of compensation by the defendant to the victim for injuries suffered as a result of the defendant's criminal act.

Restitution as we know it today can be traced to the criminal laws that authorized suspended sentences and the use of probation. By the late 1930s, several states had laws that allowed judges to order restitution as a condition of granting probation.[12] This process viewed restitution as part of the correctional process. In the late 1970s and 1980s, the victims' movement began to argue that restitution should be viewed as protecting victims from suffering financial hardship rather than as punishing or rehabilitating the offender.

The modern concept of restitution in the criminal justice system serves a variety of purposes in the administration of justice. Restitution attempts to establish a relationship between the perpetrator and the victim in an effort to make the offender aware of the financial consequences suffered by the victim as a result of the offender's acts. Another purpose of restitution is to advance the concept of personal responsibility and accountability to the victim. A third idea regarding restitution holds that though it cannot undo the wrong, it can assist the victim financially and emotionally and at the same time educate the offender. Finally, restitution serves to punish the offender. The funds used to pay restitution must come from the offender's pocketbook and thus have a continuing impact on him or her.[13]

Types of Restitution

Restitution can now be ordered for a wide variety of criminal acts, including sex crimes, child sexual abuse, telemarketing fraud, and domestic violence.[14] Restitution can also be ordered to pay for lost wages, child care, and other expenses involved in attending court hearings.[15] Additionally, there are a number of different types of restitution.[16]

The most common form of restitution is financial, which requires the offender to make payments directly to the actual victim of the crime. Financial community restitution requires the offender to make payments to a community agency such as a restitution center, which then pays the victim. Individual service restitution requires the offender to perform a service for the actual victim. For example, the offender might be required to repair or replace property he or she damaged during the commission of the crime. Community service restitution requires the offender to perform some beneficial service to the community. In this type of restitution, which is sometimes referred to as "symbolic restitution," society serves as the symbolic victim. Finally, some states authorize restitution fines. Restitution fines differ from actual restitution in that they are collected and deposited in the state's crime victim compensation fund. These monies then become part of the fund's operating expenses.

Restitution may be tied to different aspects of a defendant's sentence and is frequently imposed at the earliest possible time in the criminal process. Additionally, many plea agreements call for restitution. Imposing payment as a condition of probation is the most commonly used method of collecting restitution. A court order may also follow the defendant to the correctional institution. Many states are now imposing the requirement that inmates work while incarcerated; while working in prison, they normally receive only a minimal amount of money (usually far less than the minimum wage). Several states have passed laws requiring that a portion of that amount, no matter how small, be set aside for payment as restitution to the victim. More and more states are implementing policies that require restitution to be established as a condition of any parole. States are also passing laws that provide that any restitution order in a criminal case will also be considered as a civil order for remuneration from the defendant to the victim and may be processed in civil courts.

Problems with Restitution

Restitution is a complex process that involves a number of different professionals working in the criminal justice system. Unfortunately, these professionals are usually overworked and underbudgeted. Many of these professionals claim that collecting and disbursing restitution is someone else's job.[17] This perception leads to poor communications and diminished accountability among agencies within the criminal justice system, and in turn, causes poor consultation and communication with victims. Since there may not be one agency controlling or coordinating restitution, judges may impose insufficient or excessive restitution orders.

Many victims feel dissatisfied with the restitution process. They may believe that the amount imposed in the court order was insufficient. Other victims feel powerless as they search for answers to their questions, only to be directed from one agency to another.[18]

Occasionally, multiple perpetrators are involved in one crime against a single victim. If the prosecution grants one of the perpetrators immunity to testify against the others, the victim will not be able to receive a court order of restitution against that defendant. By the same token, there are crimes involving single perpetrators and multiple victims. Deciding which victim should receive the limited funds of the perpetrator can create great difficulties.

Another obvious problem with restitution is the socioeconomic status of the perpetrator. In a majority of cases, the offender is poor and unlikely to earn the funds necessary to make full restitution. Additionally, juvenile offenders are often incapable of obtaining or holding onto jobs that might provide them with the funds necessary to pay the court-ordered restitution.

COMPENSATION[19]

Introduction

Victims often suffer physical injury, emotional and mental trauma, and financial loss as a result of a crime. The financial loss to crime victims can cause additional stress as they worry about hospital and doctor bills being paid, physical recovery from their injuries, and their ability to return to work. Crime victim compensation programs exist to provide financial assistance to crime victims and to reduce some of these stressors. These programs exist in all fifty states, as well as the District of Columbia, and many will pay for medical care, mental health counseling, lost wages, and in the case of homicides, the funeral costs and loss of support.[20] Although no amount of money can replace the use of an arm or the loss of a loved one, it can help victims preserve their financial stability and dignity, and thereby assist in the recovery process.

As we discussed, in 1984, Congress enacted the Victims of Crime Act, which established a Crime Victims Fund, supported by revenues from federal offenders. This revenue was based upon fines, penalty assessments, and forfeited appearance bonds. When VOCA was enacted in 1984, the fund ceiling, or amount that could be allocated to the fund, was $100 million. Amendments to VOCA occurred in 1986, 1988, 1990, and in 1992, when Congress removed the ceiling. Although deposits fluctuate from year to year, the total amount deposited in the fund from its inception to 1994 was more than $1.2 billion.[21]

Some of this money is available to the Administrative Office of the U.S. Courts, which established and administers a centralized National Fine Center. This center receives all the fines, assessments, and penalties, and collects money from those who failed to pay on time. Other monies are used to improve the investigation and prosecution of child abuse cases, including those child abuse acts committed against Native Americans. However, most of the money in the fund is used to support state victim compensation and victim assistance service programs. Victim compensation is a direct payment to, or on behalf of, a crime victim for crime-related expenses such as unpaid medical bills, mental health counseling, funeral costs, and lost wages.[22] Victim assistance includes services such as crisis intervention, counseling, emergency transportation to court, temporary housing, advocacy, and criminal justice support.[23]

VOCA also established special assessments for individual crimes that are levied on every conviction. Additionally, VOCA has a "Son of Sam" provision that requires royalties from the sale of literary rights or any other profits derived from a crime to be deposited in the Crime Victims Fund and held for five years to satisfy any civil judgment that a victim may obtain. If no judgments are filed, these funds become part of the general Crime Victims Fund.[24]

Victim assistance programs include organizations that provide a wide variety of services to victims of state and federal crimes. More than eight thousand agencies or organizations provide services to victims, and nearly three thousand of those organizations received some VOCA funding.[25]

Program Operation

California established the first compensation program in 1965, and within three years, five other states created similar programs. California's is still the largest program in the nation; it pays out about a third of the total benefits paid by all programs combined.[26] The median annual payout per state is approximately $2 million.

Every state administers a crime victim compensation program through a central agency.[27] These agencies are organized and funded statewide, with administration, claims investigation, and decision making handled by each state's headquarters. There is an ongoing debate among those in the field regarding centralization versus decentralization of compensation services.[28]

Most victim compensation programs are small agencies employing only a handful of staff. The lack of personnel creates delays in processing claims, prevents the training of groups regarding their right to compensation, and does not allow for specialized services such as bilingual staff. Some agencies are using student interns or volunteers to carry out staff functions. These programs provide assistance to victims of both federal and state crimes. Although each state compensation program is independently run, most programs have similar eligibility requirements and offer the same types of benefits. The maximum state award generally ranges between $10,000 and $25,000.[29]

Victims applying for compensation must comply with certain requirements, including reporting the crime and filing claims by certain deadlines. In most states, the victim initiates the process by calling the compensation agency. Program staff then mail an application to the victim, who fills it out and returns it to the compensation agency. Once the claim form is received, it is processed by an investigator or a claims specialist. These employees do not go out into the field to obtain their information; rather, they collect data using letters, telephone calls, and other techniques. These investigators must verify a wide variety of information, including the fact that the crime was reported to the proper law enforcement agency and that there is appropriate documentation of medical expenses. They must also obtain data regarding funds paid by insurance companies and determine the amount, if any, of lost wages.

Once all pertinent information is gathered, the victim compensation agency will decide whether or not to make an award, and, if so, how much the award to the victim should be. In most states, victims may appeal a denial of benefits. These appeals are heard by a different panel from the one that made the original determination. Some states require that the appeal be heard by a judge.

Eligibility

Not all victims of every crime are eligible for state compensation. In general, the majority of states limit compensation to victims who suffered injuries as a result of the criminal conduct of another and to survivors of homicides (i.e., relatives and friends). Additionally, there is some disparity between eligibility requirements in these programs, with some states mandating that the victim suffer some sort of physical injury, and others allowing for physical or mental injures. Most of the states allow the parents of deceased victims to collect compensation.

A majority of states disallow some classes of persons from eligibility. Most states preclude firefighters and police officers from victim compensation awards. The rationale for this exclusion is that if their injuries are job related, they are eligible for other state programs, such as worker's compensation. Some states exclude convicted prisoners from filing claims while they are in jail or prison, or are serving probation or parole. VOCA has required states to provide compensation to nonresidents victimized within a state as well as to persons who are subject to federal jurisdiction, such as Native Americans. Additionally, residents of one state who are victimized in another state are eligible in their home state if the state where the crime occurred does not allow those victims compensation.

In the past, domestic violence victims were summarily denied compensation. Many states denied these claims because of the belief that the victim contributed to his or her own injuries by staying in the relationship or that any award would benefit the wrongdoer if he or she was still living with the victim. In a way similar to the change in attitudes toward victims of drunk driving, our altered perception of domestic violence victims has resulted in a change in policy in most states. The great majority of all states now include domestic violence as a compensable crime.

Some state compensation programs have very few domestic violence claims. The staff of these programs believe that is the case because victims underreport this form of violence. Additionally, cultural barriers may prevent certain minority groups from reporting because exposing male offenders to public attention violates cultural norms. Finally, many program staff believe that police add information to their reports that serves to disqualify victims of domestic violence. For instance, police officers may include details to indicate that a domestic violence victim may have contributed to his or her injuries. However, the officers might not include that same information in a barroom altercation between strangers where misconduct is far more common and likely.[30]

VICTIM IMPACT STATEMENTS

History of Victim Impact Statements[31]

A new series of rights is emerging in our judicial system. These rights confer upon the victim or upon the relatives of deceased victims the opportunity to speak out or be heard during various phases of the criminal justice process. As with many rights that converge on a single point, there is an actual or a potential conflict. How we handle this conflict is a reflection of the morals and ethics of our society. This section will review the history of these various rights and will examine the rationale behind the current status of the law as it relates to victim impact statements.

One of the most controversial "rights" bestowed upon victims is the victim impact statement. In essence, the victim impact statement presents the victim's point of view to the sentencing authority. Providing the sentencing authority with all relevant information is not a new phenomenon in the criminal justice system. For many years, courts have accepted information regarding the defendant prior to the imposition of a sentence. Traditionally, presentence reports have been used by judges to determine the proper punishment for criminal defendants. The report, which is normally prepared by a probation officer, details the defendant's background, education, and criminal record. Many of these reports also include information concerning the victim of the crime.[32]

Victim impact evidence is now admitted in sentencing for a wide variety of criminal acts, including those that fall within the realm of family violence. However, the law on admissibility and use of victim impact statements is based upon use of this evidence during death penalty cases. To understand the nature of victim impact statements, it is necessary to review how this evidence is used in the most serious types of criminal cases—those involving capital punishment.

The use of victim impact evidence during the sentencing phase of a criminal crime raises serious constitutional issues. The right to confront witnesses comes head-to-head with the right to have all relevant evidence placed before the sentencing authority. Intense feelings were aroused in the U.S. Supreme Court when it addressed this issue.

Constitutional Issues

In *Booth* v. *Maryland*, the U.S. Supreme Court initially addressed the issue of the use of victim impact statements in a sentencing jury's determination.[33] In 1983, John Booth and Willie Reed bound and gagged an elderly couple. Believing that the couple might be able to identify them, Booth stabbed the couple numerous times with a kitchen knife. The trial judge in *Booth* allowed the jury to consider a victim impact statement that detailed the family's and the community's respect and admiration for the victims as well as the impact of the murder on the victims' family.[34]

The Supreme Court, in reversing the death sentence, held that it was impermissible to allow the jury access to such evidence in the sentencing phase of a death penalty proceeding.[35] The Court listed three factors that precluded the prosecution from introducing evidence of the homicide's impact on the victim's family.

First, in holding that the victim impact statement (VIS) impermissibly allows the jury to focus on the victim rather than the defendant, the Court stated the following:

> When the full range of foreseeable consequences of a defendant's actions may be relevant in other criminal and civil contexts, we cannot agree that it is relevant in the unique circumstances of a capital sentencing hearing. In such a case, it is the function of the sentencing jury to "express the conscience of the community on the ultimate question of life or death." When carrying out this task the jury is required to focus on the defendant as a "uniquely individual being." The focus of a VIS, however, is not on the defendant, but on the character and reputation of the victim and the effect on his family. These factors may be wholly unrelated to the blame-worthiness of a particular defendant.[36]

The Court was particularly moved by the fact that the capital defendant does not typically choose his or her victim and, in fixing the punishment, there should be no correlation between the murder and the grief experienced by the victim's family.

Second, the Court held that the sentence of death should not turn on the characteristics of the victim and the victim's family. Specifically, the Court recognized that the imposition of the death penalty should not be determined on the basis of the ability of the victim's family to articulate their anguish and bereavement, whether the victim did or did not leave behind a family, or on the fact that the victim was a stellar member of the community.[37] These factors focus attention on the victim and away from the central inquiry of whether the defendant's characteristics and background are such that the death sentence is warranted.[38]

Finally, the Court stated that because a VIS contains the subjective perceptions and feelings of family members, the defendant has limited rebuttal opportunity.[39] Further, to the extent that the defendant is given an opportunity to rebut such information, "[t]he prospect of a 'mini-trial' on the victim's character is more than simply unappealing, it could well direct the sentencing jury from its constitutionally required task—determining whether the death penalty is appropriate in light of . . . the crime."[40]

In summing up the Court's holding that introduction of the VIS violates the Eighth Amendment's prohibition against cruel and unusual punishment, Justice Powell stated that such evidence would serve no other purpose than to inflame the jury and divert it from its obligation of being fair and impartial.[41] It should be apparent that at the time of the decision in *Booth* v. *Maryland*, the relevant considerations at the sentencing phase of a murder trial were those aspects of a defendant's background, or character, or those circumstances that extenuate or mitigate the defendant's culpability.

South Carolina v. *Gathers* followed the rationale of *Booth* and held unconstitutional the imposition of a death penalty based upon prosecutorial remarks that were considered inflammatory.[42] Demetrius Gathers and three companions sexually assaulted and killed Richard Haynes, a man they encountered in a park. During the incident, the perpetrators ransacked a bag the victim was carrying. The bag contained several articles pertaining to religion, including a religious tract entitled "Game Guy's Prayer." During the sentencing phase of the trial, the prosecutor's argument included references to Haynes's personal qualities and included a reading of the "Game Guy's Prayer." The Supreme Court reversed the sentence, stating that such references to the qualities of the victim were similar to the *Booth* holding prohibiting victim impact statements. The Court determined that such evidence was likely to inflame the jury and thus violated the defendant's Eighth Amendment rights. In a well-reasoned and logical dissent, Justice O'Connor stated, "Nothing in the Eighth Amendment precludes the community from considering its loss in assessing punishment nor requires that the victim remain a faceless stranger at the penalty phase of a capital case." The dissent by Justice O'Connor was a signal that the winds of judicial temperament might be changing.

In *Payne* v. *Tennessee*, the court completely reversed itself and allowed to stand the imposition of a death sentence that was based in part on evidence contained in a victim impact statement. In 1987, Pervis Tyrone Payne entered the apartment of Charisse Christopher and her two children. Payne stabbed Charisse and the two children numerous times with a butcher knife. Charisse and her daughter died; however, three-year-old Nicholas survived.

Payne was caught and convicted for the murders. During the penalty phase, four witnesses testified regarding the defendant's background, reputation, and mental state. All these witnesses urged the jury not to impose the death penalty. In rebuttal, the prosecution called the maternal grandmother, who was caring for Nicholas. She was allowed to testify, over the defendant's objection, that Nicholas continued to cry out calling for his dead mother and sister. The witness was also allowed to testify regarding her personal grief over the loss of her loved ones.

During closing arguments, the prosecutor hammered on the pain and suffering that Nicholas and his deceased family had endured, stating the following:

> But we do know that Nicholas was alive. And Nicholas was in the same room. Nicholas was still conscious. His eyes were open. He responded to the paramedics. He was able to follow their directions. He was able to hold his intestines in as he was carried to the ambulance. So he knew what happened to his mother and baby sister.
>
> There is nothing you can do to ease the pain of any of the families involved in this case. There is nothing you can do to ease the pain of Bernice or Carl Payne, and that's a tragedy. There is nothing you can do basically to ease the pain of Mr. and Mrs. Zvolanek, and that's a tragedy. They will have to live with it for the rest of their lives. There is obviously nothing you can do for Charisse and Lacie Jo. But there is something you can do for Nicholas.
>
> Somewhere down the road Nicholas is going to grow up, hopefully. He's going to want to know what happened. And he is going to know what happened to his baby sister and his mother. He is going to want to know what kind of justice was done. He is going to want to know what happened. With your verdict, you will provide the answer.[43]

The jury sentenced Payne to death, and the case was then appealed to the U.S. Supreme Court. Payne contended that the trial court erred when it allowed the maternal grandmother to testify. Relying on *Booth* and *Gathers*, Payne argued that such evidence was a violation of his Eighth Amendment rights. After reviewing the principles that have guided criminal sentencing over the ages, the court stated that the consideration of the harm caused by the crime has been an important factor in the existence of the exercise of judicial discretion. The majority opinion went on to state that neither *Booth* nor *Gathers* even suggested that a defendant, entitled as he or she is to individualized consideration, is to receive that consideration wholly apart from the crime committed. The Court stated that victim impact evidence is simply another form or method of informing the sentencing authority about the specific harm caused by the crime in question.[44]

Thus the U.S. Supreme Court overruled *Booth* and *Gathers* to the extent that they prohibited introduction of evidence or argument regarding the impact of the crime on the victim, families, and community. In addition, the Court's decision clearly stated that the decision regarding the admission of such evidence was the prerogative of the individual states. The Court ruled that it would not intervene unless the evidence introduced was so unduly prejudicial that it rendered the trial fundamentally unfair.[45] If this possibility occurred, the Court reasoned, the Due Process Clause of the Fourteenth Amendment provides a mechanism for relief.

The decision was not without heated dissent. In a dissenting opinion, Justices Marshall and Blackmun uttered words that will ring in the halls of justice and law school classrooms forevermore: "Power, not reason, is the new currency of this Court's decision making."[46] Justices Marshall and Blackmun went on to point out that the Court was disregarding the accepted judicial principle of stare decisis.[47]

The decision also generated controversy in the academic world when a series of articles appeared condemning the Court for both allowing victim impact evidence and appearing to repudiate its acceptance of stare decisis.[48] Although the dissent and certain individuals within the academic community may condemn the majority's opinion, it is now clearly the law of the land. In addition, the Supreme Court's decision enhances the victims' rights movement in the United States. It allows individual states to determine what is relevant evidence in the death penalty phase of a capital crime. Some would argue that the decision in *Payne* leaves prosecutors and defense attorneys scrambling to determine what type of evidence is admissible under the guise of victim impact statements. The answer is simply this, that evidence that does not result in rendering a trial fundamentally unfair is proper. This concept of fundamental fairness is not a new, untested, or ill-defined doctrine.

There is a long history defining acts by the state that are classified as fundamentally unfair. The doctrine of fundamental fairness has its roots in two early cases. In *Powell* v. *Alabama*, several black youths were accused of repeatedly rap-

---

LAW IN PRACTICE   *Victim's Rights Constitutional Amendment*

Section 1. To ensure that the victim is treated with fairness, dignity, and respect, from the occurrence of a crime of violence and other crimes as may be defined by law pursuant to section two of this article, and throughout the criminal, military, and juvenile justice process, as a matter of fundamental rights to liberty, justice and due process, the victim shall have the following rights: to be informed of and given the opportunity to be present at every proceeding in which those rights are extended to the accused or convicted offender; to be heard at any proceeding involving sentencing, including the right to object to a previously negotiated plea, or to a release from custody; to be informed of any release or escape; and to a speedy trial, a final conclusion free from unreasonable delay, full restitution from the convicted offender, reasonable measures to protect the victim from violence or intimidation by the accused or convicted offender, and notice of the victim's rights.

Section 2. The several States, with respect to a proceeding in a State forum, and the Congress with respect to a proceeding in a United States forum, shall have the power to implement further the rights established in this article by appropriate legislation.

Source: OVC, U.S. Department of Justice, Washington, D.C., 1996.

ing two young white girls. They were caught, tried, and convicted. Their conviction was overturned on the ground that the failure of the trial court to appoint counsel until the day of the trial was a violation of the defendant's due process.[49] In *Brown* v. *Mississippi*, a sheriff hung the defendant from a tree and whipped him until he confessed to the murder of a white man. The Supreme Court held that such actions are revolting to the sense of justice, and the confession was suppressed.[50]

The doctrine of fundamental fairness accepts the concept that due process is a generalized command that requires states to provide the defendant with a fair trial. If the admission of the victim impact evidence "revolts the sense of justice" or "shocks the conscience" of the court, such admission would be error under the Due Process Clause.

Victim impact evidence is now an accepted part of the judicial process. The ability of a victim of family violence to inform the court of the impact of the offender's acts on his or her life can only benefit the victim and continue to educate the public regarding the dynamics of violence.

REVIEW QUESTIONS

1. Explain why the historical perspective of restitution is important in understanding today's models.
2. Can you list reasons why an incarcerated prisoner should not have to make restitution to a victim? Assume that you are the prisoner's advocate and must convince a judge of your position.
3. Explain how a typical compensation program is funded and operates.
4. Describe the various eligibility requirements for receiving compensation.
5. List the various benefits that victims of crime may receive under a state compensation program.
6. Explain and give concrete examples of fundamental fairness. Can you list ways in which a victim impact statement would violate this constitutional standard?
7. Should law enforcement officers inform the victim of a crime about victim impact statements? Prepare a form that should be given to victims, outlining their rights.
8. How are we ever going to determine whether victim impact statements serve a valid purpose in the criminal justice system? How would you structure such a study? What are the pitfalls inherent in these types of studies?

LOCAL PROCEDURE

1. Who handles compensation claims in your county? Contact them, and determine whether they have handouts that explain their duties.
2. Who coordinates restitution in your court system?
3. Are different types of restitution available in your jurisdiction? List the types.
4. Attend a sentencing hearing at your local courthouse. Was the victim present? Did he or she make a victim impact statement? Do you think it had any effect on the sentencing of the offender? Explain your reasoning.

ENDNOTES

1. Portions of this chapter have been adapted from Harvey Wallace, *Victimology Legal, Psychological and Social Perspectives* (Allyn & Bacon, Boston), 1997.
2. Emilio C. Viano, *Victim/Witness Services: A Review of the Model* (GPO, Washington, D.C.), 1979.
3. M. Largen, "Grassroots Centers and National Task Forces: A History of the Anti-Rape Movement," 32 *Aegis* pp. 46–52 (Autumn 1981).
4. *President's Task Force on Victims of Crime* (Final Report, GPO, Washington, D.C.), December 1982.
5. Victims of Crime Act of 1984, 42 U.S. Code, section 10601 (1984).
6. Jeremy Travis, "Violence Against Women: Reflections on NIJ's Research Agenda," *National Institute of Justice Journal*, February 1996.
7. "Remarks by the President at Announcement of Victims' Constitutional Amendment," Press Release, The White House, Office of the Press Secretary, Washington, D.C., June 25, 1996, p. 2.
8. *Final Report, President's Task Force on Victims of Crime* (GPO, Washington, D.C.), December 1982.
9. Ibid. at 38.
10. Susan Hillenbrand, "Restitution and Victim Rights in the 1980s." In A. J. Lurigio, W. G. Skogan, and R. C. Davis (eds.), *Victims of Crime: Problems, Policies, and Programs* (Sage, Newbury Park, California), 1990.
11. Carol Shapiro, "Is Restitution Legislation the Chameleon of the Victims' Movement?" In B. Gateway and J. Hudson (eds.), *Criminal Justice, Restitution, and Reconciliation* (Willow Tree Press, Monsey, New York), 1990.
12. L. F. Frank, "The Collection of Restitution: An Overlooked Service to Crime Victims," Vol. 8, *St. John's Journal of Legal Commentary* 107 (1992).
13. *National Victim Assistance Academy Text*, pp. 21–105.
14. *Attorney General Guidelines for Victim and Witness Assistance*, 1995 (U.S. Department of Justice, Washington, D.C.), 1995.
15. 18 U.S. Code, section 3663(b) as amended by section 40504 of P.L. 103–322 (1994).
16. *National Victim Assistance Academy Text*, pp. 21–10–8, 21–10–11.
17. Michael D. Harris, "No One Wants Responsibility for Restitution," *Los Angeles Daily Transcript*, January 6, 1995, p. A-1.
18. *National Victim Assistance Academy Text*, p. 21–10–7.
19. Much of the material that appears in this section has been adapted from various federally funded projects, including NACVCB's *Crime Victim Compensation: A Fact Sheet and Crime Victim Compensation: An Overview* (National Association of Crime Victim Compensation Boards, Alexandria, Va.), July 1, 1994; *Crime Victim Compensation*, Dale G. Parent, Barbara Auerbach, and Kenneth E. Carlson, *Compensating Crime Victims: A Summary of Policies and Practices*, Office of Justice Programs (U.S. Department of Justice), January 1992; *Compensating Crime Victims and Focus on the Future: A Systems Approach to Prosecution and Victim Assistance*, National Victim Center, MADD, and American Prosecutors Research Institute (U.S. Department of Justice, Washington, D.C.), no date; hereinafter, *Focus on the Future*.
20. *Crime Victim Compensation*, p. 112.
21. "Victims of Crime Act Crime Victims Fund," *OVC Fact Sheet* (Office for Victims of Crime, Washington, D.C.), no date.
22. Ibid.

23. Ibid.
24. *Compensating Crime Victims*, p. 2.
25. Ibid.
26. *Compensating Crime Victims*, p. 2.
27. Ibid.
28. *Compensating Crime Victims*, p. 7.
29. "Victims of Crime Act Crime Victims Fund," *OVC Fact Sheet* (Office for Victims of Crime, Washington, D.C.), no date.
30. *Compensating Crime Victims*, p. 21.
31. This section has been adapted from H. Wallace, *Family Violence; Legal, Medical and Social Perspectives* (Allyn & Bacon, Boston), 1996.
32. See Phillip A. Talbert, *The Relevance of Victim Impact Statements to the Criminal Sentencing Decision*, 36 UCLA L Rev 199, 202–11 (1988), and Maureen McLeod, *Victim Participation Criminal Law Bull at Sentencing*, 22 Crim L. Bull. 501, 505–11(1986).
33. *Booth v. Maryland*, 482 U.S. 496 (1987).
34. Ibid. at 500–01.
35. Ibid. at 509. The Court did, however, carefully note that information typically contained in a victim's statement is generally admissible in noncapital cases and may be considered in capital cases if directly related to the circumstances of the crime. Id. at 508 n. 10. For example, the Court noted that the prosecution may produce evidence regarding the characteristics of the victim to rebut an argument made by the defendant (e.g., victim's peaceable nature to rebut claim of self-defense). Ibid.
36. Ibid. at 507–07 (citations omitted).
37. Ibid. at 505–07.
38. Ibid. at 507–08.
39. Ibid.
40. Ibid.
41. Ibid.
42. 490 U.S. 805 (1989).
43. 115 L.Ed.2d 728–729.
44. 115 L.Ed.2d 734–735.
45. 115 L.Ed.2d 735.
46. 115 L.Ed.2d 748.
47. 115 L.Ed.2d 756.
48. See Jimmie O. Clements, Jr., *Case Note, Criminal Law—Victim Impact Evidence: The Scope of the Eighth Amendment Does Not Include a Per Se Bar to the Use of Victim Impact Evidence in the Sentencing Phase of a Capital Trial*, Payne v. Tennessee. 23 St. Mary's L.J. 517(1991); Aida Alaka, *Note, Victim Impact Evidence, Arbitrariness and the Death Penalty: The Supreme Court Flipflops in* Payne v. Tennessee, 23 Loy. U. Chi. L.J. 581(1992); K. Elizabeth Whitehead, *Case Note, Mourning Becomes Electric:* Payne v. Tennessee's *Allowance of Victim Impact Statements During Capital Proceedings*, 45 Ark. L. Rev. 531(1992).
49. *Powell v. Alabama*, 287 U.S. 45, 53 S.C. 55, 77 L.Ed. 158 (1932).
50. U.S. 278, 56 S.Ct. 461, 80 L.Ed. 682 (1936).

Outline of Trial Procedure

In order that the reader may better understand the trial procedures, an outline of the general procedure in a criminal trial is included here. Depending upon the jurisdiction, there may be some slight deviation from the procedures set forth.

1. Selection of jury
2. Swearing in of jury (trial technically begins at this time)
3. Reading of charge and plea
4. Opening statement by prosecuting attorney
5. Opening statement by defense (this may be waived entirely or until prosecution rests)
6. Calling of first prosecution witness and administration of the oath
7. Direct examination
8. Cross-examination (may be waived)
9. Redirect examination (may be waived)
10. Recross-examination (may be waived)
11. Calling of additional prosecution witnesses, administration of oath, direct examination, and other procedure as in case of first witness
12. Prosecution rests
13. Motion for judgment of acquittal by defense (if denied, then the following procedure)
14. Opening statement by defense (if not previously given)
15. Calling of first defense witness and procedure followed as in case of first prosecution witness
16. Defense rests
17. Rebuttal presentation by prosecution
18. Closing arguments by prosecution and then by defense
19. Rebuttal closing argument by prosecution

20. Instructing the jury
21. Deliberation
22. Return of verdict (if guilty verdict returned, then the following procedure)
23. Request for new trial by defense (if denied, then the following procedure)
24. Sentencing the defendant

Psychological Report on the Issue of Insanity

APPENDIX B

Report of
Ronald J. Masters, Ph.D.
Licensed Clinical Psychologist

August 27, 1999

INSANITY AT THE TIME OF THE OFFENSE

NAME: Richard Danziger
DOB: 8/14/70
DATE OF EVALUATION: 8/14/99
REFERRAL SOURCE: Office of County Public Defender
CASE NO: 13.047

PRESENTING PROBLEM

Richard was referred for sanity evaluation in connection with a 12/3/96 charge of having a deadly weapon in a penal institution. This involved his having an eight inch metal rod weapon, commenting to his cell mate that he was going to stab him because the cell mate woke him up; but it did not involve active use of the weapon against the other inmate and Richard cooperated with the guards as he was moved and the weapon was confiscated. He refused to make a statement and refused to sign Miranda warnings. Richard suffered a severe head injury in February 1991 resulting in significant brain damage and there have subsequently been four Skyview [State hospital for criminally insane] and one Pamio [state mental institution] admissions.

EVALUATION METHODS

Prior to the evaluation Richard was reminded of his Miranda rights and the process of this evaluation was reviewed for him, including that a report of the findings would be sent to his attorney. Richard indicated that he understood and was agreeable that the evaluation would proceed.

Clinical interview and mental status exam, WAIS-R, Rorschach, and review of his inmate medical records.

FINDINGS

Richard is viewed as most probably insane at the time of the 12/3/96 offense of having a deadly weapon in a penal institution.

During this evaluation Richard stated he has no memory for the event of 12/3/96 and at the time of the event he did not make a statement to Internal Affairs (and refused to sign the Miranda warning at the time). Therefore, Richard's personal viewpoint of the events is unavailable.

During this evaluation Richard said he did not know whether it was right or wrong to hit someone, to shoot someone, or for one inmate to spit on another. His demeanor during his denials of this basic piece of knowledge was no different from all other points in the evaluation, i.e., a manifestation of cognitive limitation and inappropriate affect. It is most likely his mental status on 12/3/96 was no better than his current mental status.

Clinical records from around the time of the event indicate that on 11/29/96 he was cooperative, stable, and seizure free. The inmate involved in the incident and the apparent object for Richard's use of the weapon made a report which suggests Richard did not have aggressive feelings to accompany his verbal threat of use of the weapon, and Richard's acts seem lacking in emotion and any kind of intent.

The mental defect by which Richard is viewed as being insane at the time of the offense is dementia (with both cognitive and personality alteration) and can be distinguished from basic antisocial personality disorder.

[signed by the psychologist]

Motion for the Production and Inspection of Evidence and Information Which May Lead to Evidence

PEOPLE

V.

ROBERT LEE GRANT

Case No. 98-02145

Re: *Brady* v. *Maryland*, 373 U.S. 83, 10 L.Ed.2d 215, 83 S.Ct. 1194

Comes now, Robert Lee Grant, defendant in the above styled and numbered cause by and through his attorney of record, and respectfully requests the Court to order the prosecution to produce for inspection all evidence and information which may lead to favorable evidence as to the issue of the Defendant's guilt or innocence and punishment, including, but not limited to the following exculpatory evidence:

I.

Any major use of force paperwork, Internal Affairs Investigation paperwork, or other employer disciplinary reports involving acts of the complaining witness or any witnesses testifying on behalf of the State since their employment by the institution. Such evidence is material and exculpatory as bearing upon the witnesses's motive for testifying, their bias and prejudice against the Defendant, their credibility and is necessary in order for the Defendant to properly exercise his Sixth Amendment right to confront the witnesses against him.

II.

Any and all evidence that a witness called by the State during this trial has committed perjury or has previously made any statement or given any testimony which conflicts with or contradicts the testimony given by said witness during the trial of this cause.

III.

All statements of all persons, whether they have testified or not, who have been interviewed by the prosecution or any agent thereof and who have personal knowledge of facts of this cause which could be deemed favorable to the Defendant, as to the issues of guilt, innocence or punishment.

IV.

All exculpatory evidence and facts which are known or by the exercise of due diligence should be known by the prosecution, including facts known to investigators of the District Attorney's office, investigators or other institution employees which are relevant to have a hearing upon the guilt or innocence of the Defendant, the credibility to the State's witnesses or mitigation of punishment.

V.

The Defendant submits to the Court that the failure or refusal to produce any or all of the foregoing evidence or information by the prosecution constitutes a suppression of evidence and a violation of the Fifth, Sixth, and Fourteenth Amendments of the United States Constitution and substantially fair trial. *Brady v. Maryland*, 373 U.S. 83 (1963); *United States v. Agurs*, 427 U.S. 97 (1976); *Ashe v. Texas*, 319 E2d 80 (5th Cir. 1963); *Moore v. Illinois*, 408 U.S. 786 (1972); *United States v. Bagley*, 473 U.S. 677, 105 S.Ct. 3375, 87 L.Ed.2d 481 (1985); *United States v. McKellar*, 798 F.2d 151 (5th Cir. 1986); *Woods v. State*, 713 S.W.2d 276 (Tex.Cr.App. 1974).

WHEREFORE, PREMISES CONSIDERED, the Defendant prays that this Honorable Court will grant this motion in all things.

Respectfully submitted

Attorney for Defendant

The Judge's Instructions to the Jury in a Criminal Case

No. B-96-MO19-O-PR-B

The State of Texas	§	In the 156th District
vs.	§	Court of
Michael Runnels	§	Bee County, Texas

CHARGE OF THE COURT

LADIES AND GENTLEMEN OF THE JURY:

The Defendant, MICHAEL RUNNELS, stands charged by indictment with the offense of Assault on a Public Servant, alleged to have been made on a correctional officer on or about the 1st day of April A.D., 1996, in Bee County, Texas. The Defendant has plead not guilty.

1.

Our law provides that a person commits the offense of assault if he intentionally and knowingly causes bodily injury to another.

Such assault is aggravated assault when committed upon a guard employed by the Texas Department of Criminal Justice–Institutional Division in the lawful discharge of his official duty when the person committing the assault knows or has been informed that the person assaulted is such a guard.

2.

By the term "bodily injury" is meant physical pain, illness or any impairment of physical condition.

3.

A person acts intentionally, or with intent, with respect to a result of his conduct when it is his conscious objective or desire to cause the result.

A person acts knowingly, or with knowledge, with respect to a result of his conduct when he is aware that his conduct is reasonably certain to cause the result.

4.

Now, if you find, from the evidence, beyond a reasonable doubt that on or about the 1st day of April, 1996, in Bee County, Texas, MICHAEL RUNNELS TDCJ #698369, did then and there knowingly or intentionally cause bodily injury to Robert D. Hill, a public servant, to-wit: a Correctional officer with the Texas Department of Criminal Justice–Institutional Division, Garza East Unit, in Beeville, Bee County, Texas, by striking Robert D. Hill in the head and face with a closed fist, while Robert D. Hill was lawfully discharging an official duty and the defendant knew that Robert D. Hill was a public servant, then you will find the Defendant guilty of Aggravated Assault on a Correctional Officer.

Unless you so find beyond a reasonable doubt, or if you have a reasonable doubt thereof, you will find the defendant not guilty.

5.

A guard or Correctional Officer employed by the Texas Department of Correction is justified in using force against a person in custody when and to the degree the guard or Correctional Officer reasonably believes the force is necessary to maintain the security of the penal institution, the safety or security of other persons in custody or employed by the penal institution, or his own safety or security.

Therefore, if you find that Robert D. Hill used force against MICHAEL RUNNELS and that while doing so he did not reasonably believe that the use of force was necessary to maintain the security of the Penal Institution, the safety or security of other persons in custody or employed by the Penal Institution, or his own safety or security, you will next consider the defense of self-defense.

6.

"Reasonable Belief" as used herein means a belief that would be held by an ordinary and prudent person in the same circumstances as Robert D. Hill.

Upon the law of self-defense, a person is justified in using force against another when and to the degree he reasonably believes the force is immediately necessary to protect himself against the other's use or attempted use of unlawful force. A person is under no obligation to retreat to avoid the necessity of repelling or defending with force less than deadly force, against an attack or threatened attack. The use of force against another is not justified if the actor provoked the other's use or attempted use of unlawful force, unless the actor abandons the encounter, or clearly communicates to the other his intent to do so reasonably believing he cannot safely abandon the encounter and the other nevertheless continues or attempts to use unlawful force against the actor.

"Reasonable belief" as used herein means a belief that would be held by an ordinary and prudent person in the same circumstances as defendant.

You are instructed that it is your duty to consider all the relevant facts and circumstances surrounding the alleged assault, including the previous relationship, if any, existing between the accused and Robert D. Hill, together with all relevant facts and circumstance going to show the condition of the mind of the defendant at the time of the alleged offense. In considering all the foregoing, you should place yourself in the defendant's position and view the circumstances from his standpoint alone, at the time in question.

Now if you find and believe from the evidence beyond a reasonable doubt that on the occasion in question the defendant, MICHAEL RUNNELS, intentionally and knowingly caused bodily injury to Robert D. Hill by striking him in the head and face with his (the defendant's) closed fist and that Robert D. Hill used force against Michael Runnels without reasonably believing that the use of force was necessary to maintain the security of the Penal Institution, the safety or security of other persons in custody or employed by the Penal Institution, or his own safety or security, but you further find from the evidence, or you have a reasonable doubt thereof, that from the words or conduct, or both, of Robert D. Hill, viewed from the standpoint of the defendant at the time, it reasonably appeared to the defendant that his person was in danger of bodily injury and there was created in his mind a reasonable expectation or fear of bodily injury from the use of unlawful force at the hands of Robert D. Hill, and that acting under such apprehension and reasonably believing that the use of force on his part was immediately necessary to protect himself against such use or attempted use of unlawful force against him, the defendant struck Robert D. Hill with his fist to defend himself, then you will acquit the defendant.

7.

You are instructed that certain evidence was admitted in evidence before you in regard to the defendant's having been charged and convicted or reprimanded of offenses other than the one for which he is now on trial. Such evidence cannot be considered by you against the defendant as any evidence of guilt in this case. Said evidence was admitted before you for the purpose of aiding you, if it does aid you, in passing upon the weight you will give his testimony, and you will not consider the same for any other purposes.

8.

A grand jury indictment is the means whereby a Defendant is brought to trial in a felony case. It is not evidence of guilt nor can it be considered by you in passing upon the question of guilt of the Defendant. The burden of proof in all criminal cases rests upon the State throughout the trial, and never shifts to the Defendant.

All persons are presumed to be innocent and no person may be convicted of an offense unless each element of the offense is proved beyond a reasonable doubt. The fact that a person has been arrested, confined, or indicted for, or otherwise charged with, the offense gives rise to no inference of guilt at his trial. The law does not require a defendant to prove his innocence or produce any evidence at all. The presumption of innocence alone is sufficient to acquit the defendant unless the jurors are satisfied beyond a reasonable doubt of the defendant's guilt after careful and impartial consideration of all evidence in the case.

The prosecution has the burden of proving the defendant guilty and it must do so by proving each and every element of the offense charged beyond a reasonable doubt and if it fails to do so, you must acquit the defendant.

It is not required that the prosecution prove guilt beyond all possible doubt; it is required that the prosecution's proof excludes all "reasonable doubt" concerning the defendant's guilt.

A "reasonable doubt" is a doubt based on reason and common sense after a careful and impartial consideration of all the evidence in the case. It is the kind of doubt that would make a reasonable person hesitate to act in the most important of his own affairs.

Proof beyond a reasonable doubt, therefore, must be proof of such a convincing character that you would be willing to rely and act upon it without hesitation in the most important of your own affairs.

In the event you have a reasonable doubt as to the defendant's guilt after considering all the evidence before you, and these instructions, you will acquit him and say by your verdict, "Not guilty."

You are the exclusive judges of the facts proved, the credibility of the witnesses and the weight to be given their testimony, but the law you shall receive in these written instructions, and you must be governed thereby.

After you retire to the jury room, you should select one of your members as your presiding juror. It is his/her duty to preside at your deliberations, vote with you, and when you have unanimously agreed upon a verdict, to certify to your verdict by using the appropriate form attached hereto, and signing the same as Presiding Juror.

No one has any authority to communicate with you except the officer who has you in charge. During your deliberations in this case, you must not consider, discuss, nor relate any matters not in evidence before you. You should not consider nor mention any personal knowledge or information you may have about any fact or person connected with this case which is not shown by the evidence.

After you have retired, you may communicate with this Court in writing through the Officer who has you in charge. Do not attempt to talk to the officer, the attorneys, or the Court concerning any question you may have. After you have reached a unanimous verdict, the presiding juror will certify thereto by using the appropriate form attached to this charge and signing his/her name as Presiding Juror. You may now retire to consider your verdict after argument of counsel.

_____

Judge Presiding

No. B-96-MO19-PR-B

The State of Texas	§	In the 156th District
vs.	§	Court of
Michael Runnels	§	Bee County, Texas

VERDICT SHEET

I.

We, the Jury, find the Defendant, MICHAEL RUNNELS, guilty of the offense of Assault on a Public Servant as charged in indictment.

———————————————————
Presiding Juror

OR

II.

We, the Jury, find the Defendant, MICHAEL RUNNELS, not guilty.

———————————————————
Presiding Juror

Subject Index

Case Index